Deconstruction in Context

Deconstruction in Context
Literature and Philosophy

Edited by Mark C. Taylor

The University of Chicago Press
Chicago and London

149
0296

Mark C. Taylor, professor of religion at Williams
College, is the author of *Erring: A Postmodern
A/theology,* which is also published by the University
of Chicago Press.

The University of Chicago Press, Chicago 60637
The University of Chicago Press, Ltd., London

© 1986 by The University of Chicago
All rights reserved. Published 1986
Printed in the United States of America

95 94 93 92 91 90   5 4

Library of Congress Cataloging-in-Publication Data

Deconstruction in context.

  Bibliography: p.
  1. Philosophy. 2. Deconstruction. I. Taylor,
Mark C., 1945– . II. Title.
B29.D365 1986 149 86-4316
ISBN 0-226-79139-4
ISBN 0-226-79140-8 (pbk.)

9/95

Contents

Acknowledgments

The publication of this book involves certain risks—some avoidable, many unavoidable. In attempting to establish the philosophical context of deconstruction, it is possible to obscure precisely the difference or other that many of the texts here assembled struggle to evoke. The temptation is to make everything too coherent by suggesting that deconstruction is the result of a continuous historical process. Deconstruction, above all else, renders coherence, continuity, and even history itself suspect. As many writers and critics have long acknowledged, our narrative continuities are undeniably fictive. Why, then, take the risk entailed in gathering these texts into something that approximates a "book"? I suppose it is best to consider this volume a "strategic bet" occasioned by the continuing confusion and controversy surrounding deconstruction. This enormously complex and extremely rich critical strategy can be situated and resituated in many different ways. The readings gathered in this volume suggest *one* approach to deconstruction. Much of the controversy that continues to surround it is the result of persistent misunderstandings. Literary critics tend to be inadequately informed about the close relationship between deconstruction and modern continental philosophy, and philosophers too often are insufficiently sensitive to the literary dimensions of their own undertaking. Literature is more philosophical and philosophy is more literary than many opponents of deconstruction are willing to admit. As Derrida repeatedly insists, "one must speak several languages and produce several texts at once." By producing one text that errs in the direction of coherence and continuity, I am betting that a more errant text in which the important implications of the incoherence and discontinuity that characterize much recent writing and criticism (to say nothing of the discontinuity of experience in our incoherent world) will become at least a bit more readable, which is not to say comprehensible. Whether or not there is any return on this bet depends at least as much (and probably more) on the imagination of the reader as on the skill of the writer.

In the course of preparing this volume I have benefited from the encouragement, guidance, and support of many people. Among those who, in different ways, have contributed to the shaping and reshaping of this book are: Thomas J.J. Altizer, Emily Apter, John W. Chandler, Jacques Derrida, Kathleen East, Rodolphe Gasché, Barbara Hanrahan, Charles Karelis, H. Ganse Little, Steven Melville, Françoise Meltzer, Elizabeth Morton, Francis Oakley, George Pistorius, John Reichert, Clifford Ruprecht, Anita Sokolsky, Sara Suleri, Dinny Taylor, Lisken Van Pelt, Anthony Vidler, and Edith Wyschogrod. Their involvement makes this work something other than merely my own.

M.C.T.
Williamstown
9 September 1985

Introduction:
System . . . Structure . . . Difference . . . Other

Who will ever know what it is to know nothing?
GEORGES BATAILLE

There is an "I do not know" that is at the limit of knowledge but that belongs to knowledge. We always pronounce it too early, still knowing all—or too late, when I no longer know that I do not know . . .
MAURICE BLANCHOT

As for what "begins" then—"beyond" absolute knowledge—*unheard-of* thoughts are required, sought for across the memory of old signs. . . . In the openness of this question *we no longer know.* This does not mean that we know nothing but that we are beyond absolute knowledge (and its ethical, aesthetic, or religious system), approaching that on the basis of which its closure is announced and decided. Such a question will legitimately be understood as *meaning* nothing, as no longer belonging to the system of meaning.
JACQUES DERRIDA

THE ETERNAL RETURN OF HEGEL

How can we pass beyond absolute knowledge? How can we approach that which marks the closure of systematic thought? What remains to be written after Hegel? In an interview conducted in 1971, Jacques Derrida explains: "We will never be finished with the reading or rereading of Hegel, and, in a certain way, I do nothing other than attempt to explain myself on this point. In effect I believe that Hegel's text is necessarily fissured; that it is something more and other than the circular closure of its representation."[1]

---

1. Jacques Derrida, *Positions*, trans. A. Bass (Chicago: University of Chicago Press, 1981), 77.

In his first major work, *Of Grammatology* (1967), Derrida signals his recognition of Hegel's importance and suggests the double reading of Hegel that informs all of his writings.

The horizon of absolute knowledge is the effacement of writing in the logos, the retrieval of the trace in parousia, the reappropriation of difference, the accomplishment of what I have elsewhere called the *metaphysics of the proper*. Yet all that Hegel thought within this horizon, all, that is, except eschatology, may be reread as a meditation on writing. Hegel is *also* the thinker of irreducible difference . . . the last philosopher of the book and the first thinker of writing.[2]

Derrida's preoccupation with Hegel is not unique. During the past fifty years, Hegel has set the terms of debate for many of the most creative philosophers and critics in France as well as elsewhere. Merleau-Ponty goes so far as to insist that "all the great philosophical ideas of the past century—the philosophies of Marx and Nietzsche, phenomenology, German existentialism, and psychoanalysis—had their beginnings in Hegel; it was he who started the attempt to explore the irrational and integrate it into an expanded reason, which remains the task of our century."[3]

Hegel's influence has not always been felt so keenly in France. Reporting on the state of Hegelian studies in 1931, Alexandre Koyré notes the virtual absence of any serious interest in Hegel's work among French thinkers. Two years later this situation began to change dramatically as the result of Alexandre Kojève's celebrated lectures on Hegel delivered at the Ecole Pratique des Hautes Etudes from 1933 to 1939, and subsequently published under the title *Introduction à la lecture de Hegel*. Among those attending these lectures were many who would become leading figures in twentieth-century French intellectual life: Raymond Aron, Georges Bataille, Jacques Lacan, Merleau-Ponty, Raymond Queneau, Jean-Paul Sartre, and others. Proceeding from a careful analysis of the *Phenomenology of Spirit*, Kojève stresses what Vincent Descombes aptly describes as "*the unreasonable origins of reason*." The center of the *Phenomenology* is, for Kojève, the master-slave relation in which individuals engage in a seemingly irrational struggle for recognition. History, which grows out of violent struggle, is a dialectical process in which irrational aspects of experience gradually are rationalized. When negation itself is negated, opposition is overcome and opposites reconciled. For Kojève, this marks the end of both history and its subject—man.

2. Jacques Derrida, *Of Grammatology*, trans. G. C. Spivak (Baltimore: Johns Hopkins University Press, 1976), 26.

3. Maurice Merleau-Ponty, *Sense and Non-sense*, trans. H. L. Dreyfus and P. A. Dreyfus (Evanston, Ill: Northwestern University Press, 1964), 63.

Kojève's interpretation of Hegel echoes the early work and anticipates the later writings of another philosopher who has decisively shaped much twentieth-century French thought: Martin Heidegger. While Kojève discerns the end of history and the disappearance of man in Hegel's *Phenomenology*, Heidegger insists that Hegelian philosophy and its extension in Husserl's phenomenology bring "the end of philosophy." The trajectory of Western metaphysics, which begins in Greece, arrives at its conclusion in modern European philosophy. Modern philosophy is commonly acknowledged to have begun with Descartes's turn to the subject. Plagued by uncertainty and doubt, Descartes (1596–1650) seeks certainty through doubt. Descartes doubts everything until he reaches what he regards as indubitable—his own doubting self. He labels this self-certain subject *res cogitans*, which he distinguishes from all else, described as *res extensa*. Having radically differentiated *res cogitans* from *res extensa*, Descartes faces the problem of establishing the relationship between subjectivity and objectivity. In a move that remains decisive for all later thought, Descartes insists that the subject's relation to all otherness is mediated by and derived from its relationship to itself.

In the wake of Descartes's meditations, modern philosophy becomes a *philosophy of the subject*. The locus of certainty and truth, subjectivity is the first principle from which everything arises and to which all must be reduced or returned. With the movement from Descartes, through the Enlightenment, to Idealism and Romanticism, attributes traditionally predicated of the divine subject are gradually transferred to the human subject. Through a dialectical reversal, the creator God dies and is resurrected as the creative subject. As God created the world through the Logos, so man creates a "world" through conscious and unconscious projection. In different terms, the modern subject defines itself by its *constructive* activity. Like God, this sovereign subject relates only to what it constructs and is, therefore, unaffected by anything other than itself. What seems to be a relationship to otherness—be that other God, nature, objects, or subjects— always turns out to be an aspect of mediate self-relation that is necessary for complete self-consciousness. The absolute knowledge made possible by the phenomenological reduction of difference to identity in subjectivity's full knowledge of itself realizes Western philosophy's dream of enjoying a total presence that is undisturbed by absence or lack.

On what Derrida describes as "the eve and aftermath of philosophy," Heidegger asks: "What has always remained unasked throughout this history of thinking?"[4] What, in other words, "remains unthought in

4. Martin Heidegger, *Identity and Difference*, trans. J. Stambaugh (New York: Harper and Row, 1969), 50. Unless otherwise indicated, quotations are from the selections included in this volume.

the call 'to the thing itself' "? "Questioning in this way," Heidegger maintains, "we can become aware how something that it is no longer the matter of philosophy to think conceals itself precisely where philosophy has brought its matter to absolute knowledge and to ultimate evidence." To think this unthought, to think what remains " 'beyond' absolute knowledge" is, for Heidegger, "the task of thinking" after "the end of philosophy." Either directly or indirectly, Heidegger's questioning continues in the writings of Sartre, Merleau-Ponty, Levinas, Bataille, Blanchot, and Derrida. Each, in his own way, undertakes the impossible task of thinking the unthought by interrogating that which exceeds, escapes, and eludes philosophical reflection. This "unheard-of thought" subverts the constructive subject and thereby deconstructs Western philosophy. Those who write after the end of philosophy cannot avoid Hegel. On the one hand, Hegel's system is the culmination of the modern philosophy of the subject that brings the closure of the "metaphysics of presence"; on the other hand, Hegelian reason is fascinated by difference and is irresistibly drawn to the vertiginous question of the other. This is why Hegel is the last *philosopher* of the book and the first *thinker* of writing.

THE IDENTITY OF DIFFERENCE AND THE DIFFERENCE OF IDENTITY

Philosophy begins and ends with the question of the other. The question of the other is not, of course, *a* question; it is a complex of questions. In one of its earliest and most recurrent forms, the problem of the other is posed in terms of the relationship between the one and the many, or unity and plurality. From its inception in Greece, Western philosophy has, for the most part, privileged oneness and unity at the expense of manyness and plurality. Accordingly, the Western philosophical project can be understood as the repeated effort to overcome plurality and establish unity by reducing the many to the one. In the modern period, the problem of the one and the many takes the form of the correlative questions of the interplay between subjectivity and objectivity, and the interrelation of identity and difference. Hegel's speculative system represents the most comprehensive effort to resolve the questions of Western philosophy. While Hegel insists that his system is the logical and necessary outcome of the entire philosophical tradition, he acknowledges Kant's pivotal role in the emergence of "scientific" philosophy.

Surveying the course of modern thought, Kant asks: "What is enlightenment?" In response to his own question, he suggests that "enlightenment is man's release from his self-incurred tutelage. Tutelage is man's inability to make use of his understanding without direction from another. Self-incurred is this tutelage when its cause lies not in lack of reason but in lack of resolution and courage to use it without direction from another."[5] With the French Revolution but five years away, it is impossible not to recognize the political implications of Kant's position. While not uninterested in politics, Kant's primary concern is more philosophical than political. For Kant, freedom and reason are inseparable. Reason enables a person to overcome bondage and become the master of himself. Kant describes this process of self-mastery as a progression from heteronomy, i.e., determination by another, to autonomy, i.e., self-determination. Kantian reason is twofold—it is theoretical and practical.

In his analysis of theoretical reason, Kant attempts to establish the conditions of the possibility of knowledge. In the *Critique of Pure Reason*, he maintains that knowledge is the product of the synthetic activity of the knowing subject. Through apriori forms of intuition (space and time) and categories of understanding (unity, plurality, totality, reality, negation, limitation, substance/accident, cause/effect, action/patience, possibility/impossibility, existence/nonexistence, and necessity/contingency), the subject bestows unity and coherence upon the confusing manifold of sense data. Though always dependent on sense experience, the object of knowledge, in the strict sense of the term, is posited or constructed by the creative activity of the subject. Like Plato's demiurge, the knowing self gives form to matter. In the practical domain of experience, reason brings unity to the personality by subjecting multiple and conflicting sense inclinations to the directives of the apriori moral law. Reason, therefore, in both its theoretical and practical capacities, functions to create unity out of plurality and to reduce manyness to oneness.

Kant's account of theoretical and practical reason in the first two Critiques leaves unanswered the question of the relationship between these two rational functions. While reason synthesizes or unifies, it remains unclear whether reason itself is one. Moreover, insofar as reason *imposes* form upon nature (i.e., upon sensible intuition and natural inclination), the unification of subject and object is partial and the movement from heteronomy to autonomy incomplete. Kant addresses these problems in the *Critique of Judgment*. In his analysis of the work of art, he attempts to discern the original unity of theoretical and practical reason through which the identity of nature and reason can be secured and truth and freedom established. Anticipating arguments of many romantic philosophers and artists, Kant suggests that if subjectivity and objectivity were once identical, they can, in principle, be reunified. The

5. Immanuel Kant, *On History*, trans. L. W. Beck (New York: Bobbs-Merrill, 1965), 3.

demonstration of the primal unity of nature and reason, as well as nature and freedom, establishes the possibility of overcoming fragmentation and alienation by recovering the unity of experience, which has long been lost or hidden. The work of art opens the way to this original unity.

Since artistic activity is, according to Kant, "production through freedom," the artist cannot be subject to extraneous influences or determined by anything other than himself. The artist, in other words, is self-determining or autonomous. If, however, the work of art is to reconcile subject and object, the spontaneous activity of the artist cannot impose itself upon a nature that is alien to it and to which it is alien. The self-determination of the artist must not disrupt the integrity of nature. The unity of nature and reason in the work of art is possible only if subjectivity and objectivity are implicitly one. As the artist relates to himself in and through his object, so nature relates to itself in and through artistic activity. While the subjectivity of the artist realizes itself objectively, the objectivity of nature comes to completion in subjective artistic production.

Kant maintains that the identity of nature and freedom is actually present in artistic genius. Genius is *natural* talent. In creating the work of art, the genius acts naturally or spontaneously. Such spontaneity is not random, contingent, or arbitrary. To the contrary, the genius acts according to the rules, principles, or ideas with which he is naturally endowed. While the genius need not be conscious of the principles by which he creates, his work is always governed by rules. In Kant's terms: "*Genius* is the talent (natural endowment) which gives the rule to art. Since talent, as an innate productive faculty of the artist, belongs itself to nature, we may put it this way: *Genius* is the innate mental aptitude (*ingenium*) *through which* nature gives the rule to art." Nature, in other words, gives rules to the artist who, in turn, gives rules back to nature. These natural rules are not alien to the artist, but, as innate, are constitutive of his own subjectivity. Consequently, the artistic production of genius is autonomous activity in which all vestiges of heteronomy are overcome. Since original artistic activity is both natural and free, it is the self-realization rather than the violation of nature. While nature presents itself to itself through the artist, the genius presents himself to himself in his work.

The auto-affective character of artistic activity is mirrored in the auto-telic nature of the work of art. The art of genius is fine art, which Kant defines as "intrinsically final." Never pointing beyond itself, the work of art reconciles means and end in a harmonious, self-contained totality which, in a certain sense, is purposeless. The most complete form of fine art is poetry. Poetry—*poiēsis*—is a making that is essentially productive and creative. Kant prepares the way for the theory of poetry espoused by many romantics when he suggests that the original activity of the poet mimes the creativity of divine *poiēsis*. As Derrida points out, *"Mimesis* here is not the representation of one thing by another, the relation of resemblance or of identification between two beings, the reproduction of a product of nature by a product of art. It is not the relation of two products but of two productions. And of two freedoms. The artist does not imitate things in nature, or, if you will, in *natura natura*, but the acts of *natura naturans*, the operations of the *physis*. But since an analogy has already made *natura naturans* the art of an author-subject, and, one could even say, of an artist-god, *mimesis* displays the identification of human action with divine action—of one freedom with another freedom."[6]

The faculty of mind that constitutes genius an artist-god is *"Geist."*

Geist, in an aesthetic sense, signifies the animating principle in the mind. But that whereby this principle animates the psychic substance *Seele*—the material which it employs for that purpose—is that which sets the mental powers into a swing that is final, i.e. into a play which is self-maintaining and which strengthens those powers for such activity.

When the *Geist* of genius is put into play in the words of the poet, nature and reason—objectivity and subjectivity—are reconciled in a complex reflexive relationship. In artistic *Geist*, relation to other (i.e., the relation of subjectivity to objectivity and of objectivity to subjectivity) becomes self-relation and, thus, heteronomy gives way to autonomy. This self-relation is, for Kant, the ideal expression of truth and freedom.

In Hegel's speculative system, poet becomes philosopher as poetic representations are transformed into rational notions. From the time of his early work, *Differenzschrift*, Hegel defines the task of philosophy as the establishment of "the union of union and nonunion" or the securing of the identity of identity and difference. Though Kant recognizes the need to overcome personal, social, and intellectual fragmentation by mediating opposites, Hegel insists that each of the three Critiques fails to secure the reconciliation it promises. In the theoretical domain of experience, Kant's effort to uncover the conditions of the possibility of knowledge actually demonstrates the conditions of the *impossibility* of knowledge. Since the subjective forms of intuition and categories of understanding make it impossible to know reality as such, or, in Kant's terms, to grasp the thing-in-itself, the *Critique of Pure Reason* ends by confirming an unbridgeable gap between subject and object that undermines the very possibility of knowledge. In his consideration of moral activity, Kant does not reconcile inclination and obligation but merely

6. Jacques Derrida, 'Economimesis," *Diacritics* 11 (1981): 9.

exchanges slavery to an external overlord for a no less problematic bondage to an internal master in the form of the categorical imperative. Finally, Kant's argument in the third Critique fails to overcome the oppositions of the first two Critiques on at least three counts. In the first place, though the activity of the genius is rational, it is, nonetheless, unconscious. The artist "does not himself know how the *ideas* for [his work] have entered into his head." This lack of clear self-consciousness is related to what Hegel regards as the second shortcoming of Kant's analysis—his inadequate view of the nature of the artistic idea itself. The aesthetic idea is, according to Kant, irreducibly indeterminate and, hence, cannot be completely defined by any concept. For Hegel, free activity presupposes complete self-consciousness, which can be realized only in transparent conceptual knowledge. Third, and most importantly, the reconciliation of opposites embodied in the work of art remains an abstract ideal or "regulative idea" that guides and extends the synthetic activity of reason but is not concretely actualized in time and space. By setting idea and ideal over against nature and history, Kant's work of art deepens rather than resolves the oppositions that sunder human experience.

Hegel argues that if the impasse of Kant's critical philosophy is to be overcome, it is necessary to move beyond artistic representations and poetic images to conceptual reflection and rational knowledge. Hegel's task is, therefore, twofold: in the first place, he must give conceptual expression to Kant's aesthetic idea; secondly, he must establish the actuality of this speculative idea by uncovering its concrete embodiment in nature and history. Reformulating Kant's definition of poetic *Geist*, Hegel defines spirit as "that which *relates itself to itself* and is *determinate*, it is *other-being* and *being-for-self*, and in this determinateness, or in its self-externality, abides within itself; in other words, it is *in and for itself.*" In less technical language, Hegel explains that spirit is "*Pure* self-recognition in absolute otherness." This description of spirit reflects Hegel's conviction that the philosopher must try to discern the union of union and nonunion. Hegel presents his most complete formulation of the speculative principle that underlies his system in the account of the interrelation of identity and difference that he develops in the *Science of Logic*. Through a careful analysis of identity and difference, Hegel attempts to demonstrate that each contains *its own other* within itself and both are joined in a complex reflexive structure of identity-in-difference. In this dialectical definition of spirit, Hegel tries to avoid two opposite extremes. He wants neither to collapse difference in identity nor to dissolve identity in difference. It is, however, important to realize that Hegel remains true to the Western philosophical tradition and, thus, privileges unity over plurality. His overriding concern is to establish the *union* of union and nonunion and the *identity* of identity and difference.

Hegel's speculative concept is not merely a subjective idea or abstract ideal but is the actual Logos or concrete structure of everything that exists. Though always present from the beginning of the natural and historical process, this foundational structure is fully manifested only in absolute knowledge. Absolute knowledge emerges gradually through a complex process in which all dimensions of subjectivity and objectivity are progressively reconciled. To the gaze of the speculative philosopher, objectivity is but a moment in the self-development of an all-encompassing subject. This absolute subject, which Hegel also describes as *Geist*, is not an individual that stands over and against all else but is the entire natural-historical process comprehended as an evolving dialectical totality. Every particular existent is a member of, and moment in, this unfolding whole. Each individual both appears and disappears through what Hegel calls "determinate negation." Such negation is never merely negative, but always harbors a positive reserve that can be turned to constructive ends. Self-realization presupposes the act of self-negation in which implicit becomes explicit, potential becomes actual, abstract becomes concrete, and ideal becomes real. In a passage that is extremely important for both his supporters and critics, Hegel explains that "the life of spirit is not the life that shrinks from death and keeps itself untouched by devastation, but rather the life that endures it and maintains itself in it. It wins its truth only when, in utter dismemberment [*der absoluten Zerrissenheit; le déchirement absolu*], it finds itself." According to Hegel's notion of *Aufhebung*, every loss is turned to profit, for that which is negated is also preserved as a necessary moment in the self-realization of the totality of which it is an integral member. By comprehending the logical interrelation of each moment in and member of absolute subjectivity, the philosopher re-collects and inwardizes *(er-innern; Er-Innerung)* the externality and exteriority of spatial (natural) and temporal (historical) dispersion in a systematic totality from which nothing is excluded. Hegel presents what he regards as a complete exposition of this rational whole in his all-inclusive book, *Encyclopaedia of Philosophical Sciences*. To read and understand this book is to enjoy the absolute knowledge that marks the end (i.e., both *telos* and conclusion) of history.

By developing the manifold implications of the philosophy of the subject, Hegel's speculative system both constitutes the closure of the search for unity and identity that characterizes Western philosophy, and arrives at a form of certain knowledge that is supposed to overcome the doubt and uncertainty that occasioned Descartes's inward turn. In

Hegel's system, all consciousness is either implicitly or explicitly self-consciousness. In a manner similar to Kant's poetic *Geist*, Hegel's philosophical *Geist* reconciles opposites by returning difference to identity and other to same. In the life of spirit, alterity finally disappears in the full light of transparent self-consciousness and absolute knowledge.

To insist that Hegel's system forms the end of the Western philosophical tradition and the conclusion of the modern philosophy of the subject is not, of course, to imply that philosophical reflection built upon the assumptions of traditional metaphysics suddenly comes to an end. Many later thinkers see Hegel's work as a point of departure for an even more complete "scientific" philosophy of the subject. Nowhere is the continuation of the modern philosophy of subjectivity more evident than in the writings of Edmund Husserl. Though Husserl rarely draws directly on the work of Hegel, there are significant similarities between Hegelian and Husserlian phenomenology. Following Hegel, Husserl regards philosophy as a "universal science" that seeks perfect clarity and certainty by uncovering the "absolute foundations" of knowledge. Such apodictic knowledge is the product of phenomenological reflection. Insofar as phenomenology is the science of both "the totality of objectively existing beings" and what Husserl labels "transcendental subjectivity," "phenomenology properly carried through is the truly universal ontology." Nothing escapes the phenomenologist's grasp. As we shall see, it is precisely nothing, or "almost nothing," that returns to call into question Husserl's phenomenology.

In order not to misrepresent Husserl's project, it is necessary to understand exactly what he means by "phenomenon." A phenomenon is an entity *as it appears to consciousness*. The task of the phenomenologist is to *describe* all being as being-for-consciousness. This description entails a critical reassessment of what Husserl describes as the "natural attitude" of consciousness. According to common sense, objects exist in the world prior to and independent of the subject and impinge upon consciousness from without. Husserl brackets this "natural" understanding of experience through what he calls alternatively the "phenomenological reduction" or the "*epochē*." The *epochē* is, in effect, a version of Cartesian doubt through which Husserl tries to turn consciousness from *res extensa* to *res cogitans* in order to return or reduce objectivity to subjectivity. Natural consciousness is led into error and uncertainty by "forgetting" the origin of its world. Phenomenology involves the effort to recover this lost origin by disclosing the constructive activity of consciousness. Contrary to the natural attitude, Husserl maintains that every object of experience, as well as the world in which these objects appear, is the product of a constituting subject. This subject is the "transcendental ego" that projects the world of experience through its "intentional" activity. All objectivity is, therefore, constructed or constituted by the creative subject. In examining the object of consciousness, the phenomenologist does not look for empirical data (i.e., givens) but seeks the ideal Logos which, having been constructed by the transcendental subject, constitutes the objectivity of the object. Husserl labels the essential structure of the object its *"eidos."* This *eidos* is the unchanging form that secures the spatial and temporal presence of the object. "Eidetic phenomenology," Husserl explains, "is the presentation of invariant structural systems without which perception of a body and a synthetically concordant multiplicity of perceptions of one and the same body as such would be unthinkable." The Logos of the phenomenon (i.e., its *eidos*) "comes to its objectivity by means of language." In other words, language is the condition of the possibility of the ideality that establishes the identity of the object. Rather than the empirical language of a particular individual or historical community, the language that forms the medium of objectivity is itself ideal and must, therefore, be distinguished from the de facto existence of any historical language. The phenomenological reduction of the natural attitude of consciousness leads Husserl to conclude that the origin of the true world is the linguistic activity of transcendental subjectivity.

Husserl recognizes certain problems with his conclusion. He acknowledges that the reduction of objectivity to the constitutive activity of the subject is open to the charge of solipsism. Anticipating Wittgenstein's critique of private language, Husserl notes that solipsism would render impossible the very objectivity that language is supposed to secure. To overcome the difficulties created by the specter of solipsism, Husserl attempts to formulate a doctrine of intersubjectivity. Neither isolated nor idiosyncratic, creative subjectivity is common to or shared by a multiplicity of empirical subjects. At some points Husserl seems to approach Hegel's absolute subject by insisting that transcendental subjectivity is universal. Husserl's theory of intersubjectivity, however, finally fails to solve the puzzle of solipsism. After reducing the object to the subject, Husserl is unable to return to the other *as other*. The relation to other subjects is always mediated by the subject's self-relation and constituting activity. Husserl's subject, therefore, inevitably transforms the other into a mirror for itself. Like Hegel's phenomenology of spirit, Husserl's phenomenology of the subject remains a philosophy of self-consciousness founded upon a notion of reflexivity in which relation to other is self-relation. As Heidegger points out, "The transcendental reduction to absolute subjectivity gives and secures the possibility of grounding the objectivity of all objects (the Being of this being) in its valid structure and consistency, that is, in its constitution, in and through subjectivity. Thus transcendental subjectivity proves to be 'the sole absolute being.'"

While Husserl recognizes the importance of language for human experience, he never develops an extended account of its nature and use. Despite the preoccupation with language on the part of many twentieth-century philosophers, one of the most influential interpretations of language was presented by a linguist who was a contemporary of Husserl: Ferdinand de Saussure. In the writings of Saussure, language becomes the object of scientific investigation. Saussure's examination of language shares many of the assumptions of Hegel and Husserl. With Hegel, Saussure assumes that science is the systematic examination of structured relationships. The object of the linguist's study is the patterned set of relations that constitute any particular linguistic system. Recalling Hegel's distinction between the logical structure of the Idea and its concrete realization in space and time, Saussure differentiates synchronic and diachronic facets of the linguistic system. While the synchronic dimension of language is the form of the system considered apart from temporal change, the diachronic aspect of language is the historical development of the system. Unlike Hegel, Saussure maintains that the synchronic and diachronic aspects of language are not equally open to scientific investigation. Since Saussure regards temporal development as inescapably contingent and, hence, irreducibly irrational, he limits his scientific analysis to the description of the synchronic features of the language system and does not attempt to account for historical changes in the use of language.

As an understanding of Husserl's phenomenology is impossible apart from the recognition of his particular interpretation of the phenomenon, so Saussure's linguistics remains unintelligible without a clear grasp of what he means by a language system. Saussure no more identifies the object of his study with the actual linguistic usage of particular individuals than Husserl regards the object of his inquiry as the empirical data of experiencing subjects. We have seen that, for Husserl, the object of consciousness is the ideal structure that is articulated through language. The language by which the transcendental subject constructs the world is ideal and must not be confused with everyday speech. Drawing a distinction that is not unlike Husserl's contrast between ideal and empirical language, Saussure sets *la langue* against *la parole*. *La langue* designates the socially constituted system of language which, as the totality of formal structures, underlies and makes possible the actual speech events and concrete linguistic activity that Saussure names *la parole*. He explains that "in separating *langue* from *parole*, we are separating what is social from what is individual and what is essential from what is ancillary or accidental." In terms reminiscent of transcendental philosophy, *la langue* is the condition of the possibility of *la parole*. To the scientific investigator, *la parole* appears to be an expression of and, thus, reducible to *la langue*. In different terms, the linguist interprets individual temporal linguistic events as concrete realizations of a general (if not universal) atemporal system. It should be clear that this account of interpretation simultaneously points back to philosophers like Husserl, Hegel, Descartes, and even Plato, and anticipates various forms of structural analysis that emerge in the wake of Saussure's linguistics.

It is important to stress that the relationship between *la langue* and *la parole* remains intralinguistic. The synchronic system in which all linguistic activity is grounded is comprised of signs whose identity is a function of their differences from other signs. In what is perhaps the best-known line in his *Course in General Linguistics*, Saussure states that in the system of language, "there are only differences with no positive terms." Insofar as Saussure insists upon the differential character of identity, he appears to recall Hegel's analysis of the dialectical relation of identity and difference. Saussure's concern is, however, very different from that of Hegel. For Saussure, the differential nature of signs means that a sign never points beyond itself to an antecedent concept that it expresses, or to an independent idea that forms its essence. Within the structure of the sign, the signifier refers to a signified that is itself formed by its place within a differential system of signs. As Hegel's and Husserl's phenomenologist cannot pass beyond the constructive subject to the thing itself, so Saussure's linguist cannot move from the system of signs to a transcendental signified.

The continuity between Saussure's analysis of language and major currents in the philosophical tradition should not obscure the way in which his work subtly displaces some of the most important assumptions of Western thought. Four of Saussure's conclusions become especially important for later thinkers. First, Saussure insists that all signs are arbitrary conventions. There is no necessary connection or essential relation between signified and signifier. Signs are historically constituted and always subject to change. Since signifiers do not refer to preexisting concepts, signs have no essential meaning independent of the relative temporal network within which they are inscribed. Second, Saussure's concentration on synchronic rather than diachronic aspects of language implies an unavoidable tension between temporality and systematic thought. Since temporal change resists systematization, systems can be constructed only by *excluding* time. Time, in other words, disrupts every effort to establish a system. Third, Saussure reverses the modern philosophy of subjectivity by suggesting what later is described as the "decentering," "dissolution," or "deconstruction" of the subject. Instead of constituting the language that creates the world, the speaking

subject is constituted by its place within the linguistic system. Subject is
a function of system rather than system a function of subject. Finally,
Saussure's recognition of the differential nature of signs inverts the
traditional relation between identity and difference. As we have seen, for
most Western philosophy, unity and identity are primary and plurality
and difference secondary. The philosopher, therefore, attempts to derive
difference from, and return it to identity. Saussure reverses this relation
by insisting that since identity is derived from difference, the latter has a
certain priority over the former. The difference that constitutes identity
cannot be reduced to a more fundamental or primary identity. In the face
of Western philosophy's preoccupation with the identity of difference,
Saussure insists upon the difference of identity.

In many ways, Saussure's scientific linguistics remains limited by and
bound to traditional philosophical assumptions. But by stressing the
arbitrariness of the sign, the conventional nature of language, the
relativity of meaning, the breach between temporality and system, the
dissolution of the subject, and the irreducibility of difference to identity,
Saussure points beyond the closure of metaphysics. It is, however,
possible to detect other fissures in what Heidegger calls the "ontotheological tradition," which had begun to appear prior to Saussure and
Husserl. Before turning to more recent philosophical debates, it is
necessary to consider earlier critiques of idealistic and transcendental
philosophy and metaphysical speculation.

Unphilosophical Fragments

In the years immediately following his death, Hegel's system was
subjected to thoroughgoing criticism from a variety of perspectives. One
of the most devastating critiques of Hegelian philosophy was developed
by Søren Kierkegaard. Though not generally recognized, Kierkegaard
anticipates many of the most important insights of poststructuralism.
Kierkegaard's attack on Hegel rests upon two closely related premises:
his rejection of Hegel's speculative notion of identity, and his analysis of
the temporality of the individual.

Kierkegaard argues that Hegel's mediation of opposites both demands and destroys otherness. In terms of the foundational structure of
identity-in-difference, Kierkegaard maintains that *either* difference is
real and reconciliation with otherness is not actual, *or* reconciliation with
other is actual and difference is not real. On the one hand, if difference is
real, as it must be on Hegel's own terms, opposites cannot be mediated,
but must remain independent of and in unmediated antithesis to one
another. On the other hand, if Hegel's mediation of contraries is actual,
opposites are merely apparently opposite and are really identical. Kierkegaard insists that efforts to the contrary notwithstanding, Hegel

collapses difference in identity and thereby dissolves the tensions inherent in concrete human existence. The "I-am-I" that forms the telos of Hegelian idealism is, according to Kierkegaard, "a mathematical point that does not exist." In other words, the identity of thought and being that constitutes absolute knowledge is, for the existing individual, forever deferred. Under the guise of the pseudonym Johannes Climacus, Kierkegaard explains: "Not for a single moment is it forgotten that the subject is an existing individual, and that existence is a process of becoming, and that therefore the notion of the truth as identity of thought and being is a chimera of abstraction, in its truth only an expectation of the creature; not because truth is not such an identity, but because the knower is an existing individual for whom the truth cannot be such an identity as long as he lives in time. Unless we hold fast to this, speculative philosophy will immediately transport us into the fantastic realm of I-am-I, which modern speculative thought has not hesitated to use without explaining how a particular individual is related to it."

Kierkegaard's understanding of the temporality of the individual is implicit in his critique of Hegelian identity. For Kierkegaard, as for Saussure, temporality cannot be rationalized. Time, therefore, escapes every system that tries to assimilate it. In Kierkegaard's own words, "time cannot find a place within pure thought." Because the existing individual is thoroughly temporal, he can never be totally incorporated into any system. A system always leaves something out and this excessive remainder is what most interests Kierkegaard.

Since Kierkegaard regards "reality" as "an *inter-esse* between the moments of the hypothetical unity of thought and being that abstract thought presupposes," he maintains that truth is inaccessible and certainty unachievable. In an often-misunderstood phrase, Kierkegaard claims that "truth is subjectivity." To clarify this important point, he explains that *"an objective uncertainty held fast in an appropriation-process of the most passionate inwardness is the truth, the highest truth attainable for an existing individual."* Kierkegaard is convinced that the quest for certainty that drives modern philosophy from Descartes to Hegel inevitably ends in failure and frustration. Since the existing individual is *always* in the process of becoming, the closure required for certain knowledge of the truth is impossible. In all of his unsystematic writings and unscientific fragments, Kierkegaard attempts to force the reader to confront this impossibility.

Kierkegaard's analysis of Hegelianism anticipates many of the most significant features of the equally devastating critique of the dreams of philosophy that Nietzsche develops several decades later. The fragments in which Kierkegaard argues that truth is but a fantasy of pure thought become the aphorisms in which Nietzsche contends that truth is a fiction whose fictive status has been forgotten. In this way, Kierkegaard's subjectivism is transformed into Nietzsche's perspectivism. From Nietzsche's point of view, there is no exit from the labyrinth of interpretation; everything is "interpreted through and through." Consequently, there are no facts, "only interpretations." The notion of an independent truth or true world beyond the realm of appearances is a construction or projection that grows out of the effort to escape the flux of becoming and repress the disruptive movement of time.

In a certain sense, Nietzsche's perspectivism seems to repeat, while radicalizing, the philosophy of the subject developed in idealism and phenomenology. Insofar as we deal only with interpretations that are humanly constructed, consciousness seems to be entangled in precisely the kind of reflexive auto-affection that characterizes the philosophy of self-consciousness. The source of Nietzsche's perspectivism is, however, different from the foundation of speculative philosophy. Nietzsche maintains that consciousness is the effect of the interrelation of conflicting forces. Since force is inevitably relational, there can never be only one force, but always must be at least two forces. Nietzsche stresses this unavoidable duplicity by suggesting that force is actually a play of *differences* that cannot be reduced to unity or identity. This differential play recurs eternally and constitutes the condition of the possibility of all existence and every consciousness. Neither identical to nor coincident with itself, the play of differences is never present and, thus, cannot properly be known. Since something is forever missing, knowledge is always inadequate and identity incomplete. This unrepresentable remainder of difference is not a potential present that might eventually be comprehended but is the irreducible absence that renders possible all presence and every present.

As a result of the eternal return of difference, every thing is fissured and every consciousness duplicitous. Nietzsche believes that the search for truth is actually an exercise of "the will to power" through which one tries to master the uncertainties of the human condition by repressing the inevitability of fragmentation and dislocation. In what he describes as a "transvaluation of values," Nietzsche maintains that philosophers, priests, and moralists are really nihilists who, in affirming a world beyond this world, say "Nay" to life. He calls upon "immoralists" to reverse this denial by saying "No" to every such No. This radical "Yea-saying" subverts nihilism by negating its negation. Nietzsche's "gay wisdom" joyfully affirms the inescapability of incompletion and the impossibility of knowledge.

In his effort to address problems posed by what he calls the "uncanniest of all guests"—nihilism—Nietzsche, like Kierkegaard, ends by embracing the impossibility of certainty. Clearly this conclusion raises serious philosophical questions. One of the most important efforts to respond to the erosion of certainty is presented by Ludwig Wittgenstein. Wittgenstein develops two contrasting philosophical positions, each of which has exercised enormous influence on subsequent thinkers. Wittgenstein's later work is, in large measure, a critical refutation of the point of view he formulates in his early writings.

In his early work, most notably the *Tractatus*, Wittgenstein tries to overcome all forces of uncertainty by developing a "picture theory" of language. Though intended as a refutation of the relativism inherent in viewpoints like Saussure's theory of the arbitrary sign, Kierkegaard's subjectivism, and Nietzsche's perspectivism, Wittgenstein's account of language also calls into question the theory of the constructive subject. Language, Wittgenstein argues, is securely grounded in a world of experience that is accessible to everyone. This world consists of discrete facts that can be perfectly mirrored in language. "A proposition is a picture of reality" in which there is a one-to-one correspondence between the statement and what it represents. The transparency of thing to word renders meaning univocal and knowledge certain.

By the time of his *Philosophical Investigations*, Wittgenstein abandons the picture theory of language and the notion of representation upon which it is based. In reassessing his earlier position, he moves closer to exactly the viewpoint he previously had been struggling to avoid. He now argues that rather than representing an independent and antecedent state of affairs in the world, language is a game whose rules are constituted by the mutual consent of its players. Like Saussure's systems of signs, Wittgenstein's language games are social conventions. Instead of vainly trying to uncover a hidden essence common to all language games, the philosopher describes actual linguistic practice. In the course of such description, it becomes evident that language has no essence and words have no fixed meaning. The meaning of any term is a function of its use in a particular language game. Meaning, in other words, is thoroughly contextual, differential, and relative. Language games are always open-ended and forever subject to change. Meaning, therefore, is infinitely revisable and never secure. In direct opposition to the thrust of much modern philosophy, Wittgenstein insists that the variety of language games cannot be assembled into a systematic whole. Contrasting spheres of discourse are not reducible to an underlying or overarching unity and cannot be integrated within a comprehensive totality.

One of the common threads joining the early and late Wittgenstein is his abiding opposition to speculative philosophy and metaphysics. While Nietzsche asserts that "we are not rid of God because we still have faith in grammar,"[7] Wittgenstein contends that "a whole cloud of philosophy is condensed in a drop of grammar."[8] If philosophers gave up the dream of certainty and contented themselves with describing the everyday use of language, the cloud of philosophical unknowing would dissipate and metaphysics come to an end.

Though approaching their tasks from very different perspectives and with significantly different purposes, Kierkegaard, Nietzsche, and Wittgenstein share misgivings about Western philosophy in general and modern philosophy in particular. In their critiques of modernity, these "posthumous men" glimpse the confusing worlds of postmodernity. Their contrasting unphilosophical fragments sound the death knell for Western philosophy.

THE END OF PHILOSOPHY

Heidegger is acutely aware of this tolling. Fully persuaded that metaphysics has run its course, Heidegger asks what and how we are to think after the end of philosophy. As I have noted, he decides that the task remaining for the thinker is to try to think what philosophy has left unthought. Heidegger argues that "what characterizes metaphysical thinking which grounds the ground for beings is the fact that metaphysical thinking departs from what is present in its presence, and thus represents it in terms of its ground as something grounded." The search for grounding presence comes to its conclusion in modern philosophy. More specifically, metaphysics ends with the philosophy of the subject identified by Descartes and completed by Hegel and Husserl. But, Heidegger insists, "Hegel, as little as Husserl, as little as all metaphysics, does not ask about Being as Being, that is, does not raise the question of how there can be presence as such." This question becomes Heidegger's preoccupation.

The task of thinking is, then, to think the unthought that answers the question of how there can be presence as such. Heidegger defines this unthought as "the *difference* between Being and beings," or, more concisely, "difference *as* difference." In attempting to discover the Being common to all particular beings, metaphysics fails to ask how this grounding presence can itself be present. In a manner that indirectly recalls Nietzsche's differential play of forces, Heidegger argues that difference is the condition of the possibility of Being and beings. He describes this difference as "the Open." "Whether or not what is present

7. Friedrich Nietzsche, *The Portable Nietzsche*, trans. W. Kaufmann (New York: Viking Press, 1980), 483.

8. Ludwig Wittgenstein, *Philosophical Investigations*, trans. G.E.M. Anscombe (New York: The Macmillan Co., 1958), 224e.

is experienced, comprehended or presented, presence as lingering in openness, always remains dependent upon this prevalent opening. What is absent, too, cannot be as such unless it presences in the *free space of the opening.*" To linger in the open is to become articulate by emerging from darkness into light, by moving from concealment into unconcealment. This unconcealment is *alētheia*, which Heidegger identifies with truth. Truth, in this context, is not the adequation *(adequatio)* of subject and object but is the process of presencing through which Being as well as beings appear. It is important to realize that difference as such or the open itself never appears. Like Nietzsche's unrepresentable difference, Heidegger's difference makes possible all unconcealment and presence, yet is never unconcealed or present. As Heidegger explains: "The difference of Being and beings, as the differentiation of overwhelming and arrival, is the issue of the two in *unconcealing keeping in concealment.*"[9] *Alētheia*, therefore, always involves a paradoxical interplay of revelation and concealment. In the very act of revealing itself, difference conceals itself. This irreducible concealment implies that all presencing and every present entails a certain absence.

As Husserl's phenomena appear through language, so Heidegger's *alētheia*, in which Being and beings are presented, takes place in language. "The essential origin and character of all language is," for Heidegger, expressed in the Greek notion of Logos. As the means by which the event of unconcealment takes place, the Logos "lets lie before us what lies before us as such, it discloses what is present in its presencing."[10] It is important to realize that the unconcealment effected through the Logos includes both a centrifugal and a centripetal rhythm. On the one hand, the Logos differentiates Being and beings and establishes the differences among particular beings. On the other hand, the Logos gathers and assembles differences or "draws and joins together what is held apart."[11] Heidegger tries to capture the complementary rhythms of the Logos with his notion of the "same." The "same," Heidegger insists, solves the problem left unresolved by Hegel and the rest of the philosophical tradition. It is the mean between identity and difference in which difference does not disappear in identity and identity is not lost in difference. Heidegger argues that "the identical always moves toward the absence of difference, so that everything may be reduced to a common denominator. The same, by contrast, is the

9. Heidegger, *Identity and Difference*, 65.

10. Martin Heidegger, *Early Greek Thinking*, trans. D. Krell and F. Capuzzi (New York: Harper and Row, 1975), 70.

11. Martin Heidegger, *Poetry, Language, Thought*, trans. A. Hofstader (New York: Harper and Row, 1971), 204.

belonging together of what differs, through a gathering by way of the difference. We can only say 'the same' if we think difference."[12] To think what philosophy leaves unthought, one must think difference as difference rather than as covert or implicit identity. Difference *as* difference necessarily entails a separating that is a joining and a joining that is a separating. This difference that simultaneously divides and gathers is what Heidegger means by the "same."

The Logos achieves its fullest expression in "the speech of mortals." All speech is not, however, equally revealing. Heidegger privileges poetic language and maintains that art is the domain of truth. In rejecting Hegel's contention that truth comes to completion only when the artistic image becomes the philosophical concept, Heidegger returns to Kant's recognition of the inseparability of poetry and truth. When considering Heidegger's account of "the origin of the work of art," it is necessary to understand the word "work" in at least two ways. "Work" is both the art object and the process by which that object comes to be or originates. The origin of the work (noun) of art is the work (verb) of art. In Heidegger's apparent tautology, "the origin of art is art." The work of art, in both senses of the word, is *alētheia*. "*All art*, as the letting happen of the advent of the truth of what is, is, as such, *essentially poetry*. The nature of art, on which both the art work and the artist depend, is the setting itself-into-work of truth. It is due to the art's poetic nature that, in the midst of what is, art breaks open an open place, in whose openness everything is other than usual." By embodying what Heidegger describes as "the primal conflict" between concealment and unconcealment, (the) poetic work "holds open the Open," thereby creating the difference that allows Being and beings to appear. In this way, art "directs our thinking to the realm which the key words of metaphysics— Being and beings, the ground and what is grounded—are no longer adequate to utter."[13] Art, poetic art, allows us to think what metaphysics cannot think and what, therefore, the entire Western philosophical tradition leaves unthought. To think this "unheard-of thought" is to end philosophy.

But does philosophy really end with Heidegger? Does Heidegger, malgré lui, remain committed to the philosophical tradition he seeks to dismantle? It is clear that in struggling to think the unthought, Heidegger tries to think philosophy's other. Yet does he still think this other *philosophically* or even *metaphysically*, and, thus, not think it *as other*? Insofar as Heidegger continues to value unity over plurality, he remains

---

12. Heidegger, *Poetry, Language, Thought*, 218.
13. Heidegger, *Identity and Difference*, 71.

true to the most important assumption of Western philosophy. Though intended to overcome metaphysical notions of identity, Heidegger's concept of the same approaches the notion of identity-in-difference that Hegel develops in response to what he regards as Schelling's inadequate "philosophy of identity." The Logos that articulates Heidegger's same is, like the Hegelian Logos, a "primal phenomenon," that *draws and joins together* what is held apart in separation." By attempting to think difference as same, Heidegger seems to extend the philosophical search for origins. In exploring the difference left unthought by philosophy, Heidegger seeks what he explicitly labels an "essential origin." From this point of view, the problem with the traditional notion of Being, as well as its modern manifestation in phenomenology's "principle of principles" (i.e., transcendental subjectivity), is that both Being and subjectivity are *insufficiently* primordial, and, hence, cannot provide a proper foundation for thinking. As a more original origin, difference can answer the question of how presence becomes present.

Re-Se-Voir

The preceding remarks suggest that it is possible to read Heidegger's work as an extension rather than a subversion of metaphysical thinking. If Heideggerian thought ends with the Logos that "joins together what is held apart," then his interpretation of the task of thinking seems to be congruent with Hegel's view of the purpose of philosophy as the establishment of the union of union and nonunion. Heidegger's difference might, therefore, be understood as yet another variation of the structure of reflexivity that lies at the base of the modern philosophy of the subject and comes to full expression in the phenomenology of self-consciousness. When understood in this way, it remains unclear whether Heidegger adequately addresses the problem of difference and the question of the other.

An alternative to Heidegger's effort to step "beyond" metaphysics might be to return to the problem of subjectivity to see whether self-consciousness itself harbors conditions that make its complete realization impossible. This line of analysis is developed in different ways by Sartre and Merleau-Ponty. Though in serious disagreement on many important philosophical issues, Sartre and Merleau-Ponty are persuaded that Heidegger, like Hegel and Husserl, fails to give a satisfactory account of difference and otherness and therefore cannot solve the problem of solipsism.

Sartre devotes much of his major work, *Being and Nothingness*, to a consideration of problems raised by the relation between self and other. While sensitive to multiple dimensions of alterity, Sartre is particularly interested in dilemmas posed by the self's relation to other subjects. He argues that Heidegger's effort to respond to the difficulties in Husserl's doctrine of intersubjectivity through the analysis of "being-with [*Mitsein*]" remains caught in the impasse of solipsism. Though not immediately evident, the early Heidegger, like his teacher Husserl, takes as his point of departure the knowing subject which, through intentional activity and resolute projects, constitutes its world. This constructed world becomes the condition of the possibility of all experience. Within this world, the relationship to other subjects is always mediated by the subject's own activity.

In order to break out of this circle of self-reflection and to relate to the other subject as other, the other must be "transcendent," or, more precisely, "extramundane." Since everything "in" one's world is constituted and mediated by the self itself, the relation to the extramundane other must be "immediate." The other is immediately present to the subject in an awareness that is nonconstitutive. As soon as immediacy gives way to mediacy, other is reduced to same. Sartre's point can be put differently: in the relation to the other, the subject is never active but is absolutely passive. This passivity is most profoundly experienced in "the gaze of the other."

[I]nsofar as I experience myself as looked-at, there is realized for me a trans-mundane presence of the Other. The Other looks at me not as he is 'in the midst' of *my* world but as he comes toward the world and toward me from all his transcendence; when he looks at me, he is separated from me by no distance, by no object of the world—whether real or ideal—by no body in the world, but by the sole fact of his nature as Other. Thus the appearance of the Other's look is not an appearance *in the world*—neither in 'mine' nor in the 'Other's'—and the relation which unites me to the Other cannot be a relation of exteriority inside the world. By the Other's look I effect the concrete proof that there is a 'beyond the world.' The Other is present to me without any intermediary as a transcendence *which is not mine.* But this presence is not reciprocal.

The gaze of the other effects an alteration in the subject toward whom it is directed. Through the eyes of the other, the subject suffers objectification. In Sartre's language, the other transforms "being-for-itself" into "being-in-itself" through "being-for-others." Since it presupposes both being-for-itself and being-in-itself, self-consciousness inevitably entails relationships with others. In an effort to invert the notion of the constituting subject, Sartre contends that instead of deriving otherness from itself, the subject is, in an important sense, derived from an other over which it has no control. In contrast to Hegel, who argues that the reflexive relation to other makes self-identity concrete and self-reconciliation actual, Sartre maintains that the nonreciprocal relation to other fissures self-identity and makes self-reconciliation impossible.

In reflection in fact if I do not succeed in apprehending myself as an object but only as a quasi-object, this is because I am the object which I wish to grasp; I have to be the nothingness which separates me from myself. I can escape my selfness neither by taking a point of view on myself . . . nor by apprehending myself in the form of 'there is' (here the recovery fails because the recoverer is to himself the recovered). In the case of being-for-others, on the contrary, the scissiparity is pushed further; the (reflection-reflecting) reflected is radically distinct from the (reflection-reflecting) reflecting and thereby can be an object for it. But this time the recovery fails because the recovered is *not* the one recovering. Thus the totality which is not what it is but which is what it is not, would—as the result of a radical attempt at wrenching away from self—everywhere produce its being as an 'elsewhere.' The scattering of being-in-itself of a shattered totality, always elsewhere, always at a distance, never in itself, but always maintained in being by the perpetual explosion of this totality—such would be the being of others and of myself as other.

Within the time of human existence, this scattered totality is never re-collected (cf. Hegel's *Er-Innerung*). The perfect reconciliation of being-for-itself and being-in-itself is possible only for God. But for Sartre, unlike for Hegel, God is unreal and man is not God.

According to Merleau-Ponty, the impossibility of effecting the total coincidence of the for-itself and the in-itself is built into the very structure of self-consciousness. Merleau-Ponty's critique of the reflexive philosophy of subjectivity rests on two closely related insights: the necessary relation between self-consciousness and perception, and the irreducible temporality of self-consciousness. Building upon Sartre's insistence that the "Cartesian *cogito*" presupposes a "pre-reflective *cogito*," Merleau-Ponty proceeds to develop a careful analysis of the bodily conditions of perception. While consciousness is rooted in perception, which, in turn, is always bodily, neither perception nor the body is transparent to self-consciousness. The body remains opaque and perception can never be perceived.

The reasons for the impossibility of perceiving perception become clear in Merleau-Ponty's account of what he labels "*sur-réflexion*" or "hyper-reflection." For Merleau-Ponty, as for Heidegger, the philosophy of reflection initiated by Descartes is fully realized in Hegelian and Husserlian phenomenology. By analyzing the constructive subject, the phenomenologist attempts to turn consciousness back on itself to create true self-consciousness. The problem with this effort to return consciousness to itself as self-consciousness lies in the "re" of the turn. This "re" points to an inevitable delay that makes it impossible for consciousness to re-capture or re-collect itself. Always coming second and arriving too late, "reflection recuperates everything except itself as an effort of recuperation, it clarifies everything except its own role." In an unusually suggestive passage, Merleau-Ponty argues:

Once one is settled in it, reflection is an inexpugnable philosophical position, every obstacle, every resistance to its exercise being from the first treated not as an adversity of the things but as a simple state of non-thought, a gap in the continuous fabric of the acts of thought, which is inexplicable, but about which there is nothing to say since it is literally *nothing*. But are we to enter into reflection? In its inaugural act is concealed a decision to play a double game which, once unmasked, divests it of its apparent evidence; in one move the philosophical lie is perpetuated with which one first pays for this henceforth invulnerable method. It is essential to the reflective analysis that it start from a *de facto* situation. . . . The search for the conditions of possibility is in principle posterior to an actual experience, and from this it follows that even if subsequently one determines rigorously the *sine qua non* of that experience, it can never be washed of the original stain of having been discovered *post festum* nor ever become what positively founds that experience. . . . Never will the philosophy of reflection be able to install itself in the mind it discloses, whence to see the world as its correlative. Precisely because it is reflection, re-turn, re-conquest, or re-covery, it cannot flatter itself that it would simply coincide with a constitutive principle already at work in the spectacle of the world, that, starting with this spectacle, it would travel the very route that the constitutive principle had followed in the opposite direction.

The "re" of the re-turn, re-collection, or re-cuperation opens a gap that self-consciousness cannot close. In different terms, the re-se-voir of the subject creates an excessive reservoir that self-consciousness never exhausts. The slippage between departure and return creates a delay that opens the space of hyper-reflection. Unlike the dialectic of reflection, which reconciles opposites, hyper-reflection issues in a "hyper-dialectic," which, rather than synthesizing contraries, discloses the contradictions, antinomies, and aporia of reflection. Merleau-Ponty's "dialectic without synthesis" discloses the "blind spot" of "the mind's eye." This blind spot will reappear in a different form in what Bataille describes as "the blind spot of Hegelianism."

OTHER QUESTIONS

From Kierkegaard's attack on Hegel to Merleau-Ponty's critique of the philosophy of reflection, time threatens to fault the identity of the subject and to interrupt the presence of the present. Recognizing the importance of time for the phenomenology of subjectivity, Husserl presents a detailed investigation of temporality in *The Phenomenology of Internal Time-Consciousness*. Despite the complexity of his analysis, Husserl never really questions the traditional account of time in terms of presence and the present. Later thinkers, most notably certain French writers, develop a different interpretation of time, which eventually calls into question the entire Western metaphysics of presence. This other time can already be glimpsed in Merleau-Ponty's phenomenology of perception and analysis of hyper-reflection. The delay of consciousness's return to itself exposes a gap, which, Merleau-Ponty argues, points to "a kind of original past, a past which has never been present."[14]

In *Otherwise than Being or Beyond Essence*, Emmanuel Levinas explores a variety of questions related to the lapse of time. By drawing extensively on certain strands in the Jewish theological tradition, Levinas suggests unexpected resources and unanticipated implications of many recent philosophical and critical debates. Following Heidegger's analysis of "thrownness," Sartre's consideration of the gaze of the other, and Merleau-Ponty's account of return and delay, Levinas argues that the present of consciousness is always related to an unrecoverable past. This past is not a past present, i.e., a past that once was present, but is an absolute past—"a past more ancient than any present." Since this "unrepresentable before" remains foreign to every present, it cannot be recuperated or recovered. For Levinas, the past that never was or is present signals "a lapse of time that does not return, a diachrony refractory to all synchronization, a transcending diachrony."[15] To say that the "deep formerly" does not return is not to imply that it no longer remains. To the contrary, the absolute past is "always already there" and is, therefore, without beginning. In Levinas's terms, this past is "pre-original" and "an-archic." The anarchy of the past disrupts the present and disturbs the self.

Since this past is never present and eludes all presence, it must be thought as "otherwise than being or beyond essence." Being's "other" is not, however, nothing or nonbeing. "The statement of being's *other*, of the otherwise than being, claims to state a difference over and beyond that which separates being from nothingness—the very difference of the *beyond*, the difference of transcendence" (p. 3). This transcendent "beyond" is *radically* other or "absolutely heteronomous." As a past that can never be re-collected (*er-innern*), Levinas's other is an absolute exterior that cannot be interiorized (*er-innern*). This other, which is forever beyond being and nonbeing, constitutes subjectivity. Over against Kant, who describes self-realization as the movement from heteronomy

14. Maurice Merleau-Ponty, *Phénoménologie de la perception* (Paris: Gallimard, 1945), 71.

15. Emmanuel Levinas, *Otherwise than Being, or Beyond Essence*, trans. A. Lingis (Boston: Martinus Nijhoff, 1968), 9. Throughout the rest of this section, references to this work are cited in the text.

to autonomy, and Hegel, who sees self-fulfillment as the auto-affection of self-consciousness, Levinas insists that the subject must *patiently* suffer "hetero-affection" in "absolute passivity." This suffering is not simply the converse of the activity of the intentional subject; it is a "total passivity" that lies beyond or "beneath the level of activity and passivity" (p. 110). Rather than self-constituting, the subject is constituted by, and subject to *(sub-jacere)* an other over which it has no control. Recalling Sartre's gaze of the other, Levinas argues that "subjectivity as *the other in the same*, as an inspiration, is the putting into question of all affirmation for-oneself, all egoism born again in this very recurrence" (p. 111). The other that "inspires" and "haunts" the same cannot be interiorized or assimilated. Alterity is inside as an outside—interior as an exterior—that "obsesses" subjectivity. Neither present nor absent, the other is "proximate." The proximity of the other is, paradoxically, closer than every presence yet more remote than every absence. Such proximity is unsettling for it "is not a state, a repose, but a restlessness, null site, outside the place of rest." Never present and, thus, not re-presentable, the other is "incommensurable with consciousness" and can be glimpsed, if at all, only as "a trace of the *who knows where*" (p. 100).

The subject responds to the passing trace of the other by a "saying" that is not governed by the principle of presence and rules of representation. For Levinas, "Language permits us to utter, be it by betrayal, this *outside of being*, this *ex-ception* to being, as though being's other were an event of being" (p. 6). In saying, language, in a certain sense, "unsays itself" and by so doing utters the unutterable. "This saying . . . is bound to an irrecuperable, unrepresentable past, temporalizing according to a time with separate epochs, in a diachrony. An analysis that starts with proximity, irreducible to consciousness of. . . , and describable, if possible, as an inversion of its intentionality, will recognize this responsibility to be a substitution" (p. 47). Levinas's notion of substitution leads to an account of signification that breaks with the concept of *mimēsis* characteristic of most earlier views of language. In saying, signs are substitutions for what is never present. Signs, in other words, are always signs of signs. Levinas acknowledges that "signification, as one-for-the-other in passivity, where the other is not assumed by the one, presupposes the possibility of pure non-sense invading and threatening signification" (p. 50). For Levinas, this insignificant non-sense recalls both "Nietzsche's poetic writing" and Bataille's "laughter which refuses language" (p. 8).

It is obvious that the "pure non-sense" of saying forces a revision of the ordinary notion of communication. In this context, communication is not a closed circuit in which information passes from one self-conscious agent to another. In saying, the speaker himself becomes a sign of something that he *cannot* know and can never represent. By exposing an irreducible outside that is always inside, language turns the speaker "inside out." Saying, therefore, faults the identity of the subject by exposing self to other. "This being torn up from oneself in the core of one's unity, this absolute noncoinciding, this diachrony of the instant, signifies in the form of one-penetrated-by-the-other" (p. 49). Such openness to the other is what Levinas means by communication. "Communication," he argues, "is an adventure of subjectivity, different from that which is dominated by the concern to recover itself, different from that of coinciding in consciousness; it will involve uncertainty. It is by virtue of its eidos possible only in sacrifice, which is the approach of him for which one is responsible" (p. 120). With the recognition of the interplay between non-sensical communication and sacrifice, one approaches the transgressive domain explored by Bataille.

In Bataille's texts, Levinas's question of the other is reinscribed in a "heterology" that uncovers "the blind spot of Hegelianism." All of Bataille's writings reflect the lasting impression left upon his thinking by Kojève's lectures on Hegel. By drawing on an unusually wide range of philosophical, theological, literary, artistic, sociological, and anthropological materials, Bataille develops an extended, albeit often indirect, critique of Hegelianism and all he believes it represents. From Bataille's point of view, the heart of Hegel's philosophy is captured in a few lines in the preface to the *Phenomenology* to which I have already referred: "But the life of spirit is not the life that shrinks from death and keeps itself untouched by devastation, but rather the life that endures it and maintains itself in it. It wins its truth only when, in utter dismemberment, it finds itself." Despite this recognition of the importance of negation, Bataille insists that Hegel is unable to do justice to the radicality of negativity and, therefore, represses the experiences of death, sacrifice, expenditure, loss, and meaninglessness. In the Hegelian dialectic, every negative harbors a positive reserve. Through the process of sublation *(Aufhebung)*, negation is negated and expenditure is turned to profit. For Bataille, the history of Western theology and philosophy, of which Hegel is the culmination, represents so many efforts to exclude the negative in its multiple guises. What Hegel cannot tolerate is senseless sacrifice, meaningless loss, and profitless expenditure. Constructed upon the religious belief in crucifixion and resurrection, Hegel's dialectic *works* by transforming loss into gain. Since this dialectical process is intended to be all-encompassing, there is supposed to be nothing left out, no lingering remainder—nothing *désoeuvré*, no *hors d'oeuvre*. The closure of absolute knowledge overcomes time by a-mortizing death *(la mort)* itself.

Bataille, like his precursor, Kierkegaard, is fascinated by excessive remains that cannot be incorporated or assimilated within the system—Hegelian or otherwise. Preoccupied with what Hegel excludes (i.e., death, negation, sacrifice, expenditure, loss, meaninglessness, laughter, etc.), Bataille seeks a "Hegelianism without reserve"—a Hegelianism in which negativity is absolute and, hence, conceals neither latent positivity nor unexpended reserves. While Hegel struggles to find the way in which spirit can return from its dismemberment to itself, Bataille follows Nietzsche by gaily affirming *le déchirement absolu* in the experience of total loss or expenditure without return. Such sacrifice is realized in what Bataille calls *"l'expérience intérieure* [interior experience]." It is important to stress that the interiority of this experience does not set it against an outer world from which it is separated. *L'expérience intérieure* transgresses all boundaries and escapes the contrasts and distinctions that characterize ordinary experience. In Bataille's heterology, alterity is not simply the contrary of identity. No longer caught in the circuit of reciprocal exchange, interior experience involves a radical exteriority that is different from identity *and* difference, and is other than same *and* other. *L'expérience intérieure* is the experience of absolute difference, which can be suffered only in excesses like death, eroticism, and *le rire déchirant*.

Unlike Sartre's immediate experience of the transmundane other, Bataille's *l'expérience intérieure* is neither immediate nor mediate. Ungraspable in and unmasterable by the binary opposites that structure cognitive experience, the absolute difference of interior experience is totally unrecognizable and utterly unknowable. Like the inexplicable contingency suggested by "a throw of the die [*un coup de dés*]," *dépense* inflicts a wound *(un coup)* upon language that "ruptures discourse" by undoing thought *(dé-pense)*. While Hegel always works from the unknown to the known, which is fully comprehended in absolute knowledge, Bataille slips and slides *(glisse)* from the known to the unknown, which is incompletely experienced in absolute nonknowledge.

Nonknowledge cannot, of course, be communicated philosophically. Recalling Levinas's claim that saying utters the unutterable by unsaying itself, Bataille maintains that *poésie* is transgressive language that risks anarchy by saying nothing. In contrast to the sensible and meaningful language of the philosopher, the words of the poet are meaningless non-sense. Poetry sacrifices language itself by inscribing the irreducible absence of meaning. Unlike Heidegger's poetry and Levinas's saying, Bataille's *poésie* cannot be spoken; it must be *written*. As Derrida explains:

This writing folds itself in order to link up with classical concepts—insofar as they are inevitable. . . .—in such a way that these concepts, through a certain twist, apparently obey their habitual laws; but they do so while relating themselves, at a certain point, to the moment of sovereignty, to the absolute loss of their meaning, to expenditure without reserve, to what can no longer even be called negativity or loss of meaning except on its philosophical side; thus, they relate themselves to a nonmeaning which is beyond absolute meaning, beyond the closure or the horizon of absolute knowledge. Carried away in this calculated sliding, concepts become nonconcepts, they are unthinkable, they become *untenable*. . . . The philosopher is blind to Bataille's text because he is a philosopher only through the desire to hold on, to *maintain* his certainty of himself and the security of the concept as security against sliding. For him, Bataille's text is full of traps: it is, in the initial sense of the word, a *scandal*. The transgression of meaning is not an access to the immediate and indeterminate *identity* of a nonmeaning, nor is it an access to the possibility of *maintaining* nonmeaning. Rather, we would have to speak of an *epochē* of the epoch of meaning, of a—written—putting between brackets that suspends the epoch of meaning: the opposite of a phenomenological *epochē*, for this latter is carried out *in the name and in sight of* meaning. The phenomenological *epochē* is a reduction that pushes us back toward meaning. Sovereign transgression is a reduction of this reduction: not a reduction to meaning, but a reduction of meaning.[16]

Forever beyond the epoch of meaning, Bataille's excessive writing points to "The Absence of the Book."

THE SPACE-TIME OF LITERATURE

In 1948, Sartre asked, "What is literature?" Though few have agreed with the answer Sartre proposed, many have repeatedly returned to his question. In the years following the publication of Heidegger's highly influential essay "The End of Philosophy and the Task of Thinking," several important French writers have brought together Sartre's question about literature and Heidegger's question about thinking. It is possible, some argue, to think what philosophy leaves unthought by thinking literature. But Sartre's question remains: What *is* literature? In thinking about literature, how can one think philosophy's other? The relation between the interrogations of Sartre and Heidegger can be clarified by transposing Sartre's question: What are the space and time of literature? The answer that has emerged over the past four decades is that the space and time of literature are space and time. In literature, however, space and time are thought otherwise than philosophically or common sensically. Literary space-time is a space without presence and a time without the present. This ungraspable space and incomprehensible time are the

16. Jacques Derrida, *Writing and Difference*, trans. A. Bass (Chicago: University of Chicago Press, 1978), 267–68.

space and time of the other. In this other space and time, space is timed and time spaced. Literature inscribes "the exteriority of presence" in what Blanchot describes as "the point where time and space rejoin themselves in the original disjunction."[17] This exteriority—this disjunction that is left unthought by philosophy—is *written* in literature.

In *The Space of Literature*, Blanchot asks: *"Is Art a Thing of the Past?"* This question recalls Hegel's insistence that art *is* a thing of the past. As we have seen, Hegel transforms Kant's poetry to form a speculative system in which artistic images and representations give way to transparent philosophical concepts. For the last philosopher of the book, the total presence of the concept is realized in the *Encyclopaedia of Philosophical Sciences*. Blanchot summarizes the logic of the book:

> the book: totality or Work. But with increasing refinement and truth these forms all assume that the book contains knowledge as the presence of something virtually present and always immediately accessible, if only with the help of mediations and relays. Something is there which the book presents in presenting itself and which reading animates, which reading reestablishes—through its animation—in the life of a presence. Something that is, on the lowest level, the presence of a content or of a signified thing; then, on a higher level, the presence of a form, of a signifying thing or of an operation; and on a higher level still, the development of a system of relations that is always there already, if only as a future possibility. The book rolls up time, unrolls time, and contains this unrolling as the continuity of a presence in which past and future become actual.

While "the time of the book is determined by the beginning-end relation . . . the space of the book [is] determined by deployment from a center." The book's space is presence, its time the present. From the Bible to the *Encyclopaedia*, the book tries to master space-time.

In a certain sense, Blanchot agrees with Hegel: art *is* a thing of the past. Blanchot's past, however, differs radically from the past of Hegel. Over against Hegel, for whom the past is a past present that can be re-presented, and in agreement with Levinas, for whom the "unrepresentable before" is "more ancient than any present," Blanchot maintains that the past is the "dreadfully ancient [*l'effroyablement ancien*]," which is "always lacking the present."[18] Art, he argues, has led us "to a time before the world, before the beginning. It has cast us out of our power to begin and to end; it has turned us toward the outside where there is no intimacy, no place to rest. It has led us into the infinite migration of error. For we seek art's essence, and it lies where the nontrue admits of nothing essential. . . . It ruins the origin by returning to it the errant

17. Maurice Blanchot, *L'Entretien infini* (Paris: Gallimard, 1969) 65.
18. Maurice Blanchot, *Le Pas au-delà* (Paris: Gallimard, 1973), 25, 23.

immensity of directionless eternity."[19] This "time before time" is "outside of time in time [*hors de temps dans temps*]." As an outside that is
inside, without being interiorized (*er-innern*), the dreadfully ancient,
like Bataille's *l 'expérience intérieure*, is "the exteriority that excludes all
exterior and interior."[20] While this exterior is never present (though it is
not absent), it returns repeatedly to disrupt every present and all presence. In a fragment on Nietzsche's eternal return, Blanchot writes:

> The "re" of return inscribed as the "ex," opening of all exteriority: as if
> the return would mark, rather than putting an end to exile, the beginning
> and recommencement of the exodus. The return, this would be in coming
> again to ex-center, to err. Only *nomadic* affirmation *remains*.[21]

Excluded from the pages of the book, nomad thought "affirms itself only
in writing."

This exteriority, which is "always exterior to itself," recalls the lapse
of time described by Merleau-Ponty and Levinas. For Blanchot, the lapse
is *le dehors* that discloses the spacing of time. The "pure exteriority" of
the irreducible "before" opens a gap in time that makes presence impossible. With the recognition of the impossibility of presence, the
space of time becomes the time of space. Time faults spatial identity by
insinuating an irreducible absence in the midst of all presence. Taken
together, the spacing of time and the timing of space open the interval
where one suffers "the vertigo of spacing [*le vertige de l'espacement*]."
Blanchot defines this interval—the original disjunction of time and
space—as "*la différence*." "The exteriority thus affirmed is not tranquil
spatial and temporal continuity, the continuity of which the logic of the
logos—the discourse without discursus—gives us the key. The exteriority—time and space—is always exterior to itself. It is not correlative,
center of correlations, but institutes the relation from an interruption
that does not unify. Difference is the reservoir of the outside; the outside
is the exposition of difference; difference and outside designate the
original disjunction—the origin which is the disjunction itself and
always disjoins from itself. The disjunction, where time and space rejoin
themselves in disjoining themselves, coincides with that which does not
coincide, the noncoincident which in advance diverts [*détourne*] all
unity."[22]

The writer writes this difference "because writing is difference,

---

19. Maurice Blanchot, *The Space of Literature*, trans. A. Smock (Lincoln, Nebraska:
University of Nebraska Press, 1982), 244.
20. Blanchot, *Le Pas au-delà*, 54.
21. Ibid., 49.
22. Blanchot, *L'Entretien infini*, 242.

because difference writes."[23] "What summons us to write," Blanchot
maintains, "is the attraction of (pure) exteriority." This exteriority, this
unthought difference, cannot be comprehended by incorporation within
the philosopher's systematic work (i.e., labor as well as *oeuvre*). Like
Bataille's expenditure, the writer's labor never works. "To write is to
produce absence of the work (worklessness [*le désoeuvrement*]). Or: writing
is the absence of the work as it *produces itself* through the work and
throughout the work. Writing as worklessness (in the active sense of the
word) is the insane game, the indeterminancy that lies between reason
and unreason." With Levinas, Bataille and others, Blanchot insists that
the writer risks saying nothing. Writing, however, always seems to fail.
Though the writer represents nothing, he can only write *almost* nothing.
This inevitable failure leaves the writer in inescapable error. "Error,"
writes Blanchot, "means wandering, the inability to abide and stay. For
where the wanderer is, the conditions of a definitive here are lacking. In
this absence of here and now what happens does not clearly come to pass
as an event based upon which something solid could be achieved.
Consequently, what happens does not happen, but does not pass either,
into the past; it is never passed. It happens and recurs without cease; it is
the horror and the confusion and the uncertainty of eternal repetition. It
is not one truth or another that lacks, or truth in general; nor is it doubt
that leads us on or despair that immobilizes us. The wanderer's country
is not truth, but exile; he lives outside."[24]

Blanchot's *différence* becomes Derrida's *différance*—one of "the unheard-of thoughts" with which Derrida tries to think "beyond absolute
knowledge" by rethinking Nietzsche's and Heidegger's difference. Or
perhaps Derrida's *différance* is reinscribed as Blanchot's *différence*. One
cannot be certain. In this increasingly tangled textual labyrinth—a maze
in which work(s) overflow (*déborde*) their bounds—questions of origin,
influence, and parentage are, *in a certain sense*, irrelevant. In one of the
few essays in which Derrida (implicitly) acknowledges the legitimacy of
the genealogical question, he situates deconstruction by suggesting the
relation of his "notion" of *la différance* to various concepts or nonconcepts developed by Hegel, Nietzsche, Saussure, Freud, and Heidegger. The list is, of course, incomplete. Deconstruction is, among other
things, a critical rereading of all Western philosophy in which Derrida
tries to dismantle (the) tradition, *as if* from within, by tracing philosophy's other. When Derrida asks: "How do we conceive the outside of a
text?" he at once repeats and displaces Heidegger's question: "What has
philosophy left unthought?" Like Heidegger, Derrida responds that

23. Ibid., 247.
24. Blanchot, *The Space of Literature*, 238.

philosophy does not, indeed *cannot*, think difference. But for Derrida, as for many others, Heidegger's difference is insufficiently different from the difference of metaphysics. Along with writers like Sartre, Merleau-Ponty, Levinas, Bataille, and Blanchot, Derrida attempts to think the unthinkable by thinking difference *as* difference and other *as* other. This difference, irreducible to identity—this other, irreducible to same, is an alterity that "exceeds the alternative of presence and absence." The non-present and non-presence of *différance* are suggested by the duplicity of the word *'différer'*. *Différer* carries both temporal and spatial connotations. "To differ" is, in the first place, "to temporalize, to resort, consciously or unconsciously, to the temporal and temporalizing mediation of a detour that suspends the accomplishment or fulfillment of 'desire' or 'will,' or carries desire or will out in a way that annuls or tempers their effect. . . . The other sense of 'to differ' is the most common and most identifiable, the sense of not being identical, of being other, of being discernible, etc. And in 'differents,' whether referring to the alterity of dissimilarity or the alterity of allergy or of polemics, it is necessary that interval, distance, *spacing* occur among the different elements and occur actively, dynamically, and with a certain perseverence in repetition." For Derrida as for Blanchot, the time and space of *différance* meet (which is not to say unite) in the opening of the interval. Derrida explains:

Constituting itself, dynamically dividing itself, this interval is what could be called *spacing*; time's becoming-spatial or space's becoming-temporal *(temporalizing)*. And it is this constitution of the present as a "primordial" and irreducibly nonsimple, and, therefore, in the strict sense nonprimordial, synthesis of traces, retentions, and protensions (to reproduce here, analogically and provisionally, a phenomenological and transcendental language that will presently be revealed as inadequate) that I proposed to call protowriting, prototrace, or *différance*. The latter (is) (both) spacing (and) temporalizing.

The trace, which can be written but not spoken in the silent "a" of *différance*, shows the inadequacy of the phenomenological and transcendental language in which philosophy ends. From its beginning, Western philosophy points toward the constructive subject that is always remaking the world in its own image. As such, philosophy transforms theology into anthropology. The implications of ontotheology become explicit in Hegel's identification of man with God. By attempting to de-construct both the constructive subject and the horrifying world it has created, Derrida points beyond the certainty of absolute knowledge to the uncertainty of postmodernity. Always arriving late, forever coming second, and never returning on time, deconstruction repeatedly demonstrates the impossibility of modernity by soliciting the other which, though never present, "always already" haunts presence. As the end of modernity, deconstruction is postmodern; Derrida is the postman whose letters bear a message that never arrives. Postmodernity is not, however, another epoch in the very historical chain that deconstruction interrupts. Like the dreadfully ancient other, postmodernity is always already past. In the space-time of writing, every age is a post-age. Postmodern awareness is born of the recognition that the past that was never present eternally returns as the future that never arrives to displace all contemporaneity and defer forever the presence of the modern. As the "ex" that is the sign of this eternal re-turn, the postmodern writer cannot stop writing.

In time's absence what is new renews nothing; what is present is not contemporary; what is present presents nothing, but represents itself and belongs henceforth and always to return. It isn't, but comes back again. It comes already and forever past, so that my relation to it is not one of cognition, but of recognition, and this recognition ruins in me the power of knowing, the right to grasp. It makes what is ungraspable inescapable; it never lets me cease reaching what I cannot attain. And that which I cannot take, I must take up again, never to let go.[25]

The obsession of writing: *différance*, preface, *hors d'oeuvre*, border, limen, hymen, tympan, frame, margin . . . Literature writes the end of philosophy by writing without end

25. Ibid., 29–30.

Critique of Judgment

Analytic of the Sublime

23. TRANSITION FROM THE FACULTY OF ESTIMATING THE BEAUTIFUL TO THAT OF ESTIMATING THE SUBLIME

The beautiful and the sublime agree on the point of pleasing on their own account. Further they agree in not presupposing either a judgment of sense or one logically determinant, but one of reflection. Hence it follows that the delight does not depend upon a sensation, as with the agreeable, nor upon a definite concept, as does the delight in the good, although it has, for all that, an indeterminate reference to concepts. Consequently the delight is connected with the mere presentation or faculty of presentation, and is thus taken to express the accord, in a given intuition, of the faculty of presentation, or the imagination, with the *faculty of concepts* that belongs to understanding or reason, in the sense of the former assisting the latter. Hence both kinds of judgments are *singular*, and yet such as profess to be universally valid in respect of every Subject, despite the fact that their claims are directed merely to the feeling of pleasure and not to any knowledge of the object.

There are, however, also important and striking differences between the two. The beautiful in nature is a question of the form of the object, and this consists in limitation, whereas the sublime is to be found in an object even devoid of form, so far as it immediately involves, or else by its presence provokes, a representation of *limitlessness*, yet with a super-added thought of its totality. Accordingly the beautiful seems to be regarded as a presentation of an indeterminate concept of understanding, the sublime as a presentation of an indeterminate concept of reason. Hence the delight is in the former case coupled with the representation of *Quality*, but in this case with that of *Quantity*. Moreover, the former delight is very different from the latter in kind. For the beautiful is

Excerpted from Immanuel Kant, *Critique of Judgment*, translated by J. C. Meredith (New York: Oxford University Press, 1973), 90–94, 162–203.

directly attended with a feeling of the furtherance of life, and is thus compatible with charms and a playful imagination. On the other hand, the feeling of the sublime is a pleasure that only arises indirectly, being brought about by the feeling of a momentary check to the vital forces followed at once by a discharge all the more powerful, and so it is an emotion that seems to be no sport, but dead earnest in the affairs of the imagination. Hence charms are repugnant to it; and, since the mind is not simply attracted by the object, but is also alternately repelled thereby, the delight in the sublime does not so much involve positive pleasure as admiration or respect, i.e., merits the name of a negative pleasure.

But the most important and vital distinction between the sublime and the beautiful is certainly this: that if, as is allowable, we here confine our attention in the first instance to the sublime in Objects of nature, (that of art being always restricted by the conditions of an agreement with nature,) we observe that whereas natural beauty (such as is self-subsisting) conveys a finality in its form making the object appear, as it were, preadapted to our power of judgment, so that it thus forms of itself an object of our delight, that which, without our indulging in any refinements of thought, but, simply in our apprehension of it, excites the feeling of the sublime, may appear, indeed, in point of form to contravene the ends of our power of judgment, to be ill-adapted to our faculty of presentation, and to be, as it were, an outrage on the imagination, and yet it is judged all the more sublime on that account.

From this it may be seen at once that we express ourselves on the whole inaccurately if we term any *Object of nature* sublime, although we may with perfect propriety call many such objects beautiful. For how can that which is apprehended as inherently contra-final be noted with an expression of approval? All that we can say is that the object lends itself to the presentation of a sublimity discoverable in the mind. For the sublime, in the strict sense of the word, cannot be contained in any sensuous form, but rather concerns ideas of reason, which, although no adequate presentation of them is possible, may be excited and called into the mind by that very inadequacy itself which does admit of sensuous presentation. Thus the broad ocean agitated by storms cannot be called sublime. Its aspect is horrible, and one must have stored one's mind in advance with a rich stock of ideas, if such an intuition is to raise it to the pitch of a feeling which is itself sublime—sublime because the mind has been incited to abandon sensibility, and employ itself upon ideas involving higher finality.

Self-subsisting natural beauty reveals to us a technic of nature which shows it in the light of a system ordered in accordance with laws the principle of which is not to be found within the range of our entire faculty of understanding. This principle is that of a finality relative to the employment of judgment in respect of phenomena which have thus to be assigned, not merely to nature regarded as aimless mechanism, but also to nature regarded after the analogy of art. Hence it gives a veritable extension, not, of course, to our knowledge of Objects of nature, but to our conception of nature itself—nature as mere mechanism being enlarged to the conception of nature as art—an extension inviting profound inquiries as to the possibility of such a form. But in what we are wont to call sublime in nature there is such an absence of anything leading to particular objective principles and corresponding forms of nature, that it is rather in its chaos, or in its wildest and most irregular disorder and desolation, provided it gives signs of magnitude and power, that nature chiefly excites the ideas of the sublime. Hence we see that the concept of the sublime in nature is far less important and rich in consequences than that of its beauty. It gives on the whole no indication of anything final in nature itself, but only in the possible *employment* of our intuitions of it in inducing a feeling in our own selves of a finality quite independent of nature. For the beautiful in nature we must seek a ground external to ourselves, but for the sublime one merely in ourselves and the attitude of mind that introduces sublimity into the representation of nature. This is a very needful preliminary remark. It entirely separates the ideas of the sublime from that of a finality of *nature*, and makes the theory of the sublime a mere appendage to the aesthetic estimate of the finality of nature, because it does not give a representation of any particular form in nature, but involves no more than the development of a final employment by the imagination of its own representation.

24. SUBDIVISION OF AN INVESTIGATION OF THE FEELING OF THE SUBLIME

In the division of the moments of an aesthetic estimate of objects in respect of the feeling of the sublime, the course of the Analytic will be able to follow the same principle as in the analysis of judgments of taste. For, the judgment being one of the aesthetic reflective judgment, the delight in the sublime, just like that in the beautiful, must in its *Quantity* be shown to be universally valid, in its *Quality* independent of interest, in its *Relation* subjective finality, and the latter, in its *Modality*, necessary. Hence the method here will not depart from the lines followed in the preceding section: unless something is made of the point that there, where the aesthetic Judgment bore on the form of the Object, we began with the investigation of its Quality, whereas here, considering the formlessness that may belong to what we call Sublime, we begin with that of its Quantity, as first moment of the aesthetic judgment on the sublime—a divergence of method the reason for which is evident from § 23.

But the analysis of the sublime obliges a division not required by that of the beautiful, namely one into the *mathematically* and the *dynamically* sublime.

For the feeling of the sublime involves as its characteristic feature a mental *movement* combined with the estimate of the object, whereas taste in respect of the beautiful presupposes that the mind is in *restful* contemplation, and preserves it in this state. But this movement has to be estimated as subjectively final (since the sublime pleases). Hence it is referred through the imagination either to the *faculty of cognition* or to that of *desire*; but to whichever faculty the reference is made the finality of the given representation is estimated only in respect of these faculties (apart from end or interest). Accordingly the first is attributed to the Object as a *mathematical*, the second as a *dynamical*, affection of the imagination. Hence we get the above double mode of representing an Object as sublime. . . .

43. ART IN GENERAL

1. *Art* is distinguished from *nature* as making [*facere*] is from acting or operating in general [*agere*], and the product or the result of the former is distinguished from that of the latter as *work* [*opus*] from operation [*effectus*].

By right it is only production through freedom, i.e., through an act of will that places reason at the basis of its action, that should be termed art. For, although we are pleased to call what bees produce (their regularly constructed cells) a work of art, we only do so on the strength of an analogy with art; that is to say, as soon as we call to mind that no rational deliberation forms the basis of their labor, we say at once that it is a product of their nature (of instinct), and it is only to their Creator that we ascribe it as art.

If, as sometimes happens, in a search through a bog, we light on a piece of hewn wood, we do not say it is a product of nature but of art. Its producing cause had an end in view to which the object owes its form. Apart from such cases, we recognize an art in everything formed in such a way that its actuality must have been preceded by a representation of the thing in its cause (as even in the case of the bees), although the effect could not have been *thought* by the cause. But where anything is called absolutely a work of art, to distinguish it from a natural product, then some work of man is always understood.

2. *Art*, as human skill, is distinguished also from *science* (as *ability* from *knowledge*), as a practical from a theoretical faculty, as technic from theory (as the art of surveying from geometry). For this reason, also,

what one *can* do the moment one only *knows* what is to be done, hence without anything more than sufficient knowledge of the desired result, is not called art. To art that alone belongs for which the possession of the most complete knowledge does not involve one's having then and there the skill to do it. *Camper* describes very exactly how the best shoe must be made, but he, doubtless, was not able to turn one out himself.[1]

3. *Art* is further distinguished from *handicraft*. The first is called *free*, the other may be called *industrial art*. We look on the former as something which could only prove final (be a success) as play, i.e., an occupation which is agreeable on its own account; but on the second as labor, i.e., a business, which on its own account is disagreeable (drudgery), and is only attractive by means of what it results in (e.g., the pay), and which is consequently capable of being a compulsory imposition. Whether in the list of arts and crafts we are to rank watchmakers as artists, and smiths on the contrary as craftsmen, requires a standpoint different from that here adopted—one, that is to say, taking account of the proportion of the talents which the business undertaken in either case must necessarily involve. Whether, also, among the so-called seven free arts some may not have been included which should be reckoned as sciences, and many, too, that resemble handicraft, is a matter I will not discuss here. It is not amiss, however, to remind the reader of this: that in all free arts something of a compulsory character is still required, or, as it is called, a *mechanism*, without which the *soul*, which in art must be *free*, and which alone gives life to the work, would be bodyless and evanescent (e.g., in the poetic art there must be correctness and wealth of language, likewise prosody and meter). For not a few leaders of a newer school believe that the best way to promote a free art is to sweep away all restraint, and convert it from labor into mere play.

44. FINE ART

There is no science of the beautiful, but only a Critique. Nor, again, is there an elegant [*schöne*] science, but only a fine [*schöne*] art. For a science of the beautiful would have to determine scientifically, i.e., by means of proofs, whether a thing was to be considered beautiful or not; and the judgment upon beauty, consequently, would, if belonging to science, fail to be a judgment of taste. As for a beautiful science—a science which, as such, is to be beautiful, is a nonentity. For if, treating it as a science, we were to ask for reasons and proofs, we would be put off with

---

1. In my part of the country, if you set a common man a problem like that of Columbus and his egg, he says, "There is no art in that, it is only science," i.e., you *can* do it if you know *how*; and he says just the same of all the would-be arts of jugglers. To that of the tight-rope dancer, on the other hand, he has not the least compunction in giving the name of art.

elegant phrases *bons mots*. What has given rise to the current expression *elegant sciences* is, doubtless, no more than this, that common observation has, quite accurately, noted the fact that for fine art, in the fullness of its perfection, a large store of science is required, as, for example, knowledge of ancient languages, acquaintance with classical authors, history, antiquarian learning, etc. Hence these historical sciences, owing to the fact that they form the necessary preparation and groundwork for fine art, and partly also owing to the fact that they are taken to comprise even the knowledge of the products of fine art (rhetoric and poetry), have by a confusion of words, actually got the name of elegant sciences.

Where art, merely seeking to actualize a possible object to the *cognition* of which it is adequate, does whatever acts are required for that purpose, then it is *mechanical*. But should the feeling of pleasure be what it has immediately in view it is then termed *aesthetic* art. As such it may be either *agreeable* or *fine* art. The description "agreeable art" applies where the end of the art is that the pleasure should accompany the representations considered as mere *sensations*, the description "fine art" where it is to accompany them considered as *modes of cognition*.

Agreeable arts are those which have mere enjoyment for their object. Such are all the charms that can gratify a dinner party: entertaining narrative, the art of starting the whole table in unrestrained and sprightly conversation, or with jest and laughter inducing a certain air of gaiety. Here, as the saying goes, there may be much loose talk over the glasses, without a person wishing to be brought to book for all he utters, because it is only given out for the entertainment of the moment, and not as a lasting matter to be made the subject of reflection or repetition. (Of the same sort is also the art of arranging the table for enjoyment, or, at large banquets, the music of the orchestra—a quaint idea intended to act on the mind merely as an agreeable noise fostering a genial spirit, which, without any one paying the smallest attention to the composition, promotes the free flow of conversation between guest and guest.) In addition must be included play of every kind which is attended with no further interest than that of making the time pass by unheeded.

Fine art, on the other hand, is a mode of representation which is intrinsically final, and which, although devoid of an end, has the effect of advancing the culture of the mental powers in the interests of social communication.

The universal communicability of a pleasure involves in its very concept that the pleasure is not one of enjoyment arising out of mere sensation, but must be one of reflection. Hence aesthetic art, as art which is beautiful, is one having for its standard the reflective judgment and not organic sensation.

45. Fine Art is an Art, so Far as it Has at the Same Time the Appearance of being Nature

A product of fine art must be recognized to be art and not nature. Nevertheless the finality in its form must appear just as free from the constraint of arbitrary rules as if it were a product of mere nature. Upon this feeling of freedom in the play of our cognitive faculties—which play has at the same time to be final—rests that pleasure which alone is universally communicable without being based on concepts. Nature proved beautiful when it wore the appearance of art; and art can only be termed beautiful, where we are conscious of its being art, while yet it has the appearance of nature.

For, whether we are dealing with beauty of nature or beauty of art, we may make the universal statement: *that is beautiful which pleases in the mere estimate of it* (not in sensation or by means of a concept). Now art has always got a definite intention of producing something. Were this "something," however, to be mere sensation (something merely subjective), intended to be accompanied with pleasure, then such product would, in our estimation of it, only please through the agency of the feeling of the senses. On the other hand, were the intention one directed to the production of a definite object, then, supposing this were attained by art, the object would only please by means of a concept. But in both cases the art would please, not in *the mere estimate of it*, i.e., not as fine art, but rather as mechanical art.

Hence the finality in the product of fine art, intentional though it be, must not have the appearance of being intentional; i.e., fine art must be clothed *with the aspect* of nature, although we recognize it to be art. But the way in which a product of art seems like nature, is by the presence of perfect *exactness* in the agreement with rules prescribing how alone the product can be what it is intended to be, but with an absence of *labored effect* (without academic form betraying itself), i.e., without a trace appearing of the artist having always had the rule present to him and of its having fettered his mental powers.

46. Fine Art is the Art of Genius

Genius is the talent (natural endowment) which gives the rule to art. Since talent, as an innate productive faculty of the artist, belongs itself to nature, we may put it this way: *Genius* is the innate mental aptitude (*ingenium*) *through which* nature gives the rule to art.

Whatever may be the merits of this definition, and whether it is merely arbitrary, or whether it is adequate or not to the concept usually associated with the word *genius* (a point which the following sections have to clear up), it may still be shown at the outset that, according to this acceptation of the word, fine arts must necessarily be regarded as arts of *genius*.

For every art presupposes rules which are laid down as the foundation which first enables a product, if it is to be called one of art, to be represented as possible. The concept of fine art, however, does not permit of the judgment upon the beauty of its product being derived from any rule that has a *concept* for its determining ground, and that depends, consequently, on a concept of the way in which the product is possible. Consequently fine art cannot of its own self excogitate the rule according to which it is to effectuate its product. But since, for all that, a product can never be called art unless there is a preceding rule, it follows that nature in the individual (and by virtue of the harmony of his faculties) must give the rule to art, i.e., fine art is only possible as a product of genius.

From this it may be seen that genius (1) is a *talent* for producing that for which no definite rule can be given: and not an aptitude in the way of cleverness for what can be learned according to some rule; and that consequently *originality* must be its primary property. (2) Since there may also be original nonsense, its products must at the same time be models, i.e., be *exemplary*; and, consequently, though not themselves derived from imitation, they must serve that purpose for others, i.e., as a standard or rule of estimating. (3) It cannot indicate scientifically how it brings about its product, but rather gives the rule as *nature*. Hence, where an author owes a product to his genius, he does not himself know how the *ideas* for it have entered into his head, nor has he it in his power to invent the like at pleasure, or methodically, and communicate the same to others in such precepts as would put them in a position to produce similar products. (Hence, presumably, our word *Genie* is derived from *genius*, as the peculiar guardian and guiding spirit given to a man at his birth, by the inspiration of which those original ideas were obtained.) (4) Nature prescribes the rule through genius not to science but to art, and this also only in so far as it is to be fine art.

47. ELUCIDATION AND CONFIRMATION OF THE ABOVE EXPLANATION OF GENIUS

Everyone is agreed on the point of the complete opposition between genius and the *spirit of imitation*. Now since learning is nothing but imitation, the greatest ability, or aptness as a pupil (capacity), is still, as such, not equivalent to genius. Even though a man weaves his own thoughts or fancies, instead of merely taking in what others have thought, and even though he go so far as to bring fresh gains to art and science, this does not afford a valid reason for calling such a man of *brains*, and often great brains, a *genius*, in contradistinction to one who goes by the name of *shallow-pate*, because he can never do more than merely learn and follow a lead. For what is accomplished in this way is something that *could* have been learned. Hence it all lies in the natural path of investigation and reflection according to rules, and so is not specifically distinguishable from what may be acquired as the result of industry backed up by imitation. So all that *Newton* has set forth in his immortal work on the Principles of Natural Philosophy may well be learned, however great a mind it took to find it all out, but we cannot learn to write in a true poetic vein, no matter how complete all the precepts of the poetic art may be, or however excellent its models. The reason is that all the steps that Newton had to take from the first elements of geometry to his greatest and most profound discoveries were such as he could make intuitively evident and plain to follow, not only for himself but for every one else. On the other hand no *Homer* or *Wieland* can show how his ideas, so rich at once in fancy and in thought, enter and assemble themselves in his brain, for the good reason that he does not himself know, and so cannot teach others. In matters of science, therefore, the greatest inventor differs only in degree from the most laborious imitator and apprentice, whereas he differs specifically from one endowed by nature for fine art. No disparagement, however, of those great men, to whom the human race is so deeply indebted, is involved in this comparison of them with those who on the score of their talent for fine art are the elect of nature. The talent for science is formed for the continued advances of greater perfection in knowledge, with all its dependent practical advantages, as also for imparting the same to others. Hence scientists can boast a ground of considerable superiority over those who merit the honor of being called geniuses, since genius reaches a point at which art must make a halt, as there is a limit imposed upon it which it cannot transcend. This limit has in all probability been long since attained. In addition, such skill cannot be communicated, but requires to be bestowed directly from the hand of nature upon each individual, and so with him it dies, awaiting the day when nature once again endows another in the same way—one who needs no more than an example to set the talent of which he is conscious at work on similar lines.

Seeing, then, that the natural endowment of art (as fine art) must furnish the rule, what kind of rule must this be? It cannot be one set down in a formula and serving as a precept—for then the judgment upon the beautiful would be determinable according to concepts. Rather must the rule be gathered from the performance, i.e., from the product, which others may use to put their own talent to the test, so as to let it serve as a model, not for *imitation*, but for *following*. The possibility of this is difficult to explain. The artist's ideas arouse like ideas on the part of his pupil, presuming nature to have visited him with a like proportion of the mental powers. For this reason the models of fine art are the only means of handing down this art to posterity. This is something which cannot be done by mere descriptions (especially not in the line of the arts of speech), and in these arts, furthermore, only those models can become classical of which the ancient, dead languages, preserved as learned, are the medium.

Despite the marked difference that distinguishes mechanical art, as an art merely depending upon industry and learning, from fine art, as that of genius, there is still no fine art in which something mechanical, capable of being at once comprehended and followed in obedience to rules, and consequently something *academic*, does not constitute the essential condition of the art. For the thought of something as end must be present, or else its product would not be ascribed to an art at all, but would be a mere product of chance. But the effectuation of an end necessitates determinate rules which we cannot venture to dispense with. Now, seeing that originality of talent is one (though not the sole) essential factor that goes to make up the character of genius, shallow minds fancy that the best evidence they can give of their being full-blown geniuses is by emancipating themselves from all academic constraint of rules, in the belief that one cuts a finer figure on the back of an ill-tempered than of a trained horse. Genius can do no more than furnish rich *material* for products of fine art; its elaboration and its *form* require a talent academically trained, so that it may be employed in such a way as to stand the test of judgment. But, for a person to hold forth and pass sentence like a genius in matters that fall to the province of the most patient rational investigation, is ridiculous in the extreme. One is at a loss to know whether to laugh more at the imposter who envelops himself in such a cloud—in which we are given fuller scope to our imagination at the expense of all use of our critical faculty,—or at the simpleminded public which imagines that its inability clearly to cognize and comprehend this masterpiece of penetration is due to its being invaded by new truths *en masse*, in comparison with which, detail, due to carefully weighed exposition and an academic examination of root-principles, seems to it only the work of a tyro.

48. THE RELATION OF GENIUS TO TASTE

For *estimating* beautiful objects, as such, what is required is *taste*; but for fine art, i.e., the *production* of such objects, one needs *genius*.

If we consider genius as the talent for fine art (which the proper signification of the word imports), and if we would analyze it from this point of view into the faculties which must concur to constitute such a talent, it is imperative at the outset accurately to determine the difference between beauty of nature, which it only requires taste to estimate, and beauty of art, which requires genius for its possibility (a possibility to which regard must also be paid in estimating such an object).

A beauty of nature is a *beautiful thing*; beauty of art is a *beautiful representation* of a thing.

To enable me to estimate a beauty of nature, as such, I do not need to be previously possessed of a concept of what sort of a thing the object is intended to be, i.e., I am not obliged to know its material finality (the end), but, rather, in forming an estimate of it apart from any knowledge of the end, the mere form pleases on its own account. If, however, the object is presented as a product of art, and is as such to be declared beautiful, then, seeing that art always presupposes an end in the cause (and its causality), a concept of what the thing is intended to be must first of all be laid at its basis. And, since the agreement of the manifold in a thing with an inner character belonging to it as its end constitutes the perfection of the thing, it follows that in estimating beauty of art the perfection of the thing must be also taken into account—a matter which in estimating a beauty of nature, as beautiful, is quite irrelevant.—It is true that in forming an estimate, especially of animate objects of nature, e.g., of a man or a horse, objective finality is also commonly taken into account with a view to judgment upon their beauty; but then the judgment also ceases to be purely aesthetic, i.e., a mere judgment of taste. Nature is no longer estimated as it appears like art, but rather in so far as it actually *is* art, though superhuman art; and the teleological judgment serves as basis and condition of the aesthetic, and one which the latter must regard. In such a case, where one says, for example, "that is a beautiful woman," what one in fact thinks is only this, that in her form nature excellently portrays the ends present in the female figure. For one has to extend one's view beyond the mere form to a concept, to enable the object to be thought in such manner by means of an aesthetic judgment logically conditioned.

Where fine art evidences its superiority is in the beautiful descriptions it gives of things that in nature would be ugly or displeasing. The Furies, diseases, devastations of war, and the like, can (as evils) be very beautifully described, nay even represented in pictures. One kind of ugliness alone is incapable of being represented conformably to nature without destroying all aesthetic delight, and consequently artistic beauty, namely, that which excites *disgust*. For, as in this strange sensation, which depends purely on the imagination, the object is represented as insisting, as it were, upon our enjoying it, while we still set our face against it, the artificial representation of the object is no longer distinguishable from the nature of the object itself in our sensation, and so it cannot possibly be regarded as beautiful. The art of sculpture, again, since in its products art is almost confused with nature, has excluded from its creations the direct representation of ugly objects, and, instead, only sanctions, for example, the representation of death (in a beautiful genius), or of the warlike spirit (in Mars), by means of an allegory, or attributes which wear a pleasant guise, and so only indirectly, through an interpretation on the part of reason, and not for the pure aesthetic judgment.

So much for the beautiful representation of an object, which is properly only the form of the presentation of a concept, and the means by which the latter is universally communicated. To give this form, however, to the product of fine art, taste merely is required. By this the artist, having practiced and corrected his taste by a variety of examples from nature or art, controls his work and, after many, and often laborious, attempts to satisfy taste, finds the form which commends itself to him. Hence this form is not, as it were, a matter of inspiration, or of a free swing of the mental powers, but rather of a slow and even painful process of improvement, directed to making the form adequate to his thought without prejudice to the freedom in the play of those powers.

Taste is, however, merely a critical, not a productive faculty; and what conforms to it is not, merely on that account, a work of fine art. It may belong to useful and mechanical art, or even to science, as a product following definite rules which are capable of being learned and which must be closely followed. But the pleasing form imparted to the work is only the vehicle of communication and a mode, as it were, of execution, in respect of which one remains to a certain extent free, notwithstanding being otherwise tied down to a definite end. So we demand that table appointments, or even a moral dissertation, and, indeed, a sermon, must bear this form of fine art, yet without its appearing *studied*. But one would not call them on this account works of fine art. A poem, a musical composition, a picture-gallery, and so forth, would, however, be placed under this head; and so in a would-be work of fine art we may frequently recognize genius without taste, and in another taste without genius.

49. The Faculties of the Mind which Constitute Genius

Of certain products which are expected, partly at least, to stand on the footing of fine art, we say they are *soul*less; and this, although we find nothing to censure in them as far as taste goes. A poem may be very pretty and elegant, but is soulless. A narrative has precision and method, but is soulless. A speech on some festive occasion may be good in substance and ornate withal, but may be soulless. Conversation frequently is not devoid of entertainment, but yet soulless. Even of a woman we may well say, she is pretty, affable, and refined, but soulless. Now what do we here mean by "soul"?

"Soul" [*Geist*] in an aesthetical sense, signifies the animating principle in the mind. But that whereby this principle animates the psychic substance [*Seele*]—the material which it employs for that purpose—is that which sets the mental powers into a swing that is final, i.e., into a play which is self-maintaining and which strengthens those powers for such activity.

Now my proposition is that this principle is nothing else than the faculty of presenting *aesthetic ideas*. But, by an aesthetic idea I mean that representation of the imagination which induces much thought, yet without the possibility of any definite thought whatever, i.e., *concept*, being adequate to it, and which language, consequently, can never get quite on level terms with or render completely intelligible.—It is easily seen, that an aesthetic idea is the counterpart (pendant) of a *rational idea*, which, conversely, is a concept, to which no *intuition* (representation of the imagination) can be adequate.

The imagination (as a productive faculty of cognition) is a powerful agent for creating, as it were, a second nature out of the material supplied to it by actual nature. It affords us entertainment where experience proves too commonplace; and we even use it to remodel experience, always following, no doubt, laws that are based on analogy, but still also following principles which have a higher seat in reason (and which are every whit as natural to us as those followed by the understanding in laying hold of empirical nature). By this means we get a sense of our freedom from the law of association (which attaches to the empirical employment of the imagination), with the result that the material can be borrowed by us from nature in accordance with that law, but be worked up by us into something else—namely, what surpasses nature.

Such representations of the imagination may be termed *ideas*. This is partly because they at least strain after something lying out beyond the confines of experience, and so seek to approximate to a presentation of rational concepts (i.e., intellectual ideas), thus giving to these concepts the semblance of an objective reality. But, on the other hand, there is this most important reason, that no concept can be wholly adequate to them as internal intuitions. The poet essays the task of interpreting to sense the rational ideas of invisible beings, the kingdom of the blessed, hell, eternity, creation, etc. Or, again, as to things of which examples occur in experience, e.g., death, envy, and all vices, as also love, fame, and the like, transgressing the limits of experience he attempts with the aid of an imagination which emulates the display of reason in its attainment of a maximum, to body them forth to sense with a completeness of which nature affords no parallel; and it is in fact precisely in the poetic art that the faculty of aesthetic ideas can show itself to full advantage. This faculty, however, regarded solely on its own account, is properly no more than a talent (of the imagination).

If, now, we attach to a concept a representation of the imagination belonging to its presentation, but inducing solely on its own account such a wealth of thought as would never admit of comprehension in a definite concept, and, as a consequence, giving aesthetically an unbounded expansion to the concept itself, then the imagination here displays a creative activity, and it puts the faculty of intellectual ideas (reason) into motion—a motion, at the instance of a representation, towards an extension of thought, that, while germane, no doubt, to the concept of the object, exceeds what can be laid hold of in that representation or clearly expressed.

Those forms which do not constitute the presentation of a given concept itself, but which, as secondary representations of the imagination, express the derivatives connected with it, and its kinship with other concepts, are called (aesthetic) *attributes* of an object, the concept of which, as an idea of reason, cannot be adequately presented. In this way Jupiter's eagle, with the lightning in its claws, is an attribute of the mighty king of heaven, and the peacock of its stately queen. They do not, like *logical attributes*, represent what lies in our concepts of the sublimity and majesty of creation, but rather something else—something that gives the imagination an incentive to spread its flight over a whole host of kindred representations that provoke more thought than admits of expression in a concept determined by words. They furnish an *aesthetic idea*, which serves the above rational idea as a substitute for logical presentation, but with the proper function, however, of animating the mind by opening out for it a prospect into a field of kindred representations stretching beyond its ken. But it is not alone in the arts of painting or sculpture, where the name of attribute is customarily employed, that fine art acts in this way; poetry and rhetoric also derive the soul that animates their works wholly from the aesthetic attributes of the objects—attributes which go hand in hand with the logical, and give the imagination an impetus to bring more thought into play in the matter, though in an undeveloped manner, than allows of being brought within the embrace of a concept, or, therefore, of being definitely formulated in language.—For the sake of brevity I must confine myself to a few examples only. When the great king [Frederick the Great] expresses himself in one of his poems by saying:

> Oui, finissons sans trouble, et mourons sans regrets,
> En laissant l'Univers comblé de nos bienfaits.
> Ainsi l'Astre du jour, au bout de sa carrière,

Répand sur l'horizon une douce lumière,
Et les derniers rayons qu'il darde dans les airs
Sont les derniers soupirs qu'il donne à l'Univers;

he kindles in this way his rational idea of a cosmopolitan sentiment even at the close of life, with the help of an attribute which the imagination (in remembering all the pleasures of a fair summer's day that is over and gone—a memory of which pleasures is suggested by a serene evening) annexes to that representation, and which stirs up a crowd of sensations and secondary representations for which no expression can be found. On the other hand, even an intellectual concept may serve, conversely, as attribute for a representation of sense, and so animate the latter with the idea of the supersensible; but only by the aesthetic factor subjectively attaching to the consciousness of the supersensible being employed for the purpose. So, for example, a certain poet says in his description of a beautiful morning: "The sun arose, as out of virtue rises peace." The consciousness of virtue, even where we put ourselves only in thought in the position of a virtuous man, diffuses in the mind a multitude of sublime and tranquilizing feelings, and gives a boundless outlook into a happy future, such as no expression within the compass of a definite concept completely attains.[2]

In a word, the aesthetic idea is a representation of the imagination, annexed to a given concept, with which, in the free employment of imagination, such a multiplicity of partial representations are bound up, that no expression indicating a definite concept can be found for it—one which on that account allows a concept to be supplemented in thought by much that is indefinable in words, and the feeling of which quickens the cognitive faculties, and with language, as a mere thing of the letter, binds up the spirit (soul) also.

The mental powers whose union in a certain relation constitutes *genius* are imagination and understanding. Now, since the imagination, in its employment on behalf of cognition, is subjected to the constraint of the understanding and the restriction of having to be conformable to the concept belonging thereto, wheras aesthetically it is free to furnish of its own accord, over and above that agreement with the concept, a wealth of undeveloped material for the understanding, to which the latter paid no

2. Perhaps there has never been a more sublime utterance, or a thought more sublimely expressed, than the well-known inscription upon the Temple of *Isis* (Mother *Nature*): "I am all that is, and that was, and that shall be, and no mortal hath raised the veil from before my face." Segner made use of this idea in a suggestive vignette on the frontispiece of his *Natural Philosophy*, in order to inspire his pupil at the threshold of that temple into which he was about to lead him, with such a holy awe as would dispose his mind to serious attention.

regard in its concept, but which it can make use of, not so much objectively for cognition, as subjectively for quickening the cognitive faculties, and hence also indirectly for cognitions, it may be seen that genius properly consists in the happy relation, which science cannot teach nor industry learn, enabling one to find out ideas for a given concept, and, besides, to hit upon the *expression* for them—the expression by means of which the subjective mental condition induced by the ideas as the concomitant of a concept may be communicated to others. This latter talent is properly that which is termed soul. For to get an expression for what is indefinable in the mental state accompanying a particular representation and to make it universally communicable—be the expression in language or painting or statuary—is a thing requiring a faculty for laying hold of the rapid and transient play of the imagination, and for unifying it in a concept (which for that very reason is original, and reveals a new rule which could not have been inferred from any preceding principles or examples) that admits of communication without any constraint of rules.

If, after this analysis, we cast a glance back upon the above definition of what is called *genius*, we find: *First*, that it is a talent for art—not one for science, in which clearly known rules must take the lead and determine the procedure. *Secondly*, being a talent in the line of art, it presupposes a definite concept of the product—as its end. Hence it presupposes understanding, but, in addition, a representation, indefinite though it be, of the material, i.e., of the intuition, required for the presentation of that concept, and so a relation of the imagination to the understanding. *Thirdly*, it displays itself, not so much in the working out of the projected end in the presentation of a definite *concept*, as rather in the portrayal, or expression of *aesthetic ideas* containing a wealth of material for effecting that intention. Consequently the imagination is represented by it in its freedom from all guidance of rules, but still as final for the presentation of the given concept. *Fourthly*, and lastly, the unsought and undesigned subjective finality in the free harmonizing of the imagination with the understanding's conformity to law presupposes a proportion and accord between these faculties such as cannot be brought about by any observance of rules, whether of science or mechanical imitation, but can only be produced by the nature of the individual.

Genius, according to these presuppositions, is the exemplary originality of the natural endowments of an individual in the *free* employment of his cognitive faculties. On this showing, the product of a genius (in respect of so much in this product as is attributable to genius, and not to possible learning or academic instruction,) is an example, not for imitation (for that would mean the loss of the element of genius, and just the very soul of the work), but to be followed by another genius—one whom it arouses to a sense of his own originality in putting freedom from the constraint of rules so into force in his art, that for art itself a new rule is won—which is what shows a talent to be exemplary. Yet, since the genius is one of nature's elect—a type that must be regarded as but a rare phenomenon—for other clever minds his example gives rise to a school, that is to say a methodical instruction according to rules, collected, so far as the circumstances admit, from such products of genius and their peculiarities. And, to that extent, fine art is for such persons a matter of imitation, for which nature, through the medium of a genius, gave the rule.

But this imitation becomes *aping* when the pupil *copies* everything down to the deformities which the genius only of necessity suffered to remain, because they could hardly be removed without loss of force to the idea. This courage has merit only in the case of a genius. A certain *boldness* of expression, and, in general, many a deviation from the common rule becomes him well, but in no sense is it a thing worthy of imitation. On the contrary it remains all through intrinsically a blemish, which one is bound to try to remove, but for which the genius is, as it were, allowed to plead a privilege, on the ground that a scrupulous carefulness would spoil what is inimitable in the impetuous ardor of his soul. *Mannerism* is another kind of aping—an aping of *peculiarity* (originality) in general, for the sake of removing oneself as far as possible from imitators, while the talent requisite to enable one to be at the same time *exemplary* is absent.—There are, in fact, two modes [*modi*] in general of arranging one's thoughts for utterance. The one is called a *manner* [*modus aestheticus*], the other a *method* [*modus logicus*]. The distinction between them is this: the former possesses no standard other than the *feeling* of unity in the presentation, whereas the latter here follows definite *principles*. As a consequence the former is alone admissible for fine art. It is only, however, where the manner of carrying the idea into execution in a product of art is *aimed at* singularity instead of being made appropriate to the idea, that *mannerism* is properly ascribed to such a product. The ostentatious [*précieux*], forced, and affected styles, intended to mark one out from the common herd (though soul is wanting), resemble the behavior of a man who, as we say, hears himself talk, or who stands and moves about as if he were on a stage to be gaped at—action which invariably betrays a tyro.

50. THE COMBINATION OF TASTE AND GENIUS IN PRODUCTS OF FINE ART

To ask whether more stress should be laid in matters of fine art upon the presence of genius or upon that of taste, is equivalent to asking whether more turns upon imagination or upon judgment. Now, imagination rather entitles an art to be called an *inspired* [*geistreiche*] than a *fine* art. It is only in respect of judgment that the name of fine art is deserved. Hence it follows that judgment, being the indispensable condition [*conditio sine qua non*], is at least what one must look to as of capital importance in forming an estimate of art as fine art. So far as beauty is concerned, to be fertile and original in ideas is not such an imperative requirement as it is that the imagination in its freedom should be in accordance with the understanding's conformity to law. For in lawless freedom imagination, with all its wealth, produces nothing but nonsense; the power of judgment, on the other hand, is the faculty that makes it consonant with understanding.

Taste, like judgment in general, is the discipline (or corrective) of genius. It severely clips its wings, and makes it orderly or polished; but at the same time it gives it guidance, directing and controlling its flight, so that it may preserve its character of finality. It introduces a clearness and order into the plenitude of thought, and in so doing gives stability to the ideas, and qualifies them at once for permanent and universal approval, for being followed by others, and for a continually progressive culture. And so, where the interests of both these qualities clash in a product, and there has to be a sacrifice of something, then it should rather be on the side of genius; and judgment, which in matters of fine art bases its decision on its own proper principles, will more readily endure an abatement of the freedom and wealth of the imagination, than that the understanding should be compromised.

The requisites for fine art are, therefore, *imagination, understanding, soul,* and *taste.*[3]

51. THE DIVISION OF THE FINE ARTS

Beauty (whether it be of nature or of art) may in general be termed the *expression* of aesthetic ideas. But the proviso must be added that with beauty of art this idea must be excited through the medium of a concept of the Object, whereas with beauty of nature the bare reflection upon a given intuition, apart from any concept of what the object is intended to be, is sufficient for awakening and communicating the idea of which that Object is regarded as the *expression.*

Accordingly, if we wish to make a division of the fine arts, we can

---

3. The first three faculties are first *brought into union* by means of the fourth. *Hume,* in his history, informs the English that although they are second in their works to no other people in the world in respect of the evidences they afford to the three first qualities *separately* considered, still in what unites them they must yield to their neighbors, the French.

choose for that purpose, tentatively at least, no more convenient principle than the analogy which art bears to the mode of expression of which men avail themselves in speech, with a view to communicating themselves to one another as completely as possible, i.e., not merely in respect of their concepts but in respect of their sensations also.[4]—Such expression consists in *word, gesture,* and *tone* (articulation, gesticulation and modulation). It is the combination of these three modes of expression which alone constitutes a complete communication of the speaker. For thought, intuition, and sensation are in this way conveyed to others simultaneously and in conjunction.

Hence there are only three kinds of fine art: the art of *speech, formative* art, and the art of the *play of sensations* (as external sense impressions). This division might also be arranged as a dichotomy, so that fine art would be divided into that of the expression of thoughts or intuitions, the latter being subdivided according to the distinction between the form and the matter (sensation). It would, however, in that case appear too abstract, and less in line with popular conceptions.

1. The arts of SPEECH are *rhetoric* and *poetry. Rhetoric* is the art of transacting a serious business of the understanding as if it were a free play of the imagination; *poetry* that of conducting a free play of the imagination as if it were a serious business of the understanding.

Thus the *orator* announces a serious business, and for the purpose of entertaining his audience conducts it as if it were a mere *play* with ideas. The *poet* promises merely an entertaining *play* with ideas, and yet it has the same effect upon the understanding as if the promotion of its business had been his one intention. The combination and harmony of the two faculties of cognition, sensibility and understanding, which, though, doubtless, indispensable to one another, do not readily permit of being united without compulsion and reciprocal abatement, must have the appearance of being undesigned and a spontaneous occurrence—otherwise it is not *fine* art. For this reason what is studied and labored must be here avoided. For fine art must be free art in a double sense: i.e., not alone in a sense opposed to contract work, as not being a work the magnitude of which may be estimated, exacted, or paid for according to a definite standard, but free also in the sense that, while the mind, no doubt, occupies itelf, still it does so without ulterior regard to any other end, and yet with a feeling of satisfaction and stimulation (independent of reward).

The orator, therefore, gives something which he does not promise, viz. an entertaining play of the imagination. On the other hand, there is

---

4. The reader is not to consider this scheme for a possible division of the fine arts as a deliberate theory. It is only one of the various attempts that can and ought to be made.

something in which he fails to come up to his promise, and a thing, too, which is his avowed business, namely, the engagement of the understanding to some end. The poet's promise, on the contrary, is a modest one, and a mere play with ideas is all he holds out to us, but he accomplishes something worthy of being made a serious business, namely, the using of play to provide food for the understanding, and the giving of life to its concepts by means of the imagination. Hence the orator in reality performs less than he promises, the poet more.

2. The FORMATIVE arts, or those for the expression of ideas in *sensuous intuition* (not by means of representations of mere imagination that are excited by words) are arts either of *sensuous truth* or of *sensuous semblance*. The first is called *plastic* art, the second *painting*. Both use figures in space for the expression of ideas: the former makes figures discernible to two senses, sight and touch (though, so far as the latter sense is concerned, without regard to beauty), the latter makes them so to the former sense alone. The aesthetic idea (archetype, original) is the fundamental basis of both in the imagination; but the figure which constitutes its expression (the ectype, the copy) is given either in its bodily extension (the way the object itself exists) or else in accordance with the picture which it forms of itself in the eye (according to its appearance when projected on a flat surface). Or, whatever the archetype is, either the reference to an actual end or only the semblance of one may be imposed upon reflection as its condition.

To *plastic* art, as the first kind of formative fine art, belong *sculpture* and *architecture*. The first is that which presents concepts of things corporeally, as they *might exist in nature* (though as fine art it directs its attention to aesthetic finality). The *second* is the art of presenting concepts of things which are possible *only through art*, and the determining ground of whose form is not nature but an arbitrary end—and of presenting them both with a view of this purpose and yet, at the same time, with aesthetic finality. In architecture the chief point is a certain *use* of the artistic object to which, as the condition, the aesthetic ideas are limited. In sculpture the mere *expression* of aesthetic ideas is the main intention. Thus statues of men, gods, animals, etc., belong to sculpture; but temples, splendid buildings for public concourse, or even dwelling-houses, triumphal arches, columns, mausoleums, etc., erected as monuments, belong to architecture, and in fact all household furniture (the work of cabinet-makers, and so forth—things meant to be used) may be added to the list, on the ground that adaptation of the product to a particular use is the essential element in a *work of architecture*. On the other hand, a mere *piece of sculpture*, made simply to be looked at, and intended to please on its own account, is, as a corporeal presentation, a mere imitation of nature, though one in which regard is paid to aesthetic ideas, and in which, therefore, *sensuous truth* should not go the length of losing the appearance of being an art and a product of the elective will.

Painting, as the second kind of formative art, which presents the *sensuous semblance* in artful combination with ideas, I would divide into that of the beautiful *portrayal of nature*, and that of the beautiful *arrangement* of its *products*. The first is *painting proper*, the second *landscape gardening*. For the first gives only the semblance of bodily extension; whereas the second, giving this, no doubt, according to its truth, gives only the semblance of utility and employment for ends other than the play of the imagination in the contemplation of its forms.[5] The latter consists in no more than decking out the ground with the same manifold variety (grasses, flowers, shrubs, and trees, and even water, hills, and dales) as that with which nature presents it to our view, only arranged differently and in obedience to certain ideas. The beautiful arrangement of corporeal things, however, is also a thing for the eye only, just like painting—the sense of touch can form no intuitable representation of such a form. In addition I would place under the head of painting, in the wide sense, the decoration of rooms by means of hangings, ornamental accessories, and all beautiful furniture the sole function of which is *to be looked at*; and in the same way the art of tasteful dressing (with rings, snuff-boxes, etc.). For a *parterre* of various flowers, a room with a variety of ornaments (including even the ladies' attire) go to make at a festal gathering a sort of picture which, like pictures in the true sense of the word (those which are not intended *to teach* history or natural science), has no business beyond appealing to the eye, in order to entertain the imagination in free play with ideas, and to engage actively the aesthetic judgment independently of any definite end. No matter how heterogeneous, on the mechanical side, may be the craft involved in all this decoration, and no matter what a variety of artists may be required, still the judgment of taste, so far as it is one upon what is beautiful in this art, is determined in one and the same way: namely, as a judgment only upon

---

5. It seems strange that landscape gardening may be regarded as a kind of painting, notwithstanding that it presents its forms corporeally. But, as it takes its forms bodily from nature (the trees, shrubs, grasses, and flowers taken, originally at least, from wood and field) it is to that extent not an art such as, let us say, plastic art. Further, the arrangement which it makes is not conditioned by any concept of the object or of its end (as is the case in sculpture), but by the mere free play of the imagination in the act of contemplation. Hence it bears a degree of resemblance to simple aesthetic painting that has no definite theme (but by means of light and shade makes a pleasing composition of atmosphere, land, and water).—Throughout, the reader is to weigh the above only as an effort to connect the fine arts under a principle, which, in the present instance, is intended to be that of the expression of aesthetic ideas (following the analogy of a language), and not as a positive and deliberate derivation of the connection.

the forms (without regard to any end) as they present themselves to the eye, singly or in combination, according to their effect upon the imagination.—The justification, however, of bringing formative art (by analogy) under a common head with gesture in a speech, lies in the fact that through these figures the soul of the artist furnishes a bodily expression for the substance and character of his thought, and makes the thing itself speak, as it were, in mimic language—a very common play of our fancy, that attributes to lifeless things a soul suitable to their form, and that uses them as its mouthpiece.

3. The art of the BEAUTIFUL PLAY OF SENSATIONS, (sensations that arise from external stimulation,) which is a play of sensations that has nevertheless to permit of universal communication, can only be concerned with the proportion of the different degrees of tension in the sense to which the sensation belongs, i.e., with its tone. In this comprehensive sense of the word it may be divided into the artificial play of sensations of hearing and of sight, consequently into *music* and the *art of color*.—It is of note that these two senses, over and above such susceptibility for impressions as is required to obtain concepts of external objects by means of these impressions, also admit of a peculiar associated sensation of which we cannot well determine whether it is based on sense or reflection; and that this sensibility may at times be wanting, although the sense, in other respects, and in what concerns its employment for the cognition of objects, is by no means deficient but particularly keen. In other words, we cannot confidently assert whether a color or a tone (sound) is merely an agreeable sensation, or whether they are in themselves a beautiful play of sensations, and in being estimated aesthetically, convey, as such, a delight in their form. If we consider the velocity of the vibrations of light, or in the second case, of the air, which in all probability far outstrips any capacity on our part for forming an immediate estimate in perception of the time interval between them, we should be led to believe that it is only the *effect* of those vibrating movements upon the elastic parts of our body that can be evident to sense, but that the *time-interval* between them is not noticed nor involved in our estimate, and that, consequently, all that enters into combination with colors and tones is agreeableness, and not beauty, of their composition. But, let us consider, on the other hand, *first*, the mathematical character both of the proportion of those vibrations in music, and of our judgment upon it, and, as is reasonable, form an estimate of color contrasts on the analogy of the latter. *Secondly*, let us consult the instances, albeit rare, of men who, with the best of sight, have failed to distinguish colors, and, with the sharpest hearing, to distinguish tones, while for men who have this ability the perception of an altered quality (not merely of the degree

of the sensation) in the case of the different intensities in the scale of colors or tones is definite, as is also the number of those which may be *intelligibly* distinguished. Bearing all this in mind we may feel compelled to look upon the sensations afforded by both, not as mere sense-impressions, but as the effect of an estimate of form in the play of a number of sensations. The difference which the one opinion or the other occasions in the estimate of the basis of music would, however, only give rise to this much change in its definition, that either it is to be interpreted, as we have done, as the *beautiful* play of sensations (through hearing), or else as one of *agreeable* sensations. According to the former interpretation, alone, would music be represented out and out as a *fine* art, whereas according to the latter it would be represented as (in part at least) an *agreeable* art.

52. THE COMBINATION OF THE FINE ARTS IN ONE AND THE SAME PRODUCT

Rhetoric may in a *drama* be combined with a pictorial presentation as well of its Subjects as of objects; as may poetry with music in a *song*; and this again with a pictorial (theatrical) presentation in an *opera*; and so may the play of sensations in a piece of music with the play of figures in a *dance*, and so on. Even the presentation of the sublime, so far as it belongs to fine art, may be brought into union with beauty in a *tragedy in verse*, a *didactic poem* or an *oratorio*, and in this combination fine art is even more artistic. Whether it is also more beautiful (having regard to the multiplicity of different kinds of delight which cross one another) may in some of these instances be doubted. Still in all fine art the essential element consists in the form which is final for observation and for estimating. Here the pleasure is at the same time culture, and disposes the soul to ideas, making it thus susceptible of such pleasure and entertainment in greater abundance. The matter of sensation (charm or emotion) is not essential. Here the aim is merely enjoyment, which leaves nothing behind it in the idea, and renders the soul dull, the object in the course of time distasteful, and the mind dissatisfied with itself and ill-humored, owing to a consciousness that in the judgment of reason its disposition is perverse.

Where fine arts are not, either proximately or remotely, brought into combination with moral ideas, which alone are attended with a self-sufficing delight, the above is the fate that ultimately awaits them. They then only serve for a diversion, of which one continually feels an increasing need in proportion as one has availed oneself of it as a means of dispelling the discontent of one's mind, with the result that one makes oneself ever more and more unprofitable and dissatisfied with oneself.

With a view to the purpose first named the beauties of nature are in general the most beneficial, if one is early habituated to observe, estimate, and admire them.

53. COMPARATIVE ESTIMATE OF THE AESTHETIC WORTH OF THE FINE ARTS

Poetry (which owes its origin almost entirely to genius and is least willing to be led by precepts or example) holds the first rank among all the arts. It expands the mind by giving freedom to the imagination and by offering, from among the boundless multiplicity of possible forms accordant with a given concept, to whose bounds it is restricted, that one which couples with the presentation of the concept a wealth of thought to which no verbal expression is completely adequate, and by thus rising aesthetically to ideas. It invigorates the mind by letting it feel its faculty—free, spontaneous, and independent of determination by nature—of regarding and estimating nature as phenomenon in the light of aspects which nature of itself does not afford us in experience, either for sense or understanding, and of employing it accordingly in behalf of, and as a sort of schema for, the supersensible. It plays with semblance, which it produces at will, but not as an instrument of deception; for its avowed pursuit is merely one of play, which, however, understanding may turn to good account and employ for its own purpose.—Rhetoric, so far as this is taken to mean the art of persuasion, i.e., the art of deluding by means of a fair semblance (as *ars oratoria*), and not merely excellence of speech (eloquence and style), is a dialectic, which borrows from poetry only so much as is necessary to win over men's minds to the side of the speaker before they have weighed the matter, and to rob their verdict of its freedom. Hence it can be recommended neither for the bar nor the pulpit. For where civil laws, the right of individual persons, or the permanent instruction and determination of men's minds to a correct knowledge and a conscientious observance of their duty is at stake, then it is below the dignity of an undertaking of such moment to exhibit even a trace of the exuberance of wit and imagination, and, still more, of the art of talking men round and prejudicing them in favor of any one. For although such art is capable of being at times directed to ends intrinsically legitimate and praiseworthy, still it becomes reprehensible on account of the subjective injury done in this way to maxims and sentiments, even where objectively the action may be lawful. For it is not enough to do what is right, but we should practice it solely on the ground of its being right. Further, the simple lucid concept of human concerns of this kind, backed up with lively illustrations of it, exerts of itself, in the absence of any offense against the rules of euphony of speech or of propriety in the expression of ideas of reason (all which together make up excellence of speech), a sufficient influence upon human minds to obviate the necessity of having recourse here to the machinery of persuasion, which, being equally available for the purpose of putting a fine gloss or a cloak upon vice and error, fails to rid one completely of the lurking suspicion that one is being artfully hoodwinked. In poetry everything is straight and above board. It shows its hand: it desires to carry on a mere entertaining play with the imagination, and one consonant, in respect of form, with the laws of understanding; and it does not seek to steal upon and ensnare the understanding with a sensuous presentation.[6]

After poetry, *if we take charm and mental stimulation into account*, I would give the next place to that art which comes nearer to it than to any other art of speech, and admits of very natural union with it, namely the art of *tone*. For though it speaks by means of mere sensations without concepts, and so does not, like poetry, leave behind it any food for reflection, still it moves the mind more diversely, and, although with transient, still with intenser effect. It is certainly, however, more a matter of enjoyment than of culture—the play of thought incidentally excited by it being merely the effect of a more or less mechanical association—and it possesses less worth in the eyes of reason than any other of the fine arts. Hence, like all enjoyment, it calls for constant change, and does not stand frequent repetition without inducing weariness. Its charm, which admits of such universal communication, appears to rest on the following facts. Every expression in language has an associated tone suited to its sense. This tone indicates, more or less, a mode in which the speaker is affected, and in turn evokes it in the hearer also, in whom conversely it then also excites the idea which in language is expressed with such a tone. Further, just as modulation is, as it were, a

---

6. I must confess to the pure delight which I have ever been afforded by a beautiful poem; whereas the reading of the best speech of a Roman forensic orator, a modern parliamentary debater, or a preacher, has invariably been mingled with an unpleasant sense of disapproval of an insidious art that knows how, in matters of moment, to move men like machines to a judgment that must lose all its weight with them upon calm reflection. Force and elegance of speech (which together constitute rhetoric) belong to fine art; but oratory (*ars oratoria*), being the art of playing for one's own purpose upon the weaknesses of men (let this purpose be ever so good in intention or even in fact) merits no *respect* whatever. Besides, both at Athens and at Rome, it only attained its greatest height at a time when the state was hastening to its decay, and genuine patriotic sentiment was a thing of the past. One who sees the issue clearly, and who has a command of language in its wealth and its purity, and who is possessed of an imagination that is fertile and effective in presenting his ideas, and whose heart, withal, turns with lively sympathy to what is truly good—he is the *vir bonus dicendi peritus*, the orator without art, but of great impressiveness, as Cicero would have him, though he may not himself always have remained faithful to this ideal.

universal language of sensations intelligible to every man, so the art of tone wields the full force of this language wholly on its own account, namely, as a language of the affections, and in this way, according to the law of association, universally communicates the aesthetic ideas that are naturally combined therewith. But, further, inasmuch as those aesthetic ideas are not concepts or determinate thoughts, the form of the arrangement of these sensations (harmony and melody), taking the place of the form of a language, only serves the purpose of giving an expression to the aesthetic idea of an integral whole of an unutterable wealth of thought that fills the measure of a certain theme forming the dominant *affection* in the piece. This purpose is effectuated by means of a proportion in the accord of the sensations (an accord which may be brought mathematically under certain rules, since it rests, in the case of tones, upon the numerical relation of the vibrations of the air in the same time, so far as there is a combination of the tones simultaneously or in succession). Although this mathematical form is not represented by means of determinate concepts, to it alone belongs the delight which the mere reflection upon such a number of concomitant or consecutive sensations couples with this their play, as the universally valid condition of its beauty, and it is with reference to it alone that taste can lay claim to a right to anticipate the judgment of every man.

But mathematics, certainly, does not play the smallest part in the charm and movement of the mind produced by music. Rather is it only the indispensable condition [*conditio sine qua non*] of that proportion of the combining as well as changing impressions which makes it possible to grasp them all in one and prevent them from destroying one another, and to let them, rather, conspire towards the production of a continuous movement and quickening of the mind by affections that are in unison with it, and thus towards a serene self-enjoyment.

If, on the other hand, we estimate the worth of the fine arts by the culture they supply to the mind, and adopt for our standard the expansion of the faculties whose confluence, in judgment, is necessary for cognition, music, then, since it plays merely with sensations, has the lowest place among the fine arts—just as it has perhaps the highest among those valued at the same time for their agreeableness. Looked at in this light it is far excelled by the formative arts. For, in putting the imagination into a play which is at once free and adapted to the understanding, they all the while carry on a serious business, since they execute a product which serves the concepts of understanding as a vehicle, permanent and appealing to us on its own account, for effectuating their union with sensibility, and thus for promoting, as it were, the urbanity of the higher powers of cognition. The two kinds of art pursue completely different courses. Music advances from sensations to indefinite ideas: formative art from definite ideas to sensations. The latter gives a *lasting* impression, the former one that is only *fleeting*. The former sensations imagination can recall and agreeably entertain itself with, while the latter either vanish entirely, or else, if involuntarily repeated by the imagination, are more annoying to us than agreeable. Over and above all this, music has a certain lack of urbanity about it. For owing chiefly to the character of its instruments, it scatters its influence abroad to an uncalled-for extent (through the neighborhood), and thus, as it were, becomes obtrusive and deprives others, outside the musical circle, of their freedom. This is a thing that the arts that address themselves to the eye do not do, for if one is not disposed to give admittance to their impressions, one has only to look the other way. The case is almost on a par with the practice of regaling oneself with a perfume that exhales its odors far and wide. The man who pulls his perfumed handkerchief from his pocket gives a treat to all around whether they like it or not, and compels them, if they want to breathe at all, to be parties to the enjoyment, and so the habit has gone out of fashion.[7]

Among the formative arts I would give the palm to *painting*: partly because it is the art of design and, as such, the groundwork of all the other formative arts; partly because it can penetrate much further into the region of ideas, and in conformity with them give a greater extension to the field of intuition than it is open to the others to do.

54. REMARK

As we have often shown, an essential distinction lies between what *pleases simply in the estimate formed of it* and what *gratifies* (pleases in sensation). The latter is something which, unlike the former, we cannot demand from everyone. Gratification (no matter whether its cause has its seat even in ideas) appears always to consist in a feeling of the furtherance of the entire life of the man, and, hence, also of his bodily well-being, i.e., his health. And so, perhaps, Epicurus was not wide of the mark when he said that at bottom all gratification is bodily sensation, and only misunderstood himself in ranking intellectual and even practical delight under the head of gratification. Bearing in mind the latter distinction, it is readily explicable how even the gratification a person feels is capable of displeasing him (as the joy of a necessitous but good-natured individual on being made the heir of an affectionate but penurious father), or how deep pain may still give pleasure to the sufferer (as the sorrow of a widow

---

7. Those who have recommended the singing of hymns at family prayers have forgotten the amount of annoyance which they give to the general public by such *noisy* (and, as a rule, for that very reason, pharisaical) worship, for they compel their neighbors either to join in the singing or else abandon their meditations.

over the death of her deserving husband), or how there may be pleasure over and above gratification (as in scientific pursuits), or how a pain (as, for example, hatred, envy, and desire for revenge) may in addition be a source of displeasure. Here the delight or aversion depends upon reason, and is one with *approbation* or *disapprobation*. Gratification and pain, on the other hand, can only depend upon feeling, or upon the prospect of a possible *well-being* or the *reverse* (irrespective of source).

The changing free play of sensations (which do not follow any preconceived plan) is always a source of gratification, because it promotes the feeling of health; and it is immaterial whether or not we experience delight in the object of this play or even in the gratification itself when estimated in the light of reason. Also this gratification may amount to an affection, although we take no interest in the object itself, or none, at least, proportionate to the degree of the affection. We may divide the above play into that of *games of chance* [*Glückspiel*], *harmony* [*Tonspiel*], and *wit* [*Gedankenspiel*]. The *first* stands in need of an *interest*, be it of vanity or self-seeking, but one which falls far short of that centered in the adopted mode of procurement. All that the *second* requires is the change of *sensations*, each of which has its bearing on affection, though without attaining to the degree of an affection, and excites aesthetic ideas. The *third* springs merely from the change of the representations in the judgment, which, while unproductive of any thought conveying an interest, yet enlivens the mind.

What a fund of gratification must be afforded by play, without our having to fall back upon any consideration of interest, is a matter to which all our evening parties bear witness—for without play they hardly ever escape falling flat. But the affections of hope, fear, joy, anger, and derision here engage in play, as every moment they change their parts, and are so lively that, as by an internal motion, the whole vital function of the body seems to be furthered by the process—as is proved by a vivacity of the mind produced—although no one comes by anything in the way of profit or instruction. But as the play of chance is not one that is beautiful, we will here lay it aside. Music, on the contrary, and what provokes laughter are two kinds of play with aesthetic ideas, or even with representations of the understanding, by which, all said and done, nothing is thought. By mere force of change they yet are able to afford lively gratification. This furnishes pretty clear evidence that the quickening effect of both is physical, despite its being excited by ideas of the mind, and that the feeling of health, arising from a movement of the intestines answering to that play, makes up that entire gratification of an animated gathering upon the spirit and refinement of which we set such store. Not any estimate of harmony in tones or flashes of wit, which, with its beauty, serves only as a necessary vehicle, but rather the stimulated vital functions of the body, the affection stirring the intestines and the diaphragm, and, in a word, the feeling of health (of which we are only sensible upon some such provocation) are what constitute the gratification we experience at being able to reach the body through the soul and use the latter as the physician of the former.

In music the course of this play is from bodily sensation to aesthetic ideas (which are the Objects for the affections), and then from these back again, but with gathered strength, to the body. In jest (which just as much as the former deserves to be ranked rather as an agreeable than a fine art) the play sets out from thoughts which collectively, so far as seeking sensuous expression, engage the activity of the body. In this presentation the understanding, missing what it expected, suddenly lets go its hold, with the result that the effect of this slackening is felt in the body by the oscillation of the organs. This favors the restoration of the equilibrium of the latter, and exerts a beneficial influence upon the health.

Something absurd (something in which, therefore, the understanding can of itself find no delight) must be present in whatever is to raise a hearty convulsive laugh. *Laughter is an affection arising from a strained expectation being suddenly reduced to nothing.* This very reduction, at which certainly understanding cannot rejoice, is still indirectly a source of very lively enjoyment for a moment. Its cause must consequently lie in the influence of the representation upon the body, and the reciprocal effect of this upon the mind. This, moreover, cannot depend upon the representation being objectively an object of gratification, (for how can we derive gratification from a disappointment?) but must rest solely upon the fact that the reduction is a mere play of representations, and, as such, produces an equilibrium of the vital forces of the body.

Suppose that someone tells the following story: An Indian at an Englishman's table in Surat saw a bottle of ale opened, and all the beer turned into froth and flowing out. The repeated exclamations of the Indian showed his great astonishment. "Well, what is so wonderful in that?" asked the Englishman. "Oh, I'm not surprised myself," said the Indian, "at its getting out, but at how you ever managed to get it all in." At this we laugh, and it gives us hearty pleasure. This is not because we think ourselves, maybe, more quick-witted than this ignorant Indian, or because our understanding here brings to our notice any other ground of delight. It is rather that the bubble of our expectation was extended to the full and suddenly went off into nothing. Or, again, take the case of the heir of a wealthy relative being minded to make preparations for having the funeral obsequies on a most imposing scale, but complaining that things would not go right for him, because (as he said) "the more money I give my mourners to look sad, the more pleased they look." At this we laugh outright, and the reason lies in the fact that we had an expectation which is suddenly reduced to nothing. We must be careful to observe that the reduction is not one into the positive contrary of an expected object—for that is always something, and may frequently pain us—but must be a reduction to nothing. For where a person arouses great expectation by recounting some tale, and at the close its untruth becomes at once apparent to us, we are displeased at it. So it is, for instance, with the tale of people whose hair from excess of grief is said to have turned white in a single night. On the other hand, if a wag, wishing to cap the story, tells with the utmost circumstantiality of a merchant's grief, who, on his return journey from India to Europe with all his wealth in merchandise, was obliged by stress of storm to throw every-thing overboard, and grieved to such an extent that in the selfsame night his *wig* turned grey, we laugh and enjoy the tale. This is because we keep for a time playing on our own mistake about an object otherwise indifferent to us, or rather on the idea we ourselves were following out, and, beating it to and fro, just as if it were a ball eluding our grasp, when all we intend to do is just to get it into our hands and hold it tight. Here our gratification is not excited by a knave or a fool getting a rebuff: for, even on its own account, the latter tale told with an air of seriousness would of itself be enough to set a whole table into roars of laughter; and the other matter would ordinarily not be worth a moment's thought.

It is observable that in all such cases the joke must have something in it capable of momentarily deceiving us. Hence, when the semblance vanishes into nothing, the mind looks back in order to try it over again, and thus by a rapidly succeeding tension and relaxation it is jerked to and fro and put in oscillation. As the snapping of what was, as it were, tightening up the string takes place suddenly (not by a gradual loosen-ing), the oscillation must bring about a mental movement and a sym-pathetic internal movement of the body. This continues involuntarily and produces fatigue, but in so doing it also affords recreation (the effects of a motion conducive to health).

For supposing we assume that some movement in the bodily organs is associated sympathetically with all our thoughts, it is readily intelligible how the sudden act above referred to, of shifting the mind now to one standpoint and now to the other, to enable it to contemplate its object, may involve a corresponding and reciprocal straining and slackening of the elastic parts of our intestines, which communicates itself to the diaphragm (and resembles that felt by ticklish people), in the course of which the lungs expel the air with rapidly succeeding interruptions, resulting in a movement conducive to health. This alone, and not what goes on in the mind, is the proper cause of the gratification in a thought that at bottom represents nothing.—Voltaire said that heaven has given us two things to compensate us for the many miseries of life, *hope* and *sleep*. He might have added *laughter* to the list—if only the means of exciting it in men of intelligence were as ready to hand, and the wit or originality of humor which it requires were not just as rare as the talent is common for inventing stuff *that splits the head*, as mystic speculators do, or *that breaks your neck*, as the genius does, or that *harrows the heart* as sentimental novelists do (aye, and moralists of the same type).

We may, therefore, as I conceive, make Epicurus a present of the point that all gratification, even when occasioned by concepts that evoke aesthetic ideas, is *animal*, i.e., bodily sensation. For from this admission the *spiritual* feeling of respect for moral ideas, which is not one of gratification, but a self-esteem, (an esteem for humanity within us,) that raises us above the need of gratification, suffers not a whit—no nor even the less noble feeling of *taste*.

In *naïveté* we meet with a joint product of both the above. *Naïveté* is the breaking forth of the ingenuousness originally natural to humanity, in opposition to the art of disguising oneself that has become a second nature. We laugh at the simplicity that is as yet a stranger to dissimulation, but we rejoice the while over the simplicity of nature that thwarts that art. We await the commonplace manner of artificial utterance, thoughtfully addressed to a fair show, and lo! nature stands before us in unsullied innocence—nature that we were quite unprepared to meet, and that he who laid it bare had also no intention of revealing. That the outward appearance, fair but false, that usually assumes such importance in our judgment, is here, at a stroke, turned to a nullity, that, as it were, the rogue in us is nakedly exposed, calls forth the movement of the mind, in two successive and opposite directions, agitating the body at the same time with wholesome motion. But that something infinitely better than any accepted code of manners, namely purity of mind, (or at least a vestige of such purity,) has not become wholly extinct in human nature, infuses seriousness and reverence into this play of judgment. But since it is only a manifestation that obtrudes itself for a moment, and the veil of a dissembling art is soon drawn over it again, there enters into the above feelings a touch of pity. This is an emotion of tenderness, playful in its way, that thus readily admits of combination with this sort of genial laughter. And, in fact, this emotion is as a rule associated with it, and, at the same time, is wont to make amends to the person who provides such food for our merriment for his embarrassment at not being wise after the manner of men.—For that reason an art of being *naïf* is a contradition. But it is quite possible to give a representation of *naïveté* in a fictitious personage, and, rare as the art is, it is a fine art. With this *naïveté* we must not confuse homely simplicity, which only avoids spoiling nature by artificiality, because it has no notion of the conventions of good society.

The *humorous* manner may also be ranked as a thing which in its enlivening influence is clearly allied to the gratification provoked by laughter. It belongs to originality of mind [*des Geistes*], though not to the talent for fine art. *Humor*, in a good sense, means the talent for being able to put oneself at will into a certain frame of mind in which everything is estimated on lines that go quite off the beaten track, (a topsy-turvy view of things,) and yet on lines that follow certain principles, rational in the case of such a mental temperament. A person with whom such variations are not a matter of choice is said *to have humors*; but if a person can assume them voluntarily, and of set purpose (on behalf of a lively presentation drawn from a ludicrous contrast), he and his way of speaking are termed *humorous*. This manner belongs, however, to agreeable rather than to fine art, because the object of the latter must always have an evident intrinsic worth about it, and thus demands a certain seriousness in its presentation, as taste does in estimating it.

Phenomenology of Spirit

PREFACE: ON SCIENTIFIC COGNITION

1. It is customary to preface a work with an explanation of the author's aim, why he wrote the book, and the relationship in which he believes it to stand to other earlier or contemporary treatises on the same subject. In the case of a philosophical work, however, such an explanation seems not only superfluous but, in view of the nature of the subject matter, even inappropriate and misleading. For whatever might appropriately be said about philosophy in a preface—say a historical *statement* of the main drift and the point of view, the general content and results, a string of random assertions and assurances about truth—none of this can be accepted as the way in which to expound philosophical truth. Also, since philosophy moves essentially in the element of universality, which includes within itself the particular, it might seem that here more than in any of the other sciences the subject matter itself, and even in its complete nature, were expressed in the aim and the final results, the execution being by contrast really the unessential factor. On the other hand, in the ordinary view of anatomy, for instance (say, the knowledge of the parts of the body regarded as inanimate), we are quite sure that we do not as yet possess the subject matter itself, the content of this science, but must in addition exert ourselves to know the particulars. Further, in the case of such an aggregate of information, which has no right to bear the name of Science, an opening talk about aim and other such generalities is usually conducted in the same historical and uncomprehending way in which the content itself (these nerves, muscles, etc.) is spoken of. In the case of philosophy, on the other hand, this would give rise to the incongruity that along with the employment of such a method its inability to grasp the truth would also be demonstrated.

2. Furthermore, the very attempt to define how a philosphical work is supposed to be connected with other efforts to deal with the same

Excerpted from G. W. F. Hegel, *Phenomenology of Spirit*, translated by A. V. Miller (New York: Oxford University Press, 1977), 1–57.

subject matter drags in an extraneous concern, and what is really important for the cognition of the truth is obscured. The more conventional opinion gets fixated on the antithesis of truth and falsity, the more it tends to expect a given philosophical system to be either accepted or contradicted; and hence it finds only acceptance or rejection. It does not comprehend the diversity of philosophical systems as the progressive unfolding of truth, but rather sees in it simple disagreements. The bud disappears in the bursting-forth of the blossom, and one might say that the former is refuted by the latter; similarly, when the fruit appears, the blossom is shown up in its turn as a false manifestation of the plant, and the fruit now emerges as the truth of it instead. These forms are not just distinguished from one another, they also supplant one another as mutually incompatible. Yet at the same time their fluid nature makes them moments of an organic unity in which they not only do not conflict, but in which each is as necessary as the other; and this mutual necessity alone constitutes the life of the whole. But he who rejects a philosophical system (i.e., the new philosopher) does not usually comprehend what he is doing in this way; and he who grasps the contradiction between them (i.e., the historian of philosophy) does not, as a general rule, know how to free it from its one-sidedness, or maintain it in its freedom by recognizing the reciprocally necessary moments that take shape as a conflict and seeming incompatibility.

3. Demanding and supplying these (superficial) explanations passes readily enough as a concern with what is essential. Where could the inner meaning of a philosphical work find fuller expression than in its aims and results, and how could these be more exactly known than by distinguishing them from everything else the age brings forth in this sphere? Yet when this activity is taken for more than the mere beginnings of cognition, when it is allowed to pass for actual cognition, then it should be reckoned as no more than a device for evading the real issue [*die Sache selbst*], a way of creating an impression of hard work and serious commitment to the problem, while actually sparing oneself both. For the real issue is not exhausted by stating it as an aim, but by carrying it out, nor is the result the actual whole, but rather the result together with the process through which it came about. The aim by itself is a lifeless universal, just as the guiding tendency is a mere drive that as yet lacks an actual existence; and the bare result is the corpse which has left the guiding tendency behind it. Similarly, the specific difference of a thing is rather its limit; it is where the thing stops, or it is what the thing is not. This concern with aim or results, with differentiating and passing judgment on various thinkers is therefore an easier task than it might seem. For instead of getting involved in the real issue, this kind of activity is always away beyond it; instead of tarrying with it, and losing

itself in it, this kind of knowing is forever grasping at something new; it remains essentially preoccupied with itself instead of being preoccupied with the real issue and surrendering to it. To judge a thing that has substance and solid worth is quite easy, to comprehend it is much harder, and to blend judgment and comprehension in a definitive description is the hardest thing of all. . . .

6. To lay down that the true shape of truth is scientific—or, what is the same thing, to maintain that truth has only the Notion as the element of its existence—seems, I know, to contradict a view which is in our time as prevalent as it is pretentious, and to go against what that view implies. Some explanation therefore seems called for, even though it must for the present be no more than a bare assertion, like the view that it contradicts. If, namely, the True exists only in what, or better *as* what, is sometimes called intuition, sometimes immediate knowledge of the Absolute, religion or being—not at the center of divine love but the being of the divine love itself—then what is required in the exposition of philosophy is, from this viewpoint, rather the opposite of the form of the Notion. For the Absolute is not supposed to be comprehended, it is to be felt and intuited; not the Notion of the Absolute, but the feeling and intuition of it, must govern what is said, and must be expressed by it. . . .

11. Besides, it is not difficult to see that ours is a birth-time and a period of transition to a new era. Spirit has broken with the world it has hitherto inhabited and imagined, and is of a mind to submerge it in the past, and in the labor of its own transformation. Spirit is indeed never at rest but always engaged in moving forward. But just as the first breath drawn by a child after its long, quiet nourishment breaks the gradualness of merely quantitative growth—there is a qualitative leap, and the child is born—so likewise the Spirit in its formation matures slowly and quietly into its new shape, dissolving bit by bit the structure of its previous world, whose tottering state is only hinted at by isolated symptoms. The frivolity and boredom which unsettle the established order, the vague foreboding of something unknown, these are the heralds of approaching change. The gradual crumbling that left unaltered the face of the whole is cut short by a sunburst which, in one flash, illuminates the features of the new world.

12. But this new world is no more a complete actuality than is a newborn child; it is essential to bear this in mind. It comes on the scene for the first time in its immediacy or its Notion. Just as little as a building is finished when its foundation has been laid, so little is the achieved Notion of the whole the whole itself. When we wish to see an oak with its massive trunk and spreading branches and foliage, we are not content to be shown an acorn instead. So too, Science, the crown of a

world of Spirit, is not complete in its beginnings. The onset of the new
spirit is the product of a widespread upheaval in various forms of culture,
the prize at the end of a complicated, tortuous path and of just as
variegated and strenuous an effort. It is the whole which, having
traversed its content in time and space, has returned into itself, and is the
resultant *simple Notion* of the whole. But the actuality of this simple
whole consists in those various shapes and forms which have become its
moments, and which will now develop and take shape afresh, this time
in their new element, in their newly acquired meaning. . . .

17. In my view, which can be justified only in the exposition of the
system itself, everything turns on grasping and expressing the True, not
only as *Substance*, but equally as *Subject*. At the same time, it is to be
observed that substantiality embraces the universal, or the *immediacy of
knowledge* itself, as well as that which is *being* or immediacy *for* knowledge. If the conception of God as the one Substance shocked the age in
which it was proclaimed, the reason for this was on the one hand an
instinctive awareness that, in this definition, self-consciousness was only
submerged and not preserved. On the other hand, the opposite view,
which clings to thought as thought, to universality as such, is the very
same simplicity, is undifferentiated, unmoved substantiality. And if,
thirdly, thought does unite itself with the being of Substance, and
apprehends immediacy or intuition as thinking, the question is still
whether this intellectual intuition does not again fall back into inert
simplicity, and does not depict actuality itself in a non-actual manner.

18. Further, the living Substance is being which is in truth *Subject*,
or, what is the same, is in truth actual only in so far as it is the movement
of positing itself, or is the mediation of its self-othering with itself. This
Substance is, as Subject, pure, *simple negativity*, and is for this very reason
the bifurcation of the simple; it is the doubling which sets up opposition, and then again the negation of this indifferent diversity and of its
antithesis (the immediate simplicity). Only this self-*restoring* sameness,
or this reflection in otherness within itself—not an *original* or *immediate*
unity as such—is the True. It is the process of its own becoming, the
circle that presupposes its end as its goal, having its end also as its
beginning; and only by being worked out to its end, is it actual.

19. Thus the life of God and divine cognition may well be spoken of
as a disporting of Love with itself; but this idea sinks into mere edifica-
tion, and even insipidity, if it lacks the seriousness, the suffering, the
patience, and the labor of the negative. *In itself*, that life is indeed one of
untroubled equality and unity with itself, for which otherness and
alienation, and the overcoming of alienation, are not serious matters.
But this *in-itself* is abstract universality, in which the nature of the divine
life *to be for itself*, and so too the self-movement of the form, are altogether

left out of account. If the form is declared to be the same as the essence, then it is *ipso facto* a mistake to suppose that cognition can be satisfied with the in-itself or the essence, but can get along without the form—that the absolute principle or absolute intuition makes the working-out of the former, or the development of the latter, superfluous. Just because the form is as essential to the essence as the essence is to itself, the divine essence is not to be conceived and expressed merely as essence, i.e., as immediate substance or pure self-contemplation of the divine, but likewise as *form,* and in the whole wealth of the developed form. Only then is it conceived and expressed as an actuality.

20. The True is the whole. But the whole is nothing other than the essence consummating itself through its development. Of the Absolute it must be said that it is essentially a *result*, that only in the *end* is it what it truly is; and that precisely in this consists its nature, viz. to be actual, subject, the spontaneous becoming of itself. Though it may seem contradictory that the Absolute should be conceived essentially as a result, it needs little pondering to set this show of contradiction in its true light. The beginning, the principle, or the Absolute, as at first immediately enunciated, is only the universal. Just as when I say *"all* animals" this expression cannot pass for a zoology, so it is equally plain that the words "the Divine," "the Absolute," "the Eternal," etc., do not express what is contained in them; and only such words, in fact, do express the intuition as something immediate. Whatever is more than such a word, even the transition to a mere proposition, contains a *becoming-other* that has to be taken back, or is a mediation. But it is just this that is rejected with horror, as if absolute cognition were being surrendered when more is made of mediation than in simply saying that it is nothing absolute, and is completely absent in the Absolute.

21. But this abhorrence in fact stems from ignorance of the nature of mediation, and of absolute cognition itself. For mediation is nothing beyond self-moving selfsameness, or is reflection into self, the moment of the "I" which is for itself pure negativity or, when reduced to its pure abstraction, *simple becoming.* The "I" or becoming in general, this media- tion, on account of its simple nature, is just immediacy in the process of becoming, and is the immediate itself. Reason is, therefore, misunder- stood when reflection is excluded from the True, and is not grasped as a positive moment of the Absolute. It is reflection that makes the True a result, but it is equally reflection that overcomes the antithesis between the process of its becoming and the result, for this becoming is also simple, and therefore not different from the form of the True which shows itself as *simple* in its result; the process of becoming is rather just this return into simplicity. Though the embryo is indeed *in itself* a human being, it is not so *for itself*; this it only is as cultivated Reason,

which has *made* itself into what it is *in itself*. And that is when it for the first time is actual. But this result is itself a simple immediacy, for it is self-conscious freedom at peace with itself, which has not set the antithesis on one side and left it lying there, but has been reconciled with it.

22. What has just been said can also be expressed by saying that Reason is *purposive activity*. The exaltation of a supposed Nature over a misconceived thinking, and especially the rejection of external teleology, has brought the form of purpose in general into discredit. Still, in the sense in which Aristotle, too, defines Nature as purposive activity, purpose is what is immediate and *at rest*, the unmoved which is also *self-moving*, and as such is Subject. Its power to move, taken abstractly, is *being-for-self* or pure negativity. The result is the same as the beginning, only because the *beginning* is the *purpose*; in other words, the actual is the same as its Notion only because the immediate, as purpose, contains the self or pure actuality within itself. The realized purpose, or the existent actuality, is movement and unfolded becoming; but it is just this unrest that is the self; and the self is like that immediacy and simplicity of the beginning because it is the result, that which has returned into itself, the latter being similarly just the self. And the self is the sameness and simplicity that relates itself to itself.

23. The need to represent the Absolute as *Subject* has found expression in the propositions: *God* is the eternal, the moral world-order, love, and so on. In such propositions the True is only posited *immediately* as Subject, but is not presented as the movement of reflecting itself into itself. In a proposition of this kind one begins with the word "God." This by itself is a meaningless sound, a mere name; it is only the predicate that says *what God is*, gives Him content and meaning. Only in the end of the proposition does the empty beginning become actual knowledge. This being so, it is not clear why one does not speak merely of the eternal, of the moral world-order and so on, or, as the ancients did, of pure notions like "being," "the One," and so on, in short, of that which gives the meaning without adding the *meaningless* sound as well. But it is just this word that indicates that what is posited is not a being (i.e., something that merely *is*), or essence, or a universal in general, but rather something that is reflected into itself, a Subject. But at the same time this is only anticipated. The Subject is assumed as a fixed point to which, as their support, the predicates are affixed by a movement belonging to the knower of this Subject, and which is not regarded as belonging to the fixed point itself; yet it is only through this movement that the content could be represented as Subject. The way in which this movement has been brought about is such that it cannot belong to the fixed point; yet, after this point has been presupposed, the nature of the movement cannot really be other than what it is, it can only be external.

Hence, the mere anticipation that the Absolute is Subject is not only *not* the actuality of this Notion, but it even makes the actuality impossible; for the anticipation posits the subject as an inert point, whereas the actuality is self-movement.

24. Among the various consequences that follow from what has just been said, this one in particular can be stressed, that knowledge is only actual, and can only be expounded, as Science or as *system*; and furthermore, that a so-called basic proposition or principle of philosophy, if true, is also false, just because it is *only* a principle. It is, therefore, easy to refute it. The refutation consists in pointing out its defect; and it is defective because it is only the universal or principle, is only the beginning. If the refutation is thorough, it is derived and developed from the principle itself, not accomplished by counterassertions and random thoughts from outside. The refutation would, therefore, properly consist in the further development of the principle, and in thus remedying the defectiveness, (if it did not mistakenly pay attention solely to its *negative* action,) without awareness of its progress and result on their *positive* side too.—The genuinely *positive* exposition of the beginning is thus also, conversely, just as much a negative attitude towards it, viz. towards its initially one-sided form of being *immediate* or *purpose*. It can therefore be taken equally well as a refutation of the principle that constitutes the *basis* of the system, but it is more correct to regard it as a demonstration that the *basis* or principle of the system is, in fact, only its *beginning*.

25. That the True is actual only as system, or that Substance is essentially Subject, is expressed in the representation of the Absolute as *Spirit*—the most sublime Notion and the one which belongs to the modern age and its religion. The spiritual alone is the *actual*; it is essence, or that which has *being in itself*; it is that which *relates itself to itself* and is *determinate*, it is *other-being* and *being-for-self*, and in this determinatenes, or in its self-externality, abides within itself; in other words, it is *in and for itself*.—But this being-in-and-for-itself is at first only for us, or *in itself*, it is spiritual *Substance*. It must also be this *for itself*, it must be the knowledge of the spiritual, and the knowledge of itself as Spirit, i.e., it must be an *object* to itself, but just as immediately a sublated object, reflected into itself. It is *for itself* only for *us*, in so far as its spiritual content is generated by itself. But in so far as it is also for itself for its own self, this self-generation, the pure Notion, is for it the objective element in which it has its existence, and it is in this way, in its existence for itself, an object reflected into itself. The Spirit that, so developed, knows itself as Spirit, is *Science*; Science is its actuality and the realm which it builds for itself in its own element.

26. *Pure* self-recognition in absolute otherness, this Aether *as such*, is

the ground and soil of Science or *knowledge in general.* The beginning of philosophy presupposes or requires that consciousness should dwell in this *element.* But this element itself achieves its own perfection and transparency only through the movement of its becoming. It is pure spirituality as the *universal* that has the form of simple immediacy. This simple being in its *existential* form is the soil (of Science), it is thinking which has its being in Spirit alone. Because this element, this immediacy of Spirit, is the very substance of Spirit, it is the *transfigured essence,* reflection which is itself simple, and which is for itself immediacy as such, *being* that is reflected into itself. Science on its part requires that self-consciousness should have raised itself into this Aether in order to be able to live—and (actually) to live—with Science and in Science. Conversely, the individual has the right to demand that Science should at least provide him with the ladder to this standpoint, should show him this standpoint within himself. His right is based on his absolute independence, which he is conscious of possessing in every phase of his knowledge; for in each one, whether recognized by Science or not, and whatever the content may be, the individual is the absolute form, i.e., he is the *immediate certainty* of himself and, if this expression be preferred, he is therefore unconditioned *being.* The standpoint of consciousness which knows objects in their antithesis to itself, and itself in antithesis to them, is for Science the antithesis of its own standpoint. The situation in which consciousness knows itself to be at home is for Science one marked by the absence of Spirit. Conversely, the element of Science is for consciousness a remote beyond in which it no longer possesses itself. Each of these two aspects (of self-conscious Spirit) appears to the other as the inversion of truth. When natural consciousness entrusts itself straightway to Science, it makes an attempt, induced by it knows not what, to walk on its head too, just this once; the compulsion to assume this unwonted posture and to go about in it is a violence it is expected to do to itself, all unprepared and seemingly without necessity. Let Science be in its own self what it may, relative to immediate self-consciousness it presents itself in an inverted posture; or, because this self-consciousness has the principle of its actual existence in the certainty of itself, Science appears to it not to be actual, since self-consciousness exists on its own account outside of Science. Science must therefore unite this element of self-certainty with itself, or rather show *that* and *how* this element belongs to it. So long as Science lacks this *actual* dimension, it is only the content as the *in-itself,* the *purpose* that is as yet still something *inward,* not yet Spirit, but only spiritual Substance. This *in-itself* has to express itself outwardly and become *for itself,* and this means simply that it has to posit self-consciousness as one with itself.

27. It is this coming-to-be of *Science as such* or of *knowledge,* that is

described in this *Phenomenology* of Spirit. Knowledge in its first phase, or *immediate Spirit*, is the non-spiritual, i.e., *sense-consciousness*. In order to become genuine knowledge, to beget the element of Science which is the pure Notion of Science itself, it must travel a long way and work its passage. This process of coming-to-be (considering the content and patterns it will display therein) will not be what is commonly understood by an initiation of the unscientific consciousness into Science; it will also be quite different from the "foundation" of Science; least of all will it be like the rapturous enthusiasm which, like a shot from a pistol, begins straight away with absolute knowledge, and makes short work of other standpoints by declaring that it takes no notice of them.

28. The task of leading the individual from his uneducated standpoint to knowledge had to be seen in its universal sense, just as it was the universal individual, self-conscious Spirit, whose formative education had to be studied. As regards the relation between them, every moment, as it gains concrete form and a shape of its own, displays itself in the universal individual. The single individual is incomplete Spirit, a concrete shape in whose whole existence *one* determinateness predominates, the others being present only in blurred outline. In a Spirit that is more advanced than another, the lower concrete existence has been reduced to an inconspicuous moment; what used to be the important thing is now but a trace; its pattern is shrouded to become a mere shadowy outline. The individual whose substance is the more advanced Spirit runs through this past just as one who takes up a higher science goes through the preparatory studies he has long since absorbed, in order to bring their content to mind; he recalls them to the inward eye, but has no lasting interest in them. The single individual must also pass through the formative stages of universal Spirit so far as their content is concerned, but as shapes which Spirit has already left behind, as stages on a way that has been made level with toil. Thus, as far as factual information is concerned, we find that what in former ages engaged the attention of men of mature mind, has been reduced to the level of facts, exercises, and even games for children; and, in the child's progress through school, we shall recognize the history of the cultural development of the world traced, as it were, in a silhouette. This past existence is the already acquired property of universal Spirit which constitutes the Substance of the individual, and hence appears externally to him as his inorganic nature. In this respect formative education, regarded from the side of the individual, consists in his acquiring what thus lies at hand, devouring his inorganic nature, and taking possession of it for himself. But, regarded from the side of universal Spirit as substance, this is nothing but its own acquisition of self-consciousness, the bringing-about of its own becoming and reflection into itself.

29. Science sets forth this formative process in all its detail and
necessity, exposing the mature configuration of everything which has
already been reduced to a moment and property of Spirit. The goal is
Spirit's insight into what knowing is. Impatience demands the impossible, to wit, the attainment of the end without the means. But the *length*
of this path has to be endured, because, for one thing, each moment is
necessary; and further, each moment has to be *lingered* over, because each
is itself a complete individual shape, and one is only viewed in absolute
perspective when its determinateness is regarded as a concrete whole, or
the whole is regarded as uniquely qualified by that determination. Since
the Substance of the individual, the World-Spirit itself, has had the
patience to pass through these shapes over the long passage of time, and
to take upon itself the enormous labor of world-history, in which it
embodied in each shape as much of its entire content as that shape was
capable of holding, and since it could not have attained consciousness of
itself by any lesser effort, the individual certainly cannot by the nature of
the case comprehend his own substance more easily. Yet, at the same
time, he does have less trouble, since all this has already been *implicitly*
accomplished; the content is already the actuality reduced to a possibility, its immediacy overcome, and the embodied shape reduced to
abbreviated, simple determinations of thought. It is no longer existence
in the form of *being-in-itself*—neither still in the original form (of an
abstract concept), nor submerged in existence—but is now the *recollected
in-itself*, ready for conversion into the form of *being-for-self*. How this is
done must now be described more precisely.

30. We take up the movement of the whole from the point where the
sublation of *existence* as such is no longer necessary; what remains to be
done, and what requires a higher level of cultural reorientation, is to
represent and to get acquainted with these forms. The existence that has
been taken back into the Substance has only been *immediately* transposed
into the element of the self through that first negation. Hence this
acquired property still has the same character of uncomprehended immediacy, of passive indifference, as existence itself; existence has thus
merely passed over into *figurative representation*. At the same time it is
thus something *familiar*, something which the existent Spirit is finished
and done with, so that it is no longer active or really interested in it.
Although the activity that has finished with existence is itself only the
movement of the particular Spirit, the Spirit that does not comprehend
itself, (genuine) knowing, on the other hand, is directed against the
representation thus formed, against this (mere) familiarity; knowing is
the activity of the *universal self*, the concern of *thinking*.

31. Quite generally, the familiar, just because it is familiar, is not
cognitively understood. The commonest way in which we deceive either

ourselves or others about understanding is by assuming something as familiar, and accepting it on that account; with all its pros and cons, such knowing never gets anywhere, and it knows not why. Subject and object, God, Nature, Understanding, sensibility, and so on, are uncritically taken for granted as familiar, established as valid, and made into fixed points for starting and stopping. While these remain unmoved, the knowing activity goes back and forth between them, thus moving only on their surface. Apprehending and testing likewise consist in seeing whether everybody's impression of the matter coincides with what is asserted about these fixed points, whether it seems that way to him or not.

32. The *analysis* of an idea, as it used to be carried out, was, in fact, nothing else than ridding it of the form in which it had become familiar. To break an idea up into its original elements is to return to its moments, which at least do not have the form of the given idea, but rather constitute the immediate property of the self. This analysis, to be sure, only arrives at *thoughts* which are themselves familiar, fixed, and inert determinations. But what is thus *separated* and non-actual is an essential moment; for it is only because the concrete does divide itself, and make itself into something non-actual, that it is self-moving. The activity of dissolution is the power and work of the *Understanding*, the most astonishing and mightiest of powers, or rather the absolute power. The circle that remains self-enclosed and, like substance, holds its moments together, is an immediate relationship, one therefore which has nothing astonishing about it. But that an accident as such, detached from what circumscribes it, what is bound and is actual only in its context with others, should attain an existence of its own and a separate freedom— this is the tremendous power of the negative; it is the energy of thought, of the pure "I." Death, if that is what we want to call this non-actuality, is of all things the most dreadful, and to hold fast what is dead requires the greatest strength. Lacking strength, Beauty hates the Understanding for asking of her what it cannot do. But the life of Spirit is not the life that shrinks from death and keeps itself untouched by devastation, but rather the life that endures it and maintains itself in it. It wins its truth only when, in utter dismemberment, it finds itself. It is this power, not as something positive, which closes its eyes to the negative, as when we say of something that it is nothing or is false, and then, having done with it, turn away and pass on to something else; on the contrary, Spirit is this power only by looking the negative in the face, and tarrying with it. This tarrying with the negative is the magical power that converts it into being. This power is identical with what we earlier called the Subject, which by giving determinateness an existence in its own element supersedes abstract immediacy, i.e., the immediacy which barely is, and thus

is authentic substance: that being or immediacy whose mediation is not outside of it but which is this mediation itself.

33. The fact that the object represented becomes the property of pure self-consciousness, its elevation to universality in general, is only one aspect of formative education, not its fulfillment.—The manner of study in ancient times differed from that of the modern age in that the former was the proper and complete formation of the natural consciousness. Putting itself to the test at every point of its existence, and philosophizing about everything it came across, it made itself into a universality that was active through and through. In modern times, however, the individual finds the abstract form ready-made; the effort to grasp and appropriate it is more the direct driving-forth of what is within and the truncated generation of the universal than it is the emergence of the latter from the concrete variety of existence. Hence the task nowadays consists not so much in purging the individual of an immediate, sensuous mode of apprehension, and making him into a substance that is an object of thought and that thinks, but rather in just the opposite, in freeing determinate thoughts from their fixity so as to give actuality to the universal, and impart to it spiritual life. But it is far harder to bring fixed thoughts into a fluid state than to do so with sensuous existence. The reason for this was given above: fixed thoughts have the "I," the power of the negative, or pure actuality, for the substance and element of their existence, whereas sensuous determinations have only powerless, abstract immediacy, or being as such. Thoughts become fluid when pure thinking, this inner *immediacy*, recognizes itself as a moment, or when the pure certainty of self abstracts from itself—not by leaving itself out, or setting itself aside, but by giving up the *fixity* of its self-positing, by giving up not only the fixity of the pure concrete, which the "I" itself is, in contrast with its differentiated content, but also the fixity of the differentiated moments which, posited in the element of pure thinking, share the unconditioned nature of the "I." Through this movement the pure thoughts become *Notions*, and are only now what they are in truth, self-movements, circles, spiritual essences, which is what their substance is.

34. This movement of pure essences constitutes the nature of scientific method in general. Regarded as the connectedness of their content it is the necessary expansion of that content into an organic whole. Through this movement the path by which the Notion of knowledge is reached becomes likewise a necesasry and complete process of becoming; so that this preparatory path ceases to be a casual philosophizing that fastens on to this or that object, relationship, or thought that happens to pop up in the imperfect consciousness, or tries to base the truth on the

pros and cons, the inferences and consequences, of rigidly defined thoughts. Instead, this pathway, through the movement of the Notion, will encompass the entire sphere of secular consciousness in its necessary development.

35. Further, an exposition of this kind constitutes the *first* part of Science, because the existence of Spirit *qua* primary is nothing but the immediate or the beginning—but not yet its return into itself. The *element of immediate existence* is therefore what distinguishes this part of Science from the others. The statement of this distinction leads us into a discussion of some fixed ideas which usually crop up in this connection.

36. The immediate existence of Spirit, *consciousness*, contains the two moments of knowing and the objectivity negative to knowing. Since it is in this element (of consciousness) that Spirit develops itself and explicates its moments, these moments contain that antithesis, and they all appear as shapes of consciousness. The Science of this pathway is the Science of the *experience* which consciousness goes through; the substance and its movement are viewed as the object of consciousness. Consciousness knows and comprehends only what falls within its experience; for what is contained in this is nothing but spiritual substance, and this, too, as *object* of the self. But spirit becomes object because it is just this movement of becoming an *other to itself*, i.e., becoming an *object to itself*, and of suspending this otherness. And experience is the name we give to just this movement, in which the immediate, the unexperienced, i.e., the abstract, whether it be of sensuous (but still unsensed) being, or only thought of as simple, becomes alienated from itself and then returns to itself from this alienation, and is only then revealed for the first time in its actuality and truth, just as it then has become a property of consciousness also.

37. The disparity which exists in consciousness between the "I" and the substance which is its object is the distinction between them, the *negative* in general. This can be regarded as the *defect* of both, though it is their soul, or that which moves them. That is why some of the ancients conceived the *void* as the principle of motion, for they rightly saw the moving principle as the *negative*, though they did not as yet grasp that the negative is the self. Now, although this negative appears at first as a disparity between the "I" and its object, it is just as much the disparity of the substance with itself. Thus what seems to happen outside of it, to be an activity directed against it, is really its own doing, and Substance shows itself to be essentially Subject. When it has shown this completely, Spirit has made its existence identical with its essence; it has itself for its object just as it is, and the abstract element of immediacy,

and of the separation of knowing and truth, is overcome. Being is then absolutely mediated; it is a substantial content which is just as immediately the property of the "I," it is self-like or the Notion.

With this, the Phenomenology of Spirit is concluded. What Spirit prepares for itself in it, is the element of (true) knowing. In this element the moments of Spirit now spread themselves out in that *form of simplicity* which knows its object as its own self. They no longer fall apart into the antithesis of being and knowing, but remain in the simple oneness of knowing; they are the True in the form of the True, and their difference is only the difference of content. Their movement, which organizes itself in this element into a whole, is *Logic* or *speculative philosophy*. . . .

47. Philosophy has to do, not with *unessential* determinations, but with a determination in so far as it is essential; its element and content is not the abstract or nonactual, but the *actual*, that which posits itself and is alive within itself—existence within its own Notion. It is the process which begets and traverses its own moments, and this whole movement constitutes what is positive (in it) and its truth. This truth therefore includes the negative also, what would be called the false, if it could be regarded as something from which one might abstract. The evanescent itself must, on the contrary, be regarded as essential, not as something fixed, cut off from the True, and left lying who knows where outside it, any more than the True is to be regarded as something on the other side, positive and dead. Appearance is the arising and passing away that does not itself arise and pass away, but is 'in itself' (i.e., subsists intrinsically), and constitutes the actuality and the movement of the life of truth. The True is thus the Bacchanalian revel in which no member is not drunk; yet because each member collapses as soon as he drops out, the revel is just as much transparent and simple repose. Judged in the court of this movement, the single shapes of Spirit do not persist any more than determinate thoughts do, but they are as much positive and necessary moments, as they are negative and evanescent. In the *whole* of the movement, seen as a state of repose, what distinguishes itself therein, and gives itself particular existence, is preserved as something that *recollects* itself, whose existence is self-knowledge, and whose self-knowledge is just as immediately existence. . . .

53. Science dare only organize itself by the life of the Notion itself. The determinateness, which is taken from the schema and externally attached to an existent thing, is, in Science, the self-moving soul of the realized content. The movement of a being that immediately is, consists partly in becoming an other than itself, and thus becoming its own immanent content; partly in taking back into itself this unfolding (of its content) or this existence of it, i.e., in making *itself* into a moment, and simplifying itself into something determinate. In the former movement,

negativity is the differentiating and positing of *existence*; in this return into self, it is the becoming of the *determinate simplicity*. It is in this way that the content shows that its determinateness is not received from something else, nor externally attached to it, but that it determines itself, and ranges itself as a moment having its own place in the whole. The Understanding, in its pigeon-holing process, keeps the necessity and Notion of the content to itself—all that constitutes the concreteness, the actuality, the living movement of the reality which it arranges. Or rather, it does not keep this to itself, since it does not recognize it; for, if it had this insight, it would surely give some sign of it. It does not even recognize the need for it, else it would drop its schematizing, or at least realize that it can never hope to learn more in this fashion than one can learn from a table of contents. A table of contents is all that it offers, the content itself it does not offer at all.

Even when the specific determinateness—say one like Magnetism, for example,—is in itself concrete or real, the Understanding degrades it into something lifeless, merely predicating it of another existent thing, rather than cognizing it as the immanent life of the thing, or cognizing its native and unique way of generating and expressing itself in that thing. The formal Understanding leaves it to others to add this principal feature. Instead of entering into the immanent content of the thing, it is forever surveying the whole and standing above the particular existence of which it is speaking, i.e., it does not see it at all. Scientific cognition, on the contrary, demands surrender to the life of the object, or, what amounts to the same thing, confronting and expressing its inner necessity. Thus, absorbed in its object, scientific cognition forgets about that general survey, which is merely the reflection of the cognitive process away from the content and back into itself. Yet, immersed in the material, and advancing with its movement, scientific cognition does come back to itself, but not before its filling or content is taken back into itself, is simplified into a determinateness, and has reduced itself to *one* aspect of its own existence and passed over into its higher truth. Through this process the simple, self-surveying whole itself emerges from the wealth in which its reflection seemed to be lost.

54. In general, because, as we put it above, substance is in itself or implicitly Subject, all content is its own reflection into itself. The subsistence or substance of anything that exists is its self-identity; for a failure of self-identity would be its dissolution. Self-identity, however, is pure abstraction; but this is *thinking*. When I say "quality," I am saying simple determinateness; it is by quality that one existence is distinguished from another, or is an existence; it is for itself, or it subsists through this simple oneness with itself. But it is thereby essentially a *thought*. Comprehended in this is the fact that Being is

Thought; and this is the source of that insight which usually eludes the usual superficial [*begrifflos*] talk about the identity of Thought and Being.—Now, since the subsistence of an existent thing is a self-identity or pure abstraction, it is the abstraction of itself from itself, or it is itself its lack of self-identity and its dissolution—its own inwardness and withdrawal into itself—its own becoming. Because this is the nature of what is, and in so far as what is has this nature for (our) knowing, this knowing is not an activity that deals with the content as something alien, is not a reflection into itself away from the content. Science is not that idealism which replaced the dogmatism of assertion with a dogmatism of assurance, or a dogmatism of self-certainty. On the contrary, since (our) knowing sees the content return into its own inwardness, its activity is totally absorbed in the content, for it is the immanent self of the content; yet it has at the same time returned into itself, for it is pure self-identity in otherness. Thus it is the cunning which, while seeming to abstain from activity, looks on and watches how determinateness, with its concrete life, just where it fancies it is pursuing its own self-preservation and particular interest, is in fact doing the very opposite, is an activity that results in its own dissolution, and makes itself a moment of the whole.

55. Above we indicated the significance of the *Understanding* in reference to the self-consciousness of substance; we can now see clearly from what has been said its significance in reference to the determination of substance as being. Existence is Quality, self-identical determinateness, or determinate simplicity, determinate thought; this is the Understanding of existence (i.e., the nature of existence from the standpoint of the Understanding). Hence, it is *Noûs*, as Anaxagoras first recognized the essence of things to be. Those who came after him grasped the nature of existence more definitely as *Eidos* or *Idea*, determinate Universality, Species or Kind. It might seem as if the term *Species* or *Kind* is too commonplace, too inadequate, for Ideas such as the Beautiful, the Holy, and the Eternal that are currently in fashion. But as a matter of fact Idea expresses neither more nor less than Species or Kind. But nowadays an expression which exactly designates a Notion is often spurned in favor of one which, if only because it is of foreign extraction, shrouds the Notion in a fog, and hence sounds more edifying.

Precisely because existence is defined as Species, it is a simple thought; *Noûs*, simplicity, is substance. On account of its simplicity or self-identity it appears fixed and enduring. But this self-identity is no less negativity; therefore its fixed existence passes over into its dissolution. The determinateness seems at first to be due entirely to the fact that it is related to an *other*, and its movement seems imposed on it by an alien power; but having its otherness within itself, and being self-moving, is just what is involved in the *simplicity* of thinking itself; for this simple thinking is the self-moving and self-differentiating thought, it is its own inwardness, it is the pure Notion. Thus common understanding, too, is a becoming, and, as this becoming, it is *reason*ableness.

56. It is in this nature of what is to be in its being its own Notion, that *logical necessity* in general consists. This alone is the rational element and the rhythm of the organic whole; it is as much *knowledge* of the content, as the content is the Notion and essence—in other words, it alone is *speculative philosophy*. The self-moving concrete shape makes itself into a simple determinateness; in so doing it raises itself to logical form, and exists in its essentiality; its concrete existence is just this movement, and is directly a logical existence. It is for this reason unnecessary to clothe the content in an external (logical) formalism; the content is in its very nature the transition into such formalism, but a formalism which ceases to be external, since the form is the innate development of the concrete content itself. . . .

59. There are two aspects of the procedure of argumentation to which speculative [*begreifende*] thinking is opposed and which call for further notice. First, such reasoning adopts a negative attitude towards the content it apprehends; it knows how to refute it and destroy it. That something is *not* the case, is a merely negative insight, a dead end which does not lead to a new content beyond itself. In order to have a content once again, something new must be taken over from elsewhere. Argumentation is reflection into the empty "I," the vanity of its own knowing. This vanity, however, expresses not only the vanity of this content, but also the futility of this insight itself; for this insight is the negative that fails to see the positive within itself. Because this reflection does not get its very negativity as its content, it is never at the heart of the matter, but always beyond it. For this reason it imagines that by establishing the void it is always ahead of any insight rich in content. On the other hand, in speculative [*begreifenden*] thinking, as we have already shown, the negative belongs to the content itself, and is the *positive*, both as the *immanent* movement and determination of the content, and as the whole of this process. Looked at as a result, what emerges from this process is the *determinate* negative which is consequently a positive content as well.

60. But in view of the fact that such thinking has a content, whether of picture-thoughts or abstract thoughts or a mixture of both, argumentation has another side which makes comprehension difficult for it. The remarkable nature of this other side is closely linked with the above-mentioned essence of the Idea, or rather it expresses the Idea in the way that it appears as the movement which is thinking apprehension. For whereas, in its negative behavior, which we have just discussed, ratiocinative thinking is itself the self into which the content returns, in

its positive cognition, on the other hand, the self is a *Subject* to which the content is related as Accident and Predicate. This Subject constitutes the basis to which the content is attached, and upon which the movement runs back and forth. Speculative [*begreifendes*] thinking behaves in a different way. Since the Notion is the object's own self, which presents itself as the *coming-to-be of the object*, it is not a passive Subject inertly supporting the Accidents; it is, on the contrary, the self-moving Notion which takes its determinations back into itself. In this movement the passive Subject itself perishes; it enters into the differences and the content, and constitutes the determinateness, i.e., the differentiated content and its movement, instead of remaining inertly over against it. The solid ground which argumentation has in the passive Subject is therefore shaken, and only this movement itself becomes the object. The Subject that fills its content ceases to go beyond it, and cannot have any further Predicates or accidental properties. Conversely, the dispersion of the content is thereby bound together under the self; it is not the universal which, free from the Subject, could belong to several others. Thus the content is, in fact, no longer a Predicate of the Subject, but is the Substance, the essence and the Notion of what is under discussion. Picture-thinking, whose nature it is to run through the Accidents or Predicates and which, because they are nothing more than Predicates and Accidents, rightly goes beyond them, is checked in its progress, since that which has the form of a Predicate in a proposition is the Substance itself. It suffers, as we might put it, a counter-thrust. Starting from the Subject as though this were a permanent ground, it finds that, since the Predicate is really the Substance, the Subject has passed over into the Predicate, and, by this very fact, has been sublated; and, since in this way what seems to be the Predicate has become the whole and the independent mass, thinking cannot roam at will, but is impeded by this weight.

Usually, the Subject is first made the basis, as the *objective*, fixed self; thence the necessary movement to the multiplicity of determinations or Predicates proceeds. Here, that Subject is replaced by the knowing "I" itself, which links the Predicates with the Subject holding them. But, since that first Subject enters into the determinations themselves and is their soul, the second Subject, viz. the knowing "I," still finds in the Predicate what it thought it had finished with and got away from, and from which it hoped to return into itself; and, instead of being able to function as the determining agent in the movement of predication, arguing back and forth whether to attach this or that Predicate, it is really still occupied with the self of the content, having to remain associated with it, instead of being for itself.

61. Formally, what has been said can be expressed thus: the general

nature of the judgment or proposition, which involves the distinction of Subject and Predicate, is destroyed by the speculative proposition, and the proposition of identity which the former becomes contains the counter-thrust against that subject-predicate relationship.—This conflict between the general form of a proposition and the unity of the Notion which destroys it is similar to the conflict that occurs in rhythm between meter and accent. Rhythm results from the floating center and the unification of the two. So, too, in the philosophical proposition the identification of Subject and Predicate is not meant to destroy the difference between them, which the form of the proposition expresses; their unity, rather, is meant to emerge as a harmony. The form of the proposition is the appearance of the determinate sense, or the accent that distinguishes its fulfillment; but that the predicate expresses the Substance, and that the Subject itself falls into the universal, this is the *unity* in which the accent dies away.

62. To illustrate what has been said: in the proposition "God is being," the Predicate is "being"; it has the significance of something substantial in which the Subject is dissolved. "Being" is here meant to be not a Predicate, but rather the essence; it seems, consequently, that God ceases to be what he is from his position in the proposition, viz. a fixed Subject. Here thinking, instead of making progress in the transition from Subject to Predicate, in reality feels itself checked by the loss of the Subject, and, missing it, is thrown back on to the thought of the Subject. Or since the Predicate itself has been expressed as a Subject, as *the* being or *essence* which exhausts the nature of the Subject, thinking finds the Subject immediately in the Predicate; and now, having returned into itself in the Predicate, instead of being in a position where it has freedom for argument, it is still absorbed in the content, or at least is faced with the demand that it should be. Similarly, too, when one says: "the *actual* is the *universal*," the actual as subject disappears in its predicate. The universal is not meant to have merely the significance of a predicate, as if the proposition asserted only that the actual is universal; on the contrary, the universal is meant to express the essence of the actual.—Thinking therefore loses the firm objective basis it had in the subject when, in the predicate, it is thrown back on to the subject, and when, in the predicate, it does not return into itself, but into the subject of the content.

63. This abnormal inhibition of thought is in large measure the source of the complaints regarding the unintelligibility of philosophical writings from individuals who otherwise possess the educational requirements for understanding them. Here we see the reason behind one particular complaint so often made against them: that so much has to be read over and over before it can be understood—a complaint whose

burden is presumed to be quite outrageous, and, if justified, to admit of no defense. It is clear from the above what this amounts to. The philosophical proposition, since it *is* a proposition, leads one to believe that the usual subject-predicate relation obtains, as well as the usual attitude towards knowing. But the philosophical content destroys this attitude and this opinion. We learn by experience that we meant something other than we meant to mean; and this correction of our meaning compels our knowing to go back to the proposition, and understand it in some other way.

64. One difficulty which should be avoided comes from mixing up the speculative with the ratiocinative methods, so that what is said of the Subject at one time signifies its Notion, at another time merely its Predicate or accidental property. The one method interferes with the other, and only a philosophical exposition that rigidly excludes the usual way of relating the parts of a proposition could achieve the goal of plasticity.

65. As a matter of fact, non-speculative thinking also has its valid rights which are disregarded in the speculative way of stating a proposition. The sublation of the form of the proposition must not happen only in an *immediate* manner, through the mere content of the proposition. On the contrary, this opposite movement must find explicit expression; it must not just be the inward inhibition mentioned above. This return of the Notion into itself must be *set forth*. This movement which constitutes what formerly the proof was supposed to accomplish, is the dialectical movement of the proposition itself. This alone is the speculative *in act*, and only the expression of this movement is a speculative exposition. As a proposition, the speculative is only the *internal* inhibition and the non-*existential* return of the essence into itself. Hence we often find philosophical expositions referring us to this *inner* intuition; and in this way they evade the systematic exposition of the dialectical movement of the proposition which we have demanded.—The *proposition* should express *what* the True is; but essentially the True is Subject. As such it is merely the dialectical movement, this course that generates itself, going forth from, and returning to, itself. In non-speculative cognition proof constitutes this side of expressed inwardness. But once the dialectic has been separated from proof, the notion of philosophical demonstration has been lost. . . .

70. Should anyone ask for a royal road to Science, there is no more easy-going way than to rely on sound common sense; and for the rest, in order to keep up with the times, and with advances in philosophy, to read reviews of philosophical works, perhaps even to read their prefaces and first paragraphs. For these preliminary pages give the general principles on which everything turns, and the reviews, as well as

providing historical accounts, also provide the critical appraisal which, being a judgment, stands high above the work judged. This common road can be taken in casual dress; but the high sense for the Eternal, the Holy, the Infinite strides along in the robes of a high priest, on a road that is from the first no road, but has immediate being as its center, the genius of profound original ideas and lofty flashes of inspiration. But just as profundity of this kind still does not reveal the source of essential being, so, too, these skyrockets of inspiration are not yet the empyrean. True thoughts and scientific insight are only to be won through the labor of the Notion. Only the Notion can produce the universality of knowledge which is neither common vagueness nor the inadequacy of ordinary common sense, but a fully developed, perfected cognition; not the uncommon universality of a reason whose talents have been ruined by indolence and the conceit of genius, but a truth ripened to its properly matured form so as to be capable of being the property of all self-conscious Reason.

71. Since I hold that Science exists solely in the self-movement of the Notion, and since my view differs from, and is in fact wholly opposed to, current ideas regarding the nature and form of truth, both those referred to above and other peripheral aspects of them, it seems that any attempt to expound the system of Science from this point of view is unlikely to be favorably received. In the meantime, I can bear in mind that if at times the excellence of Plato's philosophy has been held to lie in his scientifically valueless myths, there have also been times, even called times of ecstatic dreaming, when Aristotle's philosophy was esteemed for its speculative depth, and Plato's *Parmenides* (surely the greatest artistic achievement of the ancient dialectic) was regarded as the true disclosure and positive expression of the divine life, and times when, despite the obscurity generated by ecstasy, this misunderstood ecstasy was in fact supposed to be nothing else than the pure Notion. Furthermore, what really is excellent in the philosophy of our time takes its value to lie in its scientific quality, and even though others take a different view, it is in fact only in virtue of its scientific character that it exerts any influence. Hence, I may hope, too, that this attempt to vindicate Science for the Notion, and to expound it in this its proper element, will succeed in winning acceptance through the inner truth of the subject-matter. We must hold to the conviction that it is the nature of truth to prevail when its time has come, and that it appears only when this time has come, and therefore never appears prematurely, nor finds a public not ripe to receive it; also we must accept that the individual needs that this should be so in order to verify what is as yet a matter for himself alone, and to experience the conviction, which in the first place belongs only to a particular individual, as something universally held. But in this connection the

public must often be distinguished from those who pose as its representatives and spokesmen. In many respects the attitude of the public is
quite different from, even contrary to, that of these spokesmen. Whereas
the public is inclined good-naturedly to blame itself when a philosophical work makes no appeal to it, these others, certain of their own compe-
tence, put all the blame on the author. The effect of such a work on the
public is more noiseless than the action of these dead men when they
bury their dead. The general level of insight now is altogether more
educated, its curiosity more awake, and its judgment more swiftly
reached, so that the feet of those who will carry you out are already at the
door. But from this we must often distinguish the more gradual effect
which corrects the attention extorted by imposing assurances and corrects, too, contemptuous censure, and gives some writers an audience
only after a time, while others after a time have no audience left.

72. For the rest, at a time when the universality of Spirit has gathered
such strength, and the singular detail, as is fitting, has become correspondingly less important, when, too, that universal aspect claims and
holds on to the whole range of the wealth it has developed, the share in
the total work of Spirit which falls to the individual can only be very
small. Because of this, the individual must all the more forget himself,
as the nature of Science implies and requires. Of course, he must make of
himself and achieve what he can; but less must be demanded of him, just
as he in turn can expect less of himself, and may demand less for himself.

INTRODUCTION

73. It is a natural assumption that in philosophy, before we start to deal
with its proper subject matter, viz. the actual cognition of what truly is,
one must first of all come to an understanding about cognition, which is
regarded either as the instrument to get hold of the Absolute, or as the
medium through which one discovers it. A certain uneasiness seems
justified, partly because there are different types of cognition, and one of
them might be more appropriate than another for the attainment of this
goal, so that we could make a bad choice of means; and partly because
cognition is a faculty of a definite kind and scope, and thus, without a
more precise definition of its nature and limits, we might grasp clouds of
error instead of the heaven of truth. This feeling of uneasiness is surely
bound to be transformed into the conviction that the whole project of
securing for consciousness through cognition what exists in itself is
absurd, and that there is a boundary between cognition and the Absolute
that completely separates them. For, if cognition is the instrument for
getting hold of absolute being, it is obvious that the use of an instrument
on a thing certainly does not let it be what it is for itself, but rather sets
out to reshape and alter it. If, on the other hand, cognition is not an

instrument of our activity but a more or less passive medium through which the light of truth reaches us, then again we do not receive the truth as it is in itself, but only as it exists through and in this medium. Either way we employ a means which immediately brings about the opposite of its own end; or rather, what is really absurd is that we should make use of a means at all.

It would seem, to be sure, that this evil could be remedied through an acquaintance with the way in which the *instrument* works; for this would enable us to eliminate from the representation of the Absolute which we have gained through it whatever is due to the instrument, and thus get the truth in its purity. But this "improvement" would in fact only bring us back to where we were before. If we remove from a reshaped thing what the instrument has done to it, then the thing—here the Absolute—becomes for us exactly what it was before this (accordingly) superfluous effort. On the other hand, if the Absolute is supposed merely to be brought nearer to us through this instrument, without anything in it being altered, like a bird caught by a lime-twig, it would surely laugh our little ruse to scorn, if it were not with us, in and for itself, all along, and of its own volition. For a ruse is just what cognition would be in such a case, since it would, with its manifold exertions, be giving itself the air of doing something quite different from creating a merely immediate and therefore effortless relationship. Or, if by testing cognition, which we conceive of as a *medium*, we get to know the law of its refraction, it is again useless to subtract this from the end result. For it is not the refraction of the ray, but the ray itself whereby truth reaches us, that is cognition; and if this were removed, all that would be indicated would be a pure direction or a blank space.

74. Meanwhile, if the fear of falling into error sets up a mistrust of Science, which in the absence of such scruples gets on with the work itself, and actually cognizes something, it is hard to see why we should not turn round and mistrust this very mistrust. Should we not be concerned as to whether this fear of error is not just the error itself? Indeed, this fear takes something—a great deal in fact—for granted as truth, supporting its scruples and inferences on what is itself in need of prior scrutiny to see if it is true. To be specific, it takes for granted certain ideas about cognition as an *instrument* and as a *medium*, and assumes that there is a *difference between ourselves and this cognition*. Above all, it presupposes that the Absolute stands on one side and cognition on the other, independent and separated from it, and yet is something real; or in other words, it presupposes that cognition which, since it is excluded from the Absolute, is surely outside of the truth as well, is nevertheless true, an assumption whereby what calls itself fear of error reveals itself rather as fear of the truth.

75. This conclusion stems from the fact that the Absolute alone is true, or the truth alone is absolute. One may set this aside on the grounds that there is a type of cognition which, though it does not cognize the Absolute as Science aims to, is still true, and that cognition in general, though it be incapable of grasping the Absolute, is still capable of grasping other kinds of truth. But we gradually come to see that this kind of talk which goes back and forth only leads to a hazy distinction between an absolute truth and some other kind of truth, and that words like "absolute," "cognition," etc. presuppose a meaning which has yet to be ascertained.

76. Instead of troubling ourselves with such useless ideas and locutions about cognition as "an instrument for getting hold of the Absolute," or as "a medium through which we view the truth" (relationships which surely, in the end, are what all these ideas of a cognition cut off from the Absolute, and an Absolute separated from cognition, amount to); instead of putting up with excuses which create the incapacity of Science by assuming relationships of this kind in order to be exempt from the hard work of Science, while at the same time giving the impression of working seriously and zealously; instead of bothering to refute all these ideas, we could reject them out of hand as adventitious and arbitrary, and the words associated with them like "absolute," "cognition," "objective" and "subjective," and countless others whose meaning is assumed to be generally familiar, could even be regarded as so much deception. For to give the impression that their meaning is generally well known, or that their Notion is comprehended, looks more like an attempt to avoid the main problem, which is precisely to provide this Notion. We could, with better justification, simply spare ourselves the trouble of paying any attention whatever to such ideas and locutions; for they are intended to ward off Science itself, and constitute merely an empty appearance of knowing, which vanishes immediately as soon as Science comes on the scene. But Science, just because it comes on the scene, is itself an appearance: in coming on the scene it is not yet Science in its developed and unfolded truth. In this connection it makes no difference whether we think of Science as the appearance because it comes on the scene alongside another mode of knowledge, or whether we call that other untrue knowledge its manifestation. In any case Science must liberate itself from this semblance, and it can do so only by turning against it. For, when confronted with a knowledge that is without truth, Science can neither merely reject it as an ordinary way of looking at things, while assuring us that its Science is a quite different sort of cognition for which that ordinary knowledge is of no account whatever; nor can it appeal to the vulgar view for the intimations it gives us of something better to come. By the former *assurance*, Science would be

declaring its power to lie simply in its *being*; but the untrue knowledge likewise appeals to the fact that *it is*, and *assures* us that for it Science is of no account. *One* bare assurance is worth just as much as another. Still less can Science appeal to whatever intimations of something better it may detect in the cognition that is without truth, to the signs which point in the direction of Science. For one thing, it would only be appealing again to what merely *is*; and for another, it would only be appealing to itself, and to itself in the mode in which it exists in the cognition that is without truth. In other words, it would be appealing to an inferior form of its being, to the way it appears, rather than to what it is in and for itself. It is for this reason that an exposition of how knowledge makes its appearance will here be undertaken.

77. Now, because it has only phenomenal knowledge for its object, this exposition seems not to be Science, free and self-moving in its own peculiar shape; yet from this standpoint it can be regarded as the path of the natural consciousness which presses forward to true knowledge; or as the way of the Soul which journeys through the series of its own configurations as though they were the stations appointed for it by its own nature, so that it may purify itself for the life of the Spirit, and achieve finally, through a completed experience of itself, the awareness of what it really is in itself.

78. Natural consciousness will show itself to be only the Notion of knowledge, or in other words, not to be real knowledge. But since it directly takes itself to be real knowledge, this path has a negative significance for it, and what is in fact the realization of the Notion, counts for it rather as the loss of its own self; for it does lose its truth on this path. The road can therefore be regarded as the pathway of *doubt*, or more precisely as the way of despair. For what happens on it is not what is ordinarily understood when the word "doubt" is used: shilly-shallying about this or that presumed truth, followed by a return to that truth again, after the doubt has been appropriately dispelled—so that at the end of the process the matter is taken to be what it was in the first place. On the contrary, this path is the conscious insight into the untruth of phenomenal knowledge, for which the supreme reality is what is in truth only the unrealized Notion. Therefore this thoroughgoing scepticism is also not the scepticism with which an earnest zeal for truth and Science fancies it has prepared and equipped itself in their service: the *resolve*, in Science, not to give oneself over to the thoughts of others, upon mere authority, but to examine everything for oneself and follow only one's own conviction, or better still, to produce everything oneself, and accept only one's own deed as what is true.

The series of configurations which consciousness goes through along this road is, in reality, the detailed history of the *education* of consciousness itself to the standpoint of Science. That zealous resolve represents this education simplistically as something directly over and done with in the making of the resolution; but the way of the Soul is the actual fulfillment of the resolution, in contrast to the untruth of that view. Now, following one's own conviction is, of course, more than giving oneself over to authority; but changing an opinion accepted on authority into an opinion held out of personal conviction does not necessarily alter the content of the opinion, or replace error with truth. The only difference between being caught up in a system of opinions and prejudices based on personal conviction, and being caught up in one based on the authority of others, lies in the added conceit that is innate in the latter position. The scepticism that is directed against the whole range of phenomenal consciousness, on the other hand, renders the Spirit for the first time competent to examine what truth is. For it brings about a state of despair about all the so-called natural ideas, thoughts, and opinions, regardless of whether they are called one's own or someone else's, ideas with which the consciousness that sets about the examination (of truth) *straight away* is still filled and hampered, so that it is, in fact, incapable of carrying out what it wants to undertake.

79. The necessary progression and interconnection of the forms of the unreal consciousness will by itself bring to pass the *completion* of the series. To make this more intelligible, it may be remarked, in a preliminary and general way, that the exposition of the untrue consciousness in its untruth is not a merely *negative* procedure. The natural consciousness itself normally takes this one-sided view of it; and a knowledge which makes this one-sidedness its very essence is itself one of the patterns of incomplete consciousness which occurs on the road itself, and will manifest itself in due course. This is just the scepticism which only ever sees pure nothingness in its result and abstracts from the fact that this nothingness is specifically the nothingness of that *from which it results*. For it is only when it is taken as the result of that from which it emerges, that it is, in fact, the true result; in that case it is itself a *determinate* nothingness, one which has a *content*. The scepticism that ends up with the bare abstraction of nothingness or emptiness cannot get any further from there, but must wait to see whether something new comes along and what it is, in order to throw it too into the same empty abyss. But when, on the other hand, the result is conceived as it is in truth, namely, as a *determinate* negation, a new form has thereby immediately arisen, and in the negation the transition is made through which the progress through the complete series of forms comes about of itself.

80. But the *goal* is as necessarily fixed for knowledge as the serial progression; it is the point where knowledge no longer needs to go

beyond itself, where knowledge finds itself, where Notion corresponds to object and object to Notion. Hence the progress towards this goal is also unhalting, and short of it no satisfaction is to be found at any of the stations on the way. Whatever is confined within the limits of a natural life cannot by its own efforts go beyond its immediate existence; but it is driven beyond it by something else, and this uprooting entails its death. Consciousness, however, is explicitly the *Notion* of itself. Hence it is something that goes beyond limits, and since these limits are its own, it is something that goes beyond itself. With the positing of a single particular the beyond is also established for consciousness, even if it is only *alongside* the limited object as in the case of spatial intuition. Thus consciousness suffers this violence at its own hands: it spoils its own limited satisfaction. When consciousness feels this violence, its anxiety may well make it retreat from the truth, and strive to hold on to what it is in danger of losing. But it can find no peace. If it wishes to remain in a state of unthinking inertia, then thought troubles its thoughtlessness, and its own unrest disturbs its inertia. Or, if it entrenches itself in sentimentality, which assures us that it finds everything to be *good in its kind*, then this assurance likewise suffers violence at the hands of Reason, for, precisely in so far as something is merely a kind, Reason finds it *not* to be good. Or, again, its fear of the truth may lead consciousness to hide, from itself and others, behind the pretension that its burning zeal for truth makes it difficult or even impossible to find any other truth but the unique truth of vanity—that of being at any rate cleverer than any thoughts that one gets by oneself or from others. This conceit which understands how to belittle every truth, in order to turn back into itself and gloat over its own understanding, which knows how to dissolve every thought and always find the same barren Ego instead of any content—this is a satisfaction which we must leave to itself, for it flees from the universal, and seeks only to be for itself.

81. In addition to these preliminary general remarks about the manner and the necessity of the progression, it may be useful to say something about the *method of carrying out the inquiry*. If this exposition is viewed as a way of *relating Science* to *phenomenal* knowledge, and as an investigation and *examination of the reality of cognition*, it would seem that it cannot take place without some presupposition which can serve as its underlying *criterion*. For an examination consists in applying an accepted standard, and in determining whether something is right or wrong on the basis of the resulting agreement or disagreement of the thing examined; thus the standard as such (and Science likewise if it were the criterion) is accepted as the *essence* or as the *in-itself*. But here, where Science has just begun to come on the scene, neither Science nor anything else has yet justified itself as the essence or the in-itself; and

without something of the sort it seems that no examination can take place.

82. This contradiction and its removal will become more definite if we call to mind the abstract determinations of truth and knowledge as they occur in consciousness. Consciousness simultaneously *distinguishes* itself from something, and at the same time *relates* itself to it, or, as it is said, this something exists *for* consciousness; and the determinate aspect of this *relating*, or of the *being* of something for a consciousness, is *knowing*. But we distinguish this being-for-another from *being-in-itself*; whatever is related to knowledge or knowing is also distinguished from it, and posited as existing outside of this relationship; this *being-in-itself* is called *truth*. Just what might be involved in these determinations is of no further concern to us here. Since our object is phenomenal knowledge, its determinations too will at first be taken directly as they present themselves; and they do present themselves very much as we have already apprehended them.

83. Now, if we inquire into the truth of knowledge, it seems that we are asking what knowledge is *in itself*. Yet in this inquiry knowledge is *our* object, something that exists *for us*; and the *in-itself* that would supposedly result from it would rather be the being of knowledge *for us*. What we asserted to be its essence would be not so much its truth but rather just our knowledge of it. The essence or criterion would lie within ourselves, and that which was to be compared with it and about which a decision would be reached through this comparison would not necessarily have to recognize the validity of such a standard.

84. But the dissociation, or this semblance of dissociation and presupposition, is overcome by the nature of the object we are investigating. Consciousness provides its own criterion from within itself, so that the investigation becomes a comparison of consciousness with itself; for the distinction made above falls within it. In consciousness one thing exists *for* another, i.e., consciousness regularly contains the determinateness of the moment of knowledge; at the same time, this other is to consciousness not merely *for it*, but is also outside of this relationship, or exists *in itself*; the moment of truth. Thus, in what consciousness affirms from within itself as *being-in-itself* or the *True*, we have the standard which consciousness itself sets up by which to measure what it knows. If we designate *knowledge* as the Notion, but the essence or the *True* as what exists, or the *object*, then the examination consists in seeing whether the Notion corresponds to the object. But if we call the *essence* or in-itself of the *object* the Notion, and on the other hand understand by the *object* the Notion itself as *object*, viz. as it exists *for an other*, then the examination consists in seeing whether the object corresponds to its Notion. It is evident, of course, that the two procedures are the same. But the

essential point to bear in mind throughout the whole investigation is that these two moments, "Notion" and "object," "being-for-another" and "being-in-itself," both fall *within* that knowledge which we are investigating. Consequently, we do not need to import criteria, or to make use of our own bright ideas and thoughts during the course of the inquiry; it is precisely when we leave these aside that we succeed in contemplating the matter in hand as it is *in and for itself*.

85. But not only is a contribution by us superfluous, since Notion and object, the criterion and what is to be tested, are present in consciousness itself, but we are also spared the trouble of comparing the two and really *testing* them, so that, since what consciousness examines is its own self, all that is left for us to do is simply to look on. For consciousness is, on the one hand, consciousness of the object, and on the other, consciousness of itself; consciousness of what for it is the True, and consciousness of its knowledge of the truth. Since both are *for* the same consciousness, this consciousness is itself their comparison; it is for this same consciousness to know whether its knowledge of the object corresponds to the object or not. The object, it is true, seems only to be for consciousness in the way that consciousness knows it; it seems that consciousness cannot, as it were, get behind the object as it exists for consciousness so as to examine what the object is *in itself*, and hence, too, cannot test its own knowledge by that standard. But the distinction between the in-itself and knowledge is already present in the very fact that consciousness knows an object at all. Something is *for it* the *in-itself*; and knowledge, or the being of the object for consciousness, is, *for it*, another moment. Upon this distinction, which is present as a fact, the examination rests. If the comparison shows that these two moments do not correspond to one another, it would seem that consciousness must alter its knowledge to make it conform to the object. But, in fact, in the alteration of the knowledge, the object itself alters for it too, for the knowledge that was present was essentially a knowledge of the object: as the knowledge changes, so too does the object, for it essentially belonged to this knowledge. Hence it comes to pass for consciousness that what it previously took to be the *in-itself* is not an *in-itself*, or that it was only an in-itself *for consciousness*. Since consciousness thus finds that its knowledge does not correspond to its object, the object itself does not stand the test; in other words, the criterion for testing is altered when that for which it was to have been the criterion fails to pass the test; and the testing is not only a testing of what we know, but also a testing of the criterion of what knowing is.

86. *Inasmuch as the new true object issues from it*, this *dialectical* movement which consciousness exercises on itself and which affects both its knowledge and its object, is precisely what is called *experience*

[*Erfahrung*]. In this connection there is a moment in the process just mentioned which must be brought out more clearly, for through it a new light will be thrown on the exposition which follows. Consciousness knows *something*; this object is the essence or the *in-itself*; but it is also for consciousness the in-itself. This is where the ambiguity of this truth enters. We see that consciousness now has two objects: one is the first *in-itself*, the second is the *being-for-consciousness of this in-itself*. The latter appears at first sight to be merely the reflection of consciousness into itself, i.e., what consciousness has in mind is not an object, but only its knowledge of that first object. But, as was shown previously, the first object, in being known, is altered for consciousness; it ceases to be the in-itself, and becomes something that is the *in-itself* only *for consciousness*. And this then is the True: the being-for-consciousness of this in-itself. Or, in other words, this is the *essence*, or the *object* of consciousness. This new object contains the nothingness of the first, it is what experience has made of it.

87. This exposition of the course of experience contains a moment in virtue of which it does not seem to agree with what is ordinarily understood by experience. This is the moment of transition from the first object and the knowledge of it, to the other object, which experience is said to be about. Our account implied that our knowledge of the first object, or the being-*for*-consciousness of the first in-itself, itself becomes the second object. It usually seems to be the case, on the contrary, that our experience of the untruth of our first notion comes by way of a second object which we come upon by chance and externally, so that our part in all this is simply the pure *apprehension* of what is in and for itself. From the present viewpoint, however, the new object shows itself to have come about through a *reversal of consciousness itself*. This way of looking at the matter is something contributed by *us*, by means of which the succession of experiences through which consciousness passes is raised into a scientific progression—but it is not known to the consciousness that we are observing. But, as a matter of fact, we have here the same situation as the one discussed in regard to the relation between our exposition and scepticism, viz. that in every case the result of an untrue mode of knowledge must not be allowed to run away into an empty nothing, but must necessarily be grasped as the nothing *of that from which it results*—a result which contains what was true in the preceding knowledge. It shows up here like this: since what first appeared as the object sinks for consciousness to the level of its way of knowing it, and since the in-itself becomes a *being-for-consciousness* of the in-itself, the latter is now the new object. Herewith a new pattern of consciousness comes on the scene as well, for which the essence is something different from what it was at the preceding stage. It is this fact that guides the

entire series of the patterns of consciousness in their necessary sequence. But it is just this necessity itself, or the *origination* of the new object, that presents itself to consciousness without its understanding how this happens, which proceeds for us, as it were, behind the back of consciousness. Thus in the movement of consciousness there occurs a moment of *being-in-itself* or *being-for-us* which is not present to the consciousness comprehended in the experience itself. The *content*, however, of what presents itself to us does exist *for it*; we comprehend only the formal aspect of that content, or its pure origination. *For it*, what has thus arisen exists only as an object; *for us*, it appears at the same time as movement and a process of becoming.

88. Because of this necessity, the way to Science is itself already *Science*, and hence, in virtue of its content, is the Science of the *experience of consciousness*.

89. The experience of itself which consciousness goes through can, in accordance with its Notion, comprehend nothing less than the entire system of consciousness, or the entire realm of the truth of Spirit. For this reason, the moments of this truth are exhibited in their own proper determinateness, viz. as being not abstract moments, but as they are for consciousness, or as consciousness itself stands forth in its relation to them. Thus the moments of the whole are *patterns of consciousness*. In pressing forward to its true existence, consciousness will arrive at a point at which it gets rid of its semblance of being burdened with something alien, with what is only for it, and some sort of "other," at a point where appearance becomes identical with essence, so that its exposition will coincide at just this point with the authentic Science of Spirit. And finally, when consciousness itself grasps this its own essence, it will signify the nature of absolute knowledge itself.

Alexandre Kojève

Introduction to the Reading of Hegel

In Place of an Introduction

Hegel . . . erfasst die *Arbeit* als das *Wesen*, als das
sich bewährende Wesen des Menschen.

KARL MARX

[Man is Self-Consciousness. He is conscious of himself, conscious of his
human reality and dignity; and it is in this that he is essentially different
from animals, which do not go beyond the level of simple Sentiment of
self. Man becomes conscious of himself at the moment when—for the
"first" time—he says "I." To understand man by understanding his
"origin" is, therefore, to understand the origin of the I revealed by
speech.

[Now, the analysis of "thought," "reason," "understanding," and so
on—in general, of the cognitive, contemplative, passive behavior of a
being or a "knowing subject"—never reveals the why or the how of the
birth of the word "I," and consequently of self-consciousness— that is,
of the human reality. The man who contemplates is "absorbed" by what
he contemplates; the "knowing subject" "loses" himself in the object
that is known. Contemplation reveals the object, not the subject. The
object, and not the subject, is what shows itself to him in and by—or
better, as—the act of knowing. The man who is "absorbed" by the
object that he is contemplating can be "brought back to himself" only
by a Desire; by the desire to eat, for example. The (conscious) Desire of a
being is what constitutes that being as I and reveals it as such by moving
it to say "I. . . ." Desire is what transforms Being, revealed to itself by
itself in (true) knowledge, into an "object" revealed to a "subject" by a
subject different from the object and "opposed" to it. It is in and by—or
better still, as—"his" Desire that man is formed and is revealed—to

Excerpted from Alexandre Kojève, *Introduction to the Reading of Hegel*, translated by
J. H. Nichols, edited by A. Bloom (New York: Basic Books, 1969), 3–30.
The commentary is in brackets. Words joined by hyphens correspond to a single
German word.

98

himself and to others—as an I, as the I that is essentially different from, and radically opposed to, the non-I. The (human) I is the I of a Desire or of Desire.

[The very being of man, the self-conscious being, therefore, implies and presupposes Desire. Consequently, the human reality can be formed and maintained only within a biological reality, an animal life. But, if animal Desire is the necessary condition of Self-Consciousness, it is not the sufficient condition. By itself, this Desire constitutes only the Sentiment of self.

[In contrast to the knowledge that keeps man in a passive quietude, Desire dis-quiets him and moves him to action. Born of Desire, action tends to satisfy it, and can do so only by the "negation," the destruction, or at least the transformation, of the desired object: to satisfy hunger, for example, the food must be destroyed or, in any case, transformed. Thus, all action is "negating." Far from leaving the given as it is, action destroys it; if not in its being, at least in its given form. And all "negating-negativity" with respect to the given is necessarily active. But negating action is not purely destructive, for if action destroys an objective reality, for the sake of satisfying the Desire from which it is born, it creates in its place, in and by that very destruction, a subjective reality. The being that eats, for example, creates and preserves its own reality by the overcoming of a reality other than its own, by the "transformation" of an alien reality into its own reality, by the "assimilation," the "internalization" of a "foreign," "external" reality. Generally speaking, the I of Desire is an emptiness that receives a real positive content only by negating action that satisfies Desire in destroying, transforming, and "assimilating" the desired non-I. And the positive content of the I, constituted by negation, is a function of the positive content of the negated non-I. If, then, the Desire is directed toward a "natural" non-I, the I, too, will be "natural." The I created by the active satisfaction of such a Desire will have the same nature as the things toward which that Desire is directed: it will be a "thingish" I, a merely living I, an animal I. And this natural I, a function of the natural object, can be revealed to itself and to others only as Sentiment of self. It will never attain Self-Consciousness.

[For there to be Self-Consciousness, Desire must therefore be directed toward a non-natural object, toward something that goes beyond the given reality. Now, the only thing that goes beyond the given reality is Desire itself. For Desire taken as Desire—i.e., before its satisfaction—is but a revealed nothingness, an unreal emptiness. Desire, being the revelation of an emptiness, the presence of the absence of a reality, is something essentially different from the desired thing, something other than a thing, than a static and given real being that stays eternally identical to itself. Therefore, Desire directed toward another Desire, taken as Desire, will create, by the negating and assimilating action that satisfies it, an I essentially different from the animal "I." This I, which "feeds" on Desires, will itself be Desire in its very being, created in and by the satisfaction of its Desire. And since Desire is realized as action negating the given, the very being of this I will be action. This I will not, like the animal "I," be "identity" or equality to itself, but "negating-negativity." In other words, the very being of this I will be becoming, and the universal form of this being will not be space, but time. Therefore, its continuation in existence will signify for this I: "not to be what it is (as static and given being, as natural being, as 'innate character') and to be (that is, to become) what it is not." Thus, this I will be its own product: it will be (in the future) what it has become by negation (in the present) of what it was (in the past), this negation being accomplished with a view to what it will become. In its very being this I is intentional becoming, deliberate evolution, conscious and voluntary progress; it is the act of transcending the given that is given to it and that it itself is. This I is a (human) individual, free (with respect to the given real) and historical (in relation to itself). And it is this I, and only this I, that reveals itself to itself and to others as Self-Consciousness.

[Human Desire must be directed toward another Desire. For there to be human Desire, then, there must first be a multiplicity of (animal) Desires. In other words, in order that Self-Consciousness be born from the Sentiment of self, in order that the human reality come into being within the animal reality, this reality must be essentially manifold. Therefore, man can appear on earth only within a herd. That is why the human reality can only be social. But for the herd to become a society, multiplicity of Desires is not sufficient by itself; in addition, the Desires of each member of the herd must be directed—or potentially directed— toward the Desires of the other members. If the human reality is a social reality, society is human only as a set of Desires mutually desiring one another as Desires. Human Desire, or better still, anthropogenetic Desire, produces a free and historical individual, conscious of his individuality, his freedom, his history, and finally, his historicity. Hence, anthropogenetic Desire is different from animal Desire (which produces a natural being, merely living and having only a sentiment of its life) in that it is directed, not toward a real, "positive," given object, but toward another Desire. Thus, in the relationship between man and woman, for example, Desire is human only if the one desires, not the body, but the Desire of the other; if he wants "to possess" or "to assimilate" the Desire taken as Desire—that is to say, if he wants to be "desired" or "loved," or, rather, "recognized" in his human value, in his reality as a human individual. Likewise, Desire directed toward a natural object is human only to the extent that it is "mediated" by the Desire of another directed toward the same object: it is human to desire what others desire, because they desire it. Thus, an object perfectly useless from the biological point of view (such as a medal, or the enemy's flag) can be desired because it is the object of other desires. Such a Desire can only be a human Desire, and human reality, as distinguished from animal reality, is created only by action that satisfies such Desires: human history is the history of desired Desires.

[But, apart from this difference—which is essential—human Desire is analogous to animal Desire. Human Desire, too, tends to satisfy itself by a negating—or better, a transforming and assimilating—action. Man "feeds" on Desires as an animal feeds on real things. And the human I, realized by the active satisfaction of its human Desires, is as much a function of its "food" as the body of an animal is of its food.

[For man to be truly human, for him to be essentially and really different from an animal, his human Desire must actually win out over his animal Desire. Now, all Desire is desire for a value. The supreme value for an animal is its animal life. All the Desires of an animal are in the final analysis a function of its desire to preserve its life. Human Desire, therefore, must win out over this desire for preservation. In other words, man's humanity "comes to light" only if he risks his (animal) life for the sake of his human Desire. It is in and by this risk that the human reality is created and revealed as reality; it is in and by this risk that it "comes to light," i.e., is shown, demonstrated, verified, and gives proofs of being essentially different from the animal, natural reality. And that is why to speak of the "origin" of Self-Consciousness is necessarily to speak of the risk of life (for an essentially nonvital end).

[Man's humanity "comes to light" only in risking his life to satisfy his human Desire—that is, his Desire directed toward another Desire. Now, to desire a Desire is to want to substitute oneself for the value desired by this Desire. For without this substitution, one would desire the value, the desired object, and not the Desire itself. Therefore, to desire the Desire of another is in the final analysis to desire that the value that I am or that I "represent" be the value desired by the other: I want him to "recognize" my value as his value. I want him to "recognize" me as an autonomous value. In other words, all human, anthropogenetic Desire—the Desire that generates Self-Consciousness, the human reality—is, finally, a function of the desire for "recognition." And the risk of life by which the human reality "comes to light" is a risk for the sake of such a Desire. Therefore, to speak of the "origin" of Self-Consciousness is necessarily to speak of a fight to the death for "recognition."

[Without this fight to the death for pure prestige, there would never have been human beings on earth. Indeed, the human being is formed

only in terms of a Desire directed toward another Desire, that is—
finally—in terms of a desire for recognition. Therefore, the human being
can be formed only if at least two of these Desires confront one another.
Each of the two beings endowed with such a Desire is ready to go all the
way in pursuit of its satisfaction; that is, is ready to risk its life—and,
consequently, to put the life of the other in danger—in order to be
"recognized" by the other, to impose itself on the other as the supreme
value; accordingly, their meeting can only be a fight to the death. And it
is only in and by such a fight that the human reality is begotten, formed,
realized, and revealed to itself and to others. Therefore, it is realized and
revealed only as "recognized" reality.

[However, if all men—or, more exactly, all beings in the process of
becoming human beings—behaved in the same manner, the fight would
necessarily end in the death of one of the adversaries, or of both. It would
not be possible for one to give way to the other, to give up the fight
before the death of the other, to "recognize" the other instead of being
"recognized" by him. But if this were the case, the realization and the
revelation of the human being would be impossible. This is obvious in
the case of the death of both adversaries, since the human reality—being
essentially Desire and action in terms of Desire—can be born and
maintained only within an animal life. But it is equally impossible when
only one of the adversaries is killed. For with him disappears that other
Desire toward which Desire must be directed in order to be a human
Desire. The survivor, unable to be "recognized" by the dead adversary,
cannot realize and reveal his humanity. In order that the human being be
realized and revealed as Self-Consciousness, therefore, it is not sufficient
that the nascent human reality be manifold. This multiplicity, this
"society," must in addition imply two essentially different human or
anthropogenetic behaviors.

[In order that the human reality come into being as "recognized"
reality, both adversaries must remain alive after the fight. Now, this is
possible only on the condition that they behave differently in this fight.
By irreducible, or better, by unforeseeable or "undeducible" acts of
liberty, they must constitute themselves as unequals in and by this very
fight. Without being predestined to it in any way, the one must fear the
other, must give in to the other, must refuse to risk his life for the
satisfaction of his desire for "recognition." He must give up his desire
and satisfy the desire of the other: he must "recognize" the other without
being "recognized" by him. Now, "to recognize" him thus is "to
recognize" him as his Master and to recognize himself and to be recognized as the Master's Slave.

[In other words, in his nascent state, man is never simply man. He is
always, necessarily, and essentially, either Master or Slave. If the human

reality can come into being only as a social reality, society is human—at least in its origin—only on the basis of its implying an element of Mastery and an element of Slavery, of "autonomous" existences and "dependent" existences. And that is why to speak of the origin of Self-Consciousness is necessarily to speak of "the autonomy and dependence of Self-Consciousness, of Mastery and Slavery."

[If the human being is begotten only in and by the fight that ends in the relation between Master and Slave, the progressive realization and revelation of this being can themselves be effected only in terms of this fundamental social relation. If man is nothing but his becoming, if his human existence in space is his existence in time or as time, if the revealed human reality is nothing but universal history, that history must be the history of the interaction between Mastery and Slavery: the historical "dialectic" is the "dialectic" of Master and Slave. But if the opposition of "thesis" and "antithesis" is meaningful only in the context of their reconciliation by "synthesis," if history (in the full sense of the word) necessarily has a final term, if man who becomes must culminate in man who has become, if Desire must end in satisfaction, if the science of man must possess the quality of a definitively and universally valid truth—the interaction of Master and Slave must finally end in the "dialectical overcoming" of both of them.

[However that may be, the human reality can be begotten and preserved only as "recognized" reality. It is only by being "recognized" by another, by many others, or—in the extreme—by all others, that a human being is really human, for himself as well as for others. And only in speaking of a "recognized" human reality can the term *human* be used to state a truth in the strict and full sense of the term. For only in this case can one reveal a reality in speech. That is why it is necessary to say this of Self-Consciousness, of self-conscious man:] Self-Consciousness exists *in* and *for itself* in and by the fact that it exists (in and for itself) for another Self-Consciousness; i.e., it exists only as an entity that is recognized.

This pure concept of recognition, of the doubling of Self-Consciousness within its unity, must now be considered as its evolution appears to Self-Consciousness [i.e., not to the philosopher who speaks of it, but to the self-conscious man who recognizes another man or is recognized by him].

In the first place, this evolution will make manifest the aspect of the inequality between the two Self-Consciousnesses [i.e., between the two men who confront one another for the sake of recognition], or the expansion of the middle-term [which is the mutual and reciprocal recognition] into the two extremes [which are the two who confront one another]; these are opposed to one another as extremes, the one only recognized, the other only recognizing. [To begin with, the man who wants to be recognized by another in no sense wants to recognize him in turn. If he succeeds, then, the recognition will not be mutual and reciprocal: he will be recognized but will not recognize the one who recognizes him.]

To begin with, Self-Consciousness is simple-or-undivided Being-for-itself; it is identical-to-itself by excluding from *itself* everything *other* [than itself]. Its essential-reality and its absolute object are, for it, *I* [I isolated from everything and opposed to everything that is not I]. And, in this *immediacy*, in this *given-being* [i.e., being that is not produced by an active, creative process] of its Being-for-itself, Self-Consciousness is *particular-and-isolated*. What is other for it exists as an object without essential-reality, as an object marked with the character of a negative-entity.

But [in the case we are studying] the other-entity, too, is a Self-Consciousness; a human-individual comes face to face with a human-individual. Meeting thus *immediately*, these individuals exist for one another as common objects. They are *autonomous* concrete-forms, Consciousnesses submerged in the *given-being* of *animal-life*. For it is as animal-life that the merely existing object has here presented itself. They are Consciousnesses that have not yet accomplished *for one another* the [dialectical] movement of absolute abstraction, which consists in the uprooting of all immediate given-being and in being nothing but the purely negative-or-negating given-being of the consciousness that is identical-to-itself.

Or in other words, these are entities that have not yet manifested themselves to one another as pure *Being-for-itself*—i.e., as *Self-Consciousness*. [When the "first" two men confront one another for the first time, the one sees in the other only an animal (and a dangerous and hostile one at that) that is to be destroyed, and not a self-conscious being representing an autonomous value.] Each of these two human-individuals is, to be sure, subjectively-certain of himself; but he is not certain of the other. And that is why his own subjective-certainty of himself does not yet possess truth [i.e., it does not yet reveal a reality—or, in other words, an entity that is objectively, intersubjectively, i.e., universally, recognized, and hence existing and valid]. For the truth of his subjective-certainty [of the idea that he has of himself, of the value that he attributes to himself] could have been nothing but the fact that his own Being-for-itself was manifested to him as an autonomous object; or again, to say the same thing: the fact that the object was manifested to him as this pure subjective-certainty of himself; [therefore, he must find the private idea that he has of himself in the external, objective reality]. But according to the concept of recognition, this is possible only if he accomplishes for the other (just as the other does for him) the pure abstraction of Being-for-itself; each accomplishing it in himself both by his own activity and also by the other's activity.

[The "first" man who meets another man for the first time already attributes an autonomous, absolute reality and an autonomous, absolute value to himself: we can say that he believes himself to be a man, that he has the "subjective certainty" of being a man. But his certainty is not yet knowledge. The value that he attributes to himself could be illusory; the idea that he has of himself could be false or mad. For that idea to be a truth, it must reveal an objective reality—i.e., an entity that is valid and exists not only for itself, but also for realities other than itself. In the case in question, man, to be really, truly "man," and to know that he is such, must, therefore, impose the idea that he has of himself on beings other than himself: he must be recognized by the others (in the ideal, extreme case, by all the others). Or again, he must transform the (natural and human) world in which he is not recognized into a world in which this recognition takes place. This transformation of the world that is hostile to a human project into a world in harmony with this project is called "action," "activity." This action—essentially human, because humanizing and anthropogenetic—will begin with the act of imposing oneself on the "first" other man one meets. And since this other, if he is (or more exactly, if he wants to be, and believes himself to be) a human being, must himself do the same thing, the "first" anthropogenetic action necessarily takes the form of a fight: a fight to the death between two beings that claim to be men, a fight for pure prestige carried on for the sake of "recognition" by the adversary. Indeed:]

The *manifestation* of the human-individual taken as pure abstraction of Being-for-itself consists in showing itself as being the pure negation of its objective-or-thingish mode-of-being—or, in other words, in showing that to be for oneself, or to be a man, is not to be bound to any determined *existence*, not to be bound to the universal isolated-particularity of existence as such, not to be bound to life. This manifestation is a *double* activity: activity of the other and activity by oneself. To the extent that this activity is activity *of the other,* each of the two men seeks the death of the other. But in that activity of the other is also found the second aspect, namely, the *activity by oneself*: for the activity in question implies in it the risk of the life of him who acts. The relation of the two Self-Consciousnesses, therefore, is determined in such a way that they come to light—each for itself and one for the other—through the fight for life and death.

[They "come to light"—that is, they prove themselves, they transform the purely subjective certainty that each has of his own value into objective, or universally valid and recognized, truth. Truth is the revelation of a reality. Now, the human reality is created, is constituted, only in the fight for recognition and by the risk of life that it implies. The truth of man, or the revelation of his reality, therefore, presupposes the fight to the death. And that is why] human-individuals are obliged to start this fight. For each must raise his subjective-certainty of *existing for self* to the level of truth, both in the other and in himself. And it is only through the risk of life that freedom comes to light, that it becomes clear that the essential-reality of Self-Consciousness is not *given-being* [being that is not created by conscious, voluntary action], nor the *immediate* [natural, not mediated by action (that negates the given)] mode in which it first comes to sight [in the given world], nor submersion in the extension of animal-life; but that there is, on the contrary, nothing given in Self-Consciousness that is anything but a passing constituent-element for it. In other words, only by the risk of life does it come to light that Self-Consciousness is nothing but pure *Being-for-itself*. The human-individual that *has* not dared-to-risk his life can, to be sure, be recognized as a *human-person*; but he has not attained the truth of this fact of being recognized as an autonomous Self-Consciousness. Hence, each of the two human-individuals must have the death of the other as his goal, just as he risks his own life. For the other-entity is worth no more to him than himself. His essential-reality [which is his recognized, human reality and dignity] manifests itself to him as an other-entity [or another man, who does not recognize him and is therefore independent of him]. He is outside of himself [insofar as the other has not "given him back" to himself by recognizing him, by revealing that he has recognized him, and by showing him that he (the other) depends on him and is not absolutely other than he]. He must overcome his being-outside-of-himself. The other-entity [than he] is here a Self-Consciousness existing as a given-being and involved [in the natural world] in a manifold and diverse way. Now, he must look upon his other-being as pure Being-for-itself, i.e., as absolute negating-negativity. [This means that man is human only to the extent that he wants to impose himself on another man, to be recognized by him. In the beginning, as long as he is not yet actually recognized by the other, it is the other that is the end of his action; it is on this other, it is on recognition by this other, that his human value and reality depend; it is in this other that the meaning of his life is condensed. Therefore, he is "outside of himself." But his own value and his own reality are what are important to him, and he wants to have them in himself. Hence, he must overcome his "other-being." This is to say that he must make himself recognized by the other, he must have in himself the certainty of being recognized by another. But for that recognition to satisfy him, he has to know that the other is a human being. Now, in the beginning, he sees in the other only the aspect of an

animal. To know that this aspect reveals a human reality, he must see
that the other also wants to be recognized, and that he, too is ready to
risk, "to deny," his animal life in a fight for the recognition of his human
being-for-itself. He must, therefore, "provoke" the other, force him to
start a fight to the death for pure prestige. And having done this, he is
obliged to kill the other in order not to be killed himself. In these
circumstances, then, the fight for recognition can end only in the death
of one of the adversaries—or of both together.] But this proving oneself
by death does away with the truth [or revealed objective reality] that was
supposed to come from it; and, for that very reason, it also does away
with the subjective-certainty of oneself as such. For just as animal-life is
the *natural* position of Consciousness, i.e., autonomy without absolute
negating-negativity, so is death the *natural* negation of Consciousness,
i.e., negation without autonomy, which negation, therefore, continues
to lack the significance required by recognition. [That is to say: if both
adversaries perish in the fight, "consciousness" is completely done away
with, for man is nothing more than an inanimate body after his death.
And if one of the adversaries remains alive but kills the other, he can no
longer be recognized by the other; the man who has been defeated and
killed does not recognize the victory of the conqueror. Therefore, the
victor's certainty of his being and of his value remains subjective, and
thus has no "truth."] Through death, it is true, the subjective-certainty
of the fact that both risked their lives and that each despised his own and
the other's life has been established. But this certainty has not been
established for those who underwent this struggle. Through death, they
do away with their consciousness, which resides in that foreign entity,
natural existence. That is to say, they do away with themselves. [For
man is real only to the extent that he lives in a natural world. This world
is, to be sure, "foreign" to him; he must "deny" it, transform it, fight it,
in order to realize himself in it. But without this world, outside of this
world, man is nothing.] And they are done away with as *extremes* that
want to exist for self [i.e., consciously, and independently of the rest of
the universe]. But, thereby, the essential constituent-element—i.e.,
the splitting up into extremes of opposed determinate things—disappears from the play of change. And the middle-term collapses in a
dead unity, broken up into dead extremes, which merely exist as
given-beings and are not opposed [to one another in, by, and for an
action in which one tries "to do away with" the other by "establishing"
himself and to establish himself by doing away with the other.] And the
two do not give themselves reciprocally to one another, nor do they get
themselves back in return from one another through consciousness. On
the contrary, they merely leave one another free, indifferently, as things.
[For the dead man is no longer anything more than an unconscious

thing, from which the living man turns away in indifference, since he can no longer expect anything from it for himself.] Their murderous action is abstract negation. It is not negation [carried out] by consciousness, which overcomes in such a way that it *keeps* and *preserves* the overcome-entity and, for that very reason, survives the fact of being overcome. [This "overcoming" is "dialectical." "To overcome dialectically" means to overcome while preserving what is overcome; it is sublimated in and by that overcoming which preserves or that preservation which overcomes. The dialectically overcome-entity is annulled in its contingent (stripped of sense, "senseless") aspect of natural, given ("immediate") entity, but it is preserved in its essential (and meaningful, significant) aspect; thus mediated by negation, it is sublimated or raised up to a more "comprehensive" and comprehensible mode of being than that of its immediate reality of pure and simple, positive and static given, which is not the result of creative action (i.e., of action that negates the given).

[Therefore, it does the man of the Fight no good to kill his adversary. He must overcome him "dialectically." That is, he must leave him life and consciousness, and destroy only his autonomy. He must overcome the adversary only insofar as the adversary is opposed to him and acts against him. In other words, he must enslave him.]

In that experience [of the murderous fight] it becomes clear to Self-Consciousness that animal-life is just as important to it as pure self-consciousness. In the immediate Self-Consciousness [i.e., in the "first" man, who is not yet "mediated" by this contact with the other that the fight creates], the simple-or-undivided I [of isolated man] is the absolute object. But for us or in itself [i.e., for the author and the reader of this passage, who see man as he has been definitively formed at the end of history by the accomplished social inter-action] this object, i.e., the I, is absolute mediation, and its essential constituent-element is abiding autonomy. [That is to say, real and true man is the result of his inter-action with others; his I and the idea he has of himself are "mediated" by recognition obtained as a result of his action. And his true autonomy is the autonomy that he *maintains* in the social reality by the effort of that action.] The dissolution of that simple-or-undivided unity [which is the isolated I] is the result of the first experience [which man has at the time of his "first" (murderous) fight]. By this experience are established: a pure Self-Consciousness [or an "abstract" one, since it has made the "abstraction" of its animal life by the risk of the fight—the victor], and a Consciousness that [being in fact a living corpse—the man who has been defeated and spared] does not exist purely for itself, but rather for another Consciousness [namely, for that of the victor]: i.e., a Consciousness that exists as a *given-being*, or in other words, a Consciousness that exists in the concrete-form of *thingness*. Both constituent-elements are essential—since in the beginning they are unequal and opposed to one another and their reflection into unity has not yet resulted [from their action], they exist as two opposed concrete-forms of Consciousness. The one is autonomous Consciousness, for which the essential-reality is Being-for-itself. The other is dependent Consciousness, for which the essential-reality is animal-life, i.e., given-being for an other-entity. The former is the *Master*, the latter—the *Slave*. [This Slave is the defeated adversary, who has not gone all the way in risking his life, who has not adopted the principle of the Masters: to conquer or to die. He has accepted life granted him by another. Hence, he depends on that other. He has preferred slavery to death, and that is why, by remaining alive, he lives as a Slave.]

The Master is Consciousness existing *for itself*. And he is no longer merely the [abstract] concept of Consciousness, but a [real] Consciousness existing for itself, which is mediated with itself by *another* Consciousness, namely, by a Consciousness to whose essential-reality it belongs to be synthesized with *given-being*, i.e., with thingness as such. [This "Consciousness" is the Slave who, in binding himself completely to his animal-life, is merely one with the natural world of things. By refusing to risk his life in a fight for pure prestige, he does not rise above the level of animals. Hence he considers himself as such, and as such is he considered by the Master. But the Slave, for his part, recognizes the Master in his human dignity and reality, and the Slave behaves accordingly. The Master's "certainty" is therefore not purely subjective and "immediate," but objectivized and "mediated" by another's, the Slave's, recognition. While the Slave still remains an "immediate," natural, "bestial" being, the Master—as a result of his fight—is already human, "mediated." And consequently, his behavior is also "mediated" or human, both with regard to things and with regard to other men; moreover, these other men, for him, are only slaves.] The Master is related to the following two constituent elements: on the one hand, to a *thing* taken as such, i.e., the object of Desire; and, on the other hand, to the Consciousness for which thingness is the essential-entity [i.e., to the Slave, who, by refusing the risk, binds himself completely to the things on which he depends. The Master, on the other hand, sees in these things only a simple means of satisfying his desire; and, in satisfying it, he destroys them]. Given that: (1) the Master, taken as concept of self-consciousness, is the immediate relation of *Being-for-itself*, and that (2) he now [i.e., after his victory over the Slave] exists at the same time as mediation, i.e., as a Being-for-itself that exists for itself only through an other-entity [since the Master is Master only by the fact of having a Slave who recognizes him as Master]; the Master is related (1) immediately to both [i.e., to the thing and to the Slave], and (2) in a mediated way to each of the two through the other. The Master is related *in a mediated way to the Slave*, viz., by *autonomous given-being*; for it is precisely to this given-being that the Slave is tied. This given-being is his chain, from which he could not abstract in the fight, in which fight he was re-vealed—because of that fact—as dependent, as having his autonomy in thingness. The Master, on the other hand, is the power that rules over this given-being; for he revealed in the fight that this given-being is worth nothing to him except as a negative-entity. Given that the Master is the power that rules over this given-being and that this given-being is the power that rules over the Other [i.e., over the Slave], the Master holds—in this [real or active] syllogism—that Other under his domina-tion. Likewise, the Master is related *in a mediated way to the thing*, viz., *by the Slave*. Taken as Self-Consciousness as such, the Slave, too, is related to the thing in a negative or negating way, and he overcomes it [dialecti-cally]. But—for him—the thing is autonomous at the same time. For that reason, he cannot, by his act-of-negating, finish it off to the point of the [complete] annihilation [of the thing, as does the Master who "consumes" it]. That is, he merely *transforms it by work* [i.e., he prepares it for consumption, but does not consume it himself]. For the Master, on the other hand, the *immediate* relation [to the thing] comes into being, through that mediation [i.e., through the work of the Slave who transforms the natural thing, the "raw material," with a view to its consumption (by the Master)], as pure negation of the object, that is, as *Enjoyment*. [Since all the effort is made by the Slave, the Master has only to enjoy the thing that the Slave has prepared for him, and to enjoy "negating" it, destroying it, by "consuming" it. (For example, he eats food that is completely prepared)] What Desire [i.e., isolated man "before" the Fight, who was alone with Nature and whose desires were directed without detour toward that Nature] did not achieve, the Master [whose desires are directed toward things that have been transformed by the Slave] does achieve. The Master can finish off the thing completely and satisfy himself in Enjoyment. [Therefore, it is solely thanks to the work of another (his Slave) that the Master is free with respect to Nature, and consequently, satisfied with himself. But, he is Master of the Slave only because he previously freed himself from Nature (and from his own nature) by risking his life in a fight for pure prestige, which—as such—is not at all "natural."] Desire cannot achieve this because of the autonomy of the thing. The Master, on the other hand, who introduced the Slave between the thing and himself, is consequently joined only to the aspect of the thing's dependence, and has pure enjoyment from it. As for the aspect of the thing's autonomy, he leaves it to the Slave, who transforms the thing by work.

In these two constituent-elements the Master gets his recognition through another Consciousness; for in them the latter affirms itself as unessential, both by the act of working on the thing and by the fact of being dependent on a determinate existence. In neither case can this [slavish] Consciousness become master of the given-being and achieve absolute negation. Hence it is given in this constituent-element of recognition that the other Consciousness overcomes itself as Being-for-itself and thereby does itself what the other Consciousness does to it. [That is to say, the Master is not the only one to regard the Other as his Slave; this Other also considers himself as such.] The other constituent-element of recognition is equally implied in the relation under consideration; this other constituent-element is the fact that this activity of the second Consciousness [the slavish Consciousness] is the activity proper of the first Consciousness [i.e., the Master's]. For everything that the Slave does is, properly speaking, an activity of the Master. [Since the Slave works only for the Master, only to satisfy the Master's desire and not his own, it is the Master's desire that acts in and through the Slave.] For the Master, only Being-for-itself is the essential-reality. He is pure negative-or-negating power, for which the thing is nothing; and consequently, in this relation of Master and Slave, he is the pure essential activity. The Slave, on the other hand, is not pure activity, but nonessential activity. Now, for there to be an authentic recognition, there must also be the third constituent-element, which consists in the Master's doing with respect to himself what he does with respect to the other, and in the Slave's doing with respect to the Other what he [the Slave] does with respect to himself. It is, therefore, an unequal and one-sided recognition that has been born from this relation of Master and Slave. [For although the Master treats the Other as Slave, he does not behave as Slave himself; and although the Slave treats the Other as Master, he does not behave as Master himself. The Slave does not risk his life, and the Master is idle.

[The relation between Master and Slave, therefore, is not recognition properly so-called. To see this, let us analyze the relation from the Master's point of view. The Master is not the only one to consider himself Master. The Slave, also, considers him as such. Hence, he is recognized in his human reality and dignity. But this recognition is one-sided, for he does not recognize in turn the Slave's human reality and dignity. Hence, he is recognized by someone whom he does not recognize. And this is what is insufficient—what is tragic—in his situation. The Master has fought and risked his life for a recognition without value for him. For he can be satisfied only by recognition from one whom he recognizes as worthy of recognizing him. The Master's attitude, therefore, is an existential impasse. On the one hand, the Master is Master only because his Desire was directed not toward a thing, but toward another desire—

thus, it was a desire for recognition. On the other, when he has consequently become Master, it is as Master that he must desire to be recognized; and he can be recognized as such only by making the Other his Slave. But the Slave is for him an animal or a thing. He is, therefore, "recognized" by a thing. Thus, finally, his Desire is directed toward a thing, and not—as it seemed at first—toward a (human) Desire. The Master, therefore, was on the wrong track. After the fight that made him a Master, he is not what he wanted to be in starting that fight: a man recognized by another man. Therefore: if man can be satisfied only by recognition, the man who behaves as a Master will never be satisfied. And since—in the beginning—man is either Master or Slave, the satisfied man will necessarily be a Slave; or more exactly, the man who has been a Slave, who has passed through Slavery, who has "dialectically overcome" his slavery. Indeed:]

Thus, the nonessential [or slavish] Consciousness is—for the Master—the object that forms the *truth* [or revealed reality] of the subjective-certainty he has of himself [since he can "know" he is Master only by being recognized as such by the Slave]. But it is obvious that this object does not correspond to its concept. For in the Master's fulfilling himself, something entirely different from an autonomous Consciousness has come into being [since he is faced with a Slave]. It is not such an autonomous Consciousness, but all to the contrary, a dependent Consciousness, that exists for him. Therefore, he is not subjectively certain of his *Being-for-itself* as of a truth [or of a revealed objective reality]. His truth, all to the contrary, is nonessential Consciousness, and the nonessential activity of that Consciousness. [That is to say, the Master's "truth" is the Slave and the Slave's Work. Actually, others recognize the Master as Master only because he has a Slave; and the Master's life consists in consuming the products of slavish Work, and in living on and by this Work.]

Consequently, the *truth* of autonomous Consciousness is *slavish Consciousness*. This latter first appears, it is true, as existing *outside* of itself and not as the truth of Self-Consciousness [since the Slave recognizes human dignity not in himself, but in the Master, on whom his very existence depends]. But, just as Mastery showed that its essential-reality is the reverse or perversion of what it wants to be, so much the more will Slavery, in its fulfillment, probably become the opposite of what it is immediately; as *repressed* Consciousness it will go within itself and reverse and transform itself into true autonomy.

[The complete, absolutely free man, definitively and completely satisfied by what he is, the man who is perfected and completed in and by this satisfaction, will be the Slave who has "overcome" his Slavery. If idle Mastery is an impasse, laborious Slavery, in contrast, is the source of all human, social, historical progress. History is the history of the working Slave. To see this, one need only consider the relationship between Master and Slave (that is, the first result of the "first" human, social, historical contact), no longer from the Master's point of view, but from the Slave's.]

We have seen only what Slavery is in its relation to Mastery. But Slavery is also Self-Consciousness. What it is as such, in and for itself, must now be considered. In the first place, it is the Master that is the essential-reality for Slavery. *The autonomous Consciousness existing for itself* is hence, for it, *the truth* [or a revealed reality], which, however, *for it*, does not yet exist *in it*. [The Slave is subordinated to the Master. Hence the Slave esteems, recognizes, the value and the reality of "autonomy," of human freedom. However, he does not find it realized in himself; he finds it only in the Other. And this is his advantage. The Master, unable to recognize the Other who recognizes him, finds himself at an impasse. The Slave, on the other hand, recognizes the Other (the Master) from the beginning. In order that mutual and reciprocal recognition, which alone can fully and definitively realize and satisfy man, be established, it suffices for the Slave to impose himself on the Master and be recognized by him. To be sure, for this to take place, the Slave must cease to be Slave: he must transcend himself, "overcome" himself, as Slave. But if the Master has no desire to "overcome"—and hence no possibility of "overcoming"—himself as Master (since this would mean, for him, to become a Slave), the Slave has every reason to cease to be a Slave. Moreover, the experience of the fight that made him a Slave predisposes him to that act of self-overcoming, of negation of himself (negation of his given I, which is a slavish I). To be sure, in the beginning, the Slave who binds himself to his given (slavish) I does not have this "negativity" in himself. He sees it only in the Master, who realized pure "negating-negativity" by risking his life in the fight for recognition.] However, Slavery *in fact* has *in itself* this truth [or revealed reality] of pure negating-negativity and of *Being-for-itself*. For it has *experienced* this essential-reality within itself. This slavish Consciousness was afraid not for this or that, not for this moment or that, but for its [own] entire essential-reality: it underwent the fear of death, the fear of the absolute Master. By this fear, the slavish Consciousness melted internally; it shuddered deeply and everything fixed-or-stable trembled in it. Now, this pure universal [dialectical] movement, this absolute liquefaction of every stable-support, is the simple-or-undivided essential-reality of Self-Consciousness, absolute negating-negativity, *pure Being-for-itself*. Thus, this Being-for-itself exists *in* the slavish Consciousness. [The Master is fixed in his Mastery. He cannot go beyond himself, change, progress. He must conquer—and become Master or preserve himself as such—or die.

He can be killed; he cannot be transformed, educated. He has risked his life to be Master. Therefore, Mastery is the supreme given value for him, beyond which he cannot go. The Slave, on the other hand, did not want to be a Slave. He became a Slave because he did not want to risk his life to become a Master. In his mortal terror he understood (without noticing it) that a given, fixed, and stable condition, even though it be the Master's, cannot exhaust the possibilities of human existence. He "understood" the "vanity" of the given conditions of existence. He did not want to bind himself to the Master's condition, nor does he bind himself to his condition as a Slave. There is nothing fixed in him. He is ready for change; in his very being, he is change, transcendence, transformation, "education"; he is historical becoming at his origin, in his essence, in his very existence. On the one hand, he does not bind himself to what he is; he wants to transcend himself by negation of his given state. On the other hand, he has a positive ideal to attain; the ideal of autonomy, of Being-for-itself, of which he finds the incarnation, at the very origin of his Slavery, in the Master.] This constituent-element of Being-for-itself also exists *for slavish Consciousness*. For in the Master, Being-for-itself is, for it [the slavish Consciousness], its object. [An object that it knows to be external, opposed, to it, and that it tends to appropriate for itself. The Slave knows what it is to be free. He also knows that he is not free, and that he wants to become free. And if the experience of the Fight and its result predispose the Slave to transcendence, to progress, to History, his life as a Slave working in the Master's service realizes this predisposition.] In addition, slavish Consciousness is not only this universal dissolution [of everything fixed, stable, and given], taken *as such*; in the Master's service, it accomplishes this dissolution *in an objectively real way* [i.e., concretely]. In service [in the forced work done in the service of another (the Master)], slavish Consciousness [dialectically] overcomes its attachment to natural existence in all the *particular-and-isolated* constituent-elements, and it eliminates this existence by work. [The Master forces the Slave to work. And by working, the Slave becomes master of Nature. Now, he became the Master's Slave only because—in the beginning—he was a slave of Nature, joining with it and subordinating himself to its laws by accepting the instinct of preservation. In becoming master of Nature by work, then, the Slave frees himself from his own nature, from his own instinct that tied him to Nature and made him the Master's Slave. Therefore, by freeing the Slave from Nature, work frees him from himself as well, from his Slave's nature: it frees him from the Master. In the raw, natural, given World, the Slave is slave of the Master. In the technical world transformed by his work, he rules—or, at least, will one day rule—as absolute Master. And this Mastery that arises from work, from the progressive transformation of the given World and of man given in this World, will be an entirely different thing from the "immediate" Mastery of the Master. The future and History hence belong not to the warlike Master, who either dies or preserves himself indefinitely in identity to himself, but to the working Slave. The Slave, in transforming the given World by his work, transcends the given and what is given by that given in himself; hence, he goes beyond himself, and also goes beyond the Master who is tied to the given which, not working, he leaves intact. If the fear of death, incarnated for the Slave in the person of the warlike Master, is the *sine qua non* of historical progress, it is solely the Slave's work that realizes and perfects it.]

However, the feeling of absolute power that the Slave experienced as such in the fight and also experiences in the particularities of service [for the Master whom he fears] is as yet only dissolution effected *in itself.* [Without this sense of power—i.e., without the terror and dread inspired by the Master—man would never be Slave and consequently could not attain the final perfection. But this condition "in itself"—i.e., this objectively real and necessary condition—is not sufficient. Perfection (which is always conscious of itself) can be attained only in and by work. For only in and by work does man finally become aware of the significance, the value, and the necessity of his experience of fearing absolute power, incarnated for him in the Master. Only after having worked for the Master does he understand the necessity of the fight between Master and Slave and the value of the risk and terror that it implies.] Thus, although the terror inspired by the Master is the beginning of wisdom, it can only be said that in this terror Consciousness exists *for itself*, but is not yet *Being-for-itself.* [In mortal terror man becomes aware of his reality, of the value that the simple fact of living has for him; only thus does he take account of the "seriousness" of existence. But he is not yet aware of his autonomy, of the value and the "seriousness" of his liberty, of his human dignity.] But through work Consciousness comes to itself. [In work, i.e.] in the constituent-element that corresponds to Desire in the Master's consciousness, it seemed, it is true, that the nonessential relation to the thing was what fell to the lot of the slavish Consciousness; this is because the thing preserves its autonomy. [It seemed that, in and by work, the Slave is enslaved to Nature, to the thing, to "raw material"; while the Master, who is content to consume the thing prepared by the Slave and to enjoy it, is perfectly free with respect to it. But this is not the case. To be sure] the [Master's] Desire has reserved for itself the pure act-of-negating the object [by consuming it] and has thereby reserved for itself the unmixed sentiment-of-self-and-of-one's-dignity [experienced in enjoyment]. But for the same reason this satisfaction itself is but a passing phase, for it lacks the *objective* aspect—i.e., the *stable support.*

[The Master, who does not work, produces nothing stable outside of himself. He merely destroys the products of the Slave's work. Thus his enjoyment and his satisfaction remain purely subjective: they are of interest only to him and therefore can be recognized only by him; they have no "truth," no objective reality revealed to all. Accordingly, this "consumption," this idle enjoyment of the Master's, which results from the "immediate" satisfaction of desire, can at the most procure some pleasure for man; it can never give him complete and definitive satisfaction.] Work, on the other hand, is *repressed* Desire, an *arrested* passing phase; or, in other words, it forms-and-educates. [Work transforms the World and civilizes, educates, Man. The man who wants to work—or who must work—must repress the instinct that drives him "to consume" "immediately" the "raw" object. And the Slave can work for the Master—that is, for another than himself—only by repressing his own desires. Hence, he transcends himself by working—or, perhaps better, he educates himself, he "cultivates" and "sublimates" his instincts by repressing them. On the other hand, he does not destroy the thing as it is given. He postpones the destruction of the thing by first trans-forming it through work; he prepares it for consumption—that is to say, he "forms" it. In his work, he trans-forms things and trans-forms himself at the same time: he forms things and the World by transforming himself, by educating himself; and he educates himself, he forms himself, by transforming things and the World. Thus,] the negative-or-negating relation to the object becomes a *form* of this object and gains *permanence*, precisely because, for the worker, the object has autonomy. At the same time, the *negative-or-negating* middle-term—i.e., the forming *activity* [of work]—is the *isolated-particularity* or the pure Being-for-itself of the Consciousness. And this Being-for-itself, through work, now passes into what is outside of the Consciousness, into the element of permanence. The working Consciousness thereby attains a contemplation of autonomous given-being such that it contemplates *itself* in it. [The product of work is the worker's production. It is the realization of his project, of his idea; hence, it is he that is realized in and by this product, and consequently he contemplates himself when he contemplates it. Now, this artificial product is at the same time just as "autonomous," just as objective, just as independent of man, as is the natural thing. Therefore, it is by work, and only by work, that man *realizes* himself *objectively* as man. Only after producing an artificial object is man himself really and objectively more than and different from a natural being; and only in this real and objective product does he become truly conscious of his subjective human reality. Therefore, it is only by work that man is a supernatural being that is conscious of its reality; by working, he is "incarnated" Spirit, he is historical "World," he is "objectivized" History.

[Work, then, is what "forms-or-educates" man beyond the animal. The "formed-or-educated" man, the completed man who is satisfied by his completion, is hence necessarily not Master, but Slave; or, at least, he who has passed through Slavery. Now, there is no Slave without a Master. The Master, then, is the catalyst of the historical, anthropogenetic process. He himself does not participate actively in this process; but without him, without his presence, this process would not be possible. For, if the history of man is the history of his work, and if this work is historical, social, human, only on the condition that it is carried out against the worker's instinct or "immediate interest," the work must be carried out in the service of another, and must be a forced work, stimulated by fear of death. It is this work, and only this work, that frees—i.e., humanizes—man (the Slave). On the one hand, this work creates a real objective World, which is a non-natural World, a cultural, historical, human World. And it is only in this World that man lives an essentially different life from that of animals (and "primitive" man) in the bosom of Nature. On the other hand, this work liberates the Slave from the terror that tied him to given Nature and to his own innate animal nature. It is by work in the Master's service performed in terror that the Slave frees himself from the terror that enslaved him to the Master.]

Now, the forming [of the thing by work] contains not only the positive significance that the slavish Consciousness, taken as pure *Being-for-itself*, becomes an *entity that exists as a given-being* [that is to say, work is something more than the action by which man creates an essentially human technical World that is just as real as the natural World inhabited by animals]. The forming [of the thing by work] has a further negative-or-negating significance that is directed against the first constituent-element of the slavish Consciousness; namely, against fear. For in the act of forming the thing, the negating-negativity proper of Consciousness—i.e., its Being-for-itself—comes to be an Object [i.e., a World] for Consciousness only by the fact that Consciousness [dialectically] overcomes the opposed *form* that exists as a [natural] given-being. Now, this objective *negative-entity* is precisely the foreign essential-reality before which slavish Consciousness trembled. Now, on the contrary, this Consciousness destroys that foreign negative-entity [in and by work]. Consciousness establishes *itself* as a negative-entity in the element of permanency; and thereby it becomes a thing *for itself*, an *entity-existing-for-itself*. In the Master, *Being-for-itself* is, for the slavish Consciousness, *an other* Being-for-itself; or again, Being-for-itself exists there only *for the slavish Consciousness*. In fear, Being-for-itself [already] exists *in the slavish Consciousness itself*. But in the act of forming [by work], Being-for-itself is constituted for slavish Consciousness as *its own*, and slavish Consciousness becomes aware of the fact that it itself exists in and for itself. The form [the idea or project conceived by the Consciousness], by being *established outside*]of the Consciousness, by being introduced—through work—into the objective reality of the World], does not become, for the [working] Consciousness, an other-entity than it. For it is precisely that form that is its pure Being-for-itself; and, in that form, this Being-for-itself is constituted for it [the Consciousness] as truth [or as revealed, conscious, objective reality. The man who works recognizes his own product in the World that has actually been transformed by his work: he recognizes himself in it, he sees in it his own human reality, in it he discovers and reveals to others the objective reality of his humanity, of the originally abstract and purely subjective idea he has of himself.] By this act of finding itself by itself, then, the [working] Consciousness becomes *its own meaning-or-will*; and this happens precisely in work, in which it seemed to be *alien meaning-or-will.*

[Man achieves his true autonomy, his authentic freedom, only after passing through Slavery, after surmounting fear of death by work performed in the service of another (who, for him, is the incarnation of that fear). Work that frees man is hence necessarily, in the beginning, the forced work of a Slave who serves an all-powerful Master, the holder of all real power.]

For that reflection [of Consciousness into itself], the [following] two constituent-elements [first, that] of terror, and [second, that] of service as such, as well as the educative-forming [by work], are equally necessary. And, at the same time, the two elements are necessary in a universal way. [On the one hand,] without the discipline of service and obedience, terror remains in the formal domain and is not propagated in the conscious objective-reality of existence. [It is not sufficient to be afraid, nor even to be afraid while realizing that one fears death. It is necessary to live in terms of terror. Now, to live in such a way is to serve someone whom one fears, someone who inspires or incarnates terror; it is to serve a Master (a real, that is, a human Master, or the "sublimated" Master—God). And to serve a Master is to obey his laws. Without this service, terror could not transform existence, and existence, therefore, could never go beyond its initial state of terror. It is by serving another, by externalizing oneself, by binding oneself to others, that one is liberated from the enslaving dread that the idea of death inspires. On the other hand,] without the educative-forming [by work], terror remains internal-or-private and mute, and Consciousness does not come into being for itself. [Without work that transforms the real objective World, man cannot really transform himself. If he changes, his change remains "private," purely subjective, revealed to himself alone, "mute," not communicated to others. And this "internal" change puts him at variance with the World, which has not changed, and with the others, who are bound to the unchanged World. This change, then, transforms man into a madman or a criminal, who is sooner or later annihilated by the natural and social objective reality. Only work, by finally putting the objective World into harmony with the subjective idea that at first goes beyond it, annuls the element of madness and crime that marks the attitude of every man who—driven by terror—tries to go beyond the given World of which he is afraid, in which he feels terrified, and in which, consequently, he could not be satisfied.] But, if the Consciousness forms [the thing by work] without having experienced absolute primordial terror, it is merely its vain intention or self-will; for the form or the negating-negativity of that Consciousness is not negating-negativity *in itself*; and consequently its act-of-forming cannot give it consciousness of itself as the essential-reality. If the Consciousness has not endured absolute terror, but merely some fear or other, the negative-or-negating essential-reality remains an external-entity for it, and its [own] substance is not entirely infected by this essential-reality. Since all the fulfillments-or-accomplishments of its natural consciousness have not vacillated, that Consciousness still belongs—*in itself*—to determined given-being. Its intention or self-will [*der eigene Sinn*] is then stubborn-capriciousness [*Eigensinn*]: a freedom that still remains within the bounds of Slavery. The pure form [imposed on the given by this work] cannot come into being for that Consciousness, as essential-reality. Likewise, considered as extension over particular-and-isolated entities, this form is not [a] universal educative-forming; it is not absolute Concept. This form, on the contrary, is a skillfulness that dominates only certain things, but does not dominate universal power and the totality of objective essential-reality.

[The man who has not experienced the fear of death does not know that the given natural World is hostile to him, that it tends to kill him, to destroy him, and that it is essentially unsuited to satisfy him really. This man, therefore, remains fundamentally bound to the given World. At the most, he will want to "reform" it—that is, to change its details, to make particular transformations without modifying its essential characteristics. This man will act as a "skillful" reformer, or better, a conformer, but never as a true revolutionary. Now, the given World in which he lives belongs to the (human or divine) Master, and in this World he is necessarily Slave. Therefore, it is not reform, but the "dialectical," or better, revolutionary, overcoming of the World that can free him, and—consequently—satisfy him. Now, this revolutionary transformation of the World presupposes the "negation," the nonaccepting of the given World *in its totality*. And the origin of this absolute negation can only be the absolute dread inspired by the given World, or more precisely, by that which, or by him who, dominates this World, by the Master of this World. Now, the Master who (involuntarily) engenders the desire of revolutionary negation is the Master of the Slave. Therefore, man can free himself from the given World that does not satisfy him only if this World, in its totality, belongs properly to a (real or "sublimated") Master. Now, as long as the Master lives, he himself is always enslaved by the World of which he is the Master. Since the Master transcends the given World only in and by the risk of his life, it is only his death that "realizes" his freedom. As long as he lives, therefore, he never attains the freedom that would raise him above the given World. The Master can never detach himself from the World in which he lives, and if this World perishes, he perishes with it. Only the Slave can transcend the given World (which is subjugated by the Master) and not perish. Only the Slave can transform the World that forms him and fixes him in slavery and create a World that he has formed in which he will be free. And the Slave achieves this only through forced and terrified work carried out in the Master's service. To be sure, this work by itself does not free him. But in transforming the World by this work, the Slave transforms himself, too, and thus creates the new objective conditions that permit him to take up once more the liberating Fight for recognition that he refused in the beginning for fear of death. And thus in the long run, all slavish work realizes not the Master's will, but the will—at first unconscious—of the Slave, who—finally—succeeds where the Master—necessarily—fails. Therefore, it is indeed the originally dependent, serving, and slavish Consciousness that in the end realizes and reveals the ideal of autonomous Self-Consciousness and is thus its "truth."]

Phenomenology

INTRODUCTION

The term "phenomenology" designates two things: a new kind of descriptive method which made a breakthrough in philosophy at the turn of the century, and an a priori science derived from it; a science which is intended to supply the basic instrument (*Organon*) for a rigorously scientific philosophy and, in its consequent application, to make possible a methodical reform of all the sciences. Together with this philosophical phenomenology, but not yet separated from it, however, there also came into being a new psychological discipline parallel to it in method and content: the a priori pure or "phenomenological" psychology, which raises the reformational claim to being the basic methodological foundation on which alone a scientifically rigorous empirical psychology can be established. An outline of this psychological phenomenology, standing nearer to our natural thinking, is well suited to serve as a preliminary step that will lead up to an understanding of philosophical phenomenology.

I. PURE PSYCHOLOGY: ITS FIELD OF EXPERIENCE, ITS METHOD, AND ITS FUNCTION

1. *Pure Natural Science and Pure Psychology*

Modern psychology is the science dealing with the "psychical" in the concrete context of spatio-temporal realities, being in some way so to speak what occurs in nature as egoical, with all that inseparably belongs to it as psychic processes like experiencing, thinking, feeling, willing, as capacity, and as *habitus*. Experience presents the psychical as merely a stratum of human and animal being. Accordingly, psychology is seen as a branch of the more concrete science of anthropology, or rather zoology. Animal realities are first of all, at a basic level, physical realities. As such, they belong in the closed nexus of relationships in physical nature, in Nature meant in the primary and most pregnant sense as the universal

Excerpted from Edmund Husserl, *Husserl: Shorter Works*, edited by Peter McCormick and Frederick Elliston (Notre Dame: University of Notre Dame Press, 1981), 22–55.

theme of a pure natural science; that is to say, an objective science of
nature which in deliberate one-sidedness excludes all extra-physical
predications of reality. The scientific investigation of the bodies of
animals fits within this area. By contrast, however, if the psychic aspect
of the animal world is to become the topic of investigation, the first
thing we have to ask is how far, in parallel with the pure science of
nature, a pure psychology is possible. Obviously, purely psychological
research can be done to a certain extent. To it we owe the basic concepts
of the psychical according to the properties essential and specific to it.
These concepts must be incorporated into the others, into the psychophysical foundational concepts of psychology.

It is by no means clear from the very outset, however, how far the idea
of a pure psychology—as a psychological discipline sharply separate in
itself and as a real parallel to the pure physical science of nature—has a
meaning that is legitimate and necessary of realization.

2. The Purely Psychical in Self-Experience and Community Experience. The Universal Description of Intentional Experiences.

To establish and unfold this guiding idea, the first thing that is necessary
is a clarification of what is peculiar to experience, and especially to the
pure experience of the psychical—and specifically the purely psychical
that experience reveals, which is to become the theme of a pure psychology. It is natural and appropriate that precedence will be accorded to the
most immediate types of experience, which in each case reveal to us our
own psychic being.

Focusing our experiencing gaze on our own psychic life necessarily
takes place as reflection, as a turning about of a glance which had
previously been directed elsewhere. Every experience can be subject to
such reflection, as can indeed every manner in which we occupy ourselves
with any real or ideal objects—for instance, thinking, or in the modes of
feeling and will, valuing and striving. So when we are fully engaged in
conscious activity, we focus exclusively on the specific thing, thoughts,
values, goals, or means involved, but not on the psychical experience as
such, in which these things are known *as* such. Only reflection reveals
this to us. Through reflection, instead of grasping simply the matter
straight-out—the values, goals, and instrumentalities—we grasp the
corresponding subjective experiences in which we become "conscious" of
them, in which (in the broadest sense) they "appear." For this reason,
they are called "phenomena," and their most general essential character
is to exist as the "consciousness-of" or "appearance-of" the specific
things, thoughts (judged states of affairs, grounds, conclusions), plans,
decisions, hopes, and so forth. This relatedness [of the appearing to the
object of appearance] resides in the meaning of all expressions in the

vernacular languages which relate to psychic experience—for instance, perception *of* something, recalling *of* something, thinking *of* something, hoping *for* something, fearing something, striving *for* something, deciding on something, and so on. If this realm of what we call "phenomena" proves to be the possible field for a pure psychological discipline related exclusively to phenomena, we can understand the designation of it as *phenomenological psychology*. The terminological expression, deriving from Scholasticism, for designating the basic character of being as consciousness, as consciousness of something, is *intentionality*. In unreflective holding of some object or other in consciousness, we are turned or directed towards it: our *"intentio"* goes out towards it. The phenomenological reversal of our gaze shows that this "being directed" [*Gerichtetsein*] is really an immanent essential feature of the respective experiences involved; they are "intentional" experiences.

An extremely large and variegated number of kinds of special cases fall within the general scope of this concept. Consciousness of something is not an empty holding of something; every phenomenon has its own total form of intention [*intentionale Gesamtform*], but at the same time it has a structure, which in intentional analysis leads always again to components which are themselves also intentional. So for example in starting from a perception of something (for example, a die), phenomenological reflection leads to a multiple and yet synthetically unified intentionality. There are continually varying differences in the modes of appearing of objects, which are caused by the changing of "orientation"—of right and left, nearness and farness, with the consequent differences in perspective involved. There are further differences in appearance between the "actually seen front" and the "unseeable" [*"unanschaulichen"*] and relatively "undetermined" reverse side, which is nevertheless "meant along with it." Observing the flux of modes of appearing and the manner of their "synthesis," one finds that every phase and portion [of the flux] is already in itself "consciousness-of"—but in such a manner that there is formed within the constant emerging of new phases the synthetically unified awareness that this is one and the same object. The intentional structure of any process of perception has its fixed essential type [*seine feste Wesenstypik*], which must necessarily be realized in all its extraordinary complexity just in order for a physical body simply to be perceived as such. If this same thing is intuited in other modes—for example, in the modes of recollection, fantasy or pictorial representation—to some extent the whole intentional content of the perception comes back, but all aspects peculiarly transformed to correspond to that mode. This applies similarly for every other category of psychic process: the judging, valuing, striving consciousness is not an empty having knowledge of the specific judgments, values, goals, and means. Rather, these constitute themselves, with fixed essential forms corresponding to each process, in a flowing intentionality. For psychology, the universal task presents itself: to investigate systematically the elementary intentionalities, and from out of these [unfold] the typical forms of intentional processes, their possible variants, their syntheses to new forms, their structural composition, and from this advance towards a descriptive knowledge of the totality of mental process, towards a comprehensive type of a life of the psyche [*Gesamttypus eines Lebens der Seele*]. Clearly, the consistent carrying out of this task will produce knowledge which will have validity far beyond the psychologist's own particular psychic existence.

Psychic life is accessible to us not only through self-experience but also through experience of others. This novel source of experience offers us not only what matches our self-experience but also what is new, inasmuch as, in terms of consciousness and indeed as experience, it establishes the differences between own and other, as well as the properties peculiar to the life of a community. At just this point there arises the task of also making phenomenologically understandable the mental life of the community, with all the intentionalities that pertain to it.

3. *The Self-Contained Field of the Purely Psychical.—Phenomenological Reduction and True Inner Experience.*

The idea of a phenomenological psychology encompasses the whole range of tasks arising out of the experience of self and the experience of the other founded on it. But it is not yet clear whether phenomenological experience, followed through in exclusiveness and consistency, really provides us with a kind of closed-off field of being, out of which a science can grow which is exclusively focused on it and completely free of everything psychophysical. Here [in fact] difficulties do exist, which have hidden from psychologists the possibility of such a purely phenomenological psychology even after Brentano's discovery of intentionality. They are relevant already to the construction of a really pure self-experience, and therewith of a really pure psychic datum. A particular method of access is required for the pure phenomenological field: the method of "phenomenological reduction." This *method of "phenomenological reduction"* is thus the foundational method of pure psychology and the presupposition of all its specifically theoretical methods. Ultimately the great difficulty rests on the way that already the self-experience of the psychologist is everywhere intertwined with external experience, with that of extra-psychical real things. The experienced "exterior" does not belong to one's intentional interiority, although certainly the experience itself belongs to it as experience—*of* the exterior. Exactly this same thing is true of every kind of awareness directed at something out there in the world. A consistent epoche of the phenomenologist is required, if he wishes to break through to his own consciousness as pure phenomenon or as the totality of his purely mental processes. That is to say, in the accomplishment of phenomenological reflection he must inhibit every coaccomplishment of objective positing produced in unreflective consciousness, and therewith [inhibit] every judgmental drawing-in of the world as it "exists" for him straightforwardly. The specific experience of this house, this body, of a world as such, is and remains, however, according to its own essential content and thus inseparably, experience "*of* this house," this body, this world; this is so for every mode of consciousness which is directed towards an object. It is, after all, quite impossible to describe an intentional experience—even if illusionary, an invalid judgment, or the like—without at the same time describing the object of that consciousness *as* such. The universal epoche of the world as it becomes known in consciousness (the "putting it in brackets") shuts out from the phenomenological field the world as it exists for the subject in simple absoluteness; its place, however, is taken by the world as given in *consciousness* (perceived, remembered, judged, thought, valued, etc.)—the world *as such*, the "world in brackets," or in other words, the world, or rather individual things in the world as absolute, are replaced by the respective meaning of each in *consciousness* [*Bewusstseinssinn*] in its various modes (perceptual meaning, recollected meaning, and so on).

With this, we have clarified and supplemented our initial determination of the phenomenological experience and its sphere of being. In going back from the unities posited in the natural attitude to the manifold of modes of consciousness in which they appear, the unities, as inseparable from these multiplicities—but as "bracketed"—are also to be reckoned among what is purely psychical, and always specifically in the appearance-character in which they present themselves. The method of phenomenological reduction (to the pure "phenomenon," the purely psychical) accordingly consists (1) in the methodical and rigorously consistent epoche of every objective positing in the psychic sphere, both of the individual phenomenon and of the whole psychic field in general; and (2) in the methodically practiced seizing and describing of the multiple "appearances" as appearances of their objective units and these units as units of component meanings accruing to them each time in their appearances. With this is shown a twofold direction—the *noetic* and *noematic* of phenomenological description. Phenomenological experience in the methodical form of the phenomenological reduction is the only genuine "inner experience" in the sense meant by any well-grounded science of psychology. In its own nature lies manifest the possibility of being carried out continuously in infinitum with methodical preservation of purity. The reductive method is transferred from self-experience to the experience of other insofar as there can be applied to the envisaged [*vergegen-wärtigten*] mental life of the Other the corresponding bracketing and description according to the subjective "How" of its appearance and what is appearing ("noesis" and "noema"). As a further consequence, the community that is experienced in community experience is reduced not only to the mentally particularized intentional fields but also to the unity of the community life that connects them all together, the community mental life in its phenomenological purity (intersubjective reduction). Thus results the perfect expansion of the genuine psychological concept of "inner experience."

To every mind there belongs not only the unity of its multiple *intentional life-process* [*intentionalen Lebens*] with all its inseparable unities of sense directed towards the "object." There is also, inseparable from this life-process, the experiencing *I-subject* as the identical *I-pole* giving a center for all specific intentionalities, and as the carrier of all habitualities growing out of this life-process. Likewise, then, the reduced inter-subjectivity, in pure form and concretely grasped, is a community of pure "persons" acting in the intersubjective realm of the pure life of consciousness.

4. Eidetic Reduction and Phenomenological Psychology as an Eidetic Science.

To what extent does the unity of the field of phenomenological experience assure the possibility of a psychology exclusively based on it, thus a pure phenomenological psychology? It does not automatically assure an empirically pure science of *facts* from which everything psychophysical is abstracted. But this situation is quite different with an a priori science. In it, every self-enclosed field of possible experience permits *eo ipso* the all-embracing transition from the factual to the essential form, the *eidos*. So here, too. If the phenomenological actual fact as such becomes irrelevant; if, rather, it serves only as an example and as the foundation for a free but intuitive variation of the factual mind and communities of minds *into* the a priori possible (thinkable) ones; and if now the theoretical eye directs itself to the necessarily enduring invariant in the variation; then there will arise with this systematic way of proceeding a realm of its own, of the "a priori." There emerges therewith the eidetically necessary typical form, the *eidos;* this *eidos* must manifest itself throughout all the potential forms of mental being in particular cases, must be present in all the synthetic combinations and self-enclosed wholes, if it is to be at all "thinkable," that is, intuitively conceivable. Phenomenological psychology in this manner undoubtedly must be established as an "eidetic phenomenology"; it is then exclusively directed toward the invariant essential forms. For instance, the phenomenology of perception of bodies will not be (simply) a report on the factually occurring perceptions or those to be expected; rather it will be the presentation of invariant structural systems without which perception of a body and a synthetically concordant multiplicity of perceptions of one and the same body as such would be unthinkable. If the phenomenological reduction contrived a means of access to the phenomenon of real and also potential inner experience, the method founded in it of "eidetic reduction" provides the means of access to the invariant essential structures of the total sphere of pure mental process.

5. *The Fundamental Function of Pure Phenomenological Psychology for an Exact Empirical Psychology.*

A phenomenological pure psychology is absolutely necessary as the foundation for the building up of an "exact" empirical psychology, which since its modern beginnings has been sought according to the model of the exact pure sciences of physical nature. The fundamental meaning of "exactness" in this natural science lies in its being founded on an a priori form-system—each part unfolded in a special theory (pure geometry, a theory of pure time, theory of motion, etc.)—for a Nature conceivable in these terms. It is through the utilization of this a priori form-system for factual nature that the vague, inductive empirical approach attains to a share of eidetic necessity [*Wesensnotwendigkeit*] and empirical natural science itself gains a new sense—that of working out for all vague concepts and rules their indispensable basis of rational concepts and laws. As essentially differentiated as the methods of natural science and psychology may remain, there does exist a necessary common ground: that psychology, like every science, can only draw its "rigor" ("exactness") from the rationality of the essence." The uncovering of the a priori set of types without which "I," "we," "consciousness," "the objectivity of consciousness," and therewith mental being as such would be inconceivable—with all the essentially necessary and essentially possible forms of synthesis which are inseparable from the idea of a whole comprised of individual and communal mental life—produces a prodigious field of exactness that can immediately (without the intervening link of *Limes-Idealisierung*[1]) be carried over into research on the psyche. Admittedly, the phenomenological a priori does not comprise the complete a priori of psychology, inasmuch as the psychophysical relationship as such has its own a priori. It is clear, however, that this a priori will presuppose that of a pure phenomenological psychology, just as on the

---

1. By this expression (*Limes-Idealisierung*), Husserl would seem to mean idealization to exact (mathematical) limits. [Orig. eds.]

other side it will presuppose the pure a priori of a physical (and specifically the organic) Nature as such.

The systematic construction of a phenomenological pure psychology
demands:

(1) The description of the peculiarities universally belonging to the
essence of intentional mental process, which includes the most general
law of synthesis: every connection of consciousness with consciousness
gives rise to a consciousness.

(2) The exploration of single forms of intentional mental process
which in essential necessity generally must or can present themselves in
the mind; in unity with this, also the exploration of the syntheses they
are members of for a typology of their essences: both those that are
discrete and those continuous with others, both the finitely closed and
those continuing into open infinity.

(3) The showing and eidetic description [Wesensdeskription] of the total
structure [Gesamtgestalt] of mental life as such; in other words, a description of the essential character [Wesensart] of a universal "stream of
consciousness."

(4) The term "I" designates a new direction for investigation (still in
abstraction from the social sense of this word) in reference to the
essence-forms of "habituality"; in other words, the "I" as subject of
lasting beliefs or thought-tendencies—"persuasions"—(convictions
about being, value-convictions, volitional decisions, and so on), as the
personal subject of habits, of trained knowing, of certain character
qualities.

Throughout all this, the "static" description of essences ultimately
leads to problems of genesis, and to an all-pervasive genesis that governs
the whole life and development of the personal "I" according to eidetic
laws [eidetischen Gesetzen]. So on top of the first "static phenomenology"
will be constructed in higher levels a dynamic or genetic phenomenology. As the first and founding genesis it will deal with that of passivity—genesis in which the "I" does not actively participate. Here lies the
new task, an all-embracing eidetic phenomenology of association, a
latter-day rehabilitation of David Hume's great discovery, involving an
account of the a priori genesis out of which a real spatial world constitutes itself for the mind in habitual acceptance. There follows from this
the eidetic theory dealing with the development of personal habituality,
in which the purely mental "I" within the invariant structural forms of
consciousness exists as personal "I" and is conscious of itself in habitual
continuing being and as always being transformed. For further investigation, there offers itself an especially interconnected stratum at a
higher level: the static and then the genetic phenomenology of reason.

II. Phenomenological Psychology and Transcendental Phenomenology

6. *Descartes's Transcendental Turn and Locke's Psychologism.*

The idea of a purely phenomenological psychology does not have just the function described above, of reforming empirical psychology. For deeply rooted reasons, it can also serve as a preliminary step for laying open the essence of a transcendental phenomenology. Historically, this idea too did not grow out of the peculiar needs of psychology proper. Its history leads us back to John Locke's notable basic work, and the significant development in Berkeley and Hume of the impetus it contained. Already Locke's restriction to the purely subjective was determined by extra-psychological interests: psychology here stood in the service of the transcendental problem awakened through Descartes. In Descartes's *Meditations*, the thought that had become the guiding one for "first philosophy" was that all of "reality," and finally the whole world of what exists and is so *for us*, exists only as the presentational content of our presentations, as meant in the best case and as evidently reliable in our own cognitive life. This is the motivation for all transcendental problems, genuine or false. Descartes's method of doubt was the first method of exhibiting "transcendental subjectivity," and his *ego cogito* led to its first conceptual formulation. In Locke, Descartes's transcendentally pure *mens* is changed into the "human mind," whose systematic exploration through inner experience Locke tackled out of a transcendental-philosophical interest. And so he is the founder of *psychologism*—as a transcendental philosophy founded *through* a psychology of inner experience. The fate of scientific philosophy hangs on the radical overcoming of every trace of psychologism, an overcoming which not only exposes the fundamental absurdity of psychologism but also does justice to its transcendentally significant kernel of truth. The sources of its continuous historical power are drawn from out of a double sense [an ambiguity] of all the concepts of the subjective, which arises as soon as the transcendental question is broached. The uncovering of this ambiguity involves [us in the need for] at once the sharp separation, and at the time the parallel treatment, of pure phenomenological psychology (as the scientifically rigorous form of a psychology purely of inner experience) and transcendental phenomenology as true transcendental philosophy. At the same time this will justify our advance discussion of psychology as the means of access to true philosophy. We will begin with a clarification of the true transcendental problem, which in the initially obscure unsteadiness of its sense makes one so very prone (and this applies already to Descartes) to shunt it off to a side track.

7. The Transcendental Problem.

To the essential sense of the transcendental problem belongs its all-inclusiveness, in which it places in question the world and all the sciences investigating it. It arises within a general reversal of that "natural attitude" in which everyday life as a whole as well as the positive sciences operate. In it [the natural attitude] the world is for us the self-evidently existing universe of realities which are continuously before us in unquestioned givenness. So this is the general field of our practical and theoretical activities. As soon as the theoretical interest abandons this natural attitude and in a general turning around of our regard directs itself to the life of consciousness—*in which* the "world" is for us precisely that, the world which is present *to us*—we find ourselves in a new cognitive attitude [or situation]. Every sense which the world has for us (this we now become aware of), both its general indeterminate sense and its sense determining itself according to the particular realities, is, within the internality of our own perceiving, imagining, thinking, valuing life-process, a conscious sense, and a sense which is formed in subjective genesis. Every acceptance of something as validly existing is effected within us ourselves; and every evidence in experience and theory that establishes it, is operative in us ourselves, habitually and continuously motivating us. This [principle] concerns the world in every determination, even those that are self-evident: that what belongs *in and for itself* to the world, is how it is, whether or not I, or whoever, become by chance aware of it or not. Once the world in this full universality has been related to the subjectivity of consciousness, in whose living consciousness it makes its appearance precisely as "the" world in its varying sense, then its whole mode of being acquires a dimension of unintelligibility, or rather of questionableness. This "making an appearance" [*Auftreten*], this being-for-us of the world as only subjectively having come to acceptance and only subjectively brought and to be brought to well-grounded evident presentation, requires clarification. Because of its empty generality, one's first awakening to the relatedness of the world to consciousness gives no understanding of *how* the varied life of consciousness, barely discerned and sinking back into obscurity, accomplishes such functions: how it, so to say, manages in its immanence that something which manifests itself can present itself *as* something existing in itself, and not only as something meant but as something authenticated in concordant experience. Obviously the problem extends to every kind of "ideal" world and its "being-in-itself" (for example, the world of pure numbers, or of "truths in themselves"). Unintelligibility is felt as a particularly telling affront to *our* very mode of being [as human beings]. For obviously we are the ones (individually and in community) in whose conscious life-process the real world which is present for us as such gains sense and acceptance. As human creatures, however, we ourselves are supposed to belong to the world. When we start with the sense of the world [*weltlichen Sinn*] given with our mundane existing, we are thus again referred back to ourselves and our conscious life-process as that wherein for us this sense is first formed. Is there conceivable here or anywhere another way of elucidating [it] than to interrogate consciousness itself and the "world" that becomes known in it? For it is precisely as meant by us, and from nowhere else than in us, that it has gained and can gain its sense and validity.

Next we take yet another important step, which will raise the "transcendental" problem (having to do with the being-sense of "transcendent" relative to consciousness) up to the final level. It consists in recognizing that the relativity of consciousness referred to just now applies not just to the brute fact of *our* world but in eidetic necessity to every conceivable world whatever. For if we vary our factual world in free fantasy, carrying it over into random conceivable worlds, we are implicitly varying *ourselves* whose environment the world is: we each change ourselves into a possible subjectivity, whose environment would always have to be the world that was thought of, as a world of its [the subjectivity's] possible experiences, possible theoretical evidences, possible practical life. But obviously this variation leaves untouched the pure ideal worlds of the kind which have their existence in eidetic universality, which are in their essence invariable; it becomes apparent, however, from the possible variability of the subject knowing such identical essences [*Identitäten*], that their cognizability, and thus their intentional relatedness does not simply have to do with our de facto subjectivity. With the eidetic formulation of the problem, the kind of research into consciousness that is demanded is the eidetic.

8. *The Solution by Psychologism as a Transcendental Circle.*

Our distillation of the idea of a phenomenologically pure psychology has demonstrated the possibility of uncovering by consistent phenomenological reduction what belongs to the conscious subject's own essence in eidetic, universal terms, according to all its possible forms. This includes those forms of reason [itself] which establish and authenticate validity, and with this it includes all forms of potentially appearing worlds, both those validated in themselves through concordant experiences and those determined by theoretical truth. Accordingly, the systematic carrying through of this phenomenological psychology seems to comprehend in itself from the outset in foundational (precisely, eidetic) universality the whole of correlation research on being and consciousness; thus it would seem to be the [proper] locus for all transcendental elucidation. On the other hand, we must not overlook the fact that psychology in all its empirical and eidetic disciplines remains a "positive science," a science operating within the natural attitude, in which the simply present world is the thematic ground. What it wishes to explore are the psyches and communities of psyches that are [actually] to be found in the world. Phenomenological reduction serves as psychological only to the end that it gets at the psychical aspect of animal realities in its pure own essential specificity and its pure own specific essential interconnections. Even in eidetic research [then], the psyche retains the sense of being which belongs in the realm of what is present in the world; it is merely related to possible real worlds. Even as eidetic phenomenologist, the psychologist is transcendentally naive: he takes the possible "minds" ("I"-subjects) completely according to the relative sense of the word as those of men and animals considered purely and simply as present in a possible spatial world. If, however, we allow the transcendental interest to be decisive, instead of the natural-worldly, then psychology as a whole receives the stamp of what is transcendentally problematic; and thus it can by no means supply the premises for transcendental philosophy. The subjectivity of consciousness, which, as psychic being, is its theme, cannot be that to which we go back in our questioning into the transcendental.

In order to arrive at an evident clarity at this decisive point, the thematic sense of the transcendental question is to be kept sharply in view, and we must try to judge how, in keeping with it, the regions of the problematical and unproblematical are set apart. The theme of transcendental philosophy is a concrete and systematic elucidation of those multiple intentional relationships, which in conformity with their essences belong to any possible world whatever as the surrounding world of a corresponding possible subjectivity, for which it [the world] would be the one present as practically and theoretically accessible. In regard to all the objects and structures present in the world for these subjectivities, this accessibility involves the regulations of its possible conscious life, which in their typology will have to be uncovered. [Among] such categories are "lifeless things," as well as men and animals with the internalities of their psychic life. From this starting point the full and complete being-sense of a possible world, in general and in regard to all its constitutive categories, shall be elucidated. Like every meaningful question, this transcendental question presupposes a ground of unquestioned being, in which all means of solution must be contained. This ground is here the [anonymous] subjectivity of that kind of conscious life in which a possible world, of whatever kind, is constituted as present. However, a self-evident basic requirement of any rational method is that this ground presupposed as beyond question is not confused with what the transcendental question, in its universality, puts into question. Hence the realm of this questionability includes the whole realm of the transcendentally naïve and therefore every possible world simply claimed in the natural attitude. Accordingly, all possible sciences, including all their various areas of objects, are transcendentally to be subjected to an epoche. So also psychology, and the entirety of what is considered the psychical in its sense. It would therefore be circular, a transcendental circle, to base the answer to the transcendental question on psychology, be it empirical or eidetic-phenomenological. We face at this point the paradoxical ambiguity: the subjectivity and consciousness to which the transcendental question recurs can thus really not be the subjectivity and consciousness with which psychology deals.

9. The Transcendental-Phenomenological Reduction and the Semblance of Transcendental Duplication.

Are we then supposed to be dual beings—psychological, as human objectivities in the world, the subjects of psychic life, and at the same time transcendental, as the subjects of a transcendental, world-constituting life-process? This duality can be clarified through being demonstrated with self-evidence. The psychic subjectivity, the concretely grasped "I" and "we" of ordinary conversation, is experienced in its pure psychic ownness through the method of phenomenological-psychological reduction. Modified into eidetic form it provides the ground for pure phenomenological psychology. Transcendental subjectivity, which is inquired into in the transcendental problem, and which subjectivity is presupposed in it as an existing basis, is none other than again "I myself" and "we ourselves"; not, however, as found in the natural attitude of everyday or of positive science; *i.e.*, apperceived as components of the objectively present world before us, but rather as subjects of conscious life, *in* which this world and all that is present—for "us"—"makes" itself through certain apperceptions. As men, mentally as well as bodily present in the world, we are for "ourselves"; we are appearances standing within an extremely variegated intentional life-process, "our" life, *in which* this being on hand constitutes itself "for us" apperceptively, with its entire sense-content. The (apperceived) I and we on hand presuppose and (apperceiving) I and we, *for* which they are on hand, which, however, is not itself present again in the same sense. To this transcendental subjectivity we have direct access through a transcendental experience. Just as the psychic experience requires a reductive method for purity, so does the transcendental.

We would like to proceed here by introducing the *transcendental reduction* as built on the psychological reduction—as an additional part of the purification which can be performed on it any time, a purification that is once more by means of a certain epoche. This is merely a consequence of the all-embracing epoche which belongs to the sense of the transcendental question. If the transcendental relativity of every possible world demands an all-embracing bracketing, it also postulates the bracketing of pure psyches and the pure phenomenological psychology related to them. Through this bracketing they are transformed into transcendental phenomena. Thus, while the psychologist, operating within what for him is the naturally accepted world, reduces to pure psychic subjectivity the subjectivity occurring there (but still within the world), the transcendental phenomenologist, through his absolutely all-embracing epoche, reduces this psychologically pure element to transcendental pure subjectivity, [*i.e.*,] to that which performs and posits within itself the apperception of the world and therein the objectivating apperception of a "psyche [belonging to] animal realities." For example, my actual current mental processes of pure perception, fantasy, and so forth, are, in the attitude of positivity, psychological givens [or data] of psychological inner experience. They are transmuted into my transcendental mental processes if through a radical epoche I posit as mere phenomena the world, including my own human existence, and now follow up the intentional life-process wherein the entire apperception "of" the world, and in particular the apperception of my mind, my psychologically real perception-processes, and so forth, are formed. The content of these processes, what is included in their own essences, remains in this fully preserved, although it is now visible as the core of an apperception practiced again and again psychologically but not previously considered. For the transcendental philosopher, who through a previous all-inclusive resolve of his will has instituted in himself the firm habituality of the transcendental "bracketing," even this "mundanization" [*Verweltlichung*, treating everything as part of the world] of consciousness which is omnipresent in the natural attitude is inhibited once and for all. Accordingly, the consistent reflection on consciousness yields him time after time transcendentally pure data, and more particularly it is intuitive in the mode of a new kind of experience, *transcendental "inner" experience*. Arisen out of the methodical transcendental epoche, this new kind of "inner" experience opens up the limitless transcendental field of being. This field of being is the parallel to the limitless psychological field, and the method of access [to its data] is the parallel to the purely psychological one, *i.e.*, to the psychological-phenomenological reduction. And again, the transcendental I [or ego] and the transcendental community of egos, conceived in the full concretion of transcendental life are the transcendental parallel to the I and we in the customary and psychological sense, concretely conceived as mind and community of minds, with the psychological life of consciousness that pertains to them. My transcendental ego is thus evidently "different" from the natural ego, but by no means as a second, as one *separated* from it in the natural sense of the word, just as on the contrary it is by no means bound up with it or intertwined with it, in the usual sense of these words. It is just the field of transcendental self-experience (conceived in full concreteness) which in every case can, *through mere alteration of attitude*, be changed into psychological self-experience. In this transition, an identity of the I is necessarily brought about; in transcendental reflection on this transition the psychological Objectivation becomes visible as self-objectivation of the transcendental I, and so it is as if in every moment of the natural attitude the I finds itself with an apperception imposed upon it. If the parallelism of the transcendental and psychological experience-spheres has become comprehensible out of a mere alteration of attitude, as a kind of identity of the complex interpenetration of senses of being, then there also becomes intelligible the consequence that results from it, namely the same parallelism and the interpenetration of transcendental and psychological phenomenology implied in that interpenetration, whose whole theme is pure intersubjectivity, in its dual sense. Only that in this case it has to be taken into account that the purely psychic intersubjectivity, as soon as the it is subjected to the transcendental epoche, also leads to its parallel, that is, to transcendental intersubjectivity. Manifestly this parallelism spells nothing less than theoretical equivalence. Transcendental intersubjectivity is the concretely autonomous absolute existing basis [*Seinsboden*] out of which everything transcendent (and, with it, everything that belongs to the real world) obtains its existential sense as that of something which only in a relative and therewith incomplete sense is an existing thing, namely as being an intentional unity which in truth exists from out of transcendental bestowal of sense, of harmonious confirmation, and from an habituality of lasting conviction that belongs to it by essential necessity.

10. *Pure Psychology as Propaedeutic to Transcendental Phenomenology.*

Through the elucidation of the essentially dual meaning of the subjectivity of consciousness, and also a clarification of the eidetic science to be directed to it, we begin to understand on very deep grounds the historical insurmountability of psychologism. Its power lies in an *essential transcendental semblance* which [because] undisclosed had to remain effective. Also from the clarification we have gained we begin to understand on the one hand the independence of the idea of a transcendental phenomenology, and the systematic developing of it, from the idea of a phenomenological pure psychology; and yet on the other hand the propaedeutic usefulness of the preliminary project of a pure psychology for an ascent to transcendental phenomenology, a usefulness which has guided our present discussion here. As regards this point [*i.e.*, the independence of the idea of transcendental phenomenology from a phenomenological pure psychology], clearly the phenomenological and eidetic reduction allows of being *immediately* connected to the disclosing of transcendental relativity, and in this way transcendental phenomenology springs directly out of the transcendental intuition. In point of fact, this direct path was the historical path it took. Pure phenomenological psychology as eidetic science in positivity was simply not available. As regards the second point, *i.e.*, the propaedeutic preference of the indirect approach to transcendental phenomenology through pure psychology, [it must be remembered that] the transcendental attitude involves a change of focus from one's entire form of life-style, one which goes so completely beyond all previous experiencing of life, that it must, in virtue of its absolute strangeness, needs be difficult to understand. This is also true of a transcendental science. Phenomenological psychology, although also relatively new, and in its method of intentional analysis completely novel, still has the accessibility which is possessed by all positive sciences. Once this psychology has become clear, at least according to its sharply defined idea, then only the clarification of the true sense of the transcendental-philosophical field of problems and of the transcendental reduction is required in order for it to come into possession of transcendental phenomenology as a mere reversal of its doctrinal content into transcendental terms. The basic difficulties for penetrating into the terrain of the new phenomenology fall into these two stages, namely that of understanding the true method of "inner experience," which already belongs to making possible an "exact" psychology as rational science of facts, and that of understanding the distinctive character of the transcendental methods and questioning. True, simply regarded in itself, an interest in the transcendental is the highest and ultimate scientific interest, and so it is entirely the right thing (it has been so historically and should continue) for transcendental theories to be cultivated in the autonomous, absolute system of transcendental philosophy; and to place before us, through showing the characteristic features of the natural in contrast to the transcendental attitude, the possibility within transcendental philosophy itself of reinterpreting all transcendental phenomenological doctrine [or theory] into doctrine [or theory] in the realm of natural positivity.

III. Transcendental Phenomenology and Philosophy as Universal Science with Absolute Foundations

11. *Transcendental Phenomenology as Ontology.*

Remarkable consequences arise when one weighs the significance of transcendental phenomenology. In its systematic development, it brings to realization the Leibnizian idea of a universal ontology as the systematic unity of all conceivable a priori sciences, but on a new foundation which overcomes "dogmatism" through the use of the transcendental phenomenological method. Phenomenology as the science of all conceivable transcendental phenomena and especially the synthetic total structures in which alone they are concretely possible—those of the transcendental single subjects bound to communities of subjects is *eo ipso* the a priori science of all conceivable beings. But [it is the science] then not merely of the Totality of objectively existing beings, and certainly not in an attitude of natural positivity; rather, in the full concretion of being in general which derives its sense of being and its validity from the correlative intentional constitution. This also comprises the being of transcendental subjectivity itself, whose nature it is demonstrably to be constituted transcendentally in and for itself. Accordingly, a phenomenology properly carried through is the truly universal ontology, as over against the only illusory all-embracing ontology in positivity—and precisely for this reason it overcomes the dogmatic one-sidedness and hence unintelligibility of the latter, while at the same time it comprises within itself the truly legitimate content [of an ontology in positivity] as grounded originally in intentional constitution.

12. *Phenomenology and the Crisis in the Foundations of the Exact Sciences.*

If we consider the how of this inclusion, we find that what is meant is that every a priori is ultimately prescribed in its validity of being precisely *as* a transcendental achievement; *i.e.*, it is together with the essential structures of its constitution, with the kinds and levels of its givenness and confirmation of itself, and with the appertaining habitualities. This implies that in and through the establishment of the a priori the subjective *method* of this establishing is itself made transparent, and that for the a priori disciplines which are founded within phenomenology (for example, as mathematical sciences) there can be no "paradoxes" and no "crises of the foundations." The consequence that arises [from all this] with reference to the a priori sciences that have come into being historically and in transcendental naïveté is that only a radical, phenomenological grounding can transform them into true, methodical, fully self-justifying sciences. But precisely by this they will cease to be positive (dogmatic) sciences and become dependent branches of the one phenomenology as all-encompassing eidetic ontology.

13. *The Phenomenological Grounding of the Factual Sciences*
in Relation to Empirical Phenomenology.

The unending task of presenting the complete universe of the a priori in its transcendental relatedness-back-to-itself [or self-reference], and thus in its self-sufficiency and perfect methodological clarity, is itself a function of the method for realization of an all-embracing and hence fully grounded science of empirical fact. Within [the realm of] positive reality [*Positivität*], genuine (relatively genuine) empirical science demands the methodical establishing-of-a-foundation [*Fundamentierung*] through a corresponding a priori science. If we take the universe of all possible empirical sciences whatever and demand a *radical* grounding that will be free from all "foundation crises," then we are led to the all-embracing a priori of the radical and that is [and must be] *phenomenological* grounding. The genuine form of an all-embracing science of fact is thus the phenomenological [form], and as this it is the universal science of the factual transcendental intersubjectivity, [resting] on the methodical foundation of eidetic phenomenology as knowledge applying to any possible transcendental subjectivity whatever. Hence *the idea of an empirical phenomenology* which follows after the eidetic is understood and justified. It is identical with the complete systematic universe of the positive sciences, provided that we think of them from the beginning as absolutely grounded methodologically through eidetic phenomenology.

14. *Complete Phenomenology as All-Embracing Philosophy.*

Precisely through this is restored the most primordial concept of philosophy—as all-embracing science based on radical self-justification, which is alone [truly] science in the ancient Platonic and again in the Cartesian sense. Phenomenology rigorously and systematically carried out, phenomenology in the broadened sense [which we have explained] above, is identical with this philosophy which encompasses all genuine knowledge. It is divided into eidetic phenomenology (or all-embracing ontology) as *first philosophy*, and as *second philosophy*, [it is] the science of the universe of *facta,* or of the transcendental intersubjectivity that synthetically comprises all *facta.* First philosophy is the universe of methods for the second, and is related back into itself for its methodological grounding.

15. *The "Ultimate and Highest" Problems as Phenomenological.*

In phenomenology all rational problems have their place, and thus also those that traditionally are in some special sense or other philosophically significant. For out of the absolute sources of transcendental experience, or eidetic intuiting, they first [are able to] obtain their genuine formulation and feasible means for their solution. In its universal relatedness-back-to-itself, phenomenology recognizes its particular function within a possible life of mankind [*Menschheitsleben*] at the transcendental level. It recognizes the absolute norms which are to be picked out intuitively from it [life of mankind], and also its primordial teleological-tendential structure in a directedness towards disclosure of these norms and their conscious practical operation. It recognizes itself as a function of the all-embracing reflective meditation of (transcendental) humanity, [a self-examination] in the service of an all-inclusive praxis of reason; that is, in the service of striving towards the universal ideal of absolute perfection which lies in infinity, [a striving] which becomes free through [the process of] disclosure. Or, in different words it is a striving in the direction of the idea (lying in infinity) of a humanness which in action and throughout would live and move [be, exist] in truth and genuineness. It recognizes its self-reflective function [of self-examination] for the relative realization of the correlative practical idea of a genuine human life [*Menschheitsleben*] in the second sense (whose structural forms of being and whose practical norms it is to investigate), namely as one [that is] consciously and purposively directed towards this absolute idea. In short, the metaphysically teleological, the ethical, and the problems of philosophy of history, no less than, obviously, the problems of judging reason, lie within its boundary, no differently from all significant problems whatever, and all [of them] in their inmost synthetic unity and order as [being] of transcendental spirituality [*Geistigkeit*].

16. *The Phenomenological Resolution of All Philosophical Antitheses.*

In the systematic work of phenomenology, which progresses from intuitively given [concrete] data to heights of abstraction, the old traditional ambiguous antitheses of the philosophical standpoint are resolved—by themselves and without the arts of an argumentative dialectic, and without weak efforts and compromises: oppositions such as between rationalism (Platonism) and empiricism, relativism and absolutism, subjectivism and objectivism, ontologism and transcendentalism, psychologism and anti-psychologism, positivism and metaphysics, or the teleological versus the causal interpretation of the world. Throughout all of these, [one finds] justified motives, but throughout also half-truths or impermissible absolutizing of only relatively and abstractively legitimate one-sidednesses.

Subjectivism can only be overcome by the most all-embracing and consistent subjectivism (the transcendental). In this [latter] form it is at the same time objectivism [of a deeper sort], in that it represents the claims of whatever objectivity is to be demonstrated through concordant experience, but admittedly [this is an objectivism which] also brings out its full and genuine sense, against which [sense] the supposedly realistic objectivism sins by its failure to understand transcendental constitution. *Relativism* can only be overcome through the most all-embracing relativism, that of transcendental phenomenology, which makes intelligible the relativity of all "objective" being [or existence] as transcendentally constituted; but at one with this [it makes intelligible] the most radical relativity, the relatedness of the transcendental subjectivity to itself. But just this [relatedness, subjectivity] proves its identity to be the only possible sense of [the term] "absolute" being—over against all "objective" being that is relative to it—namely, as the "for-itself"—being of transcendental subjectivity. Likewise: *Empiricism* can only be overcome by the most universal and consistent empiricism, which puts in place of the restricted [term] "experience" of the empiricists the necessarily broadened concept of experience [inclusive] of intuition which offers original data, an intuition which in all its forms (intuition of *eidos,* apodictic self-evidence, phenomenological intuition of essence, etc.) shows the manner and form of its legitimation through phenomenological clarification. Phenomenology as eidetic is, on the other hand, rationalistic: it overcomes restrictive and dogmatic rationalism, however, through the most universal rationalism of inquiry into essences, which is related uniformly to transcendental subjectivity, to the I, consciousness, and conscious objectivity. And it is the same in reference to the other antitheses bound up with them. The tracing back of all being to the transcendental subjectivity and its constitutive intentional functions leaves open, to mention one more thing, no other way of contemplating the world than the *teleological.* And yet phenomenology also acknowledges a kernel of truth in naturalism (or rather sensationism). That is, by revealing associations as intentional phenomena, indeed as a whole basic typology of forms of passive intentional synthesis with transcendental and purely passive genesis based on essential laws, phenomenology shows Humean fictionalism to contain anticipatory discoveries; particularly in his doctrine of the origin of such fictions as thing, persisting existence, causality—anticipatory discoveries all shrouded in absurd theories.

Phenomenological philosophy regards itself in its whole method as a pure outcome of methodical intentions which already animated Greek philosophy from its beginnings; above all, however, [it continues] the still vital intentions which reach, in the two lines of rationalism and empiricism, from Descartes through Kant and German idealism into our confused present day. A pure outcome of methodical intentions means real method which allows the problems to be taken in hand and completed. In the way of true science this path is endless. Accordingly, phenomenology demands that the phenomenologist foreswear the ideal of a philosophic system and yet as a humble worker in community with others, live for a perennial philosophy [*philosophia perennis*].

Course in General Linguistics

THE OBJECT OF LINGUISTICS

1. *Definition of Language*

What is both the integral and concrete object of linguistics? The question is especially difficult; later we shall see why; here I wish merely to point up the difficulty.

Other sciences work with objects that are given in advance and that can then be considered from different viewpoints; but not linguistics. Someone pronounces the French word *nu,* bare: a superficial observer would be tempted to call the word a concrete linguistic object; but a more careful examination would reveal successively three or four quite different things, depending on whether the word is considered as a sound, as the expression of an idea, as the equivalent of Latin *nudum,* etc. Far from it being the object that antedates the viewpoint, it would seem that it is the viewpoint that creates the object; besides, nothing tells us in advance that one way of considering the fact in question takes precedence over the others or is in any way superior to them.

Moreover, regardless of the viewpoint that we adopt, the linguistic phenomenon always has two related sides, each deriving its values from the other. For example:

1. Articulated syllables are acoustical impressions perceived by the ear, but the sounds would not exist without the vocal organs; an *n,* for example, exists only by virtue of the relations between the two sides. We simply cannot reduce language to sound or detach sound from oral articulation; reciprocally, we cannot define the movements of the vocal organs without taking into account the acoustical impression.

2. But suppose that sound were a simple thing: would it constitute speech? No, it is only the instrument of thought; by itself, it has no existence. At this point a new and redoubtable relationship arises: a

Excerpted from Ferdinand de Saussure, *Course in General Linguistics,* edited by Charles Bally and Albert Sechehaye in collaboration with Albert Riedlinger, translated by Wade Baskin (New York: McGraw-Hill Book Co., 1959), 7–9, 11–17, 65–74, 79–81, 88–91, 98–100, 111–22.

sound, a complex acoustical-vocal unit, combines in turn with an idea to form a complex physiological-psychological unit. But that is still not the complete picture.

3. Speech has both an individual and a social side, and we cannot conceive of one without the other. Besides:

4. Speech always implies both an established system and an evolution; at every moment it is an existing institution and a product of the past. To distinguish between the system and its history, between what it is and what it was, seems very simple at first glance; actually the two things are so closely related that we can scarcely keep them apart. Would we simplify the question by studying the linguistic phenomenon in its earliest stages—if we began, for example, by studying the speech of children? No, for in dealing with speech, it is completely misleading to assume that the problem of early characteristics differs from the problem of permanent characteristics. We are left inside the vicious circle.

From whatever direction we approach the question, nowhere do we find the integral object of linguistics. Everywhere we are confronted with a dilemma: if we fix our attention on only one side of each problem, we run the risk of failing to perceive the dualities pointed out above; on the other hand, if we study speech from several viewpoints simultaneously, the object of linguistics appears to us as a confused mass of heterogeneous and unrelated things. Either procedure opens the door to several sciences—psychology, anthropology, normative grammar, philology, etc.—which are distinct from linguistics, but which might claim speech, in view of the faulty method of linguistics, as one of their objects.

As I see it there is only one solution to all the foregoing difficulties: *from the very outset we must put both feet on the ground of language and use language as the norm of all other manifestations of speech.* Actually, among so many dualities, language alone seems to lend itself to independent definition and provide a fulcrum that satisfies the mind.

But what is language [*langue*]? It is not to be confused with human speech [*langage*], of which it is only a definite part, though certainly an essential one. It is both a social product of the faculty of speech and a collection of necessary conventions that have been adopted by a social body to permit individuals to exercise that faculty. Taken as a whole, speech is many-sided and heterogeneous; straddling several areas simultaneously—physical, physiological, and psychological—it belongs both to the individual and to society; we cannot put it into any category of human facts, for we cannot discover its unity.

Language, on the contrary, is a self-contained whole and a principle of classification. As soon as we give language first place among the facts of speech, we introduce a natural order into a mass that lends itself to no other classification. . . .

2. Place of Language in the Facts of Speech

In order to separate from the whole of speech the part that belongs to language, we must examine the individual act from which the speaking-circuit can be reconstructed. The act requires the presence of at least two persons; that is the minimum number necessary to complete the circuit. Suppose that two people, A and B, are conversing with each other:

Suppose that the opening of the circuit is in A's brain, where mental facts (concepts) are associated with representations of the linguistic sounds (sound-images) that are used for their expression. A given concept unlocks a corresponding sound-image in the brain; this purely *psychological* phenomenon is followed in turn by a *physiological* process: the brain transmits an impulse corresponding to the image to the organs used in producing sounds. Then the sound waves travel from the mouth of A to the ear of B: a purely *physical* process. Next, the circuit continues in B, but the order is reversed: from the ear to the brain, the physiological transmission of the sound-image; in the brain, the psychological association of the image with the corresponding concept. If B then speaks, the new act will follow—from his brain to A's—exactly the same course as the first act and pass through the same successive phases, which I shall diagram as follows:

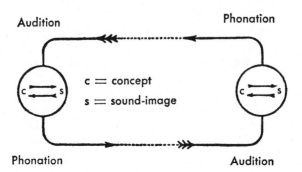

The preceding analysis does not purport to be complete. We might also single out the pure acoustical sensation, the identification of that sensation with the latent sound-image, the muscular image of phonation, etc. I have included only the elements thought to be essential, but the drawing brings out at a glance the distinction between the physical (sound waves), physiological (phonation and audition), and psychological parts (word-images and concepts). Indeed, we should not fail to note that the word-image stands apart from the sound itself and that it is just as psychological as the concept which is associated with it.

The circuit that I have outlined can be further divided into:

a. an outer part that includes the vibrations of the sounds which travel from the mouth to the ear, and an inner part that includes everything else;

b. a psychological and a nonpsychological part, the second including the physiological productions of the vocal organs as well as the physical facts that are outside the individual;

c. an active and a passive part: everything that goes from the associative center of the speaker to the ear of the listener is active, and everything that goes from the ear of the listener to his associative center is passive;

d. finally, everything that is active in the psychological part of the circuit is executive (c → s), and everything that is passive is receptive (s → c).

We should also add the associative and coordinating faculty that we find as soon as we leave isolated signs; this faculty plays the dominant role in the organization of language as a system.

But to understand clearly the role of the associative and coordinating faculty, we must leave the individual act, which is only the embryo of speech, and approach the social fact.

Among all the individuals that are linked together by speech, some sort of average will be set up: all will reproduce—not exactly of course, but approximately—the same signs united with the same concepts.

How does the social crystallization of language come about? Which parts of the circuit are involved? For all parts probably do not participate equally in it.

The nonpsychological part can be rejected from the outset. When we hear people speaking a language that we do not know, we perceive the sounds but remain outside the social fact because we do not understand them.

Neither is the psychological part of the circuit wholly responsible: the executive side is missing, for execution is never carried out by the collectivity. Execution is always individual, and the individual is always its master: I shall call the executive side *speaking* [*parole*].

Through the functioning of the receptive and coordinating faculties, impressions that are perceptibly the same for all are made on the minds of speakers. How can that social product be pictured in such a way that language will stand apart from everything else? If we could embrace the sum of word-images stored in the minds of all individuals, we could identify the social bond that constitutes language. It is a storehouse filled by the members of a given community through their active use of speaking, a grammatical system that has a potential existence in each brain, or, more specifically, in the brains of a group of individuals. For language is not complete in any speaker; it exists perfectly only within a collectivity.

In separating language from speaking we are at the same time separating: (1) what is social from what is individual; and (2) what is essential from what is accessory and more or less accidental.

Language is not a function of the speaker; it is a product that is passively assimilated by the individual. It never requires premeditation, and reflection enters in only for the purpose of classification, which we shall take up later.

Speaking, on the contrary, is an individual act. It is willful and intellectual. Within the act, we should distinguish between: (1) the combinations by which the speaker uses the language code for expressing his own thought; and (2) the psychophysical mechanism that allows him to exteriorize those combinations.

Note that I have defined things rather than words; these definitions are not endangered by certain ambiguous words that do not have identical meanings in different languages. For instance, German *Sprache* means both "language" and "speech"; *Rede* almost corresponds to "speaking" but adds the special connotation of "discourse." Latin *sermo* designates both "speech" and "speaking," while *lingua* means "language," etc. No word corresponds exactly to any of the notions specified above; that is why all definitions of words are made in vain; starting from words in defining things is a bad procedure.

To summarize, these are the characteristics of language:

1. Language is a well-defined object in the heterogeneous mass of speech facts. It can be localized in the limited segment of the speaking-circuit where an auditory image becomes associated with a concept. It is the social side of speech, outside the individual who can never create nor modify it by himself; it exists only by virtue of a sort of contract signed by the members of a community. Moreover, the individual must always serve an apprenticeship in order to learn the functioning of language; a child assimilates it only gradually. It is such a distinct thing that a man deprived of the use of speaking retains it provided that he understands the vocal signs that he hears.

2. Language, unlike speaking, is something that we can study separately. Although dead languages are no longer spoken, we can easily assimilate their linguistic organisms. We can dispense with the other elements of speech; indeed, the science of language is possible only if the other elements are excluded.

3. Whereas speech is heterogeneous, language, as defined, is homogeneous. It is a system of signs in which the only essential thing is the union of meanings and sound-images, and in which both parts of the sign are psychological.

4. Language is concrete, no less so than speaking; and this is a help in our study of it. Linguistic signs, though basically psychological, are not abstractions; associations which bear the stamp of collective approval—and which added together constitute language—are realities that have their seat in the brain. Besides, linguistic signs are tangible; it is possible to reduce them to conventional written symbols, whereas it would be impossible to provide detailed photographs of acts of speaking [*actes de parole*]; the pronunciation of even the smallest word represents an infinite number of muscular movements that could be identified and put into graphic form only with great difficulty. In language, on the contrary, there is only the sound-image, and the latter can be translated into a fixed visual image. For if we disregard the vast number of movements necessary for the realization of sound-images in speaking, we see that each sound-image is nothing more than the sum of a limited number of elements or phonemes that can in turn be called up by a corresponding number of written symbols. The very possibility of putting the things that relate to language into graphic form allows dictionaries and grammars to represent it accurately, for language is a storehouse of sound-images, and writing is the tangible form of those images.

3. Place of Language in Human Facts: Semiology

The foregoing characteristics of language reveal an even more important characteristic. Language, once its boundaries have been marked off within the speech data, can be classified among human phenomena, whereas speech cannot.

We have just seen that language is a social institution; but several features set it apart from other political, legal, etc. institutions. We must call in a new type of facts in order to illuminate the special nature of language.

Language is a system of signs that express ideas, and is therefore comparable to a system of writing, the alphabet of deaf-mutes, symbolic rites, polite formulas, military signals, etc. But it is the most important of all these systems.

A science that studies the life of signs within society is conceivable; it would be a part of social psychology and consequently of general psychology; I shall call it *semiology*[1] (from Greek *sēmeîon,* "sign"). Semiology would show what constitutes signs, what laws govern them. Since the science does not yet exist, no one can say what it would be; but it has a right to existence, a place staked out in advance. Linguistics is only a part of the general science of semiology; the laws discovered by semiology will be applicable to linguistics, and the latter will circumscribe a well-defined area within the mass of anthropological facts.

To determine the exact place of semiology is the task of the psychologist.[2] The task of the linguist is to find out what makes language a special system within the mass of semiological data. This issue will be taken up again later; here I wish merely to call attention to one thing: if I have succeeded in assigning linguistics a place among the sciences, it is because I have related it to semiology.

Why has semiology not yet been recognized as an independent science with its own object like all the other sciences? Linguists have been going around in circles: language, better than anything else, offers a basis for understanding the semiological problem; but language must, to put it correctly, be studied in itself; heretofore language has almost always been studied in connection with something else, from other viewpoints.

There is first of all the superficial notion of the general public: people see nothing more than a name-giving system in language, thereby prohibiting any research into its true nature.

Then there is the viewpoint of the psychologist, who studies the sign-mechanism in the individual; this is the easiest method, but it does not lead beyond individual execution and does not reach the sign, which is social.

Or even when signs are studied from a social viewpoint, only the traits that attach language to the other social institutions—those that are more or less voluntary—are emphasized; as a result, the goal is bypassed and the specific characteristics of semiological systems in general and of language in particular are completely ignored. For the distinguishing characteristic of the sign—but the one that is least apparent at first sight—is that in some way it always eludes the individual or social will.

In short, the characteristic that distinguishes semiological systems from all other institutions shows up clearly only in language where it

1. *Semiology* should not be confused with *semantics*, which studies changes in meaning, and which De Saussure did not treat methodically. . . . [Orig. eds.]

2. Cf. A. Naville, *Classification des Sciences*, 2d ed., p. 104. [Orig. eds.] The scope of semiology (or semiotics) is treated at length in Charles Morris, *Signs, Language and Behavior* (New York: Prentice-Hall, 1946). [Tr.]

manifests itself in the things which are studied least, and the necessity or specific value of a semiological science is therefore not clearly recognized. But to me the language problem is mainly semiological, and all developments derive their significance from that important fact. If we are to discover the true nature of language we must learn what it has in common with all other semiological systems; linguistic forces that seem very important at first glance (e.g., the role of the vocal apparatus) will receive only secondary consideration if they serve only to set language apart from the other systems. This procedure will do more than to clarify the linguistic problem. By studying rites, customs, etc. as signs, I believe that we shall throw new light on the facts and point up the need for including them in a science of semiology and explaining them by its laws. . . .

NATURE OF THE LINGUISTIC SIGN
1. *Sign, Signified, Signifier*

Some people regard language, when reduced to its elements, as a naming-process only—a list of words, each corresponding to the thing that it names. For example:

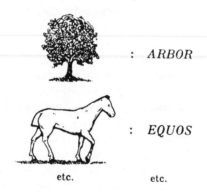

: *ARBOR*

: *EQUOS*

etc.   etc.

This conception is open to criticism at several points. It assumes that ready-made ideas exist before words (on this point, see below); it does not tell us whether a name is vocal or psychological in nature (*arbor*, for instance, can be considered from either viewpoint); finally, it lets us assume that the linking of a name and a thing is a very simple operation—an assumption that is anything but true. But this rather naive approach can bring us near the truth by showing us that the linguistic unit is a double entity, one formed by the associating of two terms.

We have seen in considering the speaking-circuit that both terms involved in the linguistic sign are psychological and are united in the brain by an associative bond. This point must be emphasized.

The linguistic sign unites, not a thing and a name, but a concept and a sound-image.[3] The latter is not the material sound, a purely physical thing, but the psychological imprint of the sound, the impression that it makes on our senses. The sound-image is sensory, and if I happen to call it "material," it is only in that sense, and by way of opposing it to the other term of the association, the concept, which is generally more abstract.

The psychological character of our sound-images becomes apparent when we observe our own speech. Without moving our lips or tongue, we can talk to ourselves or recite mentally a selection of verse. Because we regard the words of our language as sound-images, we must avoid speaking of the "phonemes" that make up the words. This term, which suggests vocal activity, is applicable to the spoken word only, to the realization of the inner image in discourse. We can avoid that misunderstanding by speaking of the *sounds* and *syllables* of a word provided we remember that the names refer to the sound-image.

The linguistic sign is then a two-sided psychological entity that can be represented by the drawing:

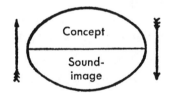

The two elements are intimately united, and each recalls the other. Whether we try to find the meaning of the Latin word *arbor* or the word that Latin uses to designate the concept "tree," it is clear that only the associations sanctioned by that language appear to us to conform to reality, and we disregard whatever others might be imagined.

Our definition of the linguistic sign poses an important question of terminology. I call the combination of a concept and a sound-image a

3. The term sound-image may seem to be too restricted inasmuch as beside the representation of the sounds of a word there is also that of its articulation, the muscular image of the phonational act. But for F. de Saussure language is essentially a depository, a thing received from without. The sound-image is par excellence the natural representation of the word as a fact of potential language, outside any actual use of it in speaking. The motor side is thus implied or, in any event, occupies only a subordinate role with respect to the sound-image. [Orig. eds.]

sign, but in current usage the term generally designates only a sound-image, a word, for example (*arbor*, etc.). One tends to forget that *arbor* is called a sign only because it carries the concept "tree," with the result that the idea of the sensory part implies the idea of the whole.

Ambiguity would disappear if the three notions involved here were designated by three names, each suggesting and opposing the others. I propose to retain the word *sign* [*signe*] to designate the whole and to replace *concept* and *sound-image* respectively by *signified* [*signifié*] and *signifier* [*significant*]; the last two terms have the advantage of indicating the opposition that separates them from each other and from the whole of which they are parts. As regards *sign*, if I am satisfied with it, this is simply because I do not know of any word to replace it, the ordinary language suggesting no other.

The linguistic sign, as defined, has two primordial characteristics. In enunciating them I am also positing the basic principles of any study of this type.

2. *Principle I: The Arbitrary Nature of the Sign*

The bond between the signifier and the signified is arbitrary. Since I mean by sign the whole that results from the associating of the signifier with the signified, I can simply say: *the linguistic sign is arbitrary.*

The idea of "sister" is not linked by any inner relationship to the succession of sounds *s-ö-r* which serves as its signifier in French; that it could be represented equally by just any other sequence is proved by differences among languages and by the very existence of different languages: the signified "ox" has as its signifier *b-ö-f* on one side of the border and *o-k-s* (*Ochs*) on the other.

No one disputes the principle of the arbitrary nature of the sign, but it is often easier to discover a truth than to assign to it its proper place. Principle I dominates all the linguistics of language; its consequences are numberless. It is true that not all of them are equally obvious at first glance; only after many detours does one discover them, and with them the primordial importance of the principle.

One remark in passing: when semiology becomes organized as a science, the question will arise whether or not it properly includes modes of expression based on completely natural signs, such as pantomime. Supposing that the new science welcomes them, its main concern will still be the whole group of systems grounded on the arbitrariness of the sign. In fact, every means of expression used in society is based, in principle, on collective behavior or—what amounts to the same thing— on convention. Polite formulas, for instance, though often imbued with a certain natural expressiveness (as in the case of a Chinese who greets his emperor by bowing down to the gound nine times), are nonetheless fixed by rule; it is this rule and not the intrinsic value of the gestures that obliges one to use them. Signs that are wholly arbitrary realize better than the others the ideal of the semiological process; that is why language, the most complex and universal of all systems of expression, is also the most characteristic; in this sense linguistics can become the master-pattern for all branches of semiology although language is only one particular semiological system.

The word *symbol* has been used to designate the linguistic sign, or more specifically, what is here called the signifier. Principle I in particular weighs against the use of this term. One characteristic of the symbol is that it is never wholly arbitrary; it is not empty, for there is the rudiment of a natural bond between the signifier and the signified. The symbol of justice, a pair of scales, could not be replaced by just any other symbol, such as a chariot.

The word *arbitrary* also calls for comment. The term should not imply that the choice of the signifier is left entirely to the speaker (we shall see below that the individual does not have the power to change a sign in any way once it has become established in the linguistic community); I mean that it is unmotivated, i.e., arbitrary in that it actually has no natural connection with the signified. . . .

The Linear Nature of the Signifier

The signifier, being auditory, is unfolded solely in time from which it gets the following characteristics: (a) it represents a span, and (b) the span is measurable in a single dimension; it is a line.

While Principle II is obvious, apparently linguists have always neglected to state it, doubtless because they found it too simple; nevertheless, it is fundamental, and its consequences are incalculable. Its importance equals that of Principle I; the whole mechanism of language depends upon it. In contrast to visual signifiers (nautical signals, etc.) which can offer simultaneous groupings in several dimensions, auditory signifiers have at their command only the dimension of time. Their elements are presented in succession; they form a chain. This feature becomes readily apparent when they are represented in writing and the spatial line of graphic marks is substituted for succession in time.

Sometimes the linear nature of the signifier is not obvious. When I accent a syllable, for instance, it seems that I am concentrating more than one significant element on the same point. But this is an illusion; the syllable and its accent constitute only one phonational act. There is no duality within the act but only different oppositions to what precedes and what follows.

IMMUTABILITY AND MUTABILITY OF THE SIGN

1. *Immutability*

The signifier, though to all appearances freely chosen with respect to the idea that it represents, is fixed, not free, with respect to the linguistic community that uses it. The masses have no voice in the matter, and the signifier chosen by language could be replaced by no other. This fact, which seems to embody a contradiction, might be called colloquially "the stacked deck." We say to language: "Choose!" but we add: "It must be this sign and no other." No individual, even if he willed it, could modify in any way at all the choice that has been made; and what is more, the community itself cannot control so much as a single word; it is bound to the existing language.

No longer can language be identified with a contract pure and simple, and it is precisely from this viewpoint that the linguistic sign is a particularly interesting object of study; for language furnishes the best proof that a law accepted by a community is a thing that is tolerated and not a rule to which all freely consent.

Let us first see why we cannot control the linguistic sign and then draw together the important consequences that issue from the phenomenon.

No matter what period we choose or how far back we go, language always appears as a heritage of the preceding period. We might conceive of an act by which, at a given moment, names were assigned to things and a contract was formed between concepts and sound-images; but such an act has never been recorded. The notion that things might have happened like that was prompted by our acute awareness of the arbitrary nature of the sign.

No society, in fact, knows or has ever known language other than as a product inherited from preceding generations, and one to be accepted as such. That is why the question of the origin of speech is not so important as it is generally assumed to be. The question is not even worth asking; the only real object of linguistics is the normal, regular life of an existing idiom. A particular language-state is always the product of historical forces, and these forces explain why the sign is unchangeable, i.e., why it resists any arbitrary substitution. . . .

1. *The arbitrary nature of the sign.* Above, we had to accept the theoretical possibility of change; further reflection suggests that the arbitrary nature of the sign is really what protects language from any attempt to modify it. Even if people were more conscious of language than they are, they would still not know how to discuss it. The reason is simply that any subject in order to be discussed must have a reasonable basis. It is possible, for instance, to discuss whether the monogamous form of marriage is more reasonable than the polygamous form and to advance arguments to support either side. One could also argue about a system of symbols, for the symbol has a rational relationship with the thing signified; but language is a system of arbitrary signs and lacks the necessary basis, the solid ground for discussion. There is no reason for preferring *soeur* to *sister*, *Ochs* to *boeuf*, etc.

2. *The multiplicity of signs necessary to form any language.* Another important deterrent to linguistic change is the great number of signs that must go into the making of any language. A system of writing comprising twenty to forty letters can in case of need be replaced by another system. The same would be true of language if it contained a limited number of elements; but linguistic signs are numberless.

3. *The over-complexity of the system.* A language constitutes a system. In this one respect (as we shall see later) language is not completely arbitrary but is ruled to some extent by logic; it is here also, however, that the inability of the masses to transform it becomes apparent. The system is a complex mechanism that can be grasped only through reflection; the very ones who use it daily are ignorant of it. We can conceive of a change only through the intervention of specialists, grammarians, logicians, etc.; but experience shows us that all such meddlings have failed.

4. *Collective inertia toward innovation.* Language—and this considera-tion surpasses all the others—is at every moment everybody's concern; spread throughout society and manipulated by it, language is something used daily by all. Here we are unable to set up any comparison between it and other institutions. The prescriptions of codes, religious rites, nautical signals, etc., involve only a certain number of individuals simultaneously and then only during a limited period of time; in language, on the contrary, everyone participates at all times, and that is why it is constantly being influenced by all. This capital fact suffices to show the impossibility of revolution. Of all social institutions, language is least amenable to initiative. It blends with the life of society, and the latter, inert by nature, is a prime conservative force.

But to say that language is a product of social forces does not suffice to show clearly that it is unfree; remembering that it is always the heritage of the preceding period, we must add that these social forces are linked with time. Language is checked not only by the weight of the collectivity but also by time. These two are inseparable. At every moment solidarity with the past checks freedom of choice. We say *man* and *dog*. This does not prevent the existence in the total phenomenon of a bond between the two antithetical forces—arbitrary convention by virtue of which choice is free and time which causes choice to be fixed. Because the sign is arbitrary, it follows no law other than that of tradition, and because it is based on tradition, it is arbitrary. . . .

STATIC AND EVOLUTIONARY LINGUISTICS

1. *Inner Duality of All Sciences Concerned with Values*

Very few linguists suspect that the intervention of the factor of time creates difficulties peculiar to linguistics and opens to their science two completely divergent paths.

Most other sciences are unaffected by this radical duality; time produces no special effects in them. Astronomy has found that the stars undergo considerable changes but has not been obliged on this account to split itself into two disciplines. Geology is concerned with successions at almost every instant, but its study of strata does not thereby become a radically distinct discipline. Law has its descriptive science and its historical science; no one opposes one to the other. The political history of states is unfolded solely in time, but a historian depicting a particular period does not work apart from history. Conversely, the science of political institutions is essentially descriptive, but if the need arises it can easily deal with a historical question without disturbing its unity.

On the contrary, that duality is already forcing itself upon the economic sciences. Here, in contrast to the other sciences, political economy and economic history constitute two clearly separated disciplines within a single science; the works that have recently appeared on these subjects point up the distinction. Proceeding as they have, economists are—without being well aware of it—obeying an inner necessity. A similar necessity obliges us to divide linguistics into two parts, each with its own principle. Here as in political economy we are confronted with the notion of *value;* both sciences are concerned with a *system for equating things of different orders*—labor and wages in one and a signified and signifier in the other.

Certainly all sciences would profit by indicating more precisely the coordinates along which their subject matter is aligned. Everywhere distinctions should be made, according to the following illustration, between (1) *the axis of simultaneities* (AB), which stands for the relations of coexisting things and from which the intervention of time is excluded;

and (2) *the axis of successions* (CD), on which only one thing can be considered at a time but upon which are located all the things on the first axis together with their changes.

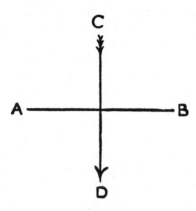

For a science concerned with values the distinction is a practical necessity and sometimes an absolute one. In these fields scholars cannot organize their research rigorously without considering both coordinates and making a distinction between the system of values per se and the same values as they relate to time.

This distinction has to be heeded by the linguist above all others, for language is a system of pure values which are determined by nothing except the momentary arrangement of its terms. A value—so long as it is somehow rooted in things and in their natural relations, as happens with economics (the value of a plot of ground, for instance, is related to its productivity)—can to some extent be traced in time if we remember that it depends at each moment upon a system of coexisting values. Its link with things gives it, perforce, a natural basis, and the judgments that we base on such values are therefore never completely arbitrary; their variability is limited. But we have just seen that natural data have no place in linguistics.

Again, the more complex and rigorously organized a system of values is, the more it is necessary, because of its very complexity, to study it according to both coordinates. No other system embodies this feature to the same extent as language. Nowhere else do we find such precise values at stake and such a great number and diversity of terms, all so rigidly interdependent. The multiplicity of signs, which we have already used to explain the continuity of language, makes it absolutely impossible to study simultaneously relations in time and relations within the system.

The reasons for distinguishing two sciences of language are clear. How should the sciences be designated? Available terms do not all bring out the distinction with equal sharpness. "Linguistic history" and "historical linguistics" are too vague. Since political history includes the description of different periods as well as the narration of events, the student might think that he is studying a language according to the axis to time when he describes its successive states, but this would require a separate study of the phenomena that make language pass from one state to another. *Evolution* and *evolutionary linguistics* are more precise, and I shall use these expressions often; in contrast, we can speak of the science of *language-states* [*états de langue*] or *static linguistics.*

But to indicate more clearly the opposition and crossing of two orders of phenomena that relate to the same object, I prefer to speak of *synchronic* and *diachronic* linguistics. Everything that relates to the static side of our science is synchronic; everything that has to do with evolution is diachronic. Similarly, *synchrony* and *diachrony* designate respectively a language-state and an evolutionary phase. . . .

But of all comparisons that might be imagined, the most fruitful is the one that might be drawn between the functioning of language and a game of chess. In both instances we are confronted with a system of values and their observable modifications. A game of chess is like an artificial realization of what language offers in a natural form.

Let us examine the matter more carefully.

First, a state of the set of chessmen corresponds closely to a state of language. The respective value of the pieces depends on their position on the chessboard just as each linguistic term derives its value from its opposition to all the other terms.

In the second place, the system is always momentary; it varies from one position to the next. It is also true that values depend above all else on an unchangeable convention, the set of rules that exists before a game begins and persists after each move. Rules that are agreed upon once and for all exist in language too; they are the constant principles of semiology.

Finally, to pass from one state of equilibrium to the next, or—according to our terminology—from one synchrony to the next, only one chesspiece has to be moved; there is no general rummage. Here we have the counterpart of the diachronic phenomenon with all its peculiarities. In fact:

a. In each play only one chesspiece is moved; in the same way in language, changes affect only isolated elements.

b. In spite of that, the move has a repercussion on the whole system; it is impossible for the player to foresee exactly the extent of the effect. Resulting changes of value will be, according to the circumstances, either nil, very serious, or of average importance. A certain move can revolutionize the whole game and even affect pieces that are not immediately involved. We have just seen that exactly the same holds for language.

c. In chess, each move is absolutely distinct from the preceding and the subsequent equilibrium. The change effected belongs to neither state: only states matter.

In a game of chess any particular position has the unique characteristic of being freed from all antecedent positions; the route used in arriving there makes absolutely no difference; one who has followed the entire match has no advantage over the curious party who comes up at a critical moment to inspect the state of the game; to describe this arrangement, it is perfectly useless to recall what had just happened ten seconds previously. All this is equally applicable to language and sharpens the radical distinction between diachrony and synchrony. Speaking operates only on a language-state, and the changes that intervene between states have no place in either state.

At only one point is the comparison weak: the chessplayer *intends* to bring about a shift and thereby to exert an action on the system, whereas language premeditates nothing. The pieces of language are shifted—or rather modified—spontaneously and fortuitously. The umlaut of *Hände* for *hanti* and *Gäste* for *gasti* produced a new system for forming the plural but also gave rise to verbal forms like *trägt* from *tragit*, etc. In order to make the game of chess seem at every point like the functioning of language, we would have to imagine an unconscious or unintelligent player. This sole difference, however, makes the comparison even more instructive by showing the absolute necessity of making a distinction between the two classes of phenomena in linguistics. For if diachronic facts cannot be reduced to the synchronic system which they condition when the change is intentional, all the more will they resist when they set a blind force against the organization of a system of signs.

5. *The Two Linguistics Contrasted According to Their Methods and Principles*

Everywhere the opposition between diachrony and synchrony stands out.

For instance—and to begin with the most apparent fact—they are not of equal importance. Here it is evident that the synchronic viewpoint predominates, for it is the true and only reality to the community of speakers. The same is true of the linguist: if he takes the diachronic perspective, he no longer observes language but rather a series of events that modify it. People often affirm that nothing is more important than understanding the genesis of a particular state; this is true in a certain sense: the forces that have shaped the state illuminate its true nature, and knowing them protects us against certain illusions; but this only goes to prove clearly that diachronic linguistics is not an end in itself. What is said of journalism applies to diachrony: it leads everywhere if one departs from it.

The methods of diachrony and synchrony also differ, and in two ways.

a. Synchrony has only one perspective, the speakers', and its whole method consists of gathering evidence from speakers; to know to just what extent a thing is a reality, it is necessary and sufficient to determine to what extent it exists in the minds of speakers. Diachronic linguistics, on the contrary, must distinguish two perspectives. One of these, the *prospective*, follows the course of time; the other, the *retrospective*, goes back in time; the result is a duplication in methodology with which we shall deal in Part Five.

b. A second difference results from delimiting the fields embraced by each of the two disciplines. Synchronic study has as its object, not everything that is simultaneous, but only the totality of facts corresponding to each language; separation will go as far as dialects and subdialects when necessary. The term *synchronic* is really not precise enough; it should be replaced by another—rather long to be sure— *idiosynchronic*. Against this, diachronic linguistics not only does not need but even rejects such specialization; the terms that it studies do not necessarily belong to the same language (compare Proto-Indo-European *esti*, Greek *esti*, German *ist*, and French *est*). The succession of diachronic events and their multiplication in space are precisely what creates the diversity of idioms. To justify the associating of two forms, it is enough to show that they are connected by a historical bond, however indirect it may be.

The foregoing oppositions are neither the most striking nor the most profound. One consequence of the radical antimony between the evolutionary and the static fact is that all notions associated with one or the other are to the same extent mutually irreducible. Any notion will point up this truth. The synchronic and diachronic "phenomenon," for example, have nothing in common. One is a relation between simultaneous elements, the other the substitution of one element for another in time, an event. . . .

9. Conclusions

Linguistics here comes to its second bifurcation. We had first to choose between language and speaking; here we are again at the intersection of two roads, one leading to diachrony and the other to synchrony.

Once in possession of this double principle of classification, we can add that everything diachronic in language is diachronic only by virtue of speaking. It is in speaking that the germ of all change is found. Each change is launched by a certain number of individuals before it is accepted for general use. Modern German uses *ich war, wir waren*, whereas until the sixteenth century the conjugation was *ich was, wir waren* (cf. English *I was, we were*). How did the substitution of *war* for *was* come about? Some speakers, influenced by *waren*, created *war* through analogy; this was a fact of speaking; the new form, repeated many times and accepted by the community, became a fact of language. But not all innovations of speaking have the same success, and so long as they remain individual, they may be ignored, for we are studying language; they do not enter into our field of observation until the community of speakers has adopted them.

An evolutionary fact is always preceded by a fact, or rather by a multitude of similar facts, in the sphere of speaking. This in no way invalidates but rather strengthens the distinction made above since in the history of any innovation there are always two distinct moments: (1) when it sprang up in individual usage; and (2) when it became a fact of language, outwardly identical but adopted by the community.

The following table indicates the rational form that linguistic study should take:

$$\text{(Human) Speech} \begin{cases} \text{Language} \begin{cases} \text{Synchrony} \\ \text{Diachrony} \end{cases} \\ \text{Speaking} \end{cases}$$

The two parts of linguistics respectively, as defined, will be the object of our study.

Synchronic linguistics will be concerned with the logical and psychological relations that bind together coexisting terms and form a system in the collective mind of speakers.

Diachronic linguistics, on the contrary, will study relations that bind together successive terms not perceived by the collective mind but substituted for each other without forming a system. . . .

LINGUISTIC VALUE

1. *Language as Organized Thought Coupled with Sound*

To prove that language is only a system of pure values, it is enough to consider the two elements involved in its functioning: ideas and sounds.

Psychologically our thought—apart from its expression in words—is only a shapeless and indistinct mass. Philosophers and linguists have always agreed in recognizing that without the help of signs we would be unable to make a clear-cut, consistent distinction between two ideas. Without language, thought is a vague, uncharted nebula. There are no preexisting ideas, and nothing is distinct before the appearance of language.

Against the floating realm of thought, would sounds by themselves yield predelimited entities? No more so than ideas. Phonic substance is neither more fixed nor more rigid than thought; it is not a mold into which thought must of necessity fit but a plastic substance divided in turn into distinct parts to furnish the signifiers needed by thought. The linguistic fact can therefore be pictured in its totality—i.e., language— as a series of contiguous subdivisions marked off on both the indefinite plane of jumbled ideas (A) and the equally vague plane of sounds (B). The following diagram gives a rough idea of it:

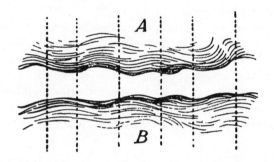

The characteristic role of language with respect to thought is not to create a material phonic means for expressing ideas but to serve as a link between thought and sound, under conditions that of necessity bring about the reciprocal delimitations of units. Thought, chaotic by nature, has to become ordered in the process of its decomposition. Neither are thoughts given material form nor are sounds transformed into mental entities; the somewhat mysterious fact is rather that "thought-sound" implies division, and that language works out its units while taking shape between two shapeless masses. Visualize the air in contact with a sheet of water; if the atmospheric pressure changes, the surface of the water will be broken up into a series of divisions, waves; the waves resemble the union or coupling of thought with phonic substance.

Language might be called the domain of articulations, using the word as it was defined earlier. Each linguistic term is a member, an *articulus* in which an idea is fixed in a sound and a sound becomes the sign of an idea.

Language can also be compared with a sheet of paper: thought is the front and the sound the back; one cannot cut the front without cutting the back at the same time; likewise in language, one can neither divide sound from thought nor thought from sound; the division could be accomplished only abstractedly, and the result would be either pure psychology or pure phonology.

Linguistics then works in the borderland where the elements of sound and thought combine; *their combination produces a form, not a substance.*

These views give a better understanding of what was said before about the arbitrariness of signs. Not only are the two domains that are linked by the linguistic fact shapeless and confused, but the choice of a given slice of sound to name a given idea is completely arbitrary. If this were not true, the notion of value would be compromised, for it would include an externally imposed element. But actually values remain entirely relative, and that is why the bond between the sound and the idea is radically arbitrary.

The arbitrary nature of the sign explains in turn why the social fact alone can create a linguistic system. The community is necessary if values that owe their existence solely to usage and general acceptance are to be set up; by himself the individual is incapable of fixing a single value.

In addition, the idea of value, as defined, shows that to consider a term as simply the union of a certain sound with a certain concept is grossly misleading. To define it in this way would isolate the term from its system; it would mean assuming that one can start from the terms and construct the system by adding them together when, on the contrary, it is from the interdependent whole that one must start and through analysis obtain its elements.

To develop this thesis, we shall study value successively from the viewpoint of the signified or concept (Section 2), the signifier (Section 3), and the complete sign (Section 4).

Being unable to seize the concrete entities or units of language directly, we shall work with words. While the word does not conform exactly to the definition of the linguistic unit, it at least bears a rough resemblance to the unit and has the advantage of being concrete; consequently, we shall use words as specimens equivalent to real terms in a synchronic system, and the principles that we evolve with respect to words will be valid for entities in general.

2. *Linguistic Value from a Conceptual Viewpoint*

When we speak of the value of a word, we generally think first of its property of standing for an idea, and this is in fact one side of linguistic value. But if this is true, how does *value* differ from *signification?* Might the two words be synonyms? I think not, although it is easy to confuse them, since the confusion results not so much from their similarity as from the subtlety of the distinction that they mark.

From a conceptual viewpoint, value is doubtless one element in signification, and it is difficult to see how signification can be dependent upon value and still be distinct from it. But we must clear up the issue or risk reducing language to a simple naming-process.

Let us first take signification as it is generally understood and as it was pictured. As the arrows in the drawing show, it is only the counterpart of the sound-image. Everything that occurs concerns only the sound-image and the concept when we look upon the word as independent and self-contained.

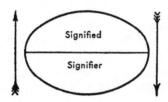

But here is the paradox: on the one hand the concept seems to be the counterpart of the sound-image, and on the other hand the sign itself is in turn the counterpart of the other signs of language.

Language is a system of interdependent terms in which the value of each term results solely from the simultaneous presence of the others, as in the diagram:

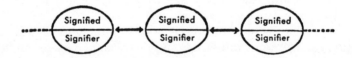

How, then, can value be confused with signification, i.e., the counterpart of the sound-image? It seems impossible to liken the relations represented here by horizontal arrows to those represented above by vertical arrows. Putting it another way—and again taking up the example of the sheet of paper that is cut in two—it is clear that the observable relation between the different pieces A, B, C, D, etc. is distinct from the relation between the front and back of the same piece as in A/A′, B/B′, etc.

To resolve the issue, let us observe from the outset that even outside language all values are apparently governed by the same paradoxical principle. They are always composed:

1. of a *dissimilar* thing that can be *exchanged* for the thing of which the value is to be determined; and

2. of *similar* things that can be *compared* with the thing of which the value is to be determined.

Both factors are necessary for the existence of a value. To determine what a five-franc piece is worth one must therefore know: (1) that it can be exchanged for a fixed quantity of a different thing, e.g., bread; and (2) that it can be compared with a similar value of the same system, e.g., a one-franc piece, or with coins of another system (a dollar, etc.). In the same way a word can be exchanged for something dissimilar, an idea; besides, it can be compared with something of the same nature, another word. Its value is therefore not fixed so long as one simply states that it can be "exchanged" for a given concept, i.e., that it has this or that signification: one must also compare it with similar values, with other words that stand in opposition to it. Its content is really fixed only by the concurrence of everything that exists outside it. Being part of a system, it is endowed not only with a signification but also and especially with a value, and this is something quite different.

A few examples will show clearly that this is true. Modern French *mouton* can have the same signification as English *sheep* but not the same value, and this for several reasons, particularly because in speaking of a piece of meat ready to be served on the table, English uses *mutton* and not *sheep*. The difference in value between *sheep* and *mouton* is due to the fact that *sheep* has beside it a second term while the French word does not.

Within the same language, all words used to express related ideas limit each other reciprocally; synonyms like French *redouter*, "dread," *craindre*, "fear," and *avoir peur*, "be afraid" have value only through their opposition: if *redouter* did not exist, all its content would go to its competitors. Conversely, some words are enriched through contact with others: e.g., the new element introduced in *décrépit* (un vieillard *décrépit*) results from the coexistence of *décrépi* (un mur *décrépi*). The value of just any term is accordingly determined by its environment; it is impossible to fix even the value of the word signifying "sun" without first considering its surroundings: in some languages it is not possible to say "sit in the *sun*."

Everything said about words applies to any term of language, e.g., to grammatical entities. The value of a French plural does not coincide with that of a Sanskrit plural even though their signification is usually identical; Sanskrit has three numbers instead of two (*my eyes, my ears, my arms, my legs,* etc. are dual);[4] it would be wrong to attribute the same

4. The use of the comparative form for two and the superlative for more than two in English (e.g., *may the* better *boxer win: the* best *boxer in the world*) is probably a remnant of the old distinction between the dual and the plural number. [Tr.]

value to the plural in Sanskrit and in French; its value clearly depends on what is outside and around it.

If words stood for preexisting concepts, they would all have exact equivalents in meaning from one language to the next; but this is not true. French uses *louer (une maison)*, "let (a house)," indifferently to mean both "pay for" and "receive payment for," whereas German uses two words, *mieten* and *vermieten;* there is obviously no exact correspondence of values. The German verbs *schätzen* and *urteilen* share a number of significations, but that correspondence does not hold at several points.

Inflection offers some particularly striking examples. Distinctions of time, which are so familiar to us, are unknown in certain languages. Hebrew does not recognize even the fundamental distinctions between the past, present, and future. Proto-Germanic has no special form for the future; to say that the future is expressed by the present is wrong, for the value of the present is not the same in Germanic as in languages that have a future along with the present. The Slavic languages regularly single out two aspects of the verb: the perfective represents action as a point, complete in its totality; the imperfective represents it as taking place, and on the line of time. The categories are difficult for a Frenchman to understand, for they are unknown in French; if they were predetermined, this would not be true. Instead of preexisting ideas then, we find in all the foregoing examples *values* emanating from the system. When they are said to correspond to concepts, it is understood that the concepts are purely differential and defined not by their positive content but negatively by their relations with the other terms of the system. Their most precise characteristic is in being what the others are not.

Now the real interpretation of the diagram of the signal becomes apparent. Thus

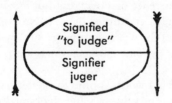

means that in French the concept "to judge" is linked to the sound-image *juger;* in short, it symbolizes signification. But it is quite clear that initially the concept is nothing, that is only a value determined by its relations with other similar values, and that without them the signification would not exist. If I state simply that a word signifies something when I have in mind the associating of a sound-image with a concept, I

am making a statement that may suggest what actually happens, but by
no means am I expressing the linguistic fact in its essence and fullness.

3. Linguistic Value from a Material Viewpoint

The conceptual side of value is made up solely of relations and differences
with respect to the other terms of language, and the same can be said of
its material side. The important thing in the word is not the sound alone
but the phonic differences that make it possible to distinguish this word
from all others, for differences carry signification.

This may seem surprising, but how indeed could the reverse be
possible? Since one vocal image is no better suited than the next for what
it is commissioned to express, it is evident, even *a priori*, that a segment
of language can never in the final analysis be based on anything except its
noncoincidence with the rest. *Arbitrary* and *differential* are two correlative qualities.

The alteration of linguistic signs clearly illustrates this. It is precisely
because the terms *a* and *b* as such are radically incapable of reaching the
level of consciousness—one is always conscious of only the *a/b* difference—that each term is free to change according to laws that are
unrelated to its signifying function. No positive sign characterizes the
genitive plural in Czech *žen*; still the two forms *žena: žen* function as well
as the earlier forms *žena: ženb; žen* has value only because it is different.

Here is another example that shows even more clearly the systematic
role of phonic differences: in Greek, *éphēn* is an imperfect and *éstēn* and
aorist although both words are formed in the same way; the first belongs
to the system of the present indicative of *phēmí*, "I say," whereas there is
no present *stēmí*; now it is precisely the relation *phēmí: éphēn* that
corresponds to the relation between the present and the imperfect (cf.
déiknūmi: edéiknūn, etc.). Signs function, then, not through their intrinsic value but through their relative position.

In addition, it is impossible for sound alone, a material element, to
belong to language. It is only a secondary thing, substance to be put to
use. All our conventional values have the characteristic of not being
confused with the tangible element which supports them. For instance,
it is not the metal in a piece of money that fixes its value. A coin
nominally worth five francs may contain less than half its worth of silver.
Its value will vary according to the amount stamped upon it and
according to its use inside or outside a political boundary. This is even
more true of the linguistic signifier, which is not phonic but incor-
poreal—constituted not by its material substance but by the differences
that separate its sound-image from all others.

The foregoing principle is so basic that it applies to all the material elements of language, including phonemes. Every language forms its words on the basis of a system of sonorous elements, each element being a clearly delimited unit and one of a fixed number of units. Phonemes are characterized not, as one might think, by their own positive quality but simply by the fact that they are distinct. Phonemes are above all else opposing, relative, and negative entities.

Proof of this is the latitude that speakers have between points of convergence in the pronunciation of distinct sounds. In French, for instance, general use of a dorsal *r* does not prevent many speakers from using a tongue-tip trill; language is not in the least disturbed by it; language requires only that the sound be different and not, as one might imagine, that it have an invariable quality. I can even pronounce the French *r* like German *ch* in *Bach*, *doch*, etc., but in German I could not use *r* instead of *ch*, for German gives recognition to both elements and must keep them apart. Similarly, in Russian there is no latitude for *t* in the direction of *t'* (palatalized *t*), for the result would be the confusing of two sounds differentiated by the language (cf. *govorit'*, "speak," and *goverit*, "he speaks"), but more freedom may be taken with respect to *th* (aspirated *t*) since this sound does not figure in the Russian system of phonemes.

Since an identical state of affairs is observable in writing, another system of signs, we shall use writing to draw some comparisons that will clarify the whole issue. In fact:

1. The signs used in writing are arbitrary; there is no connection, for example, between the letter *t* and the sound that it designates.

2. The value of letters is purely negative and differential. The same person can write *t*, for instance, in different ways: The only requirement is that the sign for *t* not be confused in his script with the signs used for *l*, *d*, etc.

3. Values in writing function only through reciprocal opposition within a fixed system that consists of a set number of letters. This third characteristic, though not identical to the second, is closely related to it, for both depend on the first. Since the graphic sign is arbitrary, its form matters little or rather matters only within the limitations imposed by the system.

4. The means by which the sign is produced is completely unimportant, for it does not affect the system (this also follows from characteristic 1). Whether I make the letters in white or black, raised or engraved, with pen or chisel—all this is of no importance with respect to their signification.

4. The Sign Considered in Its Totality

Everything that has been said up to this point boils down to this: in language there are only differences. Even more important: a difference generally implies positive terms between which the difference is set up; but in language there are only differences *without positive terms*. Whether we take the signified or the signifier, language has neither ideas nor sounds that existed before the linguistic system, but only conceptual and phonic differences that have issued from the system. The idea or phonic substance that a sign contains is of less importance than the other signs that surround it. Proof of this is that the value of a term may be modified without either its meaning or its sound being affected, solely because a neighboring term has been modified.

But the statement that everything in language is negative is true only if the signified and the signifier are considered separately; when we consider the sign in its totality, we have something that is positive in its own class. A linguistic system is a series of differences of sound combined with a series of differences of ideas; but the pairing of a certain number of acoustical signs with as many cuts made from the mass of thought engenders a system of values; and this system serves as the effective link between the phonic and psychological elements within each sign. Although both the signified and the signifier are purely differential and negative when considered separately, their combination is a positive fact; it is even the sole type of facts that language has, for maintaining the parallelism between the two classes of differences is the distinctive function of the linguistic institution.

Certain diachronic facts are typical in this respect. Take the countless instances where alteration of the signifier occasions a conceptual change and where it is obvious that the sum of the ideas distinguished corresponds in principle to the sum of the distinctive signs. When two words are confused through phonetic alteration (e.g., French *décrépit* from *décrepitus* and *décrépi* from *crispus*), the ideas that they express will also tend to become confused if only they have something in common. Or a word may have different forms (cf. *chaise* "chair" and *chaire* "desk"). Any nascent difference will tend invariably to become significant but without always succeeding or being successful on the first trial. Conversely, any conceptual difference perceived by the mind seeks to find expression through a distinct signifier, and two ideas that are no longer distinct in the mind tend to merge into the same signifier.

When we compare signs—positive terms—with each other, we can no longer speak of difference; the expression would not be fitting, for it applies only to the comparing of two sound-images, e.g., *father* and *mother*, or two ideas, e.g., the idea "father" and the idea "mother"; two signs, each having a signified and signifier, are not different but only distinct. Between them there is only *opposition*. The entire mechanism of language, with which we shall be concerned later, is based on oppositions of this kind and on the phonic and conceptual differences that they imply.

What is true of value is true also of the unit. A unit is a segment of the spoken chain that corresponds to a certain concept; both are by nature purely differential.

Applied to units, the principle of differentiation can be stated in this way: *the characteristics of the unit blend with the unit itself.* In language, as in any semiological system, whatever distinguishes one sign from the others constitutes it. Difference makes character just as it makes value and the unit.

Another rather paradoxical consequence of the same principle is this: in the last analysis what is commonly referred to as a "grammatical fact" fits the definition of the unit, for it always expresses an opposition of terms; it differs only in that the opposition is particularly significant (e.g., the formation of German plurals of the type *Nacht: Nächte*). Each term present in the grammatical fact (the singular without umlaut or final *e* in opposition to the plural with umlaut and *-e*) consists of the interplay of a number of oppositions within the system. When isolated, neither *Nacht* nor *Nächte* is anything: thus everything is opposition. Putting it another way, the *Nacht: Nächte* relation can be expressed by an algebraic formula *a/b* in which *a* and *b* are not simple terms but result from a set of relations. Language, in a manner of speaking, is a type of algebra consisting solely of complex terms. Some of its oppositions are more significant than others; but units and grammatical facts are only different names for designating diverse aspects of the same general fact: the functioning of linguistic oppositions. This statement is so true that we might very well approach the problem of units by starting from grammatical facts. Taking an opposition like *Nacht: Nächte*, we might ask what are the units involved in it. Are they only the two words, the whole series of similar words, *a* and *ä*, or all singulars and plurals, etc.?

Units and grammatical facts would not be confused if linguistic signs were made up of something besides differences. But language being what it is, we shall find nothing simple in it regardless of our approach; everywhere and always there is the same complex equilibrium of terms that mutually condition each other. Putting it another way, *language is a form and not a substance.* This truth can not be overstressed, for all the mistakes in our terminology, all our incorrect ways of naming things that pertain to language, stem from the involuntary supposition that the linguistic phenomenon must have substance.

SØREN KIERKEGAARD

Concluding Unscientific Postscript

THE SUBJECTIVE TRUTH, INWARDNESS; TRUTH IS SUBJECTIVITY

Whether truth is defined more empirically, as the conformity of thought and being, or more idealistically, as the conformity of being with thought, it is, in either case, important carefully to note what is meant by being. And in formulating the answer to this question it is likewise important to take heed lest the knowing spirit be tricked into losing itself in the indeterminate, so that it fantastically becomes a something that no existing human being ever was or can be, a sort of phantom with which the individual occupies himself upon occasion, but without making it clear to himself in terms of dialectical intermediaries how he happens to get into this fantastic realm, what significance being there has for him, and whether the entire activity that goes on out there does not resolve itself into a tautology within a recklessly fantastic venture of thought.

If being, in the two indicated definitions, is understood as empirical being, truth is at once transformed into a *desideratum*, and everything must be understood in terms of becoming; for the empirical object is unfinished and the existing cognitive spirit is itself in process of becoming. Thus the truth becomes an approximation whose beginning cannot be posited absolutely, precisely because the conclusion is lacking, the effect of which is retroactive. Whenever a beginning is *made*, on the other hand, unless through being unaware of this the procedure stamps itself as arbitrary, such a beginning is not the consequence of an immanent movement of thought, but is effected through a resolution of the will, essentially in the strength of faith. That the knowing spirit is an existing individual spirit, and that every human being is such an entity existing for himself, is a truth I cannot too often repeat; for the fantastic neglect of this is responsible for much confusion. Let no one misunderstand me. I happen to be a poor existing spirit like all other men; but if

Excerpted from Søren Kierkegaard, *Concluding Unscientific Postscript*, translated by Walter Lowrie (Princeton: Princeton University Press, 1941), 169–78, 181–82, 267–68, 270–74, 278–80, 292–95, 299–302.

there is any lawful and honest manner in which I could be helped into becoming something extraordinary, like the pure I-am-I for example, I always stand ready gratefully to accept the gift and the benefaction. But if it can only be done in the manner indicated, by saying *ein zwei drei kokolorum*, or by tying a string around the little finger, and then when the moon is full, hiding it in some secret place—in that case I prefer to remain what I am, a poor existing human being.

The term "being," as used in the above definitions, must therefore be understood (from the systematic standpoint) much more abstractly, presumably as the abstract reflection of, or the abstract prototype for, what being is as concrete empirical being. When so understood there is nothing to prevent us from abstractly determining the truth as abstractly finished and complete; for the correspondence between thought and being is, from the abstract point of view, always finished. Only with the concrete does becoming enter in, and it is from the concrete that abstract thought abstracts.

But if being is understood in this manner, the formula becomes a tautology. Thought and being mean one and the same thing, and the correspondence spoken of is merely an abstract self-identity. Neither formula says anything more than that the truth is, so understood as to accentuate the copula: the truth *is*, i.e., the truth is a reduplication. Truth is the subject of the assertion, but the assertion that it is, is the same as the subject; for this being that the truth is said to have is never its own abstract form. In this manner we give expression to the fact that truth is not something simple, but is in a wholly abstract sense a reduplication, a reduplication which is nevertheless instantly revoked.

Abstract thought may continue as long as it likes to rewrite this thought in varying phraseology, it will never get any farther. As soon as the being which corresponds to the truth comes to be empirically concrete, the truth is put in process of becoming, and is again by way of anticipation the conformity of thought with being. This conformity is actually realized for God, but it is not realized for any existing spirit, who is himself existentially in process of becoming.

For an existing spirit *qua* existing spirit, the question of the truth will again exist. The abstract answer has significance only for the abstraction into which an existing spirit is transformed when he abstracts from himself *qua* existing individual. This can be done only momentarily, and even in such moments of abstraction the abstract thinker pays his debt to existence by existing in spite of all abstraction. It is therefore an existing spirit who is now conceived as raising the question of truth, presumably in order that he may exist in it; but in any case the question is raised by someone who is conscious of being a particular existing human being. In this way I believe I can render myself intelligible to every Greek, as well as to every reasonable human being. If a German philosopher wishes to indulge a passion for making himself over, and, just as alchemists and necromancers were wont to garb themselves fantastically, first makes himself over into a superrational something for the purpose of answering this question of the truth in an extremely satisfactory manner, the affair is no concern of mine; nor is his extremely satisfactory answer, which is no doubt very satisfactory indeed—when you are fantastically transformed. On the other hand, whether it is or is not the case that a German professor behaves in this manner, can be readily determined by anyone who will concentrate enthusiastically upon seeking guidance at the hands of such a sage, without criticism but seeking merely to assimilate the wisdom in a docile spirit by proposing to shape his own life in accordance with it. Precisely when thus enthusiastically attempting to learn from such a German professor, one would realize the most apt of epigrams upon him. For such a speculative philosopher could hardly be more embarrassed than by the sincere and enthusiastic zeal of a learner who proposes to express and to realize his wisdom by appropriating it existentially. For this wisdom is something that the Herr Professor has merely imagined, and written books about, but never himself tried. Aye, it has never even occurred to him that this should be done. Like the custom clerk who writes what he could not himself read, satisfied that his responsibilities ended with the writing, so there are speculative philosophers who write what, when it is to be read in the light of action, shows itself to be nonsense, unless it is, perhaps, intended only for fantastic beings.

In that the question of truth is thus raised by an existing spirit *qua* existing, the above abstract reduplication that is involved in it again confronts him. But existence itself, namely, existence as it is in the individual who raises the question and himself exists, keeps the two moments of thought and being apart, so that reflection presents him with two alternatives. For an objective reflection the truth becomes an object, something objective, and thought must be pointed away from the subject. For a subjective reflection the truth becomes a matter of appropriation, of inwardness, of subjectivity, and thought must probe more and more deeply into the subject and his subjectivity.

But then what? Shall we be compelled to remain in this disjunction, or may we not here accept the offer of benevolent assistance from the principle of mediation, so that the truth becomes an identity of subject and object? Well, why not? But can the principle of mediation also help the existing individual while still remaining in existence himself to become the mediating principle, which is *sub specie aeterni*, whereas the poor existing individual is confined to the strait-jacket of existence? Surely it cannot do any good to mock a man, luring him on by dangling before his eyes the identity of subject and object, when his situation prevents him from making use of this identity, since he is in process of becoming in consequence of being an existing individual. How can it help to explain to a man how the eternal truth is to be understood eternally, when the supposed user of the explanation is prevented from so understanding it through being an existing individual, and merely becomes fantastic when he imagines himself to be *sub specie aeterni?* What such a man needs instead is precisely an explanation of how the eternal truth is to be understood in determinations of time by one who as existing is himself in time, which even the worshipful Herr Professor concedes, if not always, at least once a quarter when he draws his salary.

The identity of subject and object posited through an application of the principle of mediation merely carries us back to where we were before, to the abstract definition of the truth as an identity of thought and being; for to determine the truth as an identity of thought and object is precisely the same thing as saying that the truth *is*, i.e., that the truth is a reduplication. The lofty wisdom has thus again merely been absent-minded enough to forget that it was an existing spirit who asked about the truth. Or is the existing spirit himself the identity of subject and object, the subject-object? In that case I must press the question of where such an existing human being is, when he is thus at the same time also a subject-object? Or shall we perhaps here again first transform the existing spirit into something in general, and thereupon explain everything except the question asked, namely, how an existing subject is related to the truth *in concreto*; explain everything except the question that must in the next instance be asked, namely, how a particular existing spirit is related to this something in general, which seems to have not a little in common with a paper kite, or with the lump of sugar which the Dutch used to hang up under the loft for all to lick at.

So we return to the two ways of reflection; and we have not forgotten that it is an existing spirit who asks the question, a wholly individual human being. Nor can we forget that the fact that he exists is precisely what will make it impossible for him to proceed along both ways at once, while his earnest concern will prevent him from frivolously and fantastically becoming subject-object. Which of these two ways is now the way of truth for an existing spirit? For only the fantastic I-am-I is at once finished with both ways, or proceeds methodically along both ways simultaneously, a mode of ambulation which for an existing human is so inhuman that I dare not recommend it.

Since the inquirer stresses precisely the fact that he is an existing individual, then one of the above two ways which especially accentuates existence would seem to be especially worthy of commendation.

The way of objective reflection makes the subject accidental, and thereby transforms existence into something indifferent, something vanishing. Away from the subject the objective way of reflection leads to the objective truth, and while the subject and his subjectivity become indifferent, the truth also becomes indifferent, and this indifference is precisely its objective validity; for all interest, like all decisiveness, is rooted in subjectivity. The way of objective reflection leads to abstract thought, to mathematics, to historical knowledge of different kinds; and always it leads away from the subject, whose existence or non-existence, and from the objective point of view quite rightly, becomes infinitely indifferent. Quite rightly, since as Hamlet says, existence and non-existence have only subjective significance. At its maximum this way will arrive at a contradiction, and in so far as the subject does not become wholly indifferent to himself, this merely constitutes a sign that his objective striving is not objective enough. At its maximum this way will lead to the contradiction that only the objective has come into being, while the subjective has gone out; that is to say, the existing subjectivity has vanished, in that it has made an attempt to become what in the abstract sense is called subjectivity, the mere abstract form of an abstract objectivity. And yet, the objectivity which has thus come into being is, from the subjective point of view at the most, either an hypothesis or an approximation, because all eternal decisiveness is rooted in subjectivity.

However, the objective way deems itself to have a security which the subjective way does not have (and, of course, existence and existing cannot be thought in combination with objective security); it thinks to escape a danger which threatens the subjective way, and this danger is at its maximum: madness. In a merely subjective determination of the truth, madness and truth become in the last analysis indistinguishable, since they may both have inwardness.[1] Nevertheless, perhaps I may here venture to offer a little remark, one which would seem to be not wholly superfluous in an objective age. The absence of inwardness is also madness. . . .

The subjective reflection turns its attention inwardly to the subject, and desires in this intensification of inwardness to realize the truth. And it proceeds in such fashion that, just as in the preceding objective reflection, when the objectivity had come into being, the subjectivity had vanished, so here the subjectivity of the subject becomes the final

---

1. Even this is not really true, however, for madness never has the specific inwardness of the infinite. Its fixed idea is precisely some sort of objectivity, and the contradiction of madness consists in embracing this with passion. The critical point in such madness is thus again not the subjective, but the little finitude which has become a fixed idea, which is something that can never happen to the infinite.

stage, and objectivity a vanishing factor. Not for a single moment is it forgotten that the subject is an existing individual, and that existence is a process of becoming, and that therefore the notion of the truth as identity of thought and being is a chimera of abstraction, in its truth only an expectation of the creature; not because the truth is not such an identity, but because the knower is an existing individual for whom the truth cannot be such an identity as long as he lives in time. Unless we hold fast to this, speculative philosophy will immediately transport us into the fantastic realism of the I-am-I, which modern speculative thought has not hesitated to use without explaining how a particular individual is related to it; and God knows, no human being is more than such a particular individual.

If an existing individual were really able to transcend himself, the truth would be for him something final and complete; but where is the point at which he is outside himself? The I-am-I is a mathematical point which does not exist, and in so far there is nothing to prevent everyone from occupying this standpoint; the one will not be in the way of the other. It is only momentarily that the particular individual is able to realize existentially a unity of the infinite and the finite which transcends existence. This unity is realized in the moment of passion. Modern philosophy has tried anything and everything in the effort to help the individual to transcend himself objectively, which is a wholly impossible feat; existence exercises its restraining influence, and if philosophers nowadays had not become mere scribblers in the service of a fantastic thinking and its preoccupation, they would long ago have perceived that suicide was the only tolerable practical interpretation of its striving. But the scribbling modern philosophy holds passion in contempt; and yet passion is the culmination of existence for an existing individual—and we are all of us existing individuals. In passion the existing subject is rendered infinite in the eternity of the imaginative representation, and yet he is at the same time most definitely himself. The fantastic I-am-I is not an identity of the infinite and the finite, since neither the one nor the other is real; it is a fantastic rendezvous in the clouds, an unfruitful embrace, and the relationship of the individual self to this mirage is never indicated.

All essential knowledge relates to existence, or only such knowledge as has an essential relationship to existence is essential knowledge. All knowledge which does not inwardly relate itself to existence, in the reflection of inwardness, is, essentially viewed, accidental knowledge; its degree and scope is essentially indifferent. That essential knowledge is essentially related to existence does not mean the above-mentioned identity which abstract thought postulates between thought and being; nor does it signify, objectively, that knowledge corresponds to something existent as its object. But it means that knowledge has a relationship to the knower, who is essentially an existing individual, and that for this reason all essential knowledge is essentially related to existence. Only ethical and ethico-religious knowledge has an essential relationship to the existence of the knower.

Mediation is a mirage, like the I-am-I. From the abstract point of view everything is and nothing comes into being. Mediation can therefore have no place in abstract thought, because it presupposes *movement*. Objective knowledge may indeed have the existent for its object; but since the knowing subject is an existing individual, and through the fact of his existence in process of becoming, philosophy must first explain how a particular existing subject is related to a knowledge of mediation. It must explain what he is in such a moment, if not pretty nearly *distrait*; where he is, if not in the moon? There is constant talk of mediation and mediation; is mediation then a man, as Peter Deacon believes that *Imprimatur* is a man? How does a human being manage to become something of this kind? Is this dignity, this great *philosophicum*, the fruit of study, or does the magistrate give it away, like the office of deacon or grave-digger? Try merely to enter into these and other such plain questions of a plain man, who would gladly become mediation if it could be done in some lawful and honest manner, and not either by saying *ein zwei drei kokolorum*, or by forgetting that he is himself an existing human being, for whom existence is therefore something essential, and an ethico-religious existence a suitable *quantum satis*. A speculative philosopher may perhaps find it in bad taste to ask such questions. But it is important not to direct the polemic to the wrong point, and hence not to begin in a fantastic objective manner to discuss *pro* and *contra* whether there is a mediation or not, but to hold fast what it means to be a human being.

In an attempt to make clear the difference of way that exists between an objective and a subjective reflection, I shall now proceed to show how a subjective reflection makes its way inwardly in inwardness. Inwardness in an existing subject culminates in passion; corresponding to passion in the subject the truth becomes a paradox; and the fact that the truth becomes a paradox is rooted precisely in its having a relationship to an existing subject. Thus the one corresponds to the other. By forgetting that one is an existing subject, passion goes by the board and the truth is no longer a paradox; the knowing subject becomes a fantastic entity rather than a human being, and the truth becomes a fantastic object for the knowledge of this fantastic entity.

When the question of truth is raised in an objective manner, reflection is directed objectively to the truth, as an object to which the knower is related. Reflection is not focused upon the relationship, however, but upon the question of whether it is the truth to which the knower is related. If only the object to which he is related is the truth, the subject is accounted to be in the truth. When the question of the truth is raised subjectively, reflection is directed subjectively to the nature of the individual's relationship; if only the mode of this relationship is in the truth, the individual is in the truth even if he should happen to be thus related to what is not true.[2]

The objective accent falls on *WHAT* is said, the subjective accent on *HOW* it is said. This distinction holds even in the aesthetic realm, and receives definite expression in the principle that what is in itself true may in the mouth of such and such a person become untrue. In these times this distinction is particularly worthy of notice, for if we wish to express in a single sentence the difference between ancient times and our own, we should doubtless have to say: "In ancient times only an individual here and there knew the truth; now all know it, except that the inwardness of its appropriation stands in an inverse relationship to the extent of its dissemination.[3] Aesthetically the contradiction that truth becomes untruth in this or that person's mouth, is best construed comically: In the ethico-religious sphere, accent is again on the "how." But this is not to be understood as referring to demeanor, expression, or the like; rather it refers to the relationship sustained by the existing individual, in his own existence, to the content of his utterance. Objectively the interest is focused merely on the thought-content, subjectively on the inwardness. At its maximum this inward "how" is the passion of the infinite, and the passion of the infinite is the truth. But the passion of the infinite is precisely subjectivity, and thus subjectivity becomes the truth. Objectively there is no infinite decisiveness, and hence it is objectively in order to annul the difference between good and evil; together with the princi-

---

2. The reader will observe that the question here is about essential truth, or about the truth which is essentially related to existence, and that it is precisely for the sake of clarifying it as inwardness or as subjectivity that this contrast is drawn.

3. *Stages on Life's Way*, note on p. 426. Though ordinarily not wishing an expression of opinion on the part of reviewers, I might at this point almost desire it, provided such opinions, so far from flattering me, amounted to an assertion of the daring truth that what I say is something that everybody knows, even every child, and that the cultured know infinitely much better. If it only stands fast that everyone knows it, my standpoint is in order, and I shall doubtless make shift to manage with the unity of the comic and the tragic. If there were anyone who did not know it I might perhaps be in danger of being dislodged from my position of equilibrium by the thought that I might be in a position to communicate to someone the needful preliminary knowledge. It is just this which engages my interest so much, this that the cultured are accustomed to say: that everyone knows what the highest is. This was not the case in paganism, nor in Judaism, nor in the seventeen centuries of Christianity. Hail to the nineteenth century! Everyone knows it. What progress has been made since the time when only a few knew it. To make up for this, perhaps, we must assume that no one nowadays does it.

ple of contradiction, and therewith also the infinite difference between the true and the false. Only in subjectivity is there decisiveness, to seek objectivity is to be in error. It is the passion of the infinite that is the decisive factor and not its content, for its content is precisely itself. In this manner subjectivity and the subjective "how" constitute the truth.

But the "how" which is thus subjectively accentuated precisely because the subject is an existing individual, is also subject to a dialectic with respect to time. In the passionate moment of decision, where the road swings away from objective knowledge, it seems as if the infinite decision were thereby realized. But in the same moment the existing individual finds himself in the temporal order, and the subjective "how" is transformed into a striving, a striving which receives indeed its impulse and a repeated renewal from the decisive passion of the infinite, but is nevertheless a striving.

When subjectivity is the truth, the conceptual determination of the truth must include an expression for the antithesis to objectivity, a memento of the fork in the road where the way swings off; this expression will at the same time serve as an indication of the tension of the subjective inwardness. Here is such a definition of truth: *An objective uncertainty held fast in an appropriation-process of the most passionate inwardness is the truth*, the highest truth attainable for an *existing* individual. At the point where the way swings off (and where this is cannot be specified objectively, since it is a matter of subjectivity), there objective knowledge is placed in abeyance. Thus the subject merely has, objectively, the uncertainty; but it is this which precisely increases the tension of that infinite passion which constitutes his inwardness. The truth is precisely the venture which chooses an objective uncertainty with the passion of the infinite. I contemplate the order of nature in the hope of finding God, and I see omnipotence and wisdom; but I also see much else that disturbs my mind and excites anxiety. The sum of all this is an objective uncertainty. But it is for this very reason that the inwardness becomes as intense as it is, for it embraces this objective uncertainty with the entire passion of the infinite. In the case of a mathematical proposition the objectivity is given, but for this reason the truth of such a proposition is also an indifferent truth.

But the above definition of truth is an equivalent expression for faith. Without risk there is no faith. Faith is precisely the contradiction between the infinite passion of the individual's inwardness and the objective uncertainty. If I am capable of grasping God objectively, I do not believe, but precisely because I cannot do this I must believe. If I wish to preserve myself in faith I must constantly be intent upon holding fast the objective uncertainty, so as to remain out upon the deep, over seventy thousand fathoms of water, still preserving my faith. . . .

REAL OR ETHICAL SUBJECTIVITY—THE SUBJECTIVE THINKER
1. *Existence and Reality*

The difficulty that inheres in existence, with which the existing individual is confronted, is one that never really comes to expression in the
language of abstract thought, much less receives an explanation. Because
abstract thought is *sub specie aeterni* it ignores the concrete and the
temporal, the existential process, the predicament of the existing individual arising from his being a synthesis of the temporal and the eternal
situated in existence.[4] Now if we assume that abstract thought is the
highest manifestation of human activity, it follows that philosophy and
the philosophers proudly desert existence, leaving the rest of us to face
the worst. And something else, too, follows for the abstract thinker
himself, namely, that since he is an existing individual he must in one
way or another be suffering from absent-mindedness.

The abstract problem of reality (if it is permissible to treat this
problem abstractly, the particular and the accidental being constituents
of the real, and directly opposed to abstraction) is not nearly so difficult a
problem as it is to raise and to answer the question of what it means that
this definite something is a reality. This definite something is just what
abstract thought abstracts from. But the difficulty lies in bringing this
definite something and the ideality of thought together, by penetrating
the concrete particularity with thought. Abstract thought cannot even
take cognizance of this contradiction, since the very process of abstraction prevents the contradiction from arising.

This questionable character of abstract thought becomes apparent
especially in connection with all existential problems, where abstract
thought gets rid of the difficulty by leaving it out, and then proceeds to
boast of having explained everything. It explains immortality in general, and all goes quite smoothly, in that immortality is identified with
eternity, with the eternity which is essentially the medium of all
thought. But whether an existing individual human being is immortal,
which is the difficulty, abstract thought does not trouble to inquire. It is
disinterested; but the difficulty inherent in existence constitutes the
interest of the existing individual, who is infinitely interested in ex-

---

4. That Hegel in his *Logic* nevertheless permits himself to utilize a consciousness that
is only too well informed about the concrete, and what it is that the professor needs next
in spite of the necessary transition, is of course a fault, which Trendelenburg has very
effectively called to our attention. To cite an example from the field of the subject
immediately before us, how is the transition effected by which *die Existenz* becomes a
plurality of existences? *"Die Existenz ist die unmittelbare Einheit der Reflexion-in-sich und der
Reflexion-in-anders. Sie ist daher (?) die unbestimmte Menge von Existierenden."* How does the
purely abstract determination of existence come to be split up in this manner?

isting. Abstract thought thus helps me with respect to my immortality by first annihilating me as a particular existing individual and then making me immortal, about as when the doctor in Holberg killed the patient with his medicine—but also expelled the fever. Such an abstract thinker, one who neglects to take into account the relationship between his abstract thought and his own existence as an individual, not careful to clarify this relationship to himself, makes a comical impression upon the mind even if he is ever so distinguished, because he is in process of ceasing to be a human being. While a genuine human being, as a synthesis of the finite and the infinite, finds his reality in holding these two factors together, infinitely interested in existing—such an abstract thinker is a duplex being: a fantastic creature who moves in the pure being of abstract thought, and on the other hand, a sometimes pitiful professorial figure which the former deposits, about as when one sets down a walking stick. . . .

That the difficulty inherent in existence and confronting the existing individual never really comes to expression in the language of abstraction, I shall proceed to illustrate by reference to a decisive problem, about which so much has been said and written. Everyone is familiar with the fact that the Hegelian philosophy has rejected the principle of contradiction. Hegel himself has more than once sat in solemn judgment upon those thinkers who remain in the sphere of reflection and understanding, and therefore insist that there is an either-or. Since his time it has become a favorite sport for some Hegelian, as soon as anyone lets fall a hint about an *aut-aut*, to come riding *trip trap trap*, like a gamekeeper in *Kallundsborgs-Krøniken*, and after gaining a victory to ride home again. Here in Denmark the Hegelians have several times been on the warpath, especially after Bishop Mynster, to gain the brilliant victory of speculative thought. Bishop Mynster has more than once become a vanquished standpoint, though as such he seems to be doing very well, and it is rather to be feared that the tremendous exertion incident to the winning of the victory has been too much for the unvanquished victors. And yet there is perhaps a misunderstanding at the root of the controversy and the victory. Hegel is utterly and absolutely right in asserting that viewed eternally, *sub specie aeterni*, in the language of abstraction, in pure thought and pure being, there is no either-or. How in the world could there be, when abstract thought has taken away the contradiction, so that Hegel and the Hegelians ought rather be asked to explain what they mean by the hocus-pocus of introducing contradiction, movement, transition, and so forth, into the domain of logic. If the champions of an either-or invade the sphere of pure thought and there seek to defend their cause, they are quite without justification. Like the giant who wrestled with Hercules, and who lost strength as soon as he was lifted from the ground, the either-or of contradiction is *ipso facto* nullified when it is lifted out of the sphere of the existential and introduced into the eternity of abstract thought. On the other hand, Hegel is equally wrong when, forgetting the abstraction of his thought, he plunges down into the realm of existence to annul the double *aut* with might and main. It is impossible to do this in existence, for in so doing the thinker abrogates existence as well. When I take existence away, i.e., when I abstract, there is no *aut-aut*; when I take this *aut-aut* away from existence I also take existence away, and hence I do not abrogate the *aut-aut* in existence. If it is an error to say that there is something that is true in theology which is not true in philosophy, it is at any rate quite correct to say that something is true for an existing individual which is not true in abstract thought. And it is also true that from the ethical point of view, pure being is a fantastic medium, and that it is forbidden to an existing individual to forget that he exists.

One must therefore be very careful in dealing with a philosopher of the Hegelian school, and, above all, to make certain of the identity of the being with whom one has the honor to discourse. Is he a human being, an existing human being? Is he himself *sub specie aeterni*, even when he sleeps, eats, blows his nose, or whatever else a human being does? Is he himself the pure "I am I"? This is an idea that has surely never occurred to any philosopher; but if not, how does he stand existentially related to this entity, and through what intermediate determinations is the ethical responsibility resting upon him as an existing individual suitably respected? Does he in fact exist? And if he does, is he then not in process of becoming? And if he is in process of becoming, does he not face the future? And does he ever face the future by way of action? And if he never does, will he not forgive an ethical individuality for saying in passion and with dramatic truth, that he is an ass? But if he ever acts *sensu eminenti*, does he not in that case face the future with infinite passion? Is there not then for him an either-or? Is it not the case that eternity is for an existing individual not eternity, but the future, and that eternity is eternity only for the Eternal, who is not in process of becoming? Let him state whether he can answer the following question, i.e., if such a question can be addressed to him: "Is ceasing to exist so far as possible, in order to be *sub specie aeterni*, something that happens to him, or is it subject to a decision of the will, perhaps even something one ought to do?" For if I ought to do it, an *aut-aut* is established even with respect to being *sub specie aeterni*. Was he born *sub specie aeterni*, and has he lived *sub specie aeterni* ever since, so that he cannot even understand what I am asking about, never having had anything to do with the future, and never having experienced any decision? In that case I readily understand that it is not a human being I have the honor to address. But this does not quite end the matter; for it seems to me a very strange circumstance that such mysterious beings begin to make their appearance. An epidemic of cholera is usually signalized by the appearance of a certain kind of fly not otherwise observable; may it not be the case that the appearance of these fabulous pure thinkers is a sign that some misfortune threatens humanity, as for instance the loss of the ethical and the religious?

It is necessary to be thus careful in dealing with an abstract thinker who not only desires for himself to remain in the pure being of abstract thought, but insists that this is the highest goal for human life, and that a type of thought which leads to the ignoring of the ethical and a misunderstanding of the religious is the highest human thinking. But let us not on the other hand say that an *aut-aut* exists *sub specie aeterni*, where according to the Eleatic doctrine "everything is and nothing comes into being.[5] But where everything is in process of becoming, and only so much of eternity is present as to be a restraining influence in the passionate decision, where *eternity* is related as *futurity* to the individual in process of becoming, there the absolute disjunction belongs. When I put eternity and *becoming* together I do not get rest, but coming into being and futurity. It is undoubtedly for this reason that Christianity has announced eternity as the future life, namely, because it addresses itself to existing individuals, and it is for this reason also that it assumes an absolute either-or.

All logical thinking employs the language of abstraction, and is *sub specie aeterni*. To think existence logically is thus to ignore the difficulty, the difficulty, that is, of thinking the eternal as in process of becoming.

---

5. Misled by the constant reference to a continued process in which opposites are combined into a higher unity, and so again in a higher unity and so forth, a parallel has been drawn between Hegel's doctrine and that of Heraclitus, which asserts that everything is in a state of flux and nothing remains constant. But this is a misunderstanding, because everything said in Hegel's philosophy about process and becoming is illusory. This is why the System lacks an Ethic, and is the reason why it has no answer for the living when the question of becoming is raised in earnest, in the interest of action. In spite of all that Hegel says about process, he does not understand history from the point of view of becoming, but with the help of the illusion attaching to pastness understands it from the point of view of a finality that excludes all becoming. It is therefore impossible for a Hegelian to understand himself by means of his philosophy, for his philosophy helps him to understand only that which is past and finished, and a living person is surely not dead. He probably finds compensation in the thought that in comparison with an understanding of China and Persia and six thousand years of the world's history, a single individual does not much matter, even if that individual be himself. But it seems otherwise to me, and I understand it better conversely: when a man cannot understand himself, his understanding of China and Persia and the rest must surely be of a very peculiar kind.

But this difficulty is unavoidable, since the thinker himself is in process of becoming. It is easier to indulge in abstract thought than it is to exist, unless we understand by this latter term what is loosely called existing, in analogy with what is loosely called being a subject. Here we have again an example of the fact that the simplest tasks are the most difficult. Existing is ordinarily regarded as no very complex matter, much less an art, since we all exist; but abstract thinking takes rank as an accomplishment. But really to exist, so as to interpenetrate one's existence with consciousness, at one and the same time eternal and as if far removed from existence, and yet also present in existence and in the process of becoming: that is truly difficult. If philosophical reflection had not in our time become something queer, highly artificial, and capable of being learned by rote, thinkers would make quite a different impression upon people, as was the case in Greece, where a thinker was an existing individual stimulated by his reflection to a passionate enthusiasm; and as was also once the case in Christendom, when a thinker was a believer who strove enthusiastically to understand himself in the existence of faith. If anything of this sort held true of the thinkers of our own age, the enterprise of pure thought would have led to one suicide after the other. For suicide is the only tolerable existential consequence of pure thought, when this type of abstraction is not conceived as something merely partial in relation to being human, willing to strike an agreement with an ethical and religious form of personal existence, but assumes to be all and highest. This is not to praise the suicide, but to respect the passion. Nowadays a thinker is a curious creature who during certain hours of the day exhibits a very remarkable ingenuity, but has otherwise nothing in common with a human being.

To think existence *sub specie aeterni* and in abstract terms is essentially to abrogate it, and the merit of the proceeding is like the much trumpeted merit of abrogating the principle of contradiction. It is impossible to conceive existence without movement, and movement cannot be conceived *sub specie aeterni*. To leave movement out is not precisely a distinguished achievement, and to import it into logic in the form of the transition-category, and with it time and space, is only a new confusion. But inasmuch as all thought is eternal, there is here created a difficulty for the existing individual. Existence, like movement, is a difficult category to deal with; for if I think it, I abrogate it, and then I do not think it. It might therefore seem to be the proper thing to say that there is something which cannot be thought, namely, existence. But the difficulty persists, in that existence itself combines thinking with existing, in so far as the thinker exists. . . .

Abstract thought is disinterested, but for an existing individual, existence is the highest interest. An existing individual therefore has always a *telos*, and it is of this *telos* that Aristotle speaks when he says (*De Anima*, III, 10, 2) that νοῦς θεωρέτικος differs from νοῦς πρᾱκτικος τῷ τέλει. But pure thought is altogether detached, and not like the abstract thought which does indeed abstract from existence, but nevertheless preserves a relationship to it. This pure thought, hovering in mystic suspension between heaven and earth and emancipated from every relation to an existing individual, explains everything in its own terms but fails to explain itself. It explains everything in such fashion that no decisive explanation of the essential question becomes possible. Thus when an existing individual asks about the relationship between pure thought and an existing individual, pure thought makes no reply, but merely explains existence within pure thought and so confuses everything. It assigns to existence, the category upon which pure thought must suffer shipwreck, a place within pure thought itself; in this fashion everything that is said about existence is essentially revoked. When pure thought speaks of the immediate unity of reflection-in-self and reflection-in-other, and says that this immediate unity is abrogated, something must of course intervene so as to divide the two phases of this immediate unity. What can this something be? It is time. But time cannot find a place within pure thought. What then is the meaning of the talk about abrogation and transition and the new unity? And in general, what does it mean to think in such a manner as merely to pretend to think, because everything that is said is absolutely revoked? And what is the meaning of the refusal to admit that one thinks in this manner, constantly blazoning forth this pure thought as positive truth?

Just as existence has combined thought and existence by making the existing individual a thinker, so there are two media: the medium of abstract thought, and the medium of reality. But pure thought is still a third medium, quite recently discovered. It therefore begins, as the saying is, after the most exhaustive abstraction. The relation which abstract thought still sustains to that from which it abstracts, is something which pure thought innocently or thoughtlessly ignores. Here is rest for every doubt, here is the eternal positive truth, and whatever else one may be pleased to say. That is, pure thought is a phantom. If the Hegelian philosophy has emancipated itself from every presupposition, it has won this freedom by means of one lunatic postulate: the initial transition to pure thought.

Existence constitutes the highest interest of the existing individual, and his interest in his existence constitutes his reality. What reality is, cannot be expressed in the language of abstraction. Reality is an *inter-esse* between the moments of that hypothetical unity of thought and being which abstract thought presupposes. Abstract thought considers both possibility and reality, but its concept of reality is a false reflection, since the medium within which the concept is thought is not reality, but possibility. Abstract thought can get hold of reality only by nullifying it, and this nullification of reality consists in transforming it into possibility. All that is said about reality in the language of abstraction and within the sphere of abstract thought, is really said within the sphere of the possible. The entire realm of abstract thought, speaking in the language of reality, sustains the relation of possibility to the realm of reality; but this latter reality is not one which is included within abstract thought and the realm of the possible. Reality or existence is the dialectical moment in a trilogy, whose beginning and whose end cannot be for the existing individual, since *qua* existing individual he is himself in the dialectical moment. Abstract thought closes up the trilogy. Just so. But how does it close the trilogy? Is abstract thought a mystic something, or is it not the act of the abstracting individual? But the abstracting individual is the existing individual, who is as such in the dialectical moment, which he cannot close or mediate, least of all absolutely, as long as he remains in existence. So that when he closes the trilogy, this closure must be related as a possibility to the reality or existence in which he remains. And he is bound to explain how he manages to do it, i.e., how he manages to do it as an existing individual; or else he must explain whether he ceases to be an existing individual, and whether he has any right to do this.

The moment we begin to ask this sort of question, we ask ethically, and assert the claim which the ethical has upon the existing individual. This claim is not that he should abstract from existence, but rather that he should exist; and this is at the same time his highest interest.

It is not possible for an existing individual, least of all *as* an existing individual, to hold fast absolutely a suspension of the dialectical moment, namely, existence. This would require another medium than existence, which is the dialectical moment. If an existing individual can become conscious of such a suspension, it can be only as a possibility. But this possibility cannot maintain itself when the existential interest is posited, for which reason the awareness of it can exist only in a state of disinterestedness. But the existing individual can never wholly attain this state *qua* existing individual; and ethically he is not justified even in trying to attain it *approximando*, since the ethical seeks contrariwise to make the existential interest infinite, so infinite that the principle of contradiction becomes absolutely valid. . . .

The questionableness of the "Method" becomes apparent already in Hegel's relation to Kant. A scepticism which attacks thought itself cannot be vanquished by thinking it through, since the very instrument by which this would have to be done is in revolt. There is only one thing to do with such a scepticism, and that is to break with it. To answer Kant within the fantastic shadow-play of pure thought is precisely not to answer him. The only thing-in-itself which cannot be thought is existence, and this does not come within the province of thought to think. But how could pure thought possibly vanquish this difficulty, when it is abstract? And what does pure thought abstract from? Why from existence, to be sure, and hence from that which it purports to explain.

When it is impossible to think existence, and the existing individual nevertheless thinks, what does this signify? It signifies that he thinks intermittently, that he thinks before and after. His thought cannot attain to absolute continuity. It is only in a fantastic sense that an existing individual can be constantly *sub specie aeterni.*

Is thinking identical with creation, with giving existence? I am well aware of what has been said by way of reply to a stupid attack on the philosophical principle of the identity of thought and being, and am entirely willing to concede its correctness. It has been insisted quite properly that this identity must not be understood as applying to existence of an imperfect order, as if, for example, I could produce a rose by thinking it. In the same spirit it has been pointed out, over against the defenders of the principle of contradiction, that the latter principle seems most valid in connection with existence of a lower order: before and behind, right and left, up and down, and so forth. But now in connection with existences of a higher order, does it hold true that thought and being are one? Does it hold, for example, in the case of the Ideas? Aye, Hegel is quite right, and yet we have not advanced a single step. The good, the beautiful, and the other Ideas are in themselves so abstract that they are indifferent to existence, indifferent to any other than a conceptual existence. The reason why the principle of identity holds in this connection is because being means in this case the same thing as thought. But since this is so, the answer offered by pure thought is an answer to a question which cannot be raised in the sphere of the answer. A particular existing human being is surely not an Idea, and his existence is surely something quite different from the conceptual existence of the Idea. An existence as a particular human being is doubtless an imperfection in comparison with the eternal life of the Idea, but it is a perfection in comparison with not existing at all. An intermediary state like existence would seem suitable for an intermediary being like man. How is it then with the supposed identity of thought and being in connection with the kind of existence that belongs to particular human beings? Am I the good because I think the good, or am I good because I think the good? The champions of the philosophical principle of identity said themselves that it did not hold of the more imperfect existences: "Is existence as a particular human being, which is what the question is about, the same with a perfect ideal existence?" Here it is the converse principle that holds: "Because I exist and because I think, therefore I think that I exist." Existence here separates thought from being, and breaks up their ideal unity. I must exist in order to think, and I must be able to think, for example the good, in order to exist in it.

Existence as a particular human being is not so imperfect an existence as the being of a rose, for example. Hence it is that we human beings are accustomed to say that however great our unhappiness, our existence is nevertheless a good: and I remember a melancholy individual who once in the midst of his sufferings, when he wished himself dead, asked himself upon seeing a basket of potatoes if he did not after all find more happiness in existence than a potato. But existence as a particular human being is not a pure ideal existence; it is only man in general who exists in that manner, which means that this entity does not exist at all. Existence is always something particular, the abstract does not exist. From this to draw the conclusion that the abstract is without validity is a misunderstanding; but it is also a misunderstanding to confound discourse by even raising the question of existence, or of reality in the sense of existence, in connection with the abstract. When an existing individual raises the question of the relation between thought and being, thinking and existing, and philosophy explains that it is one of identity, the answer does not reply to the question because it does not reply to the questioner. Philosophy explains: "Thought and being are one; but not in connection with things that are what they are solely by virtue of existing, as for example a rose, which has no Idea within itself; and hence not in connection with things that make it most clearly evident what it means to exist, as opposed to what it means to think. But thought and being are one in connection with things whose existence is essentially indifferent, because they are so abstract as to have only conceptual existence." To answer the question in this manner is to evade it; for the question had reference to existence as a particular human being. An existence of this sort is of a different order from the existence of a potato, but neither is it the kind of existence that attaches to an Idea. Human existence has Idea in it, but it is not a purely ideal existence. Plato placed the Idea in the second rank of existence, as intermediary between God and matter; an existing human being does indeed participate in the Idea, but he is not himself an Idea.

In Greece, as in the youth of philosophy generally, it was found difficult to win through to the abstract and to leave existence, which always gives the particular; in modern times, on the other hand, it has become difficult to reach existence. The process of abstraction is easy enough for us, but we also desert existence more and more, and the realm of pure thought is the extreme limit of such desertion.

In Greece, philosophizing was a mode of action, and the philosopher was therefore an existing individual. He may not have possessed a great amount of knowledge, but what he did know he knew to some profit, because he busied himself early and late with the same thing. But nowadays, just what is it to philosophize, and what does a philosopher really know? For of course I do not deny that he knows everything.

The philosophical principle of identity is precisely the opposite of what it seems to be; it is the expression for the fact that thought has deserted existence altogether, that it has emigrated to a sixth continent where it is wholly sufficient to itself in the absolute identity of thought and being. We may finally reach the stage of identifying existence with evil, taken in a certain emasculated metaphysical sense; in the humorous sense, existence will become an extremely long dragging out of things, a ludicrous delay. But even so there remains a possibility that the ethical may impose some restraint, since it accentuates existence, and abstract thought and humor still retain a relationship to existence. But pure thought has won through to a perfect victory, and has nothing, nothing to do with existence. . . .

When thought becomes self-reflexive and seeks to think itself, there arises a familiar form of scepticism. How may this scepticism be overcome, rooted as it is in thought's refusal to pursue its proper task of thinking other things, and its selfish immersion in an attempt to think itself? When a horse bolts and runs away, we might simply say, if we disregard the damage he may do in the meanwhile, "Let him run, he will soon tire." But of the self-reflexive scepticism of thought this cannot be said, since it can continue indefinitely. Schelling put a stop to the self-reflexive process, understanding his "intellectual intuition" not as a result reached by going on with the process of self-reflection, but as a new point of departure. Hegel regarded this as a fault. He speaks contemptuously of Schelling's intellectual intuition—and then came the Method. The sceptical process of self-reflection continues until it finally abrogates itself, thought struggles through to a victory and becomes again valid, the identity of thought and being is realized in pure thought.[6] But what does it mean to say that self-reflection continues

---

6. That there is an abstract certainty tacitly presupposed in all scepticism as its ultimate ground, which gives a foothold to doubt, like the base-line on which the figure is drawn; that even the most strenuous attempts of the Greek sceptics to free the sceptical position from this latent assumption, as for example by explaining that the sceptical assertion must not be taken categorically (θητικως), fail to accomplish anything, is quite certain. But it does not follow that doubt overcomes itself. The basic certainty that

until it abrogates itself? It need not long continue to make it apparent
that there is something wrong with it; but as long as it does continue, it
is precisely the same dubious process of self-reflection. What does it
mean to say of it that it continues *so long—until?* Such speech is nothing
more than deceptive phraseology, which by the introduction of a quantitative reflection seeks to corrupt the integrity of the reader's thought,
trying to make it seem easier to understand how self-reflection can annul
itself if it only takes a long time before it happens. This quantitative
reflection is like the infinitesimally small angles of the astronomers,
which finally become so small, though still remaining angles, that their
sides are parallel. The fairy tale about the self-reflection that continues *so
long—until* distracts the attention from the dialectical issue, the question, namely, of how self-reflection comes to be abrogated. When we say
that a man continued telling a lie for so long a time in jest that he finally
came to believe it himself, the ethical accent is on the transition. But
there is something softening and distracting in the phrase, so long, so
that we almost forget the decisiveness of the transition because it takes so
long. In narrative and descriptive passages, in the rhetorical address, the
abstract *so long—until* produces a strong effect of illusion. The illusion
may have an optical form, as in the Book of Judith: "And Judith went
out, she and her maid-servant with her. But the men of the city gazed
after her until she came down the mountain, until she came through the
valley, and they were unable to see her any more." The maiden sat at the
seashore and gazed after her beloved—until she could no longer see him.
The illusion may take the form of a fantastic vanishing of time, because
there is no measure and no standard of measure in this abstract *so
long—until.* Then his passion overcame him and he deserted the way of
truth, *until* the bitterness of remorse caught up with him and stopped
him in his wild career—it would require a master of psychological
delineation to produce concretely the effect induced by this abstract
until, which leads the imagination on and on, indefinitely. But dialecti-

---

supports doubt cannot hypostasize itself as long as I doubt, because doubt consists
precisely in departing from this certainty in order to doubt. If I continue to doubt I shall
forever be unable to transcend it, since doubt consists in a false interpretation of the basic
certainty. If for a single moment I hold fast to this latent certainty as certainty, I must for
that moment cease to doubt. A doubter of very mediocre caliber will therefore soonest
find certainty; and next to him a doubter who merely puts the categories together to see
how they combine, without making the slightest attempt to realize anything of it. I
cannot refrain from returning to this point again and again, because it is so decisive. If
doubt is capable of overcoming itself, if one may find the truth in doubt simply by
doubting everything, without breach of continuity, and without an absolutely new point
of departure, not a single Christian category can be sustained, and Christianity is *ipso facto*
abolished.

cally, this fantastic length is of no significance whatever. When a Greek philosopher was asked to define religion, he asked for time to prepare an answer; when the agreed period had elapsed, he asked for another postponement, and so on. In this way he wished to express symbolically that he regarded the question as unanswerable. This was genuinely in the Greek spirit, beautiful and ingenious. But if he had argued with himself, that since it was so long that he had left the question unanswered, he must now have come nearer to the answer, this would have been a misunderstanding; just as when a debtor remains in debt so long that the debt is finally paid—through having remained so long unpaid. The *so long—until* has something strangely seductive about it. If a man were to say outright that the process of self-reflection abrogates itself, and then go on to explain how, nobody would be able to understand the explanation. But when he says that the process of self-reflection continues so long until it finally abrogates itself, one may perhaps be induced to think: "Ah, that is a different story altogether, there must be something in that." One feels a little anxious and afraid when confronting so great a lapse of time; one loses one's patience, and thinks: "Very well, let it then be so"—and so pure thought gets its beginning. In so far it may be true, as pure thought claims, that it does not begin as the older, more mediocre philosophers did, by begging or postulating its beginning; for the reader is so fearfully impressed by this terrible length of time, this *so long—until,* that he is ready to thank God for any kind of a beginning.

The sceptical process of self-reflection is consequently abrogated by the Method, and further speculative progress is assured in two ways. First and foremost by means of the magic phrase *so long—until.* Every time a transition is needed, the opposite continues so long until it finally passes over into its opposite—and so the Method marches. And, good heavens, we are all weak mortals and dearly love variety, as the proverb says; and since it cannot be otherwise, and since it would be extremely tiresome if the opposite were to continue until it passes over into its opposite, and hence were to continue forever—very well, then, let it pass; the transition is effected. And so the Method marches on—*with necessity.* But should it meet with a stubborn and extremely tiresome person who dares to make objection, saying: "It is as if the Method were a human being who had to be placated, and for whose sake something had to be done; it is as if instead of speculating methodically for the sake of the truth, one speculated for the sake of the Method, which is so great a good in itself that one must not be altogether too scrupulous—if only one gets the Method and the System"—if there is any such person let him beware, for what he represents is the *bad* infinite. The Method has all sorts of resources at its disposal, and as far as the bad infinite is concerned, the Method is stern, and will tolerate no jesting. The stubborn objector is stamped as a blockhead, presumably so long—until. And good heavens, we are all weak mortals and like to be considered intelligent by our respected contemporaries; and since it cannot be otherwise—very well, let it pass. And so the Method proceeds—with necessity. "What is that you are saying; is the Method not necessary?" Why, to be sure, that is precisely what I am saying; it proceeds with necessity, that I am willing to swear, for since it cannot be otherwise, it must be with necessity. The bad infinite is the Method's hereditary enemy; it is the Kobold that moves whenever a transition is about to take place, and prevents it from taking place. The bad infinite is infinitely tenacious of life; it can be vanquished only by a breach of continuity, a qualitative leap. But then it is all over with the Method, the facile nimbleness of its immanence, and the necessity of the transition. This is why the Method is so severe and stern; it intimidates people to the point of being as afraid to represent the bad infinite as to be Black Peter. If the System lacks an ethic otherwise, it is absolutely moral through its use of the category of the *bad* infinite; and it is so extravagantly moral that it uses this category even in logic.

FRIEDRICH NIETZSCHE

The Will to Power

1 (1885-1886): *Toward an Outline*

1. Nihilism stands at the door: whence comes this uncanniest of all guests? Point of departure: it is an error to consider "social distress" or "physiological degeneration" or, worse, corruption, as the *cause* of nihilism. Ours is the most decent and compassionate age. Distress, whether of the soul, body, or intellect, cannot of itself give birth to nihilism (i.e., the radical repudiation of value, meaning, and desirability). Such distress always permits a variety of interpretations. Rather: it is in one particular interpretation, the Christian-moral one, that nihilism is rooted.

2. The end of Christianity—at the hands of its own morality (which cannot be replaced), which turns against the Christian God (the sense of truthfulness, developed highly by Christianity, is nauseated by the falseness and mendaciousness of all Christian interpretations of the world and of history; rebound from "God is truth" to the fanatical faith "All is false"; Buddhism of *action*—).

3. Skepticism regarding morality is what is decisive. The end of the moral interpretation of the world, which no longer has any sanction after it has tried to escape into some beyond, leads to nihilism. "Everything lacks meaning" (the untenability of one interpretation of the world, upon which a tremendous amount of energy has been lavished, awakens the suspicion that *all* interpretations of the world are false). Buddhistic tendency, yearning for Nothing. (Indian Buddhism is *not* the culmination of a thoroughly moralistic development; its nihilism is therefore full of morality that is not overcome: existence as punishment, existence construed as error, error thus as a punishment—a moral valuation.) Philosophical attempts to overcome the "moral God" (Hegel, pantheism). Overcoming popular ideals: the sage; the saint; the poet. The antagonism of "true" and "beautiful" and "good"—

Excerpted from Friedrich Nietzsche, *The Will to Power*, translated by Walter Kaufmann (New York: Random House, 1968), 7–8, 12–15, 262–64, 266–71, 297–307, 314–19, 323, 326–27, 330–31, 549–50.

4. Against "meaninglessness" on the one hand, against moral value judgments on the other: to what extent has all science and philosophy so far been influenced by moral judgments? and won't this net us the hostility of science? Or an antiscientific mentality? Critique of Spinozism. Residues of Christian value judgments are found everywhere in socialistic and positivistic systems. A *critique of Christian morality* is still lacking.

5. The nihilistic consequences of contemporary natural science (together with its attempts to escape into some beyond). The industry of its pursuit eventually leads to self-disintegration, opposition, an antiscientific mentality. Since Copernicus man has been rolling from the center toward X.

6. The nihilistic consequences of the ways of thinking in politics and economics, where all "principles" are practically histrionic: the air of mediocrity, wretchedness, dishonesty, etc. Nationalism. Anarchism, etc. Punishment. The *redeeming* class and human being are lacking—the justifiers—

7. The nihilistic consequences of historiography and of the *"practical historians,"* i.e., the romantics. The position of art: its position in the modern world absolutely lacking in originality. Its decline into gloom. Goethe's allegedly Olympian stance.

8. Art and the preparation of nihilism: romanticism (the conclusion of Wagner's *Nibelungen*). . . .

12 (Nov. 1887-March 1888): *Decline of Cosmological Values*

(A)

Nihilism as a psychological state will have to be reached, *first*, when we have sought a "meaning" in all events that is not there: so the seeker eventually becomes discouraged. Nihilism, then, is the recognition of the long *waste* of strength, the agony of the "in vain," insecurity, the lack of any opportunity to recover and to regain composure—being ashamed in front of oneself, as if one had *deceived* oneself all too long.— This meaning could have been: the "fulfillment" of some highest ethical canon in all events, the moral world order; or the growth of love and harmony in the intercourse of beings; or the gradual approximation of a state of universal happiness; or even the development toward a state of universal annihilation—any goal at least constitutes some meaning. What all these notions have in common is that something is to be *achieved* through the process—and now one realizes that becoming aims at *nothing* and achieves *nothing*.— Thus, disappointment regarding an alleged aim of becoming as a cause of nihilism: whether regarding a specific aim or, universalized, the realization that all previous hypotheses about aims that concern the whole "evolution" are inadequate (man no longer the collaborator, let alone the center, of becoming).

Nihilism as a psychological state is reached, *secondly*, when one has posited a totality, a systematization, indeed any organization in all events, and underneath all events, and a soul that longs to admire and revere has wallowed in the idea of some supreme form of domination and administration (—if the soul be that of a logician, complete consistency and real dialectic are quite sufficient to reconcile it to everything). Some sort of unity, some form of "monism": this faith suffices to give man a deep feeling of standing in the context of, and being dependent on, some whole that is infinitely superior to him, and he sees himself as a mode of the deity.— "The well-being of the universal demands the devotion of the individual"—but behold, there is no such universal! At bottom, man has lost the faith in his own value when no infinitely valuable whole works through him; i.e., he conceived such a whole in order *to be able to believe in his own value.*

Nihilism as psychological state has yet a *third* and *last* form. Given these two insights, that becoming has no goal and that underneath all becoming there is no grand unity in which the individual could immerse himself completely as in an element of supreme value, an escape remains: to pass sentence on this whole world of becoming as a deception and to invent a world beyond it, a *true* world. But as soon as man finds out how that world is fabricated solely from psychological needs, and how he has absolutely no right to it, the last form of nihilism comes into being: it includes disbelief in any metaphysical world and forbids itself any belief in a *true* world. Having reached this standpoint, one grants the reality of becoming as the *only* reality, forbids oneself every kind of clandestine access to afterworlds and false divinities—but *cannot endure this world though one does not want to deny it.*

What has happened, at bottom? The feeling of valuelessness was reached with the realization that the overall character of existence may not be interpreted by means of the concept of "aim," the concept of "unity," or the concept of "truth." Existence has no goal or end; any comprehensive unity in the plurality of events is lacking: the character of existence is not "true," is *false*. One simply lacks any reason for convincing oneself that there is a *true* world. Briefly: the categories "aim," "unity," "being" which we used to project some value into the world— we *pull out* again; so the world looks *valueless.*

(B)

Suppose we realize how the world may no longer be interpreted in terms of these three categories, and that the world begins to become valueless for us after this insight: then we have to ask about the sources of

our faith in these three categories. Let us try if it is not possible to give up
our faith in them. Once we have devaluated these three categories, the
demonstration that they cannot be applied to the universe is no longer
any reason for devaluating the universe.

Conclusion: The faith in the categories of reason is the cause of
nihilism. We have measured the value of the world according to categories *that refer to a purely fictitious world.*

Final conclusion: All the values by means of which we have tried so far
to render the world estimable for ourselves and which then proved
inapplicable and therefore devaluated the world—all these values are,
psychologically considered, the results of certain perspectives of utility,
designed to maintain and increase human constructs of domination—
and they have been falsely *projected* into the essence of things. What we
find here is still the *hyperbolic naiveté* of man: positing himself as the
meaning and measure of the value of things.

13 (Spring-Fall 1887)

Nihilism represents a pathological transitional stage (what is pathological is the tremendous generalization, the inference that there is no
meaning at all): whether the productive forces are not yet strong enough,
or whether decadence still hesitates and has not yet invented its rem-
edies.

Presupposition of this hypothesis: that there is no truth, that there is
no absolute nature of things nor a "thing-in-itself." This, too, is merely
nihilism—even the most extreme nihilism. It places the value of things
precisely in the lack of any reality corresponding to these values and in
their being merely a symptom of strength on the part of the value-
positers, a simplification for the sake of life.

14 (Spring-Fall 1887)

Values and their changes are related to increases in the power of those
positing the values.

The measure of *unbelief*, of permitted "freedom of the spirit" as *an
expression of an increase in power.*

"Nihilism" an ideal of the highest degree of powerfulness of the
spirit, the over-richest life—partly destructive, partly ironic.

15 (Spring-Fall 1887)

What is a *belief*? How does it originate? Every belief is a considering-
something-true.

The most extreme form of nihilism would be the view that *every* belief,
every considering-something-true, is necessarily false because there

simply is no *true world*. Thus: a *perspectival appearance* whose origin lies in us (in so far as we continually *need* a narrower, abbreviated, simplified world).

—That it is the measure of strength to what extent we can admit to ourselves, without perishing, the merely *apparent* character, the necessity of lies.

To this extent, nihilism, as the denial of a truthful world, of being, might be *a divine way of thinking*. . . .

THE EPISTEMOLOGICAL STARTING POINT
470 (1885-1886)

Profound aversion to reposing once and for all in any one total view of the world. Fascination of the opposing point of view: refusal to be deprived of the stimulus of the enigmatic.

471 (1885-1886)

The presupposition that things are, at bottom, ordered so morally that human reason must be justified—is an ingenuous presupposition and a piece of naiveté, the after-effect of belief in God's veracity—God understood as the creator of things.— These concepts an inheritance from a former existence in a beyond——

472 (1883-1888)

Contradiction of the alleged "facts of consciousness." Observation is a thousand times more difficult, error perhaps a condition of observation in general.

473 (1886-1887)

The intellect cannot criticize itself, simply because it cannot be compared with other species of intellect and because its capacity to know would be revealed only in the presence of "true reality," i.e., because in order to criticize the intellect we should have to be a higher being with "absolute knowledge." This presupposes that, distinct from every perspective kind of outlook or sensual-spiritual appropriation, something exists, an "in-itself."— But the psychological derivation of the belief in things forbids us to speak of "things-in-themselves."

474 (Nov. 1887-March 1888)

That a sort of adequate relationship subsists between subject and object, that the object is something that if seen from within would be a subject, is a well-meant invention which, I think, has had its day. The measure of that of which we are in any way conscious is totally dependent upon the coarse utility of its becoming-conscious: how could this nook-perspective of consciousness permit us to assert anything of "subject" and "object" that touched reality!—

475 (1885-1886)

Critique of modern philosophy: erroneous starting point, as if there existed "facts of consciousness"—and no phenomenalism in introspection.

476 (1884)

"Consciousness"—to what extent the idea of an idea, the idea of will, the idea of a feeling (known to ourselves alone) are totally superficial! Our inner world, too, "appearance"!

477 (Nov. 1887-March 1888)

I maintain the phenomenality of the inner world, too: everything of which we become conscious is arranged, simplified, schematized, interpreted through and through—the actual process of inner "perception," the causal connection between thoughts, feelings, desires, between subject and object, are absolutely hidden from us—and are perhaps purely imaginary. The "apparent *inner* world" is governed by just the same forms and procedures as the "outer" world. We never encounter "facts": pleasure and displeasure are subsequent and derivative intellectual phenomena—

"Causality" eludes us; to suppose a direct causal link between thoughts, as logic does—that is the consequence of the crudest and clumsiest observation. Between two thoughts all kinds of affects play their game: but their motions are too fast, therefore we fail to recognize them, we deny them—

"Thinking," as epistemologists conceive it, simply does not occur: it is a quite arbitrary fiction, arrived at by selecting one element from the process and eliminating all the rest, an artificial arrangement for the purpose of intelligibility—

The "spirit" something that thinks: where possible even "absolute, pure spirit"—this conception is a second derivative of that false introspection which believes in "thinking": first an act is imagined which simply does not occur, "thinking," and secondly a subject-substratum in which every act of thinking, and nothing else, has its origin: that is to say, both the deed and the doer are fictions.

478 (March-June 1888)

One must not look for phenomenalism in the wrong place: nothing is more phenomenal (or, more clearly:) nothing is so much deception as this inner world which we observe with the famous "inner sense."

We have believed in the will as cause to such an extent that we have from our personal experience introduced a cause into events in general (i.e., intention a cause of events—).

We believe that thoughts as they succeed one another in our minds stand in some kind of causal relation: the logician especially, who actually speaks of nothing but instances which never occur in reality, has grown accustomed to the prejudice that thoughts *cause* thoughts—.

We believe—and even our philosophers still believe—that pleasure and pain are causes of reactions, that the purpose of pleasure and pain is to occasion reactions. For millennia, pleasure and the avoidance of displeasure have been flatly asserted as the *motives* for every action. Upon reflection, however, we should concede that everything would have taken the same course, according to exactly the same sequence of causes and effects, if these states "pleasure and displeasure" had been absent, and that one is simply deceiving oneself if one thinks they cause anything at all: they are epiphenomena with a quite different object than to evoke reactions; they are themselves effects within the instituted process of reaction.

In summa: everything of which we become conscious is a terminal phenomenon, an end—and causes nothing; every successive phenomenon in consciousness is completely atomistic— And we have sought to understand the world through the reverse conception—as if nothing were real and effective but thinking, feeling, willing!— . . .

480 (March-June 1888)

There exists neither "spirit," nor reason, nor thinking, nor consciousness, nor soul, nor will, nor truth: all are fictions that are of no use. There is no question of "subject and object," but of a particular species of animal that can prosper only through a certain relative rightness; above all, regularity of its perceptions (so that it can accumulate experience)—

Knowledge works as a tool of power. Hence it is plain that it increases with every increase of power—

The meaning of "knowledge": here, as in the case of "good" or "beautiful," the concept is to be regarded in a strict and narrow anthropocentric and biological sense. In order for a particular species to maintain itself and increase its power, its conception of reality must comprehend enough of the calculable and constant for it to base a scheme of behavior on it. The utility of preservation—not some abstract-theoretical need not to be deceived—stands as the motive behind the development of the organs of knowledge—they develop in such a way that their observations suffice for our preservation. In other words: the measure of the desire for knowledge depends upon the measure to which the will to power grows in a species: a species grasps a certain amount of reality in order to become master of it, in order to press it into service.

BELIEF IN THE "EGO." THE SUBJECT
481 (1883-1888)

Against positivism, which halts at phenomena—"There are only *facts*"—I would say: No, facts is precisely what there is not, only interpretations. We cannot establish any fact "in itself": perhaps it is folly to want to do such a thing.

"Everything is subjective," you say; but even this is interpretation. The "subject" is not something given, it is something added and invented and projected behind what there is.— Finally, is it necessary to posit an interpreter behind the interpretation? Even this is invention, hypothesis.

In so far as the word "knowledge" has any meaning, the world is knowable; but it is *interpretable* otherwise, it has no meaning behind it, but countless meanings.— "Perspectivism."

It is our needs that interpret the world; our drives and their For and Against. Every drive is a kind of lust to rule; each one has its perspective that it would like to compel all the other drives to accept as a norm.

482 (1886-1887)

We set up a word at the point at which our ignorance begins, at which we can see no further, e.g., the word "I," the word "do," the word "suffer":—these are perhaps the horizon of our knowledge, but not "truths."

483 (1885)

Through thought the ego is posited; but hitherto one believed as ordinary people do, that in "I think" there was something of immediate certainty, and that this "I" was the given *cause* of thought, from which by analogy we understood all other causal relationships. However habitual and indispensable this fiction may have become by now—that in itself proves nothing against its imaginary origin: a belief can be a condition of life and nonetheless be false.

484 (Spring-Fall 1887)

"There is thinking: therefore there is something that thinks": this is the upshot of all Descartes's argumentation. But that means positing as "true *a priori*" our belief in the concept of substance—that when there is thought there has to be something "that thinks" is simply a formulation of our grammatical custom that adds a doer to every deed. In short, this is not merely the substantiation of a fact but a logical-metaphysical postulate— Along the lines followed by Descartes one does not come upon something absolutely certain but only upon the fact of a very strong belief.

If one reduces the proposition to "There is thinking, therefore there are thoughts," one has produced a mere tautology: and precisely that which is in question, the "reality of thought," is not touched upon— that is, in this form the "apparent reality" of thought cannot be denied. But what Descartes desired was that thought should have, not an *apparent* reality, but a reality *in itself.*

485 (Spring-Fall 1887)

The concept of substance is a consequence of the concept of the subject: not the reverse! If we relinquish the soul, "the subject," the precondition for "substance" in general disappears. One acquires degrees of being, one loses that which *has* being.

Critique of "reality": where does the "more or less real," the gradation of being in which we believe, lead to?—

The degree to which we feel life and power (logic and coherence of experience) gives us our measure of "being," "reality," not-appearance.

The subject: this is the term for our belief in a unity underlying all the different impulses of the highest feeling of reality: we understand this belief as the *effect* of one cause—we believe so firmly in our belief that for its sake we imagine "truth," "reality," "substantiality" in general.— "The subject" is the fiction that many similar states in us are the effect of one substratum: but it is we who first created the "similarity" of these states; our adjusting them and making them similar is the fact, not their similarity (—which ought rather to be denied—). . . .

488 (Spring-Fall 1887)

Psychological derivation of our belief in reason—The concept "reality," "being," is taken from our feeling of the "subject."

"The subject": interpreted from within ourselves, so that the ego counts as a substance, as the cause of all deeds, as a doer.

The logical-metaphysical postulates, the belief in substance, accident, attribute, etc., derive their convincing force from our habit of regarding all our deeds as consequences of our will—so that the ego, as substance, does not vanish in the multiplicity of change.—But there is no such thing as will.—

We have no categories at all that permit us to distinguish a "world in itself" from a "world of appearance." All our categories of reason are of sensual origin: derived from the empirical world. "The soul," "the ego"—the history of these concepts shows that here, too, the oldest distinction ("breath," "life")—

If there is nothing material, there is also nothing immaterial. The concept no longer contains anything.

No subject "atoms." The sphere of a subject constantly growing or decreasing, the center of the system constantly shifting; in cases where it cannot organize the appropriate mass, it breaks into two parts. On the other hand, it can transform a weaker subject into its functionary without destroying it, and to a certain degree form a new unity with it. No "substance," rather something that in itself strives after greater strength, and that wants to "preserve" itself only indirectly (it wants to *surpass* itself—).

489 (1886-1887)

Everything that enters consciousness as "unity" is already tremendously complex: we always have only a semblance of unity.

The phenomenon of the body is the richer, clearer, more tangible phenomenon: to be discussed first, methodologically, without coming to any decision about its ultimate significance.

490 (1885)

The assumption of one single subject is perhaps unnecessary; perhaps it is just as permissible to assume a multiplicity of subjects, whose interaction and struggle is the basis of our thought and our consciousness in general? A kind of aristocracy of "cells" in which dominion resides? To be sure, an aristocracy of equals, used to ruling jointly and understanding how to command?

My hypotheses: The subject as multiplicity.

Pain intellectual and dependent upon the judgment "harmful": projected.

The effect always "unconscious": the inferred and imagined cause is projected, *follows* in time.

Pleasure is a kind of pain.

The only force that exists is of the same kind as that of the will: a commanding of other subjects, which thereupon change.

The continual transitoriness and fleetingness of the subject. "Mortal soul."

Number as perspective form. . . .

552 (Spring-Fall 1887)

Against determinism and teleology.—From the fact that something ensues regularly and ensues calculably, it does not follow that it ensues *necessarily*. That a quantum of force determines and conducts itself in every particular case in one way and manner does not make it into an "unfree will." "Mechanical necessity" is not a fact: it is we who first interpreted it into events. We have interpreted the formulatable character of events as the consequence of a necessity that rules over events. But from the fact that I do a certain thing, it by no means follows that I am compelled to do it. Compulsion in things certainly cannot be demonstrated: the rule proves only that one and the same event is not another event as well. Only because we have introduced subjects, "doers," into things does it appear that all events are the consequences of compulsion exerted upon subjects—exerted by whom? Again by a "doer." Cause and effect—a dangerous concept so long as one thinks of something that causes and something upon which an effect is produced.

a. Necessity is not a fact but an interpretation.

b. When one has grasped that the "subject" is not something that creates effects, but only a fiction, much follows.

It is only after the model of the subject that we have invented the reality of things and projected them into the medley of sensations. If we no longer believe in the effective subject, then belief also disappears in effective things, in reciprocation, cause and effect between those phenomena that we call things.

There also disappears, of course, the world of effective atoms: the assumption of which always depended on the supposition that one needed subjects.

At last, the "thing-in-itself" also disappears, because this is fundamentally the conception of a "subject-in-itself." But we have grasped that the subject is a fiction. The antithesis "thing-in-itself" and "appearance" is untenable; with that, however, the concept "appearance" also disappears.

c. If we give up the effective subject, we also give up the object upon which effects are produced. Duration, identity with itself, being are inherent neither in that which is called subject nor in that which is called object: they are complexes of events apparently durable in comparison with other complexes—e.g., through the difference in tempo of the event (rest—motion, firm—loose: opposites that do not exist in themselves and that actually express only variations in degree that from a certain perspective appear to be opposites. There are no opposites: only from those of logic do we derive the concept of opposites—and falsely transfer it to things).

d. If we give up the concept "subject" and "object," then also the concept "substance"—and as a consequence also the various modifications of it, e.g., "matter," "spirit," and other hypothetical entities, "the eternity and immutability of matter," etc. We have got rid of *materiality*.

From the standpoint of morality, the world is false. But to the extent that morality itself is a part of this world, morality is false.

Will to truth is a making firm, a making true and durable, an abolition of the false character of things, a reinterpretation of it into beings. "Truth" is therefore not something there, that might be found or discovered—but something that must be created and that gives a name to a process, or rather to a will to overcome that has in itself no end—introducing truth, as a *processus in infinitum*, an active determining—not a becoming-conscious of something that is in itself firm and determined. It is a word for the "will to power."

Life is founded upon the premise of a belief in enduring and regularly recurring things; the more powerful life is, the wider must be the knowable world to which we, as it were, attribute being. Logicizing, rationalizing, systematizing as expedients of life.

Man projects his drive to truth, his "goal" in a certain sense, outside himself as a world that has being, as a metaphysical world, as a "thing-in-itself," as a world already in existence. His needs as creator invent the world upon which he works, anticipate it; this anticipation (this "belief" in truth) is his support.

All events, all motion, all becoming, as a determination of degrees and relations of force, as a *struggle*—

As soon as we imagine someone who is responsible for our being thus and thus, etc. (God, nature), and therefore attribute to him the intention that we should exist and be happy or wretched, we corrupt for ourselves the *innocence of becoming*. We then have someone who wants to achieve something through us and with us.

The "welfare of the individual" is just as imaginary as the "welfare of the species": the former is *not* sacrificed to the latter, species viewed from a distance is just as transient as the individual. "Preservation of the species" is only a consequence of the growth of the species, i.e., the overcoming of the species on the road to a stronger type.

[Theses.—] That the apparent "purposiveness" ("that purposiveness which endlessly surpasses all the arts of man") is merely the consequence of the will to power manifest in all events; that becoming stronger involves an ordering process which looks like a sketchy purposiveness; that apparent ends are not intentional but, as soon as dominion is established over a lesser power and the latter operates as a function of the greater power, an order of rank, of organization is bound to produce the appearance of an order of means and ends.

Against apparent *"necessity"*:

—this is only an expression for the fact that a force is not also something else.

Against apparent *"purposiveness"*:

the latter only an expression for an order of spheres of power and their interplay.

THING-IN-ITSELF AND APPEARANCE
553 (1886-1887)

The sore spot of Kant's critical philosophy has gradually become visible even to dull eyes: Kant no longer has a right to his distinction "appearance" and "thing-in-itself"—he had deprived himself of the right to go on distinguishing in this old familiar way, in so far as he rejected as impermissible making inferences from phenomena to a cause of phenomena—in accordance with his conception of causality and its purely intraphenomenal validity—which conception, on the other hand, already anticipates this distinction, as if the "thing-in-self" were not only inferred but *given*.

554 (1885-1886)

Causalism.—It is obvious that things-in-themselves cannot be related to one another as cause and effect, nor can appearance be so related to appearance; from which it follows that in a philosophy that believes in things-in-themselves and appearances the concept "cause and effect" *cannot be applied*. Kant's mistakes—In fact, the concept "cause and effect" derives, psychologically speaking, only from a mode of thought that believes that always and everywhere will operates upon will—that believes only in living things and fundamentally only in *"souls"* (and *not* in things). Within the mechanistic view of the world (which is logic and its application to space and time), that concept is reduced to the formulas of mathematics—with which, as one must emphasize again and again, nothing is ever comprehended, but rather designated and distorted.

555 (1885-1886)

Against the scientific prejudice.—The biggest fable of all is the fable of knowledge. One would like to know what things-in-themselves are; but behold, there are no things-in-themselves! But even supposing there were an in-itself, an unconditioned thing, it would for that very reason be unknowable! Something unconditioned cannot be known; otherwise it would not be unconditioned! Coming to know, however, is always "placing oneself in a conditional relation to something"—one who seeks to know the unconditioned desires that it should not concern him, and that this same something should be of no concern to anyone. This involves a contradiction, first, between *wanting* to know and the desire that it not concern us (but why know at all, then?) and, secondly, because something that is of no concern to anyone *is* not at all, and thus cannot be known at all.—

Coming to know means "to place oneself in a conditional relation to something"; to feel oneself conditioned by something and oneself to condition it—it is therefore under all circumstances establishing, denoting, and making-conscious of conditions (not forthcoming entities, things, what is "in-itself").

556 (1885-1886)

A "thing-in-itself" just as perverse as a "sense-in-itself," a "meaning-in-itself." There are no "facts-in-themselves," for a sense must always be projected into them before there can be "facts."

The question "what is that?" is an imposition of meaning from some other viewpoint. "Essence," the "essential nature," is something perspective and already presupposes a multiplicity. At the bottom of it there always lies "what is that for *me?*" (for us, for all that lives, etc.)

A thing would be defined once all creatures had asked "what is that?" and had answered their question. Supposing one single creature, with its own relationships and perspectives for all things, were missing, then the thing would not yet be "defined."

In short: the essence of a thing is only an *opinion* about the "thing." Or rather: "it is considered" is the real "it is," the sole "this is."

One may not ask: "who then interprets?" for the interpretation itself is a form of the will to power, exists (but not as a "being" but as a process, a becoming) as an affect.

The origin of "things" is wholly the work of that which imagines, thinks, wills, feels. The concept "thing" itself just as much as all its qualities.—Even "the subject" is such a created entity, a "thing" like all others: a simplification with the object of defining the force which posits, invents, thinks, as distinct from all individual positing, inventing, thinking as such. Thus a capacity as distinct from all that is individual—fundamentally, action collectively considered with respect to all anticipated actions (action and the probability of similar actions).

557 (1885-1886)

The properties of a thing are effects on other "things":
if one removes other "things," then a thing has no properties,

i.e., there is no thing without other things,
i.e., there is no "thing-in-itself."

558 (Spring-Fall 1887)

The "thing-in-itself" nonsensical. If I remove all the relationships, all the "properties," all the "activities" of a thing, the thing does not remain over; because thingness has only been invented by us owing to the requirements of logic, thus with the aim of defining, communication (to bind together the multiplicity of relationships, properties, activities).

559 (Nov. 1887-March 1888)

"Things that have a constitution in themselves"—a dogmatic idea with which one must break absolutely.

560 (Spring-Fall 1887)

That things possess a constitution in themselves quite apart from interpretation and subjectivity, is a quite idle hypothesis: it presupposes that interpretation and subjectivity are not essential, that a thing freed from all relationships would still be a thing.

Conversely, the apparent *objective* character of things: could it not be merely a difference of degree within the subjective?—that perhaps that which changes slowly presents itself to us as "objectively" enduring, being, "in-itself"—that the objective is only a false concept of a genus and an antithesis *within* the subjective?

561 (1885-1886)

Suppose all unity were unity only as an organization? But the "thing" in which we believe was only invented as a foundation for the various attributes. If the thing "effects," that means: we conceive all the other properties which are present and momentarily latent, as the cause of the emergence of one single property; i.e., we take the sum of its properties—"x"—as cause of the property "x": which is utterly stupid and mad!

All unity is unity only as organization and cooperation—just as a human community is a unity—as opposed to an atomistic anarchy, as a pattern of domination that *signifies* a unity but *is* not a unity.

562 (1883-1888)

"In the development of thought a point had to be reached at which one realized that what one called the properties of things were sensations of the feeling subject: at this point the properties ceased to belong to the thing." The "thing-in-itself" remained. The distinction between the thing-in-itself and the thing-for-us is based on the older, naive form of perception which granted energy to things; but analysis revealed that even force was only projected into them, and likewise—substance. "The thing affects a subject"? Root of the idea of substance in language, not in beings outside us! The thing-in-itself is no problem at all!

Beings will have to be thought of as sensations that are no longer based on something devoid of sensation.

In motion, no new *content* is given to sensation. That which is, cannot contain motion: therefore it is a *form* of being.

> N.B. The explanation of an event can be sought firstly: through mental images of the event that precede it (aims); secondly: through mental images that succeed it (the mathematical-physical explanation).

One should not confuse the two. Thus: the physical explanation, which is a symbolization of the world by means of sensation and thought, can in itself never account for the origin of sensation and thought; rather physics must construe the world of feeling consistently as lacking feeling and aim—right up to the highest human being. And teleology is only a history of purposes and never physical!

563 (1886-1887)

Our "knowing" limits itself to establishing quantities; but we cannot help feeling these differences in quantity as qualities. Quality is a perspective truth for *us*; not an "in-itself."

Our senses have a definite quantum as a mean within which they function; i.e., we sense bigness and smallness in relation to the conditions of our existence. If we sharpened or blunted our senses tenfold, we should perish; i.e., with regard to making possible our existence we sense even relations between magnitudes as qualities.

564 (1885-1886)

Might all quantities not be signs of qualities? A greater power implies a different consciousness, feeling, desiring, a different perspective; growth itself is a desire to be more; the desire for an increase in quantum grows from a *quale*, in a purely quantitative world everything would be dead, stiff, motionless.—The reduction of all qualities to quantities is nonsense: what appears is that the one accompanies the other, an analogy—

565 (Fall 1886)

Qualities are insurmountable barriers for us; we cannot help feeling that mere quantitative differences are something fundamentally distinct from quantity, namely that they are *qualities* which can no longer be reduced to one another. But everything for which the word "knowledge" makes any sense refers to the domain of reckoning, weighing, measuring, to the domain of quantity; while, on the other hand, all our sensations of value (i.e., simply our sensations) adhere precisely to qualities, i.e., to our perspective "truths" which belong to us alone and can by no means be "known"! It is obvious that every creature different from us senses different qualities and consequently lives in a different world from that in which we live. Qualities are an idiosyncrasy peculiar to man; to demand that our human interpretations and values should be universal and perhaps constitutive values is one of the hereditary madnesses of human pride.

566 (Nov. 1887-March 1888)

The "real world," however one has hitherto conceived it—it has always been the apparent world *once again*.

567 (March-June 1888)

The apparent world, i.e., a world viewed according to values; ordered, selected according to values, i.e., in this case according to the viewpoint of utility in regard to the preservation and enhancement of the power of a certain species of animal.

The perspective therefore decides the character of the "appearance"! As if a world would still remain over after one deducted the perspective! By doing that one would deduct relativity!

Every center of force adopts a perspective toward the entire remainder, i.e., its own particular valuation, mode of action, and mode of resistance. The "apparent world," therefore, is reduced to a specific mode of action on the world, emanating from a center.

Now there is no other mode of action whatever; and the "world" is only a word for the totality of these actions. Reality consists precisely in this particular action and reaction of every individual part toward the whole—

No shadow of a right remains to speak here of *appearance*—

The specific mode of reacting is the only mode of reacting; we do not know how many and what kinds of other modes there are.

But there is no "other," no "true," no essential being—for this would be the expression of a world *without* action and reaction—

The antithesis of the apparent world and the true world is reduced to the antithesis "world" and "nothing."—

568 (March-June 1888)

Critique of the concept "true and apparent world."— Of these, the first is a mere fiction, constructed of fictitious entities.

"Appearance" itself belongs to reality: it is a form of its being; i.e., in a world where there is no being, a certain calculable world of identical cases must first be created through appearance: a tempo at which observation and comparison are possible, etc.

Appearance is an arranged and simplified world, at which our practical instincts have been at work; it is perfectly true for *us*; that is to say, we live, we are able to live in it: proof of its truth for us—

the world, apart from our condition of living in it, the world that we have not reduced to our being, our logic and psychological prejudices, does not exist as a world "in-itself"; it is essentially a world of relationships; under certain conditions it has a differing aspect from every point; its being is essentially different from every point; it presses upon every point, every point resists it—and the sum of these is in every case quite incongruent.

The measure of power determines what being possesses the other measure of power; in what form, force, constraint it acts or resists.

Our particular case is interesting enough: we have produced a conception in order to be able to live in a world, in order to perceive just enough to endure it—

569 (Spring-Fall 1887)

Our psychological perspective is determined by the following:

1. that communication is necessary, and that for there to be communication something has to be firm, simplified, capable of precision (above all in the [so-called] *identical* case). For it to be communicable, however, it must be experienced as adapted, as "recognizable." The material of the senses adapted by the understanding, reduced to rough outlines, made similar, subsumed under related matters. Thus the fuzziness and chaos of sense impressions are, as it were, logicized;

2. the world of "phenomena" is the adapted world which we feel to be real. The "reality" lies in the continual recurrence of identical, familiar, related things in their logicized character, in the belief that here we are able to reckon and calculate;

3. the antithesis of this phenomenal world is not "the true world," but the formless unformulable world of the chaos of sensations—*another kind* of phenomenal world, a kind "unknowable" for us;

4. questions, what things "in-themselves" may be like, apart from our sense receptivity and the activity of our understanding, must be rebutted with the question: how could we know that things exist? "Thingness" was first created by us. The question is whether there could not be many other ways of creating such an apparent world—and whether this creating, logicizing, adapting, falsifying is not itself the best-guaranteed reality; in short, whether that which "posits things" is

not the sole reality; and whether the "effect of the external world upon us" is not also only the result of such active subjects—The other "entities" act upon us; our adapted apparent world is an adaptation and overpowering of their actions; a kind of defensive measure. The subject alone is demonstrable; hypothesis that only subjects exist—that "object" is only a kind of effect produced by a subject upon a subject—a *modus* of *the subject.* . . .

584 (March-June 1888)

The aberration of philosophy is that, instead of seeing in logic and the categories of reason means toward the adjustment of the world for utilitarian ends (basically, toward an expedient *falsification*), one believed one possessed in them the criterion of truth and *reality.* The "criterion of truth" was in fact merely the biological utility of such a system of systematic falsification; and since a species of animals knows of nothing more important than its own preservation, one might indeed be permitted to speak here of "truth." The naiveté was to take an anthropocentric idiosyncrasy as the *measure of things*, as the rule for determining "real" and "unreal": in short, to make absolute something conditioned. And behold, suddenly the world fell apart into a "true" world and an "apparent" world: and precisely the world that man's reason had devised for him to live and settle in was discredited. Instead of employing the forms as a tool for making the world manageable and calculable, the madness of philosophers divined that in these categories is presented the concept of that world to which the one in which man lives does not correspond—The means were misunderstood as measures of value, even as a condemnation of their real intention—

The intention was to deceive oneself in a useful way; the means, the invention of formulas and signs by means of which one could reduce the confusing multiplicity to a purposive and manageable schema.

But alas! now a moral category was brought into play: no creature wants to deceive itself, no creature may deceive—consequently there is only a will to truth. What is "truth"?

The law of contradiction provided the schema: the true world, to which one seeks the way, cannot contradict itself, cannot change, cannot become, has no beginning and no end.

This is the greatest error that has ever been committed; the essential fatality of error on earth: one believed one possessed a criterion of reality in the forms of reason—while in fact one possessed them in order to become master of reality, in order to misunderstand reality in a shrewd manner—

And behold: now the world became false, and precisely on account of the properties that constitute its reality: change, becoming, multiplicity, opposition, contradiction, war. And then the entire fatality was there:

1. How can one get free from the false, merely apparent world? (—it was the real, the only one);

2. how can one become oneself as much as possible the antithesis of the character of the apparent world? (Concept of the perfect creature as an antithesis to the real creature; more clearly, as the contradiction of life—)

The whole tendency of values was toward slander of life; one created a confusion of idealist dogmatism and knowledge in general: so that the opposing party also was always attacking *science*.

The road to science was in this way doubly blocked: once by belief in the "true" world, and again by the opponents of this belief. Natural science, psychology was (1) condemned with regard to its objects, (2) deprived of its innocence—

In the actual world, in which everything is bound to and conditioned by everything else, to condemn and think away anything means to condemn and think away everything. The expression "that should not be," "that should not have been," is farcical—If one thinks out the consequences, one would ruin the source of life if one wanted to abolish whatever was in some respect harmful or destructive. Physiology teaches us better!

—We see how morality (a) poisons the entire conception of the world, (b) cuts off the road to knowledge, to science, (c) disintegrates and undermines all actual instincts (in that it teaches that their roots are immoral).

We see at work before us a dreadful tool of decadence that props itself up by the holiest names and attitudes.

585 (Spring-Fall 1887; rev. Spring-Fall 1888)

Tremendous self-examination: becoming conscious of oneself, not as individuals but as mankind. Let us reflect, let us think back; let us follow the highways and byways!

(A)

Man seeks "the truth": a world that is not self-contradictory, not deceptive, does not change, a *true* world—a world in which one does not suffer; contradiction, deception, change—causes of suffering! He does not doubt that a world as it ought to be exists; he would like to seek out the road to it. (Indian critique: even the "ego" as apparent, as not real.)

Whence does man here derive the concept *reality*?—Why is it that he derives *suffering* from change, deception, contradiction? and why not rather his happiness?—

Contempt, hatred for all that perishes, changes, varies—whence comes this valuation of that which remains constant? Obviously, the will to truth is here merely the desire for a world of the constant.

The senses deceive, reason corrects the errors; consequently, one concluded, reason is the road to the constant; the least sensual ideas must be closest to the "true world."—It is from the senses that most misfortunes come—they are deceivers, deluders, destroyers.—

Happiness can be guaranteed only by being; change and happiness exclude one another. The highest desire therefore contemplates unity with what has being. This is the formula for: the road to the highest happiness.

In summa: the world as it ought to be exists; this world, in which we live, is an error—this world of ours ought not to exist.

Belief in what has being is only a consequence: the real *primum mobile* is disbelief in becoming, mistrust of becoming, the low valuation of all that becomes—

What kind of man reflects in this way? An unproductive, suffering kind, a kind weary of life. If we imagine the opposite kind of man, he would not need to believe in what has being; more, he would despise it as dead, tedious, indifferent—

The belief that the world as it ought to be *is*, really exists, is a belief of the unproductive who do *not desire to create a world* as it ought to be. They posit it as already available, they seek ways and means of reaching it. "Will to truth"—*as the impotence of the will to create.*

To know that something *is* thus and thus: To act so that something *becomes* thus and thus:	Antagonism in the degree of power in different natures.

The fiction of a world that corresponds to our desires: psychological trick and interpretation with the aim of associating everything we honor and find pleasant with this true world.

"Will to truth" at this stage is essentially an art of interpretation: which at least requires the power to interpret.

This same species of man, grown one stage poorer, no longer possessing the strength to interpret, to create fictions, produces *nihilists*. A nihilist is a man who judges of the world as it is that it ought *not* to be, and of the world as it ought to be that it does not exist. According to this view, our existence (action, suffering, willing, feeling) has no meaning: the pathos of "in vain" is the nihilists' pathos—at the same time, as pathos, an inconsistency on the part of the nihilists.

Whoever is incapable of laying his will into things, lacking will and strength, at least lays some *meaning* into them, i.e., the faith that there is a will in them already.

It is a measure of the degree of strength of will to what extent one can do without meaning in things, to what extent one can endure to live in a meaningless world *because one organizes a small portion of it oneself*.

The philosophical objective outlook can therefore be a sign that will and strength are small. For strength organizes what is close and closest; "men of knowledge," who desire only to ascertain what is, are those who cannot *fix* anything *as it ought to be*.

Artists, an intermediary species: they at least fix an image of that which ought to be; they are productive, to the extent that they actually alter and transform; unlike men of knowledge, who leave everything as it is.

Connection between philosophers and the pessimistic religions: the same species of man (—they ascribe the highest degree of reality to the most highly valued things—).

Connection between philosophers and moral men and their evaluations (—the moral interpretation of the world as meaning: after the decline of the religious meaning—).

Overcoming of philosophers through the destruction of the world of being: intermediary period of nihilism: before there is yet present the strength to reverse values and to deify becoming and the apparent world as the only world, and to call them good.

(B)

Nihilism as a normal phenomenon can be a symptom of increasing *strength* or of increasing *weakness*:

partly, because the strength to create, to will, has so increased that it no longer requires these total interpretations and introductions of meaning ("present tasks," the state, etc.);

partly because even the creative strength to create meaning has declined and disappointment becomes the dominant condition. The incapability of believing in a "meaning," "unbelief."

What does science mean in regard to both possibilities?

1. As a sign of strength and self-control, as being able to do without healing, comforting worlds of illusion;

2. as undermining, dissecting, disappointing, weakening.

(C)

Belief in truth, the need to have a hold on something believed true, psychological reduction apart from all previous value feelings. Fear, laziness.

The same way, *unbelief*: reduction. To what extent it acquires a new value if a true world does not exist (—thus the value feelings that hitherto have been squandered on the world of being, are again set free). . . .

589 (1885-1886)

"Ends and means"	as interpretations (not as facts)
"Cause and effect"	and to what extent perhaps *nec-*
"Subject and object"	*essary* interpretations? (as re-
"Acting and suffering"	quired for "preservation")—all
"Thing-in-itself and appearance"	in the sense of a will to power.

590 (1885-1886)

Our values are interpreted *into* things.

Is there then any *meaning* in the in-itself?

Is meaning not necessarily relative meaning and perspective?

All meaning is will to power (all relative meaning resolves itself into it). . . .

600 (1885-1886)

No limit to the ways in which the world can be interpreted; every interpretation as symptom of growth or of decline.

Inertia needs unity (monism); plurality of interpretations a sign of strength. Not to desire to deprive the world of its disturbing and enigmatic character! . . .

604 (1885-1886)

"Interpretation," the introduction of meaning—not "explanation" (in most cases a new interpretation over an old interpretation that has become incomprehensible, that is now itself only a sign). There are no facts, everything is in flux, incomprehensible, elusive; what is relatively most enduring is—our opinions. . . .

617 (1883-1885)

To impose upon becoming the character of being—that is the supreme will to power.

Twofold falsification, on the part of the senses and of the spirit, to preserve a world of that which is, which abides, which is equivalent, etc.

That *everything recurs* is the closest *approximation of a world of becoming to a world of being*:—high point of the meditation.

From the values attributed to being proceed the condemnation of and discontent with becoming, after such a world of being had first been invented.

The metamorphoses of what has being (body, God, ideas, laws of nature, formulas, etc.).

"Beings" as appearance; reversal of values; appearance was that which conferred value—.

Knowledge-in-itself in a world of becoming is impossible; so how is knowledge possible? As error concerning oneself, as will to power, as will to deception.

Becoming as invention, willing, self-denial, overcoming of oneself: no subject but an action, a positing, creative, no "causes and effects."

Art as the will to overcome becoming, as "eternalization," but shortsighted, depending on the perspective: repeating in miniature, as it were, the tendency of the whole.

Regarding that which all life reveals as a diminutive formula for the total tendency; hence a new definition of the concept "life" as will to power.

Instead of "cause and effect" the mutual struggle of that which becomes, often with the absorption of one's opponent; the number of becoming elements not constant.

Uselessness of old ideals for the interpretation of the totality of events, once one knows the animal origin and utility of these ideals; all, moreover, contradictory to life.

Uselessness of the mechanistic theory—it gives the impression of meaninglessness.

The entire idealism of mankind hitherto is on the point of changing suddenly into nihilism—into the belief in absolute *worth*lessness, i.e., *meaning*lessness.

The destruction of ideals, the new desert; new arts by means of which we can endure it, we amphibians.

Presupposition: bravery, patience, no "turning back," no haste to go forward. (N.B. Zarathustra adopts a parodistic attitude toward all former values as a consequence of his abundance.). . .

1067 (1885)

And do you know what "the world" is to me? Shall I show it to you in my mirror? This world: a monster of energy, without beginning, without end; a firm, iron magnitude of force that does not grow bigger or smaller, that does not expend itself but only transforms itself; as a whole, of unalterable size, a household without expenses or losses, but likewise without increase or income; enclosed by "nothingness" as by a boundary; not something blurry or wasted, not something endlessly extended, but set in a definite space as a definite force, and not a space that might be "empty" here or there, but rather as force throughout, as a play of forces and waves of forces, at the same time one and many, increasing here and at the same time decreasing there; a sea of forces flowing and rushing together, eternally changing, eternally flooding back, with tremendous years of recurrence, with an ebb and a flood of its forms; out of the simplest forms striving toward the most complex, out of the stillest, most rigid, coldest forms toward the hottest, most turbulent, most self-contradictory, and then again returning home to the simple out of this abundance, out of the play of contradictions back to the joy of concord, still affirming itself in this uniformity of its courses and its years, blessing itself as that which must return eternally, as a becoming that knows no satiety, no disgust, no weariness: this, my *Dionysian* world of the eternally self-creating, the eternally self-destroying, this mystery world of the twofold voluptuous delight, my "beyond good and evil," without goal, unless the joy of the circle is itself a goal; without will, unless a ring feels good will toward itself—do you want a *name* for this world? A *solution* for all its riddles? A *light* for you, too, you best-concealed, strongest, most intrepid, most midnightly men?—*This world is the will to power—and nothing besides!* And you yourselves are also this will to power—and nothing besides!

On Truth and Lie in an Extra-Moral Sense

In some remote corner of the universe, poured out and glittering in innumerable solar systems, there once was a star on which clever animals invented knowledge. That was the haughtiest and most mendacious minute of "world history"—yet only a minute. After nature had drawn a few breaths the star grew cold, and the clever animals had to die.

One might invent such a fable and still not have illustrated sufficiently how wretched, how shadowy and flighty, how aimless and arbitrary, the human intellect appears in nature. There have been eternities when it did not exist; and when it is done for again, nothing will have happened. For this intellect has no further mission that would lead beyond human life. It is human, rather, and only its owner and producer gives it such importance, as if the world pivoted around it. But if we could communicate with the mosquito, then we would learn that it floats through the air with the same self-importance, feeling within itself the flying center of the world. There is nothing in nature so despicable or insignificant that it cannot immediately be blown up like a bag by a slight breath of this power of knowledge; and just as every porter wants an admirer, the proudest human being, the philosopher, thinks that he sees the eyes of the universe telescopically focused from all sides on his actions and thoughts.

It is strange that this should be the effect of the intellect, for after all it was given only as an aid to the most unfortunate, most delicate, most evanescent beings in order to hold them for a minute in existence, from which otherwise, without this gift, they would have every reason to flee as quickly as Lessing's son. That haughtiness which goes with knowledge and feeling, which shrouds the eyes and senses of man in a blinding fog, therefore deceives him about the value of existence by carrying in itself the most flattering evaluation of knowledge itself. Its most universal effect is deception; but even its most particular effects have something of the same character.

Excerpted from *The Portable Nietzsche*, edited by Walter Kaufmann (New York: Random House, 1980), 42–47.

The intellect, as a means for the preservation of the individual, unfolds its chief powers in simulation; for this is the means by which the weaker, less robust individuals preserve themselves, since they are denied the chance of waging the struggle for existence with horns or the fangs of beasts of prey. In man this art of simulation reaches its peak: here deception, flattery, lying and cheating, talking behind the back, posing, living in borrowed splendor, being masked, the disguise of convention, acting a role before others and before oneself—in short, the constant fluttering around the single flame of vanity is so much the rule and the law that almost nothing is more incomprehensible than how an honest and pure urge for truth could make its appearance among men. They are deeply immersed in illusions and dream images; their eye glides only over the surface of things and sees "forms"; their feeling nowhere leads into truth, but contents itself with the reception of stimuli, playing, as it were, a game of blindman's buff on the backs of things. Moreover, man permits himself to be lied to at night, his life long, when he dreams, and his moral sense never even tries to prevent this—although men have been said to have overcome snoring by sheer will power.

What, indeed, does man know of himself! Can he even once perceive himself completely, laid out as if in an illuminated glass case? Does not nature keep much the most from him, even about his body, to spellbind and confine him in a proud, deceptive consciousness, far from the coils of the intestines, the quick current of the blood stream, and the involved tremors of the fibers? She threw away the key; and woe to the calamitous curiosity which might peer just once through a crack in the chamber of consciousness and look down, and sense that man rests upon the merciless, the greedy, the insatiable, the murderous, in the indifference of his ignorance—hanging in dreams, as it were, upon the back of a tiger. In view of this, whence in all the world comes the urge for truth?

Insofar as the individual wants to preserve himself against other individuals, in a natural state of affairs he employs the intellect mostly for simulation alone. But because man, out of need and boredom, wants to exist socially, herd-fashion, he requires a peace pact and he endeavors to banish at least the very crudest *bellum omnium contra omnes* from his world. This peace pact brings with it something that looks like the first step toward the attainment of this enigmatic urge for truth. For now that is fixed which henceforth shall be "truth"; that is, a regularly valid and obligatory designation of things is invented, and this linguistic legislation also furnishes the first laws of truth: for it is here that the contrast between truth and lie first originates. The liar uses the valid designations, the words, to make the unreal appear as real; he says, for example, "I am rich," when the word "poor" would be the correct designation of his situation. He abuses the fixed conventions by arbitrary changes or even by reversals of the names. When he does this in a self-serving way damaging to others, then society will no longer trust him but exclude him. Thereby men do not flee from being deceived as much as from being damaged by deception: what they hate at this stage is basically not the deception but the bad, hostile consequences of certain kinds of deceptions. In a similarly limited way man wants the truth: he desires the agreeable life-preserving consequences of truth, but he is indifferent to pure knowledge, which has no consequences; he is even hostile to possibly damaging and destructive truths. And, moreover, what about these conventions of language? Are they really the products of knowledge, of the sense of truth? Do the designations and the things coincide? Is language the adequate expression of all realities?

Only through forgetfulness can man ever achieve the illusion of possessing a "truth" in the sense just designated. If he does not wish to be satisfied with truth in the form of a tautology—that is, with empty shells—then he will forever buy illusions for truths. What is a word? The image of a nerve stimulus in sounds. But to infer from the nerve stimulus, a cause outside us, that is already the result of a false and unjustified application of the principle of reason. . . . The different languages, set side by side, show that what matters with words is never the truth, never an adequate expression; else there would not be so many languages. The "thing in itself" (for that is what pure truth, without consequences, would be) is quite incomprehensible to the creators of language and not at all worth aiming for. One designates only the relations of things to man, and to express them one calls on the boldest metaphors. A nerve stimulus, first transposed into an image—first metaphor. The image, in turn, imitated by a sound—second metaphor. . . .

Let us still give special consideration to the formation of concepts. Every word immediately becomes a concept, inasmuch as it is not intended to serve as a reminder of the unique and wholly individualized original experience to which it owes its birth, but must at the same time fit innumerable, more or less similar cases—which means, strictly speaking, never equal—in other words, a lot of unequal cases. Every concept originates through our equating what is unequal. No leaf ever wholly equals another, and the concept "leaf" is formed through an arbitrary abstraction from these individual differences, through forgetting the distinctions; and now it gives rise to the idea that in nature there might be something besides the leaves which would be "leaf"—some kind of original form after which all leaves have been woven, marked, copied, colored, curled, and painted, but by unskilled hands, so that no copy turned out to be a correct, reliable, and faithful image of the original form. We call a person "honest." Why did he act so honestly today? we ask. Our answer usually sounds like this: because of his honesty. Honesty! That is to say again: the leaf is the cause of the leaves. After all, we know nothing of an essence-like quality named "honesty"; we know only numerous individualized, and thus unequal actions, which we equate by omitting the unequal and by then calling them honest actions. In the end, we distill from them a *qualitas occulta* with the name of "honesty". . . .

What, then, is truth? A mobile army of metaphors, metonyms, and anthropomorphisms—in short, a sum of human relations, which have been enhanced, transposed, and embellished poetically and rhetorically, and which after long use seem firm, canonical, and obligatory to a people: truths are illusions about which one has forgotten that this is what they are; metaphors which are worn out and without sensuous power; coins which have lost their pictures and now matter only as metal, no longer as coins.

We still do not know where the urge for truth comes from; for as yet we have heard only of the obligation imposed by society that it should exist: to be truthful means using the customary metaphors—in moral terms: the obligation to lie according to a fixed convention, to lie herd-like in a style obligatory for all. . . .

Philosophical Investigations

1. "Cum ipsi (majores homines) appellabant rem aliquam, et cum secundum eam vocem corpus ad aliquid movebant, videbam, et tenebam hoc ab eis vocari rem illam, quod sonabant, cum eam vellent ostendere. Hoc autem eos velle ex motu corporis aperiebatur: tamquam verbis naturalibus omnium gentium, quae fiunt vultu et nutu oculorum, ceterorumque membrorum actu, et sonitu vocis indicante affectionem animi in petendis, habendis, rejiciendis, fugiendisve rebus. Ita verba in variis sententiis locis suis posita, et crebro audita, quarum rerum signa essent, paulatim colligebam, measque jam voluntates, edomito in eis signis ore, per haec enuntiabam." (Augustine, *Confessions*, I. 8.)[1]

These words, it seems to me, give us a particular picture of the essence of human language. It is this: the individual words in language name objects—sentences are combinations of such names.—In this picture of language we find the roots of the following idea: Every word has a meaning. This meaning is correlated with the word. It is the object for which the word stands.

Augustine does not speak of there being any difference between kinds of word. If you describe the learning of language in this way you are, I believe, thinking primarily of nouns like "table," "chair," "bread," and of people's names, and only secondarily of the names of certain actions

Excerpted from: Ludwig Wittgenstein, *Philosophical Investigations*, translated by G. E. M. Anscombe (New York: The Macmillan Co., 1958), 2–12, 18–20, 47–51, 60–62, 79–82, 85–86.

1. "When they (my elders) named some object, and accordingly moved towards something, I saw this and I grasped that the thing was called by the sound they uttered when they meant to point it out. Their intention was shown by their bodily movements, as it were the natural language of all peoples: the expression of the face, the play of the eyes, the movement of other parts of the body, and the tone of voice which expresses our state of mind in seeking, having, rejecting, or avoiding something. Thus, as I heard words repeatedly used in their proper places in various sentences, I gradually learnt to understand what objects they signified; and after I had trained my mouth to form these signs, I used them to express my own desires."

and properties; and of the remaining kinds of word as something that will take care of itself.

Now think of the following use of language: I send someone shopping. I give him a slip marked "five red apples." He takes the slip to the shopkeeper, who opens the drawer marked "apples"; then he looks up the word "red" in a table and finds a color sample opposite it; then he says the series of cardinal numbers—I assume that he knows them by heart—up to the word "five" and for each number he takes an apple of the same color as the sample out of the drawer.——It is in this and similar ways that one operates with words.——"But how does he know where and how he is to look up the word 'red' and what he is to do with the word 'five'?"—Well, I assume that he *acts* as I have described. Explanations come to an end somewhere.—But what is the meaning of the word "five"?—No such thing was in question here, only how the word "five" is used.

2. That philosophical concept of meaning has its place in a primitive idea of the way language functions. But one can also say that it is the idea of a language more primitive than ours.

Let us imagine a language for which the description given by Augustine is right. The language is meant to serve for communication between a builder A and an assistant B. A is building with building-stones: there are blocks, pillars, slabs and beams. B has to pass the stones, and that in the order in which A needs them. For this purpose they use a language consisting of the words "block," "pillar," "slab," "beam." A calls them out;—B brings the stone which he has learnt to bring at such-and-such a call.——Conceive this as a complete primitive language.

3. Augustine, we might say, does describe a system of communication; only not everything that we call language is this system. And one has to say this in many cases where the question arises "Is this an appropriate description or not?" The answer is: "Yes, it is appropriate, but only for this narrowly circumscribed region, not for the whole of what you were claiming to describe."

It is as if someone were to say: "A game consists in moving objects about on a surface according to certain rules . . ."—and we replied: You seem to be thinking of board games, but there are others. You can make your definition correct by expressly restricting it to those games.

4. Imagine a script in which the letters were used to stand for sounds, and also as signs of emphasis and punctuation. (A script can be conceived as a language for describing sound-patterns.) Now imagine someone interpreting that script as if there were simply a correspondence of letters

to sounds and as if the letters had not also completely different functions. Augustine's conception of language is like such an over-simple conception of the script.

5. If we look at the example in §1, we may perhaps get an inkling how much this general notion of the meaning of a word surrounds the working of language with a haze which makes clear vision impossible. It disperses the fog to study the phenomena of language in primitive kinds of application in which one can command a clear view of the aim and functioning of the words.

A child uses such primitive forms of language when it learns to talk. Here the teaching of language is not explanation, but training.

6. We could imagine that the language of § 2 was the *whole* language of A and B; even the whole language of a tribe. The children are brought up to perform *these* actions, to use *these* words as they do so, and to react in *this* way to the words of others.

An important part of the training will consist in the teacher's pointing to the objects, directing the child's attention to them, and at the same time uttering a word; for instance, the word "slab" as he points to that shape. (I do not want to call this "ostensive definition," because the child cannot as yet *ask* what the name is. I will call it "ostensive teaching of words."——I say that it will form an important part of the training, because it is so with human beings; not because it could not be imagined otherwise.) This ostensive teaching of words can be said to establish an association between the word and the thing. But what does this mean? Well, it can mean various things; but one very likely thinks first of all that a picture of the object comes before the child's mind when it hears the word. But now, if this does happen—is it the purpose of the word?—Yes, it *can* be the purpose.—I can imagine such a use of words (of series of sounds). (Uttering a word is like striking a note on the keyboard of the imagination.) But in the language of § 2 it is *not* the purpose of the words to evoke images. (It may, of course, be discovered that that helps to attain the actual purpose.)

But if the ostensive teaching has this effect,—am I to say that it effects an understanding of the word? Don't you understand the call "Slab!" if you act upon it in such-and-such a way?—Doubtless the ostensive teaching helped to bring this about; but only together with a particular training. With different training the same ostensive teaching of these words would have effected a quite different understanding.

"I set the brake up by connecting up rod and lever."—Yes, given the whole of the rest of the mechanism. Only in conjunction with that is it a brake-lever, and separated from its support it is not even a lever; it may be anything, or nothing.

7. In the practice of the use of language (2) one party calls out the words, the other acts on them. In instruction in the language the following process will occur: the learner *names* the objects; that is, he utters the word when the teacher points to the stone.—And there will be this still simpler exercise: the pupil repeats the words after the teacher——both of these being processes resembling language.

We can also think of the whole process of using words in (2) as one of those games by means of which children learn their native language. I will call these games "language-games" and will sometimes speak of a primitive language as a language-game.

And the processes of naming the stones and of repeating words after someone might also be called language-games. Think of much of the use of words in games like ring-a-ring-a-roses.

I shall also call the whole, consisting of language and the actions into which it is woven, the "language-game."

8. Let us now look at an expansion of language (2). Besides the four words "block," "pillar," etc., let it contain a series of words used as the shopkeeper in (1) used the numerals (it can be the series of letters of the alphabet); further, let there be two words, which may as well be "there" and "this" (because this roughly indicates their purpose), that are used in connection with a pointing gesture; and finally a number of color samples. A gives an order like: "d—slab—there." At the same time he shows the assistant a color sample, and when he says "there" he points to a place on the building site. From the stock of slabs B takes one for each letter of the alphabet up to "d," of the same color as the sample, and brings them to the place indicated by A.—On other occasions A gives the order "this—there." At "this" he points to a building stone. And so on.

9. When a child learns this language, it has to learn the series of "numerals" a, b, c, . . . by heart. And it has to learn their use.—Will this training include ostensive teaching of the words?—Well, people will, for example, point to slabs and count: "a, b, c slabs."—Something more like the ostensive teaching of the words "block," "pillar," etc. would be the ostensive teaching of numerals that serve not to count but to refer to groups of objects that can be taken in at a glance. Children do learn the use of the first five or six cardinal numerals in this way.

Are "there" and "this" also taught ostensively?—Imagine how one might perhaps teach their use. One will point to places and things—but in this case the pointing occurs in the *use* of the words too and not merely in learning the use.—

10. Now what do the words of this language *signify?*—What is supposed to show what they signify, if not the kind of use they have? And we have already described that. So we are asking for the expression "This word signifies *this*" to be made a part of the description. In other words the description ought to take the form: "The word. . . . signifies . . . ."

Of course, one can reduce the description of the use of the word "slab" to the statement that this word signifies this object. This will be done when, for example, it is merely a matter of removing the mistaken idea that the word "slab" refers to the shape of building-stone that we in fact call a "block"—but the kind of *referring* this is, that is to say the use of these words for the rest, is already known.

Equally one can say that the signs "a," "b," etc. signify numbers; when for example this removes the mistaken idea that "a," "b," "c," play the part actually played in language by "block," "slab," "pillar." And one can also say that "c" means this number and not that one; when for example this serves to explain that the letters are to be used in the order a, b, c, d, etc. and not in the order a, b, d, c.

But assimilating the descriptions of the uses of words in this way cannot make the uses themselves any more like one another. For, as we see, they are absolutely unlike.

11. Think of the tools in a tool-box: there is a hammer, pliers, a saw, a screw-driver, a rule, a glue-pot, glue, nails and screws.—The functions of words are as diverse as the functions of these objects. (And in both cases there are similarities.)

Of course, what confuses us is the uniform appearance of words when we hear them spoken or meet them in script and print. For their *application* is not presented to us so clearly. Especially when we are doing philosophy!

12. It is like looking into the cabin of a locomotive. We see handles all looking more or less alike. (Naturally, since they are all supposed to be handled.) But one is the handle of a crank which can be moved continuously (it regulates the opening of a valve); another is the handle of a switch, which has only two effective positions, it is either off or on; a third is the handle of a brake-lever, the harder one pulls on it, the harder it brakes; a fourth, the handle of a pump: it has an effect only so long as it is moved to and fro.

13. When we say: "Every word in language signifies something" we have so far said *nothing whatever*; unless we have explained exactly *what* distinction we wish to make. (It might be, of course, that we wanted to distinguish the words of language (8) from words without meaning such as occur in Lewis Carroll's poems, or words like "Lilliburlero" in songs.)

14. Imagine someone's saying: "*All* tools serve to modify something. Thus the hammer modifies the position of the nail, the saw the shape of the board, and so on."—And what is modified by the rule, the glue-pot, the nails?—"Our knowledge of a thing's length, the temperature of the glue, and the solidity of the box."——Would anything be gained by this assimilation of expressions?—

15. The word "to signify" is perhaps used in the most straight-forward way when the object signified is marked with the sign. Suppose that the tools A uses in building bear certain marks. When A shows his assistant such a mark, he brings the tool that has that mark on it.

It is in this and more or less similar ways that a name means and is given to a thing.—It will often prove useful in philosophy to say to ourselves: naming something is like attaching a label to a thing.

16. What about the color samples that A shows to B: are they part of the *language*? Well, it is as you please. They do not belong among the words; yet when I say to someone: "Pronounce the word 'the'," you will count the second "the" as part of the sentence. Yet it has a role just like that of a color-sample in language-game (8); that is, it is a sample of what the other is meant to say.

It is most natural, and causes least confusion, to reckon the samples among the instruments of the language.

(Remark on the reflexive pronoun "*this* sentence.")

17. It will be possible to say: In language (8) we have different *kinds of word*. For the functions of the word "slab" and the word "block" are more alike than those of "slab" and "d." But how we group words into kinds will depend on the aim of the classification,—and on our own inclination.

Think of the different points of view from which one can classify tools or chessmen.

18. Do not be troubled by the fact that languages (2) and (8) consist only of orders. If you want to say that this shows them to be incomplete, ask yourself whether our language is complete;—whether it was so

before the symbolism of chemistry and the notation of the infinitesimal calculus were incorporated in it; for these are, so to speak, suburbs of our language. (And how many houses or streets does it take before a town begins to be a town?) Our language can be seen as an ancient city: a maze of little streets and squares, of old and new houses, and of houses with additions from various periods; and this surrounded by a multitude of new boroughs with straight regular streets and uniform houses.

19. It is easy to imagine a language consisting only of orders and reports in battle.—Or a language consisting only of questions and expressions for answering yes and no. And innumerable others.———And to imagine a language means to imagine a form of life.

But what about this: is the call "Slab!" in example (2) a sentence or a word?—If a word, surely it has not the same meaning as the like-sounding word of our ordinary language, for in § 2 it is a call. But if a sentence, it is surely not the elliptical sentence: "Slab!" of our language.———As far as the first question goes you can call "Slab!" a word and also a sentence; perhaps it could be appropriately called a "degenerate sentence" (as one speaks of a degenerate hyperbola); in fact it *is* our "elliptical" sentence.—But that is surely only a shortened form of the sentence "Bring me a slab," and there is no such sentence in example (2).—But why should I not on the contrary have called the sentence "Bring me a slab" a *lengthening* of the sentence "Slab!"?—Because if you shout "Slab!" you really mean: "Bring me a slab."—But how do you do this: how do you *mean that* while you *say* "Slab!"? Do you say the unshortened sentence to yourself? And why should I translate the call "Slab!" into a different expression in order to say what someone means by it? And if they mean the same thing—why should I not say: "When he says 'Slab!' he means 'Slab!'"? Again, if you can mean "Bring me the slab," why should you not be able to mean "Slab!"?—But when I call "Slab!," then what I want is, *that he should bring me a slab!*———Certainly, but does "wanting this" consist in thinking in some form or other a different sentence from the one you utter?

20. But now it looks as if when someone says "Bring me a slab" he could mean this expression as *one* long word corresponding to the single word "Slab!"———Then can one mean it sometimes as one word and sometimes as four? And how does one usually mean it?———I think we shall be inclined to say: we mean the sentence as *four* words when we use it in contrast with other sentences such as "*Hand* me a slab," "Bring *him* a slab," "Bring *two* slabs," etc.; that is, in contrast with sentences containing the separate words of our command in other combinations.———But what does using one sentence in contrast with others consist in? Do the

others, perhaps, hover before one's mind? *All* of them? And *while* one is
saying the one sentence, or before, or afterwards?—No. Even if such an
explanation rather tempts us, we need only think for a moment of what
actually happens in order to see that we are going astray here. We say
that we use the command in contrast with other sentences because *our
language* contains the possibility of those other sentences. Someone who
did not understand our language, a foreigner, who had fairly often heard
someone giving the order: "Bring me a slab!," might believe that this
whole series of sounds was one word corresponding perhaps to the word
for "building-stone" in his language. If he himself had then given this
order perhaps he would have pronounced it differently, and we should
say: he pronounces it so oddly because he takes it for a *single* word.—
—But then, is there not also something different going on in him when
he pronounces it,—something corresponding to the fact that he conceives the sentence as a *single* word?——Either the same thing may go on
in him, or something different. For what goes on in you when you give
such an order? Are you conscious of its consisting of four words *while* you
are uttering it? Of course you have a *mastery* of this language—which
contains those other sentences as well—but is this having a mastery
something that *happens* while you are uttering the sentence?—And I
have admitted that the foreigner will probably pronounce a sentence
differently if he conceives it differently; but what we call his wrong
conception *need* not lie in anything that accompanies the utterance of the
command.

   The sentence is "elliptical," not because it leaves out something that
we think when we utter it, but because it is shortened—in comparison
with a particular paradigm of our grammar.—Of course one might
object here: "You grant that the shortened and the unshortened sentence
have the same sense.—What is this sense, then? Isn't there a verbal
expression for this sense?"——But doesn't the fact that sentences have
the same sense consist in their having the same *use*?—(In Russian one
says "stone red" instead of "the stone is red"; do they feel the copula to be
missing in the sense, or attach it in *thought*?)

21. Imagine a language-game in which A asks and B reports the
number of slabs or blocks in a pile, or the colors and shapes of the
building-stones that are stacked in such-and-such a place.—Such a
report might run: "Five slabs." Now what is the difference between the
report or statement "Five slabs" and the order "Five slabs!"?—Well, it is
the part which uttering these words plays in the language-game. No
doubt the tone of voice and the look with which they are uttered, and
much else besides, will also be different. But we could also imagine the
tone's being the same—for an order and a report can be spoken in a

variety of tones of voice and with various expressions of face—the difference being only in the application. (Of course, we might use the words "statement" and "command" to stand for grammatical forms of sentence and intonations; we do in fact call "Isn't the weather glorious to-day?" a question, although it is used as a statement.) We could imagine a language in which *all* statements had the form and tone of rhetorical questions; or every command the form of the question "Would you like to. . . ?" Perhaps it will then be said: "What he says has the form of a question but is really a command,"—that is, has the function of a command in the technique of using the language. (Similarly one says "You will do this" not as a prophecy but as a command. What makes it the one or the other?)

22. Frege's idea that every assertion contains an assumption, which is the thing that is asserted, really rests on the possibility found in our language of writing every statement in the form: "It is asserted that such-and-such is the case." —But "that such-and-such is the case" is *not* a sentence in our language—so far it is not a *move* in the language-game. And if I write, not "It is asserted that. . . ," but "It is asserted: such-and-such is the case," the words "It is asserted" simply become superfluous.

We might very well also write every statement in the form of a question followed by a "Yes"; for instance: "Is it raining? Yes!" Would this show that every statement contained a question?

Of course we have the right to use an assertion sign in contrast with a question-mark, for example, or if we want to distinguish an assertion from a fiction or a supposition. It is only a mistake if one thinks that the assertion consists of two actions, entertaining and asserting (assigning the truth-value, or something of the kind), and that in performing these actions we follow the propositional sign roughly as we sing from the musical score. Reading the written sentence loud or soft is indeed comparable with singing from a musical score, but *"meaning"* (thinking) the sentence that is read is not.

Frege's assertion sign marks the *beginning of the sentence.* Thus its function is like that of the full-stop. It distinguishes the whole period from a clause *within* the period. If I hear someone say "it's raining" but do not know whether I have heard the beginning and end of the period, so far this sentence does not serve to tell me anything.[2]

2. Imagine a picture representing a boxer in a particular stance. Now, this picture can be used to tell someone how he should stand, should hold himself; or how he should not hold himself; or how a particular man did stand in such-and-such a place; and so on. One might (using the language of chemistry) call this picture a proposition-radical. This will be how Frege thought of the "assumption."

23. But how many kinds of sentence are there? Say assertion, question, and command?—There are *countless* kinds: countless different kinds of use of what we call "symbols," "words," "sentences." And this multiplicity is not something fixed, given once for all; but new types of language, new language-games, as we may say, come into existence, and others become obsolete and get forgotten. (We can get a *rough picture* of this from the changes in mathematics.)

Here the term "language-*game*" is meant to bring into prominence the fact that the *speaking* of language is part of an activity, or of a form of life.

Review the multiplicity of language-games in the following examples, and in others:

Giving orders, and obeying them—
Describing the appearance of an object, or giving its measurements—
Constructing an object from a description (a drawing)—
Reporting an event—
Speculating about an event—
Forming and testing a hypothesis—
Presenting the results of an experiment in tables and diagrams—
Making up a story; and reading it—
Play-acting—
Singing catches—
Guessing riddles—
Making a joke; telling it—
Solving a problem in practical arithmetic—
Translating from one language into another—
Asking, thanking, cursing, greeting, praying.

—It is interesting to compare the multiplicity of the tools in language and of the ways they are used, the multiplicity of kinds of word and sentence, with what logicians have said about the structure of language. (Including the author of the *Tractatus Logico-Philosophicus.*)

24. If you do not keep the multiplicity of language-games in view you will perhaps be inclined to ask questions like: "What is a question?"—Is it the statement that I do not know such-and-such, or the statement that I wish the other person would tell me. . . ? Or is it the description of my mental state of uncertainty?—And is the cry "Help!" such a description?

Think how many different kinds of thing are called "description": description of a body's position by means of its coordinates; description of a facial expression; description of a sensation of touch; of a mood.

Of course it is possible to substitute the form of statement or description for the usual form of question: "I want to know whether. . . ." or "I am in doubt whether. . . ."—but this does not bring the different language-games any closer together.

The significance of such possibilities of transformation, for example of turning all statements into sentences beginning "I think" or "I believe" (and thus, as it were, into descriptions of *my* inner life) will become clearer in another place. (Solipsism.) . . .

37. What is the relation between name and thing named?—Well, what *is* it? Look at language-game (2) or at another one: there you can see the sort of thing this relation consists in. This relation may also consist, among many other things, in the fact that hearing the name calls before our mind the picture of what is named; and it also consists, among other things, in the name's being written on the thing named or being pronounced when that thing is pointed at.

38. But what, for example, is the word "this" the name of in language-game (8) or the word "that" in the ostensive definition "that is called. . . ."?—If you do not want to produce confusion you will do best not to call these words names at all.—Yet, strange to say, the word "this" has been called the only *genuine* name; so that anything else we call a name was one only in an inexact, approximate sense.

This queer conception springs from a tendency to sublime the logic of our language—as one might put it. The proper answer to it is: we call very different things "names"; the word "name" is used to characterize many different kinds of use of a word, related to one another in many different ways;—but the kind of use that "this" has is not among them.

It is quite true that, in giving an ostensive definition for instance, we often point to the object named and say the name. And similarly, in giving an ostensive definition for instance, we say the word "this" while pointing to a thing. And also the word "this" and a name often occupy the same position in a sentence. But it is precisely characteristic of a name that it is defined by means of the demonstrative expression "That is N" (or "That is called 'N' "). But do we also give the definitions: "That is called 'this'," or "This is called 'this' "?

This is connected with the conception of naming as, so to speak, an occult process. Naming appears as a *queer* connection of a word with an object.—And you really get such a queer connection when the philosopher tries to bring out *the* relation between name and thing by staring at an object in front of him and repeating a name or even the word "this" innumerable times. For philosophical problems arise when language *goes on holiday*. And *here* we may indeed fancy naming to be some remarkable act of mind, as it were a baptism of an object. And we can also say the word "this" *to* the object, as it were *address* the object as "this"—a queer use of this word, which doubtless only occurs in doing philosophy.[3]

39. But why does it occur to one to want to make precisely this word into a name, when it evidently is *not* a name?—That is just the reason. For one is tempted to make an objection against what is ordinarily called a name. It can be put like this: *a name ought really to signify a simple.* And for this one might perhaps give the following reasons: The word "Excalibur," say, is a proper name in the ordinary sense. The sword Excalibur consists of parts combined in a particular way. If they are combined differently Excalibur does not exist. But it is clear that the sentence "Excalibur has a sharp blade" makes *sense* whether Excalibur is still whole or is broken up. But if "Excalibur" is the name of an object, this object no longer exists when Excalibur is broken in pieces; and as no object would then correspond to the name it would have no meaning. But then the sentence "Excalibur has a sharp blade" would contain a word that had no meaning, and hence the sentence would be nonsense. But it does make sense; so there must always be something corresponding to the words of which it consists. So the word "Excalibur" must disappear when the sense is analyzed and its place be taken by words which name simples. It will be reasonable to call these words the real names.

40. Let us first discuss *this* point of the argument: that a word has no meaning if nothing corresponds to it.—It is important to note that the word "meaning" is being used illicitly if it is used to signify the thing that "corresponds" to the word. That is to confound the meaning of a name with the *bearer* of the name. When Mr. N. N. dies one says that the bearer of the name dies, not that the meaning dies. And it would be nonsensical to say that, for if the name ceased to have meaning it would make no sense to say "Mr. N. N. is dead."

41. In § 15 we introduced proper names into language (8). Now

---

3. What is it to *mean* the words "*That* is blue" at one time as a statement about the object one is pointing to—at another as an explanation of the word "blue"? Well, in the second case one really means "That is called 'blue'."—Then can one at one time mean the word "is" as "is called" and the word "blue" as " 'blue'," and another time mean "is" really as "is"?

It is also possible for someone to get an explanation of the words out of what was intended as a piece of information. [Marginal note: Here lurks a crucial superstition.]

Can I say "bububu" and mean "If it doesn't rain I shall go for a walk"?—It is only in a language that I can mean something by something. This shows clearly that the grammar of "to mean" is not like that of the expression "to imagine" and the like.

suppose that the tool with the name "N" is broken. Not knowing this, A gives B the sign "N." Has this sign meaning now or not?—What is B to do when he is given it?—We have not settled anything about this. One might ask: what *will* he do? Well, perhaps he will stand there at a loss, or show A the pieces. Here one *might* say: "N" has become meaningless; and this expression would mean that the sign "N" no longer had a use in our language-game (unless we gave it a new one). "N" might also become meaningless because, for whatever reason, the tool was given another name and the sign "N" no longer used in the language-game.—But we could also imagine a convention whereby B has to shake his head in reply if A gives him the sign belonging to a tool that is broken.—In this way the command "N" might be said to be given a place in the language-game even when the tool no longer exists, and the sign "N" to have meaning even when its bearer ceases to exist. . . .

111. The problems arising through a misinterpretation of our forms of language have the character of *depth*. They are deep disquietudes; their roots are as deep in us as the forms of our langauge and their significance is as great as the importance of our language.——Let us ask ourselves: why do we feel a grammatical joke to be *deep*? (and that is what the depth of philosophy is.)

112. A simile that has been absorbed into the forms of our language produces a false appearance, and this disquiets us. "But *this* isn't how it is!"—we say. "Yet *this* is how it has to *be*!"

113. "But *this* is how it is————" I say to myself over and over again. I feel as though, if only I could fix my gaze absolutely sharply on this fact, get it in focus, I must grasp the essence of the matter.

114. (*Tractatus Logico-Philosophicus*, 4.5): "The general form of proposi-tions is: This is how things are."——That is the kind of proposition that one repeats to oneself countless times. One thinks that one is tracing the outline of the thing's nature over and over again, and one is merely tracing round the frame through which we look at it.

115. A *picture* held us captive. And we could not get outside it, for it lay in our language and language seemed to repeat it to us inexorably.

116. When philosophers use a word—"knowledge," "being," "ob-ject," "I," "proposition," "name"—and try to grasp the *essence* of the thing, one must always ask oneself: is the word ever actually used in this way in the language-game which is its original home?—

What *we* do is to bring words back from their metaphysical to their everyday use.

117. You say to me: "You understand this expression, don't you? Well then—I am using it in the sense you are familiar with."—As if the sense were an atmosphere accompanying the word, which it carried with it into every kind of application.

If, for example, someone says that the sentence "This is here" (saying which he points to an object in front of him) makes sense to him, then he should ask himself in what special circumstances this sentence is actually used. There it does make sense.

118. Where does our investigation get its importance from, since it seems only to destroy everything interesting, that is, all that is great and important? (As it were all the buildings, leaving behind only bits of stone and rubble.) What we are destroying is nothing but houses of cards and we are clearing up the ground of language on which they stand.

119. The results of philosophy are the uncovering of one, or another piece of plain nonsense and of bumps that the understanding has got by running its head up against the limits of language. These bumps make us see the value of the discovery.

120. When I talk about language (words, sentences, etc.) I must speak the language of every day. Is this language somehow too coarse and material for what we want to say? *Then how is another one to be constructed?*—And how strange that we should be able to do anything at all with the one we have!

In giving explanations I already have to use language full-blown (not some sort of preparatory, provisional one); this by itself shows that I can adduce only exterior facts about language.

Yes, but then how can these explanations satisfy us?—Well, your very questions were framed in this language; they had to be expressed in this language, if there was anything to ask!

And your scruples are misunderstandings.

Your questions refer to words; so I have to talk about words.

You say: the point isn't the word, but its meaning, and you think of the meaning as a thing of the same kind as the word, though also different from the word. Here the word, there the meaning. The money, and the cow that you can buy with it. (But contrast: money, and its use.)

121. One might think: if philosophy speaks of the use of the word "philosophy" there must be a second-order philosophy. But it is not so:

it is, rather, like the case of orthography, which deals with the word "orthography" among others without then being second-order.

122. A main source of our failure to understand is that we do not *command a clear view* of the use of our words.—Our grammar is lacking in this sort of perspicuity. A perspicuous representation produces just that understanding which consists in "seeing connections." Hence the importance of finding and inventing *intermediate cases*.

The concept of a perspicuous representation is of fundamental significance for us. It earmarks the form of account we give, the way we look at things. (Is this a Weltanschauung?)

123. A philosophical problem has the form: "I don't know my way about."

124. Philosophy may in no way interfere with the actual use of language; it can in the end only describe it.

For it cannot give it any foundation either.

It leaves everything as it is.

It also leaves mathematics as it is, and no mathematical discovery can advance it. A "leading problem of mathematical logic" is for us a problem of mathematics like any other.

125. It is the business of philosophy, not to resolve a contradiction by means of a mathematical or logico-mathematical discovery, but to make it possible for us to get a clear view of the state of mathematics that troubles us: the state of affairs *before* the contradiction is resolved. (And this does not mean that one is sidestepping a difficulty.)

The fundamental fact here is that we lay down rules, a technique, for a game, and that then when we follow the rules, things do not turn out as we had assumed. That we are therefore as it were entangled in our own rules.

This entanglement in our rules is what we want to understand (i.e., get a clear view of).

It throws light on our concept of *meaning* something. For in those cases things turn out otherwise than we had meant, foreseen. That is just what we say when, for example, a contradiction appears: "I didn't mean it like that."

The civil status of a contradiction, or its status in civil life: there is the philosophical problem.

126. Philosophy simply puts everything before us, and neither explains

nor deduces anything.—Since everything lies open to view there is nothing to explain. For what is hidden, for example, is of no interest to us.

One might also give the name "philosophy" to what is possible *before* all new discoveries and inventions.

127. The work of the philosopher consists in assembling reminders for a particular purpose.

128. If one tried to advance *theses* in philosophy, it would never be possible to debate them, because everyone would agree to them.

129. The aspects of things that are most important for us are hidden because of their simplicity and familiarity. (One is unable to notice something—because it is always before one's eyes.) The real foundations of his inquiry do not strike a man at all. Unless *that* fact has at some time struck him.—And this means: we fail to be struck by what, once seen, is most striking and most powerful.

130. Our clear and simple language-games are not preparatory studies for a future regularization of language—as it were first approximations, ignoring friction and air-resistance. The language-games are rather set up as *objects of comparison* which are meant to throw light on the facts of our language by way not only of similarities, but also of dissimilarities.

131. For we can avoid ineptness or emptiness in our assertions only by presenting the model as what it is, as an object of comparison—as, so to speak, a measuring-rod; not as a preconceived idea to which reality *must* correspond. (The dogmatism into which we fall so easily in doing philosophy.)

132. We want to establish an order in our knowledge of the use of language: an order with a particular end in view; one out of many possible orders; not *the* order. To this end we shall constantly be giving prominence to distinctions which our ordinary forms of language easily make us overlook. This may make it look as if we saw it as our task to reform language.

Such a reform for particular practical purposes, an improvement in our terminology designed to prevent misunderstandings in practice, is perfectly possible. But these are not the cases we have to do with. The confusions which occupy us arise when language is like an engine idling, not when it is doing work.

133. It is not our aim to refine or complete the system of rules for the use of our words in unheard-of ways.

For the clarity that we are aiming at is indeed *complete* clarity. But this simply means that the philosophical problems should *completely* disappear.

The real discovery is the one that makes me capable of stopping doing philosophy when I want to.—The one that gives philosophy peace, so that it is no longer tormented by questions which bring *itself* in question.—Instead, we now demonstrate a method, by examples; and the series of examples can be broken off.—Problems are solved (difficulties eliminated), not a *single* problem.

There is not *a* philosophical method, though there are indeed methods, like different therapies. . . .

153. We are trying to get hold of the mental process of understanding which seems to be hidden behind those coarser and therefore more readily visible accompaniments. But we do not succeed; or, rather, it does not get as far as a real attempt. For even supposing I had found something that happened in all those cases of understanding,—why should *it* be the understanding? And how can the process of understanding have been hidden, when I said "Now I understand" *because* I understood?! And if I say it is hidden—then how do I know what I have to look for? I am in a muddle.

154. But wait—if "Now I understand the principle" does not mean the same as "The formula . . . occurs to me" (or "I say the formula," "I write it down," etc.) —does it follow from this that I employ the sentence "Now I understand. . . ." or "Now I can go on" as a description of a process occurring behind or side by side with that of saying the formula?

If there has to be anything "behind the utterance of the formula" it is *particular circumstances*, which justify me in saying I can go on—when the formula occurs to me.

Try not to think of understanding as a mental process at all.—For *that* is the expression which confuses you. But ask yourself: in what sort of case, in what kind of circumstances, do we say, "Now I know how to go on," when, that is, the formula *has* occurred to me?—

In the sense in which there are processes (including mental processes) which are characteristic of understanding, understanding is not a mental process.

(A pain's growing more and less; the hearing of a tune or a sentence: these are mental processes.)

155. Thus what I wanted to say was: when he suddenly knew how to go

on, when he understood the principle, then possibly he had a special experience—and if he is asked: "What was it? What took place when you suddenly grasped the principle?" perhaps he will describe it much as we described it above——but for us it is *the circumstances* under which he had such an experience that justify him in saying in such a case that he understands, that he knows how to go on.

156. This will become clearer if we interpolate the consideration of another word, namely "reading." First I need to remark that I am not counting the understanding of what is read as part of "reading" for purposes of this investigation: reading is here the activity of rendering out loud what is written or printed; and also of writing from dictation, writing out something printed, playing from a score, and so on.

The use of this word in the ordinary circumstances of our life is of course extremely familiar to us. But the part the word plays in our life, and therewith the language-game in which we employ it, would be difficult to describe even in rough outline. A person, let us say an Englishman, has received at school or at home one of the kinds of education usual among us, and in the course of it has learned to read his native language. Later he reads books, letters, newspapers, and other things.

Now what takes place when, say, he reads a newspaper?——His eye passes—as we say—along the printed words, he says them out loud—or only to himself; in particular he reads certain words by taking in their printed shapes as wholes; others when his eye has taken in the first syllables; others again he reads syllable by syllable, and an occasional one perhaps letter by letter.—We should also say that he had read a sentence if he spoke neither aloud nor to himself during the reading but was afterwards able to repeat the sentence word for word or nearly so.—He may attend to what he reads, or again—as we might put it—function as a mere reading-machine: I mean, read aloud and correctly without attending to what he is reading; perhaps with his attention on something quite different (so that he is unable to say what he has been reading if he is asked about it immediately afterwards).

Now compare a beginner with this reader. The beginner reads the words by laboriously spelling them out.—Some however he guesses from the context, or perhaps he already partly knows the passage by heart. Then his teacher says that he is not really *reading* the words (and in certain cases that he is only pretending to read them).

If we think of *this* sort of reading, the reading of a beginner, and ask ourselves what *reading* consists in, we shall be inclined to say: it is a special conscious activity of mind.

We also say of the pupil: "Of course he alone knows if he is really reading or merely saying the words off by heart." (We have yet to discuss these propositions: "He alone knows. . . .")

But I want to say: we have to admit that—as far as concerns uttering any *one* of the printed words—the same thing may take place in the consciousness of the pupil who is "pretending" to read, as in that of the practiced reader who is "reading" it. The word "to read" is applied *differently* when we are speaking of the beginner and of the practiced reader.——Now we should of course like to say: What goes on in that practiced reader and in the beginner when they utter the word *can't* be the same. And if there is no difference in what they happen to be conscious of there must be one in the unconscious workings of their minds, or, again, in the brain.—So we should like to say: There are at all events two different mechanisms at work here. And what goes on in them must distinguish reading from not reading.—But these mechanisms are only hypotheses, models designed to explain, to sum up, what you observe. . . .

196. In our failure to understand the use of a word we take it as the expression of a queer *process*. (As we think of time as a queer medium, of the mind as a queer kind of being.)

197. "It's as if we could grasp the whole use of a word in a flash."—And that is just what we say we do. That is to say: we sometimes describe what we do in these words. But there is nothing astonishing, nothing queer, about what happens. It becomes queer when we are led to think that the future development must in some way already be present in the act of grasping the use and yet isn't present.—For we say that there isn't any doubt that we understand the word, and on the other hand its meaning lies in its use. There is no doubt that I now want to play chess, but chess is the game it is in virtue of all its rules (and so on). Don't I know, then, which game I want to play until I *have* played it? or are all the rules contained in my act of intending? Is it experience that tells me that this sort of game is the usual consequence of such an act of intending? so is it impossible for me to be certain what I am intending to do? And if that is nonsense—what kind of super-strong connection exists between the act of intending and the thing intended?——Where is the connection effected between the sense of the expression "Let's play a game of chess" and all the rules of the game?—Well, in the list of rules of the game, in the teaching of it, in the day-to-day practice of playing.

198. "But how can a rule show me what I have to do at *this* point? Whatever I do is, on some interpretation, in accord with the rule."— That is not what we ought to say, but rather: any interpretation still

hangs in the air along with what it interprets, and cannot give it any support. Interpretations by themselves do not determine meaning.

"Then can whatever I do be brought into accord with the rule?"—Let me ask this: what has the expression of a rule—say a sign-post—got to do with my actions? What sort of connection is there here?—Well, perhaps this one: I have been trained to react to this sign in a particular way, and now I do so react to it.

But that is only to give a causal connection; to tell how it has come about that we now go by the sign-post; not what this going-by-the-sign really consists in. On the contrary; I have further indicated that a person goes by a sign-post only in so far as there exists a regular use of sign-posts, a custom.

199. Is what we call "obeying a rule" something that it would be possible for only *one* man to do, and to do only *once* in his life?—This is of course a note on the grammar of the expression "to obey a rule."

It is not possible that there should have been only one occasion on which someone obeyed a rule. It is not possible that there should have been only one occasion on which a report was made, an order given or understood; and so on.—To obey a rule, to make a report, to give an order, to play a game of chess, are *customs* (uses, institutions).

To understand a sentence means to understand a language. To understand a language means to be master of a technique.

200. It is, of course, imaginable that two people belonging to a tribe unacquainted with games should sit at a chess-board and go through the moves of a game of chess; and even with all the appropriate mental accompaniments. And if *we* were to see it we should say they were playing chess. But now imagine a game of chess translated according to certain rules into a series of actions which we do not ordinarily associate with a *game*—say into yells and stamping of feet. And now suppose those two people to yell and stamp instead of playing the form of chess that we are used to; and this in such a way that their procedure is translatable by suitable rules into a game of chess. Should we still be inclined to say they were playing a game? What right would one have to say so?

201. This was our paradox: no course of action could be determined by a rule, because every course of action can be made out to accord with the rule. The answer was: if everything can be made out to accord with the rule, then it can also be made out to conflict with it. And so there would be neither accord nor conflict here.

It can be seen that there is a misunderstanding here from the mere fact that in the course of our argument we give one interpretation after another; as if each one contented us at least for a moment, until we thought of yet another standing behind it. What this shows is that there is a way of grasping a rule which is *not* an *interpretation*, but which is exhibited in what we call "obeying the rule" and "going against it" in actual cases.

Hence there is an inclination to say: every action according to the rule is an interpretation. But we ought to restrict the term "interpretation" to the substitution of one expression of the rule for another.

202. And hence also "obeying a rule" is a practice. And to *think* one is obeying a rule is not to obey a rule. Hence it is not possible to obey a rule "privately": otherwise thinking one was obeying a rule would be the same thing as obeying it.

203. Language is a labyrinth of paths. You approach from *one* side and know your way about; you approach the same place from another side and no longer know your way about. . . .

217. "How am I able to obey a rule?"—if this is not a question about causes, then it is about the justification for my following the rule in the way I do.

If I have exhausted the justifications I have reached bedrock, and my spade is turned. Then I am inclined to say: "This is simply what I do."

(Remember that we sometimes demand definitions for the sake not of their content, but of their form. Our requirement is an architectural one; the definition a kind of ornamental coping that supports nothing.)

218. Whence comes the idea that the beginning of a series is a visible section of rails invisibly laid to infinity? Well, we might imagine rails instead of a rule. And infinitely long rails correspond to the unlimited application of a rule.

219. "All the steps are really already taken" means: I no longer have any choice. The rule, once stamped with a particular meaning, traces the lines along which it is to be followed through the whole of space. ——But if something of this sort really were the case, how would it help?

No; my description only made sense if it was to be understood symbolically.—I should have said: *This is how it strikes me.*

When I obey a rule, I do not choose.

I obey the rule *blindly*.

220. But what is the purpose of that symbolical proposition? It was

supposed to bring into prominence a difference between being causally determined and being logically determined.

221. My symbolical expression was really a mythological description of the use of a rule.

222. "The line intimates to me the way I am to go."—But that is of course only a picture. And if I judged that it intimated this or that as it were irresponsibly, I should not say that I was obeying it like a rule.

223. One does not feel that one has always got to wait upon the nod (the whisper) of the rule. On the contrary, we are not on tenterhooks about what it will tell us next, but it always tells us the same, and we do what it tells us.

One might say to the person one was training: "Look, I always do the same thing: I. . . ."

224. The word "agreement" and the word "rule" are *related* to one another, they are cousins. If I teach anyone the use of the one word, he learns the use of the other with it.

225. The use of the word "rule" and the use of the word "same" are interwoven. (As are the use of "proposition" and the use of "true.")

The End of Philosophy and the
Task of Thinking

The title designates the attempt at a reflection which persists in questioning. The questions are paths to an answer. If the answer could be
given, the answer would consist in a transformation of thinking, not in a
propositional statement about a matter at stake.

The following text belongs to a larger context. It is the attempt
undertaken again and again ever since 1930 to shape the question of
Being and Time in a more primal way. This means: to subject the point
of departure of the question in *Being and Time* to an immanent criticism.
Thus it must become clear to what extent the *critical* question of what the
matter of thinking is, necessarily and continually belongs to thinking.
Accordingly, the name of the task of *Being and Time* will change.

We are asking:

1. What does it mean that philosophy in the present age has entered
its final stage?

2. What task is reserved for thinking at the end of philosophy?

1. *What does it mean that philosophy in the present age has entered its final
stage?*

Philosophy is metaphysics. Metaphysics thinks being as a whole—the
world, man, God—with respect to Being, with respect to the belonging
together of beings in Being. Metaphysics thinks beings as being in the
manner of representational thinking which gives reasons. For since the
beginning of philosophy and with that beginning, the Being of beings
has showed itself as the ground (*arche, aition*). The ground is from where
beings as such are what they are in their becoming, perishing and
persisting as something that can be known, handled and worked upon.
As the ground, Being brings beings to their actual presencing. The
ground shows itself as presence. The present of presence consists in the
fact that it brings what is present each in its own way to presence. In
accordance with the actual kind of presence, the ground has the character

Excerpted from Martin Heidegger, *On Time and Being*, translated by Joan Stambaugh
(New York: Harper and Row, 1972), 55–73.

of grounding as the ontic causation of the real, as the transcendental making possible of the objectivity of objects, as the dialectical mediation of the movement of the absolute Spirit, of the historical process of production, as the will to power positing values.

What characterizes metaphysical thinking which grounds the ground for beings is the fact that metaphysical thinking departs from what is present in its presence, and thus represents it in terms of its ground as something grounded.

What is meant by the talk about the end of philosophy? We understand the end of something all too easily in the negative sense as a mere stopping, as the lack of continuation, perhaps even as decline and impotence. In contrast, what we say about the end of philosophy means the completion of metaphysics. However, completion does not mean perfection as a consequence of which philosophy would have to have attained the highest perfection at its end. Not only do we lack any criterion which would permit us to evaluate the perfection of an epoch of metaphysics as compared with any other epoch. The right to this kind of evaluation does not exist. Plato's thinking is no more perfect than Parmenides'. Hegel's philosophy is no more perfect than Kant's. Each epoch of philosophy has its own necessity. We simply have to acknowledge the fact that a philosophy is the way it is. It is not our business to prefer one to the other, as can be the case with regard to various *Weltanschauungen*.

The old meaning of the word "end" means the same as place: "from one end to the other" means: from one place to the other. The end of philosophy is the place, that place in which the whole of philosophy's history is gathered in its most extreme possibility. End as completion means this gathering.

Throughout the whole history of philosophy, Plato's thinking remains decisive in changing forms. Metaphysics is Platonism. Nietszche characterizes his philosophy as reversed Platonism. With the reversal of metaphysics which was already accomplished by Karl Marx, the most extreme possibility of philosophy is attained. It has entered its final stage. To the extent that philosophical thinking is still attempted, it manages only to attain an epigonal renaissance and variations of that renaissance. Is not then the end of philosophy after all a cessation of its way of thinking? To conclude this would be premature.

As a completion, an end is the gathering into the most extreme possibilities. We think in too limited a fashion as long as we expect only a development of recent philosophies of the previous style. We forget that already in the age of Greek philosophy a decisive characteristic of philosophy appears: the development of sciences within the field which philosophy opened up. The development of the sciences is at the same time their separation from philosophy and the establishment of their independence. This process belongs to the completion of philosophy. Its development is in full swing today in all regions of beings. This development looks like the mere dissolution of philosophy, and is in truth its completion.

It suffices to refer to the independence of psychology, sociology, anthropology as cultural anthropology, to the role of logic as logistics and semantics. Philosophy turns into the empirical science of man, of all of what can become the experiential object of his technology for man, the technology by which he establishes himself in the world by working on it in the manifold modes of making and shaping. All of this happens everywhere on the basis and according to the criterion of the scientific discovery of the individual areas of beings.

No prophecy is necessary to recognize that the sciences now establishing themselves will soon be determined and guided by the new fundamental science which is called cybernetics.

This science corresponds to the determination of man as an acting social being. For it is the theory of the steering of the possible planning and arrangement of human labor. Cybernetics transforms language into an exchange of news. The arts become regulated-regulating instruments of information.

The development of philosophy into the independent sciences which, however, interdependently communicate among themselves ever more markedly, is the legitimate completion of philosophy. Philosophy is ending in the present age. It has found its place in the scientific attitude of socially active humanity. But the fundamental characteristic of this scientific attitude is its cybernetic, that is, technological character. The need to ask about modern technology is presumably dying out to the same extent that technology more definitely characterizes and regulates the appearance of the totality of the world and the position of man in it.

The sciences will interpret everything in their structure that is still reminiscent of the origin from philosophy in accordance with the rules of science, that is, technologically. Every science understands the categories upon which it remains dependent for the articulation and delineation of its area of investigation as working hypotheses. Their truth is measured not only by the effect which their application brings about within the progress of research.

Scientific truth is equated with the efficiency of these effects.

The sciences are now taking over as their own task what philosophy in the course of its history tried to present in part, and even there only inadequately, that is, the ontologies of the various regions of beings (nature, history, law, art). The interest of the sciences is directed toward the theory of the necessary structural concepts of the coordinated areas of investigation. "Theory" means now: supposition of the categories which are allowed only a cybernetical function, but denied any ontological meaning. The operational and model character of representational-calculative thinking becomes dominant.

However, the sciences still speak about the Being of beings in the unavoidable supposition of their regional categories. They just don't say so. They can deny their origin from philosophy, but never dispense with it. For in the scientific attitude of the sciences, the document of their birth from philosophy still speaks.

The end of philosophy proves to be the triumph of the manipulable arrangement of a scientific-technological world and of the social order proper to this world. The end of philosophy means: the beginning of the world civilization based upon Western European thinking.

But is the end of philosophy in the sense of its development to the sciences also already the complete realization of all the possibilities in which the thinking of philosophy was posited? Or is there a *first* possibility for thinking apart from the *last* possibility which we characterized (the dissolution of philosophy in the technologized sciences), a possibility from which the thinking of philosophy would have to start out, but which as philosophy it could nevertheless not experience and adopt?

If this were the case, then a task would still have to be reserved for thinking in a concealed way in the history of philosophy from its beginning to its end, a task accessible neither to philosophy as metaphysics nor, and even less so, to the sciences stemming from philosophy. Therefore we ask:

2. *What task is reserved for thinking at the end of philosophy?*

The mere thought of such a task of thinking must sound strange to us. A thinking which can be neither metaphysics nor science?

A task which has concealed itself from philosophy since its very beginning, even in virtue of that beginning, and thus has withdrawn itself continually and increasingly in the time to come?

A task of thinking which—so it seems—includes the assertion that philosophy has not been up to the matter of thinking and has thus become a history of mere decline?

Is there not an arrogance in these assertions which desires to put itself above the greatness of the thinkers of philosophy?

This suspicion easily suggests itself. But it can as easily be removed. For every attempt to gain insight into the supposed task of thinking finds itself moved to review the whole of the history of philosophy. Not only this, but it is even forced to think the historicity of that which grants a possible history to philosophy.

Because of this, that supposed thinking necessarily falls short of the greatness of the philosophers. It is less than philosophy. Less also because the direct or indirect effect of this thinking on the public in the industrial age, formed by technology and science, is decisively less possible to this thinking than it was in the case of philosophy.

But above all, the thinking in question remains slight because its task is only of a preparatory, not of a founding character. It is content with awakening a readiness in man for a possibility whose contour remains obscure, whose coming remains uncertain.

Thinking must first learn what remains reserved and in store for thinking to get involved in. It prepares its own transformation in this learning.

We are thinking of the possibility that the world civilization which is just now beginning might one day overcome the technological-scientific-industrial character as the sole criterion of man's world sojourn. This may happen not of and through itself, but in virtue of the readiness of man for a determination which, whether listened to or not, always speaks in the destiny of man which has not yet been decided. It is just as uncertain whether world civilization will soon be abruptly destroyed or whether it will be stabilized for a long time, in a stabilization, however, which will not rest in something enduring, but rather establish itself in a sequence of changes, each of which presenting the latest fashion.

The preparatory thinking in question does not wish and is not able to predict the future. It only attempts to say something to the present which was already said a long time ago precisely at the beginning of philosophy and for that beginning, but has not been explicitly thought. For the time being, it must be sufficient to refer to this with the brevity required. We shall take a directive which philosophy offers as an aid in our undertaking.

When we ask about the task of thinking, this means in the scope of philosophy: to determine that which concerns thinking, which is still controversial for thinking, which is the controversy. This is what the word "matter" means in the German language. It designates that with which thinking has to do in the case at hand, in Plato's language *to pragma auto.*

In recent times, philosophy has of its own accord expressly called thinking "to the things themselves." Let us mention two cases which receive particular attention today. We hear this call "to the things themselves" in the "Preface" which Hegel has placed before his work which was published in 1807, *System of Science,* first part: "The Phenomenology of Spirit." This preface is not the preface to the *Phenomenology,* but to the *System of Science,* to the whole of philosophy. The call "to the things themselves" refers ultimately—and that means: according to the matter, primarily—to the *Science of Logic.*

In the call "to the things themselves," the emphasis lies on the "themselves." Heard superficially, the call has the sense of a rejection. The inadequate relations to the matter of philosophy are rejected. Mere talk about the purpose of philosophy belongs to these relations, but so does mere reporting about the results of philosophical thinking. Both are never the real totality of philosophy. The totality shows itself only in its becoming. This occurs in the developmental presentation of the matter. In the presentation, theme and method coincide. For Hegel, this identity is called: the idea. With the idea, the matter of philosophy "itself" comes to appear. However, this matter is historically determined: subjectivity. With Descartes' *ego cogito,* says Hegel, philosophy steps on firm ground for the first time where it can be at home. If the *fundamentum absolutum* is attained with the *ego cogito* as the distinctive *subjectum,* this means: The subject is the *hypokeimenon* which is transferred to consciousness, what is truly present, what is unclearly enough called "substance" in traditional language.

When Hegel explains in the Preface "The true (in philosophy) is to be understood and expressed not as substance, but just as much as subject," then this means: The Being of beings, the presence of what is present, is only manifest and thus complete presence when it becomes present as such for itself in the absolute Idea. But since Descartes, *idea* means: *perceptio.* Being's coming to itself occurs in speculative dialectic. Only the movement of the idea, the method, is the matter itself. The call "to the thing itself" requires a philosophical method appropriate in it.

However, what the matter of philosophy should be is presumed to be decided from the outset. The matter of philosophy as metaphysics is the Being of beings, their presence in the form of substantiality and subjectivity.

A hundred years later, the call "to the thing itself" again is uttered in Husserl's treatise *Philosophy as Exact Science.* It was published in the first volume of the journal *Logos* in 1910–11. Again, the call has at first the sense of a rejection. But here it aims in another direction than Hegel's. It concerns naturalistic psychology which claims to be the genuine scientific method of investigating consciousness. For this method blocks access to the phenomena of intentional consciousness from the very beginning. But the call "to the thing itself" is at the same time directed against historicism which gets lost in treatises about the standpoints of philosophy and in the ordering of types of philosophical *Weltanschauungen.* About this Husserl says in italics: *"The stimulus for investigation must start not with philosophies, but with issues and problems."*

And what is at stake in philosophical investigation? In accordance with the same tradition, it is for Husserl as for Hegel the subjectivity of consciousness. For Husserl, the *Cartesian Meditations* were not only the topic of the Parisian lectures in February, 1920. Rather, since the time following the *Logical Investigations,* their spirit accompanied the impassioned course of his philosophical investigations to the end. In its negative and also in its positive sense, the call "to the thing itself" determines the securing and development of method. It also determines the procedure of philosophy by means of which the matter itself can be demonstrated as a datum. For Husserl, "the principle of all principles" is first of all not a principle of content, but one of method. In his work published in 1913, Husserl devoted a special section to the determination of "the principle of all principles." "No conceivable theory can upset this principle," says Husserl.

"The principle of all principles" reads:

> that very primordial dator Intuition is a source of authority (Rechtsquelle) for knowledge, that whatever presents itself in "Intuition" in primordial form (as it were in its bodily reality), is simply to be accepted as it gives itself out to be, though only within the limits in which it then presents itself.

"The principle of all principles" contains the thesis of the precedence of method. This principle decides what matter alone can suffice for the method. "The principle of principles" requires reduction to absolute subjectivity as the matter of philosophy. The transcendental reduction to absolute subjectivity gives and secures the possibility of grounding the objectivity of all objects (the Being of this being) in its valid structure and consistency, that is, in its constitution, in and through subjectivity. Thus transcendental subjectivity proves to be "the sole absolute being." At the same time, transcendental reduction as the method of "universal science" of the constitution of the Being of beings has the same mode of being as this absolute being, that is, the manner of the matter most native to philosophy. The method is not only directed toward the matter of philosophy. It does not just belong to the matter as a key belongs to a lock. Rather, it belongs to the matter because it is "the matter itself." If one wanted to ask: Where does "the principle of all principles" get its unshakable right, the answer would have to be: from transcendental subjectivity which is already presupposed as the matter of philosophy.

We have chosen a discussion of the call "to the thing itself" as our guideline. It was to bring us to the path which leads us to a determination of the task of thinking at the end of philosophy. Where are we now? We have arrived at the insight that for the call "to the thing itself," what concerns philosophy as its matter is established from the outset. From the perspective of Hegel and Husserl—and not only from their perspective—the matter of philosophy is subjectivity. It is not the matter as such that is controversial for the call, but rather its presentation by which the matter itself becomes present. Hegel's speculative dialectic is the movement in which the matter as such comes to itself, comes to its own presence. Husserl's method is supposed to bring the matter of philosophy to its ultimately originary givenness, that means: to its own presence.

The two methods are as different as they could possibly be. But the matter as such which they are to present is the same, although it is experienced in different ways.

But of what help are these discoveries to us in our attempt to bring the task of thinking to view? They don't help us at all as long as we do not go beyond a mere discussion of the call and ask what remains unthought in the call "to the thing itself." Questioning in this way, we can become aware how something which it is no longer the matter of philosophy to think conceals itself precisely where philosophy has brought its matter to absolute knowledge and to ultimate evidence.

But what remains unthought in the matter of philosophy as well as in its method? Speculative dialectic is a mode in which the matter of philosophy comes to appeal of itself and for itself, and thus becomes presence. Such appearance necessarily occurs in some light. Only by virtue of light, i.e., through brightness, can what shines show itself, that is, radiate. But brightness in its turn rests upon something open, something free which might illuminate it here and there, now and then. Brightness plays in the open and wars there with darkness. Wherever a present being encounters another present being or even only lingers near it—but also where, as with Hegel, one being mirrors itself in another speculatively—there openness already rules, open region is in play. Only this openness grants to the movement of speculative thinking the passage through that which it thinks.

We call this openness which grants a possible letting-appear and show "opening." In the history of language, the German word "opening" is a borrowed translation of the French *clairière*. It is formed in accordance with the older words *Waldung* (foresting) and *Feldung* (fielding).

The forest clearing (opening) is experienced in contrast to dense forest, called "density" (*Dickung*) in older language. The substantive "opening" goes back to the verb "to open." The adjective *licht* "open" is the same word as "light." To open something means: To make something light, free and open, e.g., to make the forest free of trees at one place. The openness thus originating is the clearing. What is light in the sense of being free and open has nothing in common with the adjective "light," meaning "bright"—neither linguistically nor factually. This is to be observed for the difference between openness and light. Still, it is possible that a factual relation between the two exists. Light can stream into the clearing, into its openness, and let brightness play with darkness in it. But light never first creates openness. Rather, light presupposes openness. However, the clearing, the opening, is not only free for brightness and darkness, but also for resonance and echo, for sounding and diminishing of sound. The clearing is the open for everything that is present and absent.

It is necessary for thinking to become explicitly aware of the matter called opening here. We are not extracting mere notions from mere words, e.g., "opening," as it might easily appear on the surface. Rather, we must observe the unique matter which is adequately named with the name "opening." What the word designates in the connection we are now thinking, free openness, is a "primal phenomenon," to use a word of Goethe's. We would have to say a primal matter. Goethe notes: "Look for nothing behind phenomena: they themselves are what is to be learned." This means: The phenomenon itself, in the present case the opening, sets us the task of learning from it while questioning it, that is, of letting it say something to us.

Accordingly, we may suggest that the day will come when we will not shun the question whether the opening, the free open, may not be that within which alone pure space and ecstatic time and everything present and absent in them have the place which gathers and protects everything.

In the same way as speculative dialectical thinking, originary intuition and its evidence remain dependent upon openness which already dominates, upon the opening. What is evident is what can be immediately intuited. *Evidentia* is the word which Cicero uses to translate the Greek *enargeia*, that is, to transform it into the Roman. *Enargeia*, which has the same root as *argentum* (silver), means that which in itself and of itself radiates and brings itself to light. In the Greek language, one is not speaking about the action of seeing, about *videre*, but about that which gleams and radiates. But it can only radiate if openness has already been granted. The beam of light does not first create the opening, openness, it only traverses it. It is only such openness that grants to giving and receiving at all what is free, that in which they can remain and must move.

All philosophical thinking which explicitly or inexplicitly follows the call "to the thing itself" is already admitted to the free space of the opening in its movement and with its method. But philosophy knows nothing of the opening. Philosophy does speak about the light of reason, but does not heed the opening of Being. The *lumen naturale*, the light of reason, throws light only on openness. It does concern the opening, but so little does it form it that it needs it in order to be able to illuminate what is present in the opening. This is true not only of philosophy's *method,* but also and primarily of its *matter,* that is, of the presence of what is present. To what extent the *subiectum,* the *hypokeimenon,* that which already lies present, thus what is present in its presence is constantly thought also in subjectivity cannot be shown here in detail.

We are concerned now with something else. Whether or not what is present is experienced, comprehended or presented, presence as lingering in openness always remains dependent upon the prevalent opening. What is absent, too, cannot be as such unless it presences in the *free space of the opening.*

All metaphysics including its opponent positivism speaks the language of Plato. The basic word of its thinking, that is, of his presentation of the Being of beings, is *eidos, idea:* the outward appearance in which beings as such show themselves. Outward appearance, however, is a manner of presence. No outward appearance without light—Plato already knew this. But there is no light and no brightness without the opening. Even darkness needs it. How else could we happen into darkness and wander through it? Still, the opening as such as it prevails through Being, through presence, remains unthought in philosophy, although the opening is spoken about in philosophy's beginning. How does this occur and with which names? Answer:

In Parmenides' reflective poem which, as far as we know, was the first to reflect explicitly upon the Being of beings, which still today, although unheard, speaks in the sciences into which philosophy dissolves. Parmenides listens to the claim:

> . . . *kreo de se panta puthestha*
> *emen aletheies eukukleos atremes etor*
> *ede broton doxas, tais ouk emi pistis alethes.*

> *Fragment 1, 28 ff.*

> . . . but you should learn all:
> the untrembling heart of unconcealment, well-rounded
> and also the opinions of mortals,
> lacking the ability to trust what is unconcealed.

Aletheia, unconcealment, is named here. It is called well-rounded because it is turned in the pure sphere of the circle in which beginning and end are everywhere the same. In this turning, there is no possibility of twisting, deceit and closure. The meditative man is to experience the untrembling heart of unconcealment. What does the word about the untrembling heart of unconcealment mean? It means unconcealment itself in what is most its own, means the place of stillness which gathers in itself what grants unconcealment to begin with. That is the opening of what is open. We ask: openness for what? We have already reflected upon the fact that the path of thinking, speculative and intuitive, needs the traversable opening. But in that opening rests possible radiance, that is, the possible presencing of presence itself.

What prior to everything else first grants unconcealment in the path on which thinking pursues one thing and perceives it: *hotos estin . . . einai:* that presence presences. The opening grants first of all the possibility of the path to presence, and grants the possible presencing of that presence itself. We must think *aletheia,* unconcealment, as the opening which first grants Being and thinking and their presencing to and for each other. The quiet heart of the opening is the place of stillness from which alone the possibility of the belonging together of Being and thinking, that is, presence and perceiving, can arise at all.

The possible claim to a binding character or commitment of thinking is grounded in this bond. Without the preceding experience of *aletheia* as the opening, all talk about committed and noncommitted thinking remains without foundation. Where does Plato's determination of presence as *idea* have its binding character from? With regard to what is Aristotle's interpretation of presencing as *energeia* binding?

Strangely enough, we cannot even ask these questions always neglected in philosophy as long as we have not experienced what Parmenides had to experience: *aletheia,* unconcealment. The path to it is distinguished from the street on which the opinion of mortals must wander around. *Aletheia* is nothing mortal, just as little as death itself.

It is not for the sake of etymology that I stubbornly translate the name *aletheia* as unconcealment, but for the matter which must be considered when we think that which is called Being and thinking adequately. Unconcealment is, so to speak, the element in which Being and thinking and their belonging together exist. *Aletheia* is named at the beginning of philosophy, but afterward it is not explicitly thought as such by philosophy. For since Aristotle it became the task of philosophy as metaphysics to think beings as such ontotheologically.

If this is so, we have no right to sit in judgment over philosophy, as though it left something unheeded, neglected it and was thus marred by some essential deficiency. The reference to what is unthought in philosophy is not a criticism of philosophy. If a criticism is necessary now, then it rather concerns the attempt which is becoming more and more urgent ever since *Being and Time* to ask about a possible task of thinking at the end of philosophy. For the question now arises, late enough: Why is *aletheia* not translated with the usual name, with the word "truth"? The answer must be:

Insofar as truth is understood in the traditional "natural" sense as the correspondence of knowledge with beings demonstrated in beings, but also insofar as truth is interpreted as the certainty of the knowledge of Being, *aletheia,* unconcealment in the sense of the opening may not be equated with truth. Rather, *aletheia,* unconcealment thought as opening, first grants the possibility of truth. For truth itself, just as Being and thinking, can only be what it is in the element of the opening. Evidence, certainty in every degree, every kind of verification of *veritas* already move *with* that *veritas* in the realm of the prevalent opening.

Aletheia, unconcealment thought as the opening of presence, is not yet truth. Is *aletheia* then less than truth? Or is it more because it first grants truth as *adequatio* and *certitudo,* because there can be no presence and presenting outside of the realm of the opening?

This question we leave to thinking as a task. Thinking must consider whether it can even raise this question at all as long as it thinks philosophically, that is, in the strict sense of metaphysics which questions what is present only with regard to its presence.

In any case, one thing becomes clear: To raise the question of *aletheia,* of unconcealment as such, is not the same as raising the question of truth. For this reason, it was inadequate and misleading to call *aletheia* in the sense of opening, truth. The talk about the "truth of Being" has a justified meaning in Hegel's *Science of Logic,* because here truth means the certainty of absolute knowledge. But Hegel also, as little as Husserl, as little as all metaphysics, does not ask about Being as Being, that is, does not raise the question how there can be presence as such. There is presence only when opening is dominant. Opening is named with *aletheia,* unconcealment, but not thought as such.

The natural concept of truth does not mean unconcealment, not in the philosophy of the Greeks either. It is often and justifiably pointed out that the word *alethes* is already used by Homer only in the *verba dicendi,* in statement and thus in the sense of correctness and reliability, not in the sense of unconcealment. But this reference means only that neither the poets nor everyday language usage, not even philosophy see themselves confronted with the task of asking how truth, that is, the correctness of statements, is granted only in the element of the opening of presence.

In the scope of this question, we must acknowledge the fact that *aletheia,* unconcealment in the sense of the opening of presence, was originally only experienced as *orthotes,* as the correctness of representations and statements. But then the assertion about the essential transformation of truth, that is, from unconcealment to correctness, is also untenable. Instead we must say: *Aletheia,* as opening of presence and presenting in thinking and saying, originally comes under the perspective of *homoiosis and adaequatio,* that is, the perspective of adequation in the sense of the correspondence of representing with what is present.

But this process inevitably provokes another question: How is it that *aletheia,* unconcealment, appears to man's natural experience and speaking *only* as correctness and dependability? Is it because man's ecstatic sojourn in the openness of presencing is turned only toward what is present and the existent presenting of what is present? But what else does this mean than that presence as such, and together with it the opening granting it, remain unheeded? Only what *aletheia* as opening grants is experienced and thought, not what it is as such.

This remains concealed. Does this happen by chance? Does it happen only as a consequence of the carelessness of human thinking? Or does it happen because self-concealing, concealment, *lethe* belongs to *a-letheia,* not just as an addition, not as shadow to light, but rather as the heart of *aletheia?* And does not even a keeping and preserving rule in this self-concealing of the opening of presence from which unconcealment can be granted to begin with, and thus what is present can appear in its presence?

If this were so, then the opening would not be the mere opening of presence, but the opening of presence concealing itself, the opening of a self-concealing sheltering.

If this were so, then with these questions we would reach the path to the task of thinking at the end of philosophy.

But isn't this all unfounded mysticism or even bad mythology, in any case a ruinous irrationalism, the denial of *ratio?*

I return to the question: What does *ratio, nous, noein,* perceiving [*Vernunft—Vernehmen*] mean? What does ground and principle and especially principle of all principles mean? Can this ever be sufficiently determined unless we experience *aletheia* in a Greek manner as unconcealment and then, above and beyond the Greek, think it as the opening of self-concealing? As long as *ratio* and the rational still remain questionable in what is their own, talk about irrationalism is unfounded. The technological scientific rationalization ruling the present age justifies itself every day more surprisingly by its immense results. But these results say nothing about what the possibility of the rational and the irrational first grants. The effect proves the correctness of technological scientific rationalization. But is the manifest character of what-is exhausted by what is demonstrable? Doesn't the insistence on what is demonstrable block the way to what-is?

Perhaps there is a thinking which is more sober than the irresistible race of rationalization and the sweeping character of cybernetics. Presumably it is precisely this sweeping quality which is extremely irrational.

Perhaps there is a thinking outside of the distinction of rational and irrational still more sober than scientific technology, more sober and thus removed, without effect and yet having its own necessity. When we ask about the task of this thinking, then not only this thinking, but also the question about it is first made questionable. In view of the whole philosophical tradition, this means:

We all still need an education in thinking, and before that first a knowledge of what being educated and uneducated in thinking means. In this respect, Aristotle gives us a hint in Book IV of his *Metaphysics*. It reads: *esti gar apaideusia to me gignoskein tinon dei zetein apodeixin kai tinon ou dei.* "For it is uneducated not to have an eye for when it is necessary to look for a proof, and when this is not necessary."

This sentence demands careful reflection. For it is not yet decided in what way that which needs no proof in order to become accessible to thinking is to be experienced. Is it dialectical mediation or originary intuition or neither of the two? Only the peculiar quality of that which demands of us above all else to be admitted can decide about that. But how is this to make the decision possible for us before we have not admitted it? In what circle are we moving here, inevitably?

Is it the *eukukleos alethein,* well-founded unconcealment itself, thought as the opening?

Does the name for the task of thinking then read instead of *Being and Time:* Opening and Presence?

But where does the opening come from and how is it given? What speaks in the "It gives"?

The task of thinking would then be the surrender of previous thinking to the determination of the matter of thinking.

MARTIN HEIDEGGER

The Origin of the Work of Art

Origin here means that from and by which something is what it is and as it is. What something is, as it is, we call its essence or nature. The origin of something is the source of its nature. The question concerning the origin of the work of art asks about the source of its nature. On the usual view, the work arises out of and by means of the activity of the artist. But by what and whence is the artist what he is? By the work; for to say that the work does credit to the master means that it is the work that first lets the artist emerge as a master of his art. The artist is the origin of the work. The work is the origin of the artist. Neither is without the other. Nevertheless, neither is the sole support of the other. In themselves and in their interrelations artist and work *are* each of them by virtue of a third thing which is prior to both, namely that which also gives artist and work of art their names—art. . . .

Whatever the decision may be, the question of the origin of the work of art becomes a question about the nature of art. Since the question whether and how art in general exists must still remain open, we shall attempt to discover the nature of art in the place where art undoubtedly prevails in a real way. Art is present in the art work. But what and how is a work of art? . . .

In order to discover the nature of the art that really prevails in the work, let us go to the actual work and ask the work what and how it is.

Works of art are familiar to everyone. Architectural and sculptural works can be seen installed in public places, in churches, and in dwellings. Art works of the most diverse periods and peoples are housed in collections and exhibitions. If we consider the works in their untouched actuality and do not deceive ourselves, the result is that the works are as naturally present as are things. The picture hangs on the wall like a rifle or a hat. A painting, e.g., the one by Van Gogh that represents a pair of peasant shoes, travels from one exhibition to another. Works of art are shipped like coal from the Ruhr and logs from the Black Forest. During

Excerpted from Martin Heidegger, *Poetry, Language, Thought* (New York: Harper and Row, 1971), 17–87.

the First World War Hölderlin's hymns were packed in the soldier's knapsack together with cleaning gear. Beethoven's quartets lie in the storerooms of the publishing house like potatoes in a cellar. . . .

Our aim is to arrive at the immediate and full reality of the work of art, for only in this way shall we discover real art also within it. Hence we must first bring to view the thingly element of the work. To this end it is necessary that we should know with sufficient clarity what a thing is. Only then can we say whether the art work is a thing, but a thing to which something else adheres; only then can we decide whether the work is at bottom something else and not a thing at all.

THING AND WORK

What in truth is the thing, so far as it is a thing? When we inquire in this way, our aim is to come to know the thing-being (thingness) of the thing. The point is to discover the thingly character of the thing. To this end we have to be acquainted with the sphere to which all those entities belong which we have long called by the name of thing. . . .

The interpretations of the thingness of the thing which, predominant in the course of Western thought, have long become self-evident and are now in everyday use, may be reduced to three.

This block of granite, for example, is a mere thing. It is hard, heavy, extended, bulky, shapeless, rough, colored, partly dull, partly shiny. We can take note of all these features in the stone. Thus we acknowledge its characteristics. But still, the traits signify something proper to the stone itself. They are its properties. The thing has them. The thing? What are we thinking of when we now have the thing in mind? Obviously a thing is not merely an aggregate of traits, nor an accumulation of properties by which that aggregate arises. A thing, as everyone thinks he knows, is that around which the properties have assembled. We speak in this connection of the core of things. The Greeks are supposed to have called it *to hupokeimenon*. For them, this core of the thing was something lying at the ground of the thing, something always already there. The characteristics, however, are called *ta sumbebekota,* that which has always turned up already along with the given core and occurs along with it.

These designations are no arbitrary names. Something that lies beyond the purview of this essay speaks in them, the basic Greek experience of the Being of beings in the sense of presence. It is by these determinations, however, that the interpretation of the thingness of the thing is established which henceforth becomes standard, and the Western interpretation of the Being of beings stabilized. The process begins with the appropriation of Greek words by Roman-Latin thought. *Hupokeimenon* becomes *subiectum; hupostasis* becomes *substantia; sumbebekos* becomes *accidens*. However, this translation of Greek names into Latin is in no way the innocent process it is considered to this day. Beneath the seemingly literal and thus faithful translation there is concealed, rather, a *trans*lation of Greek experience into a different way of thinking. *Roman thought takes over the Greek words without a corresponding, equally authentic experience of what they say, without the Greek word.* The rootlessness of Western thought begins with this translation.

According to current opinion, this definition of the thingness of the thing as the substance with its accidents seems to correspond to our natural outlook on things. No wonder that the current attitude toward things—our way of addressing ourselves to things and speaking about them—has adapted itself to this common view of the thing. A simple propositional statement consists of the subject, which is the Latin translation, hence already a reinterpretation, of *hupokeimenon* and the predicate, in which the thing's traits are stated of it. Who would have the temerity to assail these simple fundamental relations between thing and statement, between sentence structure and thing-structure? Nevertheless we must ask: Is the structure of a simple propositional statement (the combination of subject and predicate) the mirror image of the structure of the thing (of the union of substance with accidents)? Or could it be that even the structure of the thing as thus envisaged is a projection of the framework of the sentence?

What could be more obvious than that man transposes his propositional way of understanding things into the structure of the thing itself? Yet this view, seemingly critical yet actually rash and ill-considered, would have to explain first how such a transposition of propositional structure into the thing is supposed to be possible without the thing having already become visible. The question which comes first and functions as the standard, proposition structure or thing-structure remains to this hour undecided. It even remains doubtful whether in this form the question is at all decidable. . . .

That which gives things their constancy and pith but is also at the same time the source of their particular mode of sensuous pressure—colored, resonant, hard, massive—is the matter in things. In this analysis of the thing as matter (*hule*), form (*morphe*) is already coposited. What is constant in a thing, its consistency, lies in the fact that matter stands together with a form. The thing is formed matter. This interpretation appeals to the immediate view with which the thing solicits us by its looks (*eidos*). In this synthesis of matter and form a thing-concept has finally been found which applies equally to things of nature and to use-objects. . . .

Usefulness is the basic feature from which this entity regards us, that is, flashes at us and thereby is present and thus is this entity. Both the formative act and the choice of material—a choice given with the act—and therewith the dominance of the conjunction of matter and form, are all grounded in such usefulness. A being that falls under usefulness is always the product of a process of making. It is made as a piece of equipment for something. As determinations of beings, accordingly, matter and form have their proper place in the essential nature of equipment. This name designates what is produced expressly for employment and use. Matter and form are in no case original determinations of the thingness of the mere thing.

A piece of equipment, a pair of shoes for instance, when finished, is also self-contained like the mere thing, but it does not have the character of having taken shape by itself like the granite boulder. On the other hand, equipment displays an affinity with the art work insofar as it is something produced by the human hand. However, by its self-sufficient presence the work of art is similar rather to the mere thing which has taken shape by itself and is self-contained. Nevertheless we do not count such works among mere things. As a rule it is the use-objects around us that are the nearest and authentic things. Thus the piece of equipment is half thing, because characterized by thingliness, and yet it is something more; at the same time it is half art work and yet something less, because lacking the self-sufficiency of the art work. Equipment has a peculiar position intermediate between thing and work, assuming that such a calculated ordering of them is permissible.

The matter-form structure, however, by which the being of a piece of equipment is first determined, readily presents itself as the immediately intelligible constitution of every entity, because here man himself as maker participates in the way in which the piece of equipment comes into being. Because equipment takes an intermediate place between mere thing and work, the suggestion is that nonequipmental beings—things and works and ultimately everything that is—are to be comprehended with the help of the being of equipment (the matter-form structure). . . .

We choose as example a common sort of equipment—a pair of peasant shoes. We do not even need to exhibit actual pieces of this sort of useful article in order to describe them. Everyone is acquainted with them. But since it is a matter here of direct description, it may be well to facilitate the visual realization of them. For this purpose a pictorial representation suffices. We shall choose a well-known painting by Van Gogh, who painted such shoes several times. But what is there to see here? Everyone knows what shoes consist of. If they are not wooden or bast shoes, there will be leather soles and uppers, joined together by thread and nails.

Such gear serves to clothe the feet. Depending on the use to which the shoes are to be put, whether for work in the field or for dancing, matter and form will differ.

Such statements, no doubt correct, only explicate what we already know. The equipmental quality of equipment consists in its usefulness. But what about this usefulness itself? In conceiving it, do we already conceive along with it the equipmental character of equipment? In order to succeed in doing this, must we not look out for useful equipment in its use? The peasant woman wears her shoes in the field. Only here are they what they are. They are all the more genuinely so, the less the peasant woman thinks about the shoes while she is at work, or looks at them at all, or is even aware of them. She stands and walks in them. That is how shoes actually serve. It is in this process of the use of equipment that we must actually encounter the character of equipment.

As long as we only imagine a pair of shoes in general, or simply look at the empty, unused shoes as they merely stand there in the picture, we shall never discover what the equipmental being of the equipment in truth is. From Van Gogh's painting we cannot even tell where these shoes stand. There is nothing surrounding this pair of peasant shoes in or to which they might belong—only an undefined space. There are not even clods of soil from the field or the field-path sticking to them, which would at least hint at their use. A pair of peasant shoes and nothing more. And yet—

From the dark opening of the worn insides of the shoes the toilsome tread of the worker stares forth. In the stiffly rugged heaviness of the shoes there is the accumulated tenacity of her slow trudge through the far-spreading and ever-uniform furrows of the field swept by a raw wind. On the leather lie the dampness and richness of the soil. Under the soles slides the loneliness of the field-path as evening falls. In the shoes vibrates the silent call of the earth, its quiet gift of the ripening grain and its unexplained self-refusal in the fallow desolation of the wintry field. This equipment is pervaded by uncomplaining anxiety as to the certainty of bread, the wordless joy of having once more withstood want, the trembling before the impending childbed and shivering at the surrounding menace of death. This equipment belongs to the *earth,* and it is protected in the *world* of the peasant woman. From out of this protected belonging the equipment itself rises to its resting-within-itself.

But perhaps it is only in the picture that we notice all this about the shoes. The peasant woman, on the other hand, simply wears them. If only this simple wearing were so simple. When she takes off her shoes late in the evening, in deep but healthy fatigue, and reaches out for them again in the still dim dawn, or passes them by on the day of rest, she knows all this without noticing or reflecting. The equipmental quality of the equipment consists indeed in its usefulness. But this usefulness itself rests in the abundance of an essential being of the equipment. We call it reliability. By virtue of this reliability the peasant woman is made privy to the silent call of the earth; by virtue of the reliability of the equipment she is sure of her world. World and earth exist for her, and for those who are with her in her mode of being, only thus—in the equipment. We say "only" and therewith fall into error; for the reliability of the equipment first gives to the simple world its security and assures to the earth the freedom of its steady thrust.

The equipmental being of equipment, reliability, keeps gathered within itself all things according to their manner and extent. The usefulness of equipment is nevertheless only the essential consequence of reliability. The former vibrates in the latter and would be nothing without it. A single piece of equipment is worn out and used up; but at the same time the use itself also falls into disuse, wears away, and becomes usual. Thus equipmentality wastes away, sinks into mere stuff. In such wasting, reliability vanishes. This dwindling, however, to which use-things owe their boringly obtrusive usualness, is only one more testimony to the original nature of equipmental being. The worn-out usualness of the equipment then obtrudes itself as the sole mode of being, apparently peculiar to it exclusively. Only blank usefulness now remains visible. It awakens the impression that the origin of equipment lies in a mere fabricating that impresses a form upon some matter. Nevertheless, in its genuinely equipmental being, equipment stems from a more distant source. Matter and form and their distinction have a deeper origin.

The repose of equipment resting within itself consists in its reliability. Only in this reliability do we discern what equipment in truth is. But we still know nothing of what we first sought: the thing's thingly character. And we know nothing at all of what we really and solely seek: the workly character of the work in the sense of the work of art.

Or have we already learned something unwittingly, in passing so to speak, about the work-being of the work?

The equipmental quality of equipment was discovered. But how? Not by a description and explanation of a pair of shoes actually present; not by a report about the process of making shoes; and also not by the observation of the actual use of shoes occurring here and there; but only by bringing ourselves before Van Gogh's painting. This painting spoke. In the vicinity of the work we were suddenly somewhere else than we usually tend to be.

The art work let us know what shoes are in truth. It would be the worst self-deception to think that our description, as a subjective action, had first depicted everything thus and then projected it into the painting. If anything is questionable here, it is rather that we experienced too little in the neighborhood of the work and that we expressed the experience too crudely and too literally. But above all, the work did not, as it might seem at first, serve merely for a better visualizing of what a piece of equipment is. Rather, the equipmentality of equipment first genuinely arrives at its appearance through the work and only in the work.

What happens here? What is at work in the work? Van Gogh's painting is the disclosure of what the equipment, the pair of peasant shoes, *is* in truth. This entity emerges into the unconcealedness of its being. The Greeks called the unconcealedness of beings *aletheia*. We say "truth" and think little enough in using this word. If there occurs in the work a disclosure of a particular being, disclosing what and how it is, then there is here an occurring, a happening of truth at work.

In the work of art the truth of an entity has set itself to work. "To set" means here: to bring to a stand. Some particular entity, a pair of peasant shoes, comes in the work to stand in the light of its being. The being of the being comes into the steadiness of its shining.

The nature of art would then be this: the truth of beings setting itself to work. But until now art presumably has had to do with the beautiful and beauty, and not with truth. The arts that produce such works are called the beautiful or fine arts, in contrast with the applied or industrial arts that manufacture equipment. In fine art the art itself is not beautiful, but is called so because it produces the beautiful. Truth, in contrast, belongs to logic. Beauty, however, is reserved for aesthetics. . . .

Our formulation of the question of the work has been shaken because we asked, not about the work but half about a thing and half about equipment. Still, this formulation of the question was not first developed by us. It is the formulation native to aesthetics. The way in which aesthetics views the art work from the outset is dominated by the traditional interpretation of all beings. But the shaking of this accustomed formulation is not the essential point. What matters is a first opening of our vision to the fact that what is workly in the work, equipmental in equipment, and thingly in the thing comes closer to us only when we think the Being of beings. To this end it is necessary beforehand that the barriers of our preconceptions fall away and that the current pseudo concepts be set aside. That is why we had to take this detour. But it brings us directly to a road that may lead to a determination of the thingly feature in the work. The thingly feature in the work should not be denied; but if it belongs admittedly to the work-being of the work, it must be conceived by way of the work's workly nature. If this is so, then the road toward the determination of the thingly reality of the work leads not from thing to work but from work to thing.

The art work opens up in its own way the Being of beings. This opening up, i.e., this deconcealing, i.e., the truth of beings, happens in the work. In the art work, the truth of what is has set itself to work. Art is truth setting itself to work. What is truth itself, that it sometimes comes to pass as art? What is this setting-itself-to-work?

THE WORK AND TRUTH

The origin of the art work is art. But what is art? Art is real in the art work. Hence we first seek the reality of the work. In what does it consist? Art works universally display a thingly character, albeit in a wholly distinct way. The attempt to interpret this thing-character of the work with the aid of the usual thing-concepts failed—not only because these concepts do not lay hold of the thingly feature, but because, in raising the question of its thingly substructure, we force the work into a preconceived framework by which we obstruct our own access to the work-being of the work. Nothing can be discovered about the thingly aspect of the work so long as the pure self-subsistence of the work has not distinctly displayed itself.

Yet is the work ever in itself accessible? To gain access to the work, it would be necessary to remove it from all relations to something other than itself, in order to let it stand on its own for itself alone. But the artist's most peculiar intention already aims in this direction. The work is to be released by him to its pure self-subsistence. It is precisely in great art—and only such art is under consideration here—that the artist remains inconsequential as compared with the work, almost like a passageway that destroys itself in the creative process for the work to emerge. . . .

Where does a work belong? The work belongs, as work, uniquely within the realm that is opened up by itself. For the work-being of the work is present in, and only in, such opening up. We said that in the work there was a happening of truth at work. The reference to Van Gogh's picture tried to point to this happening. With regard to it there arose the question as to what truth is and how truth can happen.

We now ask the question of truth with a view to the work. But in order to become more familiar with what the question involves, it is necessary to make visible once more the happening of truth in the work. For this attempt let us deliberately select a work that cannot be ranked as representational art.

A building, a Greek temple, portrays nothing. It simply stands there in the middle of the rock-cleft valley. The building encloses the figure of the god, and in this concealment lets it stand out into the holy precinct through the open portico. By means of the temple, the god is present in the temple. This presence of the god is in itself the extension and delimitation of the precinct as a holy precinct. The temple and its precinct, however, do not fade away into the indefinite. It is the temple-work that first fits together and at the same time gathers around itself the unity of those paths and relations in which birth and death, disaster and blessing, victory and disgrace, endurance and decline acquire the shape of destiny for human being. The all-governing expanse of this open relational context is the world of this historical people. Only from and in this expanse does the nation first return to itself for the fulfillment of its vocation.

Standing there, the building rests on the rocky ground. This resting of the work draws up out of the rock the mystery of that rock's clumsy yet spontaneous support. Standing there, the building holds its ground against the storm raging above it and so first makes the storm itself manifest in its violence. The luster and gleam of the stone, though itself apparently glowing only by the grace of the sun, yet first brings to light the light of the day, the breadth of the sky, the darkness of the night. The temple's firm towering makes visible the invisible space of air. The steadfastness of the work contrasts with the surge of the surf, and its own repose brings out the raging of the sea. Tree and grass, eagle and bull, snake and cricket first enter into their distinctive shapes and thus come to appear as what they are. The Greeks early called this emerging and rising in itself and in all things *phusis*. It clears and illuminates, also, that on which and in which man bases his dwelling. We call this ground the *earth*. What this word says is not to be associated with the idea of a mass of matter deposited somewhere, or with the merely astronomical idea of a planet. Earth is that whence the arising brings back and shelters everything that arises without violation. In the things that arise, earth is present as the sheltering agent. . . .

In what, then, does the work-being of the work consist? Keeping steadily in view the points just crudely enough indicated, two essential features of the work may for the moment be brought out more distinctly. We set out here, from the long familiar foreground of the work's being, the thingly character which gives support to our customary attitude toward the work.

When a work is brought into a collection or placed in an exhibition we say also that it is "set up." But this setting up differs essentially from setting up in the sense of erecting a building, raising a statue, presenting a tragedy at a holy festival. Such setting up is erecting in the sense of dedication and praise. Here "setting up" no longer means a bare placing. To dedicate means to consecrate, in the sense that in setting up the work the holy is opened up as holy and the god is invoked into the openness of his presence. Praise belongs to dedication as doing honor to the dignity and splendor of the god. Dignity and splendor are not properties beside and behind which the god, too, stands as something distinct, but it is rather in the dignity, in the splendor that the god is present. In the reflected glory of this splendor there glows, i.e., there lightens itself, what we called the word. To e-rect means: to open the right in the sense of a guiding measure, a form in which what belongs to the nature of being gives guidance. But why is the setting up of a work an erecting that consecrates and praises? Because the work, in its work-being, demands it. How is it that the work comes to demand such a setting up? Because it itself, in its own work-being, is something that sets up. What does the work, as work, set up? Towering up within itself, the work opens up a *world* and keeps it abidingly in force.

To be a work means to set up a world. But what is it to be a world? The answer was hinted at when we referred to the temple. On the path we must follow here, the nature of world can only be indicated. What is more, this indication limits itself to warding off anything that might at first distort our view of the world's nature.

The world is not the mere collection of the countable or uncountable, familiar and unfamiliar things that are just there. But neither is it a merely imagined framework added by our representation to the sum of such given things. The *world worlds,* and is more fully in being than the tangible and perceptible realm in which we believe ourselves to be at home. World is never an object that stands before us and can be seen. World is the ever-nonobjective to which we are subject as long as the paths of birth and death, blessing and curse keep us transported into Being. Wherever those decisions of our history that relate to our very being are made, are taken up and abandoned by us, go unrecognized and are rediscovered by new inquiry, there the world worlds. A stone is worldless. Plant and animal likewise have no world; but they belong to the covert throng of a surrounding into which they are linked. The peasant woman, on the other hand, has a world because she dwells in the overtness of beings, of the things that are. Her equipment, in its reliability, gives to this world a necessity and nearness of its own. By the opening up of a world, all things gain their lingering and hastening, their remoteness and nearness, their scope and limits. In a world's worlding is gathered that spaciousness out of which the protective grace of the gods is granted or withheld. Even this doom of the god remaining absent is a way in which world worlds.

A work, by being a work, makes space for that spaciousness. "To make space for" means here especially to liberate the Open and to establish it in its structure. This in-stalling occurs through the erecting mentioned earlier. The work as work sets up a world. The work holds open the Open of the world. But the setting up of a world is only the first essential feature in the work-being of a work to be referred to here. Starting again from the foreground of the work, we shall attempt to make clear in the same way the second essential feature that belongs with the first.

When a work is created, brought forth out of this or that work-material—stone, wood, metal, color, language, tone—we say also that it is made, set forth out of it. But just as the work requires a setting up in the sense of a consecrating-praising erection, because the work's work-being consists in the setting up of a world, so a setting forth is needed because the work-being of the work itself has the character of setting forth. The work as work, in its presencing, is a setting forth, a making. But what does the work set forth? We come to know about this only when we explore what comes to the fore and is customarily spoken of as the making or production of works.

To work-being there belongs the setting up of a world. Thinking of it within this perspective, what is the nature of that in the work which is usually called the work material? Because it is determined by usefulness and serviceability, equipment takes into its service that of which it consists: the matter. In fabricating equipment—e.g., an ax—stone is used, and used up. It disappears into usefulness. The material is all the better and more suitable the less it resists perishing in the equipmental being of the equipment. By contrast the temple-work, in setting up a world, does not cause the material to disappear, but rather causes it to come forth for the very first time and to come into the Open of the work's world. The rock comes to bear and rest and so first becomes rock; metals come to glitter and shimmer, colors to glow, tones to sing, the word to speak. All this comes forth as the work sets itself back into the massiveness and heaviness of stone, into the firmness and pliancy of wood, into the hardness and luster of metal, into the lighting and darkening of color, into the clang of tone, and into the naming power of the word.

That into which the work sets itself back and which it causes to come forth in this setting back of itself we called the earth. Earth is that which comes forth and shelters. Earth, self-dependent, is effortless and untiring. Upon the earth and in it, historical man grounds his dwelling in the world. In setting up a world, the work sets forth the earth. This setting forth must be thought here in the strict sense of the word. The work moves the earth itself into the Open of a world and keeps it there. *The work lets the earth be an earth*.

But why must this setting forth of the earth happen in such a way that the work sets itself back into it? What is the earth that it attains to the unconcealed in just such a manner? A stone presses downward and manifests its heaviness. But while this heaviness exerts an opposing pressure upon us it denies us any penetration into it. If we attempt such a penetration by breaking open the rock, it still does not display in its fragments anything inward that has been disclosed. The stone has instantly withdrawn again into the same dull pressure and bulk of its fragments. If we try to lay hold of the stone's heaviness in another way, by placing the stone on a balance, we merely bring the heaviness into the form of a calculated weight. This perhaps very precise determination of the stone remains a number, but the weight's burden has escaped us. Color shines and wants only to shine. When we analyze it in rational terms by measuring its wavelengths, it is gone. It shows itself only when it remains undisclosed and unexplained. Earth thus shatters every attempt to penetrate into it. It causes every merely calculating importunity upon it to turn into a destruction. This destruction may herald itself under the appearance of mastery and of progress in the form of the technical-scientific objectivation of nature, but this mastery nevertheless remains an impotence of will. The earth appears openly cleared as itself only when it is perceived and preserved as that which is by nature undisclosable, that which shrinks from every disclosure and constantly keeps itself closed up. All things of earth, and the earth itself as a whole, flow together into a reciprocal accord. But this confluence is not a blurring of their outlines. Here there flows the stream, restful within itself, of the setting of bounds, which delimits everything present within its presence. Thus in each of the self-secluding things there is the same not-knowing-of-one-another. The earth is essentially self-secluding. To set forth the earth means to bring it into the Open as the self-secluding. . . .

The world is the self-disclosing openness of the broad paths of the simple and essential decisions in the destiny of an historical people. The earth is the spontaneous forthcoming of that which is continually self-secluding and to that extent sheltering and concealing. World and earth are essentially different from one another and yet are never separated. The world grounds itself on the earth, and earth juts through world. But the relation between world and earth does not wither away into the empty unity of opposites unconcerned with one another. The world, in resting upon the earth, strives to surmount it. As self-opening it cannot endure anything closed. The earth, however, as sheltering and concealing, tends always to draw the world into itself and keep it there.

The opposition of world and earth is a striving. But we would surely all too easily falsify its nature if we were to confound striving with discord and dispute, and thus see it only as disorder and destruction. In essential striving, rather, the opponents raise each other into the self-assertion of their natures. Self-assertion of nature, however, is never a rigid insistence upon some contingent state, but surrender to the concealed originality of the source of one's own being. In the struggle, each opponent carries the other beyond itself. Thus the striving becomes ever more intense as striving, and more authentically what it is. The more the struggle overdoes itself on its own part, the more inflexibly do the opponents let themselves go into the intimacy of simple belonging to one another. The earth cannot dispense with the Open of the world if it itself is to appear as earth in the liberated surge of its self-seclusion. The world, again, cannot soar out of the earth's sight if, as the governing breadth and path of all essential destiny, it is to ground itself on a resolute foundation.

In setting up a world and setting forth the earth, the work is an instigating of this striving. This does not happen so that the work should at the same time settle and put an end to the conflict in an insipid agreement, but so that the strife may remain a strife. Setting up a world and setting forth the earth, the work accomplishes this striving. The work-being of the work consists in the fighting of the battle between world and earth. It is because the struggle arrives at its high point in the simplicity of intimacy that the unity of the work comes about in the fighting of the battle. The fighting of the battle is the continually self-overreaching gathering of the work's agitation. The repose of the work that rests in itself thus has its presencing in the intimacy of striving. . . .

If here and elsewhere we conceive of truth as unconcealedness, we are not merely taking refuge in a more literal translation of a Greek word. We are reminding ourselves of what, unexperienced and unthought, underlies our familiar and therefore outworn nature of truth in the sense of correctness. We do, of course, occasionally take the trouble to concede that naturally, in order to understand and verify the correctness (truth) of a proposition one really should go back to something that is already evident, and that this presupposition is indeed unavoidable. As long as we talk and believe in this way, we always understand truth merely as correctness, which of course still requires a further presupposition, that we ourselves just happen to make, heaven knows how or why.

But it is not we who presuppose the unconcealedness of beings; rather, the unconcealedness of beings (Being) puts us into such a condition of being that in our representation we always remain installed within and in attendance upon unconcealedness. Not only must that in *conformity* with which a cognition orders itself be already in some way unconcealed. The entire *realm* in which this "conforming to something" goes on must already occur as a whole in the unconcealed; and this holds equally of that *for* which the conformity of a proposition to fact becomes manifest. With all our correct representations we would get nowhere, we could not even presuppose that there already is manifest something to which we can conform ourselves, unless the unconcealedness of beings had already exposed us to, placed us in that lighted realm in which every being stands for us and from which it withdraws.

But how does this take place? How does truth happen as this unconcealedness? First, however, we must say more clearly what this unconcealedness itself is.

Things are, and human beings, gifts, and sacrifices are, animals and plants are, equipment and works are. That which is, the particular being, stands in Being. Through Being there passes a veiled destiny that is ordained between the godly and the countergodly. There is much in being that man cannot master. There is but little that comes to be known. What is known remains inexact, what is mastered insecure. What is, is never of our making or even merely the product of our minds, as it might all too easily seem. When we contemplate this whole as one, then we apprehend, so it appears, all that is—though we grasp it crudely enough.

And yet—beyond what is, not away from it but before it, there is still something else that happens. In the midst of beings as a whole an open place occurs. There is a clearing, a lighting. Thought of in reference to what is, to beings, this clearing is in a greater degree than are beings. This open center is therefore not surrounded by what is; rather, the lighting center itself encircles all that is, like the Nothing which we scarcely know.

That which is can only be, as a being, if it stands within and stands out within what is lighted in this clearing. Only this clearing grants and guarantees to us humans a passage to those beings that we ourselves are not, and access to the being that we ourselves are. Thanks to this clearing, beings are unconcealed in certain changing degrees. And yet a being can be *concealed,* too, only within the sphere of what is lighted. Each being we encounter and which encounters us keeps to this curious opposition of presence in that it always withholds itself at the same time in a concealedness. The clearing in which beings stand is in itself at the same time concealment. Concealment, however, prevails in the midst of beings in a twofold way.

Beings refuse themselves to us down to that one and seemingly least feature which we touch upon most readily when we can say no more of beings than that they are. Concealment as refusal is not simply and only the limit of knowledge in any given circumstance, but the beginning of the clearing of what is lighted. But concealment, though of another sort, to be sure, at the same time also occurs within what is lighted. One being places itself in front of another being, the one helps to hide the other, the former obscures the latter, a few obstruct many, one denies all. Here concealment is not simple refusal. Rather, a being appears, but it presents itself as other than it is.

This concealment is dissembling. If one being did not simulate another, we could not make mistakes or act mistakenly in regard to beings; we could not go astray and transgress, and especially could never overreach ourselves. That a being should be able to deceive as semblance is the condition for our being able to be deceived, not conversely.

Concealment can be a refusal or merely a dissembling. We are never fully certain whether it is the one or the other. Concealment conceals and dissembles itself. This means: the open place in the midst of beings, the clearing, is never a rigid stage with a permanently raised curtain on which the play of beings runs its course. Rather, the clearing happens only as this double concealment. The unconcealedness of beings—this is never a merely existent state, but a happening. Unconcealedness (truth) is neither an attribute of factual things in the sense of beings, nor one of propositions.

We believe we are at home in the immediate circle of beings. That which is, is familiar, reliable, ordinary. Nevertheless, the clearing is pervaded by a constant concealment in the double form of refusal and dissembling. At bottom, the ordinary is not ordinary; it is extra-ordinary, uncanny. The nature of truth, that is, of unconcealedness, is dominated throughout by a denial. Yet this denial is not a defect or a fault, as though truth were an unalloyed unconcealedness that has rid itself of everything concealed. If truth could accomplish this, it would no longer be itself. *This denial, in the form of a double concealment, belongs to the nature of truth as unconcealedness.* Truth, in its nature, is un-truth. We put the matter this way in order to serve notice, with a possibly surprising trenchancy, that denial in the manner of concealment belongs to unconcealedness as clearing. The proposition, "the nature of truth is untruth," is not, however, intended to state that truth is at bottom falsehood. Nor does it mean that truth is never itself but, viewed dialectically, is always also its opposite.

Truth occurs precisely as itself in that the concealing denial, as refusal, provides its constant source to all clearing, and yet, as dissembling, it metes out to all clearing the indefeasible severity of error. Concealing denial is intended to denote that opposition in the nature of truth which subsists between clearing, or lighting, and concealing. It is the opposition of the primal conflict. The nature of truth is, in itself, the primal conflict in which that open center is won within which what is, stands, and from which it sets itself back into itself.

This Open happens in the midst of beings. It exhibits an essential feature which we have already mentioned. To the Open there belong a world and the earth. But the world is not simply the Open that corresponds to clearing, and the earth is not simply the Closed that corresponds to concealment. Rather, the world is the clearing of the paths of the essential guiding directions with which all decision complies. Every decision, however, bases itself on something not mastered, something concealed, confusing; else it would never be a decision. The earth is not simply the Closed but rather that which rises up as self-closing. World and earth are always intrinsically and essentially in conflict, belligerent by nature. Only as such do they enter into the conflict of clearing and concealing.

Earth juts through the world and world grounds itself on the earth only so far as truth happens as the primal conflict between clearing and concealing. But how does truth happen? We answer: it happens in a few essential ways. One of these ways in which truth happens is the work-being of the work. Setting up a world and setting forth the earth, the work is the fighting of the battle in which the unconcealedness of beings as a whole, or truth, is won.

Truth happens in the temple's standing where it is. This does not mean that something is correctly represented and rendered here, but that what is as a whole is brought into unconcealedness and held therein. To hold [halten] originally means to tend, keep, take care [hüten]. Truth happens in Van Gogh's painting. This does not mean that something is correctly portrayed, but rather that in the revelation of the equipmental being of the shoes, that which is as a whole—world and earth in their counterplay—attains to unconcealedness.

Thus in the work it is truth, not only something true, that is at work. The picture that shows the peasant shoes, the poem that says the Roman fountain, do not just make manifest what this isolated being as such is—if indeed they manifest anything at all; rather, they make unconcealedness as such happen in regard to what is as a whole. The more simply and authentically the shoes are engrossed in their nature, the more plainly and purely the fountain is engrossed in its nature—the more directly and engagingly do all beings attain to a greater degree of being along with them. That is how self-concealing being is illuminated. Light of this kind joins its shining to and into the work. This shining, joined in the work, is the beautiful. *Beauty is one way in which truth occurs as unconcealedness.* . . .

We must now first ask in a more essential way: how does the impulse toward such a thing as a work lie in the nature of truth? Of what nature is truth, that it can be set into work, or even under certain conditions must be set into work, in order to be *as* truth? But we defined the setting-into-a-work of truth as the nature of art. Hence our last question becomes:

What is truth, that it can happen as, or even must happen as, art? How is it that art exists at all?

TRUTH AND ART

Art is the origin of the art work and of the artist. Origin is the source of the nature in which the being of an entity is present. What is art? We seek its nature in the actual work. The actual reality of the work has been defined by that which is at work in the work, by the happening of truth. This happening we think of as the fighting of the conflict between world and earth. Repose occurs in the concentrated agitation of this conflict. The independence or self-composure of the work is grounded here. . . .

Truth is un-truth, insofar as there belongs to it the reservoir of the not-yet-uncovered, the un-uncovered, in the sense of concealment. In unconcealedness, as truth, there occurs also the other "un-" of a double restraint or refusal. Truth occurs as such in the opposition of clearing and double concealing. Truth is the primal conflict in which, always in some particular way, the Open is won within which everything stands and from which everything withholds itself that shows itself and withdraws itself as a being. Whenever and however this conflict breaks out and happens, the opponents, lighting or clearing and concealing, move apart because of it. Thus the Open of the place of conflict is won. The openness of this Open, that is, truth, can be what it is, namely, *this* openness, only if and as long as it establishes itself within its Open. Hence there must always be some being in this Open, something that is, in which the openness takes its stand and attains its constancy. In taking possession thus of the Open, the openness holds open the Open and sustains it. Setting and taking possession are here everywhere drawn from the Greek sense of *thesis*, which means a setting up in the unconcealed. . . .

Truth establishes itself in the work. Truth is present only as the conflict between lighting and concealing in the opposition of world and earth. Truth wills to be established in the work as this conflict of world and earth. The conflict is not to be resolved in a being brought forth for the purpose, nor is it to be merely housed there; the conflict, on the contrary, is started by it. This being must therefore contain within itself the essential traits of the conflict. In the strife the unity of world and earth is won. As a world opens itself, it submits to the decision of historical humanity the question of victory and defeat, blessing and curse, mastery and slavery. The dawning world brings out what is as yet undecided and measureless, and thus discloses the hidden necessity of measure and decisiveness.

But as a world opens itself the earth comes to rise up. It stands forth as that which bears all, as that which is sheltered in its own law and always wrapped up in itself. World demands its decisiveness and its measure and lets beings attain to the Open of their paths. Earth, bearing and jutting, strives to keep itself closed and to entrust everything to its law.

The conflict is not a rift [*Riss*] as a mere cleft is ripped open; rather, it is the intimacy with which opponents belong to each other. This rift carries the opponents into the source of their unity by virtue of their common ground. It is a basic design, an outline sketch, that draws the basic features of the rise of the lighting of beings. This rift does not let the opponents break apart; it brings the opposition of measure and boundary into their common outline.

Truth establishes itself as a strife within a being that is to be brought forth only in such a way that the conflict opens up in this being, that is, this being is itself brought into the rift-design. The rift-design is the drawing together, into a unity, of sketch and basic design, breach and outline. Truth establishes itself in a being in such a way, indeed, that this being itself occupies the Open of truth. This occupying, however, can happen only if what is to be brought forth, the rift, entrusts itself to the self-secluding factor that juts up in the Open. The rift must set itself back into the heavy weight of stone, the dumb hardness of wood, the dark glow of colors. As the earth takes the rift back into itself, the rift is first set forth into the Open and thus placed, that is, set, within that which towers up into the Open as self-closing and sheltering.

The strife that is brought into the rift and thus set back into the earth and thus fixed in place is *figure, shape, Gestalt*. Createdness of the work means: truth's being fixed in place in the figure. Figure is the structure in whose shape the rift composes and submits itself. This composed rift is the fitting or joining of the shining of truth. What is here called figure, *Gestalt,* is always to be thought in terms of the particular placing [*Stellen*] and framing or framework [*Ge-stell*] as which the work occurs when it sets itself up and sets itself forth. . . .

Just as a work cannot be without being created but is essentially in need of creators, so what is created cannot itself come into being without those who preserve it.

However, if a work does not find preservers, does not at once find them such as respond to the truth happening in the work, this does not at all mean that the work may also be a work without preservers. Being a work, it always remains tied to preservers, even and particularly when it is still only waiting for preservers and only pleads and waits for them to enter into its truth. Even the oblivion into which the work can sink is not nothing; it is still a preservation. It feeds on the work. Preserving the work means: standing within the openness of beings that happens in the work. This "standing-within" of preservation, however, is a knowing. Yet knowing does not consist in mere information and notions about something. He who truly knows what is, knows what he wills to do in the midst of what is. . . .

Willing is the sober resolution of that existential self-transcendence which exposes itself to the openness of beings as it is set into the work. In this way, standing-within is brought under law. Preserving the work, as knowing, is a sober standing-within the extraordinary awesomeness of the truth that is happening in the work.

This knowledge, which as a willing makes its home in the work's truth and only thus remains a knowing, does not deprive the work of its independence, does not drag it into the sphere of mere experience, and does not degrade it to the role of a stimulator of experience. Preserving the work does not reduce people to their private experiences, but brings them into affiliation with the truth happening in the work. Thus it grounds being for and with one another as the historical standing-out of human existence in reference to unconcealedness. Most of all, knowledge in the manner of preserving is far removed from that merely aestheticizing connoisseurship of the work's formal aspects, its qualities and charms. Knowing as having seen is a being resolved; it is standing within the conflict that the work has fitted into the rift. . . .

In the work, the happening of truth is at work and, indeed, at work according to the manner of a work. Accordingly the nature of art was defined to begin with as the setting-into-work of truth. Yet this definition is intentionally ambiguous. It says on the one hand: art is the fixing in place of a self-establishing truth in the figure. This happens in creation as the bringing forth of the unconcealedness of what is. Setting-into-work, however, also means: the bringing of work-being into movement and happening. This happens as preservation. Thus art is: the creative preserving of truth in the work. *Art then is the becoming and happening of truth.* Does truth, then, arise out of nothing? It does indeed if by nothing is meant the mere not of that which is, and if we here think of that which is as an object present in the ordinary way, which thereafter comes to light and is challenged by the existence of the work as only presumptively a true being. Truth is never gathered from objects that are present and ordinary. Rather, the opening up of the Open, and the clearing of what is, happens only as the openness is projected, sketched out, that makes its advent in thrownness.

Truth, as the clearing and concealing of what is, happens in being composed, as a poet composes a poem. *All art,* as the letting happen of the advent of the truth of what is, is, as such, *essentially poetry.* The nature of art, on which both the art work and the artist depend, is the setting-itself-into-work of truth. It is due to art's poetic nature that, in the midst of what is, art breaks open an open place, in whose openness everything is other than usual. By virtue of the projected sketch set into the work of the unconcealedness of what is, which casts itself toward us, everything ordinary and hitherto existing becomes an unbeing. This unbeing has lost the capacity to give and keep being as measure. The curious fact here is that the work in no way affects hitherto existing entities by causal connections. The working of the work does not consist in the taking effect of a cause. It lies in a change, happening from out of the work, of the unconcealedness of what is, and this means, of Being. . . .

If all art is in essence poetry, then the arts of architecture, painting, sculpture, and music must be traced back to poesy. That is pure arbitrariness. It certainly is, as long as we mean that those arts are varieties of the art of language, if it is permissible to characterize poesy by that easily misinterpretable title. But poesy is only one mode of the lighting projection of truth, i.e., of poetic composition in this wider sense. Nevertheless, the linguistic work, the poem in the narrower sense, has a privileged position in the domain of the arts.

To see this, only the right concept of language is needed. In the current view, language is held to be a kind of communication. It serves for verbal exchange and agreement, and in general for communicating. But language is not only and not primarily an audible and written expression of what is to be communicated. It not only puts forth in words and statements what is overtly or covertly intended to be communicated; language alone brings what is, as something that is, into the Open for the first time. Where there is no language, as in the being of stone, plant, and animal, there is also no openness of what is, and consequently no openness either of that which is not and of the empty.

Language, by naming beings for the first time, first brings beings to word and to appearance. Only this naming nominates beings *to* their being *from out of* their being. Such saying is a projecting of the clearing, in which announcement is made of what it is that beings come into the Open *as*. Projecting is the release of a throw by which unconcealedness submits and infuses itself into what is as such. This projective announcement forthwith becomes a renunciation of all the dim confusion in which what is veils and withdraws itself.

Projective saying is poetry: the saying of world and earth, the saying of the arena of their conflict and thus of the place of all nearness and remoteness of the gods. Poetry is the saying of the unconcealedness of what is. Actual language at any given moment is the happening of this saying, in which a people's world historically arises for it and the earth is preserved as that which remains closed. Projective saying is saying which, in preparing the sayable, simultaneously brings the unsayable as such into a world. In such saying, the concepts of an historical people's nature, i.e., of its belonging to world history, are formed for that folk, before it.

Poetry is thought of here in so broad a sense and at the same time in such intimate unity of being with language and word, that we must leave open whether art, in all its modes from architecture to poesy, exhausts the nature of poetry.

Language itself is poetry in the essential sense. But since language is the happening in which for man beings first disclose themselves to him each time as beings, poesy—or poetry in the narrower sense—is the most original form of poetry in the essential sense. Language is not poetry because it is the primal poesy; rather, poesy takes place in language because language preserves the original nature of poetry. Building and plastic creation, on the other hand, always happen already, and happen only, in the Open of saying and naming. It is the Open that pervades and guides them. But for this very reason they remain their own ways and modes in which truth orders itself into work. They are an ever special poetizing within the clearing of what is, which has already happened unnoticed in language.

Art, as the setting-into-work of truth, is poetry. Not only the creation of the work is poetic, but equally poetic, though in its own way, is the preserving of the work; for a work is in actual effect as a work only when we remove ourselves from our commonplace routine and move into what is disclosed by the work, so as to bring our own nature itself to take a stand in the truth of what is.

The nature of art is poetry. The nature of poetry, in turn, is the founding of truth. We understand founding here in a triple sense: founding as bestowing, founding as grounding, and founding as beginning. Founding, however, is actual only in preserving. Thus to each mode of founding there corresponds a mode of preserving. We can do no more now than to present this structure of the nature of art in a few strokes, and even this only to the extent that the earlier characterization of the nature of the work offers an initial hint.

The setting-into-work of truth thrusts up the unfamiliar and extraordinary and at the same time thrusts down the ordinary and what we believe to be such. The truth that discloses itself in the work can never be proved or derived from what went before. What went before is refuted in its exclusive reality by the work. What art founds can therefore never be compensated and made up for by what is already present and available. Founding is an overflow, an endowing, a bestowal.

The poetic projection of truth that sets itself into work as figure is also never carried out in the direction of an indeterminate void. Rather, in the work, truth is thrown toward the coming preservers, that is, toward an historical group of men. What is thus cast forth is, however, never an arbitrary demand. Genuinely poetic projection is the opening up or disclosure of that into which human being as historical is already cast. This is the earth and, for an historical people, its earth, the self-closing ground on which it rests together with everything that it already is, though still hidden from itself. It is, however, its world, which prevails in virtue of the relation of human being to the unconcealedness of Being. For this reason, everything with which man is endowed must, in the projection, be drawn up from the closed ground and expressly set upon this ground. In this way the ground is first grounded as the bearing ground.

All creation, because it is such a drawing-up, is a drawing, as of water from a spring. Modern subjectivism, to be sure, immediately misinterprets creation, taking it as the self-sovereign subject's performance of genius. The founding of truth is a founding not only in the sense of free bestowal, but at the same time foundation in the sense of this ground-laying grounding. Poetic projection comes from Nothing in this respect, that it never takes its gift from the ordinary and traditional. But it never comes from Nothing in that what is projected by it is only the withheld vocation of the historical being of man itself.

Bestowing and grounding have in themselves the unmediated character of what we call a beginning. Yet this unmediated character of a beginning, the peculiarity of a leap out of the unmediable, does not exclude but rather includes the fact that the beginning prepares itself for the longest time and wholly inconspicuously. A genuine beginning, as a leap, is always a head start, in which everything to come is already leaped over, even if as something disguised. The beginning already contains the end latent within itself. A genuine beginning, however, has nothing of the neophyte character of the primitive. The primitive, because it lacks the bestowing, grounding leap and head start, is always futureless. It is not capable of releasing anything more from itself because it contains nothing more than that in which it is caught.

A beginning, on the contrary, always contains the undisclosed abundance of the unfamiliar and extraordinary, which means that it also contains strife with the familiar and ordinary. Art as poetry is founding, in the third sense of instigation of the strife of truth: founding as beginning. Always when that which is as a whole demands, as what is, itself, a grounding in openness, art attains to its historical nature as foundation. This foundation happened in the West for the first time in Greece. What was in the future to be called Being was set into work, setting the standard. The realm of beings thus opened up was then transformed into a being in the sense of God's creation. This happened in the Middle Ages. This kind of being was again transformed at the beginning and in the course of the modern age. Beings became objects that could be controlled and seen through by calculation. At each time a new and essential world arose. At each time the openness of what is had to be established in beings themselves, by the fixing in place of truth in figure. At each time there happened unconcealedness of what is. Unconcealedness sets itself into work, a setting which is accomplished by art.

Whenever art happens—that is, whenever there is a beginning—a thrust enters history, history either begins or starts over again. History means here not a sequence in time of events of whatever sort, however important. History is the transporting of a people into its appointed task as entrance into that people's endowment.

Art is the setting-into-work of truth. In this proposition an essential ambiguity is hidden, in which truth is at once the subject and the object of the setting. But subject and object are unsuitable names here. They keep us from thinking precisely this ambiguous nature, a task that no longer belongs to this consideration. Art is historical, and as historical it is the creative preserving of truth in the work. Art happens as poetry. Poetry is founding in the triple sense of bestowing, grounding, and beginning. Art, as founding, is essentially historical. This means not only that art has a history in the external sense that in the course of time it, too, appears along with many other things, and in the process changes and passes away and offers changing aspects for historiology. Art is history in the essential sense that it grounds history.

Art lets truth originate. Art, founding preserving, is the spring that leaps to the truth of what is, in the work. To originate something by a leap, to bring something into being from out of the source of its nature in a founding leap—this is what the word origin [German *Ursprung*, literally, primal leap] means.

The origin of the work of art—that is, the origin of both the creators and the preservers, which is to say of a people's historical existence, is art. This is so because art is by nature an origin: a distinctive way in which truth comes into being, that is, becomes historical.

We inquire into the nature of art. Why do we inquire in this way? We inquire in this way in order to be able to ask more truly whether art is or is not an origin in our historical existence, whether and under what conditions it can and must be an origin.

Such reflection cannot force art and its coming-to-be. But this reflective knowledge is the preliminary and therefore indispensable preparation for the becoming of art. Only such knowledge prepares its space for art, their way for the creators, their location for the preservers.

In such knowledge, which can only grow slowly, the question is decided whether art can be an origin and then must be a head start, or whether it is to remain a mere appendix and then can only be carried along as a routine cultural phenomenon.

Are we in our existence historically at the origin? Do we know, which means do we give heed to, the nature of the origin? Or, in our relation to art, do we still merely make appeal to a cultivated acquaintance with the past?

For this either-or and its decision there is an infallible sign. Hölderlin, the poet—whose work still confronts the Germans as a test to be stood—named it in saying:

> *Schwer verlässt*
> *was nahe dem Ursprung wohnet, den Ort.*
>
> Reluctantly
> that which dwells near its origin departs.
> ("The Journey," verses 18–19)

JEAN-PAUL SARTRE

Being and Nothingness

The Existence of Others

THE PROBLEM

We have described human reality from the standpoint of negating conduct and from the standpoint of the *cogito*. Following this lead we have discovered that human reality is-for-itself. Is this *all* that it is? Without going outside our attitude of reflective description, we can encounter modes of consciousness which seem, even while themselves remaining strictly in for-itself, to point to a radically different type of ontological structure. This ontological structure is *mine*; it is in relation to myself as subject that I am concerned about myself, and yet this concern (for-myself) reveals to me a being which is *my* being without being-for-me.

Consider for example shame. Here we are dealing with a mode of consciousness which has a structure identical with all those which we have previously described. It is a non-positional self-consciousness, conscious (of) itself as shame; as such, it is an example of what the Germans call *Erlebnis,* and it is accessible to reflection. In addition its structure is intentional; it is a shameful apprehension *of* something and this something is me. I am ashamed of what I *am.* Shame therefore realizes an intimate relation of myself to myself. Through shame I have discovered an aspect of my being. Yet although certain complex forms derived from shame can appear on the reflective plane, shame is not originally a phenomenon of reflection. In fact no matter what results one can obtain in solitude by the religious *practice* of shame, it is in its primary structure shame *before somebody.* I have just made an awkward or vulgar gesture. This gesture clings to me: I neither judge it nor blame it. I simply live it. I realize it in the mode of for-itself. But now suddenly I raise my head. Somebody was there and has seen me. Suddenly I realize

Excerpted from Jean-Paul Sartre, *Being and Nothingness: An Essay on Phenomenological Ontology*, translated by Hazel Barnes (New York: Philosophical Library, 1956), 221–22; 233–39; 242–53; 256–58; 267–75; 297–301.

the vulgarity of my gesture, and I am ashamed. It is certain that my shame is not reflective, for the presence of another in my consciousness, even as a catalyst, is incompatible with the reflective attitude; in the field of my reflection I can never meet with anything but the consciousness which is mine. But the Other is the indispensable mediator between myself and me. I am ashamed of myself as I *appear* to the Other.

By the mere appearance of the Other, I am put in the position of passing judgment on myself as on an object, for it is as an object that I appear to the Other. Yet this object which has appeared to the Other is not an empty image in the mind of another. Such an image in fact, would be imputable wholly to the Other and so could not "touch" me. I could feel irritation, or anger before it as before a bad portrait of myself which gives to my expression an ugliness or baseness which I do not have, but I could not be touched to the quick. Shame is by nature *recognition*. I recognize that I *am* as the Other sees me. There is however no question of a comparison between what I am for myself and what I am for the Other as if I found in myself, in the mode of being of the For-itself, an equivalent of what I am for the Other. In the first place this comparison is not encountered in us as the result of a concrete psychic operation. Shame is an immediate shudder which runs through me from head to foot without any discursive preparation. In addition the comparison is impossible; I am unable to bring about any relation between what I am in the intimacy of the For-Itself, without distance, without recoil, without perspective, and this unjustifiable being-in-itself which I am for the Other. There is no standard here, no table of correlation. Moreover the very notion of *vulgarity* implies an inter-monad relation. Nobody can be vulgar all alone!

Thus the Other has not only revealed to me what I was; he has established me in a new type of being which can support new qualifications. This being was not in me potentially before the appearance of the Other, for it could not have found any place in the For-itself. Even if some power had been pleased to endow me with a body wholly constituted before it should be for-others, still my vulgarity and my awkwardness could not lodge there potentially; for they are meanings and as such they surpass the body and at the same time refer to a witness capable of understanding them and to the totality of my human reality. But this new being which appears *for* the other does not reside *in* the Other; I am responsible for it as is shown very well by the education system which consists in making children ashamed of what they are.

Thus shame is shame *of oneself before the Other;* these two structures are inseparable. But at the same time I need the Other in order to realize fully all the structures of my being. The For-itself refers to the For-others. Therefore if we wish to grasp in its totality the relation of man's being to being-in-itself, we can not be satisfied with the descriptions outlined in the earlier chapters of this work. We must answer two far more formidable questions: first that of the existence of the Other, then that of the relation of my *being* to the being of the Other. . . .

HUSSERL, HEGEL, HEIDEGGER

The philosophy of the nineteenth and twentieth centuries seems to have understood that once myself and the Other are considered as two separate substances, we cannot escape solipsism; any union of these substances must in fact be held to be impossible. That is why the examination of modern theories reveals to us an attempt to seize at the very heart of the consciousness a fundamental, transcending connection with the Other which would be constitutive of each consciousness in its very upsurge. But while this philosophy appears to abandon the postulate of the external negation, it nevertheless preserves its essential consequence; that is, the affirmation that my fundamental connection with the Other is realized through *knowledge*.

When Husserl in his *Cartesian Meditations* and in *Formal and Transcendental Logic* attempts to refute solipsism, he believes that he can succeed by showing that a referral to the Other is the indispensible condition for the constitution of a world. Without going into the details of his theory, we shall limit ourselves to indicating his general position. For Husserl the world as it is revealed to consciousness is inter-monadic. The Other is present in it not only as a particular concrete and empirical appearance but as a permanent condition of its unity and of its richness. Whether I consider this table or this tree or this bare wall in solitude or with companions, the Other is always there as a layer of constitutive meanings which belong to the very object which I consider; in short, he is the veritable guarantee of the object's objectivity. And since our psycho-physical self is contemporary with the world, forms a part of the world, and falls with the world under the impact of the phenomenological reduction, the Other appears as necessary to the very constitution of this self. If I am to doubt the existence of my friend Pierre or of others in general, then inasmuch as this existence is on principle outside my experience, I must of necessity doubt also my concrete being, my empirical reality as a professor having this or that tendency, these habits, this particular character. There is no privilege for *my* self: my empirical Ego and the Other's empirical Ego appear in the world at the same time. The general meaning of "Others" is necessary to the constitution of each one of these "Egos." Thus each object far from being constituted as for Kant, by a simple relation to the *subject,* appears in my concrete experience as polyvalent; it is given originally as possessing systems of reference to an indefinite plurality of consciousnesses; it is *on* the table, *on* the wall that the Other is revealed to me as that to which the object under consideration is perpetually referred—as well as on the occasion of the concrete appearances of Pierre or Paul.

To be sure, these views show progress over the classical positions. It is undeniable that the instrumental-thing from the moment of its discovery refers to a plurality of For-itselfs. We shall have to return to this point. It is also certain that the meaning of "the Other" can not come from the experience nor from a reasoning by analogy effected on the occasion of the experience; on the contrary, it is in the light of the concept of the Other that the experience is interpreted. Does that mean that the concept of the Other is *a priori*? This we shall attempt to determine later. But in spite of these undeniable advantages Husserl's theory does not seem to us perceptibly different from Kant's. This is due to the fact that while my empirical Ego is not any more sure than the Other's, Husserl has retained the transcendental subject, which is radically distinct from the Ego and which strongly resembles the Kantian subject. Now what ought to be demonstrated is that it is not the parallelism of the empirical "Egos" which throws doubt on the person but that of the transcendental subjects. This is because actually the Other is *never* that empirical person who is encountered in my experience; he is the transcendental subject to whom this person by nature refers. Thus the true problem is that of the connection of transcendental subjects who are beyond experience. If someone replies that from the start the transcendental subject refers to other subjects *for the constitution* of the noematic whole, it is easy to reply that it refers to them as to *meanings*. The Other here would be a kind of supplementary category which would allow a world to be constituted, not a real being existing beyond this world. Of course the "category" of the Other implies in its very meaning a reference from the other side of the world to a subject, but this reference could be only hypothetical. It has the pure value of the content of a unifying concept; it is valid in and for the world. Its laws are limited to the world, and the Other is by nature outside the world. Furthermore Husserl has removed the very possibility of understanding what can be meant by the extra-mundane *being* of the Other since he defines *being* as the simple indication of an infinite series of operations to be effected. There could be no better way to measure being by knowledge. Now even admitting that knowledge in general measures being, the Other's being is measured in its reality by the knowledge which the Other has of himself, not by that which I have of him. What I must attain is the Other, not as I obtain knowledge of him, but as he obtains knowledge of himself—which is impossible. This would in fact suppose the internal identification of myself with the Other. Thus we find here again that distinction on principle between the Other and myself which does not stem from the exteriority of our bodies but from the simple fact that each of us exists in interiority and that a knowledge valid for interiority can be effected only in interiority which on principle excludes all *knowledge* of the Other as he knows himself—*i.e.*, as he is. Moreover Husserl understood this since he says that "the Other" as he is revealed to our concrete experience is an *absence*. But within Husserl's philosophy, at least, how can one have a full intuition of an absence? The Other is the object of empty intentions, the Other on principle refuses himself to us and flees. The only reality which remains is therefore that of *my* intention; the Other is the empty noema which corresponds to my directing toward the Other, to the extent that he appears concretely in my experience. He is an ensemble of operations of unification and of the constitution of my experience so that he appears as a transcendental concept. Husserl replies to the solipsist that the Other's existence is as sure as that of the world, and Husserl includes in the world my psychophysical existence. But the solipsist says the same thing: it is as sure, he will say, but no more sure. The existence of the world is measured, he will add, by the knowledge which I have of it; the case will not be otherwise for the existence of the Other.

Formerly I believed that I could escape solipsism by refuting Husserl's concept of the existence of the Transcendental "Ego." At that time I thought that since I had emptied my consciousness of its subject, nothing remained there which was privileged as compared to the Other. But actually although I am still persuaded that the hypothesis of a transcendental subject is useless and disastrous, abandoning it does not help one bit to solve the question of the existence of Others. Even if outside the empirical Ego there is *nothing other* than the consciousness *of* that Ego—that is, a transcendental field without a subject—the fact remains that my affirmation of the Other demands and requires the existence beyond the world of a similar transcendental field. Consequently the only way to escape solipsism would be here again to prove that my transcendental consciousness is in its very being, affected by the extra-mundane existence of other consciousnesses of the same type. Because Husserl has reduced being to a series of meanings, the only connection which he has been able to establish between my being and that of the Other is a connection of *knowledge*. Therefore Husserl can not escape solipsism any more than Kant could.

If now instead of observing the rules of chronological succession, we are guided by those of a sort of non-temporal dialectic, we shall find that in the solution which Hegel gives to the problem in the first volume of *The Phenomenology of Mind*, he has made significant progress over Husserl. Here the appearance of the Other is indispensable not to the constitution of the world and of my empirical "Ego" but to the very existence of my consciousness as self-consciousness. In fact as self-consciousness, the Self itself apprehends itself. The equation "Myself = myself" or "I am I" is precisely the expression of this fact. At first this self-consciousness is pure self-identity, pure existence for itself. It has certitude of itself, but this certitude still lacks truth. In fact this certitude would be true only to the extent that its own existence for itself appeared to it as an independent object. Thus self-consciousness is first a syncretic relation without truth between a subject and an object, an object, which is not yet objectified and which is this subject himself. Since the impulse of this consciousness is to realize its concept by becoming conscious of itself in all respects, it tends to make itself valid externally by giving itself objectivity and manifest existence. It is concerned with making the "I am I" explicit and producing itself as an object in order to attain the ultimate stage of development. This state in another sense is naturally the prime mover for the becoming of consciousness; it is self-consciousness in general, which is recognized in other self-consciousnesses and which is identical with them and with itself. The mediator is the *Other*. The Other appears along with myself since self-consciousness is identical with itself by means of the exclusion of every Other. Thus the primary fact is the plurality of consciousnesses, and this plurality is realized in the form of a double, reciprocal relation of exclusion. Here we are then in the presence of that connection by means of an internal negation which was demanded earlier. No external nothingness in-itself separates my consciousness from the Other's consciousness; it is by the very fact of being me that I exclude the Other. The Other is the one who excludes me by being himself, the one whom I exclude by being myself. Consciousnesses are directly supported by one another in a reciprocal imbrication of their being.

This position allows us at the same time to define the way in which the Other appears to me: he is the one who is other than I; therefore he is given as a non-essential object with a character of negativity. But this Other is also a self-consciousness. As such he appears to me as an ordinary object immersed in the being of life. Similarly it is thus that I appear to the Other: as a concrete, sensible, immediate existence. Here Hegel takes his stand on the ground not of a univocal relation which goes from me (apprehended by the *cogito*) to the Other, but of the reciprocal relation which he defines as "the self-apprehension of the one in the other." In fact it is only in so far as each man is opposed to the Other that he is absolutely for himself. Opposite the Other and confronting the Other, each one asserts his right of being individual. Thus the *cogito* itself can not be a point of departure for philosophy; in fact it can be born only in consequence of my appearance for myself as an individual, and this appearance is conditioned by the recognition of the Other. The problem of the Other should not be posited in terms of the *cogito;* on the contrary, the existence of the Other renders the *cogito* possible as the abstract moment when the self is apprehended as an object. Thus the "moment" which Hegel calls *being for the Other* is a necessary stage of the development of self-consciousness; the road of interiority passes through the Other. But the Other is of interest to me only to the extent that he is another Me, a Me-object for Me, and conversely to the extent that he reflects my Me—*i.e.,* is, in so far as I am an object for him. Due to the fact that I must necessarily be an object for myself only over there in the Other, I must obtain from the Other the *recognition* of my being. But if another consciousness must mediate between my consciousness for *itself* and itself, then the being-for-itself of my consciousness—and consequently its being in general—depends on the Other. As I appear to the Other, so I am. Moreover since the Other is such as he appears to me and since my being depends upon the Other, the way in which I appear—that is, the moment of the development of my self-consciousness—depends on the way in which the Other appears to me. The value of the Other's recognition of me depends on the value of my recognition of the Other. In this sense to the extent that the Other apprehends me as bound to a body and immersed in *life*, I am myself only *an Other*. In order to make myself recognized by the Other, I must risk my own life. To risk one's life, in fact, is to reveal oneself as not-bound to the objective form or to any determined existence—as not-bound to life.

But at the same time I pursue the *death* of the Other. This means that I wish to cause myself to be mediated by an Other who is only other—that is, by a dependent consciousness whose essential characteristic is to exist only for another. This will be accomplished at the very moment when I risk my life, for in the struggle against the other I have made an abstraction of my sensible being by *risking* it. On the other hand, the Other prefers life and freedom even while showing that he has not been able to posit himself as not-bound to the objective form. Therefore he remains bound to external things in general; he appears to me and he appears to himself as *non-essential*. He is the *Slave*, I am the *Master*; for him it is I who am essence. Thus there appears the famous "Master-Slave" relation which so profoundly influenced Marx. We need not here enter into its details. It is sufficient to observe that the Slave is the Truth of the Master. But this unilateral recognition is unequal and insufficient, for the truth of his self-certitude for the Master is a non-essential consciousness; therefore the Master is not certain of *being for himself* as *truth*. In order to attain this truth there is necessary "a moment in which the master does for himself what he does as regards the Other and when the slave does as regards the Other what he does for himself." At this moment there will appear a self-consciousness in general which is recognized in other self-consciousnesses and which is identical with them and with itself.

Thus Hegel's brilliant intuition is to make me depend on the Other *in my being*. I am, he said, a being for-itself which is for-itself only through another. Therefore the Other penetrates me to the heart. I can not doubt him without doubting myself since "self-consciousness is real only in so far as it recognizes its echo (and its reflection) in another." Since the very doubt implies a consciousness which exists for itself, the Other's existence conditions my attempt to doubt it just as in the work of Descartes my existence conditions systematic doubt. Thus solipsism seems to be put out of the picture once and for all. By proceeding from Husserl to Hegel, we have realized immense progress: first the negation which constitutes the Other is direct, internal, and reciprocal; second, it calls each consciousness to account and pierces it to the deepest part of its being; the problem is posited on the level of inner being, of the universal and transcendental "I;" finally in my essential being I depend on the essential being of the Other, and instead of holding that my being-for-myself is opposed to my being-for-others, I find that being-for-others appears as a necessary condition for my being-for-myself.

Yet in spite of the wide scope of this solution, in spite of the richness and profundity of the detailed insights with which the theory of the Master and the Slave is filled to overflowing, can we be satisfied with it?

To be sure, Hegel has posed the question of the being of consciousnesses. It is being-for-itself and being-for-others which he is studying, and he holds that each consciousness includes the *reality* of the other. Nevertheless it is certain that this ontological problem remains everywhere formulated in terms of knowledge. The mainspring of the conflict of consciousnesses is the effort of each one to transform his self-certitude into *truth*. And we know that this truth can be attained only in so far as my consciousness becomes an *object* for the Other at the same time as the Other becomes an *object* for my consciousness. Thus when idealism asks, "How can the Other be an object for me?" Hegel while remaining on the same ground as idealism replies: if there is in truth a Me for whom the *Other* is an object, this is because there is an *Other* for whom the Me is object. Knowledge here is still the measure of being, and Hegel does not even conceive of the possibility of a being-for-others which is not finally reducible to a "being-as-object." Thus a universal self-consciousness which seeks to disengage itself through all these dialectical phases is by its own admission reducible to a purely empty formula—the "I am I." Yet Hegel writes, "This proposition regarding self-consciousness is void of all content." And in another place he says, "[It is] the process of absolute abstraction which consists in surpassing all immediate existence and which results in the purely negative being of consciousness identical with itself." The limiting term of this dialectical conflict, universal self-consciousness, is not enriched in the midst of its avatars; it is on the contrary entirely denuded. It is no more than the "I know that another knows me as me." Of course this is because for idealism absolute being and knowledge are identical. But what does this identification involve?

To begin with, this "I am I," a pure, universal form of identity, has nothing in common with the concrete consciousness which we have attempted to describe in our Introduction. There we established that the being of self-consciousness could not be defined in terms of knowledge. Knowledge begins with *reflection* [reflexion] but the game of "the-reflection [reflet]-reflecting" is not a subject-object dyad, not even implicitly. Its being does not depend on any transcendent consciousness; rather its mode of being is precisely to be in question for itself. We showed subsequently in the first chapter of Part Two that the relation of the reflection to the reflecting was in no way a relation of identity and could not be reduced to the "Me = Me" or to the "I *am* I" of Hegel. The reflection does not make itself be the reflecting; we are dealing here with a being which nihilates itself in its being and which seeks in vain to dissolve into itself as a *self*. If it is true that this description is the only one which allows us to understand the original fact of consciousness, then we must judge that Hegel has not succeeded in accounting for this abstract doubling of the Me which he gives as equivalent to self-consciousness. Finally we succeeded in getting rid of the pure unreflective consciousness of the transcendental "I" which obscured it and we showed that selfness, the foundation of personal existence, was altogether different from an Ego or from a reference of the Ego to itself. There can be, therefore, no question of defining consciousness in terms of a transcendental ego-ology. In short, consciousness is a concrete being *sui generis*, not an abstract, unjustifiable relation of identity. It is selfness and not the seat of an opaque, useless Ego. Its being is capable of being reached by a transcendental reflection, and there is a *truth* of consciousness which does not depend on the Other; rather the very *being* of consciousness, since it is independent of knowledge, pre-exists its truth. On this plane as for naive realism, being measures truth; for the truth of a reflective intuition is measured by its conformity to being: consciousness *was there* before it was known. Therefore if consciousness is affirmed in the face of the Other, it is because it lays claim to a recognition of its being and not of an abstract truth. In fact it would be ill conceived to think that the ardent and perilous conflict between master and slave had for its sole stake the recognition of a formula as barren and abstract as the "I am I." Moreover there would be a deception in this very conflict since the end finally attained would be universal self-consciousness, "the intuition of the existing self by the self." Here as everywhere we ought to oppose to Hegel Kierkegaard, who represents the claims of the individual as such. The individual claims his achievement as an individual, the recognition of his concrete being, and of the objective specification of a universal structure. Of course the *rights* which I demand from the Other posit the universality of *self*; respect of persons demands the recognition of my person as universal. But it is my concrete and individual being which flows into this universal and fills it; it is for that *being-there* that I demand rights. The particular is here the support and foundation of the universal; the universal in this case could have no meaning if it did not exist for the *purpose* of the individual. . . .

According to Hegel the Other is an object, and I apprehend myself as an object in the Other. But the one of these affirmations destroys the other. In order for me to be able to appear to myself as an object in the Other, I would have to apprehend the Other as subject; that is, to apprehend him in his interiority. But in so far as the Other appears to me as object, my objectivity for him can not appear to me. Of course I apprehend that the Other-as-object *refers to me* by means of intentions and acts, but due to the very fact that he is an object, the Other-as-a-mirror is clouded and no longer reflects anything. These intentions and these acts are things in the world and are apprehended in the Time of the World; they are established and contemplated, their meaning is an object for me. Thus I can only appear to myself as a transcendent quality to which the Other's acts and intentions refer; but since the Other's objectivity destroys my objectivity for him, it is as an internal subject that I apprehend myself as being that to which those intentions and those acts refer. It must be understood that this apprehension of myself by myself is in pure terms of consciousness, not of knowledge; by having to be what I am in form of an ekstatic self-consciousness, I apprehend the Other as an object pointing to me. Thus Hegel's optimism results in failure: between the Other-as-object and Me-as-subject there is no common measure, no more than between self-consciousness and consciousness of the Other. I can not know myself *in* the Other if the Other is first an object for me; neither can I apprehend the Other in his true being—that is, in his subjectivity. No universal knowledge can be derived from the relation of consciousnesses. This is what we shall call their ontological separation.

But there is in Hegel another and more fundamental form of optimism. This may be called an ontological optimism. For Hegel indeed truth is truth of the Whole. And he places himself at the vantage point of truth—*i.e.*, of the Whole—to consider the problem of the Other. Thus when Hegelian monism considers the relation of consciousnesses, it does not put itself in any particular consciousness. Although the Whole is to be realized, it is already there as the truth of all which is true. Thus when Hegel writes that every consciousness, since it is identical with itself, is other than the Other, he has established himself in the whole, outside consciousnesses, and he considers them from the point of view of the Absolute. For individual consciousnesses are moments in the whole, moments which by themselves are *unselbständig*, and the whole is a mediator between consciousnesses. Hence is derived an ontological optimism parallel to the epistemological optimism: plurality can and must be surpassed toward the totality. But if Hegel can assert the reality of this surpassing, it is because he has already given it to himself at the outset. In fact he has forgotten his own consciousness; he *is* the Whole, and consequently if he so easily resolves the problem of particular consciousnesses it is because for him there never has been any real problem in this connection. Actually he does not raise the question of the relation between his own consciousness and that of the Other. By effecting completely the abstraction of his own, he studies purely and simply the relation between the consciousnesses of others—*i.e.* the relation of consciousnesses which are already for him objects whose nature according to him, is precisely that of being a particular type of object,—the subject-object. These consciousnesses from the totalitarian point of view which he has adopted are strictly equivalent to each other although each of them is separated from the rest by a particular privilege.

But if Hegel has forgotten himself, we can not forget Hegel. This means that we are referred back to the *cogito*. In fact, if, as we have established, the being of my consciousness is strictly irreducible to knowledge, then I can not transcend my being toward a reciprocal and universal relation in which I could see my being and that of others as equivalent. On the contrary, I must establish myself *in my being* and posit the problem of the Other in terms of my being. In a word the sole point of departure is the interiority of the *cogito*. We must understand by this that each one must be able by starting out from his own interiority, to rediscover the Other's being as a transcendence which conditions the very being of that interiority. This of necessity implies that the multiplicity of consciousnesses is on principle unsurpassable, for I can undoubtedly transcend myself *toward* a Whole, but I can not establish myself in this Whole so as to contemplate myself and to contemplate the Other. No logical or epistemological optimism can cover the scandal of the plurality of consciousnesses. If Hegel believed that it could, this is because he never grasped the nature of that particular dimension of being which is self-consciousness. The task which an ontology can lay down for itself is to describe this scandal and to found it in the very nature of being, but ontology is powerless to overcome it. It is possible—as we shall see better later—that we may be able to refute solipsism and show that the Other's existence is both evident and certain for us. But even if we could succeed in making the Other's existence share in the apodictic certainty of the *cogito*—*i.e.*, of my own existence—we should not thereby "surpass" the Other toward any inter-monad totality. So long as consciousnesses exist, the separation and conflict of consciousnesses will remain; we shall simply have discovered their foundation and their true terrain.

What has this long criticism accomplished for us? Simply this: if we are to refute solipsism, then my relation to the Other is first and fundamentally a relation of being to being, not of knowledge to knowledge. We have seen Husserl's failure when on this particular level he measures being by knowledge, and Hegel's when he identifies knowledge and being. But we have equally recognized that Hegel, although his vision is obscured by the postulate of absolute idealism, has been able to put the discussion on its true plane.

In *Sein und Zeit* Heidegger seems to have profited by study of his predecessors and to have been deeply impressed with this twofold necessity: (1) the relation between "human-realities" must be a relation of being; (2) this relation must cause "human-realities" to depend on one another in their essential being. At least his theory fulfills these two requirements. In his abrupt, rather barbaric fashion of cutting Gordian knots rather than trying to untie them, he gives in answer to the question posited a pure and simple *definition.* He has discovered several moments—inseparable except by abstraction—in "being-in-the-world," which characterizes human reality. These moments are "world," "being-in," and "being." He has described the *world* as "that by which human reality makes known to itself what it is"; "being-in" he has defined as *Befindlichkeit and Verstand.* We have still to speak of *being*; that is, the mode in which human reality is its being-in-the-world. Being, Heidegger tells us, is the *Mit-Sein*—that is, "being-with." Thus human-reality the characteristic of being is that human-reality is its being *with* others. This does not come about by chance. I do not exist *first* in order that subsequently a contingency should make me *encounter* the Other. The question here is of an essential structure of my being. But this structure is not established from outside and from a totalitarian point of view as it was with Hegel. To be sure, Heidegger does not take his departure from the *cogito* in the Cartesian sense of the discovery of consciousness by itself; but the human-reality which is revealed to him and for which he seeks to fix the structures in concepts is his own. "Dasein ist je *meines*," he writes. It is by making explicit the preontological comprehension which I have of myself that I apprehend being-with-others as an essential characteristic of my being. In short I discover the transcendental relation to the Other as constituting my own being, just as I have discovered that being-in-the-world measures my human-reality. Henceforth the problem of the Other is a false problem. The Other is no longer first a particular existence which I encounter in the world—and which could not be indispensable to my own existence since I existed before encountering it. The Other is the ex-centric limit which contributes to the constitution of my being. He is the test of my being inasmuch as he throws me outside of myself toward structures which at once both escape me and define me; it is this test which originally reveals the Other to me.

Let us observe in addition that the type of connection with the Other has changed. With realism, idealism, Husserl, Hegel, the type of relation between consciousnesses was being-for; the Other appeared to me and even constituted me in so far as he was *for* me or I was *for* him. The problem was the mutual recognition of consciousnesses brought face to face which appeared *in the world* and which confronted each other. "To-be-with" has an altogether different meaning; "with" does not intend the reciprocal relation of recognition and of conflict which would result from the appearance of a human-reality other than mine *in the midst of* the world. It expresses rather a sort of ontological solidarity for the exploitation of this world. The Other is not originally bound to me as an ontic reality appearing in the midst of the world among "instruments" as a type of particular object; in that case he would be already degraded, and the relation uniting him to me could never take on reciprocity. The Other is not an *object*. In his connection with me he remains a human-reality; the being by which he determines me in my being is his pure being apprehended as "being-in-the-world." And we know that the "in" must be understood in the sense of *colo, habito,* not of *insum*; to-be-in-the-world is to haunt the world, not to be ensnared in it; and it is in my "being-in-the-world" that the Other determines me. Our relation is not a *frontal* opposition but rather an *oblique* interdependence. In so far as I make a world exist as a complex of instruments which I use for the ends of my human reality, I cause myself to be determined in my being by a being who makes the world exist as a complex of instruments for the ends of his reality. Moreover it is not necessary to understand this being-with as a pure concomitance which is passively received by my being. For Heidegger, to be is to be one's own possibilities; that is, to make oneself be. It is then a mode of being which I make myself be. And it is very true that I am responsible for my being-for the Other in so far as I realize him freely in authenticity or in unauthenticity. It is in complete freedom and by an original choice that, for example, I realize my being-with in the anonymous form of "they." And if I am asked how my "being-with" can exist for-myself, I must reply that through the world I make known to myself what I am. In particular when I am in the unauthentic mode of the "they," the world refers to me a sort of impersonal reflection of my unauthentic possibilities in the form of instruments and complexes of instruments which belong to "everybody" and which belong to me in so far as I am "everybody": ready-made clothes, common means of transportation, parks, gardens, public places, shelters made for *anyone* who may take shelter there, *etc*. Thus I make myself known as *anybody* by means of the indicative complex of instruments which indicate me as a *Worumwillen*. The unauthentic state—which is my ordinary state in so far as I have not realized my conversion to authenticity—reveals to me my "being-with," not as the relation of one unique personality with other personalities equally unique, not as the mutual connection of "most irreplaceable beings," but as a total interchangeability of the terms of the relation. The determination of the terms is still lacking; I am not opposed to the Other, for I am not "me"; instead we have the social unity of the *they*. To posit the problem on the level of the incommunicability of individual subject was to commit an ὕστερον πρότερον, to stand the world on its head. Authenticity and individuality have to be earned: I shall be my own authenticity only if under the influence of the call of conscience (*Ruf des Gewissens*) I launch out toward death with a resolute-decision (*Entschlossenheit*) as toward my own most peculiar possibility. At this moment I reveal myself to myself in authenticity, and I raise others along with myself toward the authentic.

The empirical image which may best symbolize Heidegger's intuition is not that of a conflict but rather a *crew*. The original relation of the Other and my consciousness is not the *you* and *me*; it is the *we*. Heidegger's being-with is not the clear and distinct position of an individual confronting another individual; it is not *knowledge*. It is the mute existence in common of one member of the crew with his fellows, that existence which the rhythm of the oars or the regular movements of the coxswain will render sensible to the rowers and which *will be made manifest* to them by the common goal to be attained, the boat or the yacht to be overtaken, and the entire world (spectators, performance, *etc.*) which is profiled on the horizon. It is on the common ground of this co-existence that the abrupt revelation of my "being-unto-death" will suddenly make me stand out in an absolute "common solitude" while at the same time it raises the others to that solitude.

This time we have indeed been given what we asked for: a being which in its own being implies the Other's being. And yet we can not consider ourselves satisfied. First of all, Heidegger's theory offers us the indication of the solution to be found rather than that solution itself. Even if we should without reservation accept his substitution of "being-with" for "being-for," it would still remain for us a simple affirmation without foundation. Undoubtedly we shall encounter certain empirical states of our being—in particular that to which the Germans give the untranslatable name *Stimmung*—which seem to reveal a co-existence of consciousnesses rather than a relation of opposition. But it is precisely this co-existence which must be explained. Why does it become the unique foundation of our being? Why is it the fundamental type of our relation with others? Why did Heidegger believe that he was authorized to pass from this empirical and ontic establishment of being-with to a position claiming co-existence as the ontological structure of my "being-in-the-world?" And what type of being does this co-existence have? To what extent is the negation which makes the Other *an other* and which constitutes him as non-essential maintained? If we suppress it entirely, are we not going to fall into a monism? And if we are to preserve it as an essential structure of the relation to the Other, then what modification must it undergo in order to lose the character *of opposition* which it had in being-for-others and acquire this character as a connection which creates solidarity and which is the very structure of being-with? And how shall we be able to pass from there to the concrete experience of the Other in the world, as when from my window I see a man walking in the street? To be sure it is tempting to conceive of myself as standing out on the undifferentiated ground of the human by means of the impulse of my freedom, by the choice of my unique possibilities—and perhaps this conception holds an important element of truth. But in this form at least such a view gives rise to serious objections.

First of all, the ontological point of view joins here with the abstract view of the Kantian subject. To say that human reality (even if it is my human reality) "is-with" by means of its ontological structure is to say that it is-with by nature—that is, in an essential and universal capacity. Even if this affirmation were proved, it would not enable us to explain any concrete being-with. In other words, the ontological co-existence which appears as the structure of "being-in-the-world" can in no way serve as a foundation to an ontic being-with, such as, for example, the co-existence which appears in my friendship with Pierre or in the couple which Annie and I make. In fact it would be necessary to show that "being-with-Pierre" or "being-with-Annie" is a structure constitutive of my concrete-being. But this is impossible from the point of view which Heidegger has adopted. The Other in the relation "with," taken on the ontological level, can not in fact be concretely determined any more than the directly confronted human-reality of which it is the alter ego; it is an abstract term and hence *unselbständig*, and it does not contain the power of becoming *that* Other—Pierre or Annie. Thus the relation of the *Mit-Sein* can be of absolutely no use to us in resolving the psycho-logical, concrete problem of the recognition of the Other. There are two incommunicable levels and two problems which demand separate so-lutions.

It may be said that this is only one of the difficulties which Heidegger encounters in passing in general from the ontological level to the ontic level, in passing from "being-in-the-world" in general to my relation with *this* particular instrument, in passing from my being-unto-death, which makes of my death my most essential possibility, to *this* "ontic" death which I shall experience by encountering this or that external existent. But this difficulty can be disguised, if need be, in all other cases since, for example, it is human reality which causes the existence of a world in which a threat of death to human reality is hidden. Better yet, if the world *is*, it is because it is "mortal" in the sense in which we say that a wound is mortal. But the impossibility of passing from one level to the other bursts forth when we meet the problem of the Other. In fact even if in the ekstatic upsurge of its being-in-the-world, human reality makes a world exist, one can not, for all that, say that its being-with causes another human reality to rise up. Of course I am the being by whom "there is" (*es gibt*) being. But are we to say that I am the being by whom "there is" another human-reality? If we understand by that that I am the being for whom there is *for me* another human reality, this is a pure and simple truism. If we mean that I am the being by whom *there are* in general Others, we fall back into solipsism. In fact this human reality "with whom" I am is itself "in-the-world-with-me"; it is the free foundation of a world. (How does this make it *my* world? We can not deduce from the being-with an identity of the worlds "in which" the human realities are.) Human reality is its own possibilities. It is then for itself without having to wait for me to make its being exist in the form of the "there is." Thus I can constitute a world as "mortal," but I can not constitute a human-reality as a concrete being which is its own possibili-ties. My being-with, apprehended from the standpoint of "my" being, can be considered only as a pure exigency founded in *my* being; it does not constitute the slightest proof of the Other's existence, not the slightest bridge between me and the Other.

More precisely, this ontological relation between me and an abstract Other, due to the very fact that it defines in general my relation to others, is far from facilitating a particular ontic relation between me and Pierre; in fact it renders impossible any concrete connection between my being and a particular Other given in my experience. If my relation with the Other is *a priori*, it thereby exhausts all possibility of relation with others. Empirical and contingent relations can be only the specifications of it, not particular cases. There can be specifications of a law only under two circumstances: either the law is derived inductively from empirical, particular facts, and that is not the case here; or else it is *a priori* and unifies experience, as the Kantian concepts do. Actually in this latter case, its scope is restricted to the limits of experience: I find in things only what I have put into them. Now the act of relating two concrete "beings-in-the world" can not belong to *my* experience; and it therefore escapes from the domain of *being-with*. But as the law precisely *constitutes* its own domain, it excludes *a priori* every real fact which it has not constructed. The existence of time as an *a priori* form of my sensibility would *a priori* exclude me from all connection with a noumenal time which had the characteristics of a being. Thus the existence of an ontological and hence *a priori* "being-with" renders impossible all ontic connection with a concrete human-reality which would arise *for-itself* as an absolute transcendent. The "being-with," conceived as a structure of my being, isolates me as surely as the arguments for solipsism.

The reason for this is that Heidegger's *transcendence* is a concept in bad faith: it aims, to be sure, at surpassing idealism, and it succeeds in so far as idealism presents us with a subjectivity at rest in itself and contemplating its own images. But the idealism thus surpassed is only a bastard form of idealism, a sort of empirical-critical psychologism. Undoubtedly Heidegger's human-reality "exists outside itself." But this existence outside itself is precisely Heidegger's definition of the *self*. It resembles neither the Platonic [Neo-Platonic?] ekstasis where existence is really alienation, existence in an Other, nor Malebranche's vision in God, our own conception of the ekstasis and of the internal negation. Heidegger does not escape idealism; his flight outside the self, as an *a priori* structure of his being, isolates him as surely as the Kantian reflection on the *a priori* conditions of our experience. In fact what human-reality rediscovers at the inaccessible limit of this flight outside itself is still the self: the flight outside the self is a flight toward the self, and the world appears as the pure distance between the self and the self.

Consequently it would be in vain to look in *Sein und Zeit* for a simultaneous surpassing of all idealism and of all realism. Heidegger's attempt to bring human-reality out of its solitude raises those same difficulties which idealism generally encounters when it tries to found the existence of concrete beings which are similar to us and which as such escape our experience, which even as they are being constituted do not arise from our *a priori*. He seems to escape isolation because he takes the "outside of self" sometimes as being "outside-of-self-toward-self" and sometimes as "outside-self-in-others." But the second interpretation of "outside-of-self," which Heidegger surreptitiously slides in through his devious reasoning, is strictly incompatible with the first. Human-reality at the very heart of its ekstases remains alone. It is here that we can derive a new and valid insight as the result of our critical examination of Heidegger's teaching: Human-reality remains alone because the Other's existence has the nature of a contingent and irreducible fact. We *encounter* the Other; we do not constitute him. And if this fact still appears to us in the form of a necessity, yet it does not belong with those "conditions of the possibility of our experience" or—if you prefer—with ontological necessity. If the Other's existence is a necessity, it is a "contingent necessity"; that is, it is of the same type as the factual necessity which is imposed on the *cogito*. If the Other is to be capable of being given to us, it is by means of a direct apprehension which leaves to the encounter its character as facticity, just as the *cogito* itself leaves all its facticity to my own thought, a facticity which nevertheless shares in the apodicity of the *cogito* itself—*i.e.,* in its indubitability.

This long exposition of doctrine will not therefore have been useless if it enables us to formulate the necessary and sufficient conditions under which a theory of the existence of others can be valid.

1. Such a theory can not offer a new *proof* of the existence of others, or an argument better than any other against solipsism. Actually if solipsism is to be rejected, this can not be because it is impossible or, if you prefer, because nobody is truly solipsistic. The Other's existence will always be subject to doubt, at least if one doubts the Other only in words and abstractly, in the same way that without really being able to conceive of it, I can write, "I doubt my own existence." In short the Other's existence can not be a *probability*. Probability can concern only objects which appear in our experience and from which new effects can appear in our experience. There is probability only if a validation or invalidation of it is at every moment possible. Thus since the Other on principle and in its "For-itself" is outside my experience, the probability of his existence as *Another Self* can never be either validated or invalidated; it can be neither believed nor disbelieved, it can not even be measured; it loses therefore its very being as probability and becomes a pure fictional conjecture. In the same way M. Lalande has effectively shown that a hypothesis concerning the existence of living beings on the planet Mars will remain purely conjectural with no chance of being either true or false so long as we do not have at our disposal instruments or scientific theories enabling us to produce facts validating or invalidating this hypothesis. But the structure of the Other is on principle such that no new experiment will ever be able to be conceived, that no new theory will come to validate or invalidate the hypothesis of his existence, that no instrument will come to reveal new facts inspiring me to affirm or to reject this hypothesis. Therefore if the Other is not immediately present to me, and if his existence is not as sure as my own, all conjecture concerning him is entirely lacking in meaning. But if I do not conjecture about the Other, then, precisely, I affirm him. A theory of the Other's existence must therefore simply question me in my being, must make

clear and precise the meaning of that affirmation; in particular, far from inventing a proof, it must make explicit the very foundation of that certainty. In other words Descartes has not *proved* his existence. Actually I have always known that I existed, I have never ceased to practice the *cogito*. Similarly my resistance to solipsism—which is as lively as any I should offer to an attempt to doubt the *cogito*—proves that I have always known that the Other existed, that I have always had a total though implicit *comprehension* of his existence, that this "pre-ontological" comprehension comprises a surer and deeper understanding of the nature of the Other and the relation of his being to my being than all the theories which have been built around it. If the Other's existence is not a vain conjecture, a pure fiction, this is because there is a sort of *cogito* concerning it. It is this *cogito* which we must bring to light by specifying its structures and determining its scope and its laws.

2. On the other hand, Hegel's failure has shown us that the only point of departure possible is the Cartesian *cogito*. Moreover the *cogito* alone establishes us on the ground of that factual necessity which is the necessity of the Other's existence. Thus what for lack of a better term we called the *cogito* of the Other's existence is merged with my own *cogito*. The *cogito* examined once again, must throw me outside it and onto the Other, just as it threw me outside upon the In-itself; and this must be done not by revealing to me an *a priori* structure of myself which would point toward an equally *a priori* Other but by disclosing to me the concrete, indubitable presence of a particular, concrete Other, just as it has already revealed to me my own incomparable, contingent but necessary, and concrete existence. Thus we must ask the For-itself to deliver to us the For-others; we must ask absolute immanence to throw us into absolute transcendence. In my own inmost depths I must find not *reasons for believing* that the Other exists but the Other himself as not being me.

3. What the *cogito* must reveal to us is not the-Other-as-object. For a long time now it must have been obvious that what is called an *object* is said to be *probable*. If the Other is an object for me, he refers me to probability. But probability is founded solely on the infinite congruity of our representations. Since the Other is neither a representation nor a system of representations nor a necessary unity of our representations, he can not be probable: he can not *at first* be an object. Therefore if he is *for us*, this can be neither as a constitutive factor of our knowledge of the self, but as one who "interests" our being, and that not as he contributes *a priori* to constitute our being but as he interests it concretely and "ontically" in the empirical circumstances of our facticity.

4. If we attempt somehow regarding the Other what Descartes attempted to do for God with that extraordinary "proof by the idea of

perfection" which is wholly animated by the intuition of transcendence, then for our apprehension of the Other qua Other we are compelled to reject a certain type of negation which we have called an external negation. The Other must appear to the *cogito* as *not being* me. This negation can be conceived in two ways: either it is a pure, external negation, and it will separate the Other from myself as one substance from another substance—and in this case all apprehension of the Other is by definition impossible; or else it will be an internal negation, which means a synthetic, active connection of the two terms, each one of which constitutes itself by denying that it is the other. This negative relation will therefore be reciprocal and will possess a two fold interiority: This means first that the multiplicity of "Others" will not be a *collection* but a *totality* (in this sense we admit that Hegel is right) since each Other finds his being in the Other. It also means that this Totality is such that it is on principle impossible for us to adopt "the point of view of the whole." In fact we have seen that no abstract concept of consciousness can result from the comparison of my being-for-myself with my object-state for the Other. Furthermore this totality—like that of the For-itself—is a detotalized totality; for since existence-for-others is a radical refusal of the Other, no totalitarian and unifying synthesis of "Others" is possible.

It is in the light of these few observations that we in turn shall now attack the question of The Other.

THE LOOK

This woman whom I see coming toward me, this man who is passing by in the street, the beggar whom I hear calling before my window, all are for me *objects*—of that there is no doubt. Thus it is true that at least one of the modalities of the Other's presence to me is *object-ness*. But we have seen that if this relation of object-ness is the fundamental relation between the Other and myself, then the Other's existence remains purely conjectural. Now it is not only conjectural but *probable* that this voice which I hear is that of a man and not a song on a phonograph; it is infinitely *probable* that the passerby whom I see is a man and not a perfected robot. This means that without going beyond the limits of probability and indeed because of this very probability, my apprehension of the Other as an object essentially refers me to a fundamental apprehension of the Other in which he will not be revealed to me as an object but as a "presence in person." In short, if the Other is to be a probable object and not a dream of an object, then his object-ness must of necessity refer not to an original solitude beyond my reach, but to a fundamental connection in which the Other is manifested in some way other than through the knowledge which I have of him. The classical theories are right in considering that every perceived human organism *refers* to something and that this to which it refers is the foundation and guarantee of its probability. Their mistake lies in believing that this reference indicates a separate existence, a consciousness which would be behind its perceptible manifestations as the noumenon is behind the Kantian *Empfindung*. Whether or not this consciousness exists in a separate state, the face which I see does not refer to it; it is not this consciousness which is the *truth* of the probable object which I perceive. In actual fact the reference to a twin upsurge in which the Other is presence for me is to a "being-in-a-pair-with-the-Other," and this is given outside of knowledge proper even if the latter be conceived as an obscure and unexpressible form on the order of intuition. In other words, the problem of Others has generally been treated as if the primary relation by which the Other is discovered is object-ness; that is, as if the Other were first revealed—directly or indirectly—to our perception. But since this perception by its very nature *refers* to something other than to itself and since it can refer neither to an infinite series of appearances of the same type—as in idealism the perception of the table or of the chair does—nor to an isolated entity located on principle outside my reach, its essence must be to refer to a primary relation between my consciousness and the Other's. This relation, in which the Other must be given to me directly as a subject although in connection with me, is the fundamental relation, the very type of my being-for-others.

Nevertheless the reference here cannot be to any mystic or ineffable experience. It is in the reality of everyday life that the Other appears to us, and his probability refers to everyday reality. The problem is precisely this: there is in everyday reality an original relation to the Other which can be constantly pointed to and which consequently can be revealed to me outside all reference to a religious or mystic unknowable. In order to understand it I must question more exactly this ordinary appearance of the Other in the field of my perception; since this appearance refers to that fundamental relation, the appearance must be capable of revealing to us at least as a reality aimed at, the relation to which it refers. . . .

None of this enables us to leave the level on which the Other is an *object*. At most we are dealing with a particular type of objectivity akin to that which Husserl designated by the term *absence* without, however, his noting that the Other is defined not as the absence of a consciousness in relation to the body which I see but by the absence of the world which I perceive, an absence discovered at the very heart of my perception of this world. On this level the Other is an object in the world, an object which can be defined by the world. But this relation of flight and of absence on the part of the world in relation to me is only probable. If it is this which defines the objectivity of the Other, then to what original presence of the

Other does it refer? At present we can give this answer: if the Other-as-object is defined in connection with the world as the object which sees what I see, then my fundamental connection with the Other-as-subject must be able to be referred back to my permanent possibility of *being seen* by the Other. It is in and through the revelation of my being-as-object for the Other that I must be able to apprehend the presence of his being-as-subject. For just as the Other is a probable object for me-as-subject, so I can discover myself in the process of becoming a probable object for only a certain subject. This revelation can not derive from the fact that *my universe is an object for the Other-as-object*, as *if* the Other's look after having wandered over the lawn and the surrounding objects came following a definite path to place itself on me. I have observed that I can not be an object for an object. A radical conversion of the Other is necessary if he is to escape objectivity. Therefore I can not consider the look which the Other directs on me as one of the possible manifestations of his objective being; the Other can not look at *me* as he looks at the grass. Furthermore my objectivity can not itself derive *for me* from the objectivity of the world since I am precisely the one by whom *there is* a world; that is, the one who on principle can not be an object for himself.

Thus this relation which I call "being-seen-by-another," far from being merely one of the relations signified by the word *man*, represents an irreducible fact which can not be deduced either from the essence of the Other-as-object, or from my being-as-subject. On the contrary, if the concept of the Other-as-object is to have any meaning, this can be only as the result of the conversion and the degradation of that original relation. In a word, my apprehension of the Other in the world as *probably being* a man refers to my permanent possibility of *being-seen-by-him*; that is, to the permanent possibility that a subject who sees me may be substituted for the object seen by me. "Being-seen-by-the-Other" is the *truth* of "seeing-the-Other." Thus the notion of the Other can not under any circumstances aim at a solitary, extra-mundane consciousness which I can not even think. The man is defined by his relation to the world and by his relation to myself. He is that object in the world which determines an internal flow of the universe, an internal hemorrhage. He is the subject who is revealed to me in that flight of myself toward objectivation. But the original relation of myself to the Other is not only an absent truth aimed at across the concrete presence of an object in my universe; it is also a concrete, daily relation which at each instant I experience. At each instant the Other *is looking at me*. It is easy therefore for us to attempt with concrete examples to describe this fundamental connection which must form the basis of any theory concerning the Other. If the Other is on principle the *one who looks at me*, then we must be able to explain the meaning of the Other's look.

Every look directed toward me is manifested in connection with the appearance of a sensible form in our perceptive field, but contrary to what might be expected, it is not connected with any determined form. Of course what *most often* manifests a look is the convergence of two ocular globes in my direction. But the look will be given just as well on occasion when there is a rustling of branches, or the sound of a footstep followed by silence, or the slight opening of a shutter, or a light movement of a curtain. During an attack men who are crawling through the brush apprehend as a *look to be avoided*, not two eyes, but a white farm-house which is outlined against the sky at the top of a little hill. It is obvious that the object thus constituted still manifests the look as being probable. It is only probable that behind the bush which has just moved there is someone hiding who is watching me. But this probability need not detain us for the moment; we shall return to this point later. What is important first is to define the look in itself. Now the bush, the farmhouse are not the look; they only represent the eye, for the eye is not at first apprehended as a sensible organ of vision but as the support for the look. They never refer therefore to the actual eye of the watcher hidden behind the curtain, behind a window in the farmhouse. In themselves they are already eyes. On the other hand neither is the look one quality among others of the object which functions as an eye, nor is it the total form of that object, nor a "worldly" relation which is established between that object and me. On the contrary, far from perceiving the look on the objects which manifest it, my apprehension of a look turned toward me appears on the ground of the destruction of the eyes which "look at me." If I apprehend the look, I cease to perceive the eyes; they are there, they remain in the field of my perception as pure *presentations*, but I do not make any use of them; they are neutralized, put out of play; they are no longer the object of a thesis but remain in that state of "disconnection" in which the world is put by a consciousness practicing the phenomenological reduction prescribed by Husserl. It is never when eyes are looking at you that you can find them beautiful or ugly, that you can remark on their color. The Other's look hides his eyes; he seems to go *in front of them*. This illusion stems from the fact that eyes as objects of my perception remain at a precise distance which unfolds from me to them (in a word, I am present to the eyes without distance, but they are distant from the place where I "find myself") whereas the look is upon me without distance while at the same time it holds me at a distance—that is, its immediate presence to me unfolds a distance which removes me from it. I can not therefore direct my attention on the look without at the same stroke causing my perception to decompose and pass into the background. There is produced here something analogous to what I attempted to show elsewhere in connection with the subject of the imagination. We can not, I said then, perceive and imagine simultaneously; it must be either one or the other. I should willingly say here: we can not perceive the world and at the same time apprehend a look fastened upon us; it must be either one or the other. This is because to perceive is to *look at,* and to apprehend a look is not to apprehend a look-as-object in the world (unless the look is not directed upon us); it is to be conscious of *being looked at.* The look which the *eyes* manifest, no matter what kind of eyes they are is a pure reference to myself. What I apprehend immediately when I hear the branches crackling behind me is not that *there is someone there;* it is that I am vulnerable, that I have a body which can be hurt, that I occupy a place and that I can not in any case escape from the space in which I am without defense—in short, that I *am seen.* Thus the look is first an intermediary which refers from me to myself. . . .

But the Other's look is not only apprehended as spatializing; it is also *temporalizing.* The appearance of the Other's look is manifested for me through an *Erlebnis* which was on principle impossible for me to get in solitude—that of simultaneity. A world for a single for-itself could not comprehend simultaneity but only co-presences, for the for-itself is lost outside itself everywhere in the world, and it links all beings by the unity of its single presence. But simultaneity supposes the temporal connection of two existents which are not bound by any other relation. Two existents which exercise a reciprocal action on one another are not simultaneous because they belong to the same system. Simultaneity therefore does not belong to the existents of the world, it supposes the co-presence to the world of two presents considered as *presences-to.* Pierre's presence *to the* world is simultaneous *with* my presence. In this sense the original phenomenon of simultaneity is the fact that this glass is for Paul *at the same time* that it is for me. This supposes therefore a foundation for all simultaneity which must of necessity be the presence of an Other who is temporalized by my own temporalization. But to be exact, in so far as the other temporalizes *himself,* he temporalizes *me* with him; in so far as he launches out toward his own time, I appear to him in universal time. The *Other's look* in so far as I apprehend it comes to give to *my* time a new dimension. My presence, in so far as it is a present grasped by another as *my* present, has an outside; this presence which makes-itself-present *for me* is alienated for me in a present to which the Other makes himself present. I am thrown into the universal present in so far as the Other makes himself be a presence to me. But the universal present in which I come to take my place is a pure alienation of my universal present; physical time flows toward a pure and free temporalization which I am not; what is outlined on the horizon of that simultaneity which I live is an absolute temporalization from which I am separated by a nothingness.

As a temporal-spatial object in the world, as an essential structure of a temporal-spatial situation in the world, I offer myself to the Other's appraisal. This also I apprehend by the pure exercise of the *cogito*. To be looked at is to apprehend oneself as the unknown object of unknowable appraisals—in particular, of value judgments. But at the same time that in shame or pride I recognize the justice of these appraisals, I do not cease to take them for what they are—a free surpassing of the given toward possibilities. A judgment is the transcendental act of a free being. Thus being-seen constitutes me as a defenseless being for a freedom which is not my freedom. It is in this sense that we can consider ourselves as "slaves" in so far as we appear to the Other. But this slavery is not a historical result—capable of being surmounted—of a *life* in the abstract form of consciousness. I am a slave to the degree that my being is dependent at the center of a freedom which is not mine and which is the very condition of my being. In so far as I am the object of values which come to qualify me without my being able to act on this qualification or even to know it, I am enslaved. By the same token in so far as I am the instrument of possibilities which are not my possibilities, whose pure presence beyond my being I can not even glimpse, and which deny my transcendence in order to constitute me as a means to ends of which I am ignorant—I am *in danger*. This danger is not an accident but the permanent structure of my being-for-others.

This brings us to the end of our description. Yet before we can make use of it to discover just what the Other is, we must note that this description *has been worked out entirely on the level of the cogito*. We have only made explicit the meaning of those subjective reactions to the Other's look which are fear (the feeling of being in danger before the Other's freedom), pride, or shame (the feeling of being finally what I am but elsewhere, over there for the Other), the recognition of my slavery (the feeling of the alienation of all my possibilities). In addition this specification is not merely a conceptual fixing of bits of knowledge more or less obscure. Let each one refer to his own experience. There is no one who has not at some time been surprised in an attitude which was guilty or simply ridiculous. The abrupt modification then experienced was in no way provoked by the irruption of knowledge. It is rather in itself a solidification and an abrupt stratification of myself which leaves intact my possibilities and my structures "for-myself," but which suddenly pushes me into a new dimension of existence—the dimension of the *unrevealed*. Thus the appearance of the look is apprehended by me as the upsurge of an ekstatic relation of being, of which one term is the "me" as for-itself which is what it is not and which is not what it is, and of which other term is still the "me" but outside my reach, outside my action, outside my knowledge. This term, since it is directly connected with the infinite possibilities of a free Other, is itself an infinite and inexhaustible synthesis of unrevealed properties. Through the Other's look I *live* myself as fixed in the midst of the world, as in danger, as irremediable. But I *know* neither what I am nor what is my place in the world, not what face this world in which I am turns toward the Other.

Now at last we can make precise the meaning of this upsurge of the Other in and through his look. The Other is in no way given to us as an object. The objectivation of the Other would be the collapse of his being-as-a-look. Furthermore as we have seen, the Other's look is the disappearance of the Other's eyes as objects which manifest the look. The Other can not even be the object aimed at emptily at the horizon of my being for the Other. The objectivation of the Other, as we shall see, is a defence on the part of my being which, precisely by conferring on the Other a being for-me, frees me from my being-for the Other. In the phenomenon of the look, the Other is on principle that which can not be an object. At the same time we see that he can not be a *limiting term* of that relation of myself to myself which makes me arise for myself as the *unrevealed*. Neither can the Other be the goal of my *attention*; if in the upsurge of the Other's look, I *paid attention* to the look or to the Other, this could be only as to objects, for attention is an intentional direction toward objects. But it is not necessary to conclude that the Other is an abstract condition, a conceptual structure of the ekstatic relation; there is here in fact no object really thought, of which the Other could be a universal, formal structure. The Other is, to be sure, the condition of my being-unrevealed. But he is the concrete, particular condition of it. He is not engaged in my being in the midst of the world as one of its integral parts since he is precisely that which transcends this world in the midst of which I am as non-revealed; as such he can therefore be neither an object nor the formal, constituent element of an object. He can not appear to me, as we have seen, as a unifying or regulative category of my experience since he comes to me through an encounter. Then what is the Other?

In the first place, he is the being toward whom I do not turn my attention. He is the one who looks at me and at whom I am not yet looking, the one who delivers me to myself as *unrevealed* but without revealing himself, the one who is present to me as directing at me but never as the object of my direction; he is the concrete pole (though out of reach) of my flight, of the alienation of my possibles, and of the flow of the world toward another world which is *the same* world and yet lacks all communication with it. But he can not be distinct from this same alienation and flow; he is the meaning and the direction of them; he haunts this flow not as a *real or categorial* element but as a presence which is fixed and made part of the world if I attempt to "make-it-present" and which is never more present, more urgent than when I am not aware of it. For example if I am wholly engulfed in my shame, the Other is the immense, invisible presence which supports this shame and embraces it on every side; he is the supporting environment of my being-unrevealed. Let us see what it is which the Other manifests as *unrevealable* across my lived experience of the unrevealed.

First, the *Other's look* as the necessary condition of my objectivity is the destruction of all objectivity for me. The Other's look touches me across the world and is not only a transformation of myself but a total metamorphosis of the *world.* I am looked-at in a world which is looked-at. In particular the Other's look, which is a look-looking and not a look-looked-at, denies my distances from objects and unfolds its own distances. This look of the Other is given immediately as that by which distance comes to the world at the heart of a presence without distance. I withdraw; I am stripped of my distanceless presence to my world, and I am provided with a distance from the Other. There I am fifteen paces from the door, six yards from the window. But the Other comes searching for me so as to constitute me at a certain distance from him. As the Other constitutes me as at six yards from him, it is necessary that he be present to me without distance. Thus within the very experience of my distance from things and from the Other, I experience the distanceless presence of the Other to me.

Anyone may recognize in this abstract description that immediate and burning presence of the Other's look which has so often filled him with shame. In other words, in so far as I experience myself as looked-at, there is realized for me a trans-mundane presence of the Other. The Other looks as me not as he is "in the midst of" *my* world but as he comes toward the world and toward me from all his transcendence; when he looks at me, he is separated from me by no distance, by no object of the world—whether real or ideal—by no body in the world, but the sole fact of his nature as Other. Thus the appearance of the Other's look is not an appearance *in the world*—neither in "mine" nor in the "Other's"—and the relation which unites me to the Other cannot be a relation of exteriority inside the world. By the Other's look I effect the concrete proof that there is a "beyond the world." The Other is present to me without any intermediary as a transcendence *which is not mine.* But this presence is not reciprocal. All of the world's density is necessary in order that I may myself be present to the Other. An omnipresent and inapprehensible transcendence, posited upon me without intermediary as I am my being-unrevealed, a transcendence separated from me by the infinity of being, as I am plunged by this look into the heart of a world complete with its distances and its instruments—such is the Other's look when first I experience it as a look.

Furthermore by fixing my possibilities the Other reveals to me the impossibility of my being an object except for another freedom. I can not be an object for myself, for I am what I am; thrown back on its own resources, the reflective effort toward a dissociation results in failure; I am always reapprehended by myself. And when I naively assume that it is possible for me to be an objective being without being responsible for it, I thereby implicitly suppose the Other's existence; for how could I be an object if not for a subject. Thus for me the Other is first the being for whom I am an object; that is, the being *through whom* I gain my objectness. If I am to be able to conceive of even one of my properties in the objective mode, then the Other is already given. He is given not as a being of my universe but as a pure subject. Thus this pure subject which by definition I am unable to know—*i.e.*, to posit as object—is always *there* out of reach and without distance whenever I try to grasp myself as object. In experiencing the look, in experiencing myself as an unrevealed object-ness, I experience the inapprehensible subjectivity of the Other directly and with my being.

At the same time I experience the Other's infinite freedom. It is for and by means of a freedom and only for and by means of it that my possibles can be limited and fixed. A material obstacle can not fix my possibilities; it is only the occasion for my projecting myself toward other possibles and can not confer upon them an *outside*. To remain at home because it is raining and to remain at home because one has been forbidden to go out are by no means the same thing. In the first case I myself determine to stay inside in consideration of the consequences of my acts; I surpass the obstacle "rain" toward myself and I make an instrument of it. In the second case it is my very possibilities of going out of or staying inside which are presented to me as surpassed and fixed and which a freedom simultaneously forsees and prevents. It is not mere caprice which causes us often to do very naturally and without annoyance what would irritate us if another commanded it. This is because the order and the prohibition cause us to experience the Other's freedom across our own slavery. Thus in the look the death of my possibilities causes me to experience the Other's freedom. This death is realized only at the heart of that freedom; I am inaccessible to myself and yet myself, thrown, abandoned at the heart of the Other's freedom. In connection with this experience my belonging to universal time can appear to me only as contained and realized by an autonomous temporalization; only a for-itself which temporalizes itself can throw me into time.

Thus through the look I experience the Other concretely as a free,

conscious subject who causes there to be a world by temporalizing
himself toward his own possibilities. That subject's presence without
intermediary is the necessary condition of all thought which I would
attempt to form concerning myself. The Other is that "myself" from
which nothing separates me, absolutely nothing except his pure and
total freedom; that is, that indetermination of himself which he has to be
for and through himself.

We know enough at present to attempt to explain that unshakable
resistance which common sense has always opposed to the solipsistic
argument. This resistance indeed is based on the fact that the Other is
given to me as a concrete evident presence which I can in no way derive
from myself and which can in no way be placed in doubt nor made the
object of a phenomenological reduction or of any other ἐποχή.

If someone looks at me, I am conscious *of being* an object. But this
consciousness can be produced only in and through the existence of the
Other. In this respect Hegel was right. However *that other* consciousness
and *that other* freedom are never *given* to me; for if they were, they would
be *known* and would therefore be an object, which would cause me to
cease being an object. Neither can I derive the concept or the representation of them from my own background. First because I do not "conceive"
them nor "represent" them to myself; expressions like these would refer
us again to "knowing," which on principle is removed from consideration. In addition this concrete proof of freedom which I can effect by
myself is the proof of *my* freedom; every concrete apprehension of a
consciousness is consciousness (of) *my* consciousness; the very notion of
consciousness makes reference only to *my* possible consciousnesses. Indeed we established in our Introduction that the *existence* of freedom and
of consciousness precedes and conditions their *essence*; consequently these
essences can subsume only concrete exemplifications of *my* consciousness
or of *my* freedom. In the third place the Other's freedom and consciousness can not be categories serving for the unification of my representations. To be sure, as Husserl has shown, the ontological structure of
"my" world demands that it be also a *world for others*. But to the extent
that the Other confers a particular type of objectivity on the objects of *my*
world, this is because he is already in this world in the capacity of an
object. If it is correct that Pierre, who is reading before me, gives a
particular type of objectivity to the face of the book which is turned
toward him, then this objectivity is conferred on a face which on
principle I can see (although as we have said, it escapes me in so far as it is
read), on a face which belongs to the world where I am and which
consequently by a magic bond is connected beyond distance to Pierre-as-
object. Under these conditions the concept of the Other can in fact be

fixed as an empty form and employed constantly as a reinforcement of objectivity for the world which is mine. But the Other's presence in his look-looking can not contribute to reinforce the world, for on the contrary it undoes the world by the very fact that it causes the world to escape me. The escape of the world from me when it is *relative* and when it is an escape toward the Other-as-object, reinforces objectivity. The escape of the world and of my self from me when it is absolute and when it is effected toward a freedom which is not mine, is a dissolution of my knowledge. The world disintegrates in order to be reintegrated over there as a world; but this disintegration is not given to me; I can not know it nor even think it. The presence to me of the Other-as-a-look is therefore neither a knowledge nor a projection of my being nor a form of unification nor a category. It *is* and I can not derive it from me.

At the same time I can not make it fall beneath the stroke of the phenomenological ἐποχή. The latter indeed has for its goal putting the world within brackets so as to reveal transcendental consciousness in its absolute reality. Whether in general this operation is possible or not is something which is not for us to decide here. But in the case which concerns us the *Other* can not be put out of consideration since as a look-looking he definitely does not belong to the world. I am ashamed *of* myself *before* the Other, we said. The phenomenological reduction must result in removing from consideration the object of shame in order better to make shame itself stand out in its absolute subjectivity. But the Other is not the *object* of the shame; the object is my act or my situation in the world. They alone can be strictly "reduced." The Other is not even an objective condition of my shame. Yet he is as the very-being of it. Shame is the revelation of the Other not in the way in which a consciousness reveals an object but in the way in which one moment of consciousness implies on the side another moment as its motivation. If we should have attained pure consciousness by means of the *cogito,* and if this pure consciousness were only a consciousness (of being) shame, the Other's consciousness would still haunt it as an inapprehensible presence and would thereby escape all reduction. This demonstrates sufficiently that it is not in the world that the Other is first to be sought but at the side of consciousness as a consciousness in which and by which consciousness makes itself be what it is. Just as my consciousness apprehended by the *cogito* bears indubitable witness of itself and of its own existence, so certain particular consciousnesses—for example, "shame-conscious-ness"—bear indubitable witness to the *cogito* both of themselves and of the existence of the Other.

But, someone may object, is this not simply because of the Other's look as *meaning* of my objectivity-for-myself. If so, we shall fall back into solipsism; when I integrate myself as an object in the concrete system of representations, the meaning of this objectivation would be projected outside me and hypostasized as *the Other*.

But we must note the following:

1. My object-ness for myself is in no way a specification of Hegel's *Ich bin Ich*. We are not dealing with a formal identity, and my being-as-object or being-for-others is profoundly different from my being-for-myself. In fact the notion of *objectivity,* as we observed in Part One, requires an explicit negation. The object is that which is not my consciousness; consequently it is that which does not have the characteristics of consciousness since the only existent which has for me the characteristics of consciousness is the consciousness which is *mine.* Thus the Me-as-object-for-myself is a Me which *is not* Me; that is, which does not have the characteristics of consciousness. It is a *degraded* consciousness; objectivation is a radical metamorphosis. Even if I could see myself clearly and distinctly as an object, what I should see would not be the adequate representation of what I am in myself and for myself, of that "incomparable monster preferable to all," as Malraux puts it, but the apprehension of my being-outside-myself, for the Other; that is, the objective apprehension of my being-other, which is radically different from my being-for-myself, and which does not refer to myself at all.

To apprehend myself as *evil*, for example, could not be to refer myself to what I am for myself, for I am not and can not be evil for myself for two reasons. In the first place, I *am* not evil any more than I *am* a civil servant or a physician. In fact I am in the mode of not being what I am and of being what I am not. The qualification "evil," on the contrary, characterizes me as an *in-itself.* In the second place, if I were *to be* evil for myself, I should of necessity be so in the mode of *having* to be so and would have to apprehend myself and will myself as evil. But this would mean that I must discover myself as willing what appears to myself as the opposite of my Good and precisely because it is the Evil or the opposite of my Good. It is therefore expressly necessary that I will the contrary of what I desire at one and the same moment and in the same relation; that is, I would have to hate myself precisely as I am myself. If on the level of the for-itself I am to realize fully this essence of evil, it would be necessary for me to assume myself as evil; that is, I would have to approve myself by the same act which makes me blame myself. We can see that this notion of evil can in no way derive its origin from me in so far as I am Me. It would be in vain for me to push the ekstasis to its extreme limits or to effect a detachment from self which would constitute me for myself; I shall never succeed in conferring evil on myself or even in conceiving it for myself if I am thrown on my own resources.

This is because I *am* my own detachment, I *am* my own nothingness; simply because I am my own mediator between Me and Me, all objectivity disappears. I can not *be* this nothingness which separates me from me-as-object, for there must of necessity be a *presentation* to me of the object which I am. Thus I can not confer on myself any quality without mediation or an objectifying power which is not my own power and which I can neither pretend nor forge. Of course this has been said before; it was said a long time ago that the Other teaches me who I am. But the same people who uphold this thesis affirm on the other hand that I derive the concept of the Other from myself by reflecting on my own powers and by projection or analogy. Therefore they remain at the center of a vicious circle from which they can not get out. Actually the Other can not be the meaning of my objectivity; he is the concrete, transcending condition of it. This is because such qualities as "evil," "jealous," "sympathetic" or "antipathetic" and the like are not empty imaginings; when I use them to qualify the Other, I am well aware that I want to touch him in his being. Yet I can not live them as my own realities. If the Other confers them on me, they are admitted by what I am for-myself; when the Other describes my character, I do not "recognize" myself and yet I know that "it is me." I accept the responsibility for this stranger who is presented to me, but he does not cease to be a stranger. This is because he is neither a simple unification of my subjective representations, not a "Me" which I am in the sense of the *Ich bin Ich*, nor an empty image which the Other makes of me for himself and for which he alone bears the responsibility. This Me, which is not to be compared to the Me which I have to be, is still Me but metamorphosed by a new setting and adapted to that setting; it is a being, *my* being but with entirely new dimensions of being and new modalities. It is Me separated from Me by an impassible nothingness, for I *am* this me but I am not this nothingness which separates me from myself. It is the Me which I am by an ultimate ekstasis which transcends all my *ekstases* since it is not the ekstasis which I have to be. My being for-others is a fall through absolute emptiness toward objectivity. And since this fall is an *alienation*, I can not make myself be for myself as an object; for in no case can I ever alienate myself from myself.

2.   Furthermore the Other does not constitute me as an object for myself but *for him.* In other words he does not serve as a regulative or constitutive concept for the pieces of knowledge which I may have of myself. Therefore the Other's presence does not cause me-as-object to "appear." I apprehend nothing but an escape from myself toward ———. Even when language has revealed that the Other considers me evil or jealous, I shall never have a concrete intuition of my evil or of my

jealousy. These will never be more than fleeting notions whose very nature will be to escape me. I shall not apprehend my evil, but in relation to this or that particular act I shall escape myself, I shall feel my alienation or my flow towards . . . a being which I shall only be able to think emptily as evil and which nevertheless I shall *feel that I am,* which I shall live at a distance through shame or fear.

Thus myself-as-object is neither knowledge nor a unity of knowledge but an uneasiness, a lived wrenching away from the ekstatic unity of the for-itself, a limit which I can not reach and which yet I am. The Other through whom this Me *comes to me* is neither knowledge nor category but the fact of the presence of a strange freedom. In fact my wrenching away from myself and the upsurge of the Other's freedom are one; I can feel them and live them only as an ensemble; I cannot even try to conceive of one without the other. The fact of the Other is incontestable and touches me to the heart. I realize him through *uneasiness;* through him I am perpetually *in danger* in a world which is *this* world and which nevertheless I can only glimpse. The Other does not appear to me as a being who is constituted first so as to encounter me later; he appears as a being who arises in an original relation of being with me and whose indubitability and *factual necessity* are those of my own consciousness. . . . At this point in our investigation now we have elucidated the essential structures of being-for-others, there is an obvious temptation to raise the metaphysical question: "Why are there Others?" As we have seen, the existence of Others is not a consequence which can derive from the ontological structure of the for-itself. It is a primary event, to be sure, but of a *metaphysical* order; that is, it results from the contingency of being. The question "why" is essentially connected with these metaphysical existences.

We know very well that the answer to the "why" can only refer us to an original contingency, but still it is necessary to prove that the metaphysical phenomenon which we are considering is an irreducible contingency. In this sense ontology appears to us capable of being defined as the specification of the structures of being of the existent taken as a totality, and we shall define metaphysics rather as raising the question of the existence of the existent. This is why in view of the absolute contingency of the existent, we are convinced that any metaphysics must conclude with a "that is"—*i.e.*, in a direct intuition of that contingency.

Is it possible to posit the question of the existence of Others? Is this existence an irreducible fact, or is it to be derived from a fundamental contingency? Such are the preliminary questions which we can in turn pose to the metaphysician who questions us concerning the existence of Others.

Let us examine more closely the possibility of the metaphysical question. What appears to us first is the fact that the being-for-others represents the third ekstasis of the for-itself. The first ekstasis is indeed the tridimensional projection on the part of the for-itself toward a being which it has to be in the mode of non-being. It represents the first fissure, the nihilation which the for-itself has to be, the wrenching away on the part of the for-itself from everything which it is, and this wrenching away is constitutive of its being. The second ekstasis or reflective ekstasis is the wrenching away from this very wrenching away. The reflective scissiparity corresponds to a vain attempt to take a point of view on the nihilation which the for-itself has to be, in order that this nihilation as a simply given phenomenon may be a nihilation *which is*. But at the same time reflection wants to recover this wrenching away, which it attempts to contemplate as a pure given, by affirming concerning itself that it *is* this nihilation which is. This is a flagrant contradiciton: in order to be able to apprehend my transcendence, I should have to transcend it. But my own transcendence can only transcend. I *am* my own transcendence; I can not make use of it so as to constitute it as a transcendence-transcended. I am condemned to be forever my own nihilation. In short reflection [reflexion] *is* the reflected-on.

The reflective nihilation, however, is pushed further than that of the pure for-itself as a simple self-consciousness. In self-consciousness, in fact, the two terms of the dyad "reflected-reflecting" [*reflété-reflétant*] were so incapable of presenting themselves separately that the duality remained perpetually evanescent and each term while positing itself for the other *became* the other. But with reflection the case is different since the "reflection-reflecting" which is reflected-on exists for a "reflection-reflecting" which is reflective. Reflected-on and reflective, therefore, each tend toward independence, and the *nothing* which separates them tends to divide them more profoundly than the *nothingness* which the For-itself has to be separates the reflection from the reflecting. Yet neither the reflective nor the reflected-on can secrete this separating nothingness, for in that case reflection [*reflexion*] would be an autonomous for-itself coming to direct itself on the reflected-on, which would be to suppose an external negation as the preliminary condition of an internal negation. There can be no reflection if it is not entirely a *being*, a being which has to be its own nothingness.

Thus the reflective ekstasis is found on the path to a more radical ekstasis—the being-for-others. The final term of the nihilation, the ideal pole should be in fact the external negation—that is, a scissiparity in-itself or the spatial exteriority of indifference. In relation to this external negation the three ekstases are ranked in the order which we have just presented, but the goal is never achieved. It remains on principle ideal; in fact the for-itself—without running the risk of ceasing by the same stroke to be-for-itself—can not by itself realize in relation to any being a negation which would be in-itself. The constitutive negation of being-for-others is therefore an *internal negation*; it is a nihilation which the for-itself has to be, just like the reflective nihilation. But here the scissiparity attacks the very negation; it is no longer only the negation which divides being into reflected and reflecting and in turn divides the dyad reflected-reflecting into (reflected-reflecting) reflected and (reflected-reflecting) reflecting. Here the negation is divided into two internal and opposed negations; each is an internal negation, but they are nevertheless separated from one another by an inapprehensible external nothingness. In fact since each of them is exhausted in denying that one for-itself is the other and since each negation is wholly engaged in that being which it has to be, it is no longer in command of itself so as to deny concerning itself that it is the opposite negation. Here suddenly appears the *given*, not as the result of an identity of being-in-itself but as a sort of phantom of exteriority which neither of the negations has to be and which yet separates them. Actually in the reflective being we have already found the beginning of this negative inversion. In fact the reflective as a witness is profoundly affected in its being by its reflectivity, and consequently in so far as it makes itself reflective, it aims at not being the reflected-on. But reciprocally the reflected-on is self-consciousness as the reflected-on consciousness *of* this or that transcendent phenomenon. We said of it that it knows itself looked-at. In this sense it aims on its part at not-being the reflective since every consciousness is defined by its negativity. But this tendency to a double schism was recovered and stifled by the fact that in spite of everything the reflective had to be the reflected-on and that the reflected-on had to be the reflective. The double negation remained evanescent.

In the case of the third ekstasis we behold a reflective scissiparity pushed further. The results may surprise us: on the one hand, since the negations are effected in interiority, the Other and myself can not come to one another from the outside. It is necessary that there be a *being* "I-and-the-Other" which has to be the reciprocal scissiparity of the for-others just as the totality "reflective-reflected-on" is a being which has to be its own nothingness; that is, my selfness and that of the Other are structures of one and the same totality of being. Thus Hegel appears to be right: the point of view of the totality is the point of view of being, the *true* point of view. Everything happens as if my selfness confronting that of the Other were produced and maintained by a totality which would push its own nihilation to the extreme; being-for-others appears to be the prolongation of the pure reflective scissiparity. In this sense everything happens as if the Other and myself indicated the vain effort of a totality of for-itself to reapprehend itself and to envelop what it *has to be* in the pure and simple mode of the in-itself. This effort to reapprehend itself as object is pushed here to the limit—that is, well beyond the reflective division—and would produce a result precisely the reverse of the end toward which this totality would project itself. By its effort to be self-consciousness the totality-for-itself would be constituted in the face *of* the self as a self-as-consciousness which has to not-be the self of which it is consciousness. Conversely the self-as-object in order to *be* would have to experience itself as made-to-be by and for a consciousness which it has to not-be if it wishes to be. Thus would be born the schism of the for-others, and this dichotomic division would be repeated to infinity in order to constitute a plurality of consciousnesses as fragments of a radical explosion. "There would be" numerous *Others* as the result of a failure the reverse of the reflective failure. In reflection in fact if I do not succeed in apprehending myself as an object but only as a quasi-object, this is because I am the object which I wish to grasp; I have to be the nothingness which separates me from myself. I can escape my selfness neither by taking a point of view on myself (for thus I do not succeed in realizing myself as being) nor by apprehending myself in the form of the "there is" (here the recovery fails because the recoverer is to himself the recovered). In the case of being-for-others, on the contrary, the scissiparity is pushed further; the (reflection-reflecting) reflected is radically distinct from the (reflection-reflecting) reflecting and thereby can be an object for it. But this time the recovery fails because the recovered is *not* the one recovering. Thus the totality which is not what it is but which is what it is not, would—as the result of a radical attempt at wrenching away from self—everywhere produce its being as an "elsewhere." The scattering of being-in-itself of a shattered totality, always elsewhere, always at a distance, never in itself, but always maintained in being by the perpetual explosion of this totality—such would be the being of others and of myself as other.

But on the other hand, *simultaneously* with my negation of myself, the Other denies concerning himself that he is me. These two negations are equally indispensible to being-for-others, and they can not be reunited by any synthesis. This is not because an external nothingness would have separated them at the start but rather because the in-itself would recapture each one in relation to the other by the mere fact that each one *is not* the other without having to not-be the other. There is here a kind of limit of the for-itself which stems from the for-itself itself but which qua limit is independent of the for-itself. We rediscover something like *facticity* and we can not conceive how the totality of which we were speaking earlier would have been able at the very heart of the most radical wrenching away to produce in its being a nothingness which it in no way has to be. In fact it seems that this nothingness has slipped into this totality in order to shatter it just as in the atomism of Leucippus non-being slips into the Parmenidean totality of being and makes it explode into atoms. Therefore it represents the negation of any synthetic totality in terms of which one might claim to understand the plurality of consciousnesses. Of course it is inapprehensible since it is produced neither by the Other nor by myself, nor by any intermediary, for we have established that consciousnesses experience one another without intermediary. Of course where we directed our sight, we encountered as the object of our description only a pure and simple internal negation. Yet it is there in the irreducible fact that there is a *duality* of negations. It is not, to be sure, the *foundation* of the multiplicity of consciousnesses, for if it existed before this multiplicity, it would make all *being-for* others impossible. On the contrary, we must conceive of it as the expression of this multiplicity; it appears with this multiplicity. But since there is *nothing* which can found it, neither a particular consciousness nor a totality exploding into consciousnesses, it appears as a pure, irreducible contingency. It is *the fact that my denial that I am the Other is not sufficient to make the Other exist, but that the Other must simultaneously with my own negation deny that he is me.* This is the *facticity* of being-for-others.

Thus we arrive at this contradictory conclusion: being-for-others can be only if it *is made-to-be* by a totality which is lost so that being-for-others may arise, a position which would lead us to postulate the existence and directing power of the *mind.* But on the other hand, this being-for-others can exist only if it involves an inapprehensible and external non-being which no totality, not even the mind, can produce or found. In one sense the existence of a plurality of consciousnesses can not be a primary fact and it refers us to an original fact of a wrenching away from self, a fact of the mind. Thus the question "Why is there a plurality of consciousnesses?" could receive an answer. But in another sense the facticity of this plurality seems to be irreducible; and if the mind is considered from the standpoint of the *fact* of the plurality, it vanishes. Then the metaphysical question no longer has meaning; we have encountered a fundamental contingency, and we can answer only by "So it is." Thus the original ekstasis is deepened; it appears that we can not make it a part of nothingness. The for-itself has appeared to us as a being which exists in so far as it is not what it is and is what it is not. The ekstatic totality of the mind is not simply a totality detotalized; it appears to us as a shattered being concerning which we can neither say that it exists or that it does not exist. Thus our description has enabled us to satisfy the preliminary conditions which we have posited for any theory about the existence of the Other. The multiplicity of consciousnesses appears to us as a *synthesis* and not as a *collection*, but it is a synthesis whose totality is inconceivable.

Is this to say that the antinomic character of the totality is itself an irreducible? Or from a higher point of view can we make it disappear? Ought we to posit that the mind is the *being which is and is not* just as we posited that the for-itself is what it is not and is not what it is? The question has no meaning. It is supposing that it is possible for us to *take a point of view* on the totality; that is, to consider it from outside. But this is impossible precisely because I exist as myself on the foundation of this totality and to the extent that I am engaged in it. No consciousness, not even God's, can "see the underside"—that is, apprehend the totality as such. For if God is consciousness, he is integrated in the totality. And if by his nature, he is a being *beyond consciousness* (that is, an in-itself which would be its own foundation) still the totality can appear to him only as *object* (in that case he lacks the totality's internal disintegration as the subjective effort to reapprehend the self) or as subject (then since God *is not* this subject, he can only experience it without knowing it). Thus no point of view on the totality is conceivable; the totality has no "outside," and the very question of the meaning of the "underside" is stripped of meaning. We cannot go further.

Maurice Merleau-Ponty

The Visible and the Invisible

Reflection and Interrogation

THE PERCEPTUAL FAITH AND ITS OBSCURITY

We see the things themselves, the world is what we see: formulae of this kind express a faith common to the natural man and the philosopher—the moment he opens his eyes; they refer to a deep-seated set of mute "opinions" implicated in our lives. But what is strange about this faith is that if we seek to articulate it into theses or statements, if we ask ourselves what is this *we*, what *seeing* is, and what *thing* or *world* is, we enter into a labyrinth of difficulties and contradictions.

What Saint Augustine said of time—that it is perfectly familiar to each, but that none of us can explain it to the others—must be said of the world. [Ceaselessly the philosopher finds himself] obliged to reinspect and redefine the most well-grounded notions, to create new ones, with new words to designate them, to undertake a true reform of the understanding—at whose term the evidence of the world, which seemed indeed to be the clearest of truths, is supported by the seemingly most sophisticated thoughts, before which the natural man now no longer recognizes where he stood. Whence the age-old ill-humor against philosophy is reanimated, the grievance always brought against it that it reverses the roles of the clear and the obscure. The fact that the philosopher claims to speak in the very name of the naïve evidence of the world, that he refrains from adding anything to it, that he limits himself to drawing out all its consequences, does not excuse him; on the contrary he dispossesses [humanity] only the more completely, inviting it to think of itself as an enigma.

This is the way things are and nobody can do anything about it. It is at the same time true that the world is *what we see* and that, nonetheless, we must learn to see it—first in the sense that we must match this vision

Excerpted from Maurice Merleau-Ponty, *The Visible and the Invisible*, translated by A. Lingis, edited by C. Lefort (Evanston: Northwestern University Press, 1968), 3–14, 28–49.

with knowledge, take possession of it, *say* what *we* and what *seeing* are, act therefore as if we knew nothing about it, as if here we still had everything to learn. But philosophy is not a lexicon, it is not concerned with "word-meanings," it does not seek a verbal substitute for the world we see, it does not transform it into something said, it does not install itself in the order of the said or of the written as does the logician in the proposition, the poet in the word, or the musician in the music. It is the things themselves, from the depths of their silence, that it wishes to bring to expression. If the philosopher questions, and hence feigns ignorance of the world and of the vision of the world which are operative and take form continually within him, he does so precisely in order to make them speak, because he believes in them and expects from them all his future science. The questioning here is not a beginning of negation, a perhaps put in the place of being. It is for philosophy the only way to conform itself with the vision we have in fact, to correspond with what, in that vision, provides for thought, with the paradoxes of which that vision is made, the only way to adjust itself to those figured enigmas, the thing and the world, whose massive being and truth teem with incompossible details.

For after all, sure as it is that I see my table, that my vision terminates in it, that it holds and stops my gaze with its insurmountable density, as sure even as it is that when, seated before my table, I think of the Pont de la Concorde, I am not then in my thoughts but am at the Pont de la Concorde, and finally sure as it is that at the horizon of all these visions or quasi-visions it is the world itself I inhabit, the natural world and the historical world, with all the human traces of which it is made—still as soon as I attend to it this conviction is just as strongly contested, by the very fact that this visions is *mine*. We are not so much thinking here of the age-old argument from dreams, delirium, or illusions, inviting us to consider whether what we see is not "false." For to do so the argument makes use of that faith in the world it seems to be unsettling: we would not know even what the false is, if there were not times when we had distinguished it from the true. The argument therefore postulates the world in general, the true in itself; this is secretly invoked in order to disqualify our perceptions and cast them pell-mell back into our "interior life" along with our dreams, in spite of all observable differences, for the sole reason that our dreams were, at the time, as convincing as they—forgetting that the "falsity" of dreams cannot be extended to perceptions since it appears only relative to perceptions and that if we are to be able to speak of falsity, we do have to have experiences of truth. Valid against naïveté, against the idea of a perception that would plunge forth to surprise the things beyond all experience, as the light draws them from the night wherein they pre-existed, the argument does not [elucidate?]; it is marked with this same naïveté itself, since it equalizes the perception and the dream only by setting opposite them a Being that would be in itself only. If, however, as the argument, in the measure that it has validity, shows, we must completely reject this phantasm, then the intrinsic, descriptive differences between the dream and the perceived take on ontological value. And we answer Pyrrhonism sufficiently by showing that there is a difference of structure and, as it were, of grain between the perception or true vision, which gives rise to an open series of concordant explorations, and the dream, which is not *observable* and, upon examination, is almost nothing but blanks. To be sure, this does not terminate the problem of our access to the world; on the contrary it is only beginning. For there remains the problem of how we can be under the illusion of seeing what we do not see, how the rags of the dream can, before the dreamer, be worth the close-woven fabric of the true world, how the unconsciousness of not having observed can, in the fascinated man, take the place of the consciousness of having observed. If one says that the void of the imaginary remains forever what it is, is never equivalent to the plenum of the perceived and never gives rise to the *same* certitude, that it is *not taken to be worth* the perceived, that the sleeping man has lost every reference mark, every model, every canon of the clear and the articulate, and that one sole particle of the perceived world introduced in it would instantaneously dissipate the enchantment, the fact remains that if we can lose our reference marks *unbeknownst to ourselves* we are never sure of *having* them when we think we have them; if we can withdraw from the world of perception without knowing it, nothing proves to us that we are ever in it, nor that the observable is ever entirely observable, nor that it is made of another fabric than the dream. Then, the difference between perception and dream not being absolute, one is justified in counting them both among "our experiences," and it is above perception itself that we must seek the guarantee and the sense of its ontological function. We will stake out that route, which is that of the philosophy of reflection [*la philosphie réflexive*], when it opens. But it begins well beyond the Pyrrhonian arguments; by themselves they would deter us from any elucidation, since they refer vaguely to the idea of a Being wholly in itself and by contrast count the perceived and the imaginary indiscriminately among our "states of consciousness." At bottom, Pyrrhonism shares the illusions of the naïve man. It is the naïveté that rends itself asunder in the night. Between Being in itself and the "interior life" it does not even catch sight of the *problem of the world*. Whereas it is toward that problem that we are making our way. What interests us is not the reasons one can have to consider the existence of the world "uncertain"—as if one already knew what to exist is and as if the whole question were to apply this concept appropriately. For us the essential is to know precisely what the being of the world means. Here we must presuppose nothing—neither the naïve idea of being in itself, therefore, nor the correlative idea of a being of representation, of a being for the consciousness, of a being for man: these, along with the being of the world, are all notions that we have to rethink with regard to our experience of the world. We have to reformulate the sceptical arguments outside of every ontological preconception and reformulate them precisely so as to know what world-being, thing-being, imaginary being, and conscious being are.

Now that I have in perception the thing itself, and not a representation, I will only add that the thing is at the end of my gaze and, in general, at the end of my exploration. Without assuming anything from what the science of the body of the other can teach me, I must acknowledge that the table before me sustains a singular relation with my eyes and my body: I see it only if it is within their radius of action; above it there is the dark mass of my forehead, beneath it the more indecisive contour of my cheeks—both of these visible at the limit and capable of hiding the table, as if my vision of the world itself were formed from a certain point of the world. What is more, my movements and the movements of my eyes make the world vibrate—as one rocks a dolmen with one's finger without disturbing its fundamental solidity. With each flutter of my eyelashes a curtain lowers and rises, though I do not think for an instant of imputing this eclipse to the things themselves; with each movement of my eyes that sweep the space before me the things suffer a brief torsion, which I also ascribe to myself; and when I walk in the street with eyes fixed on the horizon of the houses, the whole of the setting near at hand quivers with each footfall on the asphalt, then settles down in its place. I would express what takes place badly indeed in saying that here a "subjective component" or a "corporeal constituent" comes to cover over the things themselves: it is not a matter of another layer or a veil that would have come to pose itself between them and me. The stirring of the "appearance" does not disrupt the evidence of the thing—any more than monocular images interfere when my two eyes operate in synergy. The binocular perception is not made up of two monocular perceptions surmounted; it is of another order. The monocular images *are* not in the same sense that the thing perceived with both eyes *is*. They are phantoms and it is the real; they are pre-things and it is the thing: they vanish when we pass to normal vision and re-enter into the thing as into their daylight truth. They are too far from having its density to enter into competition with it: they are only a certain divergence from the imminent true vision, absolutely bereft of its [prestiges?] and therefore drafts for or residues of the true vision, which accomplishes them by reabsorbing them. The monocular images cannot be *compared* with the synergic perception: one cannot put them side by side; it is necessary to choose between the thing and the floating pre-things. We can effect the passage by *looking*, by awakening to the world; we cannot witness it as spectators. It is not a *synthesis*; it is a metamorphosis by which the appearances are instantaneously stripped of a value they owed merely to the absence of a true perception. Thus in perception we witness the miracle of a totality that surpasses what one thinks to be its conditions or its parts, that from afar holds them under its power, as if they existed only on its threshold and were destined to lose themselves in it. But if it is to displace them as it does, it is necessary that the perception maintain in its depth all their corporeal ties: it is by *looking*, it is still with my eyes that I arrive at the true thing, with these same eyes that a moment ago gave me monocular images—now they simply function *together* and as though *for good*. Thus the relation between the things and my body is decidedly singular: it is what makes me sometimes remain in appearances, and it is also what sometimes brings me to the things themselves; it is what produces the buzzing of appearances, it is also what silences them and casts me fully into the world. Everything comes to pass as though my power to reach the world and my power to entrench myself in phantasms only came one with the other; even more: as though the access to the world were but the other face of a withdrawal and this retreat to the margin of the world a servitude and another expression of my natural power to enter into it. The world is what I perceive, but as soon as we examine and express its absolute proximity, it also becomes, inexplicably, irremediable distance. The "natural" man holds on to both ends of the chain, thinks *at the same time* that his perception enters into the things and that it is formed this side of his body. Yet coexist as the two convictions do without difficulty in the exercise of life, once reduced to theses and to propositions they destroy one another and leave us in confusion.

What if I took not only my own views of myself into account but also the other's views of himself and of me? Already my body as stage director of my perception has shattered the illusion of a coinciding of my perception with the things themselves. Between them and me there are henceforth hidden powers, that whole vegetation of possible phantasms which it holds in check only in the fragile act of the look. No doubt, it is not entirely my body that perceives: I know only that it can prevent me from perceiving, that I cannot perceive without its permission; the moment perception comes my body effaces itself before it and never does the perception grasp the body in the act of perceiving. If my left hand is touching my right hand, and if I should suddenly wish to apprehend with my right hand the work of my left hand as it touches, this reflection of the body upon itself always miscarries at the last moment: the moment I feel my left hand with my right hand, I correspondingly cease touching my right hand with my left hand. But this last-minute failure does not

drain all truth from that presentiment I had of being able to touch myself
touching: my body does not perceive, but it is as if it were built around
the perception that dawns through it; through its whole internal
arrangement, its sensory-motor circuits, the return ways that control
and release movements, it is, as it were, prepared for a self-perception,
even though it is never itself that is perceived nor itself that perceives.
Before the science of the body (which involves the relation with the
other) the experience of my flesh as gangue of my perception has taught
me that perception does not come to birth just anywhere, that it emerges
in the recess of a body. The other men who see "as we do," whom we see
seeing and who see us seeing, present us with but an amplification of the
same paradox. If it is already difficult to say that my perception, such as I
live it, goes unto the things themselves, it is indeed impossible to grant
access to the world to the others' perception; and, by a sort of backlash,
they also refuse me this access which I deny to them. For where the others
(or myself seen by them) are concerned, one must not only say that the
thing is caught up by the vortex of exploratory movements and perceptual behaviors and drawn inward. If perhaps there is for me no sense in
saying that my perception and the thing it aims at are "in my head" (it is
certain only that they are *"not elsewhere"*), I cannot help putting the
other, and the perception he has, *behind his body*. More exactly, the thing
perceived by the other is doubled: there is *the one he perceives*, God knows
where, and there is the one I see, outside of his body, and which I call the
true thing—as he calls true thing the table *he sees* and consigns to the
category of appearances the one I see. The true things and the perceiving
bodies are this time no longer in the ambiguous relation which a
moment ago we found between *my* things and *my* body. Now the true
things and the perceiving bodies, whether close-up or distant, are in any
case juxtaposed in the world, and perception, which perhaps is not "in
my head," is nowhere else than in my body as a thing of the world. From
now on it seems impossible to remain in the inner certitude of him who
perceives: seen from without perception glides over the things and does
not touch them. At most one will say, if one wishes to admit the
perception's own perspective upon itself, that each of us has a private
world: these private worlds are "worlds" only for their titulars; they are
not the world. The sole world, that is, the unique world, would be a
κοίνος κόσμος, and our perceptions do not open upon it.

But upon what then do they open? How are we to name, to describe,
such as I see it from my place, that *lived by another* which yet for me is not
nothing, since I believe in the other—and that which furthermore
concerns me myself, since it is there as another's view upon me? Here is
this well-known countenance, this smile, these modulations of voice,
whose style is as familiar to me as myself. Perhaps in many moments of

my life the other is for me reduced to this spectacle, which can be a charm. But should the voice alter, should the unwonted appear in the score of the dialogue, or, on the contrary, should a response respond too well to what I thought without having really said it—and suddenly there breaks forth the evidence that yonder also, minute by minute, life is being lived: somewhere behind those eyes, behind those gestures, or rather before them, or again about them, coming from I know not what double ground of space, another private world shows through, through the fabric of my own, and for a moment I live in it; I am no more than the respondent for the interpellation that is made to me. To be sure, the least recovery of attention persuades me that this other who invades me is made only of my own substance: how could I conceive, precisely as *his*, *his* colors, *his* pain, *his* world, except as in accordance with the colors I see, the pains I have had, the world wherein I live? But at least my private world has ceased to be mine only; it is now the instrument which another plays, the dimension of a generalized life which is grafted onto my own.

But at the very moment that I think I share the life of another, I am rejoining it only in its ends, its exterior poles. It is in the world that we communicate, through what, in our life, is articulate. It is from this lawn before me that I think I catch sight of the impact of the green on the vision of another, it is through the music that I enter into his musical emotion, it is the thing itself that opens unto me the access to the private world of another. But the thing itself, we have seen, is always for me the thing that *I* see. The intervention of the other does not resolve the internal paradox of my perception: it adds to it this other enigma: of the propagation of my own most secret life in another—another enigma, but yet the same one, since, from all the evidence, it is only through the world that I can leave myself. It is therefore indeed true that the "private worlds" communicate, that each of them is given to its incumbent as a variant of one common world. The communication makes us the witnesses of one sole world, as the synergy of our eyes suspends them on one unique thing. But in both cases, the certitude, entirely irresistible as it may be, remains absolutely obscure; we can live it, we can neither think it nor formulate it nor set it up in theses. Every attempt at elucidation brings us back to the dilemmas.

And it is this unjustifiable certitude of a sensible world common to us that is the seat of truth within us. That a child perceives before he thinks, that he begins by putting his dreams in the things, his thoughts in the others, forming with them, as it were, one block of common life wherein the perspectives of each are not yet distinguished—these genetic facts cannot be simply ignored by philosophy in the name of the exigencies of the intrinsic analysis. Thought cannot ignore its apparent history, it is not to install itself beneath the whole of our experience, in a pre-empirical order where it would no longer merit its name; it must put to itself the problem of the genesis of its own meaning. It is in terms of its intrinsic meaning and structure that the sensible world is "older" than the universe of thought, because the sensible world is visible and relatively continuous, and because the universe of thought, which is invisible and contains gaps, constitutes at first sight a whole and has its truth only on condition that it be supported on the canonical structures of the sensible world. If we reconstitute the way in which our experiences, according to their ownmost meaning, depend on one another, and if, in order to better lay bare the essential relations of dependency, we try to break them apart in our thought, we come to realize that all that for us is called thought requires that distance from oneself, that initial openness which a field of vision and a field of future and of past are for us. . . . In any case, since we are here only trying to take a first look at our natural certitudes, there is no doubt that, in what concerns the mind and truth, they rest on the primary stratum of the sensible world and that our assurance of being in the truth is one with our assurance of being in the world. We speak and we understand speech long before learning from Descartes (or rediscovering for ourselves) that thought is our reality. We learn to meaningfully handle language [*language*], in which we install ourselves, long before learning from linguistics the intelligible principles upon which our tongue [*langue*] and every tongue are "based" (supposing that it does teach them). Our experience of the true, when it is not immediately reducible to that of the thing we see, is at first not distinct from the tensions that arise between the others and ourselves, and from their resolution. As the thing, as the other, the true dawns through an emotional and almost carnal experience, where the "ideas"— the other's and our own—are rather traits of his physiognomy and of our own, are less understood than welcomed or spurned in love or hatred. To be sure, there are motifs, quite abstract categories, that function very precociously in this wild thought, as the extraordinary anticipations of adult life in childhood show sufficiently; and one can say that the whole of man is already there in his infancy. The child understands well beyond what he knows how to say, responds well beyond what he could define, and this after all is as true of the adult. A genuine conversation gives me access to thoughts that I did not know myself capable of, that I *was* not capable of, and sometimes I feel myself *followed* in a route unknown to myself which my words, cast back by the other, are in the process of tracing out for me. To suppose here that an *intelligible world* sustains the exchange would be to take a name for a solution—and furthermore it would be to grant us what we are maintaining: that it is by borrowing from the world structure that the universe of truth and of thought is constructed for us. When we want to express strongly the consciousness we have of a truth, we find nothing better than to invoke a τόπος νοητός that would be common to minds or to men, as the sensible world is common to the sensible bodies. And this is not only an analogy: it is the same world that contains our bodies and our minds, provided that we understand by world not only the sum of things that fall or could fall under our eyes, but also the locus of their compossibility, the invariable style they observe, which connects our perspectives, permits transition from one to the other, and—whether in describing a detail of the landscape or in coming to agreement about an invisible truth—makes us feel we are two witnesses capable of hovering over the same true object, or at least of exchanging our situations relative to it, as we can exchange our standpoints in the visible world in the strict sense. But here again, more than ever, the naïve certitude of the world, the anticipation of an intelligible world, is as weak when it wishes to convert itself into theses as it is strong in practice. As long as we are dealing with the visible, a mass of facts comes to support it: beyond the divergence of the witnesses it is often easy to re-establish the unity and concordance of the world. But as soon as one goes beyond the circle of *instituted* opinions, which are undivided among us as are the Madeleine or the Palais de Justice, much less thoughts than monuments of our historical landscape, as soon as one reaches the true, that is, the invisible, it seems rather that each man inhabits his own islet, without there being transition from one to the other, and we should rather be astonished that sometimes men come to agreement about anything whatever. For after all each of them has begun by being a fragile mass of living jelly, and it is already a great deal that they would have taken the same route of ontogenesis; it is still more of a wonder that all, from the bottom of their retreats, would have let themselves be caught up by the same social functioning and the same language; but, when it comes to using these according to their own wills and to saying what no one sees, neither the type of the species nor that of the society guarantees that they should come to compatible propositions. When one thinks of the mass of contingencies that can alter both, nothing is more improbable than the extrapolation that treats the universe of the truth as one world also, without fissures and without incompossibles. . . .

THE PERCEPTUAL FAITH AND REFLECTION

The methods of *proof* and of *cognition* invented by a thought already established in the world, the concepts of *object* and *subject* it introduces, do not enable us to understand what the perceptual faith is, precisely because it is a faith, that is, an adherence that knows itself to be beyond proofs, not necessary, interwoven with incredulity, at each instant menanced by non-faith. Belief and incredulity are here so closely bound up that we always find the one in the other, and in particular a germ of non-truth in the truth: the certitude I have of being connected up with the world by my look already promises me a pseudo-world of phantasms if I let it wander. It is said that to cover one's eyes so as to not see a danger is to not believe in the things, to believe only in the private world; but this is rather to believe that what is for us is absolutely, that a world we have succeeded in seeing as without danger is without danger. It is therefore the greatest degree of belief that our vision goes to the things themselves. Perhaps this experience teaches us better than any other what the perceptual presence of the world is: not affirmation and negation of the same thing in the same respect, positive and negative judgment, or, as we said a moment ago, belief and incredulity—which would be impossible; beneath affirmation and negation, beneath judgment (those critical opinions, ulterior operations), it is our experience, prior to every opinion, of inhabiting the world by our body, of inhabiting the truth by our whole selves, without there being need to choose nor even to distinguish between the assurance of seeing and the assurance of seeing the true, because in principle they are one and the same thing— faith, therefore, and not knowledge, since the world is here not separated from our hold on it, since, rather than affirmed, it is taken for granted, rather than disclosed, it is non-dissimulated, non-refuted.

If philosophy is to appropriate to itself and to understand this initial openness upon the world which does not exclude a possible occultation, it cannot be content with describing it; it must tell us how there is openness without the occultation of the world being excluded, how the occultation remains at each instant possible even though we be naturally endowed with light. The philosopher must understand how it is that these two possibilities, which the perceptual faith keeps side by side within itself, do not nullify one another. He will not succeed if he remains at their level, oscillating from the one to the other, saying in turn that my vision is at the thing itself and that my vision is my own or "in me." He must abandon these two views, he must eschew the one as well as the other; since taken literally they are incompossible, he must appeal beyond them to himself who is their titular and therefore must know what motivates them from within; he must lose them as a state of fact in order to reconstruct them as his own possibilities, in order to learn from himself what they mean in truth, what delivers him over to both perception and to phantasms—in a word, he must *reflect*. But as soon as he does so, beyond the world itself and beyond what is only "in us," beyond being in itself and being for us, a third dimension seems to open up, wherein their discordance is effaced. With the conversion to reflection, perceiving and imagining are now only two modes of *thinking*.

From vision and feeling [*sentir*] will be retained only what animates them
and sustains them indubitably, the pure thought of seeing or of feeling.
It is possible to describe that thought, to show that it is made of a strict
correlation between my exploration of the world and the sensorial
responses it arouses. The imaginary will be submitted to a parallel
analysis, and we will come to realize that the thought of which it is made
is not in this precise sense a thought of seeing or of feeling, that it is
rather the intent to not apply and even forget the criteria of verification
and to take as "good" what is not and could not be seen. Thus the
antinomies of the perceptual faith seem to be lifted; it is true indeed that
we perceive the thing itself, since the thing is nothing but what we
see—but not by the occult power of our eyes. For our eyes are no longer
the subjects of vision; they have joined the number of things seen. And
what we call vision rises from the power of thought that certifies that the
appearance here has responded to the movements of our eyes according to
a rule. When perception is full or effective, it is the thought of perceiving. If therefore it reaches the thing itself, it is necessary to say, without
this being a contradiction, that it is entirely our work, and our own
through and through, like all our thoughts. Open upon the thing itself,
the perception is no less our own work, because the thing is henceforth
exactly what we think we see—*cogitatum* or noema. It no more leaves the
circle of our thoughts than does the imagination, which is also a thought
of seeing, but a thought that does not seek the exercise, the proof, the
plenitude, that therefore presumes on itself and is only half-thought.
Thus the real becomes the correlative of thought, and the imaginary is,
within the same sphere, the narrow circle of objects of thought that are
only half-thought, half-objects or phantoms that have no consistency, no
place of their own, disappearing before the sun of thought like the mists
of dawn, and that are, between the thought and what it thinks, only a
thin layer of the unthought. The reflection retains everything contained
in the perceptual faith: the conviction that there is something, that there
is the world, the idea of truth, the true idea given. It simply reduces that
crude [*barbare*] conviction of going to the things themselves—which is
incompatible with the fact of illusion—to what it means or signifies. It
converts it into its truth; it discovers in it the adequation and assent of
the thought with thought, the transparency of what I think for myself
who thinks it. The brute and prior existence of the world I thought I
found already there by opening my eyes is only the symbol of a being that
is for itself as soon as it is because appearing, and therefore appearing to
itself, is its whole being—that is the being we call mind. Through the
conversion to reflection, which leaves nothing but ideates, *cogitata*, or
noemata subsisting before the pure subject, we finally leave the
equivocations of the perceptual faith, which paradoxically assured us

that we have access to the things themselves and that we gain access to them through the intermediary of the body, which therefore opened us to the world only by sealing us up in the succession of our private events. From now on everything seems clear; the blend of dogmatism and scepticism, the confused convictions of the perceptual faith, are called into question. I no longer think I see with my eyes things exterior to myself who sees them: they are exterior only to my body, not to my thought, which soars over it as well as them. Nor do I any longer allow myself to be impressed by that evidence that the other perceiving subjects do not go to the things themselves, that their perception takes place within them—an evidence that ends by rebounding upon my own perception, since after all I am "an other" in their eyes, and my dogmatism, communicated to the others, returns to me as scepticism. For if it is true that, seen from the outside, the perception of each seems to be shut up in some retreat "behind" his body, reflection precisely relegates this exterior view to the number of phantasms without consistency and confused thoughts: one does not think a thought from the outside, by definition thought is thought only inwardly. If then the others are thoughts, as such they are not behind their body which I see—they are, like myself, nowhere; they are, like myself, coextensive with being, and there is no problem of incarnation. At the same time that the reflection liberates us from the false problems posed by bastard and unthinkable experiences, it also accounts for them through the simple transposition of the incarnate subject into a transcendental subject and of the reality of the world into an ideality: we all reach the world, and the same world, and it belongs wholly to each of us, without division or loss, because it is *that which* we think we perceive, the undivided object of all our thoughts. Its unity, if it is not the numerical unity, is not the specific unity either: it is that ideal unity or unity of signification that makes the triangle of the geometer be the same in Tokyo and in Paris, the same in the fifth century before Christ and now. This unity suffices and it untangles every problem, because the divisions that can be opposed to it, the plurality of the fields of perception and of lives, are as nothing before it, do not belong to the universe of ideality and of meaning, and cannot even be formulated or articulated into distinct thoughts, and finally, because we have through reflection recognized at the heart of all the situated, bogged-down, and incarnated thoughts the pure appearing of thought to itself, the universe of internal adequation, where everything *true* that we have is integrated without difficulty. . . .

This movement of reflection will always at first sight be convincing: in a sense it is imperative, it is truth itself, and one does not see how philosophy could dispense with it. The question is whether it has brought philosophy to the harbor, whether the universe of thought to which it leads is really an order that suffices to itself and puts an end to every question. Since the perceptual faith is a paradox, how could I remain with it? And if I do not remain with it, what else can I do except re-enter into myself and seek there the abode of truth? Is it not evident that, precisely if my perception is a perception of the world, I must find in my commerce with the world the reasons that induce me to see it, and in my vision the meaning of my vision? From whom would I, who am in the world [*suis au monde*], learn what it is to be in the world if not from myself, and how could I say that I am in the world if I did not know it? Without even presuming that I know everything of myself, it is certain at least that, among other things, I am a knowing; this attribute assuredly belongs to me, even if I have others. I cannot imagine that the world irrupts into me or I into it: the world can present itself to this knowing which I am only by offering it a meaning, only in the form of a thought of the world. The secret of the world we are seeking must necessarily be contained in my contact with it. Inasmuch as I live it, I possess the meaning of everything I live, otherwise I would not live it; and I can seek no light concerning the world except by consulting, by making explicit, my frequenting of the world, by comprehending it from within. What will always make of the philosophy of reflection not only a temptation but a route that must be followed is that it is true in what it denies, that is, the exterior relation between a world in itself and myself, conceived as a process of the same type as those that unfold within the world—whether one imagines an intrusion of the world in myself, or, on the contrary, some excursion of my look among the things. But does it conceive properly the natal bond between me who perceives and what I perceive? And because we assuredly must reject the idea of an exterior relation between the perceiving and the perceived, must we pass to the antithesis of immanence, be it wholly ideal and spiritual, and say that I who perceives am the thought of perceiving, and the perceived world a thing thought? Because perception is not an entering of the world into myself and is not centripetal, must it be centrifugal, as is a thought I form or the signification I give by judgment to an indecisive appearance? The philosophy of reflection practices the philosophical interrogation and the resultant effort toward explicitness in a style that is not the sole possible one; it mixes in presuppositions which we have to examine and which in the end reveal themselves to be contrary to what inspires the reflection. It thinks it can comprehend our natal bond with the world only by *undoing* it in order to *remake* it, only by constituting it, by fabricating it. It thinks it finds clarity through analysis, that is, if not in the most simple elements, at least in the most fundamental conditions implicated in the brute product, in the premises from which it results as a consequence, in a *source of meaning* from which it is derived.[1] It is therefore essential to the philosophy of reflection that it bring us back, this side of our *de facto* situation, to a center of things from which we proceeded, but from which we were decentered, that it retravel this time starting from us a route already traced out from that center to us. The very effort toward internal adequation, the enterprise to reconquer explicitly all that we are and do implicitly, signifies that what we are finally as *naturata* we first are actively as *naturans*, that the world is our birthplace only because first we as minds are the cradle of the world. But, in this, if the reflection confines itself to this first movement, if it installs us by regression in the immanent universe of our thoughts and strips whatever may be left over of any probative power with respect to itself, dismissing it as confused, mutilated, or naïve thought, the reflection then falls short of its task and of the radicalism that is its law. For the movement of recovery, of recuperation, of return to self, the progression toward internal adequation, the very effort to coincide with a *naturans* which is already ourselves and which is supposed to unfold the things and the world before itself—precisely inasmuch as they are a return or a reconquest, these operations of reconstitution or of reestablishment which come second cannot by principle be the mirror image of its internal constitution and its establishment, as the route from the Etoile to the Notre-Dame is the inverse of the route from the Notre-Dame to the Etoile: the reflection recuperates everything except itself as an effort of recuperation, it clarifies everything except its own role. The mind's eye too has its blind spot, but, because it is of the mind, cannot be unaware of it, nor treat as a simple state of non-vision, which requires no particular mention, the very act of reflection which is *quoad nos* its act of birth. If it is not unaware of itself—which would be contrary to its definition—the reflection cannot feign to unravel the same thread that the mind would first have woven, to be the mind returning to itself within me, when by definition it is I who reflect. The reflection must appear to itself as a progression toward a subject X, an appeal to a subject X. As the reflection's very assurance that it rejoin a universal *naturans* cannot come from some prior contact with it (since precisely it is still ignorance), reflection evokes it and does not coincide with it. That assurance can come only from the world—or from my thoughts insofar as they form a world, insofar as their cohesion, their vanishing lines, designate beneath reflection a virtual focus with which I do not yet

1. Idea of return—of the latent: idea of the reflection coming back over the traces of a constitution. Idea of intrinsic possibility of which the constituted is its unfolding. Idea of a *naturans* of which it is the *naturata*. Idea of the originating as intrinsic. Hence the reflective thought is an anticipation of the whole; it performs all its operations under the guarantee of the totality that it claims to engender. Cf. Kant: if a world is to be possible. . . . This reflection does not find the originating.

coincide. As an effort to found the existing world upon a *thought* of the world, the reflection at each instant draws its inspiration from the prior presence of the world, of which it is tributary, from which it derives all its energy. When Kant justifies each step of his Analytic with the famous refrain "if a world is to be possible," he emphasizes the fact that his guideline is furnished him by the unreflected image of the world, that the necessity of the steps taken by the reflection is suspended upon the hypothesis "world," and that the thought of the world which the Analytic is charged with disclosing is not so much the foundation as the second expression of the fact that for me there has been an experience of a world—in other words, that the intrinsic possibility of the world as a thought rests upon the fact that I can see the world, that is, upon a possibility of a wholly different type, which we have seen borders on the impossible. It is by a secret and constant appeal to this impossible-possible that reflection can maintain the illusion of being a return to oneself and of establishing itself in immanence, and our power to re-enter into ourselves is exactly measured by a power to leave ourselves, which is neither older nor more recent than it, which is exactly synony-mous with it. The whole reflective analysis is not false, but still naïve, as long as it dissimulates from itself its own mainspring and as long as, in order to constitute the world, it is necessary to have a notion of the world as preconstituted—as long as the procedure is in principle delayed behind itself. The reply will perhaps be that the great philosophies of reflection know this very well, as the reference to the true idea given in Spinoza or the very conscious reference to a pre-critical experience of the world in Kant shows, but that the circle of the unreflected and the reflection is deliberate in these philosophies—that one begins with the unreflected, because one does have to begin, but that the universe of thought that is opened up by reflection contains everything necessary to account for the mutilated thought of the beginning, which is only the ladder one pulls up after oneself after having climbed it. . . . But if this is so, there is no longer any philosophy of reflection, for there is no longer the originating and the derived; there is a thought traveling a circle where the condition and the conditioned, the reflection and the un-reflected, are in a reciprocal, if not symmetrical, relationship, and where the end is in the beginning as much as the beginning is in the end. We are not saying anything different. The remarks we made concerning reflection were nowise intended to disqualify it for the profit of the unreflected or the immediate (which we know only through reflection). It is a question not of putting the perceptual faith in place of reflection, but on the contrary of taking into account the total situation, which involves reference from the one to the other. What is given is not a massive and opaque world, or a universe of adequate thought; it is a reflection which turns back over the density of the world in order to clarify it, but which, coming second, reflects back to it only its own light.

It is indeed true that, in order to disentangle myself from the perplexities in which the perceptual faith casts me, I can address myself only to my experience of the world, to that blending with the world that recommences for me each morning as soon as I open my eyes, to that flux of perceptual life between it and myself which beats unceasingly from morning to night, and which makes my own secret thoughts change the aspect of faces and landscapes for me, as, conversely, the faces and landscapes bring me the help sometimes and the menace sometimes of a manner of being a man which they infuse into my life. But it is just as sure that the relation between a thought and its object, between the *cogito* and the *cogitatum*, contains neither the whole nor even the essential of our commerce with the world and that we have to situate that relation back within a more muted relationship with the world, within an initiation into the world upon which it rests and which is always already accomplished when the reflective return intervenes. We will miss that relationship—which we shall here call the openness upon the world [*ouverture au monde*]—the moment that the reflective effort tries to capture it, and we will then be able to catch sight of the reasons that prevent it from succeeding, and of the way through which we would reach it. I see, I feel [*sens*], and it is certain that for me to account for what seeing and feeling are I must cease accompanying the seeing and the feeling into the visible and the sensible into which they throw themselves, and I must contrive, on this side of them, a sphere they do not occupy and whence they would become comprehensible according to their sense and their essence. To understand them is to suspend them, since the naïve vision occupies me completely, and since the attention to vision that is added on subtracts something from this total gift, and especially since to understand is to translate into disposable significations a meaning first held captive in the thing and in the world itself. But this translation aims to convey the text; or rather the visible and the philosophical explicitation of the visible are not side by side as two sets of signs, as a text and its version in another tongue. If it were a text, it would be a strange text, which is directly given to us all, so that we are not restricted to the philosopher's translation and can compare the two. And philosophy for its part is more and less than a translation: more, since it alone tells us what the text means; less, since it is useless if one does not have the text at one's disposal. The philosopher therefore suspends the brute vision only in order to make it pass into the order of the expressed: that vision remains his model or measure, and it is upon that vision that the network of significations which philosophy organizes in order to reconquer it must open. Hence the philosopher does not have to *consider as inexistent* what was seen or felt, and the vision or the feeling themselves, to replace them, according to the words of Descartes, with the "thought of seeing and of feeling," which for its part is considered unshakable only because it presumes nothing about what effectively is, only because it entrenches itself in the apparition to the thought of what is thought—from which it is indeed inexpugnable. To reduce perception to the thought of perceiving, under the pretext that immanence alone is sure, is to take out an insurance against doubt whose premiums are more onerous than the loss for which it is to indemnify us: for it is to forego comprehending the effective world and move to a type of certitude that will never restore to us the "there is" of the world. Either the doubt is only a state of rending and obscurity, in which case it teaches me nothing—or if it teaches me something, it is because it is deliberate, militant, systematic, and then it is an act, and then, even if subsequently its own existence imposes itself upon me as a limit to the doubt, as a something that is not nothing, this something is of the order of acts, within which I am henceforth confined. The illusion of illusions is to think now that to tell the truth we have never been certain of anything but our own acts, that from the beginning perception has been an inspection of the mind, and that reflection is only the perception returning to itself, the conversion from the knowing of the thing to a knowing of oneself of which the thing was made, the emergence of a "binding" that was the bond itself. We think we prove this Cartesian "spirituality," this *identity* of space with the mind, by saying that it is obvious that the "far-off" object is far-off only by virtue of its relation with other objects "further off" or "less distant"—which relation belongs properly to neither of them and *is* the immediate presence of the mind to all; the doctrine finally replaces our belongingness to the world with a view of the world from above. But it gets its apparent evidence only from a very naïve postulate (and one suggested to us precisely by the world) according to which it is always *the same* thing I think when the gaze of attention is displaced and looks back from itself to what conditions it. This is a massive conviction drawn from external experience, where I have indeed the assurance that the things under my eyes remain *the same* while I approach them to better inspect them, but this is because the functioning of my body as a possibility for changing point of view, a "seeing apparatus," or a sedimented science of the "point of view," assures me that I am approaching the same thing I saw a moment ago from further off. It is the perceptual life of my body that here sustains and guarantees the perceptual explicitation, and far from it itself being a cognition of intra-mundane or inter-objective relations between my body and the exterior things, it is presupposed in every notion of an object, and it is this life that accomplishes the primary openness to the world. My conviction that I see the thing itself does not *result* from the perceptual exploration, it is not a word to designate the proximal vision; on the contrary it is what gives me the notion of the "proximal," of the "best" point of observation, and of the "thing itself." Having therefore learned through perceptual experience what it is to "see well" the thing, that to do so one must and one can approach it, and that the new data thus acquired are determinations of the *same* thing, we transfer this certitude to the interior, we resort to the fiction of a "little man in the man," and in this way we come to think that to reflect on perception is, *the perceived thing and the perception remaining what they were,* to disclose the true subject that inhabits and has always inhabited them. But in fact I should say that there was there a thing perceived and an openness upon this thing which the reflection has neutralized and transformed into perception-reflected-on and thing-perceived-within-a-perception-reflected-on. And that the functioning of reflection, like the functioning of the exploring body, makes use of powers obscure to me, spans the cycle of duration that separates the brute perception from the reflective examination, and during this time maintains the permanence of the perceived and the permanence of the perception under the gaze of the mind only because my mental inspection and my attitudes of mind prolong the "I can" of my sensorial and corporeal exploration. To found the latter on the former, and the *de facto* perception on the essence of perception such as it appears to reflection, is to forget the reflection itself as a distinct act of recovery. In other words, we are catching sight of the necessity of another operation besides the conversion to reflection, more fundamental than it, of a sort of *hyper-reflection* [*sur-réflexion*] that would also take itself and the changes it introduces into the spectacle into account. It accordingly would not lose sight of the brute thing and the brute perception and would not finally efface them, would not cut the organic bonds between the perception and the thing perceived with a hypothesis of inexistence. On the contrary, it would set itself the task of thinking about them, of reflecting on the transcendence of the world as transcendence, speaking of it not according to the law of the word-meanings inherent in the given language, but with a perhaps difficult effort that uses the significations of words to express, beyond themselves, our mute contact with the things, when they are not yet things said. If therefore the reflection is not to presume upon what it finds and condemn itself to putting into the things what it will then pretend to find in them, it must suspend the faith in the world only so as to *see it*, only so as to read in it the route it has followed in becoming a world for us; it must seek in the world itself the secret of our perceptual bond with it. It must use words not according to their pre-established signification, but *in order to state* this prelogical bond. It must plunge into the world instead of surveying it, it must descend toward it such as it is instead of working its way back up toward a prior possibility of thinking it—which would impose upon the world in advance the conditions for our control over it. It must question the world, it must enter into the forest of references that our interrogation arouses in it, it must make it say, finally, what in its silence *it means to say.* . . . We know neither what exactly is this order and this concordance of the world to which we thus entrust ourselves, nor therefore what the enterprise will result in, nor even if it is really possible. But the choice is between it and a dogmatism of reflection concerning which we know only too well where it goes, since with it philosophy concludes the moment it begins and, for this very reason, does not make us comprehend our own obscurity.

A philosophy of reflection, as methodic doubt and as a reduction of the openness upon the world to "spiritual acts," to intrinsic relations between the idea and *its* ideate, is thrice untrue to what it means to elucidate: untrue to the visible world, to him who sees it, and to his relations with the other "visionaries." To say that perception is and has always been an "inspection of the mind" is to define it not by what it gives us, but by what in it *withstands* the hypothesis of *non-existence*; it is to identify from the first the positive with a negation of negation; it is to require of the innocent the proof of his non-culpability, and to reduce in advance our contact with Being to the discursive operations with which we defend ourselves against illusion, to reduce the true to the credible, the real to the probable. It has often been pointed out that even the most credible imagination, the most conformable to the context of experience, does not bring us one step closer to "reality" and is immediately ascribed by us to the imaginary—and that conversely an even absolutely unexpected and unforeseeable noise is from the first perceived as real, however weak be its links with the context. This simple fact imposes upon us the idea that with the "real" and the "imaginary" we are dealing with two "orders," two "stages," or two "theaters"—that of space and that of phantasms—which are set up within us before the acts of discrimination (which intervene only in the equivocal cases), and in which what we live comes to settle of itself, outside of all criteriological control. The fact that sometimes the controls become necessary and result in judgments of reality which rectify the naïve experience does not prove that judgments of this sort are at the origin of this distinction, or constitute it, and therefore does not dispense us from understanding it for itself. If we do so, we then will have to not define the real by its coherence and the imaginary by its incoherence or its lacunae: the real is coherent and probable because it is real, and not real because it is coherent; the imaginary is incoherent or improbable because it is imaginary, and not imaginary because it is incoherent. The least particle of the perceived incorporates it from the first into the "perceived," the most credible phantasm glances off at the surface of the world; it is this presence of the whole world in one reflection, its irremediable absence in the richest and most systematic deliriums, that we have to understand, and this difference is not a difference of the more and the less. It is true that it gives rise to mistakes or to illusions, whence the conclusion is sometimes drawn that it therefore cannot be a difference of nature, and that the real, after all, is only the less improbable or the more probable. This is to think the true by the false, the positive by the negative—and it is to ill-describe indeed the experience of dis-illusion, wherein precisely we learn to know the fragility of the "real." For when an illusion dissipates, when an appearance suddenly breaks up, it is always for the profit of a new appearance which takes up again for its own account the ontological function of the first. I thought I saw on the sands a piece of wood polished by the sea, and *it was* a clayey rock. The breakup and the destruction of the first appearance do not authorize me to define henceforth the "real" as a simple probable, since *they are only another name for the new apparition*, which must therefore figure in our analysis of the *dis-illusion*. The dis-illusion is the loss of one evidence only because it is the acquisition of *another evidence*. If, out of prudence, I decide to say that this new evidence is "in itself" doubtful or only probable (in itself—that is: for me, in a moment, when I will have gotten a little closer to it or looked more closely), the fact remains that at the moment I speak it incontestably gives itself as "real" and not as "very possible" or probable; and if subsequently it breaks up in its turn, it will do so only under the pressure of a new "reality." What I can conclude from these disillusions or deceptions, therefore, is that perhaps "reality" does not belong definitely to any particular perception, that in this sense it lies *always further on*; but this does not authorize me to break or to ignore the bond that joins them one after the other to the real, a bond that cannot be broken with the one without first having been established with the following, so that there is no *Schein* without an *Erscheinung*, that every *Schein* is the counterpart of an *Erscheinung*, and that the meaning of the "real" is not reduced to that of the "probable," but on the contrary the "probable" evokes a definitive experience of the "real" whose accomplishment is only deferred. When faced with a perceptual appearance we not only know that it can subsequently "break up," we also know that it will do so only for having been so well replaced by another that there remains no trace of it, and that we seek in vain in this chalky rock what a moment ago *was* a piece of wood polished by the sea. Each perception is mutable and only probable—it is, if one likes, only an *opinion*; but what is not opinion, what each perception, even if false, verifies, is the belongingness of each

experience to the same world, their equal power to manifest it, as *possibilities of the same world*. If the one takes the place of the other so well—to the point that one no longer finds any trace of it a moment after the illusion—it is precisely because they are not successive hypotheses about an unknowable Being, but perspectives upon the same familiar Being, which we know cannot exclude the one without including the other and which we know in any case to be itself beyond contestation. And this is why the very fragility of a perception, attested by its breakup and by the substitution of another perception, far from authorizing us to efface the index of "reality" from them all, obliges us to concede it to all of them, to recognize all of them to be variants of the same world, and finally to consider them not as all false but as "all true," not as repeated failures in the determination of the world but as progressive approximations. Each perception envelops the possibility of its own replacement by another, and thus of a sort of disavowal from the things. But this also means that each perception is the term of an approach, of a series of "illusions" that were not merely simple "thoughts" in the restrictive sense of Being-for-itself and the "merely thought of," but possibilities that could have been, radiations of this unique world that "there is" . . .
—and which, as such, never revert to nothingness or to subjectivity as if they had never appeared, but are rather, as Husserl puts it well, "crossed out" or "cancelled" by the "new" reality. The philosophy of reflection is not wrong in considering the false as a mutilated or partial truth: its error is rather to act as if the partial were only a *de facto* absence of the totality, which does not need to be accounted for. This finally destroys any consistency proper to the appearance, integrates it in advance into Being, deprives it of its tenor of truth because it is partial, makes it disappear into an internal adequation where Being and the reasons for being are one. The movement toward adequation, to which the facts of dis-illusion bear witness, is not the returning to itself of an adequate Thought that would have inexplicably lost sight of itself—nor is it a blind progress of probability, founded on the number of signs and concordances. It is the prepossession of a totality which is there before one knows how and why, whose realizations are never what we would have imagined them to be, and which nonetheless fulfills a secret expectation within us, since we believe in it tirelessly.

The reply will no doubt be that if, in order to save what is original in the "world" as a preobjective theme, we refuse to make of it the immanent correlative of a spiritual act, then the natural light, the openness of my perception upon the world, can result only from a preordination whose effects I record, a finality to whose law I am subjected, as I undergo the law of finality of all my organs. And that moreover once this passivity is introduced in me, it will vitiate everything when I proceed, as one must, to the order of thought and will have to explain how I think about my perceptions. Either I reinstate at this level the autonomy I renounced at the level of the perceived—but then one does not see how this active thinker could recover possession of the reasons of a perception that is given to him ready-made—or (as in Malebranche) the passivity overtakes the order of thought also, which, like the perception, loses every efficacity of its own and has to await its light from a causality that functions in it without it, as the perception obtains its light only through the play of the laws of the union of the soul and the body—and consequently the thought's grasp upon itself and the light of the intelligible become an incomprehensible mystery, in a being for whom the true is at the term of a natural inclination, conformable to the pre-established system according to which his mind functions, and is not *truth*, conformity of self with self, light. . . . And it is indeed certain that every attempt to fit a passivity upon an activity ends up either in extending the passivity to the whole—which amounts to detaching us from Being, since, for lack of a contact of myself with myself, I am in every operation of knowledge delivered over to an organization of my thoughts whose premises are masked from me, to a mental constitution which is given to me as a fact—or ends up by restoring the activity to the whole. This is in particular the flaw in the philosophies of reflection that do not follow themselves through; after having defined the requirements for thought, they add that these do not impose any law upon the things and evoke an order of the things themselves which, in contradistinction to the order of our thoughts, could receive only exterior rules. But we are not opposing to an interior light an order of the things in themselves into which it could not penetrate. There can be no question of fitting together passivity before a transcendent with an activity of immanent thought. It is a question of reconsidering the interdependent notions of the active and the passive in such a way that they no longer place us before the antinomy of a philosophy that accounts for being and the truth, but does not take the world into account, and a philosophy that takes the world into account, but uproots us from being and the truth. The philosophy of reflection replaces the "world" with the "being-thought." One cannot, while recognizing this deficiency, justify it in spite of everything because of the untenable consequences of an exterior regulation of our thoughts, for only from the point of view of a philosophy of reflection is this the alternative, and it is the reflective analysis that we find questionable. What we propose is not to stop the philosophy of reflection after having started as it does—this is indeed impossible, and, all things considered, a philosophy of total reflection seems to us to go further, be it only in circumscribing what in our experience resists it; what we propose is to take another point of departure.

To remove all equivocation on this point, let us repeat that we reproach the philosophy of reflection not only for transforming the world into a noema, but also for distorting the being of the reflecting "subject" by conceiving it as "thought"—and finally for rendering unthinkable its relations with other "subjects" in the world that is common to them. The philosophy of reflection starts with the principle that if a perception is to be able to be my own it must from the start be one of my "representations"—in other words, that I, qua "thought," must be what effects the connection between the aspects under which the object presents itself and their synthesis into an object. The reflection, the return to the interior, would not modify the perception, since it would limit itself to bringing out what from the first made up its framework or its joints, and since the thing perceived, if it is not nothing, is the set of connecting operations which the reflection enumerates and makes explicit. One is barely permitted to say that the reflective gaze turns back from the object toward me, since I qua thought am what makes there be a distance and in general any relation whatever from one point of the object to another. With one stroke the philosophy of reflection metamorphoses the effective world into a transcendental field; in doing so it only puts me back at the origin of a spectacle that I could never have had unless, unbeknownst to myself, I organized it. It only makes me be consciously what I have always been distractedly; it only makes me give its name to a dimension behind myself, a depth whence, in fact, already my vision was formed. Through the reflection, the *I* lost in its perceptions rediscovers itself by rediscovering them as thoughts. It thought it had quit itself for them, spread itself out in them; it comes to realize that if it had quit itself they would not be and that the very outspread of the distances and the things was only the "outside" of its own inward intimacy with itself, that the unfolding of the world was the coiling up upon itself of a thought which thinks anything whatever only because it thinks itself first.

Once one is settled in it, reflection is an inexpugnable philosophical position, every obstacle, every resistance to its exercise being from the first treated not as an adversity of the things but as a simple state of non-thought, a gap in the continuous fabric of the acts of thought, which is inexplicable, but about which there is nothing to say since it is literally *nothing*. But are we to enter into reflection? In its inaugural act is concealed a decision to play a double game which, once unmasked, divests it of its apparent evidence; in one move the philosophical lie is perpetrated with which one first pays for this henceforth invulnerable method. It is essential to the reflective analysis that it start from a *de facto* situation. If it did not from the first take as given the true idea, the internal adequation of my thought with what I think, or the thought in act of the world, it should have to suspend every "I think" upon an "I think that I think," and this upon an "I think that I think that I think," and so on. . . . . The search for the conditions of possibility is in principle posterior to an actual experience, and from this it follows that even if subsequently one determines rigorously the *sine qua non* of that experience, it can never be washed of the original stain of having been discovered *post festum* nor ever become what positively founds that experience. This is why we must say not that it precedes the experience (even in the transcendental sense) but that it must be able to accompany it, that is, that it translates or expresses its essential character but does not indicate a prior possibility whence it would have issued. Never therefore will the philosophy of reflection be able to install itself in the mind it discloses, whence to see the world as its correlative. Precisely because it is reflection, re-turn, re-conquest, or re-covery, it cannot flatter itself that it would simply coincide with a constitutive principle already at work in the spectacle of the world, that, starting with this spectacle, it would travel the very route that the constitutive principle had followed in the opposite direction. But this is what it would have to do if it is really a *return*, that is, if its point of arrival were also the starting point—and this exigency is no optional clause, since if it were not fulfilled the regressive analysis, declining to make any progressive synthesis, would be abandoning the pretension to disclose the sources to us and would be nothing more than the technique of a philosophical quietism. The reflection finds itself therefore in the strange situation of simultaneously requiring and excluding an inverse movement of constitution. It requires it in that, without this centrifugal movement, it should have to acknowledge itself to be a retrospective construction; it excludes it in that, coming in principle after an experience of the world or of the true which it seeks to render explicit, it thereby establishes itself in an order of idealization and of the "after-the-fact" which is not that wherein the world is formed. This is what Husserl brought frankly into the open when he said that every transcendental reduction is also an eidetic reduction, that is: every effort to comprehend the spectacle of the world from within and from the sources demands that we detach ourselves from the effective unfolding of our perceptions and from our perception of the world, that we cease being one with the concrete flux of our life in order to retrace the total bearing and principal articulations of the world upon which it opens. To reflect is not to coincide with the flux from its source unto its last ramifications; it is to disengage from the things, perceptions, world, and perception of the world, by submitting them to a systematic variation, the intelligible nuclei that resist, and to proceed from one intelligible nucleus to the next in a way that is not belied by experience but gives us only its universal contours. It therefore by principle leaves untouched the twofold problem of the genesis of the existent world and of the genesis of the idealization performed by reflection and finally evokes and requires as its foundation a *hyper-reflection* where the ultimate problems would be taken seriously. To tell the truth, it is not even certain that the reflection that proceeds by way of the essences can accomplish its propaedeutic task and fulfill its role of being a discipline of the understanding. For there is no guarantee that the whole of experience can be expressed in essential invariants, that certain beings—for example, the being of time—do not in principle elude this fixation and do not require from the start, if they are to be able to be thought by us, the consideration of the fact, the dimension of facticity and the hyper-reflection, which would then become, at least in regard to them, not a superior degree at the ultimate level of philosophy, but philosophy itself. But if time should elude the reflection, space too would be involved in this secession, since time is bound to the present through all its fibers, and, through the present, to the simultaneous; one would also have to describe in terms of facticity, and not in terms of essences, a subjectivity situated in space and in time. Little by little it is the whole of experience—the essence itself, and the subject of the essences, and the reflection itself as eidetic—that would require reconsideration. The legitimate function of the fixing of the eidetic invariants would be no longer to confine us within the consideration of the *what*, but to make evident the divergence between the eidetic invariants and the effective functioning and to invite us to bring the experience itself forth from its obstinate silence. . . . In recognizing that every reflection is eidetic and, as such, leaves untouched the problem of our unreflected being and that of the world, Husserl simply agrees to take up the problem which the reflective attitude ordinarily avoids—the discordance between its initial situation and its ends.

Confronting the mind, focus of all clarity, with the world reduced to its intelligible schema, a consistent rflection dissipates every question concerning the relationship between them. Henceforth their relationship will be one of pure correlation: the mind is what thinks, the world what is thought; one could conceive neither of encroachment of the one upon the other, nor of confusion of one with the other, nor of passage from one to the other, nor even of contact between them. Since they are related to one another as the bound to the binding or the *naturata* to the *naturans*, they are too perfectly coextensive for the one to ever be able to be preceded by the other, too irremediably distinct for the one ever to be able to envelop the other. Philosophy therefore impugns as meaningless every encroachment of the world upon the mind, or of the mind upon the world. That the world could pre-exist my consciousness of the world is out of the question: is it not obvious that every world without me that I could think of becomes, by the very fact that I think of it, a world for me; that the private world I divine at the origin of another's gaze is not so private as to prevent me from becoming at that very moment its quasi-spectator? What we express by saying that the world is in itself, or that it is beyond the perception I and the others have of it, is simply the signification "world," which is the same for all and independent of our phantasms, just as the properties of the triangle are the same in all places and at all times and do not begin to be true the day they are recognized. There is a pre-existence of the world with regard to our perception, of the aspects of the world which the other perceives to the perception I will have of them later, of my world to that of men yet to be born, and all these "worlds" make one unique world, but do so only in that the things and the world are objects of thought with their intrinsic properties, are of the order of the true, of the valid, of the signification, and are not of the order of events. The question whether the world be unique for all the subjects loses all meaning once one has admitted the ideality of the world; it no longer makes any sense to ask if my world and that of the other are numerically or specifically the same, since, as an intelligible structure, the world lies always beyond my thoughts as events, but also beyond those of the others, so that it is not divided by the knowledge we acquire of it, nor unique in the sense that each of us is unique. In all that they signify, my perception and the perception another man has of the world are the same, even though our lives be incommensurable, because the *signification*, the meaning—being an internal adequation, a relation of self with self, pure interiority and total openness all at once—never descend into us as subjected to a perspective (for as such we are never our own light to ourselves), and because thus all our truths as truths rejoin of themselves and form by right one sole system. Thus, with the correlation between thought and the object of thought set up as a principle, there is established a philosophy that knows neither difficulties nor problems nor paradoxes nor reversals: once and for all, I have grasped within myself, with the pure correlation between him who thinks and what he thinks, the truth of my life, which is also the truth of the world and of the other lives. Once and for all, the being-object is placed before me as alone meaningful for me, and every inherence of the others in their bodies, and of myself in my own, is impugned as a confusion—once and for all, the being-self is given to me in the adequation of my thought with itself, and, from this side also, there is no question of taking seriously the compound of the mind with the body. I am forever subjected to the centrifugal movement that makes an object of thought be for a thought, and there is no question of my quitting this position and examining what Being can indeed be before it be thought by me or (what amounts to the same thing) by another, what indeed can be the intermundane space [*l'intermonde*] where our gazes cross and our perceptions overlap: there is no brute world, there is only an elaborated world; there is no intermundane space, there is only a signification "world". . . . And here too the reflective attitude would be inexpugnable if it did not belie in the hypothesis and as reflection what it affirms in the thesis about what is reflected on. For before the reflection I thought myself situated in an actual world by my body, in the midst of other men situated in it by their bodies; I thought I saw them perceive the same world I perceive, and thought I was one of them occupied in seeing their world—and where else have I found, if not in this naïve initiation and in these confused perceptions, the meaning first sighted that I wanted to approach by the reflection? How was I able to appeal to myself as to the universal source of meaning—which is to reflect—if not because the spectacle had meaning for me before I discovered that I am he who gives it meaning, that is—since a philosophy of reflection identifies my being with what I think of it—before being this? My access to a universal mind via reflection, far from finally discovering what I always was, is motivated by the intertwining of my life with the other lives, of my body with the visible things, by the intersection of my perceptual field with that of the others, by the blending in of my duration with the other durations. If I pretend to find, through reflection, in the universal mind the premise that had always backed up my experience, I can do so only by forgetting this non-knowing of the beginning which is not nothing, and which is not the reflective truth either, and which also must be accounted for. I was able to appeal from the world and the others to myself and take the route of reflection, only because first I was outside of myself, in the world, among the others, and constantly this experience feeds my reflection. Such is the total stuation that a philosophy must account for. It will do so only by admitting the double polarity of reflection and by admitting that, as Hegel said, to retire into oneself is also to leave oneself.

The Trace of the Other

1. BEING AND THE SAME

The I is identification in the strong sense; it is the origin of the very phenomenon of identity. The identity of the I is not the permanence of an unalterable quality; I am myself not because of some character trait which I first identify, and then find myself to be the same. It is because I am from the first the same—*me ipse*, an ipseity—that I can identify every object, every character trait, and every being.

This identification is not a simple "restating" of the self: The "A is A" that characterizes the I is an "A anxious for A," or an "A enjoying A," always an "A bent over A." The *outside of me* solicits it in need: the *outside of me* is *for me*. The tautology of ipseity is an egoism.

The true cognition where the I "leaves it to him" and lets an alien being shine forth does not interrupt this original identification, does not draw the I out of itself without return. The being *enters* into the sphere of true knowledge. In becoming a theme, it does indeed retain a foreignness with respect to the thinker that embraces it. But it at once ceases to strike up against thought. The alien being is as it were naturalized as soon as it commits itself with knowledge. In itself—and consequently *elsewhere* than in thought, *other* than it—it does not have the wild barbarian character of alterity. It has a meaning. The being is propagated in infinite images which emanate from it; it dilates in a kind of ubiquity and penetrates the inwardness of men. It shows itself and radiates, as though the very plenitude of its alterity overflowed the mystery that harbors it, and pro-duces itself. Though it surprised the I, a being that is in truth does not alter the identity of the I. The obscurity from which it comes is promised to research. It thus opens a future whose night is but the opacity produced by the density of the superimposed transparencies. Memory brings back the past itself and puts it into this future in which research and historical interpretation wander. The traces of the irreversible past are taken as signs that ensure the discovery and unity of a world.

Excerpted from Emmanuel Levinas, "La Trace de L'Autre," translated by A. Lingis, *Tijdschrift voor Philosophie* (Sept. 1963), 605–23.

The priority of the future among the "ecstasies" of time constitutes knowledge as comprehension of being. This priority bears witness to the adequateness of being with thought. The idea of being with which philosophers interpret the irreducible alienness of the non-I is thus cut to the measure of the same. It is the idea that is of itself adequate.

The being of beings—difference in itself, and consequently alterity—enlightens, according to Heidegger, inasmuch as it is buried and always already forgotten. But the poets and philosophers force, for a moment, its inexpressible essence. For it is still in terms of light and obscurity, disclosure and veiling, truth and nontruth—that is, in the priority of the future—that the being of beings is approached.

The intentionality caught sight of, by the phenomenological movement, at the core of practice and affectivity confirms the fact that self-consciousness, or the identification of the self, is not incompatible with consciousness of . . . , that is, consciousness of being. And, conversely, the whole weight of being can be resolved into a play of inwardness and stand on the brink of illusion, so rigorous is the adequation. The apparition of being is possibly but appearance. The shadow is taken for a prey; the prey is let loose for the shadow. Descartes thought that I could have accounted for the heavens and the sun out of myself—despite all their magnificence. Every experience, however passive it be, however welcoming, is at once converted into a "constitution of being" which it receives, as though the *given* were drawn from oneself, as though the meaning it brings were ascribed to it by me. Being bears in itself the possibility of idealism.

Western philosophy coincides with the disclosure of the other where the other, in manifesting itself as a being, loses its alterity. From its infancy philosophy has been struck with a horror of the other that remains other—with an insurmountable allergy. It is for this reason that it is essentially a philosophy of being, that the comprehension of being is its last word, and the fundamental structure of man. It is for this reason that it becomes philosophy of immanence and of autonomy, or atheism. The God of the philosophers, from Aristotle to Leibniz, by way of the God of the scholastics, is a god adequate to reason, a comprehended god who could not trouble the autonomy of consciousness, which finds itself again in all its adventures, returning home to itself like Ulysses, who through all his peregrinations is only on the way to his native island.

The philosophy handed down to us reduces to this return not only theoretical thought, but every spontaneous movement of consciousness. Not only the world understood by reason ceases to be other, for consciousness finds itself in that world, but everything that is an *attitude* of consciousness, that is, valorization, feeling, action, labor, and, in general commitment, is in the last analysis self-consciousness, that is,

identity and autonomy. Hegel's philosophy represents the logical outcome of this underlying allergy of philosophy. One of the most profound
modern interpreters of Hegelianism, Eric Weil, has expressed this
admirably in his *Logique de la philosophie*, showing how every attitude of
the rational being turns into a category, that is, grasps itself in a new
attitude. But, in conformity with philosophical tradition, he thinks that
the outcome is a category reabsorbing all the attitudes.

Even if life precedes philosophy, even if contemporary philosophy,
which wishes to be anti-intellectualist, insists on this antecedence of
existence with respect to essence, of life with respect to understanding,
even if Heidegger conceives the comprehension of being as gratitude and
obedience, the complacency of modern philosophy for the multiplicity
of cultural significations and for the games of art lightens being of its
alterity and represents the form in which philosophy prefers expectation
to action, remaining indifferent to the other and to others, refusing every
movement without return. It mistrusts every inconsiderate gesture, as if
a lucidity of old age had to repair all the imprudence of youth. Action
recuperated in advance in the light that should guide it—is perhaps the
very definition of philosophy.

2. MOVEMENT WITHOUT RETURN

Yet the transcendence of being which is described by immanence is not
the only transcendence the philosophers themselves speak of. The philosophers bring us also the enigmatic message of the beyond being.

The transcendence of the Good with respect to being *epekeina tēs ousias*
is a transcendence to the second degree, and we are not obliged to make it
immediately reenter into the Heideggerian interpretation of being that
transcends beings. The One in Plotinus is posited beyond being, and
also *epekeina nou* The One of which Plato speaks in the first hypothesis of
the Parmenides is foreign to definition and limit, place and time,
self-identity and difference with respect to oneself, resemblance and
dissemblance, foreign to being and to knowledge—for which all these
attributes constitute the categories of knowledge. It is something else
than all that, *other* absolutely and not with respect to some relative term.
It is the Unrevealed, but not unrevealed because all knowledge would be
too limited or too narrow to receive its light. It is unrevealed because it is
One, and because making oneself known implies a duality which already
clashes with the unity of the One. The One is not beyond being because
it is buried and hidden; it is buried because it is beyond being, wholly
other than being.

In what sense, then, does the *absolutely other* concern me? Must we
with the—from the first unthinkable—contact with transcendence and
alterity renounce philosophy? Would transcendence be possible only for

a completely blind touch, or for a faith attached to non-signification? Or, on the contrary, if the Platonic hypothesis concerning the One, which is One above being and knowledge, is not the development of a sophism, is there not an experience of it, an experience different from that in which the other is transmuted into the same? It would be an experience, for it would be a movement toward the transcendent, but also because in this movement the same does not lose itself ecstatically in the other, and resists the sirens' song, does not dissolve into the rumble of an anonymous event. This experience would still remain a movement of the same, a movement of an I; it consequently approaches the transcendent in a signification which it will not have ascribed to it. Does there exist a signifyingness of signification which would not be equivalent to the transmutation of the other into the same? Can there be something as strange as an experience of the absolutely exterior, as contradictory in its terms as a heteronomous experience? In the affirmative case, we will, to be sure, not succumb to the temptation and the illusion that would consist in finding again by philosophy the empirical data of positive religions, but we will disengage a movement of transcendence that is ensured like the bridgehead of the "other shore," without which the simple coexistence of philosophy and religion in souls and even in civilizations is but an inadmissible weakness of the mind. We will also put into question the thesis according to which the ultimate essence of man and of truth is the *comprehension of the being of beings*, a thesis to which, we must agree, theory, experience, and discourse seem to lead.

The heteronomous experience we seek would be an attitude that cannot be converted into a category, and whose movement unto the other is not recuperated in identification, does not return to its point of departure. Is it not furnished us by what we call quite simply goodness, and works, without which goodness is but a dream without transcendence, a pure wish (*blosser Wunsch*), as Kant put it?

But then we must not conceive of a work as an apparent agitation of a ground which afterwards remains identical with itself, like an energy which, in all its transformations, remains equal to itself. Nor must we conceive it as a technical operation, which through its much-proclaimed negativity reduces an alien world to a world whose alterity is converted into my idea. Both conceptions continue to affirm being as identical with itself and reduce its fundamental event to thought which is (and this is the ineffaceable lesson of idealism) thought of itself, thought of thought. *A work conceived radically is a movement of the same unto the other which never returns to the same.* To the myth of Ulysses returning to Ithaca, we wish to oppose the story of Abraham who leaves his fatherland forever for a yet unknown land, and forbids his servant to even bring back his son to the point of departure.

A work conceived in its ultimate nature requires a radical generosity of the same who in the work goes unto the other. It then requires an *ingratitude* of the other. Gratitude would in fact be the *return* of the movement to its origin. On the other hand, a work differs from a game or pure expenditure. It is not realized in pure loss, and it is not enough for it to affirm the same in its identity circumvented with nothingness. A work is neither a pure acquiring of merits nor a pure nihilism. Beneath the apparent gratuity of his action, both he who chases after merits and the nihilist agent forthwith takes himself as the goal. A work is thus a relationship with the other who is reached without showing himself touched. It forms outside of the morose delectation of failure, and outside of the consolations with which Nietzsche defines religion.

The departure without return, which does not go forth into the void, would also lose its absolute goodness if the work sought for its recompense in the immediacy of its triumph, if it impatiently awaited the triumph of its cause. The one-way movement would be inverted into a reciprocity. The work, confronting its departure and its end, would be absorbed again in calculations of deficits and compensations, in accountable operations. It would be subordinated to thought. The one-way action is possible only in patience, which, pushed to the limit, means for the agent to renounce being the contemporary of its outcome, to act without entering the promised land.

The future for which the work is undertaken must be posited from the start as indifferent to my death. A work, distinguished from games and from calculation, is being-for-beyond-my-death. Patience does not consist in the agent belying his generosity by giving himself the time of a *personal immortality*. To renounce being the contemporary of the triumph of one's work is to have this triumph in a time *without me*, to aim at this world without me, to aim at a time beyond the horizon of my time. It works in an eschatology without hope for oneself, an eschatology of liberation from my own time.

To be for a time that would be without me, to be for a time after my time, for a future beyond the celebrated "being-for-death," to-be-for-after-my-death—"Let the future and the most far-off things be the rule for all the present days"—is not a banal thought that extrapolates one's own duration; it is passage to the time of the other. Do we have to call what makes such a passage possible eternity? But perhaps the possibility of sacrifice goes unto the end of this passage, and discovers the non-inoffensive character of this extrapolation: to-be-for-death in order to be for-what-is-after-me.

I should like to fix the work of the same as a movement without return of the same to the other with a Greek term which in its primary meaning indicates the exercise of an office that is not only completely gratuitous, but that requires, on the part of him that exercises it, a putting out of funds at a loss. I would like to fix it with the term "liturgy." We must for the moment remove from this term every religious signification, even if a certain idea of God should become visible, as a trace, at the end of our analysis. Liturgy, as an absolutely patient action, does not take its place as a cult alongside of works and of ethics. It is ethics itself.

3. NEED AND DESIRE

The liturgical orientation of a work does not proceed from need. Need opens upon a world that is for-me; it returns to the self. Even when sublime, as the need for salvation, it is still nostalgia, homesickness. Need is the return itself, the anxiety of an ego for itself, the original form of identification which we have called egoism. It is an assimilation of the world in view of coincidence with oneself, or happiness.

In the "Canticle of the Columns," Valéry speaks of a "desire without lack." He refers, no doubt, to Plato, who, in his analysis of the pure pleasures, discovered an aspiration that is conditioned by no preexisting lack. I shall take up this term desire. To a subject turned to himself, which according to the Stoic formula is characterized by *ornē* or the tendency to persist in his being, or for whom, according to Heidegger's formula, "in his existence this very existence is in question," to a subject that is thus defined by concern for himself and who in happiness fulfills his "for himself"—we oppose the desire for the other which proceeds from a being already replenished to overflowing and independent, and who does not desire for himself. Desire is the need of him who has no more needs. We can recognize it in the desire for an other who is another [*autrui*], neither my enemy (as he is in Hobbes and in Hegel) nor my complement (as is still the case in Plato's *Republic*, which is constituted because something would be lacking for the subsistence of each individual). The desire for another is born in a being that lacks nothing, or, more exactly, it comes to birth on the other side of all that can be lacking him or can satisfy him. This desire for another, which is our very sociality, is not a simple relationship with a being where, according to our formulas at the beginning, the other is converted into the same.

In desire the ego is borne unto another in such a way as to compromise the sovereign identification of the I with itself, an identification of which need is but the nostalgia, and which the consciousness of need anticipates. The movement unto another, instead of completing and contenting me, implicates me in a situation which by one side should not concern me and should leave me indifferent: "What then was I looking for in this convict-ship?" Whence comes to me this shock when I pass, indifferent, under the gaze of another? The relationship with another puts me into question, empties me of myself, and does not let off emptying me—uncovering for me ever new resources. I did not know myself so rich, but I have no longer any right to keep anything. Is the desire for another an appetite or a generosity? The desirable does not fill up my desire but hollows it out, nourishing me as it were with new hungers. Desire is revealed to be goodness. There is a scene in Dostoyevski's *Crime and Punishment* where, apropos of Sonia Marmeladova who looks at Raskolnikov in his despair, Dostoyevski speaks of "insatiable compassion." He does not say "inexhaustible compassion." It is as though the compassion that goes from Sonia to Raskolnikov were a hunger which the presence of Raskolnikov nourished beyond all saturation, increasing this hunger ad infinitum.

The analysis of desire, which it was important to us to first distinguish from need, will be specified by the analysis of the other toward which desire bears.

The manifestation of the other is, to be sure, first produced in conformity with the way every signification is produced. The other is present in a cultural whole and is illuminated by this whole, like a text by its context. The manifestation of the whole ensures this presence and this present; they are illuminated by the light of the world. The comprehension of the other is thus a hermeneutics and an exegesis. The other is given in the concept of the totality to which he is immanent, and which, in conformity with Merleau-Ponty's remarkable analyses, our own cultural initiative, the corporeal, linguistic, or artistic gesture, expresses and discloses.

But the epiphany of the other involves a signifyingness of its own, independently of this signification received from the world. The other does not only come to us out of a context, but comes without mediation; he signifies by himself. His cultural signification is revealed and reveals as it were *horizontally*, on the basis of the historical world to which it belongs. According to the phenomenological expression, it reveals the horizons of this world. But this mundane signification is found to be disturbed and shaken by another presence, abstract, not integrated into the world. His presence consists in coming unto us, *making an entry*. This can be stated in this way: the phenomenon which is the apparition of the other is also a *face*. Again, to show this entry at every moment into the immanence and historicity of the phenomenon, we can say: the epiphany of a face is alive. Its life consists in undoing the form in which every entity, when it enters into immanence, that is, when it exposes itself as a theme, is already dissimulated.

The other who manifests himself in the face as it were breaks through his own plastic essence, like someone who opens a window on which his figure is outlined. His presence consists in *divesting* himself of the form which, however, manifests him. His manifestation is a surplus over the inevitable paralysis of manifestation. This is what the formula "the face speaks" expresses. The manifestation of a face is the first discourse. To speak is before all this way of coming from behind one's appearance, behind one's form—an opening in the openness.

4. DIACONATE

The visitation of a face is then not the disclosure of a world. In the concreteness of the world the face is abstract or naked. It is denuded of its own image. Through the nudity of the face nudity in itself is first possible in the world.

The nudity of the face is a destitution without any cultural ornament, an absolution—a detaching in the midst of its very production. A face *enters* our world from an absolutely alien sphere—that is, precisely out of an absoluteness, which in fact is the name for fundamental strangeness. The signification of a face in its abstractness is, in the literal sense of the term, extra-ordinary. How is such a production possible? How can the coming of the other out of the absolute, in the visitation of a face, be in no way convertible into a revelation—not even by a symbolism or a suggestion? How is a face not simply a true *representation*, in which the other renounces his alterity? To answer, we will have to study the exceptional signifyingness of a trace, and the personal order in which such a signifyingness is possible.

For the moment let us emphasize the sense involved in the abstract-ness or the nudity of a face which opens to us this order, and works the overwhelming of consciousness, which answers to this abstractness. Stripped of its very form, a face is benumbed in its nudity. It is a wretchedness. The nudity of a face is a denuding, and already a supplica-tion in the uprightness that aims at me. But this supplication is an exigency; in it humbleness is joined with height. Here the ethical dimension of the visitation is announced. While a true representation remains the possibility of a mere appearance, while the world that strikes up against thought can do nothing against the free thought which is capable of refusing it inwardly, taking refuge in itself, remaining precisely a free thought before the true and existing as "there first," the origin of what it receives, mastering by memory what precedes it, while free thought remains "the same"—a face is imposed on me without my being able to be deaf to its appeal nor to forget it, that is, without my being able to cease to be held responsible for its wretchedness. Con-sciousness loses its first place.

The presence of a face thus signifies an irrecusable order, a command, which calls a halt to the availability of consciousness. Consciousness is put into question by a face. The putting into question is not reducible to becoming aware of this being put into question. The absolutely other is not reflected in consciousness. It resists it to the point that even its resistance is not converted into a content of consciousness. The visitation consists in overwhelming the very egoism of the I; a face disconcerts the intentionality that aims at it.

It is a matter of the putting into question of consciousness, and not of a consciousness of a being put into question. The I loses its sovereign coincidence with itself, its identification, in which consciousness returned triumphally to itself and rested on itself. Before the exigency of the other, the I is expelled from this rest, and is not the consciousness of this exile, already glorious. Every complacency would destroy the uprightness of the ethical movement.

But the putting into question of this wild and naive freedom, sure of its refuge in itself, is not reducible to this negative movement. The putting into question of the self is precisely the welcome of the absolutely other. The epiphany of the absolutely other is a face in which the other calls to me and signifies an order to me by its nudity, its denuding. Its presence is a summation to respond. The I does not simply become conscious of this necessity to answer, as if it were a matter of an obligation or a duty which it would have to decide of. In its very position it is completely responsibility or diaconate, as said in Isaiah 53.

To be an I then signifies not to be able to slip away from responsibility. This surplus of being, this exaggeration which we call to be an I, this upsurgence of ipseity in being, is realized as a turgescence of responsibility. The putting into question of the I by the other makes me solidary with the other in an incomparable and unique way—not solidary as matter is solidary with the block which it is a part of, or as an organ is solidary with the organism in which it has its function. Solidarity here is responsibility—as though the whole edifice of creation rested on my shoulders. The unicity of the I is the fact that no one can answer in my place. Responsibility which empties the I of its imperialism and its egoism, be it the egoism of salvation, does not transform it into a moment of the universal order. It confirms it in its ipseity, in its function of being a support for the universe.

To discover in the I such an orientation is to identify the I and morality. The I before another is infinitely responsible. The other who provokes this ethical movement in consciousness, and who disorders the good conscience of the coinciding of the same with itself involves a surplus for which intentionality is inadequate. To desire is to burn with another fire than that of need which saturation puts out, to think beyond what one conceives. Because of this unassimilable surplus, this beyond, we have called the relationship which attaches the I to the other the idea of infinity.

The idea of infinity is desire. It consists, paradoxically, in thinking more than what is thought while conserving it still in its inordinateness relative to thought, entering into relationship with the ungraspable while certifying its status of being ungraspable. Infinity is then not the correlate of the idea of infinity, as though this idea were an intentionality that is fulfilled in its object. The marvel of infinity in the finite is the overwhelming of intentionality, the overwhelming of this appetite for light; unlike the saturation in which intentionality is appeased, infinity disconnects its idea. The I in relationship with infinity is an impossibility of stopping one's march forward, the impossibility, to say it with Plato's expression in the *Phaedo*, of deserting one's post; it is literally not to have time to turn back. *The attitude irreducible to a category* is not to be able to slip away from responsibility, not to have a hiding place in inwardness in which one can return into oneself, to go forward without regard for oneself. There is continual increase of demands put on one: the more I face my responsibilities the more I am responsible. Responsible is a power made of impotencies. Such is the putting into question of consciousness and its entry into a confluence of relationships which break with disclosure.

5. THE TRACE

But is the *beyond* from which a face comes an idea understood and disclosed in its turn? If the extraordinary experience of entry and visitation retains its signifyingness, it is because the *beyond* is not a simple background from which a face solicits us, is not "another world" behind the world. The *beyond* is precisely beyond the "world," that is, beyond every disclosure—like the One of the first hypothesis of the *Parmenides*, which transcends all cognition, be it symbolic or signified. The One is "neither similar nor dissimilar, neither identical nor non-identical," Plato says, thus excluding it from every even indirect revelation. A symbol still brings the symbolized back to the world in which it appears.

What then can be this relationship with an absence radically withdrawn from disclosure and from dissimulation? And what is this absence that renders visitation possible, an absence not reducible to hiddenness, since it involves a signifyingness—a signifyingness in which the other is not converted into the same?

A face is abstract. This abstractness is not, to be sure, like the brute sensible datum of the empiricists. Nor is it an instantaneous cross-section of the world in which time would cross with eternity. It is an incision made in time that does not bleed. But the abstractness of a face is a visitation and a coming. It disturbs immanence without settling into the horizons of the world. Its abstractness is not obtained by a logical process starting from the substance of beings and going from the particular to the general. On the contrary, it goes toward those beings, but does not compromise itself with them, withdraws from them, ab-solves itself. Its wonder is due to the elsewhere from which it comes and into which it already withdraws. This coming from elsewhere is not a symbolic reference to that elsewhere as to a term. A face presents itself in its nudity; it is not a form concealing, but thereby indicating, a ground, a phenomenon that hides, but thereby betrays a thing itself. Otherwise, a face would be one with a mask—but a mask presupposes a face. If *signifying* were equivalent to *indicating* a face would be insignificant. Sartre says that the other is a pure hole in the world—a most noteworthy insight, but he stops his analysis too soon. The other proceeds from the absolutely absent. His relationship with the absolutely absent from which he comes *does not indicate, does not reveal* this absent; and yet the absent has a meaning in a face. This signifyingness is not a way for the absent to be given in a blank in the presence of a face—which would again bring us back to a mode of disclosure. The relationship which goes from a face to the absent is outside every revelation and dissimulation, a third way excluded by these contradictories. How is this third way possible? But—are we not still seeking that from which a face proceeds as though it were a sphere, a place, a world? Have we been attentive enough to the interdiction against seeking the *beyond* as a world behind our world? The order of being would still seem to be presupposed, an order which contains no other status but that of the revealed and of the dissimulated. Within being, a transcendence revealed is inverted into immanence, the extra-ordinary is inserted into an order, the other is absorbed into the same. In the presence of the other do we not respond to an "order" in which signifyingness remains an irremissible disturbance, an utterly bygone past? Such is the signifyingness of a trace. The beyond from which a face comes signifies as a trace. A face is in the trace of the utterly bygone, utterly passed absent, withdrawn into what Paul Valéry calls "the deep yore, never long ago enough," which cannot be discovered in the self by an introspection. For a face is the unique openness in which the signifyingness of the transcendent does not nullify the transcendence and make it enter into an immanent *order*; here on the contrary transcendence refuses immanence precisely as the ever bygone transcendence of the transcendent. In a trace the relationship between the signified and the signification is not a correlation, but *unrightness* itself. The allegedly mediated and indirect relationship between a sign and the signified is thus still a rightness, for it is a disclosure which neutralizes transcendence. The signifyingness of a trace places us in a lateral relationship, unconvertible into rightness (something inconceivable in the order of disclosure and being), answering to an irreversible past. No memory could follow the traces of this past. It is an immemorial past—and this also is perhaps eternity, whose signifyingness is not foreign to the past. Eternity is the very irreversibility of time, the source and refuge of the past.

But if the signifyingness of a trace is not immediately transformed into the straightforwardness which still marks signs, which reveal the signified absent and bring it into immanence, it is because a trace signifies beyond being. The personal order to which a face obliges us is beyond being. *Beyond being is a third person*, which is not definable by the oneself, by ipseity. It is the possibility of this third direction of radical *unrightness* which escapes the bipolar play of immanence and transcendence proper to being, where immanence always wins against transcendence. Through a trace the irreversible past takes on the profile of a "He." The *beyond* from which a face comes is in the third person. The pronoun *He* expresses exactly its inexpressible irreversibility, already escaping every relation as well as every dissimulation, and in this sense absolutely unencompassable or absolute, a transcendence in an ab-solute past. The *illeity* of the third person is the condition for the irreversibility.

This third person who in a face has already withdrawn from every relation and every dissimulation, who has passed, this illeity, is not a "less than being" by comparison with the world in which a face enters; it is the whole enormity, the inordinateness, the infinity of the absolutely other, which eludes treatment by ontology. The supreme presence of a face is inseparable from this supreme and irreversible absence which founds the eminence of visitation.

6. TRACES AND "ILLEITY"

If the signifyingness of a trace consists in signifying without making appear, if it establishes a relationship with illeity, a relationship which is personal and ethical—is an obligation and does not disclose, and if, consequently, a trace does not belong to phenomenology, to the comprehension of the "appearing" and the "self-dissimulating," we can at least approach this signifyingness in another way by situating it with respect to the phenomenology it interrupts.

A trace is not a sign like any other. But every trace also plays the role of a sign; it can be taken for a sign. A detective examines everything in the area where a crime took place, as revealing signs which betoken the voluntary or involuntary work of the criminal; a hunter follows the traces of the game, which reflect the activity and movement of the animal the hunter is after; a historian discovers ancient civilizations which form the horizon of our world on the basis of the vestiges left by their existence. Everything is arranged in an order, in a world, where each thing reveals another or is revealed in function of another.

But when a trace is thus taken as a sign, it is exceptional with respect to other signs in that it signifies outside of every intention of signaling and outside of every project of which it would be the aim. When in transactions one "pays by check" so that there will be a trace of the payment, the trace is inscribed in the very order of the world. But a trace in the strict sense disturbs the order of the world. It occurs by overprinting. Its original signifyingness is sketched out in, for example, the fingerprints left by someone who wanted to wipe away his traces and commit a perfect crime. He who left traces in wiping out his traces did not mean to say or do anything by the traces he left. He disturbed the order in an irreparable way. He has passed absolutely. *To be* qua *leaving a trace* is to pass, to depart, to absolve oneself.

But in this sense every sign is a trace. In addition to what the sign signifies, it is the past of him who delivered the sign. The signifyingness of a trace doubles up this signifyingness proper to a sign issued in view of communication. A sign stands in this trace. This signifyingness lies in, for example, the writing and the style of a letter, in all that brings it about that during the emission of a message, which we capture on the basis of the letter's language and its sincerity, someone passes, purely and simply. This trace can be taken in its turn as a sign. A graphologist, an expert in writing styles, or a psychoanalyst could interpret a trace's singular signifyingness, and seek in it the sealed and unconscious, but real, intentions of him who delivered the message. But then what remains in the specific sense a trace in the writing and style of the letter does not signal any of these intentions, any of these qualities, reveals and hides nothing. In a trace has passed a past absolutely bygone. In a trace its irreversible lapse is sealed. Disclosure, which reinstates the world and leads back to the world, and is proper to a sign or a signification, is suppressed in traces.

But then is not a trace the weight of being itself outside of its acts and its language, weighing not through its presence, which fits it into the world, but by its very irreversibility, its ab-soluteness?

A trace would seem to be the very indelibility of being, its omnipotence before all negativity, its immensity incapable of being self-enclosed, somehow too great for discretion, inwardness, or a self. And it was indeed important for us to say that a trace does not effect a relationship with what would be less than being, but obliges with regard to the infinite, the absolutely other.

But this superiority of the superlative, this height, this constant elevation to power, this exaggeration, or this infinite overbidding— and, let us say the word, this divinity—are not deducible from the being of beings nor its revelation, even if it is contemporary with a concealment, nor deducible from "concrete duration." These signify something on the basis of a past which, in a trace, is neither *indicated* nor signaled, but yet disturbs order, while coinciding neither with revelation nor with dissimulation. A trace is the insertion of space in time, the point at which the world inclines toward a past and a time. This time is a withdrawal of the other, and, consequently, nowise a degradation of duration, which, in memory, is still complete. Superiority does not reside in a presence in the world, but in an irreversible transcendence. It is not a modulation of the being of entities. As He and third person it is somehow outside the distinction between being and entities. Only a being that transcends the world can leave a trace. A trace is a presence of that which properly speaking has never been there, of what is always past. Plotinus conceived the procession from the One as compromising neither the immutability nor the ab-solute separation of the One. It is in this situation, at first purely dialectical and quasi-verbal (and which is also the case for Intelligence and the Soul, which remain with their principle in their higher parts and are inclined only through their lower parts—a structure which still belongs to iconography), that the exceptional signifyingness of a trace delineates in the world. "Much more then does the unit, The One, remain intact in the principle which is before all beings; especially since the entities produced in its likeness, while it thus remains intact, owe their existence to no other, but to its own all-sufficient power . . . in the realm of Being, the trace of the One establishes reality; existence is a trace of The One . . ." (Enneads 5.5).

That which preserves the specific signifyingness of a trace in each trace of an empirical passage, over and above the sign it can become, is possible only through its situation in the trace of this transcendence. This position in a trace, which we have called *illeity*, does not begin in things, which by themselves do not leave traces but produce effects, that is, remain in the world. When a stone has scratched another stone, the scratch can, to be sure, be taken as a trace, but in fact without the man who held the stone this scratch is but an effect. It is as little a trace as the forest fire is a trace of the lightning. A cause and an effect, even separated by time, belong to the same world. Everything in things is exposed, even what is unknown in them. The traces that mark them are part of this plenitude of presence; their history is without a past. A trace qua trace does not simply lead to the past, but is the very *passing* toward a past more remote than any past and any future which still are set in my time—the past of the other, in which eternity takes form, an absolute past which unites all times.

The absoluteness of the presence of the other, which has justified our interpreting the exceptional uprightness of thou-saying as an epiphany of this absoluteness, is not the simple presence in which in the last analysis things are also present. Their presence belongs to the present of *my* life. Everything that constitutes my life with its past and its future is assembled in the present in which things come to me. But it is in the trace of the other that a face shines; what is presented there is absolving itself from my life and visits me as already ab-solute. Someone has already passed. His trace does not *signify* his past, as it does not *signify* his labor or his enjoyment in the world; it is a disturbance imprinting itself (we are tempted to say *engraving* itself) with an unexceptionable gravity.

The illeity of this *He* is not the *it* of things which are at our disposal, and to which Buber and Gabriel Marcel rightly prefer the *thou* to describe a human encounter. The movement of an encounter is not something added to an immobile face; it is in the face itself. A face is of itself a visitation and transcendence. But a face, wholly open, can at the same time be in itself because it is in the trace of illeity. Illeity is the origin of the alterity of being in which the in itself of objectivity participates, while also betraying it.

The God who passed is not the model of which the face would be an image. To be in the image of God does not mean to be an icon of God, but to find oneself in his trace. The revealed God of our Judeo-Christian spirituality maintains all the infinity of his absence, which is in the personal order itself. He shows himself only by his trace, as is said in Exodus 33. To go toward Him is not to follow this trace which is not a sign; it is to go toward the others who stand in the trace of illeity.

GEORGES BATAILLE

The Notion of Expenditure

I. THE INSUFFICIENCY OF THE PRINCIPLE OF CLASSICAL UTILITY

Every time the meaning of a discussion depends on the fundamental value of the word *useful*—in other words, every time the essential question touching on the life of human societies is raised, no matter who intervenes and what opinions are represented—it is possible to affirm that the debate is necessarily warped and that the fundamental question is eluded. In fact, given the more or less divergent collection of present ideas, there is nothing that permits one to define what is useful to man. This lacuna is made fairly prominent by the fact that it is constantly necessary to return, in the most unjustifiable way, to principles that one would like to situate beyond utility and pleasure: *honor* and *duty* are hypocritically employed in schemes of pecuniary interest and, without speaking of God, *Spirit* serves to mask the intellectual disarray of the few people who refuse to accept a closed system.

Current practice, however, is not deterred by these elementary difficulties, and common awareness at first seems able to raise only verbal objections to the principles of classical utility—in other words, to supposedly material utility. The goal of the latter is, theoretically, pleasure—but only in a moderate form, since violent pleasure is seen as *pathological*. On the one hand, this material utility is limited to acquisition (in practice, to production) and to the conservation of goods; on the other, it is limited to reproduction and to the conservation of human life (to which is added, it is true, the struggle against pain, whose importance itself suffices to indicate the negative character of the pleasure principle instituted, in theory, as the basis of utility). In the series of quantitative representations linked to this flat and untenable conception of existence only the question of reproduction seriously lends itself to controversy, because an exaggerated increase in the number of the living

Excerpted from Georges Bataille, *Visions of Excess: Selected Writings, 1927–1939*, translated by Allan Stoekl, with C. R. Lovitt and D. M. Leslie (Minneapolis: University of Minnesota Press, 1985), 116–29.

threatens to diminish the individual share. But on the whole, any general judgment of social activity implies the principle that all individual effort, in order to be valid, must be reducible to the fundamental necessities of production and conservation. Pleasure, whether art, permissible debauchery, or play, is definitively reduced, in the intellectual representations *in circulation*, to a concession; in other words it is reduced to a diversion whose role is subsidiary. The most appreciable share of life is given as the condition—sometimes even as the regrettable condition—of productive social activity.

It is true that personal experience—if it is a question of a useful man, capable of wasting and destroying without reason—each time gives the lie to this miserable conception. But even when he does not spare himself and destroys himself while making allowance for nothing, the most lucid man will understand nothing, or imagine himself sick; he is incapable of a *utilitarian* justification for his actions, and it does not occur to him that a human society can have, just as he does, an *interest* in considerable losses, in catastrophes that, *while conforming to well-defined needs*, provoke tumultuous depressions, crises of dread, and, in the final analysis, a certain orgiastic state.

In the most crushing way, the contradiction between current social conceptions and the real needs of society recalls the narrowness of judgment that puts the father in opposition to the satisfaction of his son's needs. This narrowness is such that it is impossible for the son to express his will. The father's partially malevolent solicitude is manifested in the things he provides for his son: lodgings, clothes, food, and, when absolutely necessary, a little harmless recreation. But the son does not even have the right to speak about what really gives him a fever; he is obliged to give people the impression that for him no *horror* can enter into consideration. In this respect, it is sad to say that *conscious humanity has remained a minor*; humanity recognizes the right to acquire, to conserve, and to consume rationally, but it excludes in principle *nonproductive expenditure*.

It is true that this exclusion is superficial and that it no more modifies practical activities than prohibitions limit the son, who indulges in his unavowed pleasures as soon as he is no longer in his father's presence. Humanity can allow itself the pleasure of expressing, in the father's interest, conceptions marked with flat paternal sufficiency and blindness. In the practice of life, however, humanity acts in a way that allows for the satisfaction of disarmingly savage needs, and it seems able to subsist only at the limits of horror. Moreover, to the small extent that a man is incapable of yielding to considerations that either are official or are susceptible of becoming so, to the small extent that he is inclined to feel the attraction of a life devoted to the destruction of established authority, it is difficult to believe that a peaceful world, conforming to his interests, could be for him anything other than a convenient illusion.

The difficulties met with in the development of a conception that is not guided by the servile mode of father-son relations are thus not insurmountable. It is possible to admit the historical necessity of vague and disappointing images, used by a majority of people, who do not act without a minimum of error (which they use as if it were a drug)—and who, moreover, in all circumstances refuse to find their way in a labyrinth resulting from human inconsistencies. An extreme simplification represents, for the uncultivated or barely cultivated segments of the population, the only chance to avoid a diminution of aggressive force. But it would be cowardly to accept, as a limit to understanding, the conditions of poverty and necessity in which such simplified images are formed. And if a less arbitrary conception is condemned to remain esoteric, and if as such, in the present circumstances, it comes into conflict with an unhealthy repulsion, then one must stress that this repulsion is precisely the shame of a generation whose rebels are afraid of the noise of their own words. Thus one cannot take it into account.

II. THE PRINCIPLE OF LOSS

Human activity is not entirely reducible to processes of production and conservation, and consumption must be divided into two distinct parts. The first, reducible part is represented by the use of the minimum necessary for the conservation of life and the continuation of individuals' productive activity in a given society; it is therefore a question simply of the fundamental condition of productive activity. The second part is represented by so-called unproductive expenditures: luxury, mourning, war, cults, the construction of sumptuary monuments, games, spectacles, arts, perverse sexual activity (i.e., deflected from genital finality)— all these represent activities which, at least in primitive circumstances, have no end beyond themselves. Now it is necessary to reserve the use of the word *expenditure* for the designation of these unproductive forms, and not for the designation of all the modes of consumption that serve as a means to the end of production. Even though it is always possible to set the various forms of expenditure in opposition to each other, they constitute a group characterized by the fact that in each case the accent is placed on a *loss* that must be as great as possible in order for that activity to take on its true meaning.

This principle of loss, in other words, of unconditional expenditure, no matter how contrary it might be to the economic principle of balanced accounts (expenditure regularly compensated for by acquisition), only *rational* in the narrow sense of the word, can be illustrated through a small number of examples taken from common experience:

1. Jewels must not only be beautiful and dazzling (which would make the substitution of imitations possible): one sacrifices a fortune, preferring a diamond necklace; such a sacrifice is necessary for the constitution of this necklace's fascinating character. This fact must be seen in relation to the symbolic value of jewels, universal in psychoanalysis. When in a dream a diamond signifies excrement, it is not only a question of association by contrast; in the unconscious, jewels, like excrement, are cursed matter that flows from a wound: they are a part of oneself destined for open sacrifice (they serve, in fact, as sumptuous gifts charged with sexual love). The functional character of jewels requires their immense material value and alone explains the inconsequence of the most beautiful imitations, which are very nearly useless.

2. Cults require a bloody wasting of men and animals in *sacrifice*. In the etymological sense of the word, sacrifice is nothing other than the production of *sacred* things.

From the very first, it appears that sacred things are constituted by an operation of loss: in particular, the success of Christianity must be explained by the value of the theme of the Son of God's ignominious crucifixion, which carries human dread to a representation of loss and limitless degradation.

3. In various competitive games, loss in general is produced under complex conditions. Considerable sums of money are spent for the maintenance of quarters, animals, equipment, or men. As much energy as possible is squandered in order to produce a feeling of stupefaction— in any case with an intensity infinitely greater than in productive enterprises. The danger of death is not avoided; on the contrary, it is the object of a strong unconscious attraction. Besides, competitions are sometimes the occasion for the public distribution of prizes. Immense crowds are present; their passions most often burst forth beyond any restraint, and the loss of insane sums of money is set in motion in the form of wagers. It is true that this circulation of money profits a small number of professional bettors, but it is no less true that this circulation can be considered to be a real *charge* of the passions unleashed by competition and that, among a large number of bettors, it leads to losses disproportionate to their means; these even attain such a level of madness that often the only way out for gamblers is prison or death. Beyond this, various modes of unproductive expenditure can be linked, depending on the circumstances, to great competitive spectacles, just as elements moving separately are caught up in a mightier whirlwind. Thus horse races are associated with a sumptuary process of social classification (the existence of Jockey Clubs need only be mentioned) and the ostentatious display of the latest luxurious fashions. It is necessary in any case to observe that the complex of expenditure represented by present-day

racing is insignificant when compared to the extravagance of the Byzantines, who tied the totality of their public activity to equestrian competition.

4. From the point of view of expenditure, artistic productions must be divided into two main categories, the first constituted by architectural construction, music, and dance. This category is comprised of *real* expenditures. Nevertheless, sculpture and painting, not to mention the use of sites for ceremonies and spectacles, introduces even into architecture the principle of the second category, that of *symbolic* expenditure. For their part, music and dance can easily be charged with external significations.

In their major form, literature and theater, which constitute the second category, provoke dread and horror through symbolic representations of tragic loss (degradation or death); in their minor form, they provoke laughter through representations which, though analogously structured, exclude certain seductive elements. The term poetry, applied to the least degraded and least intellectualized forms of the expression of a state of loss, can be considered synonymous with expenditure; it in fact signifies, in the most precise way, creation by means of loss. Its meaning is therefore close to that of *sacrifice*. It is true that the word "poetry" can only be appropriately applied to an extremely rare residue of what it commonly signifies and that, without a preliminary reduction, the worst confusions could result; it is, however, impossible in a first, rapid exposition to speak of the infinitely variable limits separating subsidiary formations from the residual element of poetry. It is easier to indicate that, for the rare human beings who have this element at their disposal, poetic expenditure ceases to be symbolic in its consequences; thus, to a certain extent, the function of representation engages the very life of the one who assumes it. It condemns him to the most disappointing forms of activity, to misery, to despair, to the pursuit of inconsistent shadows that provide nothing but vertigo or rage. The poet frequently can use words only for his own loss; he is often forced to choose between the destiny of a reprobate, who is as profoundly separated from society as dejecta are from apparent life, and a renunciation whose price is a mediocre activity, subordinated to vulgar and superficial needs.

III. PRODUCTION, EXCHANGE, AND UNPRODUCTIVE ACTIVITY

Once the existence of expenditure as a social function has been established, it is then necessary to consider the relations between this function and those of production and acquisition that are opposed to it. These relations immediately present themselves as those of an *end* with *utility*. And if it is true that production and acquisition in their development and changes of form introduce a variable that must be understood in order to comprehend historical processes, they are, however, still only means subordinated to expenditure. As dreadful as it is, human poverty has never had a strong enough hold on societies to cause the concern for conservation—which gives production the appearance of an end—to dominate the concern for unproductive expenditure. In order to maintain this preeminence, since power is exercised by the classes that expend, poverty was excluded from all social activity. And the poor have no other way of reentering the circle of power than through the revolutionary destruction of the classes occupying that circle—in other words, through a bloody and in no way limited social expenditure.

The secondary character of production and acquisition in relation to expenditure appears most clearly in primitive economic institutions, since exchange is still treated as a sumptuary loss of ceded objects: thus at its *base* exchange presents itself as a process of expenditure, over which a process of acquisition has developed. Classical economics imagined that primitive exchange occurred in the form of barter; it had no reason to assume, in fact, that a means of acquisition such as exchange might have as its origin not the need to acquire that it satisfies today, but the contrary need, the need to destroy and to lose. The traditional conceptions of the origins of economy have only recently been disproved—even so recently that a great number of economists continue arbitrarily to represent barter as the ancestor of commerce.

In opposition to the artificial notion of barter, the archaic form of exchange has been identified by Mauss under the name *potlatch*,[1] borrowed from the Northwestern American Indians who provided such a remarkable example of it. Institutions analogous to the Indian *potlatch*, or their traces, have been very widely found.

The *potlatch* of the Tlingit, the Haida, the Tsimshian, and the Kwakiutl of the northwestern coast has been studied in detail since the end of the nineteenth century (but at that time it was not compared with the archaic forms of exchange of other countries). The least advanced of these American tribes practice *potlatch* on the occasion of a person's change in situation—initiations, marriages, funerals—and, even in a more evolved form, it can never be separated from a festival; whether it provides the occasion for this festival, or whether it takes place on the festival's occasion. *Potlatch* excludes all bargaining and, in general, it is constituted by a considerable gift of riches, offered openly and with the goal of humiliating, defying, and *obligating* a rival. The exchange value of the gift results from the fact that the donee, in order to efface the

---

1. On *potlatch*, see above all Marcel Mauss, "Essai sur le don, form archaïque de l'échange" in *Année Sociologique* (1925). [Translated as *The Gift: Forms and Functions of Exchange in Archaic Societies*, trans. I. Cunnison (New York: Norton, 1967). Tr.]

humiliation and respond to the challenge, must satisfy the obligation (incurred by him at the time of acceptance) to respond later with a more valuable gift, in other words, to return with interest.

But the gift is not the only form of *potlatch*; it is equally possible to defy rivals through the spectacular destruction of wealth. It is through the intermediary of this last form that *potlatch* is reunited with religious sacrifice, since what is destroyed is theoretically offered to the mythical ancestors of the donees. Relatively recently a Tlingit chief appeared before his rival to slash the throats of some of his own slaves. This destruction was repaid at a given date by the slaughter of a greater number of slaves. The Tchoukchi of far northwestern Siberia, who have institutions analogous to *potlatch*, slaughter dog teams in order to stifle and humiliate another group. In northwestern America, destruction goes as far as the burning of villages and the smashing of flotillas of canoes. Emblazoned copper ingots, a kind of money on which the fictive value of an immense fortune is sometimes placed, are broken or thrown into the sea. The delirium of the festival can be associated equally with hecatombs of property and with gifts accumulated with the intention of stunning and humiliating.

Usury, which regularly intervenes in these operations as obligatory surplus at the time of the returned *potlatch*, gives rise to the observation that the loan with interest must be substituted for barter in the history of the origins of exchange. It must be recognized, in fact, that wealth is multiplied in *potlatch* civilizations in a way that recalls the inflation of credit in banking civilizations; in other words, it would be impossible to realize at once all the wealth possessed by the total number of donors resulting from the obligations contracted by the total number of donees. But this comparison applies only to a secondary characteristic of *potlatch*.

It is the constitution of a positive property of loss—from which spring nobility, honor, and rank in a hierarchy—that gives the institution its significant value. The gift must be considered as a loss and thus as a partial destruction, since the desire to destroy is in part transferred onto the recipient. In unconscious forms, such as those described by psychoanalysis, it symbolizes excretion, which itself is linked to death, in conformity with the fundamental connection between anal eroticism and sadism. The excremental symbolism of emblazoned coppers, which on the Northwest Coast are the gift objects *par excellence*, is based on a very rich mythology. In Melanesia, the donor designates as his excrement magnificent gifts, which he deposits at the feet of the rival chief.

The consequences in the realm of acquisition are only the unwanted result—at least to the extent that the drives that govern the operation have remained primitive—of a process oriented in the opposite direction. "The ideal," indicates Mauss, "would be to give a *potlatch* and not have it returned." This ideal is realized in certain forms of destruction to which custom allows no possible response. On the other hand, since the yields of *potlatch* are in some ways pledged in advance in a new *potlatch*, the archaic principle of wealth is displayed with none of the attenuations that result from the avarice developed at later stages; wealth appears as an acquisition to the extent that power is acquired by a rich man, but it is entirely directed toward loss in the sense that this power is characterized as power to lose. It is only through loss that glory and honor are linked to wealth.

As a game, *potlatch* is the opposite of a principle of conservation: it puts an end to the stability of fortunes as it existed within the totemic economy, where possession was hereditary. An activity of excessive exchange replaced heredity (as source of possession) with a kind of deliriously formed ritual poker. But the players can never retire from the game, their fortunes made; they remain at the mercy of provocation. At no time does a fortune serve to *shelter its owner from need*. On the contrary, it functionally remains—as does its possessor—*at the mercy of a need for limitless loss*, which exists endemically in a social group.

The nonsumptuary production and consumption upon which wealth depends thus appear as relative utility.

IV. The Functional Expenditure of the Wealthy Classes

The notion of *potlatch*, strictly speaking, should be reserved for expenditures of an agonistic type, which are instigated by challenges and which lead to responses. More precisely, it should be reserved for forms which, for archaic societies, are not distinguishable from *exchange*.

It is important to know that exchange, at its origin, was *immediately* subordinated to a human *end*; nevertheless it is evident that its development, linked to progress in the modes of production, only started at the stage at which this subordination ceased to be immediate. The very principle of the function of production requires that products be exempt from loss, at least provisionally.

In the market economy, the processes of exchange have an acquisitive sense. Fortunes are no longer placed on a gambling table; they have become relatively stable. It is only to the extent that stability is assured and can no longer be compromised by even considerable losses that these losses are submitted to the regime of unproductive expenditure. Under these new conditions, the elementary components of *potlatch* are found in forms that are no longer as directly agonistic.[2] Expenditure is still destined to acquire or maintain rank, but in principle it no longer has the goal of causing another to lose his rank.

2. In other words: involving rivalry and struggle.

In spite of these attenuations, ostentatious loss remains universally linked to wealth, as its ultimate function.

More or less narrowly, social rank is linked to the possession of a fortune, but only on the condition that the fortune be partially sacrificed in unproductive social expenditures such as festivals, spectacles, and games. One notes that in primitive societies, where the exploitation of man by man is still fairly weak, the products of human activity not only flow in great quantities to rich men because of the protection or social leadership services these men supposedly provide, but also because of the spectacular collective expenditures for which they must pay. In so-called civilized societies, the fundamental *obligation* of wealth disappeared only in a fairly recent period. The decline of paganism led to a decline of the games and cults for which wealthy Romans were obliged to pay; thus it has been said that Christianity individualized property, giving its possessor total control over his products and abrogating his social function. It abrogated at least the obligation of this expenditure, for Christianity replaced pagan expenditure prescribed by custom with voluntary alms, either in the form of distributions from the rich to the poor, or (and above all) in the form of extremely significant contributions to churches and later to monasteries. And these churches and monasteries precisely assumed, in the Middle Ages, the major part of the spectacular function.

Today the great and free forms of unproductive social expenditure have disappeared. One must not conclude from this, however, that the very principle of expenditure is no longer the end of economic activity.

A certain evolution of wealth, whose symptoms indicate sickness and exhaustion, leads to shame in oneself accompanied by petty hypocrisy. Everything that was generous, orgiastic, and excessive has disappeared; the themes of rivalry upon which individual activity still depends develop in obscurity, and are as shameful as belching. The representatives of the bourgeoisie have adopted an effaced manner; wealth is now displayed behind closed doors, in accordance with depressing and boring conventions. In addition, people in the middle class—employees and small shopkeepers—having attained mediocre or minute fortunes, have managed to debase and subdivide ostentatious expenditure, of which nothing remains but vain efforts tied to tiresome rancor.

Such trickery has become the principle reason for living, working, and suffering for those who lack the courage to condemn this moldy society to revolutionary destruction. Around modern banks, as around the totem poles of the Kwakiutl, the same desire to dazzle animates individuals and leads them into a system of petty displays that blinds them to each other, as if they were staring into a blinding light. A few steps from the bank, jewels, dresses, and cars wait behind shop windows for the day when they will serve to establish the augmented splendor of a sinister industrialist and his even more sinister old wife. At a lower level, gilded clocks, dining room buffets, and artificial flowers render equally shameful service to a grocer and his wife. Jealousy arises between human beings, as it does among the savages, and with an equivalent brutality; only generosity and nobility have disappeared, and with them the dazzling contrast that the rich provided to the poor.

As the class that possesses the wealth—having received with wealth the obligation of functional expenditure—the modern bourgeoisie is characterized by the refusal in principle of this obligation. It has distinguished itself from the aristocracy through the fact that it has consented only to *spend for itself*, and within itself—in other words, by hiding its expenditures as much as possible from the eyes of the other classes. This particular form was originally due to the development of its wealth in the shadow of a more powerful noble class. The rationalist conceptions developed by the bourgeosie, starting in the seventeenth century, were a response to these humiliating conceptions of restrained expenditure; this rationalism meant nothing other than the strictly economic representation of the world—economic in the vulgar sense, the bourgeois sense, of the word. The hatred of expenditure is the *raison d'être* of and the justification for the bourgeoisie; it is at the same time the principle of its horrifying hypocrisy. A fundamental grievance of the bourgeois was the prodigality of feudal society and, after coming to power, they believed that, because of their habits of accumulation, they were capable of acceptably dominating the poorer classes. And it is right to recognize that the people are incapable of hating them as much as their former masters, to the extent that they are incapable of loving them, for the bourgeois are incapable of concealing a sordid face, a face so rapacious and lacking in nobility, so frighteningly small, that all human life, upon seeing it, seems degraded.

In opposition, the people's consciousness is reduced to maintaining profoundly the principle of expenditure by representing bourgeois existence as the shame of man and as a sinister cancellation.

V. Class Struggle

In trying to maintain sterility in regard to expenditure, in conformity with a reasoning that balances *accounts,* bourgeois society has only managed to develop a universal meanness. Human life only rediscovers agitation on the scale of irreducible needs through the efforts of those who push the consequences of current rationalist conceptions as far as they will go. What remains of the traditional modes of expenditure has become atrophied, and living sumptuary tumult has been lost in the unprecedented explosion of *class struggle.*

The components of *class struggle* are seen in the process of expenditure, dating back to the archaic period. In *potlatch*, the rich man distributes products furnished him by other, impoverished, men. He tries to rise above a rival who is rich like himself, but the ultimate stage of his foreseen elevation has no more necessary a goal than his further separation from the nature of destitute men. Thus expenditure, even though it might be a social function, immediately leads to an agonistic and apparently antisocial act of separation. The rich man consumes the poor man's losses, creating for him a category of degradation and abjection that leads to slavery. Now it is evident that, from the endlessly transmitted heritage of the sumptuary world, the modern world has received slavery, and has reserved it for the proletariat. Without a doubt bourgeois society, which pretends to govern according to rational principles, and which, through its own actions, moreover, tends to realize a certain human homogeneity, does not accept without protest a division that seems destructive to man himself; it is incapable, however, of pushing this resistance further than theoretical negation. It gives the workers rights equal to those of the masters, and it announces this *equality* by inscribing that word on walls. But the masters, who act as if they were the expression of society itself, are preoccupied—more seriously than with any other concern—with showing that they do not in any way share the abjection of the men they employ. *The end of the workers' activity is to produce in order to live, but the bosses' activity is to produce in order to condemn the working producers to a hideous degradation*—for there is no disjunction possible between, on the one hand, the characterization the bosses seek through their modes of expenditure, which tend to elevate them high above human baseness, and on the other hand this baseness itself, of which this characterization is a function.

In opposition to this conception of agonistic social expenditure, there is the representation of numerous bourgeois efforts to ameliorate the lot of the workers—but this representation is only the expression of the cowardice of the modern upper classes, who no longer have the force to recognize the results of their own destructive acts. The expenditures taken on by the capitalists in order to aid the proletarians and give them a chance to pull themselves up on the social ladder only bear witness to their inability (due to exhaustion) to carry out thoroughly a sumptuary process. Once the loss of the poor man is accomplished, little by little the pleasure of the rich man is emptied and neutralized; it gives way to a kind of apathetic indifference. Under these conditions, in order to maintain a neutral state rendered relatively agreeable by apathy (and which exists in spite of troublesome elements such as sadism and pity), it can be useful to compensate for the expenditure that engenders abjection with a new expenditure, which tends to attenuate it. The bosses' political sense, together with certain partial developments of prosperity, has allowed this process of compensation to be, at times, quite extensive. Thus in the Anglo-Saxon countries, and in particular in the United States of America, the primary process takes place at the expense of only a relatively small portion of the population: to a certain extent, the working class itself has been led to participate in it (above all when this was facilitated by the preliminary existence of a class held to be abject by common accord, as in the case of the blacks). But these subterfuges, whose importance is in any case strictly limited, do not modify in any way the fundamental division between noble and ignoble men. The cruel game of social life does not vary among the different civilized countries, where the insulting splendor of the rich loses and degrades the human nature of the lower class.

It must be added that the attenuation of the masters' brutality—which in any case has less to do with destruction itself than with the psychological tendencies to destroy—corresponds to the general atrophy of the ancient sumptuary processes that characterizes the modern era.

Class struggle, on the contrary, becomes the grandest form of social expenditure when it is taken up again and developed, this time on the part of the workers, and on such a scale that it threatens the very existence of the masters.

VI. CHRISTIANITY AND REVOLUTION

Short of revolt, it has been possible for the provoked poor to refuse all moral participation in a system in which men oppress men; in certain historical circumstances, they succeeded, through the use of symbols even more striking than reality, in lowering all of "human nature" to such a horrifying ignominy that the pleasure found by the rich in measuring the poverty of others suddenly became too acute to be endured without vertigo. Thus, independently of all ritual forms, an exchange of exasperated challenges was established, exacerbated above all by the poor, a *potlatch* in which real refuse and revealed moral filth entered into a rivalry of horrible grandeur with everything in the world that was rich, pure, and brilliant; and an exceptional outlet was found for this form of spasmodic convulsion in religious despair, which was its unreserved exploitation.

In Christianity, the alternations between the exaltation and dread, tortures and orgies constituting religious life were conjoined in a more tragic way and were merged with a sick social structure, which was tearing itself apart with the dirtiest cruelty. The triumphal song of the Christians glorifies God because he has entered into the bloody game of social war, and because he has "hurled the powerful from the heights of their grandeur and has exalted the miserably poor." Their myths associate social ignominy and the cadaverous degradation of the torture victim with divine splendor. In this way religion assumes the total oppositional function manifested by contrary forces, which up to this point had been divided between the rich and the poor, with the one group condemning the other to ruin. It is closely tied to terrestrial despair, since it itself is only an epiphenomenon of the measureless hate that divides men—but an epiphenomenon that tends to substitute itself for the totality of divergent processes it summarizes. In conformity with the words attributed to Christ, who said he came to divide and not to reign, religion thus does not at all try to do away with what others consider the scourge of man. On the contrary, in its immediate form, it wallows in a revolting impurity that is indispensable to its ecstatic torment.

The meaning of Christianity is given in the development of the delirious consequences of the expenditure of classes, in a mental agonistic orgy practiced at the expense of the real struggle.

However, in spite of the importance that it has had in human activity, Christian *humiliation* is only an episode in the historic struggle of the ignoble against the noble, of the impure against the pure. It is as if society, conscious of its own intolerable splitting, had become for a time dead drunk in order to enjoy it sadistically. But the heaviest drunkenness has not done away with the consequences of human poverty, and, with the exploited classes opposing the superior classes with greater lucidity, no conceivable limit can be assigned to hatred. In historical agitation, only the word Revolution dominates the customary confusion and carries with it the promise that answers the unlimited demands of the masses. As for the masters and the exploiters, whose function is to create the contemptuous forms that exclude human nature—causing this nature to exist at the limits of the earth, in other words in mud—a simple law of reciprocity requires that they be condemned to fear, to the *great night* when their beautiful phrases will be drowned out by death screams in riots. That is the bloody hope which, each day, is one with the existence of the people, and which sums up the insubordinate content of the class struggle.

Class struggle has only one possible end: the loss of those who have worked to lose "human nature."

But whatever form of development is foreseen, be it revolutionary or servile, the general convulsions constituted eighteen hundred years ago by the religious ecstasy of the Christians, and today by the workers' movement, must equally be represented as a decisive impulse *constraining* society to use the exclusion of one class by another to realize a mode of expenditure as tragic and as free as possible, and at the same time *constraining* it to introduce sacred forms so human that the traditional forms become relatively contemptible. It is the tropic character of such movements that accounts for the total human value of the workers'

Revolution, a Revolution capable of exerting a force of attraction as strong as the force that directs simple organisms toward the sun.

VII. THE INSUBORDINATION OF MATERIAL FACTS

Human life, distinct from juridical existence, existing as it does on a globe isolated in celestial space, from night to day and from one country to another—human life cannot in any way be limited to the closed systems assigned to it by reasonable conceptions. The immense travail of recklessness, discharge, and upheaval that constitutes life could be expressed by stating that life starts only with the deficit of these systems; at least what it allows in the way of order and reserve has meaning only from the moment when the ordered and reserved forces liberate and lose themselves for ends that cannot be subordinated to anything one can account for. It is only by such insubordination—even if it is impoverished—that the human race ceases to be isolated in the unconditional splendor of material things.

In fact, in the most universal way, isolated or in groups, men find themselves constantly engaged in processes of expenditure. Variations in form do not in any way alter the fundamental characteristics of these processes, whose principle is loss. A certain excitation, whose sum total is maintained at a noticeably constant level, animates collectivities and individuals. In their intensified form, the *states of excitation*, which are comparable to toxic states, can be defined as the illogical and irresistible impulse to reject material or moral goods that it would have been possible to utilize rationally (in conformity with the balancing of accounts). Connected to the losses that are realized in this way—in the case of the "lost woman" as well as in the case of military expenditure—is the creation of unproductive values; the most absurd of these values, and the one that makes people the most rapacious, is *glory*. Made complete through degradation, glory, appearing in a sometimes sinister and sometimes brilliant form, has never ceased to dominate social existence; it is impossible to attempt to do anything without it when it is dependent on the blind practice of personal or social loss.

In this way the boundless refuse of activity pushes human plans—including those associated with economic operations—into the game of characterizing universal matter; matter, in fact, can only be defined as the *nonlogical difference* that represents in relation to the *economy* of the universe what *crime* represents in relation to the law. The glory that sums up or symbolizes (without exhausting) the object of free expenditure, while it can never exclude crime, cannot be distinguished—at least if one takes into account the only characterization that has a value comparable to matter—from the *insubordinate characterization*, which is not the condition for anything else.

If on the other hand one demonstrates the interest, concurrent with glory (as well as with degradation), which the human community necessarily sees in the qualitative change constantly realized by the movement of history, and if, finally, one demonstrates that this movement is impossible to contain or direct toward a limited end, it becomes possible, having abandoned all reserves, to assign a *relative* value to utility. Men assure their own subsistence or avoid suffering, not because these functions themselves lead to a sufficient result, but in order to accede to the insubordinate function of free expenditure.

The Labyrinth

> Negativity, in other words, the integrity of deter-
> mination.
>
> HEGEL

I. THE INSUFFICIENCY OF BEINGS

Men act in order to be. This must not be understood in the negative sense
of conservation (conserving in order not to be thrown out of existence by
death), but in the positive sense of a tragic and incessant combat for a
satisfaction that is almost beyond reach. From incoherent agitation to
crushing sleep, from chatter to turning inward, from overwhelming love
to hardening hate, existence sometimes weakens and sometimes
accomplishes "being." And not only do states have a variable intensity,
but different beings "are" unequally. A dog that runs and barks seems
"to be" more than a mute and clinging sponge, the sponge more than the
water in which it lives, an influential man more than a vacant passerby.

In the first movement, where the force that the master has at his
disposal puts the slave at his mercy, the master deprives the slave of a
part of his being. Much later, in return, the "existence" of the master is
impoverished to the extent that it distances itself from the material
elements of life. The slave enriches his being to the extent that he
enslaves these elements by the work to which his impotence condemns
him.

The contradictory movements of degradation and growth attain, in
the diffuse development of human existence, a bewildering complexity.
The fundamental separation of men into masters and slaves is only the
crossed threshold, the entry into the world of specialized functions where
personal "existence" empties itself of its contents; a man is no longer
anything but a part of being, and his life, engaged in the game of

Excerpted from Georges Bataille, *Visions of Excess: Selected Writings, 1927–1939*,
translated by Allan Stoekl, with C. R. Lovitt and D. M. Leslie (Minneapolis: University
of Minnesota Press, 1985), 171–77.

creation and destruction that goes beyond it, appears as a degraded particle lacking reality. The very fact of assuming that knowledge is a function throws the philosopher back into the world of petty inconsistencies and dissections of lifeless organs. Isolated as much from action as from the dreams that turn action away and echo it in the strange depths of animated life, he led astray the very being that he chose as the object of his uneasy comprehension. "Being" increases in the tumultuous agitation of a life that knows no limits; it wastes away and disappears if he who is at the same time "being" and knowledge mutilates himself by reducing himself to knowledge.

This deficiency can grow even greater if the object of knowledge is no longer being in general but a narrow domain, such as an organ, a mathematical question, a juridical form. Action and dreams do not escape this poverty (each time they are confused with the totality of being), and, in the multicolored immensity of human lives, a limitless insufficiency is revealed; life, finding its endpoint in the happiness of a bugle blower or the snickering of a village chair-renter, is no longer the fulfillment of itself, but is its own ludicrous degradation—its fall is comparable to that of a king onto the floor.

At the basis of human life there exists a *principle of insufficiency*. In isolation, each man sees the majority of others as incapable or unworthy of "being." There is found, in all free and slanderous conversation, as an animating theme, the awareness of the vanity and the emptiness of our fellowmen; an apparently stagnant conversation betrays the blind and impotent flight of all life toward an indefinable summit.

The sufficiency of each being is endlessly contested by every other. Even the look that expresses love and admiration comes to me as a doubt concerning my reality. A burst of laughter or the expression of repugnance greets each gesture, each sentence or each oversight through which my profound insufficiency is betrayed—just as sobs would be the response to my sudden death, to a total and irremediable omission.

This uneasiness on the part of everyone grows and reverberates, since at each detour, with a kind of nausea, men discover their solitude in empty night. The universal night in which everything finds itself—and soon loses itself—would appear to be existence for nothing, without influence, equivalent to the absence of being, were it not for human nature that emerges within it to give a dramatic importance to being and life. But this absurd night manages to empty itself of "being" and meaning each time a man discovers within it human destiny, itself locked in turn in a comic impasse, like a hideous and discordant trumpet blast. That which, in me, demands that there be "being" in the world, "being" and not just the manifest insufficiency of human or nonhuman nature, necessarily projects (at one time or another and in reply to human chatter) divine sufficiency across space, like the reflection of an impotence, of a servilely accepted malady of being.

II. The Composite Character of Beings and the Impossibility of Fixing Existence in Any Given *Ipse*

Being in the world is so *uncertain* that I can project it where I want—outside of me. It is a clumsy man, still incapable of eluding the intrigues of nature, who locks being in the me. Being in fact is found NOWHERE and it was an easy game for a sickly malice to discover it to be divine, at the summit of a pyramid formed by the multitude of beings, which has at its base the immensity of the simplest matter.

Being could be confined to the electron if *ipseity* were precisely not lacking in this simple element. The atom itself has a complexity that is too elementary to be determined *ipsely*.[1] The number of particles that make up a being intervene in a sufficiently heavy and clear way in the constitution of its *ipseity*; if a knife has its handle and blade indefinitely replaced, it loses even the shadow of *ipseity*; it is not the same for a machine which, after five or six years, loses each of the *numerous* elements that constituted it when new. But the *ipseity* that is finally apprehended with difficulty in the machine is still only shadowlike.

Starting from an extreme complexity, being imposes on reflection more than the precariousness of a fugitive appearance, but this complexity—displaced little by little—becomes in turn the labyrinth where what had suddenly come forward strangely loses its way.

A sponge is reduced by pounding to a dust of cells; this living dust is formed by a multitude of isolated beings, and is lost in the new sponge that it reconstitutes. A siphonophore fragment is by itself an autonomous being, yet the whole siphonophore, to which this fragment belongs, is itself hardly different from a being possessing unity. Only with linear animals (worms, insects, fish, reptiles, birds, and mammals) do the living individual forms definitively lose the faculty of constituting aggregates bound together in a single body. But while *societies* of nonlinear animals do not exist, superior animals form aggregates without ever giving rise to corporeal links; men as well as beavers or ants form societies of individuals whose bodies are autonomous. But in regard to being, is this autonomy the final appearance, or is it simply error?

In men, all existence is tied in particular to language, whose terms determine its modes of appearance within each person. Each person can only represent his total existence, if only in his own eyes, through the

---

1. See Paul Langevin, *La Notion de corpuscules et d'atomes* (Paris: Hermann, 1934), p. 35.

medium of words. Words spring forth in his head, laden with a host of human or superhuman lives *in relation* to which he privately exists. Being depends on the mediation of words, which cannot merely present it arbitrarily as "autonomous being," but which must present it profoundly as "being in relation." One need only follow, for a short time, the traces of the repeated circuits of words to discover, in a disconcerting vision, the labyrinthine structure of the human being. What is commonly called *knowing*—when a man *knows* his neighbor—is never anything but existence *composed* for an instant (in the sense that all existence composes itself—thus the atom composes its unity from variable electrons), which *once* made of these two beings a *whole* every bit as real as its parts. A limited number of exchanged phrases, no matter how conventional, sufficed to create the banal interpenetration of two existing juxtaposed regions. The fact that after this short exchange the man is aware of *knowing* his neighbor is opposed to a meeting without recognition in the street, as well as to the ignorance of the multitude of beings that one never meets, in the same way that life is opposed to death. The *knowledge* of human beings thus appears as a mode of biological connection, unstable but just as real as the connections between cells in tissue. The exchange between two human particles in fact possesses the faculty of surviving momentary separation.

A man is only a particle inserted in unstable and entangled wholes. These wholes are composed in personal life in the form of multiple possibilities, starting with a *knowledge* that is crossed like a threshold—and the existence of the particle can in no way be isolated from this composition, which agitates it in the midst of a whirlwind of ephemerids. This extreme instability of connections alone permits one to introduce, as a puerile but convenient illusion, a representation of isolated existence turning in on itself.

In the most general way, *every isolable element of the universe always appears as a particle that can enter into composition with a whole that transcends it. Being is only found as a whole composed of particles whose relative autonomy is maintained.* These two principles dominate the uncertain presence of an *ipse* being across a distance that never ceases to put *everything* in question. Emerging in universal play as unforeseeable chance, with extreme dread imperatively becoming the demand for universality, carried away to vertigo by the movement that composes it, the *ipse* being that presents itself as a universal is only a challenge to the diffuse immensity that escapes its precarious violence, the tragic negation of all that is not its own bewildered phantom's chance. But, as a man, this being falls into the meanders of the *knowledge* of his fellowmen, which absorbs his substance in order to reduce it to a component of what goes beyond the virulent madness of his autonomy in the total night of the world.

Abdication and inevitable fatigue—due to the fact that "being" is, *par excellence,* that which, desired to the point of dread, cannot be endured—plunge human beings into a foggy labyrinth formed by the multitude of "acquaintances" with which signs of life and phrases can be exchanged. But when he escapes the dread of "being" through this flight—a "being" that is autonomous and isolated in night—a man is thrown back into insufficiency, at least if he cannot find outside of himself the blinding flash that he had been unable to endure within himself, without whose intensity his life is but an impoverishment, of which he feels obscurely ashamed.

III. The Structure of the Labyrinth

Emerging out of an inconceivable void into the play of beings, as a lost satellite of two phantoms (one with a bristly beard, the other softer, her head decorated with a bun), it is in the father and mother who transcend him that the minuscule human being first encountered the illusion of sufficiency. In the complexity and entanglement of wholes, to which the human particle belongs, this satellite-like mode of existence never entirely disappears. A particular being not only acts as an element of a shapeless and structureless whole (a part of the world of unimportant "acquaintances" and chatter), but also as a peripheral element orbiting around a nucleus where being hardens. What the lost child had found in the self-assured existence of the all-powerful beings who took care of him is now sought by the abandoned man wherever knots and concentrations are formed throughout a vast incoherence. Each particular being delegates to the group of those situated at the center of the multitudes the task of realizing the inherent totality of "being." He is content to be a part of a total existence, which even in the simplest cases retains a diffuse character. Thus relatively stable wholes are produced, whose center is a city, in its early form a corolla that encloses a double pistil of sovereign and god. In the case where many cities abdicate their central function in favor of a single city, an empire forms around a capital where sovereignty and the gods are concentrated; the gravitation around a center then degrades the existence of peripheral cities, where the organs that constituted the totality of being wilt. By degrees, a more and more complex movement of group composition raises to the point of universality the human race, but it seems that universality, at the summit, causes all existence to explode and decomposes it with violence. The universal god destroys rather than supports the human aggregates that raise his ghost. He himself is only dead, whether a mythical delirium set him up to be adored as a cadaver covered with wounds, or whether through his very universality he becomes, more than any other, incapable of stopping the loss of being with the cracked partitions of *ipseity*.

IV. THE MODALITIES OF COMPOSITION AND DECOMPOSITION OF BEING

The city that little by little empties itself of life, in favor of a more brilliant and attractive city, is the expressive image of the play of existence engaged in composition. Because of the composing attraction, *composition empties elements of the greatest part of their being, and this benefits the center*—in other words, it benefits composite being. There is the added fact that, in a given domain, *if the attraction of a certain center is stronger than that of a neighboring center, the second center then goes into decline.* The action of powerful poles of attraction across the human world thus reduces, depending on their force of resistance, a multitude of personal beings to the state of empty shadows, especially when the pole of attraction on which they depend itself declines, due to the action of another more powerful pole. Thus if one imagines the effects of an influential current of attraction on a more or less arbitrarily isolated form of activity, a style of clothing created in a certain city devalues the clothes worn up to that time and, consequently, it devalues those who wear them within the limits of the influence of this city. This devaluation is stronger if, in a neighboring country, the fashions of a more brilliant city have already outclassed those of the first city. The objective character of these relations is registered in reality when the contempt and laughter manifested in a given center are not compensated for by anything elsewhere, and when they exert an effective fascination. The effort made on the periphery to "keep up with fashion" demonstrates the inability of the peripheral particles to exist by themselves.

Laughter intervenes in these value determinations of being as the expression of the circuit of movements of attraction across a human field. It manifests itself each time a change in level suddenly occurs: it characterizes all vacant lives as *ridiculous*. A kind of incandescent joy— the explosive and sudden revelation of the presence of being—is liberated each time a striking appearance is contrasted with its absence, with the human void. Laughter casts a glance, charged with the mortal violence of being, into the void of life.

But laughter is not only the composition of those it assembles into a unique convulsion; it most often decomposes without consequence, and sometimes with a virulence that is so pernicious that it even puts in question composition itself, and the wholes across which it functions. Laughter attains not only the peripheral regions of existence, and its object is not only the existence of fools and children (of those who remain vacant); through a necessary reversal, it is sent back from the child to its father and from the periphery to the center, each time the father or the center in turn reveals an insufficiency comparable to that of the particles that orbit around it. Such a central insufficiency can be ritually revealed (in saturnalia or in a festival of the ass as well as in the puerile grimaces of the father amusing his child). It can be revealed by the very action of children or the "poor" each time exhaustion withers and weakens authority, allowing its precarious character to be seen. In both cases, a dominant necessity manifests itself, and the profound nature of being is disclosed. Being can complete itself and attain the menacing grandeur of imperative totality; this accomplishment only serves to project it with a greater violence into the vacant night. The relative insufficiency of peripheral existences is absolute insufficiency in total existence. Above knowable existences, laughter traverses the human pyramid like a network of endless waves that renew themselves in all directions. This reverberated convulsion chokes, from one end to the other, the innumerable being of man—opened at the summit by the agony of God in a black night.

V. The Monster in the Night of the Labyrinth

Being attains the blinding flash in tragic annihilation. Laughter only assumes its fullest impact on being at the moment when, in the fall that it unleashes, a representation of death is cynically recognized. It is not only the composition of elements that constitutes the incandescence of being, but its decomposition in its mortal form. The difference in levels that provokes common laughter—which opposes the lack of an absurd life to the plenitude of successful being—can be replaced by that which opposes the summit of imperative elevation to the dark abyss that obliterates all existence. Laughter is thus assumed by the totality of being. Renouncing the avaricious malice of the scapegoat, being itself, to the extent that it is the sum of existences at the limits of the night, is spasmodically shaken by the idea of the ground giving way beneath its feet. It is in *universality* (where, due to solitude, the possibility of facing death through war disappears) that the necessity of engaging in a struggle, no longer with an equal group but with nothingness, becomes clear. THE UNIVERSAL resembles a bull, sometimes absorbed in the nonchalance of animality and abandoned to the secret paleness of death, and sometimes hurled by the rage of ruin into the void ceaselessly opened before it by a skeletal torero. But the void it meets is also the nudity it espouses TO THE EXTENT THAT IT IS A MONSTER lightly assuming many crimes, and it is no longer, like the bull, the plaything of nothingness, because nothingness itself is its plaything; it only throws itself into nothingness in order to tear it apart and to illuminate the night for an instant, with an immense laugh—a laugh it never would have attained if this nothingness had not totally opened beneath its feet.

The Absence of the Book

Let us try to question ourselves, that is, admit in the form of a question
something that cannot reach the point of questioning.

1. *"This insane game of writing."* With these words, simple as they are,
Mallarmé opens up writing to writing. The words are very simple, but
their nature is also such that we will need a great deal of time—a great
variety of experiments, the work of the world, countless misunderstandings, works lost and scattered, the movement of knowledge, and finally
the turning point of an infinite crisis—if we are to begin to understand
what decision is being prepared on the basis of this end of writing that is
foretold by its coming.

2. Apparently we only read because the writing is already there, laid out
before our eyes. Apparently. But the first person who ever wrote, who
cut into stone and wood under ancient skies, was far from responding to
the demands of a view that required a reference point and gave it
meaning, changed all relations between seeing and the visible. What he
left behind him was not something more, something added to other
things; it was not even something less—a subtraction of matter, a
hollow in the relation to the relief. Then what was it? A hole in the
universe: nothing that was visible, nothing that was invisible. I suppose
the first reader was engulfed by that non-absent absence, but without
knowing anything about it, and there was no second reader because
reading, from then on understood to be the vision of an immediately
visible—that is, intelligible—presence, was affirmed for the very purpose of making this disappearance into *the absence of the book* impossible.

3. Culture is linked to the book. The book as repository and receptacle
of knowledge is identified with knowledge. The book is not only the

Excerpted from Maurice Blanchot, *The Gaze of Orpheus and Other Literary Essays*,
translated by Lydia Davis (New York: Station Hill Press, 1981), 145–60.

book that sits in libraries—that labyrinth in which all combinations of forms, words and letters are rolled up in volumes. The book is the Book. Still to be read, still to be written, always already written, always already paralyzed by reading, the book constitutes the condition for every possibility of reading and writing.

The book admits of three distinct investigations. There is the empirical book; the book acts as vehicle of knowledge; a given determinate book receives and gathers a given determinate form of knowledge. But the book as book is never simply empirical. The book is the *a priori* of knowledge. We would know nothing if there did not always exist in advance the impersonal memory of the book and, more importantly, the prior inclination to write and read contained in every book and affirming itself only in the book. The absolute of the book, then, is the isolation of a possibility that claims not to have originated in any other anteriority. An absolute that will later tend to assert itself in the Romantics (Novalis), then more rigorously in Hegel, then more radically—though in a different way—in Mallarmé, as the totality of relations (absolute knowledge or the Work), in which would be achieved either consciousness, which knows itself and returns to itself after having been exteriorized in all its dialectically linked figures, or language, closed around its own statement and already dispersed.

Let us recapitulate: the empirical book; the book: condition for all reading and all writing; the book: totality or Work. But with increasing refinement and truth these forms all assume that the book contains knowledge as the presence of something virtually present and always immediately accessible, if only with the help of mediations and relays. Something is there which the book presents in presenting itself and which reading animates, which reading reestablishes—through its animation—in the life of a presence. Something that is, on the lowest level, the presence of a content or of a signified thing; then, on a higher level, the presence of a form, of a signifying thing or of an operation; and, on a higher level still, the development of a system of relations that is always there already, if only as a future possibility. The book rolls up time, unrolls time, and contains this unrolling as the continuity of a presence in which present, past, and future become actual.

4. *The absence of the book* revokes all continuity of presence, just as it evades the questioning conveyed by the book. It is not the interiority of the book, nor its continuously evaded Meaning. Rather it is outside the book, though it is enclosed in it, not so much its exterior as a reference to an outside that does not concern the book.

The more the Work assumes meaning and acquires ambition, retaining in itself not only all works, but all the forms of discourse and all the powers of discourse, the more the absence of the work seems about to propose itself, though without ever allowing itself to be designated. This happens with Mallarmé. With Mallarmé, the Work becomes aware of itself and so knows itself as something coinciding with the absence of the work, the latter then deflecting it from ever coinciding with itself, and dooming it to impossibility. A deviation in which the work disappears into the absence of the work, but in which the absence of the work always escapes the more it reduces itself to being nothing but the Work that has always disappeared already.

5. The act of writing is related to the absence of the work, but is invested in the Work as book. The insanity of writing—*the insane game*—is the relationship of writing, a relationship established not between writing and the production of the book, but, through the production of the book, between the act of writing and the absence of the work.

To write is to produce absence of the work (worklessness). Or: writing is the absence of the work as it *produces itself* through the work and throughout the work. Writing as worklessness (in the active sense of the word) is the insane game, the indeterminacy that lies between reason and unreason.

What happens to the book during this "game," in which worklessness is set loose during the operation of writing? The book: the passage of an infinite movement, a movement that goes from writing as an operation to writing as worklessness; a passage that immediately impedes. Writing passes through the book, but the book is not that to which it is destined (its destiny). Writing passes through the book, completing itself there even as it disappears in the book; and yet, we do not write for the book. The book: a ruse by which writing goes towards *the absence of the book.*

6. Let us try to gain a clearer understanding of the relation of the book to *the absence of the book.*

a) The book plays a dialectical role. In some sense it is there so that not only the dialectic of discourse can take place, but also discourse as dialectic. The book is the work language performs on itself: as though the book were necessary in order for language to become aware of language, for it to know itself and complete itself in its incompleteness.

b) Yet the book that has become a work—the whole literary process, whether it asserts itself as a long succession of books or is manifested in one unique book or in the space that takes the place of that book—is both more of a book than the others and already beyond the book, outside its category and outside its dialectic. *More* a book: a book of knowledge scarcely exists as a book, as a developed volume; the work, on the other hand, makes a claim to be singular: unique, irreplaceable, it is almost a person; this is why there is a dangerous tendency for the work to promote itself into a masterpiece, and also to make itself essential, that is, to designate itself by a signature (it is not only signed by the author, but also somehow by itself, which is more serious). And yet it is already outside the book process: as though the work only indicated the opening—the interruption—through which the neutrality of writing passes, as though the work were oscillating suspended between itself (the totality of language) and an affirmation that had not yet been made.

What is more, in the work, language is already changing direction—or place: place of direction—no longer the logos that participates in a dialectic and knows itself, rather, it is engaged in a different relationship. So that one can say the work hesitates between the book, vehicle of knowledge and fleeting moment of language, and the Book, raised to the Capital Letter, Idea, and Absolute of the book—and then between the work as presence and the absence of the work that is constantly escaping and in which time as time is disturbed.

7. The end of the act of writing does not lie in the book or in the work. As we write the work, we are drawn by the absence of the work. We necessarily fall short of the work, but this does not mean that because of this deficiency we fall under the necessity of the absence of the work.

8. The book: a ruse by which the energy of writing, relying on discourse and allowing itself to be carried along by the vast continuity of discourse, separating itself from it at the limit, is also the use of discourse, restoring to culture that alteration which threatens it and opens it to the absence of the book. Or the book is a labor through which writing, changing the givens of a culture, of "experience," of knowledge, that is to say of discourse, obtains another product that will constitute a new modality of discourse as a whole and will integrate itself with it even as it claims to disintegrate it.

The absence of the book: reader, you would like to be its author, and then you would be nothing more than the plural reader of the Work.

How long will it last—this lack that is sustained by the book and that expels the book from itself as book? Produce the book, then, so that it will detach itself, disengage itself as it scatters: this will not mean that you have produced *the absence of the book.*

9. The book (the civilization of the book) declares: there is a memory

that transmits things, there is a system of relations that arranges things; time becomes entangled in the book, where the void still belongs to a structure. But the absence of the book is not based on writing that leaves a mark and determines a directed movement, whether this movement develops linearly from a beginning toward an end, or is deployed from a center toward the surface of a sphere. The absence of the book makes an appeal to writing that does not commit itself, that does not settle out, is not satisfied with disavowing itself, nor with going back over its tracks to erase them.

What summons us to write, when the time of the book determined by the beginning-end relation, and the space of the book determined by deployment from a center, cease to impose themselves? The attraction of (pure) exteriority.

The time of the book, determined by the beginning-end (past-future) relation based on a presence. The space of the book determined by deployment from a center, itself conceived as the search for a source.

Everywhere that there is a system of relations that arranges, a memory that transmits, everywhere that writing gathers in the substance of a mark that reading regards in the light of a meaning (tracing it back to an origin whose sign it is), when emptiness itself belongs to a structure and allows itself to be adjusted, then there is the book: the *law* of the book.

As we write, we always write in the name of the exteriority of writing and against the exteriority of the law, and always the law uses what is written as a resource.

The attraction of (pure) exteriority—the place where, since the outside "precedes" any interior, writing does not deposit itself in the manner of a spiritual or ideal presence subsequently inscribing itself and then leaving a mark, a mark or a sedimentary deposit that would allow one to track it down, in other words to restore it—on the basis of that mark as deficiency—to its ideal presence or ideality, its fullness, its integrity as presence.

Writing marks but leaves no mark; it does not allow us to work our way back from some vestige or sign to anything more than itself as (pure) exteriority and, as such, never given as either forming itself, or being gathered in a unifying relationship with a presence (to be seen, to be heard), or with the whole of presence or the Unique, present-absence.

When we begin to write, either we are not beginning or we are not writing: writing does not accompany beginning.

10. In the book, the uneasiness of writing—the energy—tries to come to rest in the favor of the work (*ergon*), but the absence of the work always summons it immediately to respond to the deflection of the outside,

where what is affirmed no longer finds its measure in a relationship of unity.

We have no "idea" of the absence of the work, certainly not as a presence, but also not as the destruction of the thing that would prevent this absence, if only in the form of absence itself. To destroy the work, which itself is not, to destroy at least the affirmation of the work and the dream of the work, to destroy the indestructible, to destroy nothing so that an idea that is out of place here will not impose itself—the idea that to destroy would be enough. The negative can no longer be operative where an affirmation has been made that affirms the work. And in no case can the negative lead to the absence of the work.

Reading would be reading in the book the absence of the book, and as a consequence producing this absence where there is no question of the book being absent or present (defined by an absence or a presence).

The absence of the book: never contemporaneous with the book, not because it emerges from another time, but because it is the source of noncontemporaneity from which it, too, comes. The absence of the book: always diverging, always lacking a present relationship with itself, so that it is never received in its fragmentary plurality by a single reader in the present of his reading, unless, at the limit, with the present torn apart, dissuaded—

The attraction of (pure) exteriority or the vertigo of space as distance, fragmentation that only drives us back to the fragmentary.

The absence of the book: the prior deterioration of the book, the game of dissidence it plays with reference to the space in which it is inscribed; the preliminary dying of the book. Writing, the relation to every book's *other*, to what is de-scription in the book, a scripturary demand beyond discourse, beyond language. The act of writing at the edge of the book, outside the book.

Writing outside language, writing which would be in some sense originally language making it impossible for there to be any object (present or absent) of language. Then writing would never be man's writing, which is to say it would never be God's writing either; at most it would be the writing of the other, of dying itself.

11. The book begins with the Bible, in which the logos is inscribed as law. Here the book achieves its unsurpassable meaning, including what extends beyond it everywhere and cannot be surpassed. The Bible takes language back to its origin: whether this language is written or spoken, it is always the theological era that opens with this language and lasts as long as biblical space and time. The Bible not only offers us the highest model of a book, the specimen that will never be superceded; the Bible

also encompasses all books, no matter how alien they are to biblical revelation, knowledge, poetry, prophecy, proverbs, because it contains the spirit of the book; the books that follow it are always contemporaneous with the Bible: the Bible certainly grows, expands with itself in an infinite growth that leaves it identical, permanently sanctioned by the relationship of Unity, just as the ten Laws set forth and contain the monologos, the One Law, the law of Unity that cannot be transgressed and never can be denied by negation alone.

The Bible: a testamentary book in which the alliance is declared, that is to say, the destiny of speech bound to the one who bestows language, and in which he consents to remain through this gift that is the gift of his name, that is to say, also the destiny of this relationship of speech to language, which is dialectic. It is not because the Bible is a sacred book that the books which spring from it—the whole literary process—are marked with the theological sign and cause us to belong to the realm of the theological. It is just the opposite: it was because the testament—the alliance of speech—was rolled up in a book, took the form and structure of a book, that the "sacred" (what is separated from writing) found its place in theology. The book is in essence theological. This is why the first manifestation of the theological (and the only one that continues to unfold and to develop) could only have been in the form of a book. In some sense God does not remain God (does not become divine) except as He speaks through the book.

Mallarmé, confronting the Bible in which God is God, establishes a work in which *the insane game of writing* sets to work and already disowns itself, encountering indeterminacy with its double game: necessity, accident. The Work, the absolute of the voice and of writing, is unworked even before it has been accomplished, before it ruins the possibility of accomplishment by being accomplished. The Work still belongs to the book, and because of this it helps sustain the biblical aspect of every Work, and yet designates the disjunction of a time and a space that are *something other*, precisely that which can no longer assert that it is in a relationship of unity. The Work as book leads Mallarmé outside his name. The Work in which the absence of the work is in effect leads the man who is no longer called Mallarmé to madness: let us understand, if we can, that this *to* means the limit which would be decisive madness if it were crossed; and this obliges us to conclude that the limit—"the edge of madness"—if conceived as indecision that cannot decide, or as nonmadness, is more essentially mad: would be abyss, not the abyss, but the edge of the abyss.

Suicide: what is written as necessity in the book is denounced as chance in the absence of the book. What one says, the other repeats, and this statement that reiterates, by virtue of this reiteration encompasses death—the death of self.

12. The anonymity of the book is such that in order to sustain the book it calls for the dignity of a name. The name is that of a temporary particularity that supports reason and that reason authorizes by raising it to itself. The relationship of the Book and the name is always contained in the historical relationship that linked absolute knowledge of system with Hegel's name: this relationship of the Book and of Hegel, identifying the latter with the book, carrying him along in its development, made Hegel into post-Hegel, Hegel-Marx, and then Marx radically estranged from Hegel, who continues to write, to correct, to know, to assert the absolute law of written discourse.

Just as the Book takes the name of Hegel, the work, in its more essential (more uncertain) anonymity, takes the name of Mallarmé, with the difference that Mallarmé not only recognizes the anonymity of the Work as his own trait and the indication of his own place, not only withdraws into this manner of being anonymous, but does not call himself the author of the Work, suggesting at the very most, hyperbolically, that he is the capacity—never a unique or a unifiable capacity—to read the nonpresent Work, that is, the capacity to respond, by his absence, to the work that continues to be absent (but the absent work is not *the absence of the work*, is even separated from it by a radical break).

In this sense, there is already a decisive distance between Hegel's book and Mallarmé's work, a difference evidenced by their different ways of being anonymous in the naming and signing of their works. Hegel does not die, even if he disavows himself in the displacement or reversal of the System: every system still names him, Hegel is never altogether without a name. Mallarmé and the work have no relationship, and this lack of relationship is played out in the Work, establishing the work as what would be forbidden to this particular Mallarmé as to anyone else with a name, and ultimately forbidden to the work when conceived as capable of completing itself by and through itself. The Work is not freed of the name because it could be produced without someone producing it, but because anonymity affirms that it is constantly already beyond whatever could name it. The book is the whole, whatever the form of that totality, whether or not the structure of that totality is completely different from that which a belated reading assigns to Hegel. The Work is not everything, it is already outside everything, but, in its resignation, it is still designated as absolute. The Work is not bound up with success (with completion) as the book is, but with disaster: but this disaster is yet another affirmation of the absolute.

Let us say briefly that the book can always be signed, it remains indifferent to who signs it; the work—Festivity as disaster—requires resignation, requires that whoever claims to write it renounce himself and cease to designate himself.

Then why do we sign our books? Out of modesty, as a way of saying: these are still only books, indifferent to signatures.

13. The "absence of the book"—which the written thing provokes as the future of writing, a future that has never come to pass—does not form a concept anymore than the word "outside" does, or the word "fragment," or the word "neuter," but it helps conceptualize the word "book." It is not some contemporary expositor who gives Hegel's philosophy its coherence and conceives of it as a book, thus conceiving of the book as the finality of absolute Knowledge; beginning at the end of the 19th century, it is Mallarmé. But Mallarmé, through the very force of his experience, immediately pierces through the book to designate (dangerously) the Work whose center of attraction—a center that is always off center—would be writing. The act of writing, *the insane game.* But the act of writing has a relationship, a relationship of otherness, with the absence of the Work, and it is precisely because he senses this radical alteration that comes to writing and through writing with the absence of the Work that Mallarmé is able to name the Book, naming it as the thing that gives meaning to becoming by suggesting a place and a time for it: first and last concept. But Mallarmé does not yet name the absence of the book or he only recognizes it as a way of thinking the Work, the Work as failure or impossibility.

14. *The absence of the book* is not the book coming apart, even though in some sense coming apart lies at the origin of the book and is its opposing principle. The fact that the book is always coming apart (disordering itself) still only leads to another book or to a possibility other than the book, but not to the absence of the book. Let us admit that what obsesses the book (what haunts it) would be the absence of the book that it always lacks, contenting itself with containing it (holding it at a distance) without containing it (transforming it into content). Let us also admit the opposite, that the book encloses the absence of the book that excludes it, but that the absence of the book is never conceived only on the basis of the book and only as its negation. Let us admit that if the book carries meaning, the absence of the book is so alien to meaning that nonmeaning does not concern it either.

It is very striking that within a certain tradition of the book (the one derived from the kabbalists' formulation, although there it is a question of sanctioning the mystical signification of the literal presence), what is called the "written Torah" preceded the "oral Torah," the latter then giving rise to the edited version that alone constitutes the Book. Here, thought is confronted with an enigmatic proposition: Nothing precedes writing. Yet the writing on the first tablets does not become readable until after they are broken and because they are broken—after and because of the resumption of the oral decision, which brings us to the second writing, the one we know, rich in meaning, capable of issuing commandments, always equal to the law it transmits.

Let us try to examine this surprising proposition by relating it to what might be a future experiment of writing. There are two kinds of writing, one white, the other black; one makes the invisibility of a colorless flame invisible, the other is made accessible in the form of letters, characters, and articulations by the power of the black fire. Between the two there is orality, which, however, is not independent, but always involved with the second kind of writing, because it is the black fire itself, the measured darkness that limits, defines all light, makes all light visible. Thus, what we call oral is designation in a temporal present and a presence of space, but also, at first, development or mediation as it is guaranteed by a discourse that explains, welcomes and defines the neutrality of the initial inarticulation. The "oral Torah" is therefore no less written, but is called oral in the sense that as discourse it alone allows there to be communication, otherwise known as *commentary,* speech that both teaches and declares, authorizes and justifies: as though language (discourse) were necessary for writing to give rise to common legibility and perhaps also to the Law understood as prohibition and limit; and also as though the first writing, in its configuration of invisibility, had to be considered *outside speech* and directed only towards the *outside,* an absence or a fracture so primordial that it will have to be broken to escape the savagery of what Hölderlin calls the aorgic.

15. Writing is absent from the Book, being the nonabsent absence on the basis of which the Book, having absented itself from this absence, makes itself readable (on both its levels—the oral and the written, the Law and its exegesis, the forbidden and the thought of the forbidden) and comments on itself by enclosing history: the closing of the book, the severity of the letter, the authority of knowledge. What we can say about this writing, which is absent from the book and yet stands in a relationship of otherness with it, is that it remains alien to readability, that it is unreadable insofar as to read is necessarily to enter through one's gaze into a relationship of meaning or nonmeaning with a presence. There would, therefore, be a writing exterior to the kind of knowledge

that is gained through reading, and also exterior to the form and the requirements of the Law. Writing, (pure) exteriority, alien to every relationship of presence, and to all legality.

The moment the exteriority of writing *slackens*, that is, responds to the appeal of the oral force, agreeing to be informed in language giving rise to the book—the written discourse—this exteriority tends to appear as the exteriority of the Law, on the highest level, and on the lowest level as the interiority of meaning. The Law is writing itself which has renounced the exteriority of interlocution to designate the place of the interdicted. The illegitimacy of writing, always rebellious towards the Law, hides the asymmetrical illegitimacy of the Law in relation to writing.

Writing: exteriority. Perhaps there is a "pure" exteriority of writing, but this is only a postulate, a postulate that is already disloyal to the neutrality of writing. In the book that signs our alliance with every Book, exteriority does not succeed in authorizing itself on its own, and as it writes down its name, it does so under the space of the Law. The exteriority of writing, spreading itself out in layers in the book, becomes exteriority as law. The Book speaks as Law. Reading it, we read in it that everything which is, is either forbidden or allowed. But isn't this structure of permission and prohibition a result of our level of reading? Isn't there perhaps another reading of the Book in which the book's other would cease to be proclaimed in precepts? And if we were to read this way, would we read yet another book? Wouldn't we be about to read *the absence of the book?*

The initial exteriority: perhaps we should assume that its nature is such that we should not be able to tolerate it except under the sanction of the Law. What would happen if the system of prohibition and limitations stopped protecting it? Or might it simply be there, at the limit of possibility, just to make the limit possible? Is this exteriority nothing more than a requirement of limit? Is limit itself conceived only through a definition that is necessary at the approach of the unlimited and that would disappear if it was ever passed—for that reason impassable, yet always passed because it is impassable?

16. Writing contains exteriority. The exteriority that becomes Law falls henceforth under the protection of the Law—which, in turn, is written; that is, once again under the protection of writing. We must assume that this reduplication of writing, which immediately designates it as difference, only affirms, through this duplicity, the quality of exteriority itself, which is always developing, always exterior to itself, in a relationship of discontinuity. There is a "first" writing, but since this writing is the first writing, it is already distinct from itself, separated

because of what marks it, being at the same time nothing but that mark and also different from it, if the mark is made there, and broken, outdistanced, and denounced to such a degree—in that outside, that disjunction where it is revealed—that a new rupture will be necessary, a break that is violent but human (and, in this sense, defined and delimited), so that, having become an explosive text—and the initial fragmentation having been replaced by a determined act of rupture—the law may, under the mask of the forbidden, redeem a promise of unity.

In other words, the breaking of the first tablets is not a break with an original state of undivided harmony; on the contrary, what it initiates is the substitution of a limited exteriority (in which the possibility of a limit is intimated) for an exteriority without limitation, the substitution of a lack for an absence, of a break for a gap, of an infraction for the pure-impure fraction of the fragmentary, the fraction that falls short of the sacred separation, crowding into the scission of the neuter (which is the neuter). To put it yet another way, we must break with the first exteriority so that language, henceforth regularly divided, in a reciprocal bond of mastery with itself, grammatically constructed, will engage us in mediate and immediate relationships with the second exteriority, in which the logos is law and the law logos—relationships that guarantee discourse and then dialectic, where the law in turn will dissolve.

The "first" writing, far from being more immediate than the second, is alien to all these categories. It does not bestow its gifts generously through some ecstatic participation in which the law that protects the One merges with it and ensures confusion with it. The first writing is otherness itself, a severity and austerity that never grant authority, the burning of a parching breeze, infinitely more rigorous than any law. The law is what saves us from writing by forcing writing to act indirectly through the rupture—the transitiveness—of speech. A salvation that introduces us to knowledge and, through our desire for knowledge, even to the Book, where knowledge maintains desire by hiding it from itself.

17. The nature of the Law: it is infringed upon even before it has been stated; from that time on, certainly, it is promulgated in a high place, at a distance and in the name of what is distant, but without any relationship of direct knowledge with those for whom it is destined. From this we could conclude that the law, as it is transmitted, tolerates transmission, becomes a law of transmission, is only constituted as a law by the decision to fail to do so: there would be no limit if the limit were not passed, revealed as impassable by being passed.

Yet doesn't the law precede all knowledge (including knowledge of the law), knowledge which it alone opens, preparing it for its conditions by a preliminary "it must be," even if only from the Book in which the law attests to itself through the order—the structure—that it looms over as it establishes it?

Always anterior to the law, neither founded in nor determined by the necessity of being brought to knowledge, never endangered by someone's misunderstanding, always essentially affirmed by the infraction that implies reference to it, attracting in its trial the authority that submits itself to it, and all the more firm because it is open to easy transgression: the law.

The law's "it must be" is not primarily a "thou shalt." "It must be" applies to no one or, more deliberately, applies only to no one. The nonapplicability of the law is not only a sign of its abstract force, of its inexhaustible authority, of the reserve it maintains. Incapable of saying *thou*, the law is never directed at anyone in particular: not because it is universal, but because it separates in the name of unity, being separation itself that prescribes for the sake of what is unique. This is perhaps the law's august lie: itself having "legalized" the outside in order to make it possible (or real), it frees itself of all determination and all content in order to preserve itself as pure inapplicable form, pure exigency to which no presence is able to respond, yet immediately particularized in multiple norms and, through the code of alliance, in ritual forms so as to allow for the discreet interiority of a return to self, where the infrangible intimacy of the "thou shalt" will be affirmed.

18. The ten laws are only laws with reference to Unity. God—the name that cannot be spoken in vain because no language can contain it—is only God so that He can carry the Unity and designate its sovereign finality. No one will try to attack the One. And then the Other bears witness, bears witness for none other than the Unique, a reference that unites all thought to what is *un*thought, keeping it turned towards the One as towards something upon which thought cannot infringe. It is therefore important to say: not the unique God, but Unity is necessarily God, transcendence itself.

The exteriority of the law finds its measure in responsibility towards the One, it is an alliance of the One and the many that thrusts aside as impious the primordiality of difference. Yet in the law itself there is still a clause that retains some memory of the exteriority of writing, when it is said: thou shalt make no images, thou shalt not represent, thou shalt reject presence in the form of resemblance, sign, and mark. What does that mean? First, and almost too clearly, the prohibition of the sign as mode of presence. The act of writing—if that act is relating oneself to the image and naming the idol—makes its mark outside the exteriority proper to it, an exteriority that writing then repels in its effort to overwhelm it, both by the void of words and by the pure signification of the sign. "Thou shalt make no idol" is thus, in the form of the law, not a statement about the law, but about the exigency of writing that precedes any law.

19. Let us admit that the law is obsessed by exteriority, that this obsession haunts it and that it separates itself from this obsession, in the name of the very separation that establishes it as a form, in the movement in which this obsession formulates it as law. Let us admit that exteriority as writing, a relation always without relation, can be called exteriority that *slackens* into law, precisely when it is *more tense,* when it has the tension of a gathering form. We need to know that as soon as the law exists (finds its place), everything changes, and it is the so-called "initial" exteriority that—in the name of a law that from now on cannot be denounced—is presented as slackness, as undemanding neutrality, in the same way that writing outside the law, outside the book, seems at that point to be nothing more than the return to a spontaneity without rules, an automatism of ignorance, an irresponsible gesture, an immoral game. To put it another way, one cannot climb back up from exteriority as law to exteriority as writing; going back up, in this context, would be going down. That is to say: one cannot "go back up" save by accepting the fall—though one is incapable of consenting to it—an essentially indeterminate fall into inessential chance (what the law disdainfully calls a game—a game in which everything is risked each time, and everything is lost: the necessity of law, the chance of writing). The law is the summit, there is no other. Writing remains outside the arbitration between high and low.[1]

1. I dedicate *(and disavow)* these uncertain pages to the books in which the absence of the book is already being produced by being promised; these books were written by _____ _____ , but will only be designated here by the lack of a name, for the sake of friendship.

Différance

I will speak, therefore, of a letter.

Of the first letter, if the alphabet, and most of the speculations which have ventured into it, are to be believed.

I will speak, therefore, of the letter *a*, this initial letter which it apparently has been necessary to insinuate, here and there, into the writing of the word *difference;* and to do so in the course of a writing on writing, and also of a writing within writing whose different trajectories thereby find themselves, at certain very determined points, intersecting with a kind of gross spelling mistake, a lapse in the discipline and law which regulate writing and keep it seemly. One can always, de facto or de jure, erase or reduce this lapse in spelling, and find it (according to situations to be analyzed each time, although amounting to the same), grave or unseemly, that is, to follow the most ingenuous hypothesis, amusing. Thus, even if one seeks to pass over such an infraction in silence, the interest that one takes in it can be recognized and situated in advance as prescribed by the mute irony, the inaudible misplacement, of this literal permutation. One can always act as if it made no difference. And I must state here and now that today's discourse will be less a justification of, and even less an apology for, this silent lapse in spelling, than a kind of insistent intensification of its play.

On the other hand, I will have to be excused if I refer, at least implicitly, to some of the texts I have ventured to publish. This is precisely because I would like to attempt, to a certain extent, and even though in principle and in the last analysis this is impossible, and impossible for essential reasons, to reassemble in a *sheaf* the different directions in which I have been able to utilize what I would call provisionally the word or concept of *différance,* or rather to let it impose itself upon me in its neographism, although as we shall see, *différance* is literally neither a word nor a concept. And I insist upon the word *sheaf* for two reasons. On the one hand, I will not be concerned, as I might

Excerpted from Jacques Derrida, *Margins of Philosophy*, translated by Alan Bass (Chicago: University of Chicago Press, 1982), 3–27.

have been, with describing a history and narrating its stages, text by text, context by context, demonstrating the economy that each time imposed this graphic disorder; rather, I will be concerned with the *general system of this economy*. On the other hand, the word *sheaf* seems to mark more appropriately that the assemblage to be proposed has the complex structure of a weaving, an interlacing which permits the different threads and different lines of meaning—or of force—to go off again in different directions, just as it is always ready to tie itself up with others.

Therefore, preliminarily, let me recall that this discreet graphic intervention, which neither primarily nor simply aims to shock the reader or the grammarian, came to be formulated in the course of a written investigation of a question about writing. Now it happens, I would say in effect, that this graphic difference (*a* instead of *e*), this marked difference between two apparently vocal notations, between two vowels, remains purely graphic: it is read, or it is written, but it cannot be heard. It cannot be apprehended in speech, and we will see why it also bypasses the order of apprehension in general. It is offered by a mute mark, by a tacit monument, I would even say by a pyramid, thinking not only of the form of the letter when it is printed as a capital, but also of the text in Hegel's *Encyclopedia* in which the body of the sign is compared to the Egyptian Pyramid. The *a* of *différance*, thus, is not heard; it remains silent, secret and discreet as a tomb: *oikēsis*. And thereby let us anticipate the delineation of a site, the familial residence and tomb of the proper in which is produced, by *différance*, the *economy of death*. This stone—provided that one knows how to decipher its inscription—is not far from announcing the death of the tyrant.

And it is a tomb that cannot even be made to resonate. In effect, I cannot let you know through my discourse, through the speech being addressed at this moment to the French Society of Philosophy, what difference I am talking about when I talk about it. I can speak of this graphic difference only through a very indirect discourse on writing, and on the condition that I specify, each time, whether I am referring to difference with an *e* or *différance* with an *a*. Which will not simplify things today, and will give us all, you and me, a great deal of trouble, if, at least, we wish to understand each other. In any event, the oral specifications that I will provide—when I say "with an *e*" or "with an *a*"—will refer uncircumventably to a *written text* that keeps watch over my discourse, to a text that I am holding in front of me, that I will read, and toward which I necessarily will attempt to direct your hands and your eyes. We will be able neither to do without the passage through a written text, nor to avoid the order of the disorder produced within it—and this, first of all, is what counts for me.

The pyramidal silence of the graphic difference between the *e* and the *a* can function, of course, only within the system of phonetic writing, and within the language and grammar which is as historically linked to phonetic writing as it is to the entire culture inseparable from phonetic writing. But I would say that this in itself—the silence that functions within only a so-called phonetic writing—quite opportunely conveys or reminds us that, contrary to a very widespread prejudice, there is no phonetic writing. There is no purely and rigorously phonetic writing. So-called phonetic writing, by all rights and in principle, and not only due to an empirical or technical insufficiency, can function only by admitting into its system nonphonetic "signs" (punctuation, spacing, etc.). And an examination of the structure and necessity of these non-phonetic signs quickly reveals that they can barely tolerate the concept of the sign itself. Better, the play of difference, which, as Saussure re-minded us, is the condition for the possibility and functioning of every sign, is in itself a silent play. Inaudible is the difference between two phonemes which alone permits them to be and to operate as such. The inaudible opens up the apprehension of two present phonemes such as they present themselves. If there is no purely phonetic writing, it is that there is no purely phonetic *phōnē*. The difference which establishes phonemes and lets them be heard remains in and of itself inaudible, in every sense of the word.

It will be objected, for the same reasons, that graphic difference itself vanishes into the night, can never be sensed as a full term, but rather extends an invisible relationship, the mark of an inapparent relationship between two spectacles. Doubtless. But, from this point of view, that the difference marked in "differ()nce" between the *e* and the *a* eludes both vision and hearing perhaps happily suggests that here we must be permitted to refer to an order which no longer belongs to sensibility. But neither can it belong to intelligibility, to the ideality which is not fortuitously affiliated with the objectivity of *theōrein* or understanding. Here, therefore, we must let ourselves refer to an order that resists the opposition, one of the founding oppositions of philosophy, between the sensible and the intelligible. The order which resists this opposition, and resists it because it transports it, is announced in a movement of *différance* (with an *a*) between two differences or two letters, a *différance* which belongs neither to the voice nor to writing in the usual sense, and which is located, as the strange space that will keep us together here for an hour, *between* speech and writing, and beyond the tranquil familiarity which links us to one and the other, occasionally reassuring us in our illusion that they are two.

What am I to do in order to speak of the *a* of *différance?* It goes without saying that it cannot be *exposed*. One can expose only that which at a certain moment can become *present,* manifest, that which can be shown, presented as something present, a being-present in its truth, in the truth of a present or the presence of the present. Now if *différance* ̶i̶s̶ (and I also cross out the " ̶i̶s̶") what makes possible the presentation of the being-present, it is never presented as such. It is never offered to the present. Or to anyone. Reserving itself, not exposing itself, in regular fashion it exceeds the order of truth at a certain precise point, but without dissimulating itself as something, as a mysterious being, in the occult of a nonknowledge or in a hole with indeterminable borders (for example, in a topology of castration). In every exposition it would be exposed to disappearing as disappearance. It would risk appearing: disappearing.

So much so that the detours, locutions, and syntax in which I will often have to take recourse will resemble those of negative theology, occasionally even to the point of being indistinguishable from negative theology. Already we have had to delineate *that différance is not,* does not exist, is not a present-being (*on*) in any form; and we will be led to delineate also everything *that* it *is not,* that is, *everything;* and consequently that it has neither existence nor essence. It derives from no category of being, whether present or absent. And yet those aspects of *différance* which are thereby delineated are not theological, not even in the order of the most negative of negative theologies, which are always concerned with disengaging a superessentiality beyond the finite categories of essence and existence, that is, of presence, and always hastening to recall that God is refused the predicate of existence, only in order to acknowledge his superior, inconceivable, and ineffable mode of being. Such a development is not in question here, and this will be confirmed progressively. *Différance* is not only irreducible to any ontological or theological—ontotheological—reappropriation, but as the very opening of the space in which ontotheology—philosophy—produces its system and its history, it includes ontotheology, inscribing it and exceeding it without return.

For the same reason there is nowhere to *begin* to trace the sheaf or the graphics of *différance.* For what is put into question is precisely the quest for a rightful beginning, an absolute point of departure, a principal responsibility. The problematic of writing is opened by putting into question the value *arkhē.* What I will propose here will not be elaborated simply as a philosophical discourse, operating according to principles, postulates, axioms or definitions, and proceeding along the discursive lines of a linear order of reasons. In the delineation of *différance* everything is strategic and adventurous. Strategic because no transcendent truth present outside the field of writing can govern theologically the totality of the field. Adventurous because this strategy is not a simple strategy in the sense that strategy orients tactics according to a final goal, a *telos* or theme of domination, a mastery and ultimate reappropriation of the development of the field. Finally, a strategy without finality, what might be called blind tactics, or empirical wandering if the value of empiricism did not itself acquire its entire meaning in its opposition to philosophical responsibility. If there is a certain wandering in the tracing of *différance*, it no more follows the lines of philosophical-logical discourse than that of its symmetrical and integral inverse, empirical-logical discourse. The concept of *play* keeps itself beyond this opposition, announcing, on the eve of philosophy and beyond it, the unity of chance and necessity in calculations without end.

Also, by decision and as a rule of the game, if you will, turning these propositions back on themselves, we will be introduced to the thought of *différance* by the theme of strategy or the strategem. By means of this solely strategic justification, I wish to underline that the efficacy of the thematic of *différance* may very well, indeed must, one day be superseded, lending itself if not to its own replacement, at least to enmeshing itself in a chain that in truth it never will have governed. Whereby, once again, it is not theological.

I would say, first off, that *différance*, which is neither a word nor a concept, strategically seemed to me the most proper one to think, if not to master—thought, here, being that which is maintained in a certain necessary relationship with the structural limits of mastery—what is most irreducible about our "era." Therefore I am starting, strategically, from the place and the time in which "we" are, even though in the last analysis my opening is not justifiable, since it is only on the basis of *différance* and its "history" that we can allegedly know who and where "we" are, and what the limits of an "era" might be.

Even though *différance* is neither a word nor a concept, let us nevertheless attempt a simple and approximate semantic analysis that will take us to within sight of what is at stake.

We know that the verb *différer* (Latin verb *differre*) has two meanings which seem quite distinct; for example in Littré they are the object of two separate articles. In this sense the Latin *differre* is not simply a translation of the Greek *diapherein*, and this will not be without consequences for us, linking our discourse to a particular language, and to a language that passes as less philosophical, less originally philosophical than the other. For the distribution of meaning in the Greek *diapherein* does not comport one of the two motifs of the Latin *differre*, to wit, the action of putting off until later, of taking into account, of taking account of time and of the forces of an operation that implies an economical calculation, a detour, a delay, a relay, a reserve, a representation—concepts that I would summarize here in a word I have never used but that could be inscribed in this chain: *temporization. Différer* in this sense is to temporize, to take recourse, consciously or unconsciously, in the temporal and temporizing mediation of a detour that suspends the accomplishment or fulfillment of "desire" or "will," and equally effects this suspension in a mode that annuls or tempers its own effect. And we will see, later, how this temporization is also temporalization and spacing, the becoming-time of space and the becoming-space of time, the "originary constitution" of time and space, as metaphysics or transcendental phenomenology would say, to use the language that here is criticized and displaced.

The other sense of *différer* is the more common and identifiable one: to be not identical, to be other, discernible, etc. When dealing with *differen(ts)(ds)*, a word that can be written with a final *ts* or a final *ds*, as you will, whether it is a question of dissimilar otherness or of allergic and polemical otherness, an interval, a distance, *spacing*, must be produced between the elements other, and be produced with a certain perseverence in repetition.

Now the word *différence* (with an *e*) can never refer either to *différer* as temporization or to *différends* as *polemos*. Thus the word *différance* (with an *a*) is to compensate—economically—this loss of meaning, for *différance* can refer simultaneously to the entire configuration of its meanings. It is immediately and irreducibly polysemic, which will not be indifferent to the economy of my discourse here. In its polysemia this word, of course, like any meaning, must defer to the discourse in which it occurs, its interpretive context; but in a way it defers itself, or at least does so more readily than any other word, the *a* immediately deriving from the present participle (*différant*), thereby bringing us close to the very action of the verb *différer*, before it has even produced an effect constituted as something different or as *différence* (with an *e*). In a conceptuality adhering to classical strictures *"différance"* would be said to designate a constitutive, productive, and originary causality, the process of scission and division which would produce or constitute different things or differences. But, because it brings us close to the infinitive and active kernel of *différer*, *différance* (with an *a*) neutralizes what the infinitive denotes as simply active, just as *mouvance* in our language does not simply mean the fact of moving, of moving oneself or of being moved. No more is resonance the act of resonating. We must consider that in the usage of our language the ending *-ance* remains undecided *between* the active and the passive. And we will see why that which lets itself be designated *différance* is neither simply active nor simply passive, announcing or rather recalling something like the middle voice, saying an operation that is not an operation, an operation that cannot be conceived either as passion or as the action of a subject on an object, or on the basis of the categories of agent or patient, neither on the basis of nor moving toward any of these *terms*. For the middle voice, a certain nontransitivity, may be what philosophy, at its outset, distributed into an active and a passive voice, thereby constituting itself by means of this repression.

Différance as temporization, *différance* as spacing. How are they to be joined?

Let us start, since we are already there, from the problematic of the sign and of writing. The sign is usually said to be put in the place of the thing itself, the present thing, "thing" here standing equally for meaning or referent. The sign represents the present in its absence. It takes the place of the present. When we cannot grasp or show the thing, state the present, the being-present, when the present cannot be presented, we signify, we go through the detour of the sign. We take or give signs. We signal. The sign, in this sense, is deferred presence. Whether we are concerned with the verbal or the written sign, with the monetary sign, or with electoral delegation and political representation, the circulation of signs defers the moment in which we can encounter the thing itself, make it ours, consume or expend it, touch it, see it, intuit its presence. What I am describing here in order to define it is the classically determined structure of the sign in all the banality of its characteristics—signification as the *différance* of temporization. And this structure presupposes that the sign, which defers presence, is conceivable only on the *basis* of the presence that it defers and *moving toward* the deferred presence that it aims to reappropriate. According to this classical semiology, the substitution of the sign for the thing itself is both *secondary* and *provisional:* secondary due to an original and lost presence from which the sign thus derives; provisional as concerns this final and missing presence toward which the sign in this sense is a movement of mediation.

In attempting to put into question these traits of the provisional secondariness of the substitute, one would come to see something like an originary *différance;* but one could no longer call it originary or final in the extent to which the values of origin, archi-, *telos, eskhaton,* etc. have always denoted presence—*ousia, parousia.* To put into question the secondary and provisional characteristics of the sign, to oppose to them an "originary" *différance,* therefore would have two consequences.

1. One could no longer include *différance* in the concept of the sign, which always has meant the representation of a presence, and has been constituted in a system (thought or language) governed by and moving toward presence.

2. And thereby one puts into question the authority of presence, or of its simple symmetrical opposite, absence or lack. Thus one questions the limit which has always constrained us, which still constrains us—as inhabitants of a language and a system of thought—to formulate the meaning of Being in general as presence or absence, in the categories of

being or beingness (*ousia*). Already it appears that the type of question to which we are redirected is, let us say, of the Heideggerian type, and that *différance seems* to lead back to the ontico-ontological difference. I will be permitted to hold off on this reference. I will note only that between difference as temporization-temporalization, which can no longer be conceived within the horizon of the present, and what Heidegger says in *Being and Time* about temporalization as the transcendental horizon of the question of Being, which must be liberated from its traditional, metaphysical domination by the present and the now, there is a strict communication, even though not an exhaustive and irreducibly necessary one.

But first let us remain within the semiological problematic in order to see *différance* as temporization and *différance* as spacing conjoined. Most of the semiological or linguistic researches that dominate the field of thought today, whether due to their own results or to the regulatory model that they find themselves acknowledging everywhere, refer genealogically to Saussure (correctly or incorrectly) as their common inaugurator. Now Saussure first of all is the thinker who put the *arbitrary character of the sign* and the *differential character* of the sign at the very foundation of general semiology, particularly linguistics. And, as we know, these two motifs—arbitrary and differential—are inseparable in his view. There can be arbitrariness only because the system of signs is constituted solely by the differences in terms, and not by their plenitude. The elements of signification function due not to the compact force of their nuclei but rather to the network of oppositions that distinguishes them, and then relates them one to another. "Arbitrary and differential," says Saussure, "are two correlative characteristics."

Now this principle of difference, as the condition for signification, affects the *totality* of the sign, that is the sign as both signified and signifier. The signified is the concept, the ideal meaning; and the signifier is what Saussure calls the "image," the "psychical imprint" of a material, physical—for example, acoustical—phenomenon. We do not have to go into all the problems posed by these definitions here. Let us cite Saussure only at the point which interests us: "The conceptual side of value is made up solely of relations and differences with respect to the other terms of language, and the same can be said of its material side . . . Everything that has been said up to this point boils down to this: in language there are only differences. Even more important: a difference generally implies positive terms between which the difference is set up; but in language there are only differences *without positive terms*. Whether we take the signified or the signifier, language has neither ideas nor sounds that existed before the linguistic system, but only conceptual and phonic differences that have issued from the system. The idea or phonic substance that a sign contains is of less importance than the other signs that surround it."

The first consequence to be drawn from this is that the signified concept is never present in and of itself, in a sufficient presence that would refer only to itself. Essentially and lawfully, every concept is inscribed in a chain or in a system within which it refers to the other, to other concepts, by means of the systematic play of differences. Such a play, *différance*, is thus no longer simply a concept, but rather the possibility of conceptuality, of a conceptual process and system in general. For the same reason, *différance*, which is not a concept, is not simply a word, that is, what is generally represented as the calm, present, and self-referential unity of concept and phonic material. Later we will look into the word in general.

The difference of which Saussure speaks is itself, therefore, neither a concept nor a word among others. The same can be said, a fortiori, of *différance*. And we are thereby led to explicate the relation of one to the other.

In a language, in the *system* of language, there are only differences. Therefore a taxonomical operation can undertake the systematic, statistical, and classificatory inventory of a language. But, on the one hand, these differences *play*: in language, in speech too, and in the exchange between language and speech. On the other hand, these differences are themselves *effects*. They have not fallen from the sky fully formed, and are no more inscribed in a *topos noētos*, than they are prescribed in the gray matter of the brain. If the word "history" did not in and of itself convey the motif of a final repression of difference, one could say that only differences can be "historical" from the outset and in each of their aspects.

What is written as *différance*, then, will be the playing movement that "produces"—by means of something that is not simply an activity— these differences, these effects of difference. This does not mean that the *différance* that produces differences is somehow before them, in a simple and unmodified—in-different—present. *Différance* is the non-full, non-simple, structured and differentiating origin of differences. Thus, the name "origin" no longer suits it.

Since language, which Saussure says is a classification, has not fallen from the sky, its differences have been produced, are produced effects, but they are effects which do not find their cause in a subject or a substance, in a thing in general, a being that is somewhere present, thereby eluding the play of *différance*. If such a presence were implied in the concept of cause in general, in the most classical fashion, we then would have to speak of an effect without a cause, which very quickly would lead to speaking of no effect at all. I have attempted to indicate a

way out of the closure of this framework via the "trace," which is no more
an effect than it has a cause, but which in and of itself, outside its text, is
not sufficient to operate the necessary transgression.

Since there is no presence before and outside semiological difference,
what Saussure has written about language can be extended to the sign in
general: "Language is necessary in order for speech to be intelligible and
to produce all of its effects; but the latter is necessary in order for
language to be established; historically, the fact of speech always comes
first."

Retaining at least the framework, if not the content, of this requirement formulated by Saussure, we will designate as *différance* the movement according to which language, or any code, any system of referral in
general, is constituted "historically" as a weave of differences. "Is
constituted," "is produced," "is created," "movement," "historically,"
etc., necessarily being understood beyond the metaphysical language in
which they are retained, along with all their implications. We ought to
demonstrate why concepts like *production,* constitution, and history
remain in complicity with what is at issue here. But this would take me
too far today—toward the theory of the representation of the "circle" in
which we appear to be enclosed—and I utilize such concepts, like many
others, only for their strategic convenience and in order to undertake
their deconstruction at the currently most decisive point. In any event, it
will be understood, by means of the circle in which we appear to be
engaged, that as it is written here, *différance* is no more static than it is
genetic, no more structural than historical. Or is no less so; and to object
to this on the basis of the oldest of metaphysical oppositions (for
example, by setting some generative point of view against a structural-
taxonomical point of view, or vice versa) would be, above all, not to read
what here is missing from orthographical ethics. Such oppositions have
not the least pertinence to *différance,* which makes the thinking of it
uneasy and uncomfortable.

Now if we consider the chain in which *différance* lends itself to a
certain number of nonsynonymous substitutions, according to the
necessity of the context, why have recourse to the "reserve," to "archi-writing," to the "archi-trace," to spacing," that is, to the "supple-
ment," or to the *pharmakon,* and soon to the hymen, to the mar-
gin-mark-march, etc.

Let us go on. It is because of *différance* that the movement of signification is possible only if each so-called "present" element, each element
appearing on the scene of presence, is related to something other than
itself, thereby keeping within itself the mark of the past element, and
already letting itself be vitiated by the mark of its relation to the future
element, this trace being related no less to what is called the future than

to what is called the past, and constituting what is called the present by means of this very relation to what it is not: what it absolutely is not, not even a past or a future as a modified present. An interval must separate the present from what it is not in order for the present to be itself, but this interval that constitutes it as present must, by the same token, divide the present in and of itself, thereby also dividing, along with the present, everything that is thought on the basis of the present, that is, in our metaphysical language, every being, and singularly substance or the subject. In constituting itself, in dividing itself dynamically, this interval is what might be called *spacing,* the becoming-space of time or the becoming-time of space (*temporization*). And it is this constitution of the present, as an "originary" and irreducibly nonsimple (and therefore, *stricto sensu* nonoriginary) synthesis of marks, or traces of retentions and protentions (to reproduce analogically and provisionally a phenomenological and transcendental language that soon will reveal itself to be inadequate), that I propose to call archi-writing, archi-trace, or *différance.* Which (is) (simultaneously) spacing (and) temporization.

Could not this (active) movement of (the production of) *différance* without origin be called simply, and without neographism, *differentiation?* Such a word, among other confusions, would have left open the possibility of an organic, original, and homogeneous unity that eventually would come to be divided, to receive difference as an event. And above all, since it is formed from the verb "to differentiate," it would negate the economic signification of the detour, the temporizing delay, "deferral." Here, a remark in passing, which I owe to a recent reading of a text that Koyré (in 1934, in *Revue d'histoire et de philosophie réligieuse,* and reprinted in his *Etudes d'histoire de la pensée philosophique*) devoted to "Hegel in Jena." In this text Koyré gives long citations, in German, of the Jena *Logic,* and proposes their translation. On two occasions he encounters the expression *differente Beziehung* in Hegel's text. This word (*different*), with its Latin root, is rare in German and, I believe, in Hegel, who prefers *verschieden* or *ungleich,* calling difference *Unterschied* and qualitative variety *Verschiedenheit.* In the Jena *Logic* he uses the word *different* precisely where he treats of time and the present. Before getting to a valuable comment of Koyré's, let us look at some sentences from Hegel, such as Koyré translates them: "The infinite, in this simplicity, is, as a moment opposed to the equal-to-itself, the negative, and in its moments, although it is (itself) presented to and in itself the totality, (it is) what excludes in general, the point or limit; but in its own (action of) negating, it is related immediately to the other and negates itself by itself. The limit or moment of the present (*der Gegen-wart*), the absolute 'this' of time, or the now, is of an absolutely negative simplicity, which absolutely excludes from itself all multiplicity, and, by virtue of this, is absolutely determined; it is not whole or a *quantum* which would be extended in itself (and) which, in itself, also would have an undetermined moment, a diversity which, as indifferent (*gleichgultig*) or exterior in itself, would be related to an other (*auf ein anderes bezöge*), but in this is a relation absolutely different from the simple (*sondern es ist absolut differente Beziehung*)." And Koyré most remarkably specifies in a note: "different Relation: *differente Beziehung*. One might say: 'differentiating relation.' " And on the next page, another text of Hegel's in which one can read this: "*Diese Beziehung ist Gegenwart, als eine differente Beziehung* (This relationship is [the] present as a different relationship)." Another note of Koyré's: "The term *different* here is taken in an active sense."

Writing "*différant* or "*différance*" (with an *a*) would have had the advantage of making it possible to translate Hegel at that particular point—which is also an absolutely decisive point in his discourse—without further notes or specifications. And the translation would be, as it always must be, a transformation of one language by another. I contend, of course, that the word *différance* can also serve other purposes: first, because it marks not only the activity of "originary" difference, but also the temporizing detour of deferral; and above all because *différance* thus written, although maintaining relations of profound affinity with Hegelian discourse (such as it must be read), is also, up to a certain point, unable to break with that discourse (which has no kind of meaning or chance); but it can operate a kind of infinitesimal and radical displacement of it, whose space I attempt to delineate elsewhere but of which it would be difficult to speak briefly here.

Differences, thus, are "produced"—deferred—by *différance*. But *what* defers or *who* defers? In other words, *what is différance?* With this question we reach another level and another resource of our problematic.

What differs? Who differs? What is *différance?*

If we answered these questions before examining them as questions, before turning them back on themselves, and before suspecting their very form, including what seems most natural and necessary about them, we would immediately fall back into what we have just disengaged ourselves from. In effect, if we accepted the form of the question, in its meaning and its syntax ("what is?" "who is?" "who is it that?"), we would have to conclude that *différance* has been derived, has happened, is to be mastered and governed on the basis of the point of a present being, which itself could be some thing, a form, a state, a power in the world to which all kinds of names might be given, a *what*, or a present being as a *subject*, a *who*. And in this last case, notably, one would conclude implicitly that this present being, for example a being present to itself, as consciousness, eventually would come to defer or to differ: whether by delaying and turning away from the fulfillment of a "need" or a "desire," or by differing from itself. But in neither of these cases would such a present being be "constituted" by this *différance*.

Now if we refer, once again, to semiological difference, of what does Saussure, in particular, remind us? That "language [which only consists of differences] is not a function of the speaking subject." This implies that the subject (in its identity with itself, or eventually in its consciousness of its identity with itself, its self-consciousness) is inscribed in language, is a "function" of language, becomes a *speaking* subject only by making its speech conform—even in so-called "creation," or in so-called "transgression"—to the system of the rules of language as a system of differences, or at very least by conforming to the general law of *différance*, or by adhering to the principle of language which Saussure says is "spoken language minus speech." "Language is necessary for the spoken word to be intelligible and so that it can produce all of its effects."

If, by hypothesis, we maintain that the opposition of speech to language is absolutely rigorous, then *différance* would be not only the play of differences within language but also the relation of speech to language, the detour through which I must pass in order to speak, the silent promise I must make; and this is equally valid for semiology in general, governing all the relations of usage to schemata, of message to code, etc. (Elsewhere I have attempted to suggest that this *différance* in language, and in the relation of speech and language, forbids the essential dissociation of speech and language that Saussure, at another level of his discourse, traditionally wished to delineate. The practice of a language or of a code supposing a play of forms without a determined and invariable substance, and also supposing in the practice of this play a retention and protention of differences, a spacing and a temporization, a play of traces—all this must be a kind of writing before the letter, an archi-writing without a present origin, without archi-. Whence the regular erasure of the archi-, and the transformation of general semiology into grammatology, this latter executing a critical labor on everything within semiology, including the central concept of the sign, that maintained metaphysical presuppositions incompatible with the motif of *différance*.)

One might be tempted by an objection: certainly the subject becomes a *speaking* subject only in its commerce with the system of linguistic differences; or yet, the subject becomes a *signifying* (signifying in general, by means of speech or any other sign) subject only by inscribing itself in the system of differences. Certainly in this sense the speaking or signifying subject could not be present to itself, as speaking or signifying, without the play of linguistic or semiological *différance*. But can one not conceive of a presence, and of a presence to itself of the subject before speech or signs, a presence to itself of the subject in a silent and intuitive consciousness?

Such a question therefore supposes that, prior to the sign and outside it, excluding any trace and any *différance*, something like consciousness is possible. And that consciousness, before distributing its signs in space and in the world, can gather itself into its presence. But what is consciousness? What does "consciousness" mean? Most often, in the very form of meaning, in all its modifications, consciousness offers itself to thought only as self-presence, as the perception of self in presence. And what holds for consciousness holds here for so-called subjective existence in general. Just as the category of the subject cannot be, and never has been, thought without the reference to presence as *hupokeimenon* or as *ousia*, etc., so the subject as consciousness has never manifested itself except as self-presence. The privilege granted to consciousness therefore signifies the privilege granted to the present; and even if one describes the transcendental temporality of consciousness, and at the depth at which Husserl does so, one grants to the "living present" the power of synthesizing traces, and of incessantly reassembling them.

This privilege is the ether of metaphysics, the element of our thought that is caught in the language of metaphysics. One can delimit such a closure today only by soliciting the value of presence that Heidegger has shown to be the ontotheological determination of Being; and in thus soliciting the value of presence, by means of an interrogation whose status must be completely exceptional, we are also examining the absolute privilege of this form or epoch of presence in general that is consciousness as meaning" in self-presence.

Thus one comes to posit presence—and specifically consciousness, the being beside itself of consciousness—no longer as the absolutely central form of Being but as a "determination" and as an "effect." A determination or an effect within a system which is no longer that of presence but of *différance*, a system that no longer tolerates the opposition of activity and passivity, nor that of cause and effect, or of indetermination and determination, etc., such that in designating consciousness as an effect or a determination, one continues—for strategic reasons that can be more or less lucidly deliberated and systematically calculated—to operate according to the lexicon of that which one is de-limiting.

Before being so radically and purposely the gesture of Heidegger, this gesture was also made by Nietzsche and Freud, both of whom, as is well known, and sometimes in very similar fashion, put consciousness into question in its assured certainty of itself. Now is it not remarkable that they both did so on the basis of the motif of *différance*?

Différance appears almost by name in their texts, and in those places where everything is at stake. I cannot expand upon this here; I will only recall that for Nietzsche "the great principal activity is unconscious," and that consciousness is the effect of forces whose essence, byways, and modalities are not proper to it. Force itself is never present; it is only a play of differences and quantities. There would be no force in general without the difference between forces; and here the difference of quantity counts more than the content of the quantity, more than absolute size itself. "Quantity itself, therefore, is not separable from the difference of quantity. The difference of quantity is the essence of force, the relation of force to force. The dream of two equal forces, even if they are granted an opposition of meaning, is an approximate and crude dream, a statistical dream, plunged into by the living but dispelled by chemistry." Is not all of Nietzsche's thought a critique of philosophy as an active indifference to difference, as the system of adiaphoristic reduction or repression? Which according to the same logic, according to logic itself, does not exclude that philosophy lives *in* and *on différance,* thereby blinding itself to the *same,* which is not the identical. The same, precisely, is *différance* (with an *a*) as the displaced and equivocal passage of one different thing to another, from one term of an opposition to the other. Thus one could reconsider all the pairs of opposites on which philosophy is constructed and on which our discourse lives, not in order to see opposition erase itself but to see what indicates that each of the terms must appear as the *différance* of the other, as the other different and deferred in the economy of the same (the intelligible as differing-deferring the sensible, as the sensible different and deferred; the concept as different and deferred, differing-deferring intuition; culture as nature different and deferred, differing-deferring; all the others of *physis—tekhnē, nomos, thesis,* society, freedom, history, mind, etc.—as *physis* different and deferred, or as *physis* differing and deferring. *Physis* in *différance.* And in this we may see the site of a reinterpretation of *mimēsis* in its alleged opposition to *physis*). And on the basis of this unfolding of the same as *différance,* we see announced the sameness of *différance* and repetition in the eternal return. Themes in Nietzsche's work that are linked to the symptomatology that always diagnoses the detour or ruse of an agency disguised in its *différance;* or further, to the entire thematic of active interpretation, which substitutes incessant deciphering for the unveiling of truth as the presentation of the thing itself in its presence, etc. Figures without truth, or at least a system of figures not dominated by the value of truth, which then becomes only an included, inscribed, circumscribed function.

Thus, *différance* is the name we might give to the "active," moving discord of different forces, and of differences of forces, that Nietzsche sets up against the entire system of metaphysical grammar, wherever this system governs culture, philosophy, and science.

It is historically significant that this diaphoristics, which, as an energetics or economics of forces, commits itself to putting into question the primacy of presence as consciousness, is also the major motif of Freud's thought: another diaphoristics, which in its entirety is both a theory of the figure (or of the trace) and an energetics. The putting into question of the authority of consciousness is first and always differential.

The two apparently different values of *différance* are tied together in Freudian theory: to differ as discernibility, distinction, separation, diastem, *spacing;* and to defer as detour, relay, reserve, *temporization.*

1. The concepts of trace (*Spur*), of breaching (*Bahnung*), and of the forces of breaching, from the *Project* on, are inseparable from the concept of difference. The origin of memory, and of the psyche as (conscious or unconscious) memory in general, can be described only by taking into account the difference between breaches. Freud says so overtly. There is no breach without difference and no difference without trace.

2. All the differences in the production of unconscious traces and in the processes of inscription (*Niederschrift*) can also be interpreted as moments of *différance*, in the sense of putting into reserve. According to a schema that never ceased to guide Freud's thought, the movement of the trace is described as an effort of life to protect itself by *deferring* the dangerous investment, by constituting a reserve (*Vorrat*). And all the oppositions that furrow Freudian thought relate each of his concepts one to another as moments of a detour in the economy of *différance*. One is but the other different and deferred, one differing and deferring the other. One is the other in *différance*, one is the *différance* of the other. This is why every apparently rigorous and irreducible *opposition* (for example the opposition of the secondary to the primary) comes to be qualified, at one moment or another, as a "theoretical fiction." Again, it is thereby, for example (but such an example governs, and communicates with, everything), that the difference between the pleasure principle and the reality principle is only *différance* as detour. In *Beyond the Pleasure Principle* Freud writes: "Under the influence of the ego's instincts of self-preservation, the pleasure principle is replaced by the reality principle. This latter principle does not abandon the intention of ultimately obtaining pleasure, but it nevertheless demands and carries into effect the postponement of satisfaction, the abandonment of a number of possibilities of gaining satisfaction and the temporary toleration of unpleasure as a step on the long indirect road (*Aufschub*) to pleasure."

Here we are touching upon the point of greatest obscurity, on the very enigma of *différance*, on precisely that which divides its very concept by means of a strange cleavage. We must not hasten to decide. How are we to think *simultaneously*, on the one hand, *différance* as the economic detour which, in the element of the same, always aims at coming back to the

pleasure or the presence that have been deferred by (conscious or unconscious) calculation, and, on the other hand, *différance* as the relation to an
impossible presence, as expenditure without reserve, as the irreparable
loss of presence, the irreversible usage of energy, that is, as the death
instinct, and as the entirely other relationship that apparently interrupts
every economy? It is evident—and this is the evident itself—that the
economical and the noneconomical, the same and the entirely other,
etc., cannot be thought *together*. If *différance* is unthinkable in this way,
perhaps we should not hasten to make it evident, in the philosophical
element of evidentiality which would make short work of dissipating the
mirage and illogicalness of *différance* and would do so with the infallibil-
ity of calculations that we are well acquainted with, having precisely
recognized their place, necessity, and function in the structure of *differance*. Elsewhere, in a reading of Bataille, I have attempted to indicate
what might come of a rigorous and, in a new sense, "scientific" *relating* of
the "restricted economy" that takes no part in expenditure without
reserve, death, opening itself to nonmeaning, etc., to a general economy
that *takes into account* the nonreserve, that keeps in reserve the nonreserve,
if it can be put thus. I am speaking of a relationship between a *différance*
that can make a profit on its investment and a *différance* that misses its
profit, the *investiture* of a presence that is pure and without loss here being
confused with absolute loss, with death. Through such a relating of a
restricted and a general economy the very project of philosophy, under
the privileged heading of Hegelianism, is displaced and reinscribed. The
Aufhebung—la relève—is constrained into writing itself otherwise. Or
perhaps simply into writing itself. Or, better, into taking account of its
consumption of writing.

For the economic character of *différance* in no way implies that the
deferred presence can always be found again, that we have here only an
investment that provisionally and calculatedly delays the perception of
its profit or the profit of its perception. Contrary to the metaphysical,
dialectical, "Hegelian" interpretation of the economic movement of
différance, we must conceive of a play in which whoever loses wins, and in
which one loses and wins on every turn. If the displaced presentation
remains definitively and implacably postponed, it is not that a certain
present remains absent or hidden. Rather, *différance* maintains our
relationship with that which we necessarily misconstrue, and which
exceeds the alternative of presence and absence. A certain alterity—to
which Freud gives the metaphysical name of the unconscious—is definitively exempt from every process of presentation by means of which
we would call upon it to show itself in person. In this context, and
beneath this guise, the unconscious is not, as we know, a hidden,
virtual, or potential self-presence. It differs from, and defers, itself;

which doubtless means that it is woven of differences, and also that it sends out delegates, representatives, proxies; but without any chance that the giver of proxies might "exist," might be present, be "itself" somewhere, and with even less chance that it might become conscious. In this sense, contrary to the terms of an old debate full of the metaphysical investments that it has always assumed, the "unconscious" is no more a "thing" than it is any other thing, is no more a thing than it is a virtual or masked consciousness. This radical alterity as concerns every possible mode of presence is marked by the irreducibility of the aftereffect, the delay. In order to describe traces, in order to read the traces of "unconscious" traces (there are no "conscious" traces), the language of presence and absence, the metaphysical discourse of phenomenology, is inadequate. (Although the phenomenologist is not the only one to speak this language.)

The structure of delay (*Nachträglichkeit*) in effect forbids that one make of temporalization (temporization) a simple dialectical complication of the living present as an originary and unceasing synthesis—a synthesis constantly directed back on itself, gathered in on itself and gathering—of retentional traces and protentional openings. The alterity of the "unconscious" makes us concerned not with horizons of modified—past or future—presents, but with a "past" that has never been present, and which never will be, whose future to come will never be a *production* or a reproduction in the form of presence. Therefore the concept of trace is incompatible with the concept of retention, of the becoming-past of what has been present. One cannot think the trace—and therefore, *différance*—on the basis of the present, or of the presence of the present.

A past that has never been present: this formula is the one that Emmanuel Levinas uses, although certainly in a nonpsychoanalytic way, to qualify the trace and enigma of absolute alterity: the Other. Within these limits, and from this point of view at least, the thought of *différance* implies the entire critique of classical ontology undertaken by Levinas. And the concept of the trace, like that of *différance* thereby organizes, along the lines of these different traces and differences of traces, in Nietzsche's sense, in Freud's sense, in Levinas's sense—these "names of authors" here being only indices—the network which reassembles and traverses our "era" as the delimitation of the ontology of presence.

Which is to say the ontology of beings and beingness. It is the domination of beings that *différance* everywhere comes to solicit, in the sense that *sollicitare,* in old Latin, means to shake as a whole, to make tremble in entirety. Therefore, it is the determination of Being as presence or as beingness that is interrogated by the thought of *différance*. Such a question could not emerge and be understood unless the difference between Being and beings were somewhere to be broached. First consequence: *différance* is not. It is not a present being, however excellent, unique, principal, or transcendent. It governs nothing, reigns over nothing, and nowhere exercises any authority. It is not announced by any capital letter. Not only is there no kingdom of *différance*, but *différance* instigates the subversion of every kingdom. Which makes it obviously threatening and infallibly dreaded by everything within us that desires a kingdom, the past or future presence of a kingdom. And it is always in the name of a kingdom that one may reproach *différance* with wishing to reign, believing that one sees it aggrandize itself with a capital letter.

Can *différance,* for these reasons, settle down into the division of the ontico-ontological difference, such as it is thought, such as its "epoch" in particular is thought, "through," if it may still be expressed such, Heidegger's uncircumventable meditation?

There is no simple answer to such a question.

In a certain aspect of itself, *différance* is certainly but the historical and epochal *unfolding* of Being or of the ontological difference. The *a* of *différance* marks the *movement* of this unfolding.

And yet, are not the thought of the *meaning* or *truth* of Being, the determination of *différance* as the ontico-ontological difference, difference thought within the horizon of the question *of Being,* still intrametaphysical effects of *différance*? The unfolding of *différance* is perhaps not solely the truth of Being, or of the epochality of Being. Perhaps we must attempt to think this unheard-of thought, this silent tracing: that the history of Being, whose thought engages the Greco-Western *logos* such as it is produced via the ontological difference, is but an epoch of the *diapherein.* Henceforth one could no longer even call this an "epoch," the concept of epochality belonging to what is within history as the history of Being. Since Being has never had a "meaning," has never been thought or said as such, except by dissimulating itself in beings, then *différance*, in a certain and very strange way, (is) "older" than the ontological difference or than the truth of Being. When it has this age it can be called the play of the trace. The play of a trace which no longer belongs to the horizon of Being, but whose play transports and encloses the meaning of Being: the play of the trace, or the *différance*, which has no meaning and is not. Which does not belong. There is no maintaining, and no depth to, this bottomless chessboard on which Being is put into play.

Perhaps this is why the Heraclitean play of the *hen diapheron heautōi*, of the one differing from itself, the one in difference with itself, already is lost like a trace in the determination of the *diapherein* as ontological difference.

To think the ontological difference doubtless remains a difficult task, and any statement of it has remained almost inaudible. Further, to prepare, beyond our *logos,* for a *différance* so violent that it can be interpellated neither as the epochality of Being nor as ontological difference, is not in any way to dispense with the passage through the truth of Being, or to "criticize," "contest," or misconstrue its incessant necessity. On the contrary, we must stay within the difficulty of this passage, and repeat it in the rigorous reading of metaphysics, wherever metaphysics normalizes Western discourse, and not only in the texts of the "history of philosophy." As rigorously as possible we must permit to appear/disappear the trace of what exceeds the truth of Being. The trace (of that) which can never be presented, the trace which itself can never be presented: that is, appear and manifest itself, as such, in its phenomenon. The trace beyond that which profoundly links fundamental ontology and phenomenology. Always differing and deferring, the trace is never as it is in the presentation of itself. It erases itself in presenting itself, muffles itself in resonating, like the *a* writing itself, inscribing its pyramid in *différance.*

The annunciating and reserved trace of this movement can always be disclosed in metaphysical discourse, and especially in the contemporary discourse which states, through the attempts to which we just referred (Nietzsche, Freud, Levinas), the closure of ontology. And especially through the Heideggerean text.

This text prompts us to examine the essence of the present, the presence of the present.

What is the present? What is it to think the present in its presence?

Let us consider, for example, the 1946 text entitled *Der Spruch des Anaximander* ("The Anaximander Fragment"). In this text Heidegger recalls that the forgetting of Being forgets the difference between Being and beings: ". . . to be the Being *of* beings is the matter of Being (*die Sache des Seins*). The grammatical form of this enigmatic, ambiguous genitive indicates a genesis (*Genesis*), the emergence (*Herkunft*) of what is present from presencing (*des Anwesenden aus dem Anwesen*). Yet the essence (*Wesen*) of this emergence remains concealed (*verbogen*) along with the essence of these two words. Not only that, but even the very relation between presencing and what is present (*Anwesen und Anwesendem*) remains unthought. From early on it seems as though presencing and what is present were each something for itself. Presencing itself unnoticeably becomes something present . . . The essence of presencing (*Das Wesen des Anwesens*), and with it the distinction between presencing and what is present, remains forgotten. *The oblivion of Being is oblivion of the distinction between Being and beings.*"

In recalling the difference between Being and beings (the ontological

difference) as the difference between presence and the present, Heidegger advances a proposition, a body of propositions, that we are not going
to use as a subject for criticism. This would be foolishly precipitate;
rather, what we shall try to do is to return to this proposition its power to
provoke.

Let us proceed slowly. What Heidegger wants to mark is this: the
difference between Being and beings, the forgotten of metaphysics, has
disappeared without leaving a trace. The very trace of difference has been
submerged. If we maintain the *différance* (is) (itself) other than absence
and presence, if it *traces,* then when it is a matter of the forgetting of the
difference (between Being and beings), we would have to speak of a
disappearance of the trace of the trace. Which is indeed what the
following passage from "The Anaximander Fragment" seems to imply:
"Oblivion of Being belongs to the self-veiling essence of Being. It
belongs so essentially to the destiny of Being that the dawn of this
destiny rises as the unveiling of what is present in its presencing. This
means that the history of Being begins with the oblivion of Being, since
Being—together with its essence, its distinction from beings—keeps to
itself. The distinction collapses. It remains forgotten. Although the two
parties to the distinction, what is present and presencing (*das Anwesende
und das Anwesen*), reveal themselves, they do not do so as distinguished.
Rather, even the early trace (*die frühe Spur*) of the distinction is obliter-
ated when presencing appears as something present (*das Anwesen wie ein
Anwesendes erscheint*) and finds itself in the position of being the highest
being present (*in einem höchsten Anwesenden*)."

Since the trace is not a presence but the simulacrum of a presence that
dislocates itself, displaces itself, refers itself, it properly has no site—
erasure belongs to its structure. And not only the erasure which must
always be able to overtake it (without which it would not be a trace but
an indestructible and monumental substance), but also the erasure
which constitutes it from the outset as a trace, which situates it as the
change of site, and makes it disappear in its appearance, makes it emerge
from itself in its production. The erasure of the early trace (*die frühe Spur*)
of difference is therefore the "same" as its tracing in the text of metaphysics. This latter must have maintained the mark of what it has lost,
reserved, put aside. The paradox of such a structure, in the language of
metaphysics, is an inversion of metaphysical concepts, which produces
the following effect: the present becomes the sign of the sign, the trace of
the trace. It is no longer what every reference refers to in the last analysis.
It becomes a function in a structure of generalized reference. It is a trace,
and a trace of the erasure of the trace.

Thereby the text of metaphysics is *comprehended.* Still legible; and to be
read. It is not surrounded but rather traversed by its limit, marked in its

interior by the multiple furrow of its margin. Proposing *all at once* the monument and the mirage of the trace, the trace simultaneously traced and erased, simultaneously living and dead, and, as always, living in its simulation of life's preserved inscription. A pyramid. Not a stone fence to be jumped over but itself stonelike, on a wall, to be deciphered otherwise, a text without voice.

Thus one can think without contradiction, or at least without granting any pertinence to such a contradiction, what is perceptible and imperceptible in the trace. The "early trace" of difference is lost in an invisibility without return, and yet its very loss is sheltered, retained, seen, delayed. In a text. In the form of presence. In the form of the proper. Which itself is only an effect of writing.

Having stated the erasure of the early trace, Heidegger can therefore, in a contradiction without contradiction, consign, countersign, the sealing of the trace. A bit further on: "However, the distinction between Being and beings, as something forgotten, can invade our experience only if it has already unveiled itself with the presencing of what is present (*mit dem Anwesen des Anwesenden*); only if it has left a trace (*eine Spur geprägt hat*) which remains preserved (*gewahrt bleibt*) in the language to which Being comes."

Still further on, while meditating on Anaximander's *to khreon*, which he translates as *Brauch* (usage), Heidegger writes this: "Enjoining order and reck (*Fug und Ruch verfügend*), usage delivers to each present being (*Anwesende*) the while into which it is released. But accompanying this process is the constant danger that lingering will petrify into mere persistence (*in das blosse Beharren verhärtet*). Thus usage essentially remains at the same time the distribution (*Aushändigung:* dis-maintenance) of presencing (*des Anwesens*) into disorder (*in den Un-fug*). Usage conjoins the dis (*Der Brauch fügt das Un-*)."

And it is at the moment when Heidegger recognizes *usage* as *trace* that the question must be asked: can we, and to what extent, think this trace and the *dis* of *différance* as *Wesen des Seins*? Does not the *dis* of *différance* refer us beyond the history of Being, and also beyond our language, and everything that can be named in it? In the language of Being, does it not call for a necessarily violent transformation of this language by an entirely other language?

Let us make this question more specific. And to force the "trace" out of it (and has anyone thought that we have been tracking something down, something other than tracks themselves to be tracked down?), let us read this passage: "The translation of *to khreon* as 'usage' has not resulted from a preoccupation with etymologies and dictionary meanings. The choice of the word stems from a prior crossing *over (Über-setzen;* trans-lation) of a thinking which tries to think the distinction in the essence of Being (*im Wesen des Seins*) in the fateful beginning of Being's oblivion. The word 'usage' is dictated to thinking in the experience (*Erfahrung*) of Being's oblivion. What properly remains to be thought in the word 'usage' has presumably left a trace (*Spur*) in *to khreon*. This trace quickly vanishes (*alsbald verschwindet*) in the destiny of Being which unfolds in world history as Western metaphysics."

How to conceive what is outside a text? That which is more or less than a text's *own, proper* margin? For example, what is other than the text of Western metaphysics? It is certain that the trace which "quickly vanishes in the destiny of Being (and) which unfolds . . . as Western metaphysics" excapes every determination, every name it might receive in the metaphysical text. It is sheltered, and therefore dissimulated, in these names. It does not appear in them as the trace "itself." But this is because it could never appear itself, *as such*. Heidegger also says that difference cannot appear as such: "Lichtung des Unterschiedes kann deshalb auch nicht bedeuten, dass der Unterschied als der Unterschied erscheint." There is no essence of *différance;* it (is) that which not only could never be appropriated in the *as such* of its name or its appearing, but also that which threatens the authority of the *as such* in general, of the presence of the thing itself in its essence. That there is not a proper essence[1] of *différance* at this point, implies that there is neither a Being nor truth of the play of writing such as it engages *différance*.

---

1. *Différance* is not a "species" of the genus *ontological difference*. If the "gift of presence is the property of Appropriating *(Die Gabe von Anwesen ist Eigentum des Ereignens)"* [Martin Heidegger, "Time and Being," in *On Time and Being*, trans. Joan Stambaugh (New York: Harper and Row, 1972), p. 22.], *différance* is not a process of propriation in any sense whatever. It is neither position (appropriation) nor negation (expropriation), but rather other. Hence it seems—but here, rather, we are marking the necessity of a future itinerary—that *différance* would be no more a species of the genus *Ereignis* than Being. Heidegger: ". . . then Being belongs into Appropriating *(Dann gehort das Sein in das Ereignen).* Giving and its gift receive their determination from Appropriating. In that case, Being would be a species of Appropriation *(Ereignis)*, and not the other way around. To take refuge in such an inversion would be too cheap. Such thinking misses the matter at stake *(Sie denkt am Sachverhalt vorbei).* Appropriation *(Ereignis)* is not the encompassing general concept under which Being and time could be subsumed. Logical classifications mean nothing here. For as we think Being itself and follow what is its own *(seinem Eigenen folgen)*, Being proves to be destiny's gift of presence *(gewahrte Gabe des Geschickes von Anwesenheit)*, the gift granted by the giving *(Reichen)* of time. The gift of presence is the property of Appropriating *(Die Gabe von Anwesen ist Eigentum des Ereignens)."* (Heidegger, *On Time and Being*, pp. 21–22.

Without a displaced reinscription of this chain (Being, presence, -propriation, etc.) the relation between general or fundamental onto-logy and whatever ontology masters or makes subordinate under the rubric of a regional or particular science will never be transformed rigorously and irreversibly. Such regional sciences include not only political economy, psychoanalysis, semiolinguistics—in all of which, and perhaps more than

For us, *différance* remains a metaphysical name, and all the names that it receives in our language are still, as names, metaphysical. And this is particularly the case when these names state the determination of *différance* as the difference between presence and the present (*Anwesen/ Anwesend*), and above all, and is already the case when they state the determination of *différance* as the difference of Being and beings.

"Older" than Being itself, such a *différance* has no name in our language. But we "already know" that if it is unnameable, it is not provisionally so, not because our language has not yet found or received this *name*, or because we would have to seek it in another language, outside the finite system of our own. It is rather because there is no *name* for it at all, not even the name of essence or of Being, not even that of "*différance*," which is not a name, which is not a pure nominal unity, and unceasingly dislocates itself in a chain of differing and deferring substitutions.

"There is no name for it": a proposition to be read in its *platitude*. This unnameable is not an ineffable Being which no name could approach: God, for example. This unnameable is the play which makes possible nominal effects, the relatively unitary and atomic structures that are called names, the chains of substitutions of names in which, for example, the nominal effect *différance* is itself *enmeshed*, carried off, reinscribed, just as a false entry or a false exit is still part of the game, a function of the system.

What we know, or what we would know if it were simply a question here of something to know, is that there has never been, never will be, a unique word, a master-name. This is why the thought of the letter *a* in *différance* is not the primary prescription or the prophetic annunciation of an imminent and as yet unheard-of nomination. There is nothing kerygmatic about this "word," provided that one perceives its decapita-(liza)tion. And that one puts into question the name of the name.

There will be no unique name, even if it were the name of Being. And we must think this without *nostalgia*, that is, outside of the myth of a purely maternal or paternal language, a lost native country of thought. On the contrary, we must *affirm* this, in the sense in which Nietzsche puts affirmation into play, in a certain laughter and a certain step of the dance.

From the vantage of this laughter and this dance, from the vantage of

elsewhere, the value of the *proper* plays an irreducible role—but equally all spiritualist or materialist metaphysics. The analyses articulated in this volume aim at such a preliminary articulation. It goes without saying that such a reinscription will never be contained in theoretical or philosophical discourse, or generally in any discourse or writing, but only on the scene of what I have called elsewhere the text in general (1972).

this affirmation foreign to all dialectics, the other side of nostalgia, what I will call Heideggerian *hope,* comes into question. I am not unaware how shocking this word might seem here. Nevertheless I am venturing it, without excluding any of its implications, and I relate it to what still seems to me to be the metaphysical part of "The Anaximander Fragment": the quest for the proper word and the unique name. Speaking of the first word of Being (*das frühe Wort des Seins: to khreon*), Heidegger writes: "The relation to what is present that rules in the essence of presencing itself is a unique one (*ist eine einzige*), altogether incomparable to any other relation. It belongs to the uniqueness of Being itself (*Sie gehört zur Einzigkeit des Seins selbst*). Therefore, in order to name the essential nature of Being (*das wesende Seins*), language would have to find a single word, the unique word (*ein einziges, das einzige Wort*). From this we can gather how daring every thoughtful word (*denkende Wort*) addressed to Being is (*das dem Sein zugesprochen wird*). Nevertheless such daring is not impossible, since Being speaks always and everywhere throughout language."

Such is the question: the alliance of speech and Being in the unique word, in the finally proper name. And such is the question inscribed in the simulated affirmation of *différance.* It bears (on) each member of this sentence: "Being / speaks / always and everywhere / throughout / language."

Bibliography

GENERAL STUDIES

Altizer, Thomas J. J.; Myers, Max; Raschke, Carl; Scharlemann, Robert; Taylor, Mark; and Winquist, Charles. *Deconstruction and Theology*. New York: Crossroad, 1982.

Arac, Jonathan; Godzich, Wlad; and Wallace, Martin. *The Yale Critics: Deconstruction in America*. Minneapolis: University of Minnesota Press, 1983.

Bloom, Harold; de Man, Paul; Derrida, Jacques; Hartman, Geoffrey; and Miller, J. Hillis. *Deconstruction and Criticism*. New York: Seabury Press, 1979.

Booth, Wayne. *Critical Understanding: The Powers and Limits of Pluralism*. Chicago: University of Chicago Press, 1979.

Cohen, Ralph, ed. *New Directions in Literary History*. Baltimore: Johns Hopkins University Press, 1974.

Culler, Jonathan. *On Deconstruction: Theory and Criticism after Structuralism*. Ithaca: Cornell University Press, 1983.

DeMan, Paul. *Blindness and Insight*. New York: Oxford University Press, 1971.

Descombes, Vincent. *Modern French Philosophy*. Translated by L. Scott-Fox and J. M. Harding. Cambridge: Cambridge University Press, 1982.

Doubrovsky, Serge. *The New Criticism in France*. Translated by Derek Coltman. Chicago: University of Chicago Press, 1973.

Graff, Gerald. *Literature against Itself: Literary Ideas in Modern Society*. Chicago: University of Chicago Press, 1979.

Harari, Josué, ed. *Textual Strategies: Perspectives in Post-Structuralist Criticism*. Ithaca: Cornell University Press, 1979.

Hartman, Geoffrey. *Criticism in the Wilderness: The Study of Literature Today*. New Haven: Yale University Press, 1979.

———. *The Fate of Reading and Other Essays*. Chicago: University of Chicago Press, 1975.

Jameson, Fredric. *The Prison-House of Language: A Critical Account of Structuralism and Russian Formalism*. Princeton: Princeton University Press, 1972.

Krupnick, Mark, ed. *Displacement: Derrida and After*. Bloomington: Indiana University Press, 1983.

Lacoue-Labarthe, Philippe, and Nancy, Jean-Luc, eds. *Les Finis de l'homme: A partir du travail de Jacques Derrida*. Paris: Galilée, 1981.

Lentricchia, Frank. *After the New Criticism*. Chicago: University of Chicago Press, 1980.

Lyotard, Jean-François. *The Postmodern Condition: A Report on Knowledge*. Translated by G. Bennington and B. Massumi. Minneapolis: University of Minnesota Press, 1984.

Montefiore, Alan, ed. *Philosophy in France Today*. New York: Cambridge University Press, 1983.

Norris, Christopher. *Deconstruction: Theory and Practice*. New York: Methuen and Company, 1982.

———. *The Deconstructive Turn: Essays in the Rhetoric of Philosophy*. New York: Methuen and Company, 1983.

Said, Edward. *Beginnings: Intention and Method*. New York: Basic Books, 1975.

Simon, John K., ed. *Modern French Criticism: From Proust and Valéry to Structuralism*. Chicago: University of Chicago Press, 1972.

Spanos, William, ed. *The Question of Textuality: Strategies of Reading in Contemporary American Criticism*. Bloomington: Indiana University Press, 1982.

Taylor, Mark C. "Deconstruction: What's the Difference?" *Soundings* 66, no. 4 (1983): 387–403.

Young, Robert, ed. *Untying the Text: A Post-Structuralist Reader*. Boston: Routledge & Kegan Paul, 1981.

IMMANUEL KANT

Kant, Immanuel. *Anthropology from a Pragmatic Point of View*. Translated by M. J. Gregar. The Hague: Nijhoff, 1974.

———. *Critique of Practical Reason*. Translated by L. W. Beck. Chicago: University of Chicago Press, 1949.

———. *Critique of Pure Reason*. Translated by N. K. Smith. New York: St. Martin's Press, 1965.

———. *On History*. Translated by L. W. Beck, R. E. Anchar, and E. L. Fackenheim. New York: Bobbs-Merrill, 1963.

———. *Religion within the Limits of Reason Alone*. Translated by T. M. Greene and H. H. Hudson. New York: Harper Torchbooks, 1960.

Aquila, Richard. *Representational Mind: A Study of Kant's Theory of Knowledge*. Bloomington: Indiana University Press, 1983.

Cassirer, Ernst. *Rousseau, Kant, Goethe*. Translated by J. Gutmann, P. O. Kristeller, and J. H. Randall. Princeton: Princeton University Press, 1945.

Cohen, Ted, and Guyer, Paul. *Essays in Kant's Aesthetics*. Chicago: University of Chicago Press, 1982.

Crawford, Donald. *Kant's Aesthetic Theory*. Madison: University of Wisconsin Press, 1974.

Deleuze, Gilles. *Kant's Critical Philosophy: The Doctrine of the Faculties*. Translated by H. Tomlinson and B. Habberjam. Minneapolis: University of Minnesota Press, 1984.

Derrida, Jacques. "The Conflict of Faculties." In *Languages of Knowledge and of Inquiry*, edited by Michael Riffaterre. New York: Columbia University Press, 1982.

———. "Economimesis." *Diacritics* 11, no. 2 (1981): 3–25.

———. "Of an Apocalyptic Tone Recently Adopted in Philosophy." *Semeia* 23 (1982): 61–97.

———. *La Verité en peinture.* Paris: Flammarion, 1978.

Guyer, Paul. *Kant and the Claims of Taste.* Cambridge: Harvard University Press, 1979.

Hegel, G. W. F. *Faith and Knowledge.* Translated by W. Cerf and H. S. Harris. Albany: State University of New York Press, 1977.

Heidegger, Martin. *Kant and the Problem of Metaphysics.* Translated by J. S. Churchill. Bloomington: Indiana University Press, 1962.

———. *What Is a Thing?* Translated by W. Barton and V. Deutsch. Chicago: H. Regnery Co., 1968.

Kern, Iso. *Husserl und Kant: Eine Unterschung über Husserls Verhältnis zu Kant und Neukantianismus.* The Hague: Nijhoff, 1964.

Klein, Richard. "Kant's Sunshine." *Diacritics* 11, no. 2 (1981): 26–41.

Morrison, Ronald P. "Kant, Husserl, and Heidegger on Time and the Unity of 'Consciousness.'" *Philosophy and Phenomenological Research* 39, no. 2 (1978): 182–98.

Nancy, Jean-Luc. *Le Discours de la syncope.* Vol. I: *Logodaedalus.* Paris: Aubier-Flammarion, 1976.

———. *L'Impératif catégorique.* Paris: Flammarion, 1983.

Shapiro, Gary, and Sica, Alan. *Hermeneutics: Questions and Prospects.* Amherst: University of Massachusetts Press, 1984.

Sherover, Charles. *Heidegger, Kant, and Time.* Bloomington: Indiana University Press, 1971.

G. W. F. HEGEL

Hegel, G. W. F. *Aesthetics: Lectures on Fine Art.* Translated by T. M. Knox. 3 vols. New York: Oxford University Press, 1975.

———. *The Difference between Fichte's and Schelling's System of Philosophy.* Translated by H. S. Harris and W. Cerf. Albany: State University of New York Press, 1977.

———. *Lectures on the Philosophy of Religion.* Translated by E. B. Speirs and J. B. Sanderson. 3 vols. New York: Humanities Press, 1968.

———. *The Logic of Hegel.* Translated by W. Wallace. New York: Oxford University Press, 1968.

———. *Philosophy of History.* Translated by C. J. Friedrich. New York: Dover Publications, 1956.

———. *Philosophy of Mind.* Translated by W. Wallace. New York: Oxford University Press, 1971.

———. *Philosophy of Nature.* Translated by A. V. Miller. New York: Oxford University Press, 1970.

———. *Philosophy of Right.* Translated by T. M. Knox. New York: Oxford University Press, 1967.

———. *Science of Logic.* Translated by A. V. Miller. New York: Humanities Press, 1969.

Bahti, Timothy. "The Indifferent Reader: The Performance of Hegel's Introduction to the *Phenomenology.*" *Diacritics* 11, no. 2 (1981): 68–82.

DeMan, Paul. "Sign and Symbol in Hegel's Aesthetics." *Critical Inquiry* 8
(1981): 761–75.

Derrida, Jacques. "L'Age de Hegel." In *GREPH, Qui a peur de la philosophie?*,
73–107. Paris: Flammarion, 1977.

———. *Glas.* Paris: Galilée, 1979.

———. "Outwork, prefacing." In *Dissemination*, translated by B. Johnson,
1–59. Chicago: University of Chicago Press, 1981.

———. "The Pit and the Pyramid: Introduction to Hegel's Semiology." In
Margins of Philosophy, translated by A. Bass, 69–108. Chicago: University of
Chicago Press, 1982.

———. "White Mythology: Metaphor in the Text of Philosophy." In *Margins
of Philosophy*, translated by A. Bass, 207–271. Chicago: University of
Chicago Press, 1982.

Donougho, Martin. "The Semiotics of Hegel." *CLIO* 11, no. 4 (1982): 415–
30.

Gasché, Rodolphe. "'*Setzung*' and '*Übersetzung*': Notes on Paul DeMan." *Diacritics* 11, no. 4 (1981): 36–57.

Hamacher, Werner. "The Reader's Supper: A Piece of Hegel." *Diacritics* 11,
no. 2 (1981): 52–67.

Heidegger, Martin. *Hegel's Concept of Experience.* Translated by K. R. Dove.
New York: Harper and Row, 1970.

———. *Identity and Difference.* Translated by J. Stambaugh. New York:
Harper & Row, 1969.

Hyppolite, Jean. *Etudes sur Marx et Hegel.* Paris: Librairie Marcel Rivière, 1955.

———. *Genesis and Structure of Hegel's "Phenomenology of Spirit."* Translated by S.
Cherniak and J. Heckman. Evanston, Ill.: Northwestern University Press,
1974.

———. "Hegel's Phenomenology and Psychoanalysis." In *New Studies in
Hegel's Philosphy*, edited by W. E. Steinkraus, 55–70. New York: Holt,
Rinehart and Winston, 1971.

Lacoue-Labarthe, Philippe. "The Caesura of the Speculative." *Glyph* 4 (1978):
57–84.

Lacoue-Labarthe, Philippe, and Nancy, Jean-Luc. *L'Absolu littéraire: Theorie de
la littérature du romantisme allemande.* Paris: Editions du Seuil, 1978.

Lauer, Quentin. *A Reading of Hegel's Phenomenology of Spirit.* New York: Ford-
ham University Press, 1976.

Lyotard, Jean-François. "Analyzing Speculative Discourse as Language Game."
The Oxford Literary Review 4, no. 3 (1981): 59–67.

Marx, Werner, *Hegel's Phenomenology of Spirit.* Translated by P. Heath. New
York: Harper & Row, 1975.

Merleau-Ponty, Maurice. "Hegel's Existentialism." In *Sense and Non-Sense*,
translated by H. L. Dreyfus and P. A. Dreyfus, 63–70. Evanston, Ill.:
Northwestern University Press, 1964.

Nancy, Jean-Luc. *La Remarque speculative.* Paris: Galilée, 1973.

Queneau, Raymond. "Premières confrontations avec Hegel." *Critique* 195/96 (1963): 695–700.
Solomon, Robert. *In the Spirit of Hegel: A Study of G. W. F. Hegel's Phenomenology of Spirit.* New York: Oxford University Press, 1983.
Taylor, Mark C. *Journeys to Selfhood: Hegel and Kierkegaard.* Berkeley: University of California Press, 1980.
Warminski, Andrzej. "Pre-positional By-play." *Glyph* 3 (1978): 98–117.
———. "Reading for Example: Sense-Certainty in Hegel's Phenomenology of Spirit." *Diacritics* 11, no. 2 (1981): 83–94.

ALEXANDRE KOJÈVE

Brée, Germaine. *Twentieth-Century French Literature.* Translated by L. Guiney. Chicago: University of Chicago Press, 1983.
Darby, Tom. *The Feast: Meditations on Politics and Time.* Toronto: Toronto University Press, 1982.
Descombes, Vincent. *Modern French Philosophy.* Translated by L. Scott-Fox and J. M. Harding. Cambridge: Cambridge University Press, 1982.
Donato, Eugenio. "Historical Imagination and the Idioms of Criticism." *Boundary 2* 8, no. 1 (1979): 39–56.
Goldford, Dennis. "Kojève's Reading of Hegel." *International Philosophical Quarterly* 22 (1982): 275–94.
Harris, H. S. "From Hegel to Marx via Heidegger." *Philosophy of the Social Sciences* 13 (1983): 247–52.
Lacan, Jacques. *Ecrits.* Paris: Editions du Seuil, 1966.
Macherey, Pierre. "Queneau scribe et lecteur de Kojève." *Revue Littéraire Mensuelle* 650–51 (1983): 82–91.
Riley, Patrick. "Introduction to the Reading of Alexandre Kojève." *Political Theory* 9 (1981): 5–48.
Roth, Michael. "A Note on Kojève's Phenomenology of Right." *Political Theory* 11 (1983): 447–50.

EDMUND HUSSERL

Husserl, Edmund. *Cartesian Meditations.* Translated by D. Cairns. The Hague: M. Nijhoff, 1960.
———. *The Crisis of European Sciences and Transcendental Phenomenology: An Introduction to Phenomenological Philosophy.* Translated by D. Carr. Evanston, Ill. Northwestern University Press, 1970.
———. *Ideas.* Translated by W. R. Boyce-Gibson. New York: Macmillan Publishing Co., 1962.
———. *Paris Lectures.* Translated by P. Koestenbaum. The Hague: M. Nijhoff, 1964.
———. *The Phenomenology of Internal Time-Consciousness.* Edited by Martin Heidegger. Translated by J. S. Churchill. Bloomington: Indiana University Press, 1964.

Dauenhauer, Bernard. "On Speech and Temporality: Derrida and Husserl."
    Philosophy Today 18 (1974): 171–80.
Derrida, Jacques. *Edmund Husserl's Origin of Geometry*. Translated by John
    Leavey. Stonybrook, N.Y.: Nicholas Hays, 1978.
———. "Form and Meaning: A Note on the Phenomenology of Language."
    In *Margins of Philosophy*, translated by A. Bass, 155–173. Chicago: Univer-
    sity of Chicago Press, 1982.
———. "'Genesis and Structure' and Phenomenology." In *Writing and Differ-
    ence*, translated by A. Bass, 154–168. Chicago: University of Chicago Press,
    1978.
———. *Speech and Phenomena and Other Essays on Husserl's Theory of Signs*.
    Translated by D. B. Allison. Evanston, Ill.: Northwestern University Press,
    1973.
Farber, Marvin. *The Aims of Phenomenology: The Motives, Methods, and Impact of
    Husserl's Thought*. New York: Harper & Row, 1966.
Heidegger, Martin. *The Basic Problems of Phenomenology*. Translated by A.
    Hofstadter. Bloomington: Indiana University Press, 1982.
Kockelmans, Joseph J. *On Heidegger and Language*. Evanston, Ill.: Northwestern
    University Press, 1972.
Lauer, Quentin. *The Triumph of Subjectivity: An Introduction to Transcendental
    Phenomenology*. New York: Fordham University Press, 1958.
Lawall, Sarah N. *Critics of Consciousness: The Existentialist Structures of Literature*.
    Cambridge: Harvard University Press, 1968.
Levinas, Emmanuel. *En découvrant l'existence avec Husserl et Heidegger*. Paris: Vrin,
    1967.
———. "Sur les Ideen de E. Husserl." *Revue Philosophique de la France et de
    l'Etrange* 54 (1929): 230–65.
———. *The Theory of Intuition in Husserl's Phenomenology*. Translated by A.
    Orianne. Evanston, Ill.: Northwestern University Press, 1973.
Miller, J. Hillis. "Geneva or Paris? The Recent Work of Georges Poulet."
    University of Toronto Quarterly 39 (1970): 212–38.
Poulet, Georges. *The Interior Distance*. Translated by E. Coleman. Ann Arbor:
    University of Michigan Press, 1964.
———. "The Self and the Other in Critical Consciousness." *Diacritics* 2, no. 1
    (1972): 46–50.
———. *Studies in Human Time*. Translated by E. Coleman. Baltimore: Johns
    Hopkins University Press, 1956.
Ricoeur, Paul. *The Conflict of Interpretations: Essays in Hermeneutics*. Edited by D.
    Idhe. Evanston, Ill.: Northwestern University Press, 1974.
Sefler, George F. *Language and the World: A Methodological Synthesis within the
    Writings of Martin Heidegger and Ludwig Wittgenstein*. Atlantic Highlands, N.
    J.: Humanities Press, 1974.
Theunissen, Michael. *The Other: Studies in the Social Ontology of Husserl, Heidegger,
    Sartre, and Buber*. Translated by C. Macann. Cambridge, Mass.: MIT Press,
    1984.
Tran, duc-Thao. *Phénoménologie et matérialisme dialectique*. Paris: Editions Minh-
    Tan, 1951.

FERDINAND DE SAUSSURE

Aron, Thomas. "Une seconde révolution saussurienne?" *Langue française* 7 (1970): 56–62.

Barthes, Roland. *Elements of Semiology*. New York: Hill & Wang, 1968.

Benveniste, Emile. *Problems in General Linguistics*. Miami: University of Miami Press, 1971.

Cassirer, Ernst. "Structuralism in Modern Linguistics." *Word* 1, no. 1 (1945): 99–120.

Caws, Peter. "Structuralism." *Partisan Review* 35, no. 1 (1968): 75–91.

———. *Structuralism: The Art of the Intelligible*. Atlantic Highlands, N.J.: Humanities Press, 1985.

Chomsky, Noam. *Cartesian Linguistics*. New York: Harper & Row, 1966.

———. *Current Issues in Linguistic Theory*. The Hague: Mouton, 1964.

———. *Syntactic Structures*. The Hague: Mouton, 1957.

Culler, Jonathan. *Ferdinand de Saussure*. New York: Penguin Books, 1979.

———. *Structuralist Poetics: Structuralism, Linguistics, and the Study of Literature*. Ithaca: Cornell University Press, 1975.

Deguy, Michel. "La Folie de Saussure." *Critique* 260 (1969): 20–26.

Derrida, Jacques. "The Linguistic Circle of Geneva." In *Margins of Philosophy*, translated by A. Bass, 137–153. Chicago: University of Chicago Press, 1982.

———. *Of Grammatology*. Translated by G. C. Spivak. Baltimore: Johns Hopkins University Press, 1976.

Eco, Umberto. *A Theory of Semiotics*. Bloomington: Indiana University Press, 1976.

Foucault, Michel. *The Order of Things: An Archaeology of the Human Sciences*. Westminster, Md.: Pantheon, 1971.

Jakobson, Roman. *Essais de linguistique générale*. 2 vols. Paris. Editions de Minuit, 1973.

———. *Fundamentals of Language*. The Hague: Mouton, 1956.

Kristeva, Julia. "La Mutation sémiotique." *Annales* 25 (1970): 1497–1522.

———. *Semiotexte: Recherches pour une semanalyse*. Paris: Editions du Seuil, 1969.

Lévi-Strauss, Claude. *The Elementary Structures of Kinship*. Translated by J. H. Bell, J. R. von Sturmen, and R. Needham. Boston: Beacon Press, 1969.

———. *The Raw and the Cooked*. Translated by J. D. Weightman. New York: Harper & Row, 1969.

———. *The Savage Mind*. Chicago: University of Chicago Press, 1966.

———. *Structural Anthropology*. New York: Basic Books, 1963.

Macksey, Richard, and Donato, Eugenio, eds. *The Structuralist Controversy: The Languages of Criticism and the Sciences of Man*. Baltimore: Johns Hopkins University Press, 1970.

Mounin, Georges. *Saussure ou le structuraliste sans le savoir*. Paris: Seghers, 1968.

Pariente, Jacques, ed. *Essais sur le langage*. Paris: Editions de Minuit, 1969.

Propp, Vladimir. *Morphology of the Folktale*. Bloomington: Indiana Research Center in Anthropology, 1958.

Riffaterre, Michael. *Semiotics of Poetry.* Bloomington: Indiana University Press, 1978.

Ruegg, Maria. "Metaphor and Metonymy: The Logic of Structuralist Rhetoric." *Glyph* 6 (1979): 141–57.

Starobinski, Jean. *Words upon Words: The Anagrams of Ferdinand de Saussure.* Translated by O. Emmet. New Haven: Yale University Press, 1979.

Todorov, Tzvetan. *Introduction à la littérature fantastique.* Paris: Editions du Seuil, 1970.

———. *Littérature et signification.* Paris: Larousse, 1967.

Weber, Samuel. "Saussure and the Apparition of Language." *Modern Language Notes* 91 (1976): 913–38.

Søren Kierkegaard

Kierkegaard, Søren. *The Concept of Irony.* Translated by L. M. Capel. Bloomington: Indiana University Press, 1968.

———. *Concluding Unscientific Postscript.* Translated by D. F. Swenson and W. Lowrie. Princeton: Princeton University Press, 1968.

———. *Fear and Trembling.* Translated by Howard Hong and Edna Hong. Princeton: Princeton University Press, 1983.

———. *Philosophical Fragments.* Translated by D. F. Swenson. Princeton: Princeton University Press, 1967.

———. *Repetition.* Translated by W. Lowrie. New York: Harper & Row, 1964.

Agacinski, Sylviane. *Aparté: Conceptions et morts de Søren Kierkegaard.* Paris: Aubier-Flammarion, 1977.

Bigelow, Patrick. *Kierkegaard and the Problem of Writing.* Tallahassee: Florida State University Press, 1986.

Blanchot, Maurice. "From Dread to Language." In *The Gaze of Orpheus*, translated by L. Davis, 3–20. Barrytown, N.Y.: Station Hill Press, 1981.

Booth, Wayne C. *A Rhetoric of Irony.* Chicago: University of Chicago Press, 1974.

Bové, Paul. "The Penitentiary of Reflection: Søren Kierkegaard and Critical Activity." *Boundary 2* 8, no. 3 (1980).

Mackie, Louis. *Points of View: Readings of Søren Kierkegaard.* Tallahassee: Florida State University Press, 1986.

———. "A Ram in the Afternoon: Kierkegaard's Discourse of the Other." In *Kierkegaard's Truth: The Disclosure of the Self*, edited by J. H. Smith, 193–234. New Haven: Yale University Press, 1981.

Norris, Christopher. "Fictions of Authority: Narrative and Viewpoint in Kierkegaard's Writing." In *The Deconstructive Turn: Essays in the Rhetoric of Philosophy*, 85–106. New York: Methuen and Co., 1983.

Schleifer, Roland, and Markley, Robert, eds. *Kierkegaard and Literature: Irony, Repetition, and Criticism.* Norman: University of Oklahoma Press, 1984.

Smyth, John. *A Question of Eros: Irony in Kierkegaard, Sterne, and Barthes.* Tallahassee: Florida State University Press, 1986.

Sussman, Henry. *The Hegelian Aftermath: Readings in Hegel, Kierkegaard, Freud, Proust, and James*. Baltimore: Johns Hopkins University Press, 1982.

Taylor, Mark C. "Aesthetic Therapy: Hegel and Kierkegaard." In *Kierkegaard's Truth: The Disclosure of the Self*, edited by J. H. Smith, 44–80. New Haven: Yale University Press, 1981.

———. *Journeys to Selfhood: Hegel and Kierkegaard*. Berkeley: University of California Press, 1980.

———. *Kierkegaard's Pseudonymous Authorship: A Study of Time and the Self*. Princeton: Princeton University Press, 1975.

———. "Self in/as Other." *Kierkegaardiana* 13 (1984): 63–71.

Theunissen, Michael. "Kierkegaard's Negativisitic Method." In *Kierkegaard's Truth: The Disclosure of the Self*, edited by J. H. Smith, 380–423. New Haven: Yale University Press, 1981.

Thompson, Josiah. "The Master of Irony." In *A Collection of Critical Essays*, edited by J. Thompson, 103–163. New York: Doubleday and Co., 1972.

Thompson, Josiah, ed. *Kierkegaard: A Collection of Critical Essays*. New York: Doubleday and Co., 1972.

Ussher, Arland. *Journey through Dread: A Study of Kierkegaard, Heidegger and Sartre*. New York: Devin-Adair Co., 1955.

Wyschogrod, Michael. *Kierkegaard and Heidegger: The Ontology of Existence*. London: Routledge & Kegan Paul, 1984.

FRIEDRICH NIETZSCHE

Nietzsche, Friedrich. *Beyond Good and Evil*. Translated by W. Kaufmann. New York: Random House, 1966.

———. *The Birth of Tragedy and the Genealogy of Morals*. Translated by F. Golfting. New York: Doubleday and Co., 1956.

———. *The Gay Science*. Translated by W. Kaufmann. New York: Random House, 1974.

———. *Thus Spoke Zarathustra*. Translated by M. Cowan. Chicago: Henry Regnery Co., 1957.

———. *The Will To Power*. Translated by W. Kaufmann. New York: Random House, 1968.

———. *Nietzsche aujourd'hui?* Paris: Union Générale d'Editions, 1973. Contributions by: Gilles Deleuze, Jacques Derrida, Pierre Klossowski, Sarah Kofman, Philippe Lacoue-Labarthe, Jean-François Lyotard, Jean-Luc Nancy, and others.

Allison, David B., ed. *The New Nietzsche: Contemporary Styles of Interpretation*. New York: Delta, 1979. Contributions by Martin Heidegger, Gilles Deleuze, Pierre Klossowski, Maurice Blanchot, Jacques Derrida, Sarah Kofman, and others.

Blanchot, Maurice. "L'Exigence du retour." *L'Arc* 43 (1970): 48–53.

———. "Nietzsche et l'écriture fragmentaire." *La Nouvelle Revue Française* 168 (1966): 966–83; 169 (1967): 19–32.

Blondel, Eric. *Nietzsche: Le 5° Evangile?* Paris: Les Bergers et les Mages, 1980.

Corngold, Stanley. "Error in Paul deMan." In *The Yale Critics: Deconstruction in America*, edited by J. Arac; Wlad Godzich; and Wallace Martin. 90–108. Minneapolis: University of Minnesota Press, 1983.

Critique, 333 (1974). Devoted to Nietzsche.

Deleuze, Gilles. *Différence et répétition*. Paris: Presses Universitaires de France, 1968.

―――. *Nietzsche and Philosophy*. Translated by H. Tomlinson. New York: Columbia University Press, 1983.

Deleuze, Gilles, and Guattari, Felix. *Anti-Oedipus: Capitalism and Schizophrenia*. Translated by R. Hurley, M. Seem, and H. R. Lane. New York: Viking, 1977.

DeMan, Paul. "Action and Identity in Nietzsche." *Yale French Studies* 52 (1975): 16–30.

―――. *Allegories of Reading: Figural Language in Rousseau, Nietzsche, Rilke, and Proust*. New Haven: Yale University Press, 1979.

―――. "Genesis and Genealogy in Nietzsche's *The Birth of Tragedy*." *Diacritics* 2 (1972): 44–53.

―――. "Nietzsche's Theory of Rhetoric." *Symposium* 28 (1974): 49–50.

Derrida, Jacques. *The Ear of the Other: Otobiography, Transference, Translation*. Translated by Peggy Kamuf. New York: Schocken Books, 1985.

―――. *Spurs: Nietzsche's Styles*. Translated by B. Harlow. Chicago: University of Chicago Press, 1978.

Foucault, Michel. "Nietzsche, Genealogy, History." In *Language, Counter-Memory, Practice*, translated by D. F. Bouchard and S. Simon, 139–64. Ithaca: Cornell University Press, 1977.

Gasché, Rodolphe. "Autobiography as Gestalt in Nietzsche's *Ecce Homo*." *Boundary* 2, no. 9 (1981): 271–94.

Heidegger, Martin. *Nietzsche*. 4 vols. Translated by D. Krell and F. Capuzzi. New York: Harper & Row, 1979–85.

Jacobs, Carol. *The Dissimulating Harmony: The Image of Interpretation in Nietzsche, Rilke, Artaud, and Benjamin*. Baltimore: Johns Hopkins University Press, 1978.

Klossowski, Pierre. *Nietzsche et le cercle vicieux*. Paris: Mercure, 1969.

―――. *Un Si Funestre Désir*. Paris: Gallimard, 1963.

Kofman, Sarah. *Nietzsche et la métaphore*. Paris: Payot, 1972.

―――. *Nietzsche et la scène philosophique*. Paris: Union Générale d'Editions, 1979.

Lévesque, Claude. *L'Etrangeté du texte: Essai sur Nietzsche, Freud, Blanchot et Derrida*. Paris: Union Générale d'Editions, 1978.

Löwith, Karl. *From Hegel to Nietzsche: The Revolution in Nineteenth-Century Thought*. Translated by D. E. Green. New York: Doubleday and Co., 1972.

Miller, J. Hillis. "The Disarticulation of the Self in Nietzsche." *Monist* 64 (1981): 247–61.

―――. "Dismembering and Disremembering in Nietzsche's 'Truth and Lie in a Non-moral Sense.'" *Boundary 2* 9, no. 3 (1981): 41–54.

O'Hara, Daniel, ed. "Why Nietzsche Now?" *Boundary 2* 9, no. 3; X, no. 1 (1981).

Pautrat, Bernard. *Versions du soleil: Figures et système de Nietzsche.* Paris: Editions du Seuil, 1971.
Rey, Jean-Michel. *L'Enjeu des signes: Lecture de Nietzsche.* Paris: Seuil, 1965.
Schutte, Ofelia. *Beyond Nihilism: Nietzsche without Masks.* Chicago: University of Chicago Press, 1984.
Solomon, Robert C., ed. *Nietzsche: A Collection of Critical Essays.* Notre Dame, Ind.: University of Notre Dame Press, 1973.
White, Hayden. *Metahistory: The Historical Imagination in Nineteenth-Century Europe.* Baltimore: Johns Hopkins University Press, 1973.

LUDWIG WITTGENSTEIN

Wittgenstein, Ludwig. *Lectures and Conversations on Aesthetics, Psychology and Religious Belief.* Oxford: Blackwell, 1966.
————. *On Certainty.* Oxford: Blackwell, 1969.
————. *Tractatus Logico-Philosophicus.* Translated by D. F. Pears and B. F. McGuinnes. New York: Humanities Press, 1961.

Agacinski, Sylviane. "Découpages du *Tractatus.*" In *Mimesis: Des Articulations*, 19–53. Paris: Flammarion, 1975.
Allison, David B. "Derrida and Wittgenstein: Playing the Game." *Research in Phenomenology* 8 (1978): 93–109.
Altieri, Charles. *Act and Quality: A Theory of Literary Meaning and Humanistic Understanding.* Amherst: University of Massachusetts Press, 1981.
————. "Wittgenstein on Consciousness and Language: A Challenge to Derridean Literary Theory." *Modern Language Notes* 91, no. 6 (1976): 1409.
Austin, J. L. *How to Do Things with Words.* Cambridge: Harvard University Press, 1975.
Black, Max. *The Labyrinth of Language.* New York: Praeger, 1968.
————. *Models and Metaphors.* Ithaca: Cornell University Press, 1962.
Blanchot, Maurice. "Wittgenstein's Problem." In *The Gaze of Orpheus*, translated by L. Davis, 123–32. Barrytown, N.Y.: Station Hill Press, 1981.
Cavell, Stanley. *The Claim of Reason: Wittgenstein, Skepticism, Morality and Tragedy.* New York: Oxford University Press, 1979.
————. *Must We Mean What We Say?* New York: Charles Scribner's Sons, 1969.
————. *Themes Out of School: Effects and Causes.* San Francisco: North Point Press, 1984.
Culler, Jonathan. "Problems in the Theory of Fiction." *Diacritics* 14, no. 1 (1984): 2–11.
Derrida, Jacques. "Limited Inc abc . . ." *Glyph* 2 (1970): 167–251.
————. "Signature Event Context." In *Margins of Philosophy*, translated by A. Bass, 307–30. Chicago: University of Chicago Press, 1983.
Fish, Stanley. "How to do Things with Austin and Searle: Speech Act Theory and Literary Criticism." *Modern Language Notes* 91, no. 5 (1976): 983–1025.
Gier, Nicholas. *Wittgenstein and Phenomenology.* Dordrecht, Holland: D. Reidel, 1979.

Gil, Fernando. *La Logique du nom.* Paris: L'Herne, 1971.

Greene, Marjorie. "Life, Death, and Language: Some Thoughts on Wittgenstein and Derrida." In *Philosophy In and Out of Europe.* Berkeley: University of California Press, 1976.

Hester, Marcus. *The Meaning of Poetic Metaphor: An Analysis in Light of Wittgenstein's Claim That Meaning Is Use.* The Hague: Mouton, 1967.

Idhe, Don. *Sense and Significance.* Pittsburgh: Dusquesne University Press, 1973.

Naess, Arne. *Four Modern Philosophers: Carnap, Wittgenstein, Heidegger, Sartre.* Translated by A. Hannay. Chicago: University of Chicago Press, 1968.

Norris, Christopher. "The Insistence of the Letter: Textuality and Metaphor in Wittgenstein's Later Philosophy." In *The Deconstructive Turn: Essays in the Rhetoric of Philosophy,* 34–58. New York: Methuen and Co., 1983.

Pettit, Philip. "Wittgenstein and the Case for Structuralism." *Journal of the British Society for Phenomenology* 3, no. 1 (1972): 46–57.

Rorty, Richard. *Philosophy and the Mirror of Nature.* Princeton: Princeton University Press, 1980.

Searle, John. *Speech Acts: An Essay in the Philosophy of Language.* Cambridge: Cambridge University Press, 1969.

Sefler, George. *Language and the World: A Methodological Synthesis within the Writings of Martin Heidegger and Ludwig Wittgenstein.* New York: Humanities Press, 1974.

Staten, Henry, *Wittgenstein And Derrida.* Lincoln: University of Nebraska Press, 1984.

Turbayne, Colin. *The Myth of Metaphor.* New Haven: Yale University Press, 1962.

Willett-Shoptaw, Cynthia. "A Deconstruction of Wittgenstein." *Auslegung* 10 (1983): 75–81.

MARTIN HEIDEGGER

Heidegger, Martin. *Being and Time.* Translated by J. Macquarrie and E. Robinson. New York: Harper & Row, 1962.

———. *Discourse on Thinking.* Translated by J. M. Anderson and E. H. Freund. New York: Harper & Row, 1975.

———. *Early Greek Thinking.* Translated by D. F. Krell and F. A. Capuzzi. New York: Harper & Row, 1975.

———. *Kant and the Problem of Metaphysics.* Translated by James Churchill. Bloomington: Indiana University Press, 1962.

———. *Nietzsche.* 4 vols. Translated by D. Krell and F. Capuzzi. New York: Harper & Row, 1979–84.

———. *On Time and Being.* Translated by J. Stambaugh. New York: Harper & Row, 1972.

———. *The Question Concerning Technology and Other Essays.* Translated by W. Lovitt. New York: Harper & Row, 1977.

———. *What is Called Thinking?* Translated by J. G. Gray. New York: Harper & Row, 1968.

Bernasconi, Robert. *The Question of Language in Heidegger's History of Being.* Atlantic Highlands, N.J.: Humanities Press, 1985.

Bové, Paul. *Destructive Poetics: Heidegger and Modern American Poetry.* New York: Columbia University Press, 1980.

Corngold, Stanley. "*Sein und Zeit*: Implications for Poetics." *Boundary 2* 4, no. 2 (1976): 99–148.

Cumming, Robert. "The Odd Couple: Heidegger and Derrida." *Review of Metaphysics* 34 (1981): 487–522.

DeMan, Paul. "Heidegger Reconsidered." *New York Review of Books*, 2 April 1974, pp. 14–16.

———. "Heidegger's Exegesis of Hölderlin." In *Blindness and Insight: Essays in the Rhetoric of Contemporary Criticism*, 246–66. Minneapolis: University of Minnesota Press, 1983.

Derrida, Jacques. "The Ends of Man." In *Margins of Philosophy*, translated by A. Bass, 109–36. Chicago: University of Chicago Press, 1982.

———. "*Ousia* and *Grammē*: Note on a Note from *Being and Time*." In *Margins of Philosophy*, translated by A. Bass, 29–68. Chicago: University of Chicago Press, 1982.

———. "The Principle of Reason: The University in the Eyes of Its Pupils." *Diacritics* 13, no. 3 (1983): 3–20.

———. "Le Retrait de la métaphore." *Poésie* 7 (1978): 103–26.

Duroche, L. L. *Aspects of Criticism: Literary Study in Present-Day Germany.* The Hague: Mouton, 1967.

Fell, Joseph P. *Heidegger and Sartre: An Essay on Being and Place.* New York: Columbia University Press, 1979.

Ferguson, Frances C. "Reading Heidegger: Paul DeMan and Jacques Derrida." *Boundary 2* 4 (1976): 593–610.

Fynsk, Christopher. "The Self and Its Witness: On Heidegger's *Being and Time*." *Boundary 2* 10 (1982): 185–207.

Gadamer, Hans Georg. *Philosophical Hermeneutics.* Translated by D. Linge. Berkeley: University of California Press, 1976.

———. *Truth and Method.* Translated by G. Barden and J. Cumming. New York: Seabury Press, 1975.

Gillespie, Michael. *Hegel, Heidegger, and the Ground of History.* Chicago: University of Chicago Press, 1984.

Halliburton, David. *Poetic Thinking: An Approach to Heidegger.* Chicago: University of Chicago Press, 1981.

Howey, Richard. *Heidegger and Jaspers on Nietzsche: A Critical Examination of Heidegger's and Jaspers' Interpretations of Nietzsche.* The Hague: Nijhoff, 1973.

Kaelin, Eugene. *Art and Existence: A Phenomenological Aesthetics.* Lewisburg, Pa.: Bucknell University Press, 1971.

Krell, David. *On the Verge: Of Memory, Reminiscence, and Writing.* Atlantic Highlands, N.J.: Humanities Press, 1985.

Lacoue-Labarthe, Philippe. *Le Sujet de la philosophie: Typographies I* Paris: Flammarion 1979.

Levinas, Emmanuel. *En découvrant l'existence avec Husserl et Heidegger.* Paris: Vrin, 1977.

———. "Martin Heidegger et l'ontologie." *Revue Philosophique de la France et de l'Etranger* 57 (1932): 395–431.

Magliola, Robert, *Phenomenology and Literature: An Introduction.* West Lafayette, Ind.: Purdue University Press, 1977.

Marshall, Donald G. "The Ontology of the Literary Sign: Notes toward a Heideggerian Revision of Semiology." *Boundary 2* 4, no. 2 (1976): 271–94.

Marx, Werner. *Heidegger and the Tradition.* Translated by T. Kisiel and M. Greene. Evanston, Ill.: Northwestern University Press, 1971.

———. *Reason and World: Between Tradition and Another Beginning.* The Hague: Nijhoff, 1971.

Palmer, Richard. *Hermeneutics: Interpretation Theory in Schleiermacher, Dilthey, Heidegger, and Gadamer.* Evanston, Ill.: Northwestern University Press, 1969.

Pöggeler, Otto. *Martin Heidegger's Path of Thinking.* Translated by D. Magurshak and S. Barber. Atlantic Highlands, N.J.: Humanities Press, 1985.

Raschke, Carl. *The Alchemy of the Word: Language and the End of Theology.* Chico, Calif.: Scholars Press, 1979.

Ricoeur, Paul. *Interpretation Theory: Discourse and the Surplus of Meaning.* Fort Worth: Texas Christian University Press, 1976.

Riddel, Joseph N. "From Heidegger to Derrida to Chance: Doubling and (Poetic) Language." *Boundary 2,* no. 4 (1976): 571–92.

Spanos, William, ed. *Martin Heidegger and the Question of Literature.* Bloomington: Indiana University Press, 1976.

———. *Toward a Post-Modern Literary Hermeneutics.* Bloomington: Indiana University Press, 1980.

Steiner, George. *Martin Heidegger.* New York: Viking Press, 1979.

White, David. *Heidegger and the Language of Poetry.* Lincoln: University of Nebraska Press, 1970.

JEAN-PAUL SARTRE

Sartre, Jean-Paul. *Between Existentialism and Marxism.* Translated by J. Mathews. New York: Pantheon Books, 1975.

———. *Critique of Dialectical Reason.* Translated by A. Sheridan-Smith. London: NLB, 1976.

———. *Essays in Aesthetics.* Translated by W. Baskin. New York: Philosophical Library, 1963.

———. *Literary and Philosophical Essays.* Translated by Annette Michelson. New York: Collier Books, 1962.

———. *Saint Genet: Actor and Martyr.* New York: New American Library, 1963.

———. *What Is Literature?* Translated by W. Fowlie. Gloucester, Mass.: P. Smith, 1978.

L'Arc 30 (1966). Devoted to Sartre.

Aron, Raymond. *History and the Dialectic of Violence: An Analysis of Sartre's*

"Critique de la raison dialectique." Translated by Barry Cooper. Oxford: Blackwell, 1975.

Barnes, Hazel E. *Sartre and Flaubert.* Chicago: University of Chicago Press, 1981.

Bauer, George M. *Sartre and the Artist.* Chicago: University of Chicago Press, 1969.

Brée, Germaine. *Camus and Sartre: Crisis and Commitment.* New York: Delacorte Press, 1972.

Caws, Peter. *Sartre.* London: Routledge & Kegan Paul, 1979.

DeMan, Paul. "Sartre's Confessions." *New York Review of Books* 5 Nov. 1964, pp. 10–13.

Garner, Sebastian. "Splitting the Subject: An Overview of Sartre, Lacan and Derrida." *Auslegung* 10 (1983): 57–64.

Goldthorpe, Rhiannon. *Sartre, Literature, and Theory.* New York: Cambridge University Press, 1984.

Hollier, Denis. *Politique de la prose: Jean-Paul Sartre et l'an quarante.* Paris: Gallimard, 1982.

Howells, Christina. "Sartre and Derrida: Qui Perde Gagne." *Journal of the British Society of Phenomenology* 13 (1982): 26–34.

Kern, Edith. *Existentialist Thought and Fictional Technique: Kierkegaard, Sartre, Beckett.* New Haven: Yale University Press, 1970.

LaCapra, Dominick. *A Preface to Sartre.* Ithaca: Cornell University Press, 1978.

Mehlman, Jeffrey. *A Structural Study of Autobiography: Proust, Leiris, Sartre, Lévi-Strauss.* Ithaca: Cornell University Press, 1974.

Poster, Mark. *Existential Marxism in Postwar France: From Sartre to Althusser.* Princeton: Princeton University Press, 1975.

Sicard, Michel, ed. *Sartre et les arts.* Paris: Librairie Obliques, 1981.

Spanos, William. "The Un-Naming of the Beasts: The Postmodernity of Sartre's 'La Nausée.'" *Criticism* 20 (1978): 223–80.

Ungar, Steven R. "Sartre as Critic." *Diacritics* 1, no. 1 (1971): 32–36.

MAURICE MERLEAU-PONTY

Merleau-Ponty, Maurice. *Adventures of the Dialectic.* Translated by J. Bien. Evanston, Ill. Northwestern University Press, 1973.

———. *Consciousness and the Acquisition of Language.* Translated by H. Silverman. Evanston, Ill. Northwestern University Press, 1973.

———. *Humanism and Terror: An Essay on the Communist Problem.* Evanston, Ill. Northwestern University Press, 1969.

———. *Phenomenology of Perception.* Translated by C. Smith. London: Routledge and Kegan Paul, 1962.

———. *The Prose of the World.* Translated by J. O'Neill. Evanston, Ill.: Northwestern University Press, 1973.

———. *Sense and Non-Sense.* Translated by H. L. Dreyfus and P. A. Dreyfus. Evanston, Ill. Northwestern University Press, 1964.

———. *Signs.* Translated by R. C. McCleary. Evanston, Ill. Northwestern University Press, 1964.

———. *The Visible and the Invisible*. Translated by A. Lingis. Evanston, Ill.: Northwestern University Press, 1968.

L'Arc, 46. (1972). Devoted to Merleau-Ponty.
Aron, Raymond. *Marxism and the Existentialists*. New York: Harper & Row, 1969.
Blanchot, Maurice. "Le Discours philosophique." *L'Arc* 46 (1972): 1–4.
Clemens, Eric. "L'Histoire (comme) inachèvement." *Revue Métaphysique Morale* 76 (1971): 206–25.
Flynn, Bernard C. "Textuality and the Flesh: Derrida and Merleau-Ponty." *Journal of the British Society of Phenomenlogy* 15 (1984): 164–79.
Kaelin, Eugene F. *An Existentialist Aesthetic: The Theories of Sartre and Merleau-Ponty*. Madison: University of Wisconsin Press, 1962.
Kruks, Sonia. "Merleau-Ponty, Hegel and the Dialectic." *Journal of the British Society of Phenomenology* 7 (1976): 96–110.
Kwant, Remiguis. *From Phenomenology to Metaphysics: An Inquiry into the Last Period of Merleau-Ponty's Philosophical Life*. Pittsburgh: Dusquesne University Press, 1966.
Langan, Thomas. *Merleau-Ponty's Critique of Reason*. New Haven: Yale University Press, 1966.
Lévi-Strauss, Claude. "De quelques rencontres." *L'Arc* 46 (1972): 43–47.
Lyotard, Jean-François. *La Phénoménologie*. Paris: Presses Universitaires de France, 1969.
Pingaud, Bernard. "Merleau-Ponty, Sartre et la littérature." *L'Arc* 46 (1972): 80–87.
Schmidt, James. "Lordship and Bondage in Merleau-Ponty and Sartre." *Political theory* 7 (1979): 201–27.
Simeon, J. P. "Vérité et ideologie." *L'Arc* 46 (1972): 48–55.
Spiegelberg, Herbert. *The Phenomenological Movement: An Historical Introduction*. 2 vols. The Hague: Nijhoff, 1960.

EMMANUEL LEVINAS

Levinas, Emmanuel. *En découvrant l'existence avec Husserl et Heidegger*. Paris: Vrin, 1967.
———. *Existence and Existents*. Translated by A. Lingis. The Hague: Nijhoff, 1978.
———. "Il y a." *Deucalion* 1 (1946): 141–54.
———. *Noms propres*. Paris: Fata Morgana, 1976.
———. "La Pensée de l'être et la question de l'Autre." *Critique* 34 (1978): 187–97.
———. *Le Temps et l'Autre*. Montpellier: Fata Morgana, 1979.
———. *Totality and Infinity: An Essay on Exteriority*. Translated by A. Lingis. Pittsburgh: Dusquesne University Press, 1979.
Blanchot, Maurice. "Connaissance de l'inconnu." In *L'Entretien infini*. Paris: Gallimard, 1969.

————. "Tenir parole." In *L'Entretien infini*. Paris: Gallimard, 1969.

Bouckaert, Luk. "Ontology and Ethics: Reflections on Levinas' Critique of Heidegger." *International Philosophical Quarterly* 10 (1970): 402–19.

Derrida, Jacques. "En ce moment même dans cet ouvrage me voici." In *Textes pour Emmanuel Levinas*, edited by Francois Laruelle, 21–60. Paris: Editions Jean-Michel Place, 1980.

————. "Violence and Metaphysics: An Essay on the Thought of Emmanuel Levinas." In *Writing and Difference*, translated by A. Bass, 79–153. Chicago: University of Chicago Press, 1978.

Exercises de la patience. Volume 1. Paris: Obisdiane, 1981.

Gans, Stephen. "Ethics or Ontology: Levinas and Heidegger." *Philosophy Today* 16 (1971): 117–21.

Keyes, Charles D. "An Evaluation of Levinas' Critique of Heidegger." *Research in Phenomenology* 2 (1972): 121–42.

Laruelle, François, ed. *Textes pour Emmanuel Levinas*. Paris: Editions Jean-Michel Place, 1980
    Includes essays by: Maurice Blanchot, Jacques Derrida, Edmond Jabès, Jean-François Lyotard, Paul Ricoeur, and others.

Wolosky, Shira. "Derrida, Jabès, Levinas: Sign-Theory as Ethical Discourse." *Prooftexts* 2, no. 3 (1982): 283–302.

Wyschogrod, Edith. *Emmanuel Levinas: The Problem of Ethical Metaphysics*. The Hague: Nijhoff, 1974.

GEORGES BATAILLE

Bataille, Georges. *L'Abbé C*. Translated by P. A. Facey. New York: Marion Boyars, 1983.

————. "Ce Monde où nous mourons." *Critique* 123–24 (1957): 675–84.

————. *Death and Sensuality: A Study of Eroticism and the Taboo*. Edited by Robert Kastenbaum. New York: Arno, 1977.

————. *Eroticism*. Translated by Mary Dalwood. London: John Calder, 1962.

————. *L'Expérience intérieure*. Paris: Gallimard, 1954.

————. "Lautréamont et Sade par Maurice Blanchot." *Critique* 35 (1949): 291–306; 36 (1949): 401–11.

————. *Literature and Evil*. Translated by A. Hamilton. New York: Urizen, 1981.

————. *Oeuvres complètes*. Paris: Gallimard, 1970.

————. "Silence et littérature." *Critique* 57 (1952): 99–104.

————. *Story of the Eye*. Translated by Joachim Neugroschel. New York: Urizen Books, 1977.

————. *Sur Nietzsche*. Paris: Gallimard, 1945.

————. *Visions of Excess: Selected Writings, 1927–1939*. Translated by A. Stoekl. Minneapolis: University of Minnesota Press, 1985.

L'Arc 44 (1971). Devoted to Bataille.

Barthes, Roland. "La Métaphore de l'oeil." *Critique* 195–96 (1962): 770–77.

438   Bibliography

———. "Les sorties du texte." In *Bataille*, edited by P. Sollers, 63–73. Paris: Union Générale d'Editions, 1974.

Baudry, Jean-Louis. "Bataille et l'expérience intérieure." *Tel Quel* 55 (1973): 63–76.

Beaujour, Michel. "Eros and Nonsense: Georges Bataille." In *Modern French Criticism: From Proust and Valéry to Structuralism*, edited by J. K. Simon, 149–73. Chicago: University of Chicago Press, 1972.

Blanchot, Maurice. "L'Expérience-limite." *La Nouvelle Revue Française* 118 (1962): 577–92.

———. "Le Jeu de la pensée." *Critique* 195–96 (1963): 734–41.

———. "Pour Georges Bataille: l'amitié." *Les Lettres Nouvelles* 29 (1962): 7–12.

Caillois, Roger. *L'Homme et le sacré*. Paris: Gallimard, 1950.

Creech, James. "Julia Kristeva's Bataille: Reading as Triumph." *Diacritics* 5, no. 1 (1975): 62–68.

Derrida, Jacques. "From Restricted to General Economy: A Hegelianism Without Reserve." In *Writing and Difference*, translated by A. Bass, 251–77. Chicago: University of Chicago Press, 1978.

Foucault, Michel. "A Preface to Transgression." In *Language, Counter-Memory, Practice*, translated by D. F. Bouchard and S. Simon, 29–52. Ithaca: Cornell University Press, 1977.

Gallop, Jane. *Intersections: A Reading of Sade with Bataille, Blanchot, and Klossowski*. Lincoln: University of Nebraska Press, 1981.

Gasché, Rodolphe. "L'Almanach héterologique." *Nuovo Corrente* 66 (1975): 3–60.

———. "L'Avorton de la pensée." *L'Arc* 44 (1971): 11–26.

———. *System und Metaphorik in der Philosophie von Georges Bataille*. Frankfurt: Peter Lang, 1978.

Gueunier, Nicole. "*L'Impossible* de Georges Battaille." In *Essais de sémiotique poétique*, edited by A. J. Greimas, 107–24. Paris: Larousse, 1972.

Hawley, Daniel. *L'Oeuvre insolite de Georges Bataille*. Geneva: Slatkine, 1978.

Hollier, Denis. "De l'au-delà de Hegel à l'absence de Nietzsche." In Bataille, edited by P. Sollers, 97–105. Paris: Union Générale d'Editions, 1974.

———. "Le Dispositif Hegel/Nietzsche dans la bibliothèque de Bataille." *L'Arc* 38 (1968): 35–47.

———. "Le Matérialisme dualiste de Georges Bataille." *Tel Quel* (1967: 41–54.

———. *La Prise de la Concorde: Essais sur Georges Bataille*. Paris: Gallimard, 1974.

———. ed. *Le Collège de sociologie*. Paris: Gallimard, 1974.

Klossowski, Pierre. "A propos du simulacre dans la communication de Georges Bataille." *Critique* 195–96 (1963): 742–50.

———. *Sade mon prochain*. Paris: Seuil, 1947.

Kojève, Alexandre. "Preface à l'oeuvre de Georges Bataille." *L'Arc* 44 (1971): 36.

Kristeva, Julia. "Bataille: l'expérience et la pratique." In *Bataille*, edited by P. Sollers, 302–16. Paris: Union Générale d'Editions, 1974.

———. *Desire in Language*. New York: Columbia University Press, 1980.

———. *Polylogue*. Paris: Seuil, 1977.

———. *Revolution in Poetic Language*. Translated by M. Waller. New York: Columbia University Press, 1984.

Leiris, Michel. "Du temps de Lord Auch." *L'Arc* 32 (1967): 6–16.

Limousin, Christian. *Bataille*. Paris: Editions Universitaires, 1974.

Lingis, Alphonso. *Excesses: Eros and Culture*. Albany: State University of New York Press, 1983.

Mauss, Marcel. *The Gift: Forms and Functions of Exchange in Archaic Societies*. Translated by I. Cunnison. New York: Norton, 1967.

Mehlman, Jeffrey. "Ruse de Rivoli: Politics and Deconstruction." *Modern Language Notes* 91 (1976): 1061–72.

Merleau-Ponty, Maurice. "From Mauss to Lévi-Strauss." In *Signs*, translated by R. C. McCleary, Evanston, Ill.: Northwestern University Press, 1964, 114–25.

Richman, Michele. *Reading Georges Bataille: Beyond the Gift*. Baltimore: Johns Hopkins University Press, 1982.

Sartre, Jean-Paul. "Un Nouveau Mystique." In *Situations* 1 143–88. Paris: Gallimard, 1947.

Sasso, Robert. "Bataille-Hegel, ou l'enjeu philosophique." *Etudes philosophiques* 33 (1978): 465–79.

———. *Georges Bataille: Le Système du non-savoir: Une Ontologie du jeu*. Paris: Editions de Minuit, 1978.

Semiotext(e) 2, no. 2. Devoted to Bataille.

Sollers, Philippe. "De grandes irregularites du langage." *Critique* 195–96 (1962): 796–801.

———. *L'Ecriture et l'expérience des limites*. Paris: Editions de Seuil, 1971.

Sollers, Philippe, ed. *Bataille*. Paris: Union Générale d'Editions, 1973.

Sontag, Susan. "The Pornographic Imagination." In *Styles of Radical Will*, 35–73. New York: Dell, 1966.

Stoekl, Allan. "The Death of *Acephale* and the Will to Chance: Nietzsche in the Text of Bataille." *Glyph* 6 (1979): 42–67.

Sub-stance 5–6 (1973). Devoted to Bataille.

Titmuss, Richard M. *The Gift Relationship*. New York: Vintage, 1972.

MAURICE BLANCHOT

Blanchot, Maurice. *L'Attente l'oubli*. Paris: Gallimard, 1962.

———. "Connaissance de l'inconnu." *La Nouvelle Revue Française* 108 (1961): 1081–95.

———. *Death Sentence*. Translated by L. Davis. Barrytown, N.Y.: Station Hill Press, 1978.

———. *L'Ecriture du désastre*. Paris: Gallimard, 1980.

———. *L'Entretien infini*. Paris: Gallimard, 1969.

————. *The Gaze of Orpheus and Other Literary Essays*. Translated by L. Davis. Barrytown, N.Y.: Station Hill Press, 1981.

————. "L'Indéstructible." *La Nouvelle Revue Française* 112 (1962): 671–80.

————. *Lautréamont et Sade*. Paris: Les Editions de Minuit, 1963.

————. *Le Livre à venir*. Paris: Gallimard, 1959.

————. *The Madness of the Day*. Translated by L. Davis. Barrytown, N.Y.: Station Hill Press, 1981.

————. *Le Pas au-delà*. Paris: Gallimard, 1973.

————. *The Space of Literature*. Translated by A. Smock. Lincoln: University of Nebraska Press, 1982.

————. *Thomas the Obscure*. Translated by Robert Lamberton. New York: David Lewis, 1973.

Balladur, Jean. "Le Dedans et le dehors." *Les Temps Modernes* 49 (1949): 896–912.

Bataille, Georges. "*Lautréamont et Sade* par Maurice Blanchot." *Critique* 35 (1949): 291–306; 36 (1949): 401–11.

————. "Maurice Blanchot." *Gramma* 3–4 (1976): 217–22.

————. "Silence et littérature." *Critique* 57 (1952): 99–104.

Blegen, John. "Writing the Question: About Maurice Blanchot." *Diacritics* 2, no. 2 (1972); 13–17.

Bonnefoy, Claude. "A la limite de l'écriture." *Les Nouvelles Littéraires* 2409 (1973): 7.

Collin, Françoise. "Ecriture et matérialité." *Critique* 179–80 (1970): 747–58.

————. *Maurice Blanchot et la question de l'écriture*. Paris: Gallimard, 1971.

Critique 229 (1966). Devoted to Blanchot.

Cronel, Herve. "Maurice Blanchot: l'impossible silence." *La Nouvelle Revue Française* 244 (1973): 103–7.

Culler, Jonathan. "Maurice Blanchot et la question de l'écriture." *French Studies* 27 (1973): 231–32.

Dalmas, André. "E. Levinas parle de Blanchot." *La Quinzaine Littéraire* 115 (1971): 14–15.

De Dieguez, Manual. *L'Ecrivain et son langage*. Paris: Gallimard, 1960.

DeMan, Paul. "Impersonality in the Criticism of Maurice Blanchot." In *Blindness and Insight: Essays in the Rhetoric of Contemporary Criticism*, 60–78. Minneapolis: University of Minnesota Press, 1983.

Derrida, Jacques. "La Loi du genre." *Glyph* 7 (1980): 176–201.

————. "Pas." *Gramma* 3–4 (1976): 111–215.

Douglas, Kenneth. "Blanchot and Sartre." *Yale French Studies* 3 (1949): 85–89.

Exercises de la patience. Volume 2. Paris: Obisdiance, 1981.

Foucault, Michel. "La Pensée du dehors." *Critique* 229 (1966): 523–46.

Gallop, Jane. *Intersections: A Reading of Sade with Bataille, Blanchot, and Klossowski*. Lincoln: University of Nebraska Press, 1981.

Garth, Gillian. "About Blanchot: An Interview [with Georges Bataille]." *Sub-stance* 14 (1976): 54–57.

Gasché, Rodolphe. "L'Almanach héterologique." *Nuova Corrente* 66 (1975): 3–60.

Gramma 3–5 (1976). Devoted to Blanchot.

Hartman, Geoffrey H. "The Fullness and Nothingness of Literature." *Yale French Studies* 16 (1955–56): 63–78.

Jabès, Edmond. "L'Inconditionnel." *Le Nouveau Commerce* 27–28 (1974): 41–63.

Klossowski, Pierre. "Sur Maurice Blanchot." *Les Temps Modernes* 4, no. 40 (1949): 298–314.

Laporte, Roger. "Le oui, le non, le neutre." *Critique* 229 (1966): 579–90.

Laporte, Roger, and Noel, Bernard. *Deux Lectures de Maurice Blanchot.* Montpellier: Fata Morgana, 1973.

Lawall, Sarah N. "The Negative Consciousness." In *Critics of Consciousness: The Existential Structures of Literature*, 221–65. Cambridge: Harvard University Press, 1968.

Lecomte, Marcel. "Robbe-Grillet, Blanchot and Henry Miller." *Synthèses* 132 (1957): 430–36.

Lévesque, Claude. *L'Etrangeté du texte: Essai sur Nietzsche, Freud, Blanchot, et Derrida.* Paris: Union Générale d'Editions, 1978.

Levinas, Emmanuel. "Maurice Blanchot et le regard du poète." *Monde Nouveau* 98 (1956): 6–19.

———. "Sans identité." In *Humanisme de l'autre homme*, 83–102 Montpellier: Fata Morgana, 1972.

———. "La Servante et son maître." *Critique* 229 (1966): 514–22.

———. *Sur Maurice Blanchot.* Montpellier: Fata Morgana, 1975.

Libertson, Joseph. *Proximity: Blanchot, Bataille, Levinas.* The Hague: Nijhoff, 1982.

Marshall, Donald. "History, Theory, and Influence: Yale Critics as Readers of Maurice Blanchot." In *The Yale Critics: Deconstruction in America*, edited by J. Arac, Wlad Godzich, and Wallace Martin. pp. 135–155. Minneapolis: University of Minnesota Press, 1983.

Mauriac, Claude. "Pascal avant Hegel, Blanchot après Bataille." *Le Figaro Littéraire* 1328 (1971): 15.

Mehlman, Jeffrey. "Orphée scripteur: Blanchot, Rilke, Derrida." *Poétique* 20 (1974): 458–82.

Meschonnic, Henri. "Blanchot ou l'écriture hors langage." *Les Cahiers du Chemin* 20 (1974): 79–116.

Nancy, Jean-Luc. *Le Partage des voix.* Paris: Galilée, 1982.

Oxenhandler, Neal. "Paradox and Negation in the Criticism of Maurice Blanchot." *Symposium* 16, no. 1 (1962): 36–44.

Poulet, Georges. "Maurice Blanchot as a Novelist." *Yale French Studies* 8 (1951): 77–81.

Roudiez, Leon S. "Maurice Blanchot." In *French Fiction Today: A New Direction*, 58–80. New Brunswick: Rutgers University Press, 1972.

Sartre, Jean-Paul. "*Aminadab* or the Fantastic Considered as a Language." In *Literary Essays*, 56–72. New York: Wisdom Library, 1957.

Starobinski, Jean. *"Thomas l'obscur*, chapitre premier." *Critique* 229 (1966):
498–513.
Steiner, George. *Language and Silence: Essays on Language, Literature, and the
Inhuman.* New York: Atheneum, 1967.
Strauss, Walter A. *Descent and Return: The Orphic Theme in Modern Literature.*
Cambridge: Harvard University Press, 1971.
Sub-stance 14 (1976). Devoted to Blanchot.
Ungar, Steven. "Waiting for Blanchot." *Diacritics* 5, no. 2 (1975): 32–36.
Wilhem, Daniel. *Maurice Blanchot: La voix narrative.* Paris; Union Générale
d'Editions, 1974.

JACQUES DERRIDA

Derrida, Jacques. "Limited Inc abc . . ." *Glyph* 2 (1977): 167–251.
———. "No Apocalypse, Not Now (full speed ahead, seven missiles, seven
missives)." *Diacritics* 14, no. 2 (1984): 20–31.
———. *Of Grammatology.* Translated by Gayatri Chakravorty Spivak. Balti-
more: Johns Hopkins University Press, 1976.
———. "The Retrait of Metaphor." *Enclitic* 2, no. 2 (1978): 5–34.
———. "Sending: On Representation." *Social Research* 49 (1982): 294–326.
———. *Writing and Difference.* Translated by A. Bass. Chicago: University of
Chicago Press, 1978.

Abrams, M. H. "The Deconstructive Angel." *Critical Inquiry* 3 (1977): 425–
38.
———. "How to Do Things with Texts." *Partisan Review* 46 (1979): 566–88.
Agacinski, Sylviane. "La Philosophie à l'affiche." *Revue des Sciences Humaines* 1,
no. 185 (1982): 13–24.
Agacinski, Sylviane; Jacques Derrida; Sarah Kofman; Ph. Lacoue-Labarthe;
Jean-Luc Nancy; and Bernald Pautrat. *Mimesis: Des Articulations.* Paris:
Flammarion, 1975.
Allison, David B. "Destruction/Deconstruction in the Text of Nietzsche."
Boundary 8, no. 1 (1979): 197–222.
Arac, Jonathan; Wlad Godzichi; and Wallace Martin. *The Yale Critics: Decon-
struction in America.* Minneapolis: University of Minnesota Press, 1983.
Bandera, Cesareo. "Notes on Derrida, Tombstones, and the Representational
Game." *Stanford French Review* 6, nos. 2–3 (1982): 311–25.
Barthes, Roland. "To Write: An Intransitive Verb." In *The Languages of
Criticism and the Sciences of Man*, edited by R. Macksey and E. Donato,
134–45. Baltimore: Johns Hopkins Press, 1970.
Benoist, Jean-Marie. *Tyrannie du logos.* Paris: Minuit, 1975.
Bloom, Harold. *The Anxiety of Influence: A Theory of Poetry.* New York: Oxford
University Press, 1973.
Boyne, Roy. "Alcibiades as Hero: Derrida/Nietzsche?" *Sub-stance* 28 (1980):
25–36.
Carroll, David. "The Alterity of Discourse: Form, History, and the Question of
the Political in M. M. Bakhtin." *Diacritics* 13, no. 2 (1983): 65–83.

Caws, Mary Ann. "Tel Quel: Text and Revolution." *Diacritics* 3, no. 1 (1973): 2–8.

Culler, Jonathan. "Convention and Meaning: Derrida and Austin." *New Literary History* 8, no. 1 (1981): 15–30.

———. *On Deconstruction: Theory and Criticism after Structuralism.* Ithaca: Cornell University Press, 1982.

———. *The Pursuit of Signs: Semiotics, Literature, Deconstruction.* Ithaca: Cornell University Press, 1981.

———. "Structuralism and Grammatology." *Boundary* 8, no. 1 (1979): 75–85.

DeMan, Paul. "Autobiography as De-facement." *Modern Language Notes* 94 (1979): 919–30.

———. "The Epistemology of Metaphor." *Critical Inquiry* 5 (1978): 13–30.

———. "The Rhetoric of Temporality." In *Interpretation: Theory and Practice,* edited by Charles Singleton, 173–209. Baltimore: Johns Hopkins University Press, 1969.

———. "Semiology and Rhetoric." *Diacritics* 3, no. 3 (1973): 27–33.

Donato, Eugenio. "'Here, Now'/'Always, Already': Incidental Remarks on some Recent Characterizations of the Text," *Diacritics* 6, no. 3 (1976): 24–29.

———. "The Idioms of the *Text*: Notes on the Language of Philosophy and the Fictions of Literature." *Glyph* 2 (1977): 1–13.

Eagleton, Terry. "Marxism and Deconstruction." *Contemporary Literature* 22, no. 4 (1981): 477–88.

Felman, Shoshana. "Madness and Philosophy or Literature's Reason." *Yale French Studies* 52 (1975): 206–28.

———. "Turning the Screw of Interpretation." *Yale French Studies* 55–56 (1977): 94–207.

Fish, Stanley E. "With the Compliments of the Author: Reflections on Derrida." *Critical Inquiry* 8, no. 4 (1982): 693–721.

Flores, Ralph. *The Rhetoric of Doubtful Authority: Deconstructive Readings of Self-Questioning Narratives: St. Augustine to Faulkner.* Ithaca: Cornell University Press, 1984.

Frank, Manfred. "The Infinite Text." *Glyph* 7 (1980): 70–101.

Fynsk, Christopher I. "A Decelebration of Philosophy." *Diacritics* 8, no. 2 (1978): 80.

Gasché, Rodolphe. "Deconstruction as Criticism." *Glyph* 6 (1979): 177–215.

———. "Joining the Text: From Heidegger to Derrida." In *The Yale Critics: Deconstruction in America,* edited by J. Arac, Wlad Godzich, and Wallace Martin. 156–175. Minneapolis: University of Minnesota Press, 1983.

———. "'Setzung' and 'Übersetzung': Notes on Paul de Man." *Diacritics* 11 (1981): 36–57.

Graff, Gerald. "Textual Leftism." *Partisan Review* 49, no 1 (1982): 558–75.

Grisoni, Dominique, ed. *Politiques de la philosophie.* Paris: Grasset, 1976.

Hartman, Geoffrey. *Saving the Text: Literature/Derrida/Philosophy.* Baltimore: Johns Hopkins University Press, 1978.

444   Bibliography

Henning, E. M. "Foucault and Derrida: Archaeology and Deconstruction."
   Stanford French Review 5, no. 2 (1981): 247–64.
Hoy, David. "Forgetting the Text: Derrida's Critique of Heidegger." *Boundary*
   8, no. 1 (1983): 223–35.
――――. "Must We Say What We Mean?" *Revue Université d'Ottawa* 50 (1980):
   411–26.
Itzkowitz, Kenneth. "Differance and Identity." *Research in Phenomenology* 8
   (1978): 127–43.
Jacobson, Richard. "Absence, Authority, and the Text." *Glyph* 3 (1978):
   137–47.
Johnson, Barbara. "The Critical Difference." *Diacritics* 8, no. 2 (1978): 2–9.
――――. *The Critical Difference: Essays in the Contemporary Rhetoric of Reading*.
   Baltimore: Johns Hopkins University Press, 1980.
Kemp, Peter. "Death and Gift." *Journal of the American Academy of Religion* 50,
   no. 1 (1982): 459–71.
――――. *Døden og Maskinen: Introduktion til Derrida*. Copenhagen: Bibliotek
   Rhodos, 1981.
Klein, Richard. "Prolegomenon to Derrida." *Diacritics* 2 (1972): 29–34.
Lacoue-Labarthe, Philippe. "Le Détour." *Poétique* 5 (1971).
――――. "La Fable." *Poétique* 1 (1974).
――――. "L'Imprésentable." *Poétique* 21 (1975).
――――. "Theatrum Analyticum." *Glyph* 3 (1977): 122–43.
Lacoue-Labarthe, Philippe, and Nancy, Jean-Luc. "Genre." *Glyph* 7 (1980):
   1–14.
――――. *L'Absolue littéraire: Theorie de la littérature du romantisme allemand*. Paris:
   Éditions du Seuil, 1978.
Lang, Candace. "Aberrance in Criticism?" *Sub-stance* 12, no. 4 (1983): 3–16.
Lentricchia, Frank. Derrida, History, and Intellectuals." *Salmagundi* 50–51
   (1980–81): 284–301.
Lingis, Alphonso. "Differance in the Eternal Recurrence of the Same." *Research
   in Phenomenology* 8 (1978): 77–91.
Llewelyn, John. *Beyond Metaphysics?: The Hermeneutic Circle in Contemporary
   Continental Philosophy*. Atlantic Highlands, N.J.: Humanities Press, 1985.
Loselle, Andrea. "Freud/Derrida as Fort/Da and the Repetitive Eponym."
   Modern Language Notes 97, no. 5 (1982): 1180–85.
Miller, J. Hillis. "Ariadne's Thread: Repetitions and the Narrative Line."
   Critical Inquiry 3 (1976): 57–77.
――――. "Deconstructing the Deconstructors." *Diacritics* 5, no. 2 (1975):
   30–31.
――――. *Fiction and Repetition: Seven English Novels*. Cambridge: Harvard Uni-
   versity Press, 1982.
――――. "Stevens' Rock and Criticism as Cure." *Georgia Review* 30 (1976):
   5–33 (part I), 330–48 (part II).
――――. "Tradition and Difference." *Diacritics* 2, no. 4 (1972): 6–13.
Mulligan, Kevin. "Inscriptions and Speaking's Place: Derrida and Wittgen-
   stein." *The Oxford Literary Review* 3, no. 2 (1978): 62–67.

Nancy, Jean-Luc. "Larvatus Pro Deo." *Glyph* 2 (1977): 14–36.
Norris, Christopher. "Deconstruction and the Limits of Sense." *Essays in Criticism* 30 (1980): 281–92.
The Oxford Literary Review 3, no. 2 (1978). Devoted to Derrida.
Parker, Andrew. "Taking Sides (On History): Derrida Re-Marx." *Diacritics* 11, no. 3 (1981): 57–73
Raschke, Carl, ed. *New Directions in Philosophical Theology.* Chico, Calif.: Scholars Press, 1982.
Riffaterre, Michael. "Syllepsis." *Critical Inquiry* 6 (1980): 625–38.
Rorty, Richard. *Consequences of Pragmatism.* Minneapolis: University of Minnesota Press, 1982.
———. "Derrida on Language, Being and Abnormal Philosophy." *Journal of Philosophy* 74 (1977): 673–81.
———. "Philosophy as a Kind of Writing: An Essay on Derrida." *New Literary History* 10 (1978): 141–60.
———. "The World Well Lost." *Journal of Philosophy* 69 (1972): 649–65.
Ryan, Michael. *Marxism and Deconstruction.* Baltimore: Johns Hopkins University Press, 1982.
Said, Edward W. "Abecedarium Culturae: Structuralism, Absence, Writing." In *Modern French Criticism*, edited by J. Simon, 341–92. Chicago: University of Chicago Press, 1972.
———. *Beginnings: Intention and Method.* New York: Basic Books, 1975.
———. "Eclecticism and Orthodoxy in Criticism." *Diacritics* 2, no. 1 (1972): 2–8.
———. "The Problem of Textuality: Two Exemplary Positions." *Critical Inquiry* 4 (1978): 673–714.
Searle, John. "Reiterating the Differences: A Reply to Derrida." *Glyph* 1 (1977): 198–208.
Smith, Barbara Hernstein. *On the Margins of Discourse: The Relation of Literature to Language.* Chicago: University of Chicago Press, 1979.
Spivak, Gayatri. "*Glas*-Piece: A Compte Rendu." *Diacritics* 7 (1977): 22–43.
———. "Revolutions That as Yet Have No Model: Derrida's Limited Inc." *Diacritics* 10, no. 4 (1980): 29–49.
Sprinker, Michael. "Textual Politics: Foucault and Derrida." *Boundary 2* 8, no. 3 (1980): 75–98.
Sussman, Henry. "The Deconstructor as Politician: Melville's Confidence-Man." *Glyph* 4 (1978): 32–56.
Taminiaux, Jacques. *Dialectic and Difference: Finitude in Modern Thought.* Translated by J. Decker and R. Crease. Atlantic Highlands, N.J.: Humanities Press, 1985.
Taylor, Mark C. *Deconstructing Theology.* New York: Crossroad, 1982.
———. *Erring: A Postmodern A/theology.* Chicago: University of Chicago Press, 1984.
Terdiman, Richard. "Deconstruction/Mediation: A Dialectical Critique of 'Derrideanism.'" *The Minnesota Review* 19 (1983): 103–11.

Ulmer, Gregory. *Applied Grammatology: Post(e)-Pedagogy from Jacques Derrida to Joseph Beuys.* Baltimore: Johns Hopkins University Press, 1985.

——. "The Post-Age." *Diacritics* 11, no. 3 (1981): 39–56.

Weber, Samuel. "A Stroke of Luck." *Enclitic* 6, no. 2 (1982): 29–31.

——. "It." *Glyph* 4 (1978): 1–29.

White, Hayden. *Tropics of Discourse.* Baltimore: Johns Hopkins University Press, 1978.

Wills, David, and McHoul, Alec. "'Die Welt ist alles was der Fall ist' (Wittgenstein, Weissman, Pynchon)/'Le Signe est toujours le signe de la Chute.'" *Southern Review* 16, no. 2 (1983): 274–91.

Winquist, Charles E. "Theology, Deconstruction, and Ritual Process." *Zygon* 18 (1983): 295–310.

Wolosky, Shire. "Derrida, Jabès, Levinas: Sign-Theory as Ethical Discourse." *Prooftexts* 2, no. 3 (1982): 283–302.

Wood, David. *The Structures of Time.* Atlantic Highlands, N.J.: Humanities Press, 1985.

——. "Style and Strategy at the Limits of Philosophy." *Monist* 63 (1980): 494–511.

——. "Time and the Sign." *Journal of the British Society of Phenomenology* 13 (1982): 143–53.

Wordsworth, Ann. "Derrida and Criticism." *The Oxford Literary Review* 3, no. 2 (1978): 47–52.

Wright, Edmond. "Derrida, Searle, Contexts, Games, Riddles." *New Literary History* 13, no. 3 (1982): 463–77.

Wyschogrod, Edith. "Time and Non-Being in Derrida and Quine." *Journal of the British Society of Phenomenology* 14 (1983): 112–26.

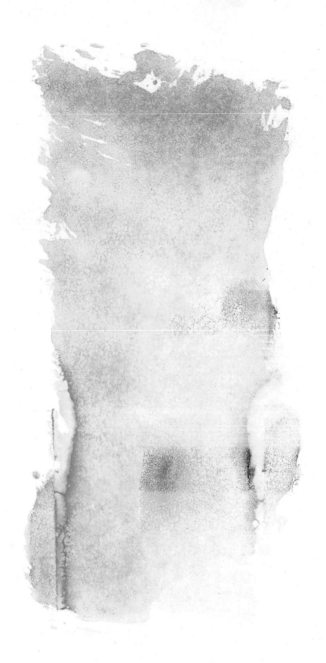